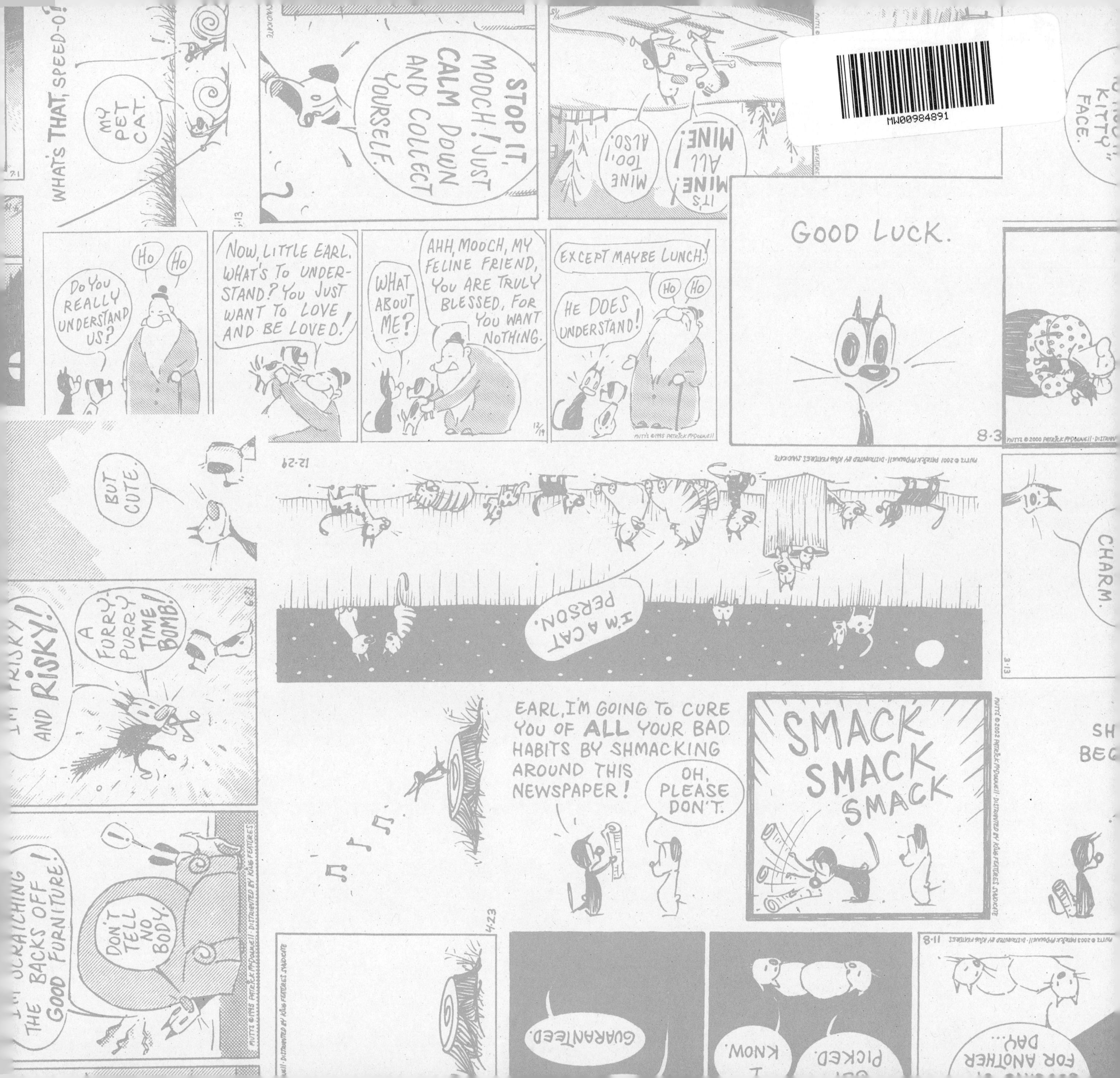

WHAT'S THAT, SPEED-O?
MY PET CAT.
STOP IT, MOOCH! JUST CALM DOWN AND COLLECT YOURSELF.
IT'S MINE! ALL MINE!
MINE TOO! ALSO.
KITTY FACE.
GOOD LUCK.
DO YOU REALLY UNDERSTAND US?
HO HO
NOW, LITTLE EARL. WHAT'S TO UNDER-STAND? YOU JUST WANT TO LOVE AND BE LOVED!
WHAT ABOUT ME?
AHH, MOOCH, MY FELINE FRIEND, YOU ARE TRULY BLESSED, FOR YOU WANT NOTHING.
EXCEPT MAYBE LUNCH!
HE DOES UNDERSTAND!
BUT CUTE.
CHARM.
I'M A CAT PERSON.
AND RISKY!
A FURRY PURRY TIME BOMB!
EARL, I'M GOING TO CURE YOU OF ALL YOUR BAD HABITS BY SHMACKING AROUND THIS NEWSPAPER!
OH, PLEASE DON'T.
SMACK SMACK SMACK SMACK
THE BACKS OFF GOOD FURNITURE!
DON'T TELL NO BODY.
GUARANTEED.
PICKED.
KNOW.
FOR ANOTHER DAY...

# THE BEST OF MUTTS 1994–2004

By **Patrick McDonnell**

Introduction by **Alice Sebold** and **Glen David Gold**

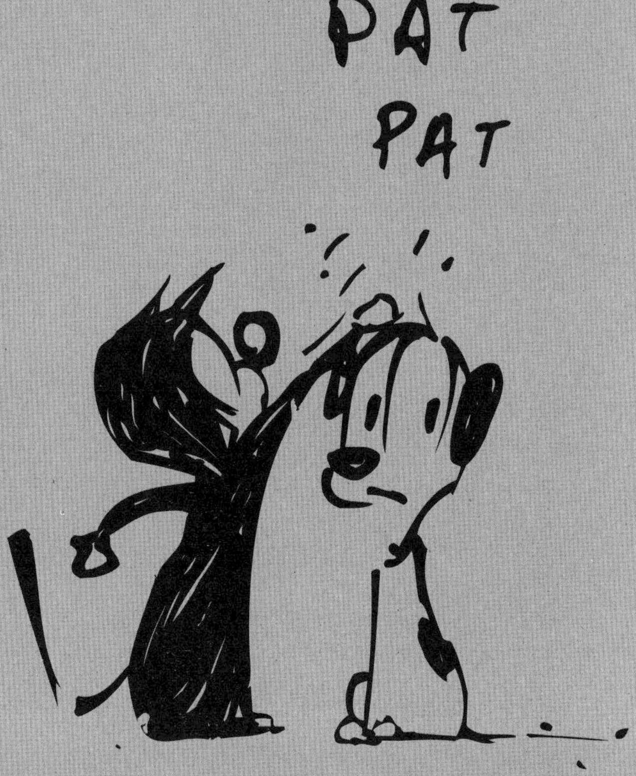
PAT
PAT

Andrews McMeel Publishing, LLC
Kansas City

For Jay Kennedy

**I want to thank:**
Rocky Shepard, Frank Caruso, Glenn Mott, Evelyn Smith, Todd X Chen, and everyone at King Features Syndicate
John McMeel, Hugh Andrews, Dorothy O'Brien, Stephanie Bennett, Erin Friedrich, and everyone at Andrews McMeel
Alice Sebold and Glen David Gold
Jen and Jeff Schulz
Rich Mansfield and everyone at muttscomics.com
The newspapers that carry *Mutts*
My family, friends, and my nest of Karen, Earl, and MeeMow.

Editor: Erin Friedrich
Design: Jeff Schulz @ Command-Z-Design

**Other Books by Patrick McDonnell**
*MUTTS, CATS AND DOGS: MUTTS II, MORE SHTUFF: MUTTS III, YESH!: MUTTS IV, OUR MUTTS: FIVE, A LITTLE LOOK-SEE: MUTTS VI,*
*WHAT NOW: MUTTS VII, I WANT TO BE THE KITTY: MUTTS NO. EIGHT, DOG-EARED: MUTTS IX, WHO LET THE CAT OUT?: MUTTS X, MUTTS SUNDAYS,*
*MUTTS SUNDAY MORNINGS, MUTTS SUNDAY AFTERNOONS, MUTTS SUNDAY EVENINGS, EVERYDAY MUTTS, ANIMAL FRIENDLY*

All color Sunday strips in this book have been reproduced from newspaper tear sheets. The black-and-white daily strips were reproduced from digital archives.

**MUTTS** is distributed internationally by King Features Syndicate, Inc. For information, write King Features Syndicate, Inc., 300 West Fifty-seventh Street, New York, New York 10019.

07 08 09 10 11 TWP 10 9 8 7 6 5 4 3

**THE BEST OF MUTTS** © 2007 Patrick McDonnell. All rights reserved. Printed in Singapore. No part of this book may be used or reproduced in any manner whatsoever without written permission except in the case of reprints in the context of reviews. For information, write Andrews McMeel Publishing, LLC, an Andrews McMeel Universal company, 4520 Main Street, Kansas City, Missouri 64111.

ISBN-13: 978-0-7407-6844-6
ISBN-10: 0-7407-6844-1

**THE BEST OF MUTTS** is printed on recycled paper | **MUTTS** can be found on the Internet at www.muttscomics.com

Library of Congress Control Number: 200792

**ATTENTION: SCHOOLS AND BUSINESSES** Andrews McMeel books are available at quantity discounts with bulk purchase for educational, business, or sales promotional use.
For information, please write to: Special Sales Department, Andrews McMeel Publishing, LLC, 4520 Main Street, Kansas City, Missouri 64111.

www.andrewsmcmeel.com

# Dogs can't make their dreams come true. So it's up to us. —Lithuanian proverb

For such a simple-looking strip, *Mutts*, the adventures of a cat, a dog, their guardians, and the world around them, turns out to be about more than you might imagine. This book contains the best comic strips in the *Mutts* series, but "the best" of *Mutts* is something a little different.

On a recent afternoon at an exhibition in the New York Public Library, Patrick McDonnell stopped in his tracks before a display case of 18th- and 19th-century illustrated Japanese books. He hunched over the way only a cartoonist can (it looks natural), and you could see him taking in the drawings of dancing flowers, the birds in flight, the cats in windows, the dogs in the street, the lightning whelks and conch shells on the beach, and realizing he had wandered into a room of kindred spirits. Edo-period Japan—that time of reflective Shinto and Buddhist worldviews—took such an intense delight in nature that a single falling leaf could provoke tears and six stanzas of poetry.

And they celebrated simplicity. The most famous haiku in literature is Bashō's, which translates into English something like this:

Old pond
Frog jumps in
Water sound

It has never been clear whether courtiers of 1686, upon reading this poem, wanted to tape it to the refrigerator or hand it over the top of the cubicle to the courtesans next door. Perhaps it just seemed *cute*, an image that reminded people of their own ponds. "I've seen that. Frogs do things like that." Its depths likely sneaked up on everyone.

Its brevity, its soul, its seventeen syllables more or less demand to be reread until it makes us swim with that frog. The mysteries of eternity, the frog vanishing, the ephemeral sound, oh, wait, it's not just about frogs, is it?

So it is with *Mutts*, which is the finest comic strip currently running. It is as quick as haiku, but it also resonates in ways not so easily understood. Its quickest pleasure is the daily visit with Mooch and Earl among their friends somewhere in the suburbs. They eat, they sleep, they play, they behave like real animals (except for the talking—well, maybe that's real; who knows yet?) and they're very, very funny. Over the years, the strip has built up recurrent gags and motif—the little pink sock, the trips to the beach, the Sphinx, the search for tigers, the Shelter Stories—whose appearances are as welcome as old friends.

Further, McDonnell is a scholar of art history, both the kind one sees on the walls of a museum and the kind that gets taped to the refrigerator. His work comments on his predecessors in a way that allows people who need to throw the word "postmodern" into a conversation to enjoy a strip about cats and dogs. Good for Patrick! What those scholars really want to do is get on their bellies and squeeze a toy hamburger to get their dogs to play with them.

But *Mutts* has a secret agenda, or perhaps not so secret, if you have read enough of the strips to feel your heart breaking. At a recent comic convention, a woman found McDonnell sitting quietly to the side of all the action (the natural habitat of the cartoonist). She wanted to talk about *Mutts*, but not so much about how adorable it was. Instead, almost whispering, as if he might find her crazy, she said it was the strip's spiritual side that moved her most. Does McDonnell intend that?

Oh yes.

His insights are as ephemeral and eternal as Bashō's frog disappearing into that old pond. *Mutts* is spiritual in the way *Peanuts* was—but coming from a different tradition, less biblical than Zen, but equally concerned with how to live as our best selves on this beautiful, unjust planet.

And what about that planet? The current mood is troubling. We live in awful times, and every day the skies are a little more sickly, the weather is a little more terrible (even on nice days—especially on nice days), and every day the sea is lapping a little more closely at our toes. We could be excused for turning to the funny papers for a good laugh. Which *Mutts* provides. But what *Mutts* knows, and dares to say every day, is that we do not own the world—we share it. It's our job to keep it going for those who rely on us.

This is a radical idea.

Its effect is still to come. In two hundred years, perhaps, in a city, maybe even Manhattan, a cartoonist will be in an exhibit celebrating the antique grace of *Mutts*. He will have the cartoonist's hunch and the cartoonist's sharp eye, and he will recognize—again—a kindred spirit. If we are still around then, it is likely that the strip's basic wisdom will not just have survived, but will have saved us. And *that* is the best of *Mutts*.

**—Alice Sebold and Glen David Gold**

T

This is a collection of dailies and Sundays that I chose from
the first ten years of my comic strip *Mutts*. These are the strips
that spoke to me most strongly. The criteria varied (art, humor,
layout, theme, character), but mainly it came down to the ones
that just "felt right." Art is mostly intuitive.

I hope these feel right to you, too.

PATRICK McDONNEll

**I've always felt at home** sitting at a desk and drawing. I scribbled through grade school, went on to graduate from the School of Visual Arts in New York City, and became a professional doodler as a magazine illustrator.

I was, and still am, mesmerized by the pen-and-ink dreams of McCay's *Little Nemo*, Herriman's *Krazy Kat*, Segar's *Popeye*, Kelly's *Pogo*, and Schulz's *Peanuts*. I believe that the comic strip is an important and underappreciated art form that, when done right, is visual and literal poetry. Art that can also make you laugh. For as long as I can remember, I had wanted to draw a daily comic strip that would give back some of this joy and comfort. And, after many years at the drawing table, I thought I would give it a try.

On Monday, September 5, 1994, the first *Mutts* comic strip (page 7) appeared in seventy-five newspapers. In its third panel, Ozzie announces to his dog, Earl, "We're home!" I felt I was, too.

The strip all started with Earl, a sweet little dog based on my own Jack Russell terrier, Earl. He truly is a best friend. I often find myself wondering what he is thinking, and I am always trying to capture his playful spirit on paper. The basic premise of *Mutts* is the world as seen though the eyes of our companion animals, and the special bond we share with them. Animals are one with life and help us to link back to nature. My mantra for the strip was—and is—simplicity and compassion.

In developing my "dog strip," I sketched some ideas about Earl meeting a cat next door. I had hoped this would be good fodder for a week-or-two's worth of gags. But that's not how cats work in my life. In the style of most felines, Mooch wandered into our comic strip home and took over.

My inspiration for Mooch was the many cats I've had the pleasure to know. He has his own way of thinking (and talking), and became yang to Earl's yin. This unique friendship of supposed natural enemies became the heart of the strip.

In those last four months of 1994, we were introduced (I include myself because it was all new to me as well) to the main cast of Earl and his Ozzie, Mooch and his guardians, Frank and Millie, and the sad goldfish Sid. We visited for the first time Earl and Mooch's favorite hangout, the Fatty Snax Deli, and its proprietor, Butchie. And we heard Mooch's first "Yesh!"

You'll see that just as Earl and Mooch were trying to get their bearings, so was this novice cartoonist. This very early work was sketchy, drawn freehand (no T-squares here), and its lettering and coloring back then were a bit of an adventure. *Mutts*' puppy stage.

On a personal note, the original for the December 25 strip (page 20) was given as a gift to my boyhood idol and good friend Sparky, and now has a home in his Charles M. Schulz Museum in Santa Rosa, California.

OKAY, WE'RE HOME!
9-5

YOU KNOW, EARL, I SOMETIMES SEE YOU AS MY NOBLE PROTECTOR.
I WONDER HOW YOU SEE ME?
9-7

YOU START AT THE BOTTOM...
BUT EVENTUALLY...
MAKE IT TO THE TOP.
IT'S THE SUREST WAY TO GET A HEAD.
9-9

EARL WATCHES THE WORLD GO BY.
YES, SIR.
NO DIFFERENT SIDEWAYS.
McDONNELL
9-10

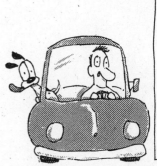

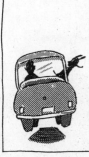

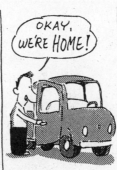

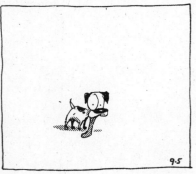

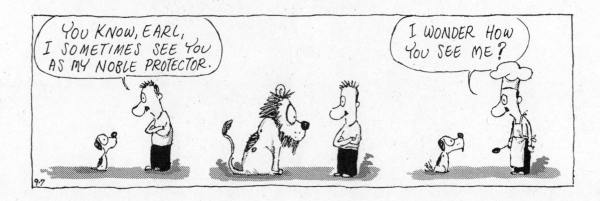

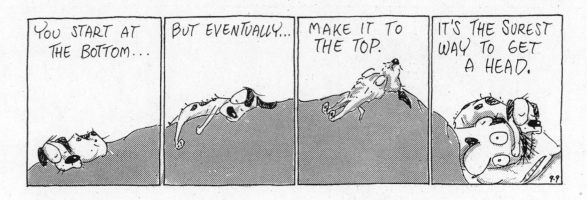

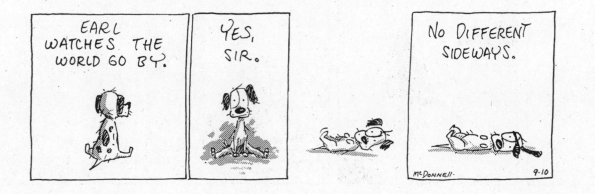

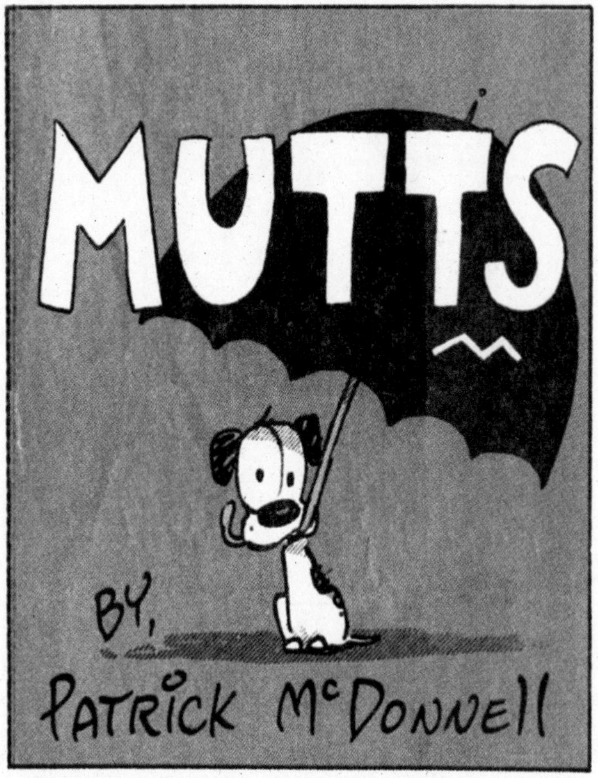
MUTTS
BY,
PATRICK McDONNELL

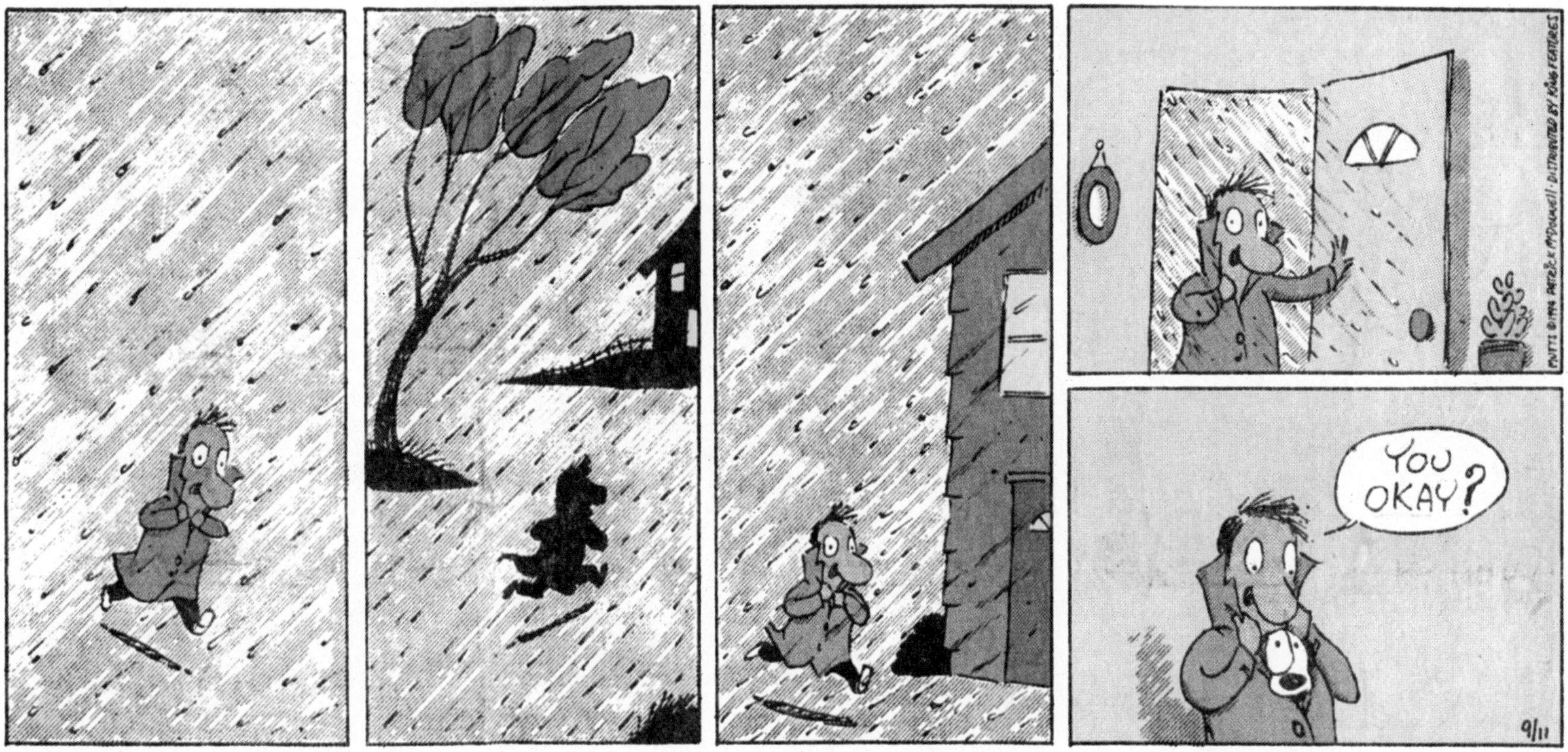
YOU OKAY?
9/11

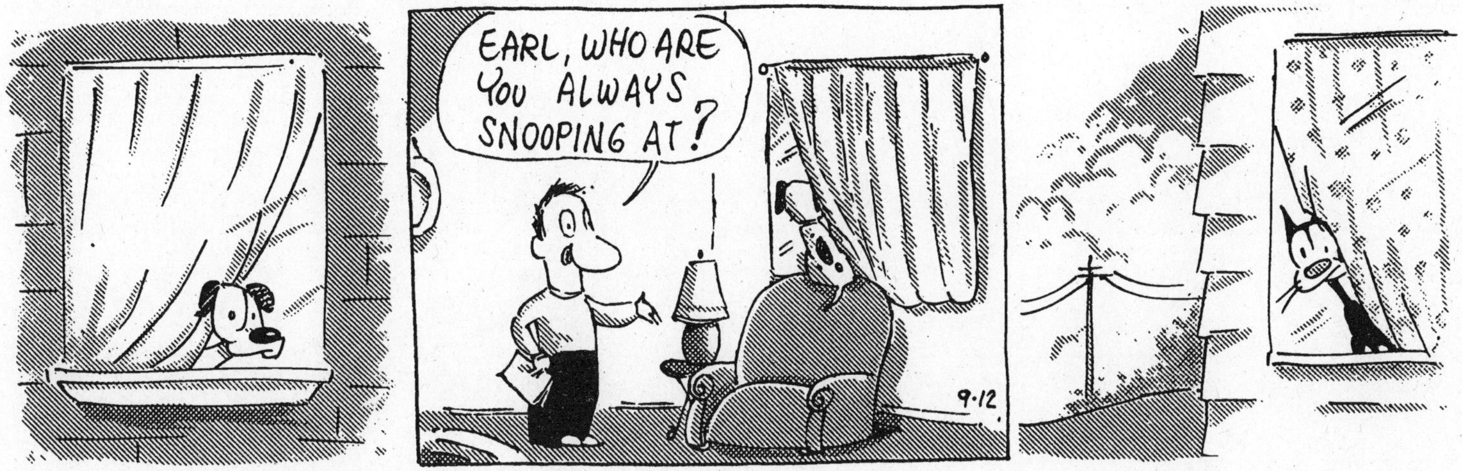
EARL, WHO ARE YOU ALWAYS SNOOPING AT?
9.12

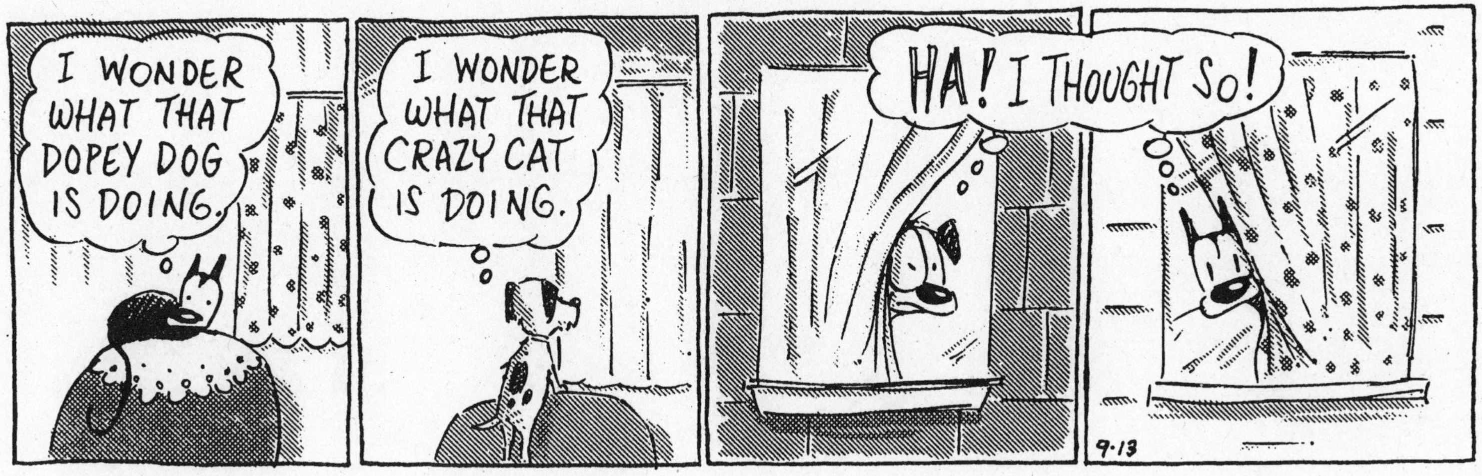
I WONDER WHAT THAT DOPEY DOG IS DOING.
I WONDER WHAT THAT CRAZY CAT IS DOING.
HA! I THOUGHT SO!
9.13

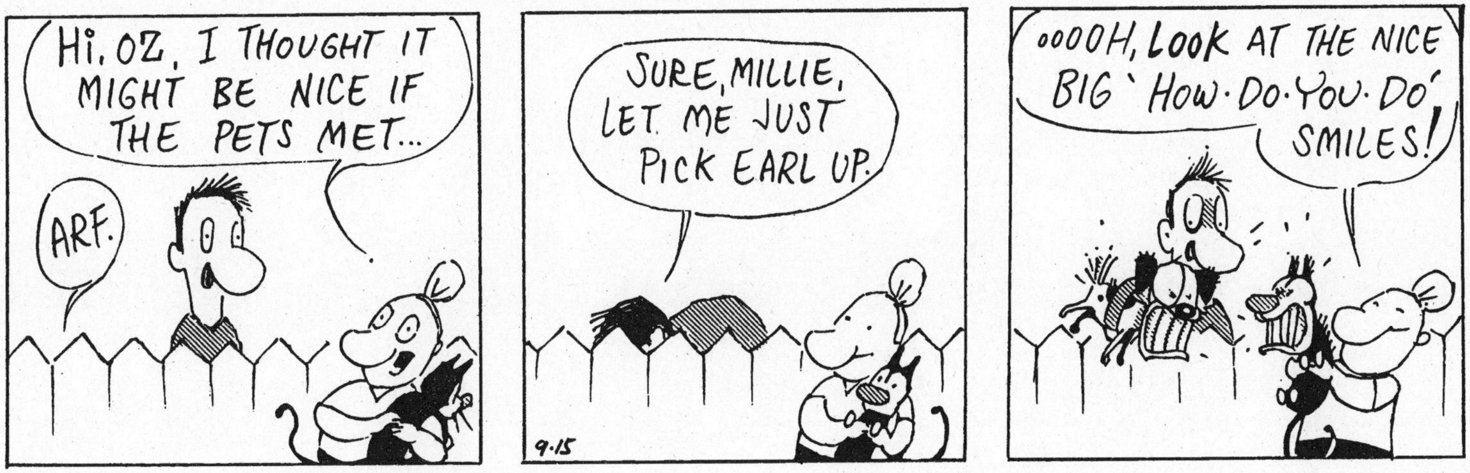
Hi, OZ, I THOUGHT IT MIGHT BE NICE IF THE PETS MET...
ARF.
SURE, MILLIE, LET ME JUST PICK EARL UP.
9.15
oooOH, LOOK AT THE NICE BIG 'HOW-DO-YOU-DO' SMILES!

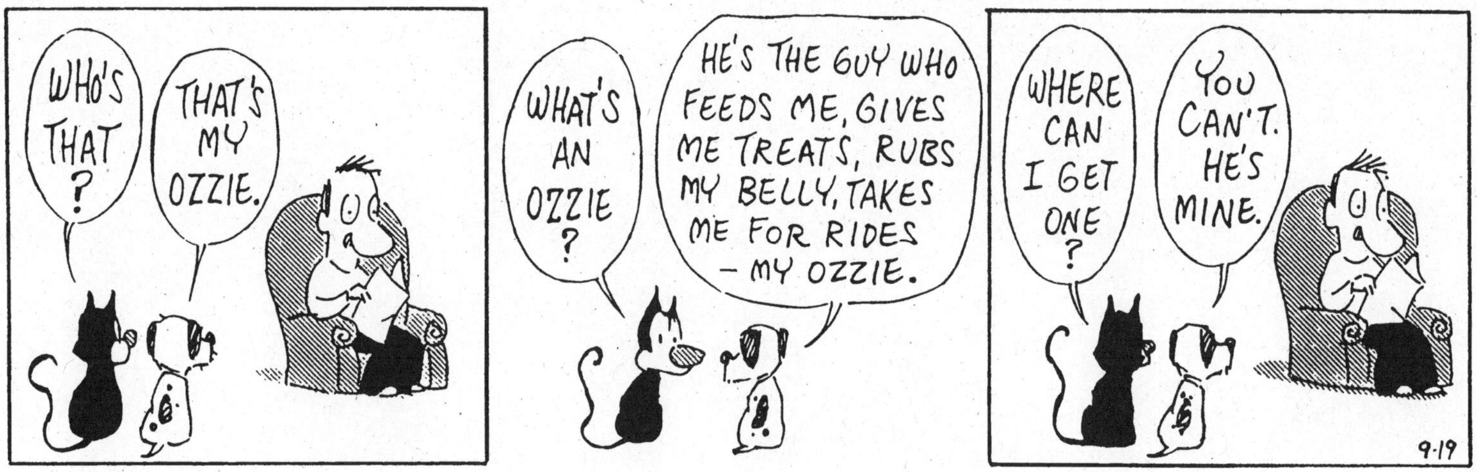
WHO'S THAT?
THAT'S MY OZZIE.
WHAT'S AN OZZIE?
HE'S THE GUY WHO FEEDS ME, GIVES ME TREATS, RUBS MY BELLY, TAKES ME FOR RIDES – MY OZZIE.
WHERE CAN I GET ONE?
YOU CAN'T. HE'S MINE.
9·19

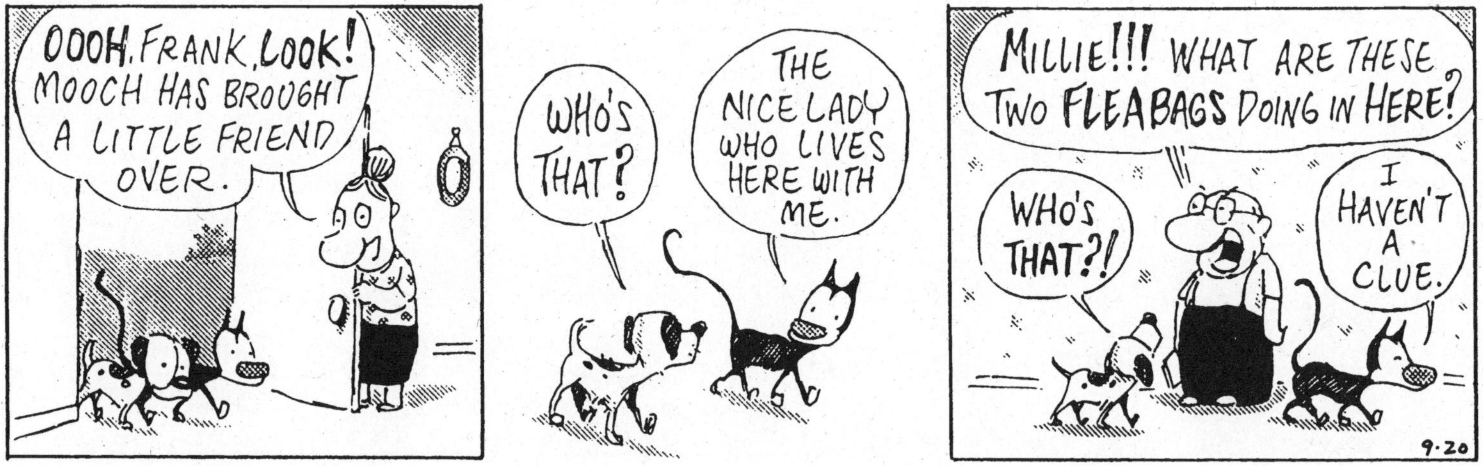
OOOH, FRANK, LOOK! MOOCH HAS BROUGHT A LITTLE FRIEND OVER.
WHO'S THAT?
THE NICE LADY WHO LIVES HERE WITH ME.
MILLIE!!! WHAT ARE THESE TWO FLEABAGS DOING IN HERE?
WHO'S THAT?!
I HAVEN'T A CLUE.
9·20

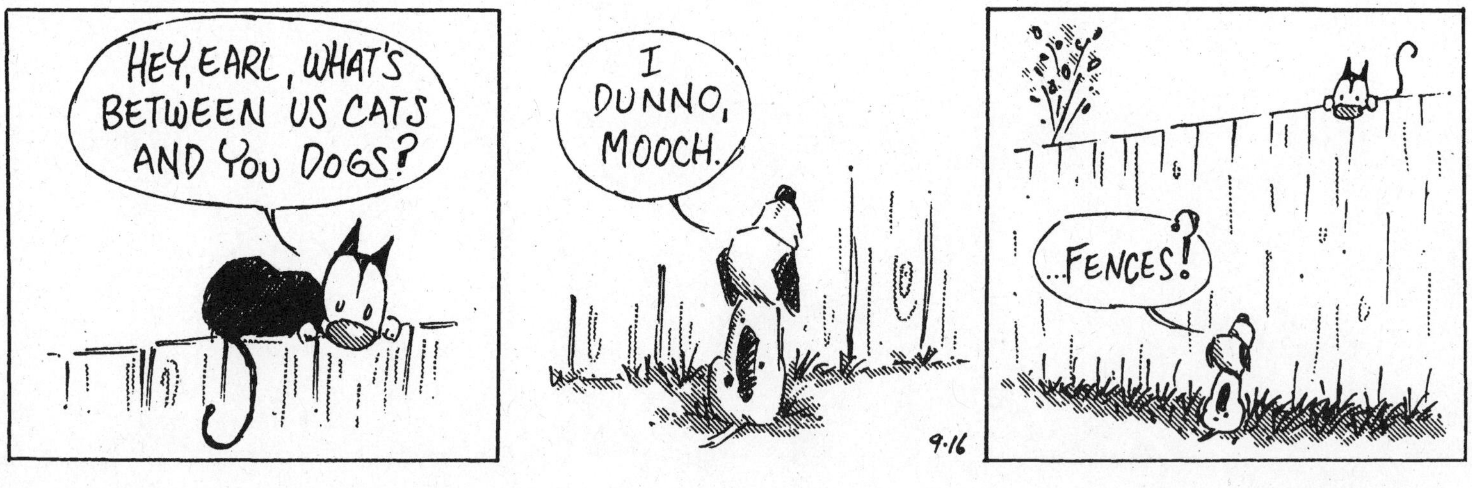
HEY, EARL, WHAT'S BETWEEN US CATS AND YOU DOGS?
I DUNNO, MOOCH.
9·16
...FENCES?

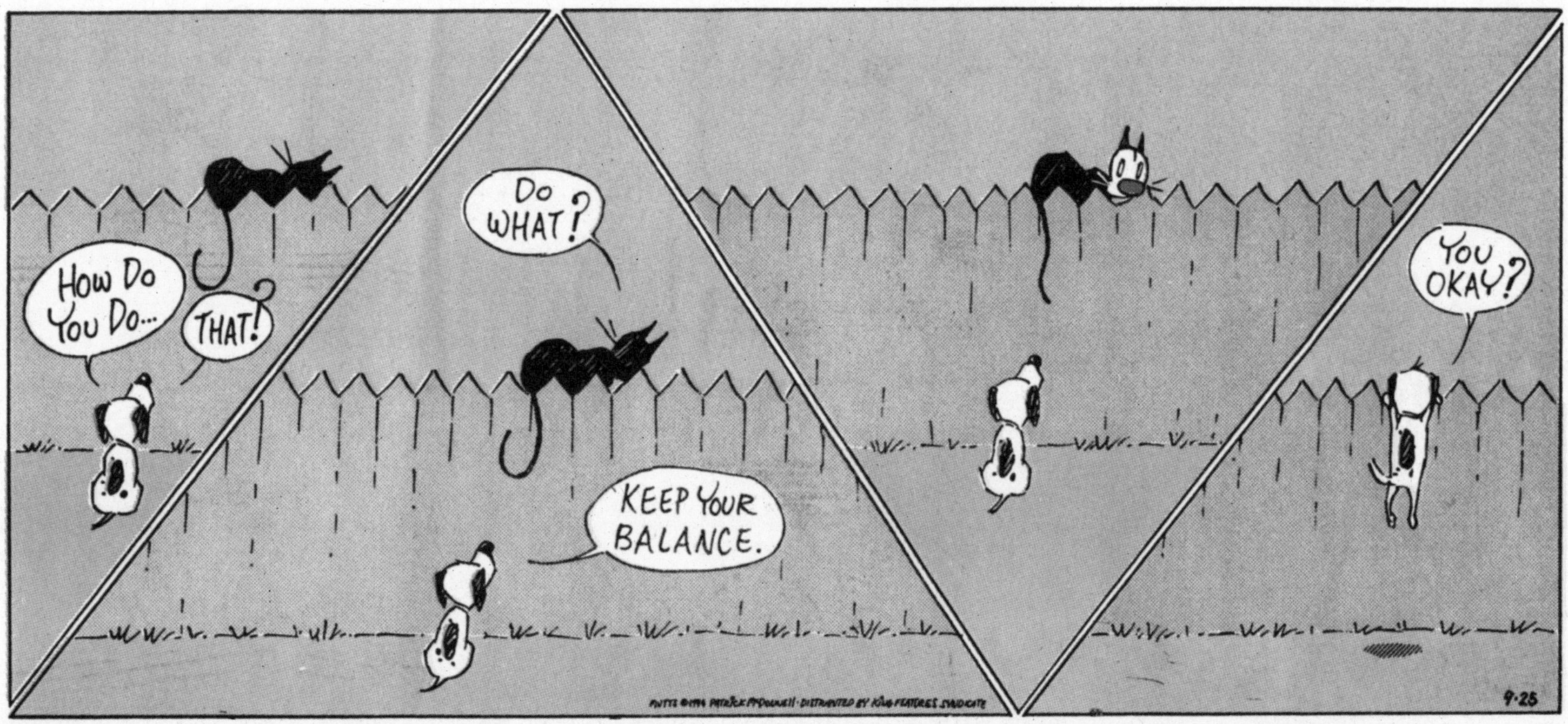
HOW DO YOU DO...
THAT!
DO WHAT?
KEEP YOUR BALANCE.
YOU OKAY?
9·25

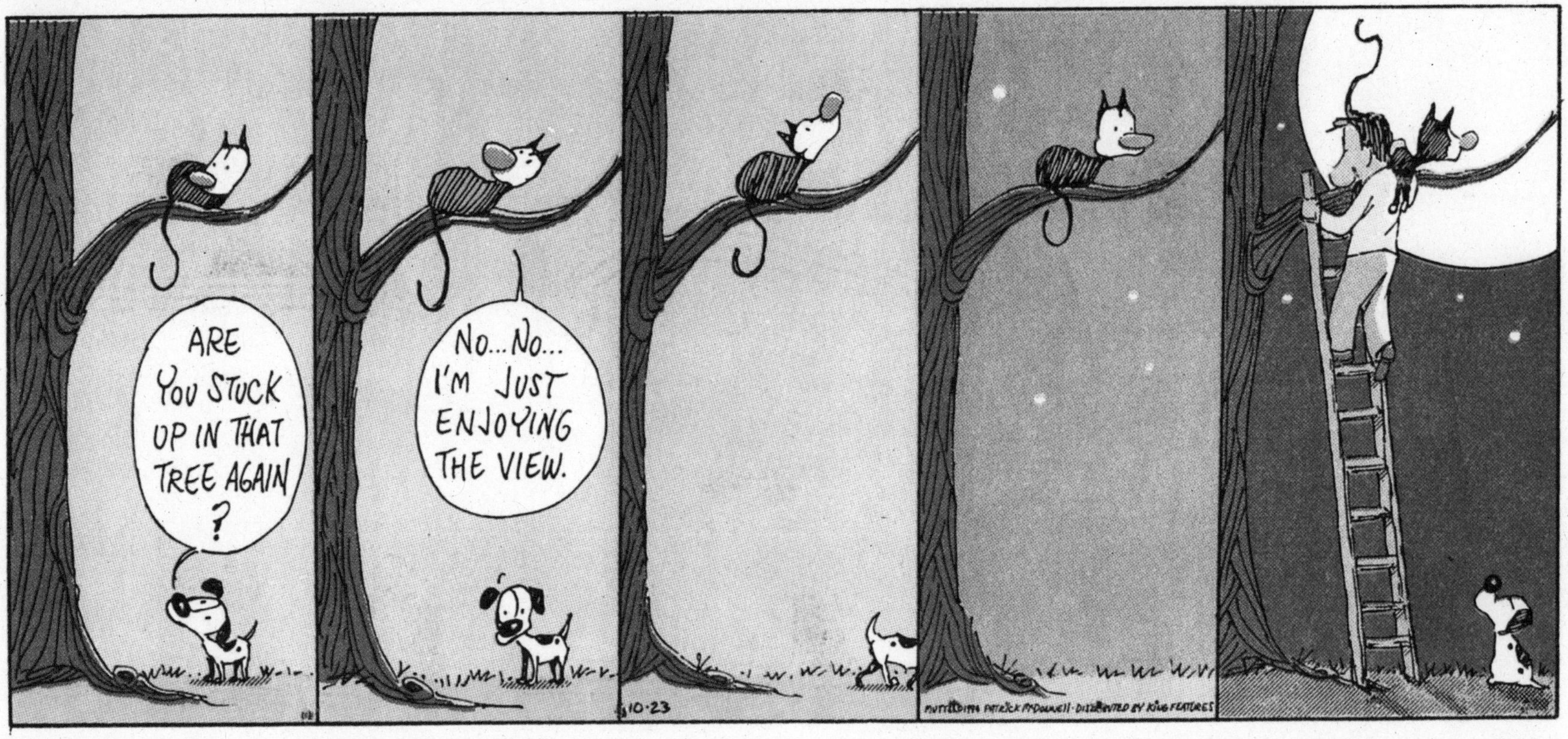
ARE YOU STUCK UP IN THAT TREE AGAIN ?
NO... NO... I'M JUST ENJOYING THE VIEW.
10·23

DOG THERMOMETER:

70°       80°       90°       100°

CAT THERMOMETER:

30°       50°       70°       90°

PAT
PAT
PAT
PAT
PAT
PAT
PAT
PAT
PAT
9·29

How Do You STAY SO CLEAN?
I WASH MYSELF.
How Do You TURN ON THE FAUCET?
9·28

SLAM!
THEY'RE GONE!
THE HOUSE is MINE!
ALL MINE
YESH
HA HA
PURR
WHAT DO I BUST FIRST?
9·29

FLEA.
10·8

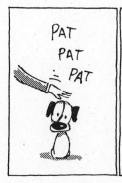

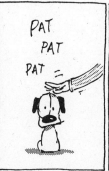

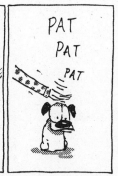

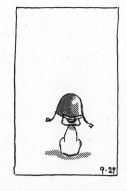

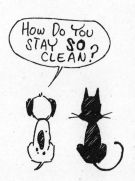

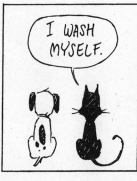

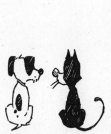

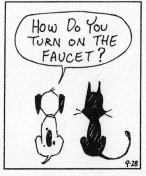

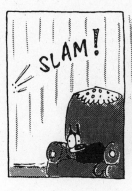

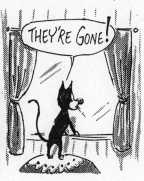

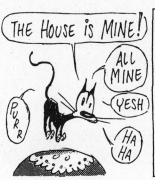

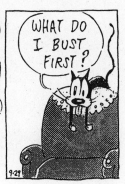

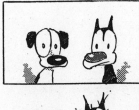

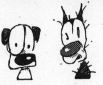

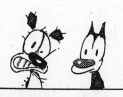

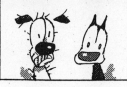

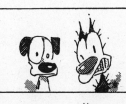

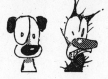

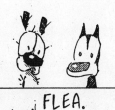

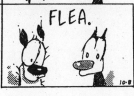

FATTY SNAX DELI
SORRY, FELLAS-NO LEFTOVERS TODAY.
WHO WANTED 'LEFTOVERS'!?!
10·4

SOME SAY HE'S "ALWAYS LOOKING FOR TROUBLE".
SOME CALL HIM "NOSY"
WE LEAN TOWARD HE HAS A "LUST FOR LIFE."
MCDONNELL
10·22

WAIT UP... YOU MEAN ALL YOU DO IS WADDLE AROUND THIS PARK AND COMPLETE STRANGERS, COME UP AND FEED YOU!?! THAT'S SURVIVAL OF THE FITTEST!?!
QUAK.
QUACK.
QUAK.
10·27

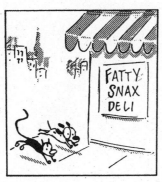

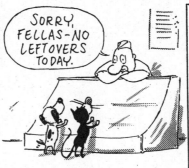

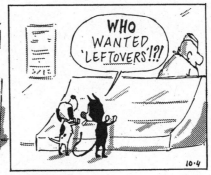

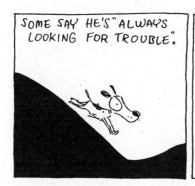

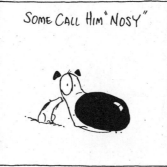

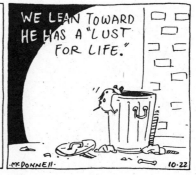

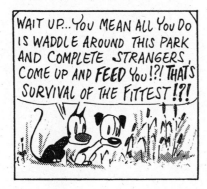

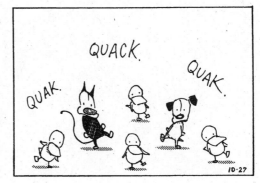

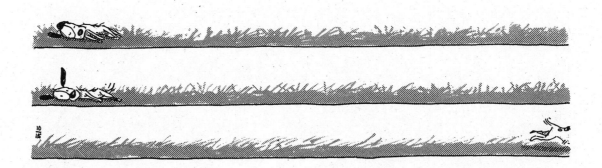

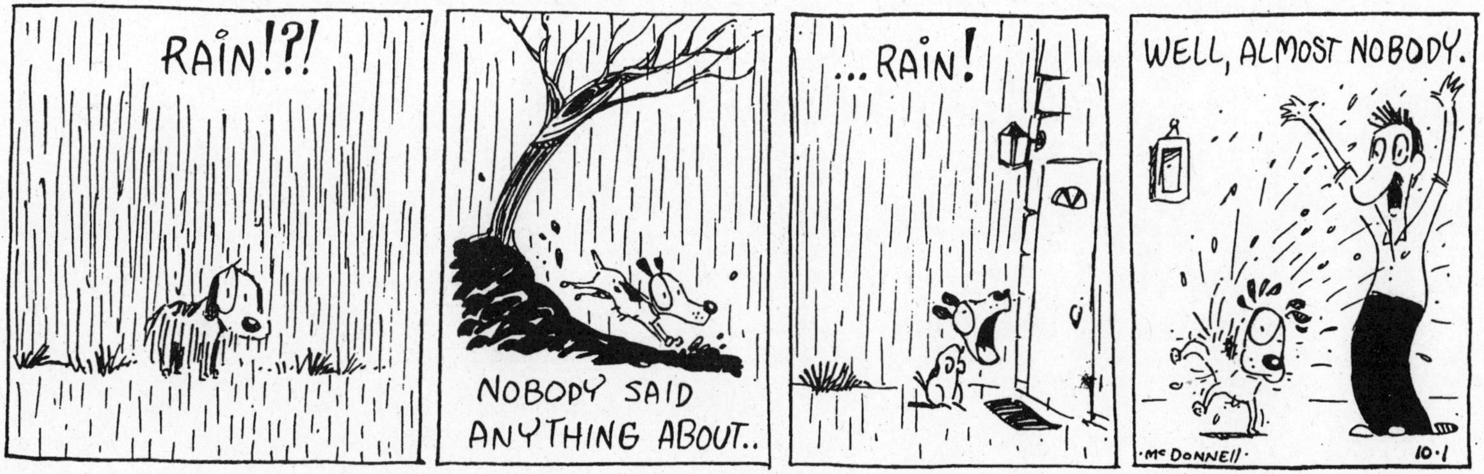
RAIN!?!
NOBODY SAID ANYTHING ABOUT..
...RAIN!
WELL, ALMOST NOBODY.
MCDONNELL
10·1

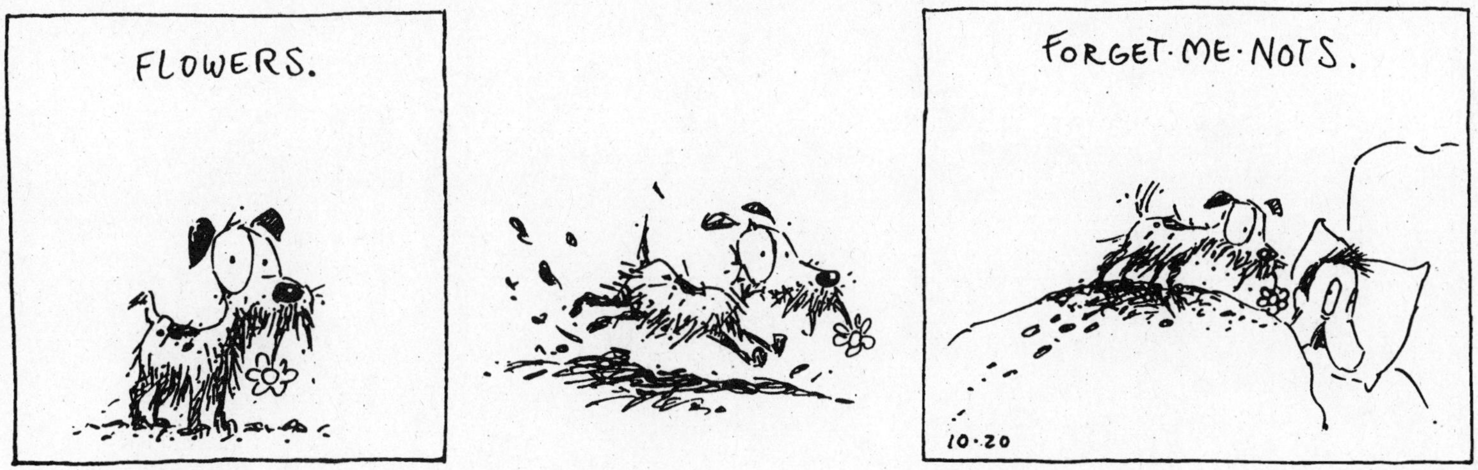
FLOWERS.
FORGET·ME·NOTS.
10·20

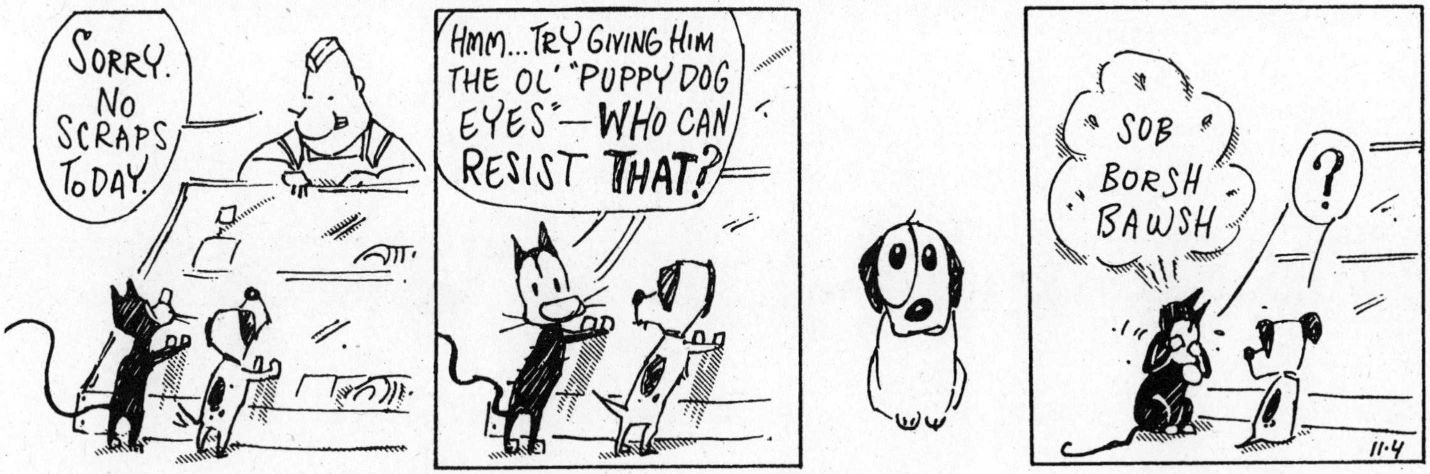
SORRY. NO SCRAPS TODAY.
HMM...TRY GIVING HIM THE OL' "PUPPY DOG EYES"—WHO CAN RESIST THAT?
SOB BORSH BAWSH
?
11·4

How Do You REMEMBER THOSE TRICKS?
E-Z
I CAN'T LEARN NUTHIN'. IT'S NOT IN MY NATURE! JUST TRY! JUST TRY TO TEACH ME A TRICK!
SIT.
10·12

SIT.
THAT'S A TRICK!?!
YUP.
10·13
AND YOU GET A TREAT FOR THAT?
SOME TIMES TWO.
ARF
ARF

HEY, EARL! WATCH THIS! I KNOW A DOGGY TRICK!
SIT.
HA! HA! AIN'T I GREAT!?! DUH! WOOF WOOF WHAT A TRICKSTER! BOW·WOW
10·14
O.K., WHAT CAN I LEARN NEXT?
PLAY DEAD?

How DO CATS LAND ON THEIR FEET?
EASY.
10·21

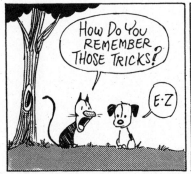

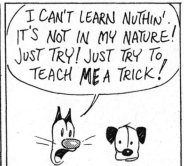

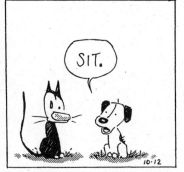

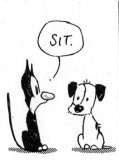

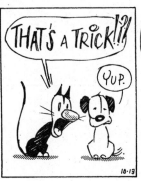

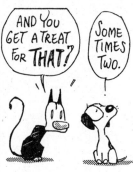

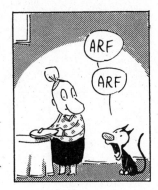

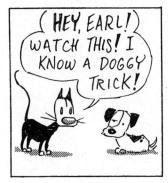

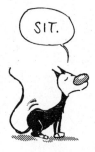

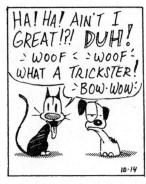

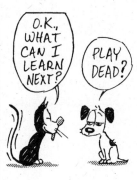

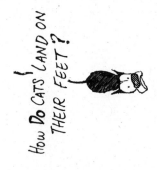

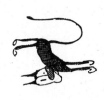

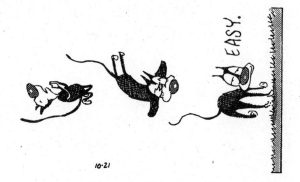

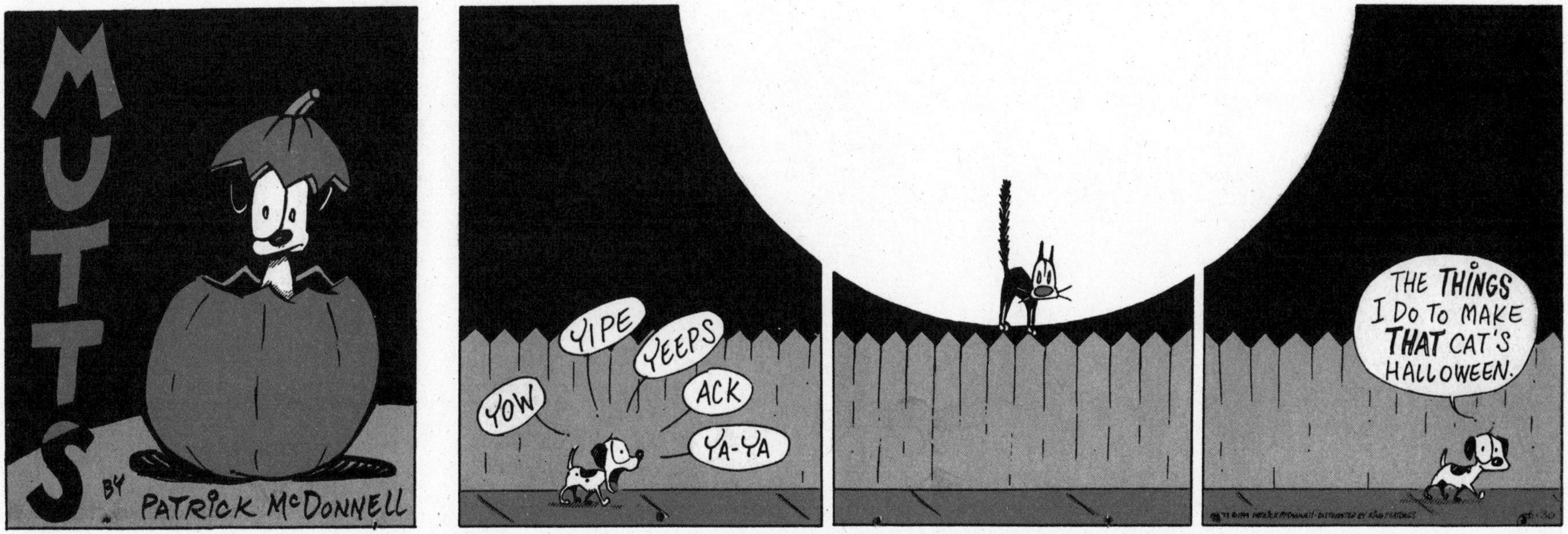
MUTTS
BY PATRICK McDONNELL
YOW
YIPE
YEEPS
ACK
YA-YA
THE THINGS I DO TO MAKE THAT CAT'S HALLOWEEN.

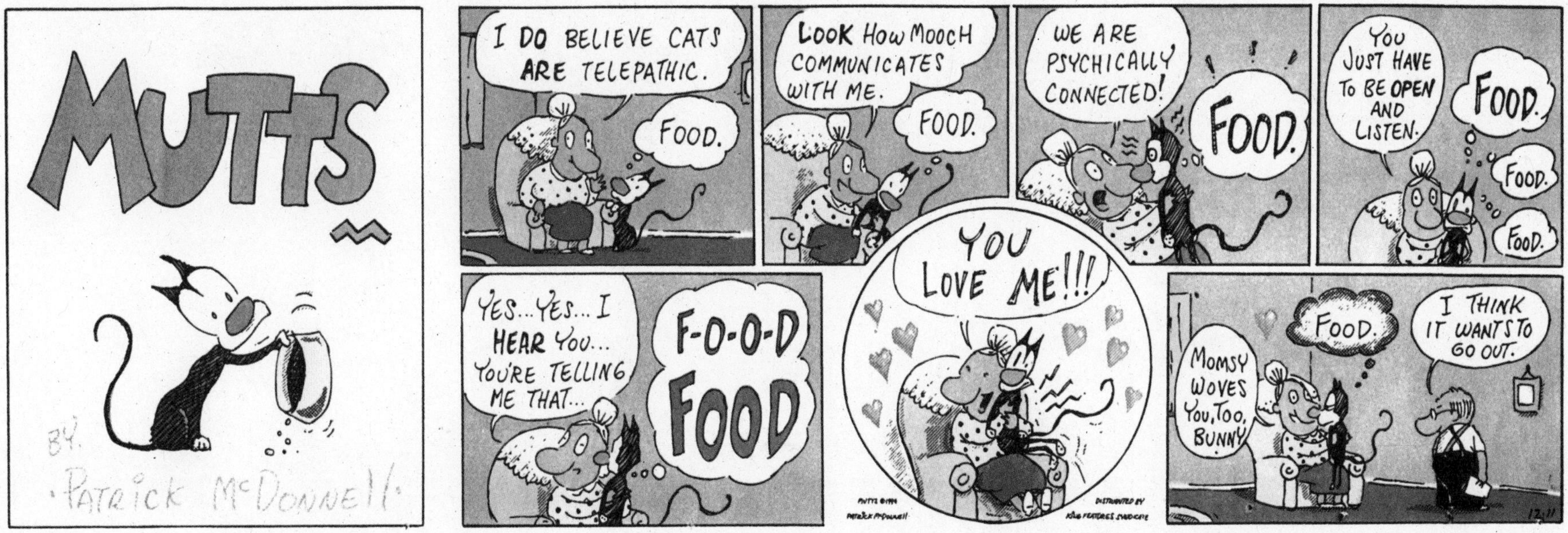
MUTTS
BY. PATRICK McDONNELL
I DO BELIEVE CATS ARE TELEPATHIC.
FOOD.
LOOK HOW MOOCH COMMUNICATES WITH ME.
FOOD.
WE ARE PSYCHICALLY CONNECTED!
FOOD.
YOU JUST HAVE TO BE OPEN AND LISTEN.
FOOD.
FOOD.
FOOD.
YES...YES...I HEAR YOU... YOU'RE TELLING ME THAT...
F-O-O-D FOOD
YOU LOVE ME!!!
FOOD.
MOMSY WOVES YOU, TOO, BUNNY
I THINK IT WANTS TO GO OUT.

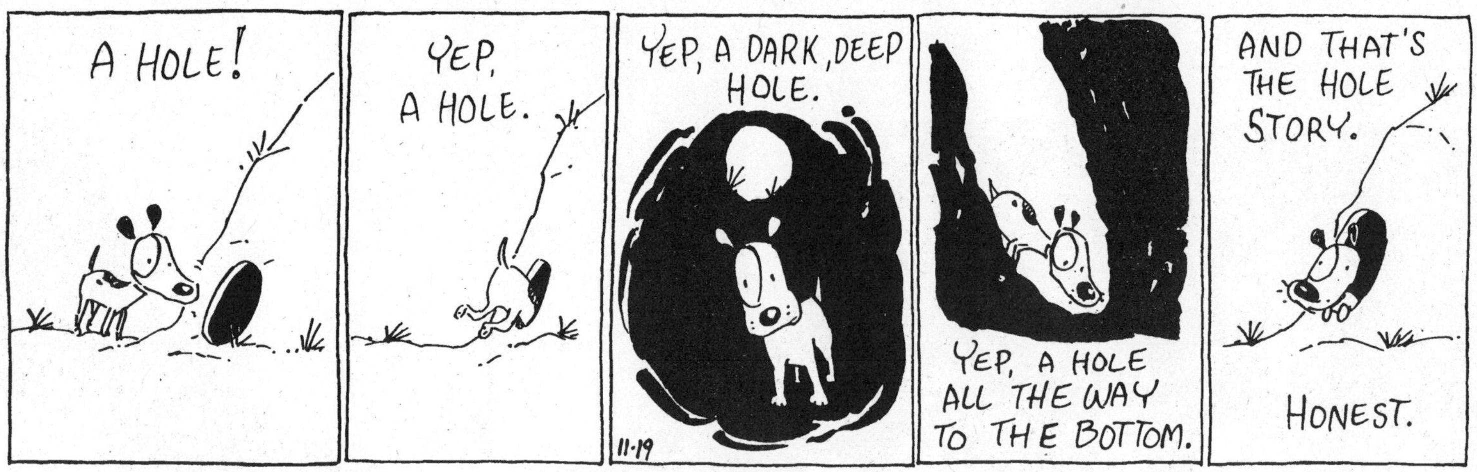
A HOLE!
YEP, A HOLE.
YEP, A DARK, DEEP HOLE.
11·19
YEP, A HOLE ALL THE WAY TO THE BOTTOM.
AND THAT'S THE HOLE STORY.
HONEST.

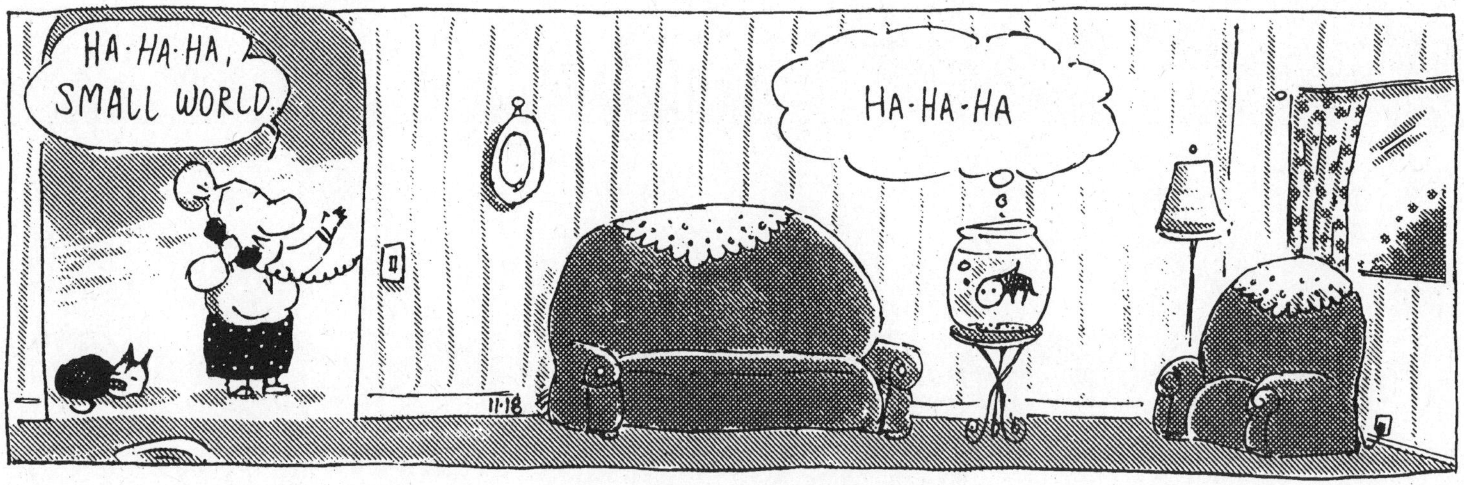
HA·HA·HA, SMALL WORLD.
HA·HA·HA
11·18

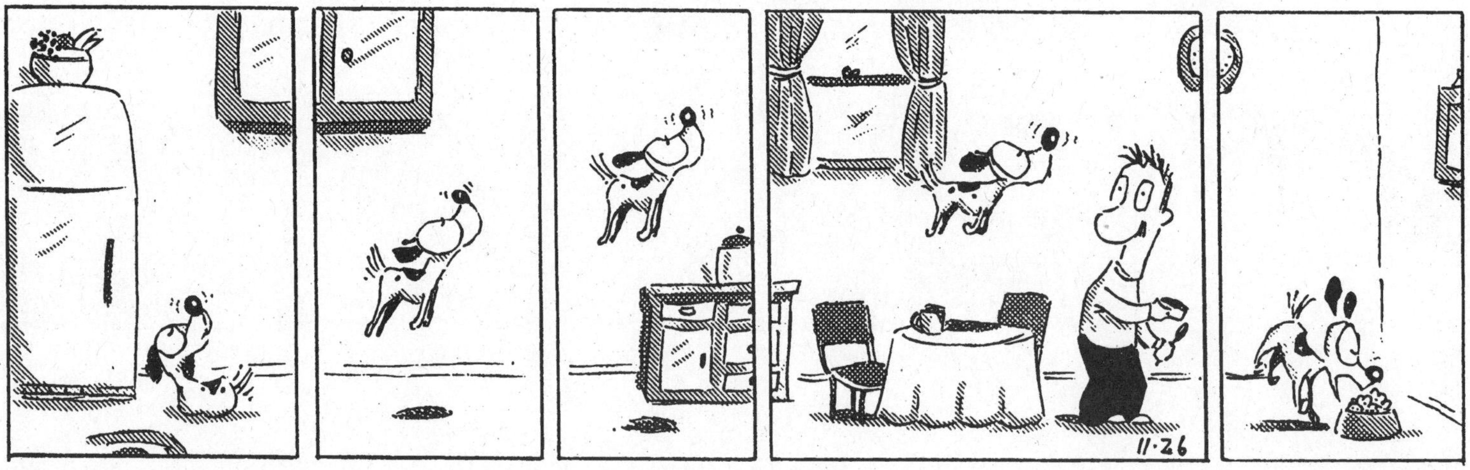
11·26

YAP
YAP
YAP
YAP
YAP
12·2

HEY, CAT, WE'RE REALLY NOT SUPPOSE TO GET ALONG.
SEZ WHO?
MOTHER NATURE
WHO'S SHE?
I'M NOT SURE... I GUESS SHE SORT OF RUNS THE WORLD.
I NEED TO TALK TO HER.
12·1

MY HOUSE.
MY BED.
MY SPOT.
MY LIFE.
12·3

SNIFF
SNIFF
CHOMP
CHOMP
EARL!
12·17

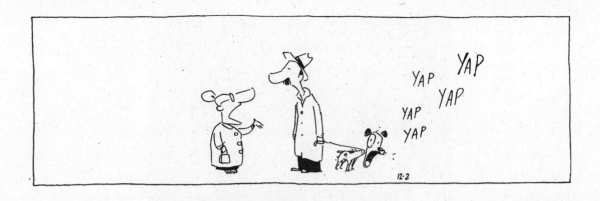

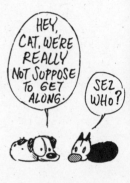

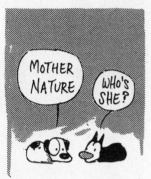

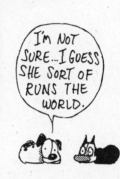

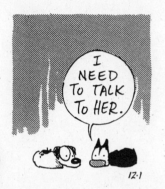

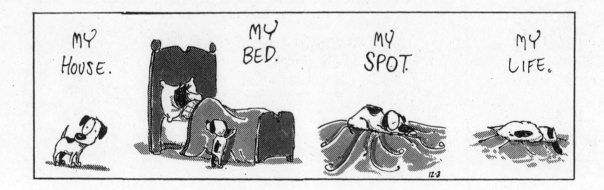

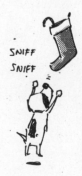

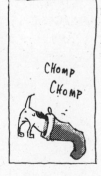

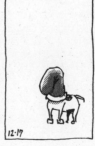

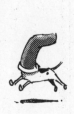

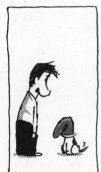

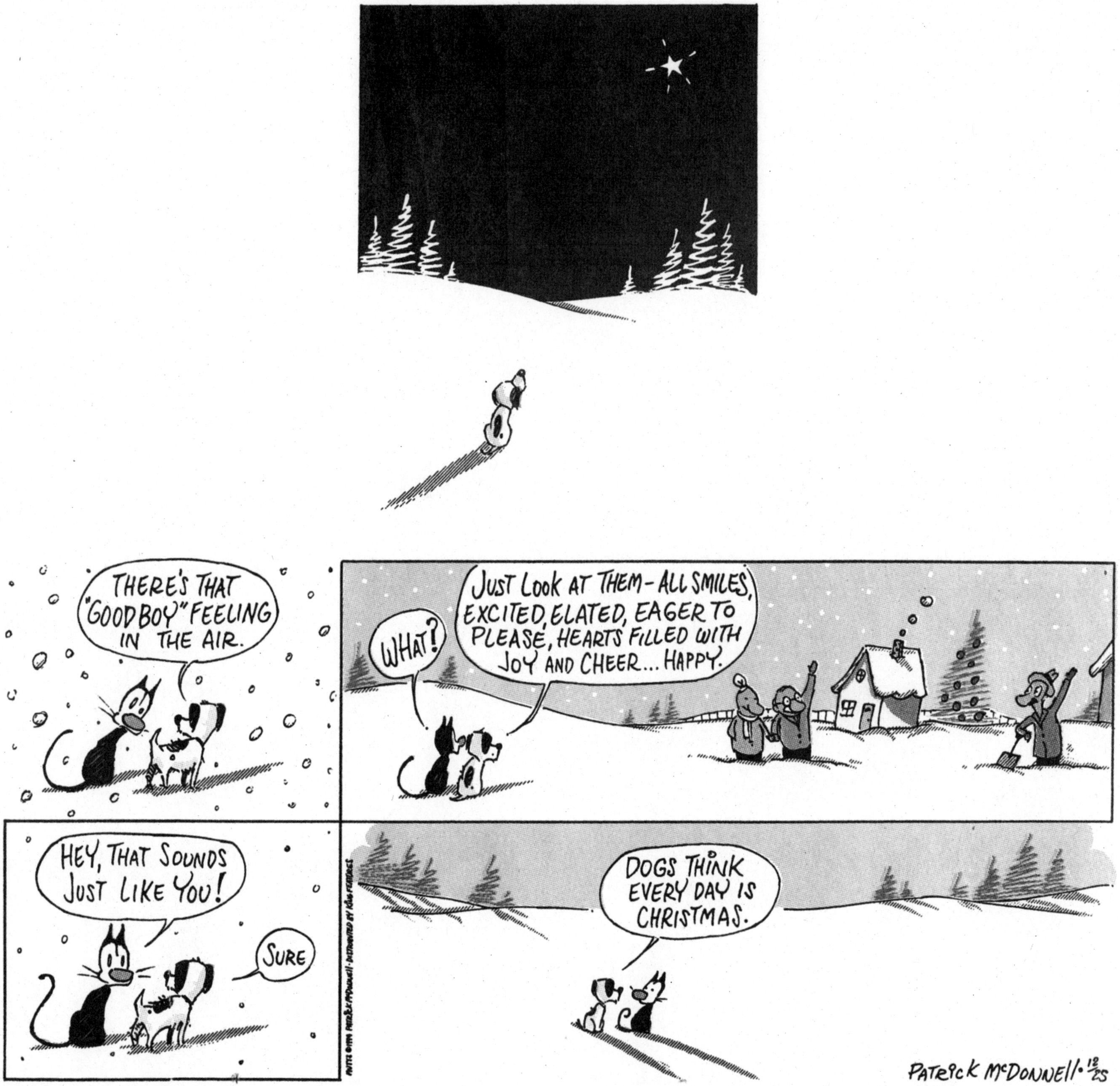
THERE'S THAT "GOOD BOY" FEELING IN THE AIR.
WHAT?
JUST LOOK AT THEM - ALL SMILES, EXCITED, ELATED, EAGER TO PLEASE, HEARTS FILLED WITH JOY AND CHEER... HAPPY.
HEY, THAT SOUNDS JUST LIKE YOU!
SURE
DOGS THINK EVERY DAY IS CHRISTMAS.
PATRICK McDONNELL 12/25

95

**After the first few months** of doing a daily comic strip, its reality sets in. Your small stockpile of jokes has evaporated into the newsprint ether and you're staring blankly at the never-ending deadline. This is where the real art of cartooning begins: learning to float in a sea of uncertainty. It takes some getting used to. You just take it strip by strip, day by day. You begin to have faith in the creative process. The secret is in getting out of the way and letting the ideas come.

In 1995 I was still discovering the nuances of my characters and the art form. My appreciation for all my favorite cartoonists grew by leaps and bounds as I experienced the actualities of the job. *Mutts* is typically a gag-a-day strip with occasional week-long themes and stories. But being a fan of the lost art of adventure/continuity strips, I created my first four-week-long story line: Earl and Mooch getting lost in the woods.

From the beginning, *Mutts* has celebrated the natural world: the beauty of glorious sunsets, luminescent full moons, slow moving clouds, gentle rains, quiet flurries. The ever-changing seasons and the weather they bring play a big part in the strip. The environment and how we treat it is a topic I often find myself going back to again and again.

That fall, the acorn-tossing, head-bonking squirrels Bip and Bop made their first appearance.

We were also introduced to Guard Dog. Here he's a big rough bulldog who I thought could be somewhat of the "bad guy" to the innocent Earl and Mooch. Later, leaning on some cartoon clichés, I drew a chain around his neck to make him appear tougher. I stared at that drawing and thought of the horrible lives these poor, innocent chained dogs endure. My "villain" became a tragic character and, hopefully, a light to shine in this dark area of the human-animal relationship.

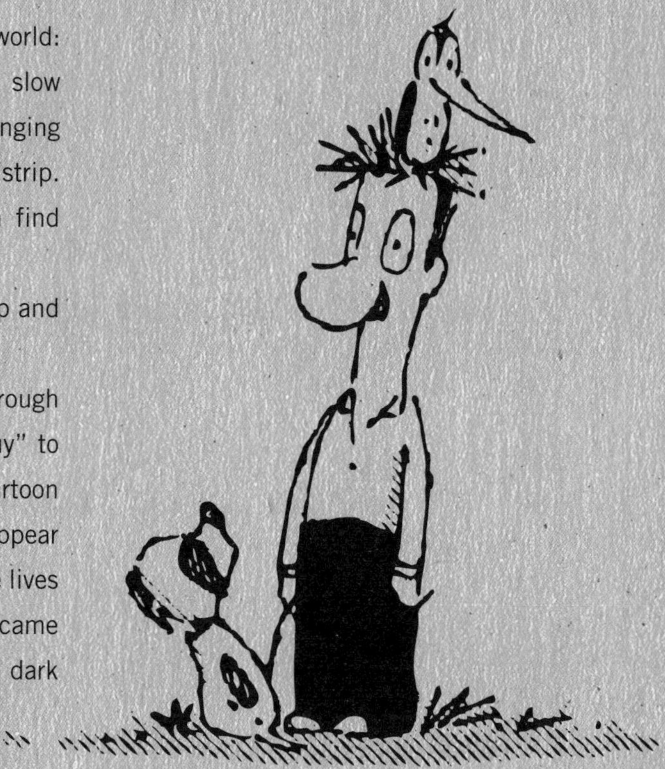

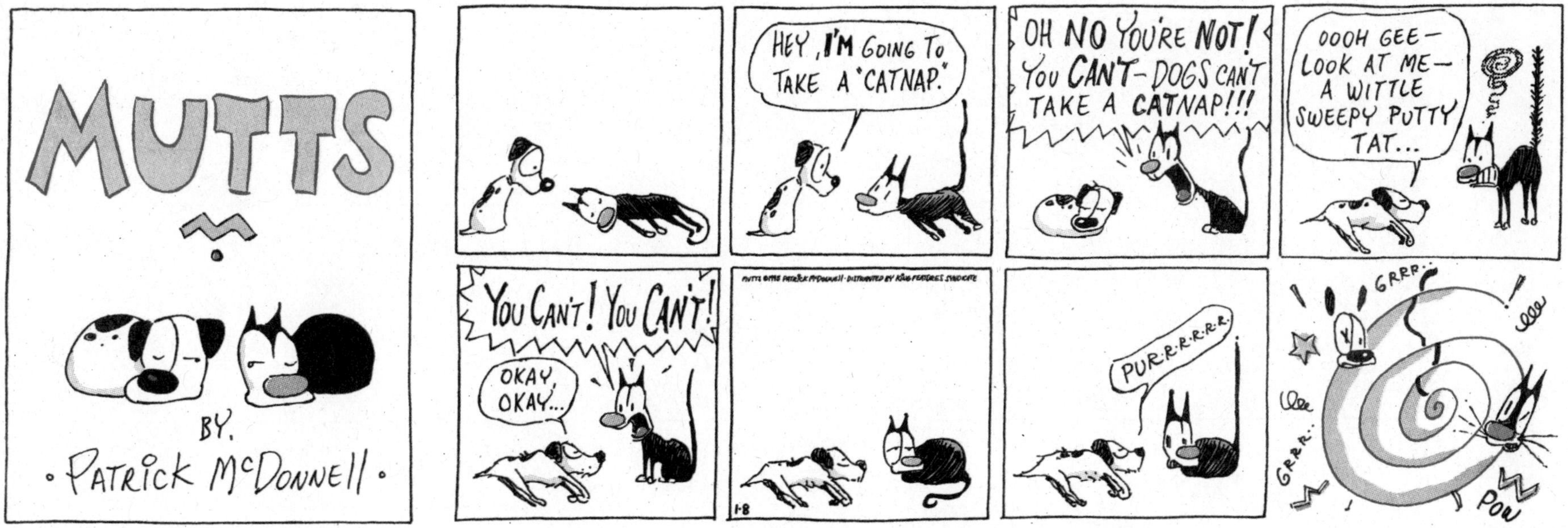
MUTTS
BY, PATRICK McDONNELL
HEY, I'M GOING TO TAKE A "CATNAP."
OH NO YOU'RE NOT! YOU CAN'T- DOGS CAN'T TAKE A CATNAP!!!
OOOH GEE— LOOK AT ME— A WITTLE SWEEPY PUTTY TAT...
YOU CAN'T! YOU CAN'T!
OKAY, OKAY...
1-8
PUR-R-R-R-R-R.
GRRR..
GRRR..
POW

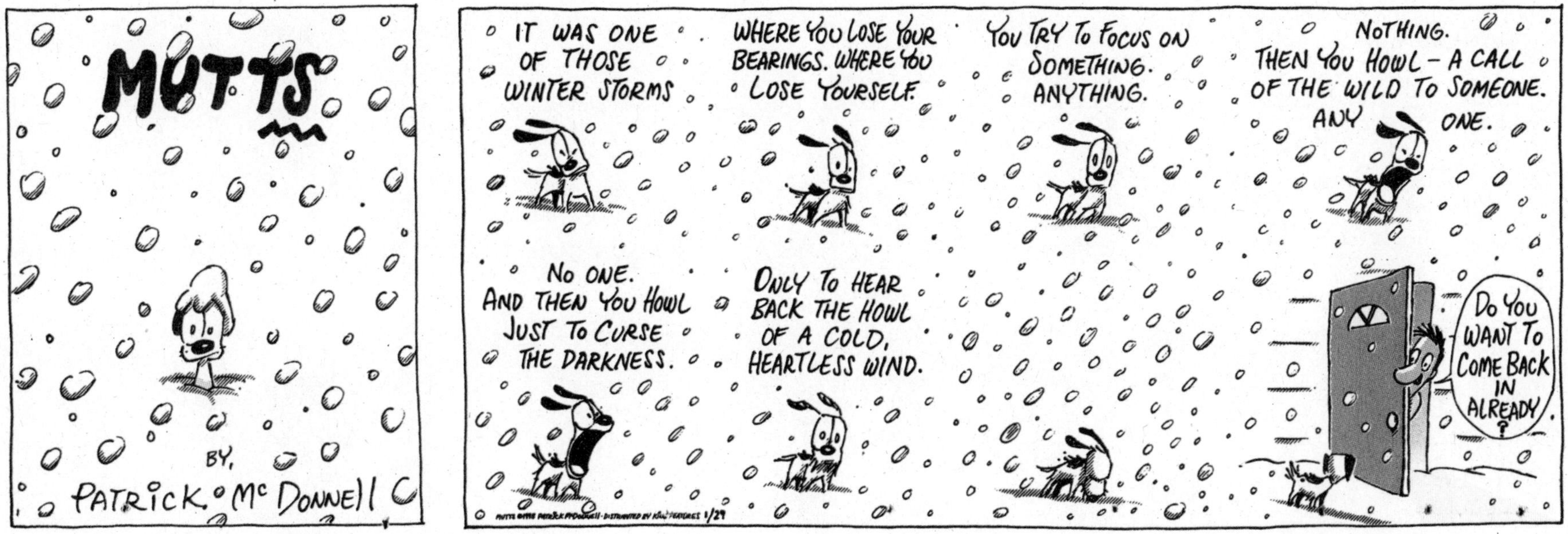
MUTTS
BY, PATRICK McDONNELL
IT WAS ONE OF THOSE WINTER STORMS
WHERE YOU LOSE YOUR BEARINGS. WHERE YOU LOSE YOURSELF.
YOU TRY TO FOCUS ON SOMETHING. ANYTHING.
NOTHING. THEN YOU HOWL – A CALL OF THE WILD TO SOMEONE. ANY ONE.
NO ONE. AND THEN YOU HOWL JUST TO CURSE THE DARKNESS.
ONLY TO HEAR BACK THE HOWL OF A COLD, HEARTLESS WIND.
DO YOU WANT TO COME BACK IN ALREADY?
1/29

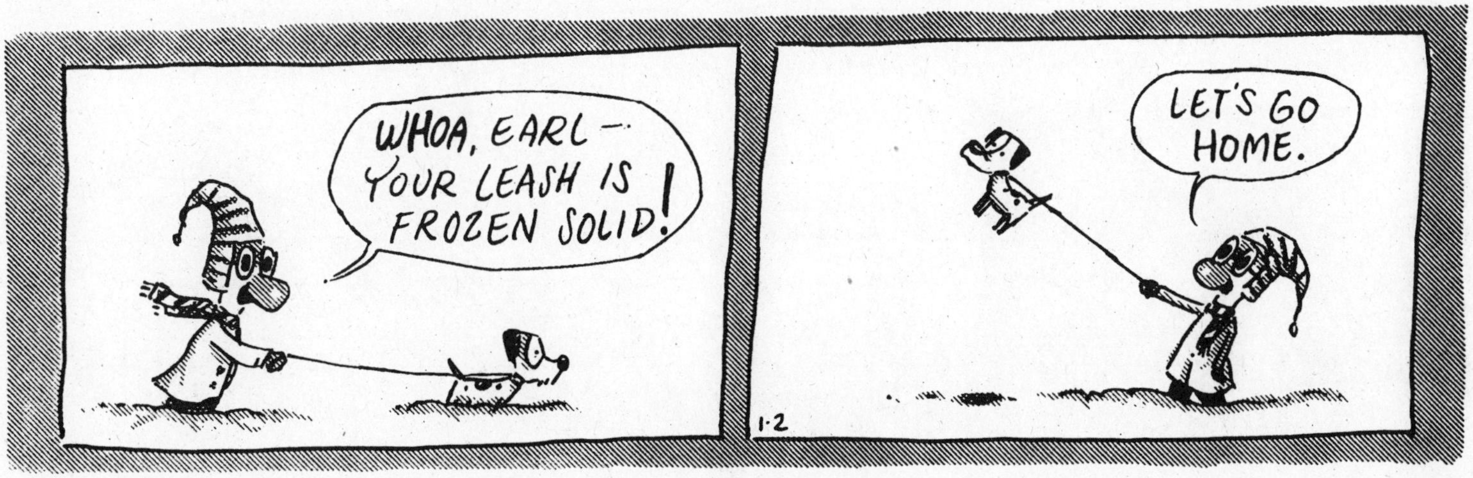
WHOA, EARL— YOUR LEASH IS FROZEN SOLID!
LET'S GO HOME.
1·2

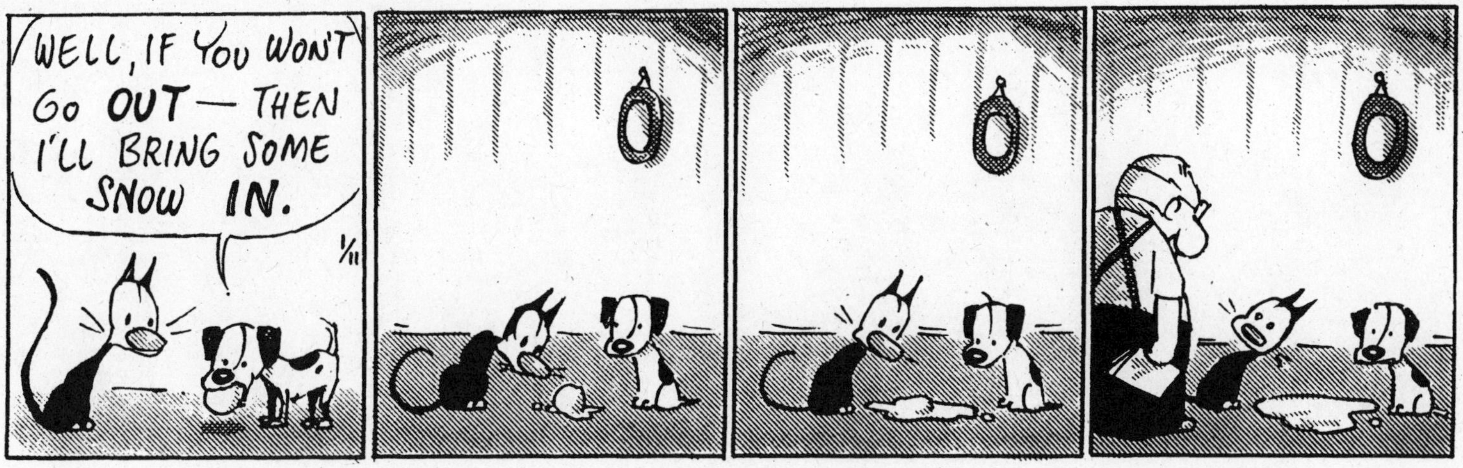
WELL, IF YOU WON'T GO OUT— THEN I'LL BRING SOME SNOW IN.
1/11

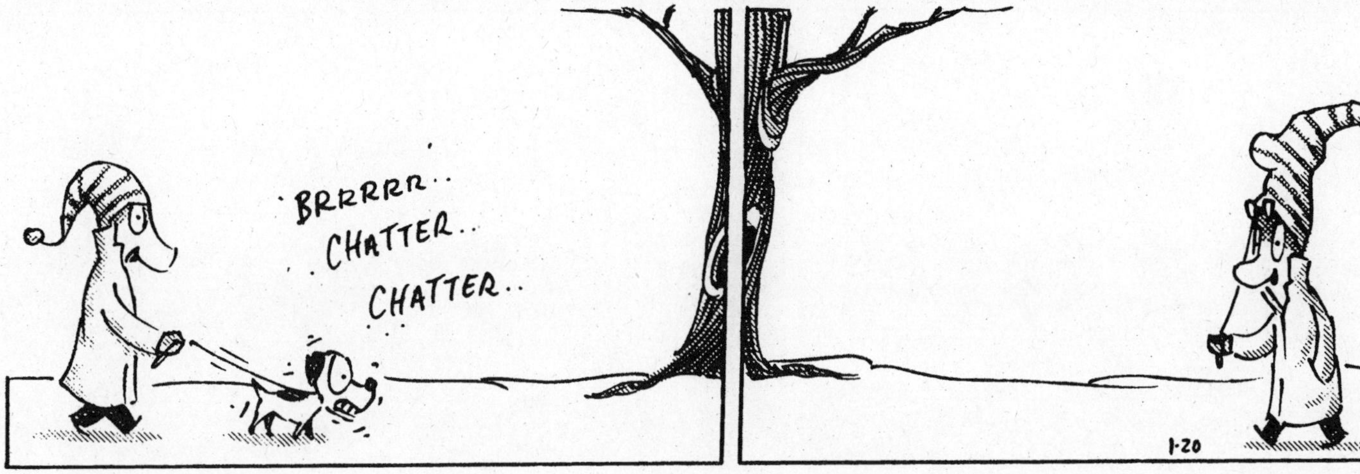
BRRRRR..
CHATTER..
CHATTER..
1·20

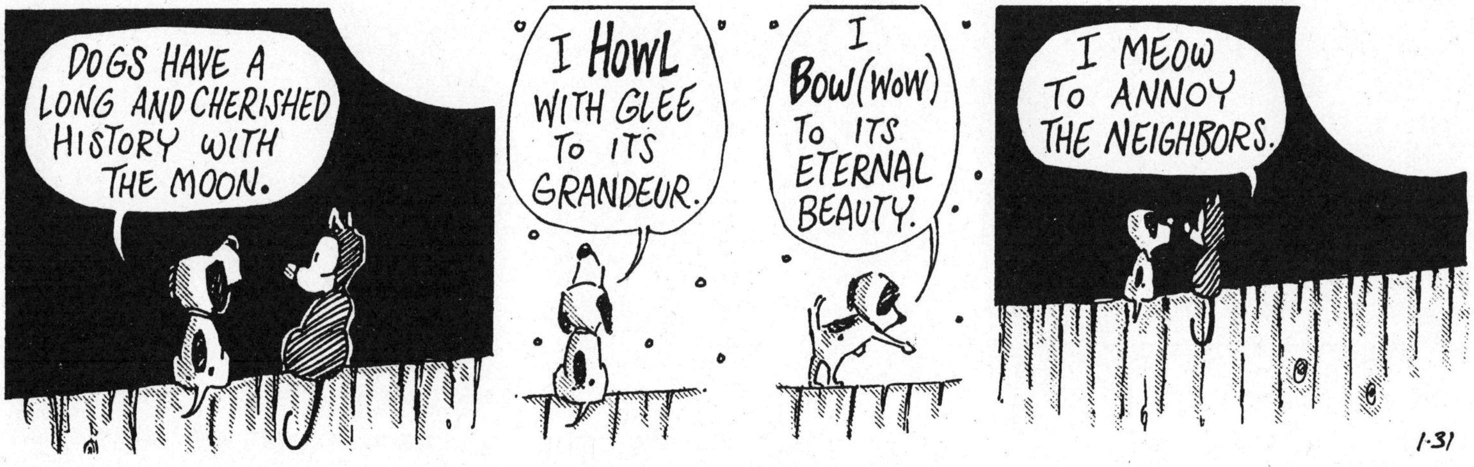
DOGS HAVE A LONG AND CHERISHED HISTORY WITH THE MOON.
I HOWL WITH GLEE TO ITS GRANDEUR.
I BOW(WOW) TO ITS ETERNAL BEAUTY.
I MEOW TO ANNOY THE NEIGHBORS.
1-31

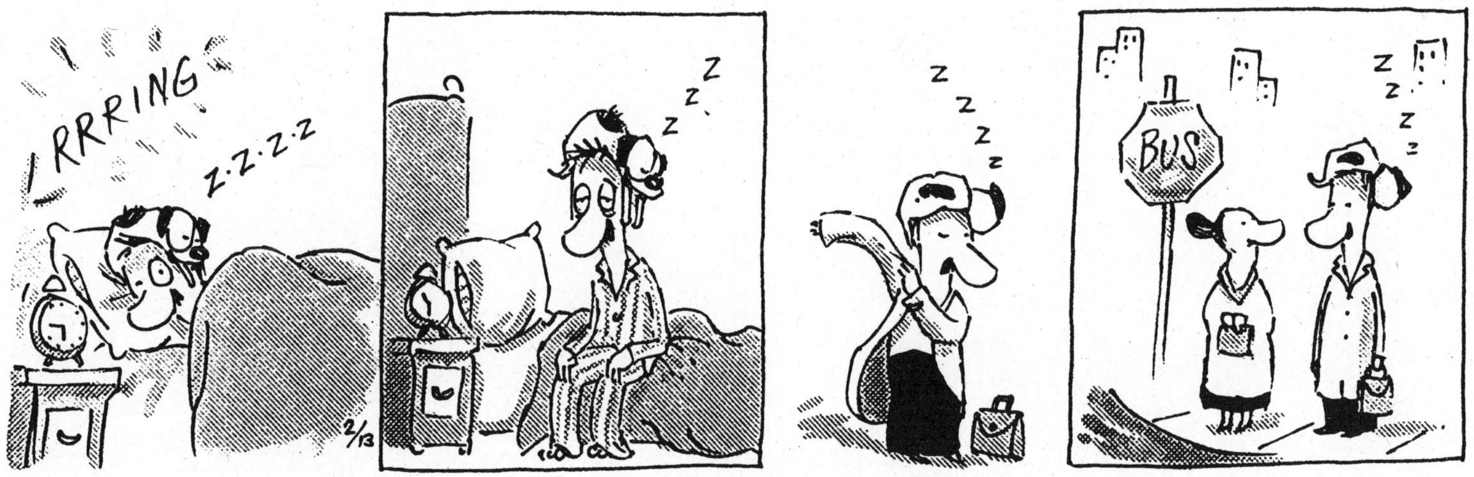
RRRING
Z·Z·Z·Z
2/13
Z Z Z
Z Z Z Z
BUS
Z Z Z Z

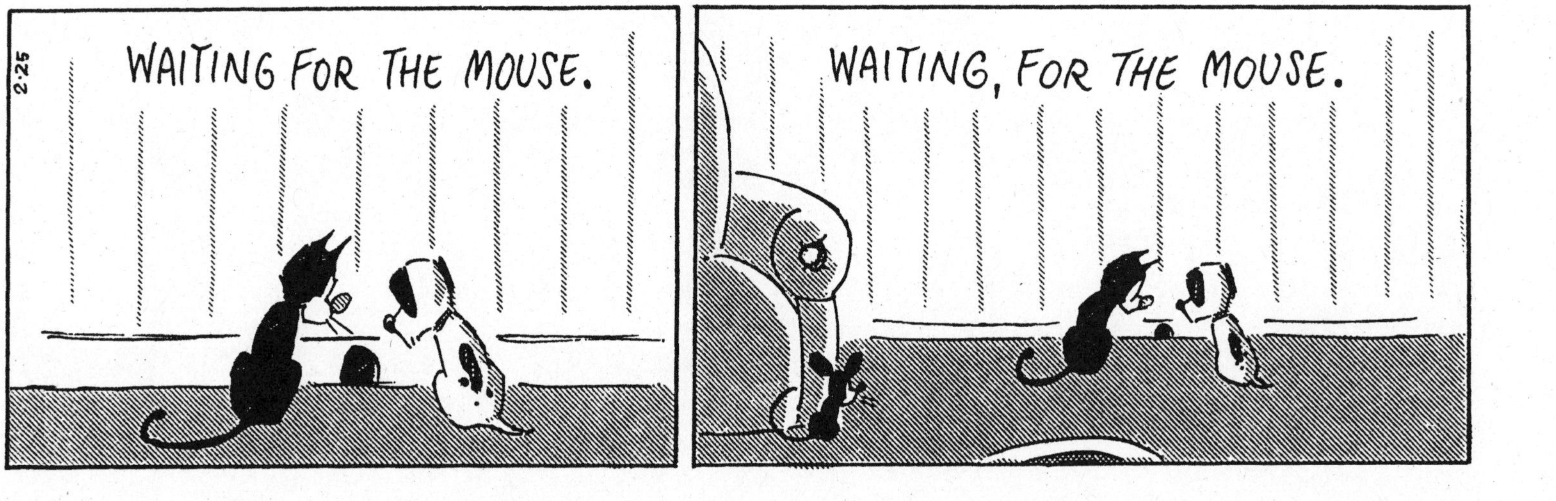
2·25
WAITING FOR THE MOUSE.
WAITING, FOR THE MOUSE.

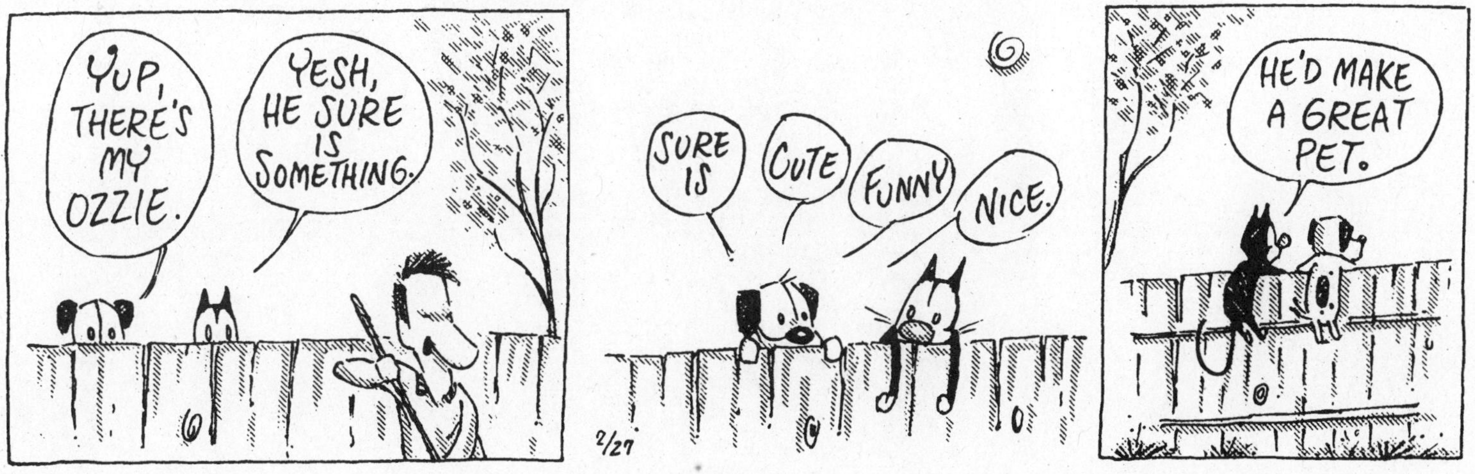
YUP, THERE'S MY OZZIE.
YESH, HE SURE IS SOMETHING.
SURE IS
CUTE
FUNNY
NICE.
HE'D MAKE A GREAT PET.
2/27

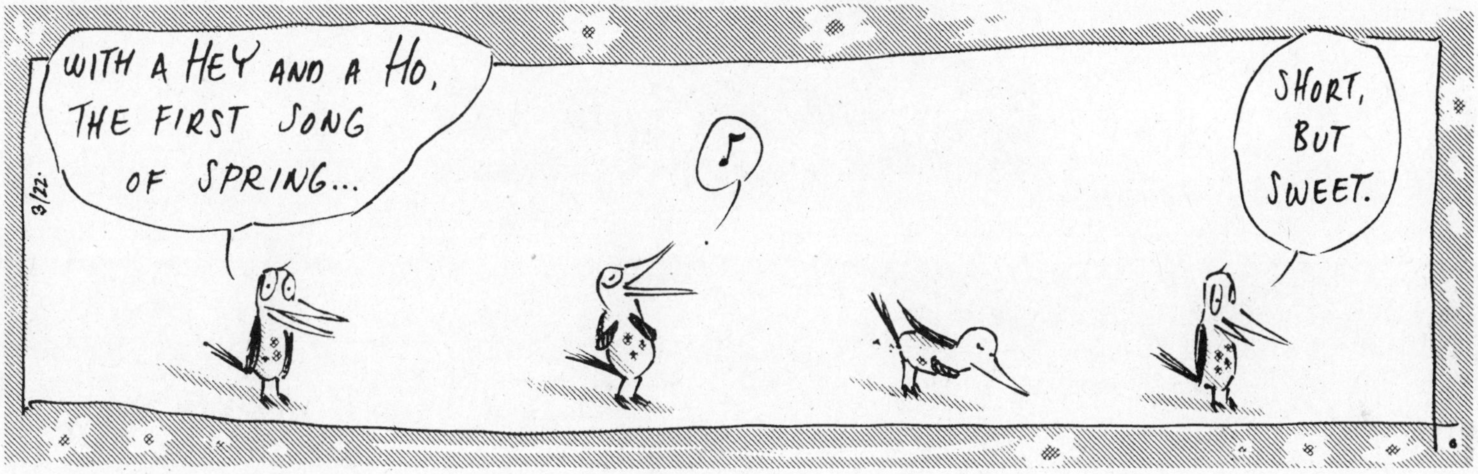
WITH A HEY AND A HO, THE FIRST SONG OF SPRING...
SHORT, BUT SWEET.
3/22

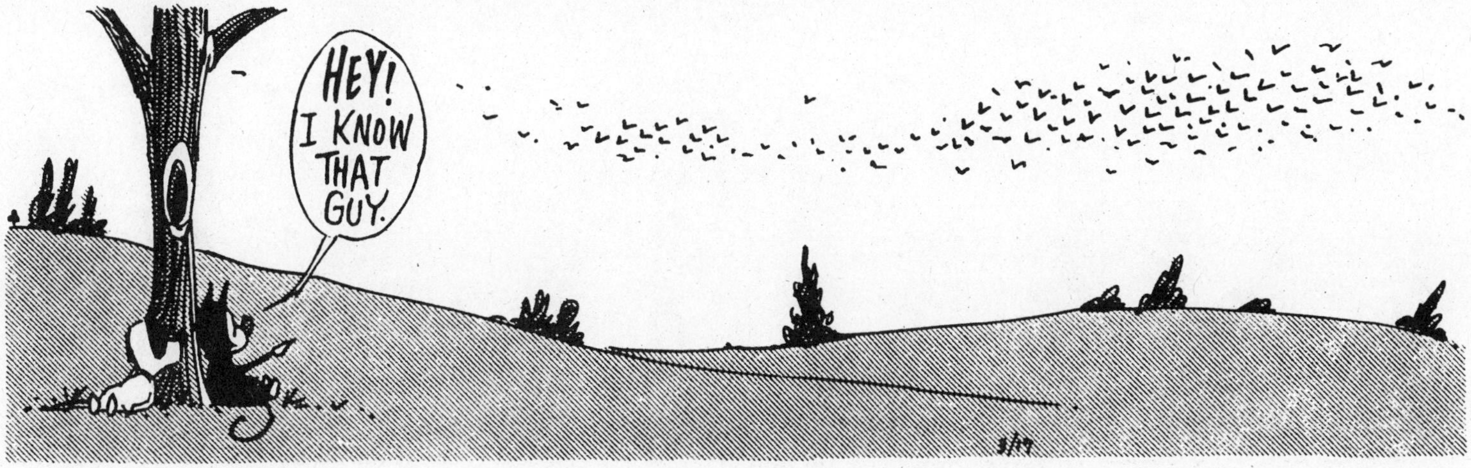
HEY! I KNOW THAT GUY.
3/19

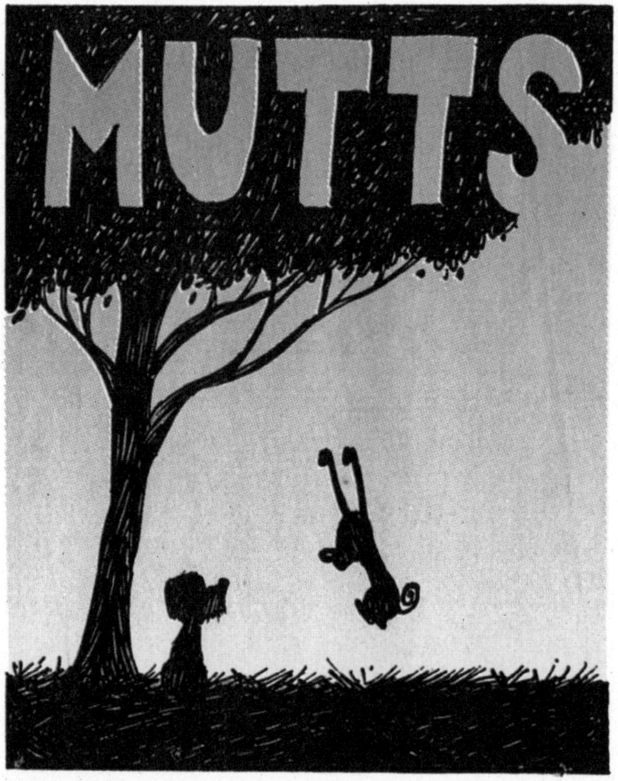
MUTTS

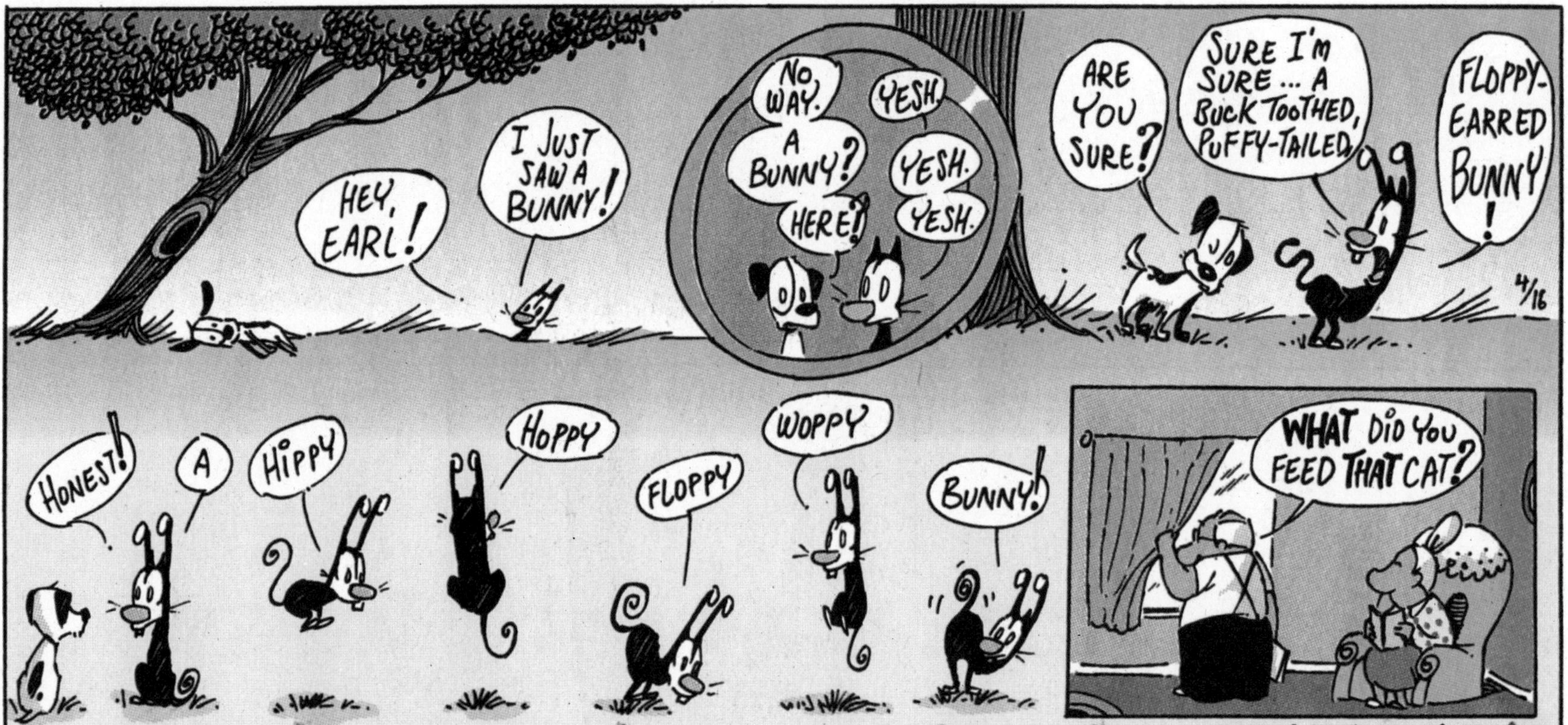
HEY, EARL!
I JUST SAW A BUNNY!
NO WAY.
A BUNNY?
HERE!
YESH.
YESH.
YESH.
ARE YOU SURE?
SURE I'M SURE ... A BUCK TOOTHED, PUFFY-TAILED,
FLOPPY-EARRED BUNNY!
4/16
HONEST!
A
HIPPY
HOPPY
FLOPPY
WOPPY
BUNNY!
WHAT DID YOU FEED THAT CAT?

WHOA-IT LOOKS LIKE RAIN-LET'S GET OUT OF HERE!
WHY?
4/10
CATS DO NOT LIKE TO GET WET. WE HATE WATER!
THEN HOW COME YOU'RE ALWAYS WASHING YOURSELVES?
WE LIKE SPIT.

BUS

EARL, ARE YOU ASLEEP?
YES
4-20
LET SLEEPING DOGS LIE.

PAT
PAT
PAT
4/21
Z.Z.Z.Z.
PAT
PAT
PAT

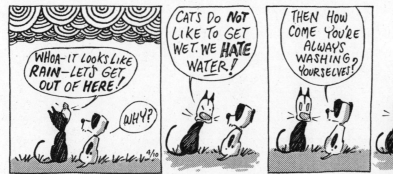

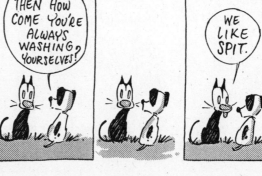

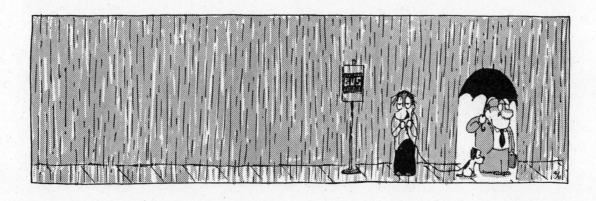

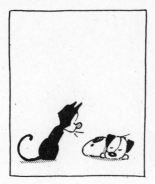

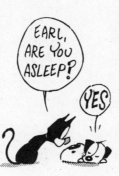

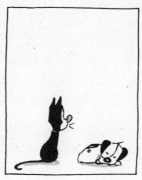

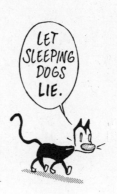

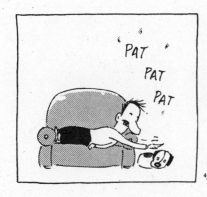

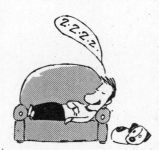

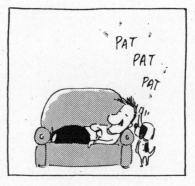

MOOCH! LOOK AT YOU!! YOU LAZY CAT!!! ALWAYS NAPPING!
WHO RAISED YOU LIKE THAT!?! WHERE DID YOU COME FROM!?!
THAT TOP BRANCH.

MOOCH! THAT WAS SOME NASTY FALL YOU TOOK. ARE YOU OKAY? IS THERE ANYTHING I CAN DO!?!
ANYTHING
YESH
GET OFF MY TAIL.

GEEZ, THAT WAS SOME FALL!
YESH.
OOOOOH, I THINK I SEE ONE OF MY NINE LIVES PASSING BEFORE ME...
I WONDER WHICH ONE IT IS?
THE SMART ONE?

IF YOU FALL OFF A HORSE- YOU GET RIGHT BACK ON.
TO FALL AGAIN? DON'T BE STUPID!
HEY! I CAN SEE YOUR HOUSE FROM HERE.

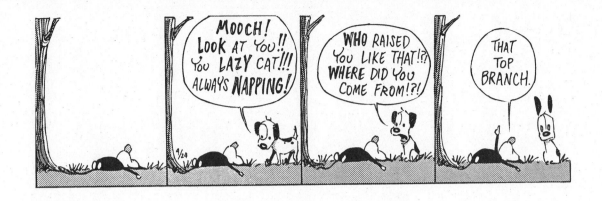

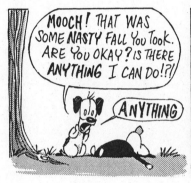

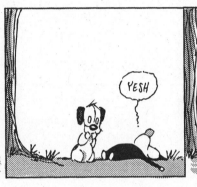

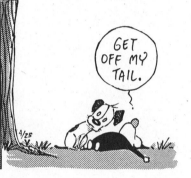

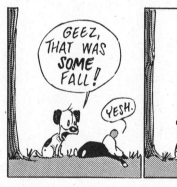

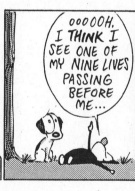

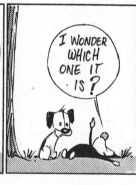

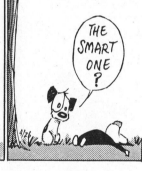

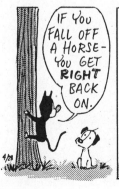

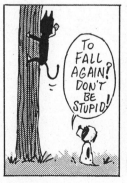

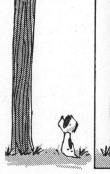

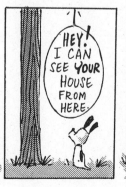

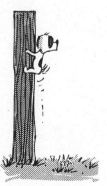

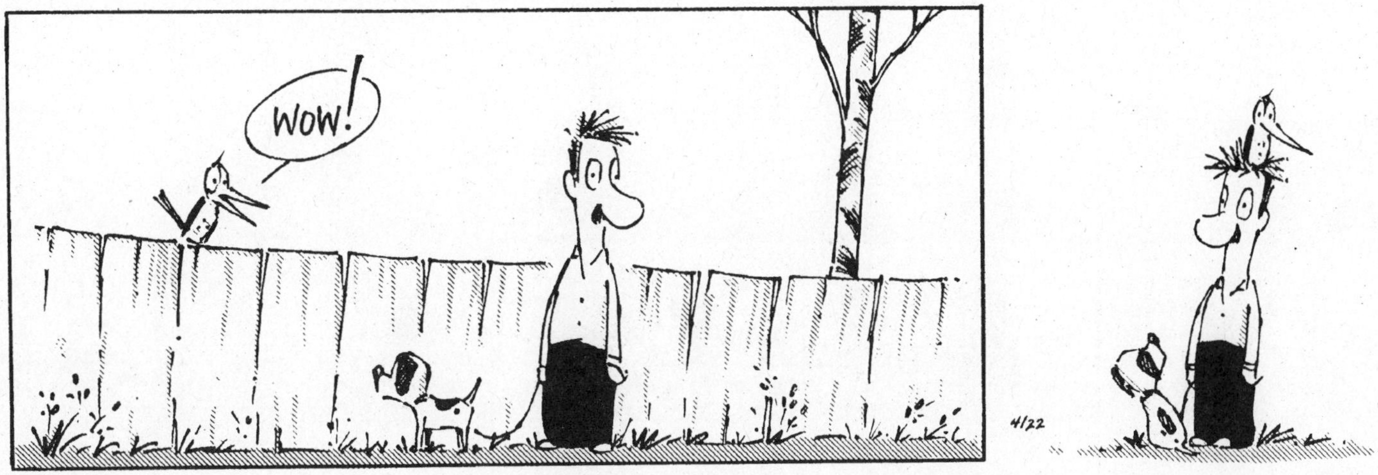
WOW!
4/22

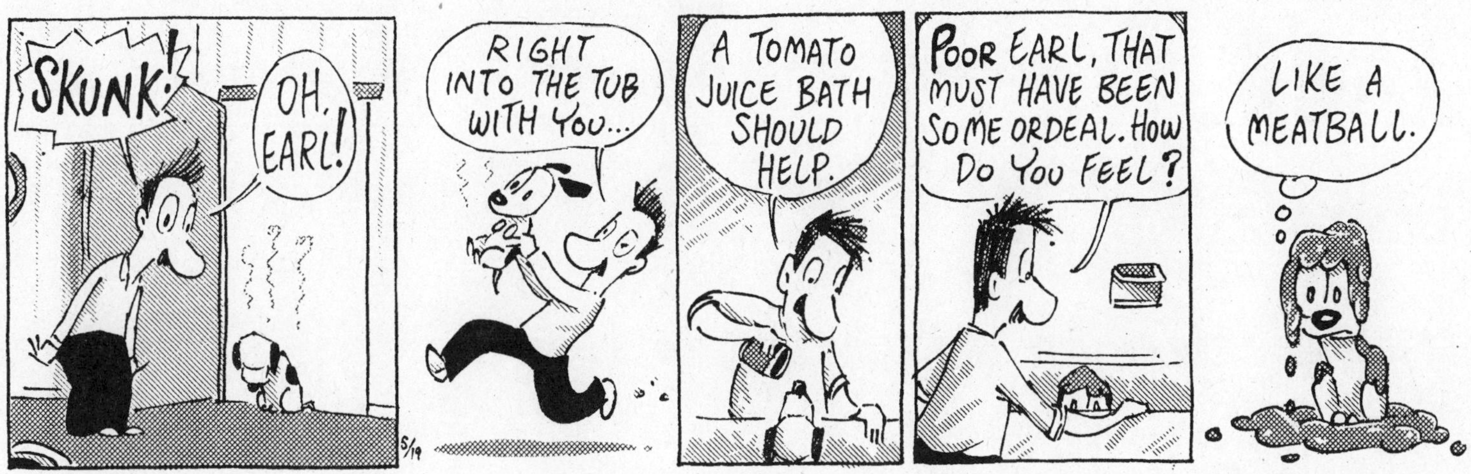
SKUNK!
OH, EARL!
5/19
RIGHT INTO THE TUB WITH YOU...
A TOMATO JUICE BATH SHOULD HELP.
POOR EARL, THAT MUST HAVE BEEN SOME ORDEAL. HOW DO YOU FEEL?
LIKE A MEATBALL.

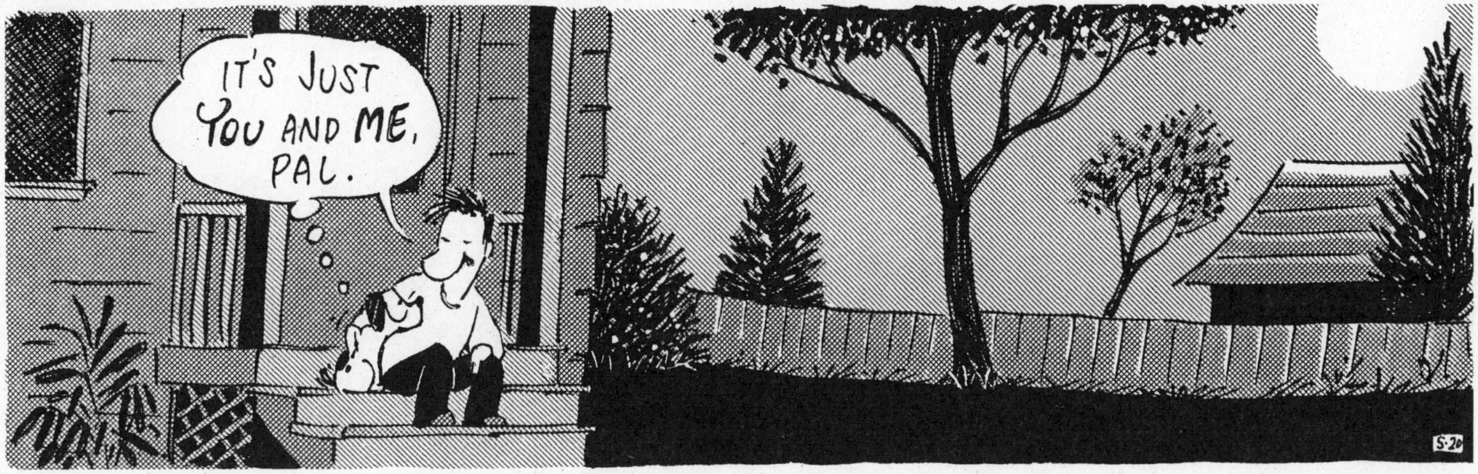
IT'S JUST YOU AND ME, PAL.
5-20

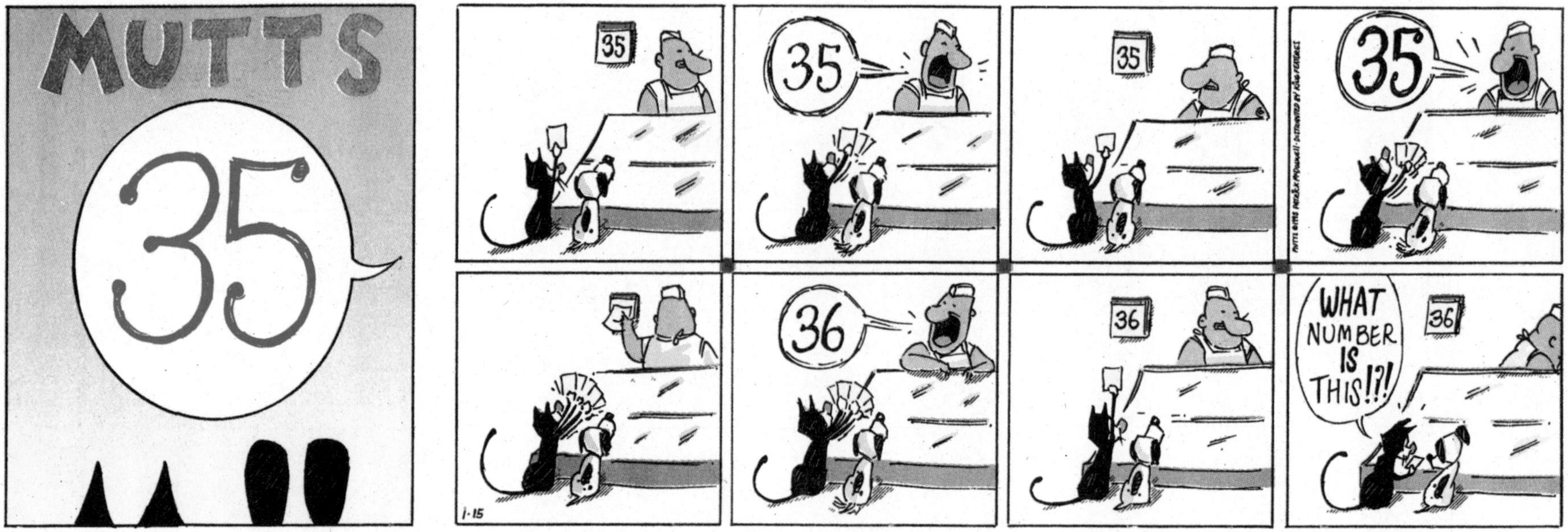
MUTTS
35
35
35
35
35
36
36
WHAT NUMBER IS THIS!?!
36
1-15

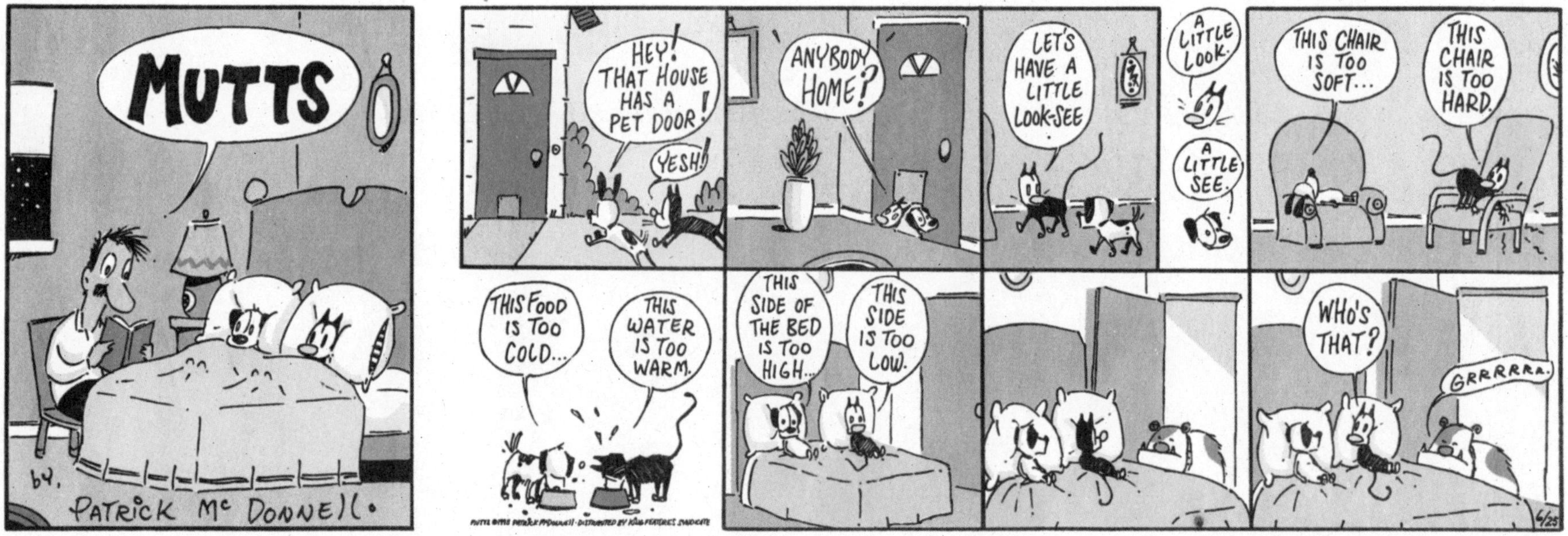
MUTTS
by, PATRICK Mc DONNELL.
HEY! THAT HOUSE HAS A PET DOOR!
YESH!
ANYBODY HOME?
LET'S HAVE A LITTLE LOOK-SEE
A LITTLE LOOK.
A LITTLE SEE.
THIS CHAIR IS TOO SOFT...
THIS CHAIR IS TOO HARD.
THIS FOOD IS TOO COLD...
THIS WATER IS TOO WARM.
THIS SIDE OF THE BED IS TOO HIGH...
THIS SIDE IS TOO LOW.
WHO'S THAT?
GRRRRRA.
6/25

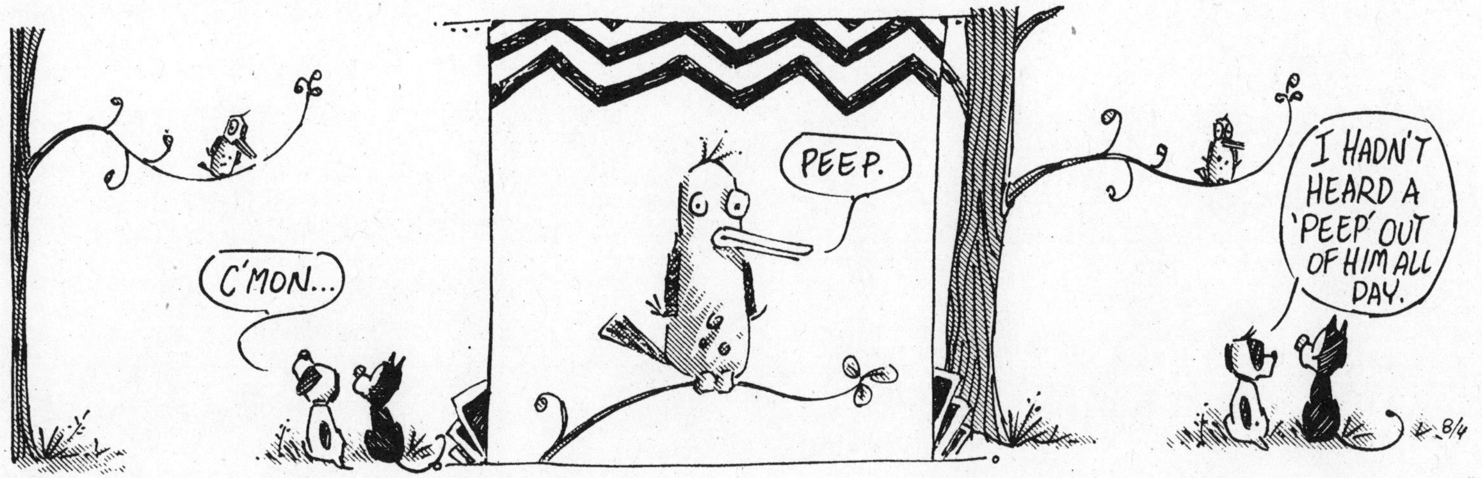
C'MON...
PEEP.
I HADN'T HEARD A 'PEEP' OUT OF HIM ALL DAY.

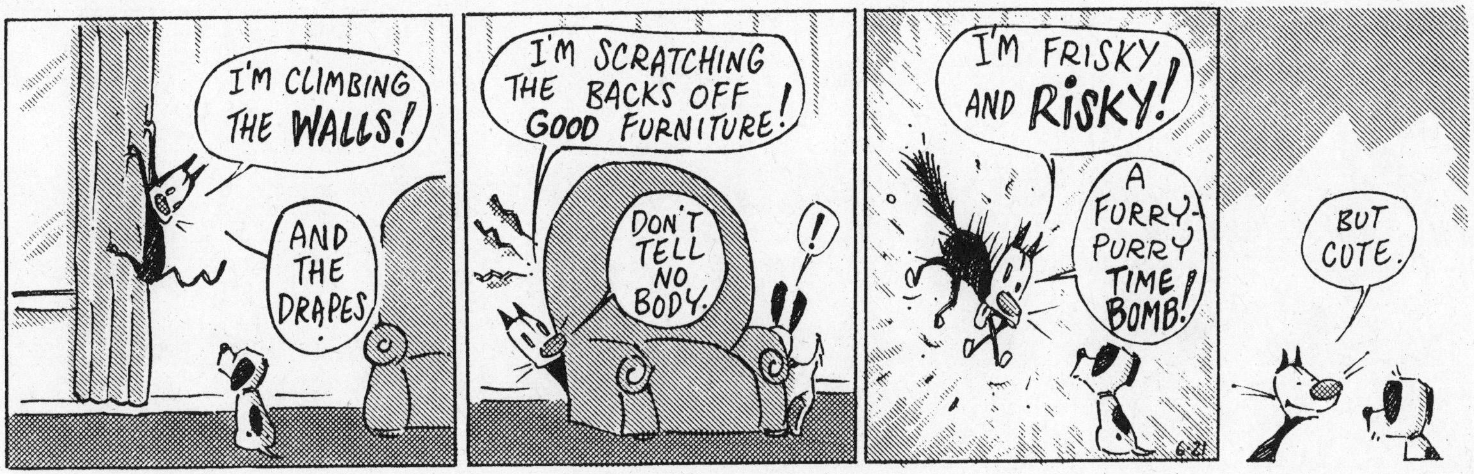
I'M CLIMBING THE WALLS!
AND THE DRAPES.
I'M SCRATCHING THE BACKS OFF GOOD FURNITURE!
DON'T TELL NO BODY.
!
I'M FRISKY AND RISKY!
A FURRY-PURRY TIME BOMB!
BUT CUTE.

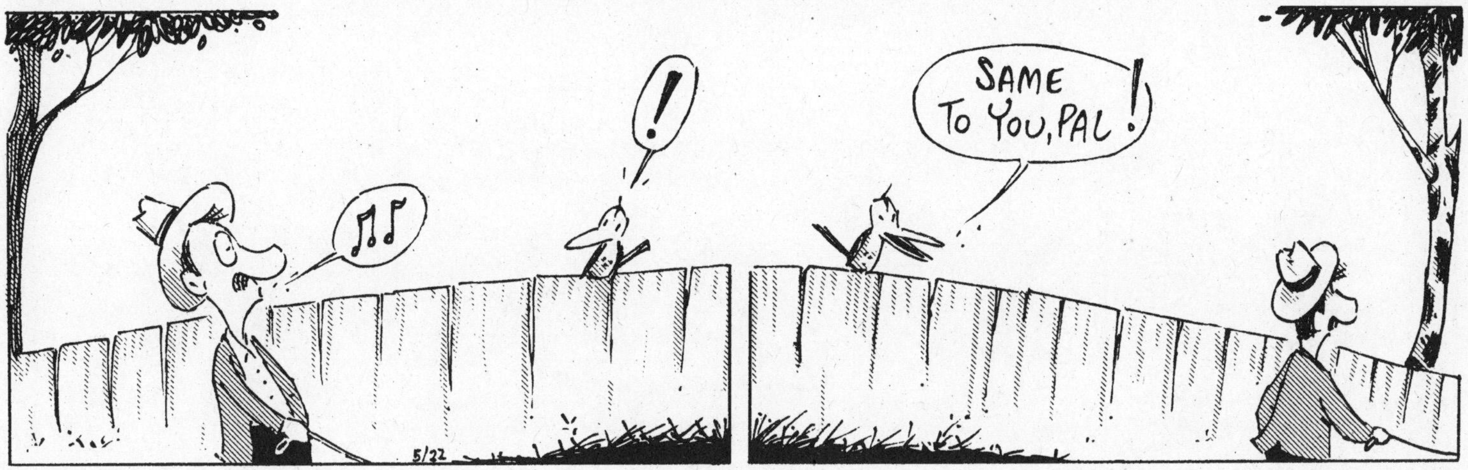
!
SAME TO YOU, PAL!

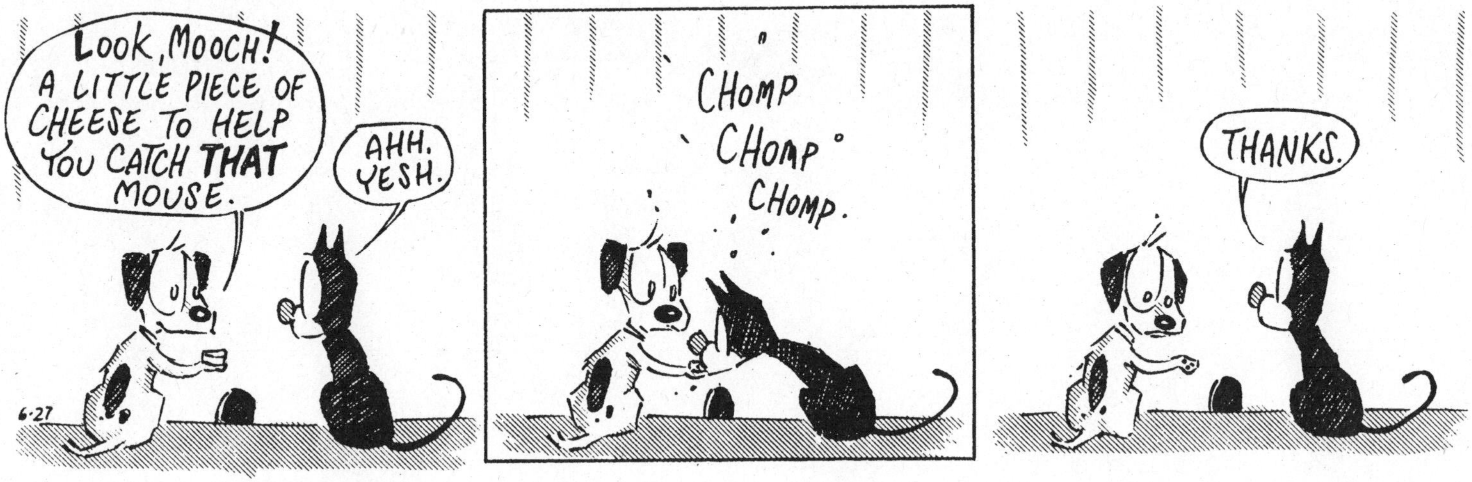
LOOK, MOOCH! A LITTLE PIECE OF CHEESE TO HELP YOU CATCH THAT MOUSE.
AHH. YESH.
6·27
CHOMP
CHOMP
CHOMP.
THANKS.

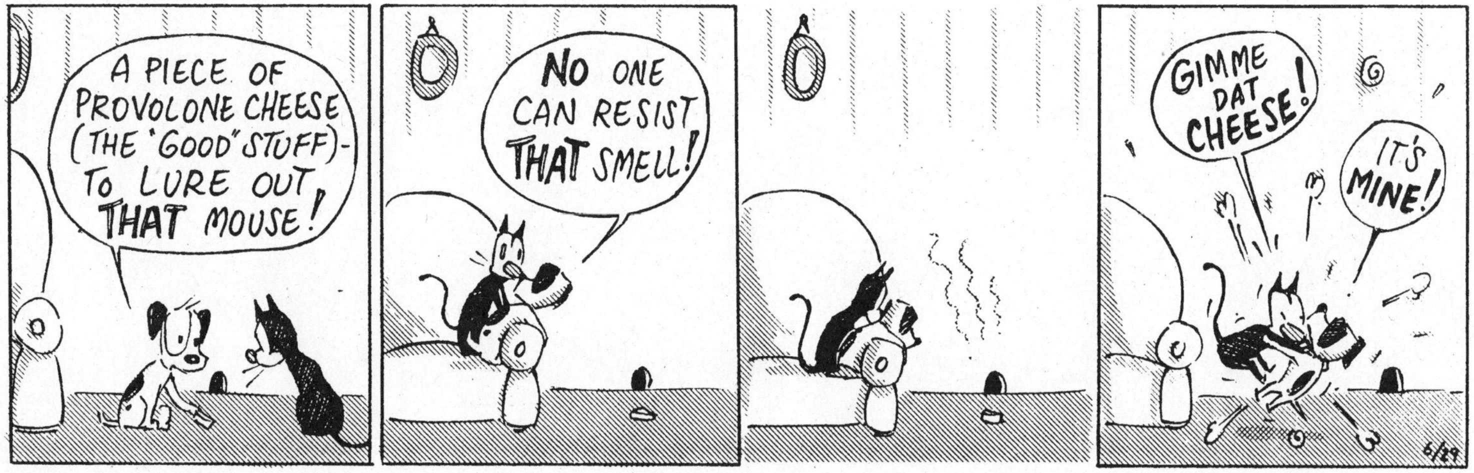
A PIECE OF PROVOLONE CHEESE (THE "GOOD" STUFF)- TO LURE OUT THAT MOUSE!
NO ONE CAN RESIST THAT SMELL!
GIMME DAT CHEESE!
IT'S MINE!
6/29

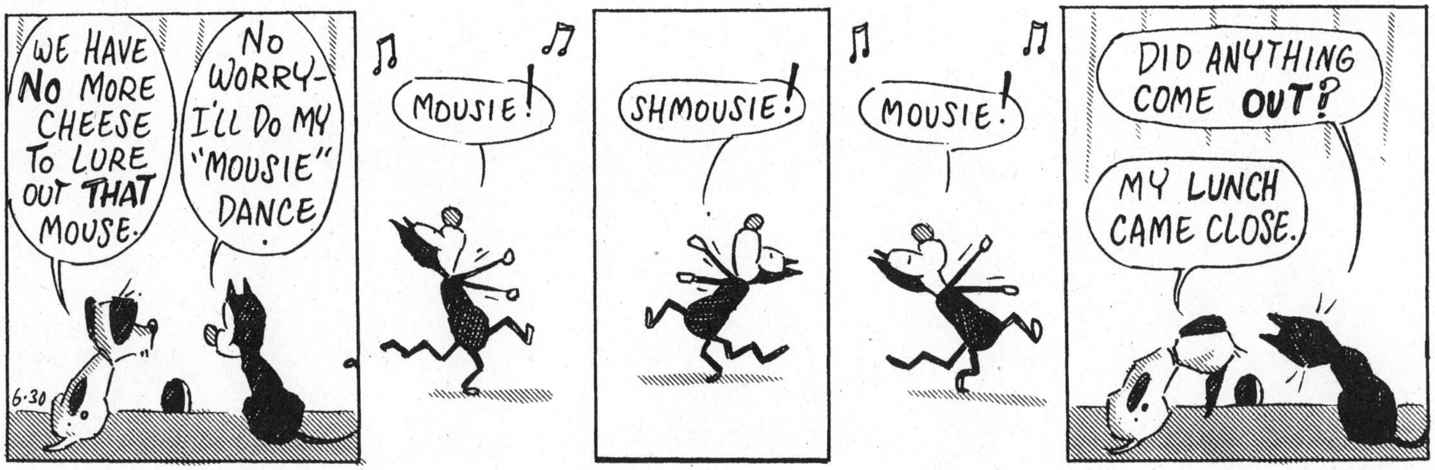
WE HAVE NO MORE CHEESE TO LURE OUT THAT MOUSE.
NO WORRY- I'LL DO MY "MOUSIE" DANCE.
6·30
MOUSIE!
SHMOUSIE!
MOUSIE!
DID ANYTHING COME OUT?
MY LUNCH CAME CLOSE.

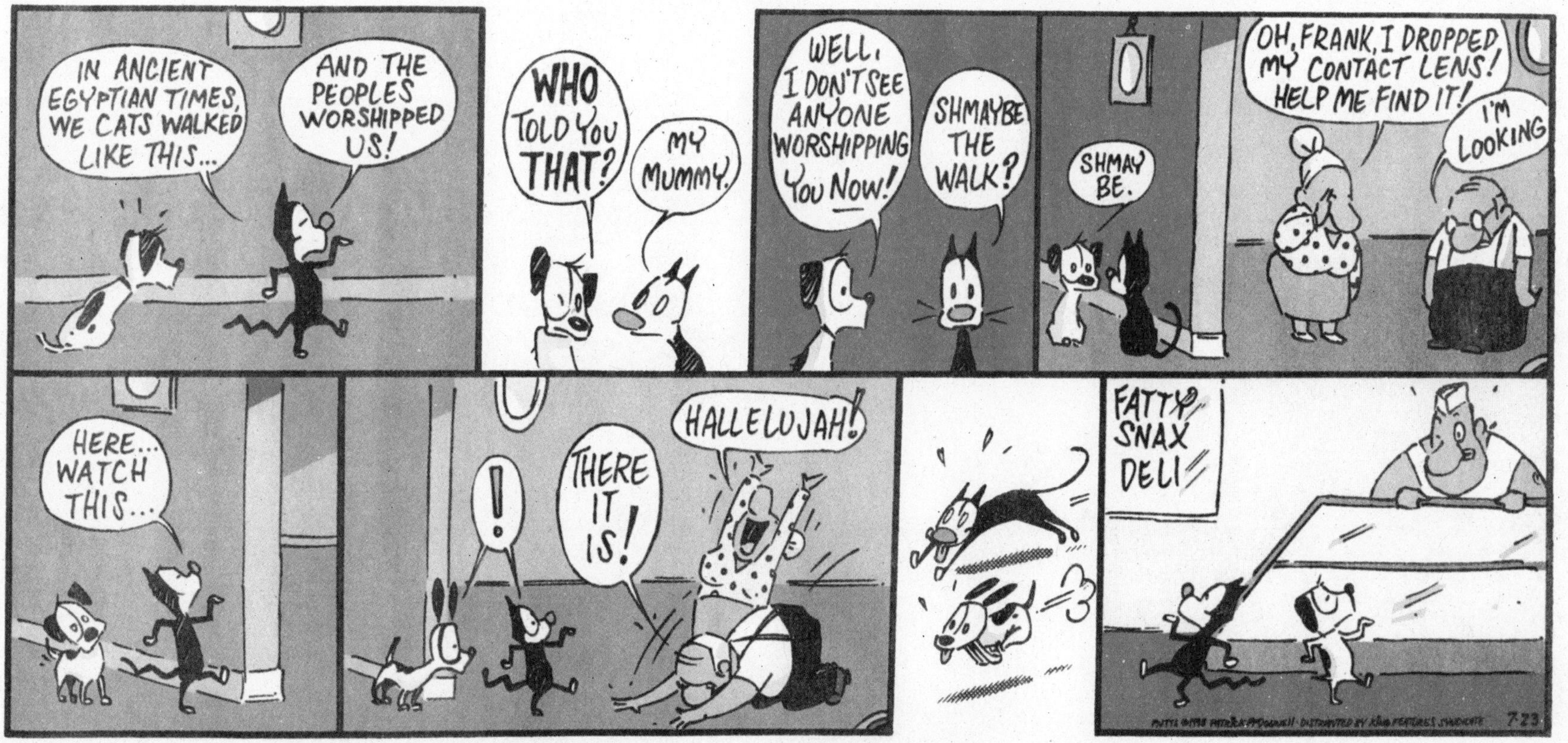
IN ANCIENT EGYPTIAN TIMES, WE CATS WALKED LIKE THIS...
AND THE PEOPLES WORSHIPPED US!
WHO TOLD YOU THAT?
MY MUMMY.
WELL, I DON'T SEE ANYONE WORSHIPPING YOU NOW!
SHMAYBE THE WALK?
SHMAY BE.
OH, FRANK, I DROPPED MY CONTACT LENS! HELP ME FIND IT!
I'M LOOKING
HERE... WATCH THIS...
!
THERE IT IS!
HALLELUJAH!
FATTY SNAX DELI

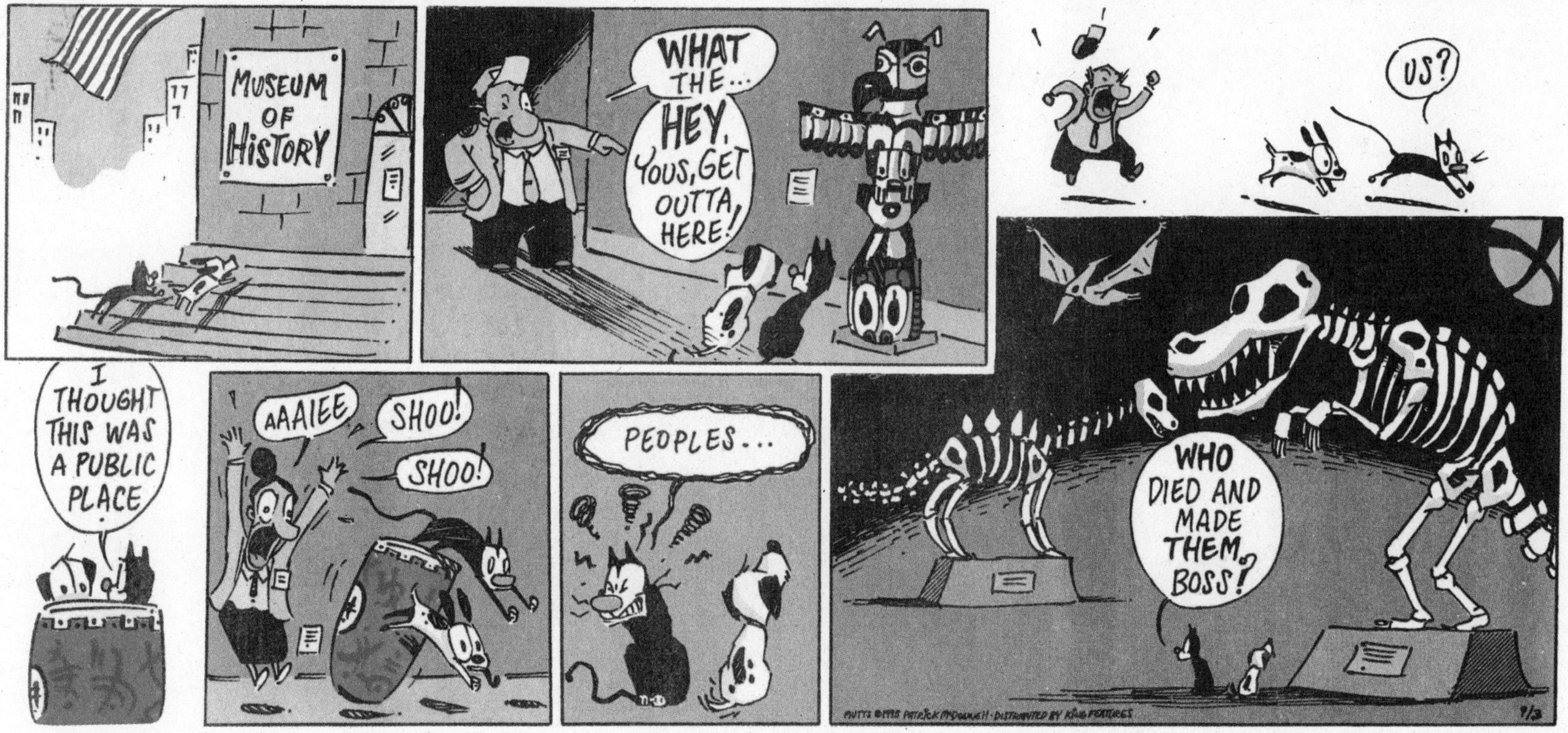
MUSEUM OF HISTORY
WHAT THE...
HEY, YOUS, GET OUTTA HERE!
US?
I THOUGHT THIS WAS A PUBLIC PLACE
AAAIEE
SHOO!
SHOO!
PEOPLES...
WHO DIED AND MADE THEM BOSS?

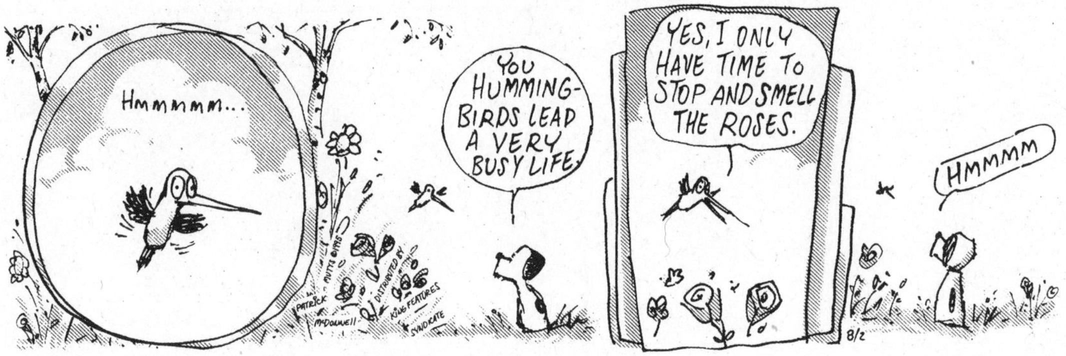
Hmmmmm...
YOU HUMMING-BIRDS LEAD A VERY BUSY LIFE.
YES, I ONLY HAVE TIME TO STOP AND SMELL THE ROSES.
HMMMM
8/2

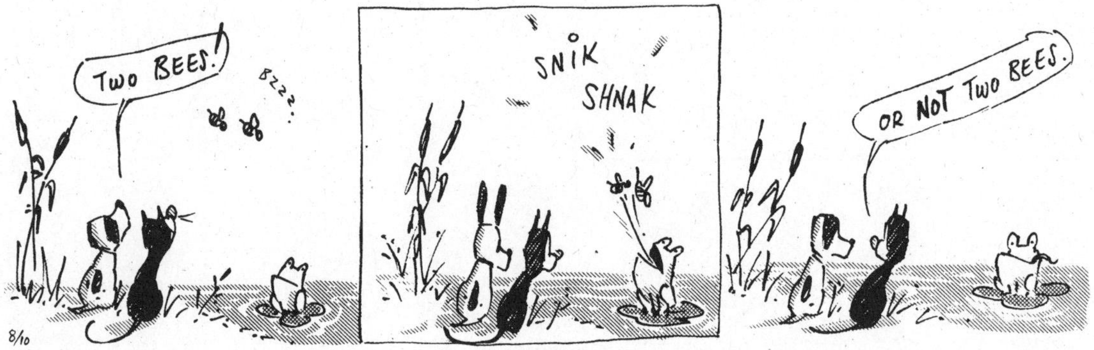
TWO BEES!
BZZZ.
8/10
SNIK
SHNAK
OR NOT TWO BEES.

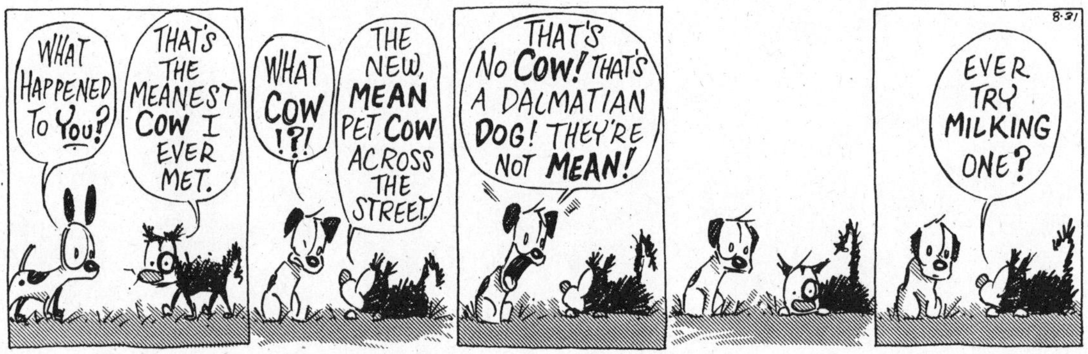
WHAT HAPPENED TO YOU?
THAT'S THE MEANEST COW I EVER MET.
WHAT COW !?!
THE NEW, MEAN PET COW ACROSS THE STREET.
THAT'S NO COW! THAT'S A DALMATIAN DOG! THEY'RE NOT MEAN!
8·31
EVER TRY MILKING ONE?

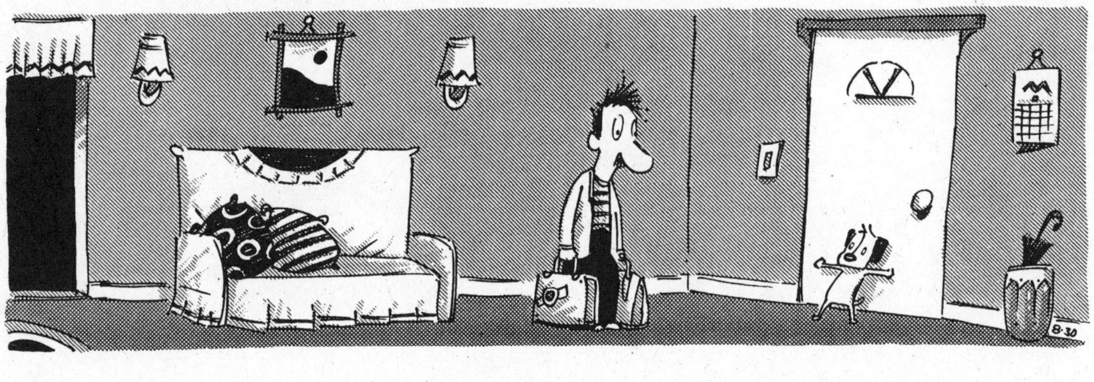
8·30

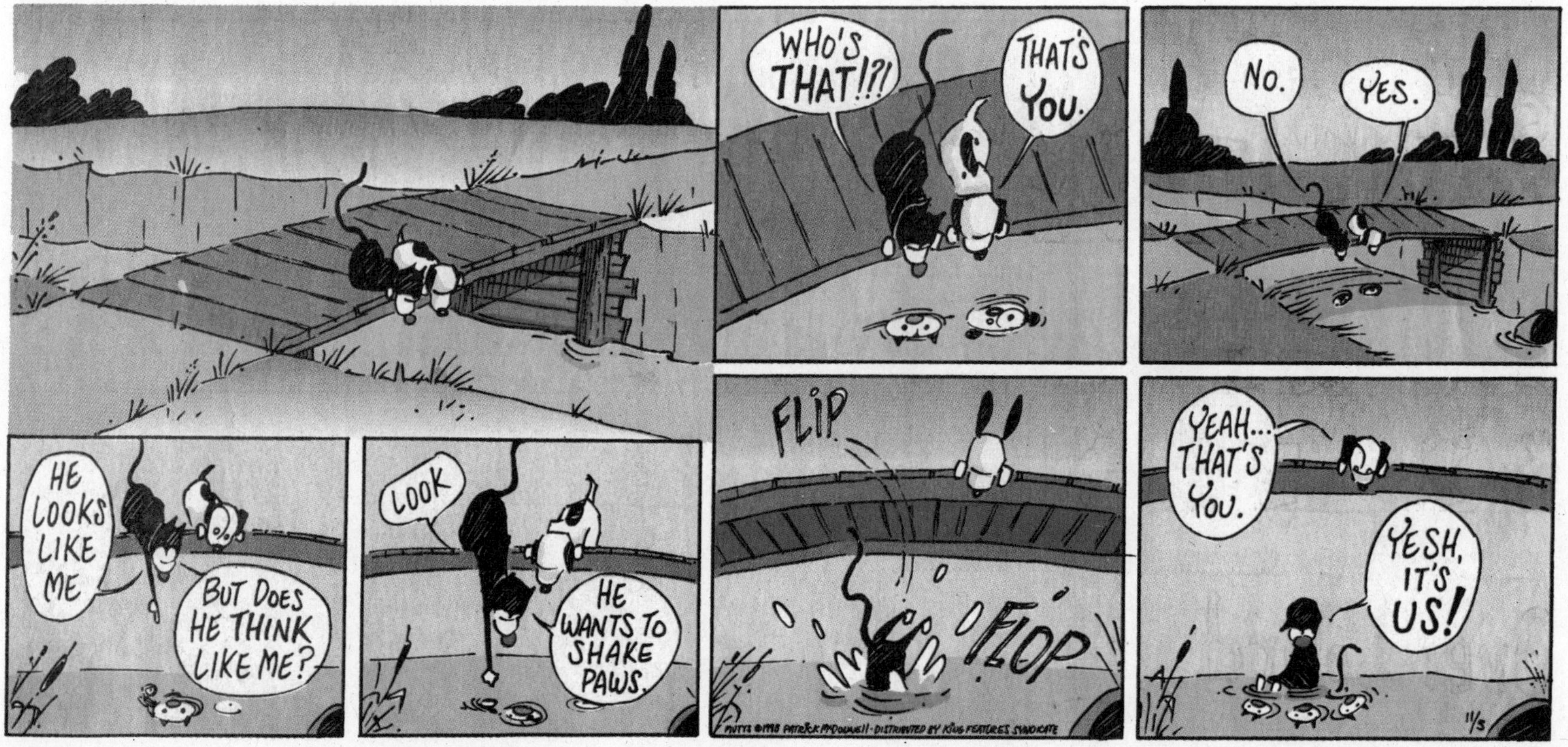
WHO'S THAT!?!
THAT'S YOU.
NO.
YES.
HE LOOKS LIKE ME
BUT DOES HE THINK LIKE ME?
LOOK
HE WANTS TO SHAKE PAWS.
FLIP
FLOP
YEAH... THAT'S YOU.
YESH, IT'S US!
11/3

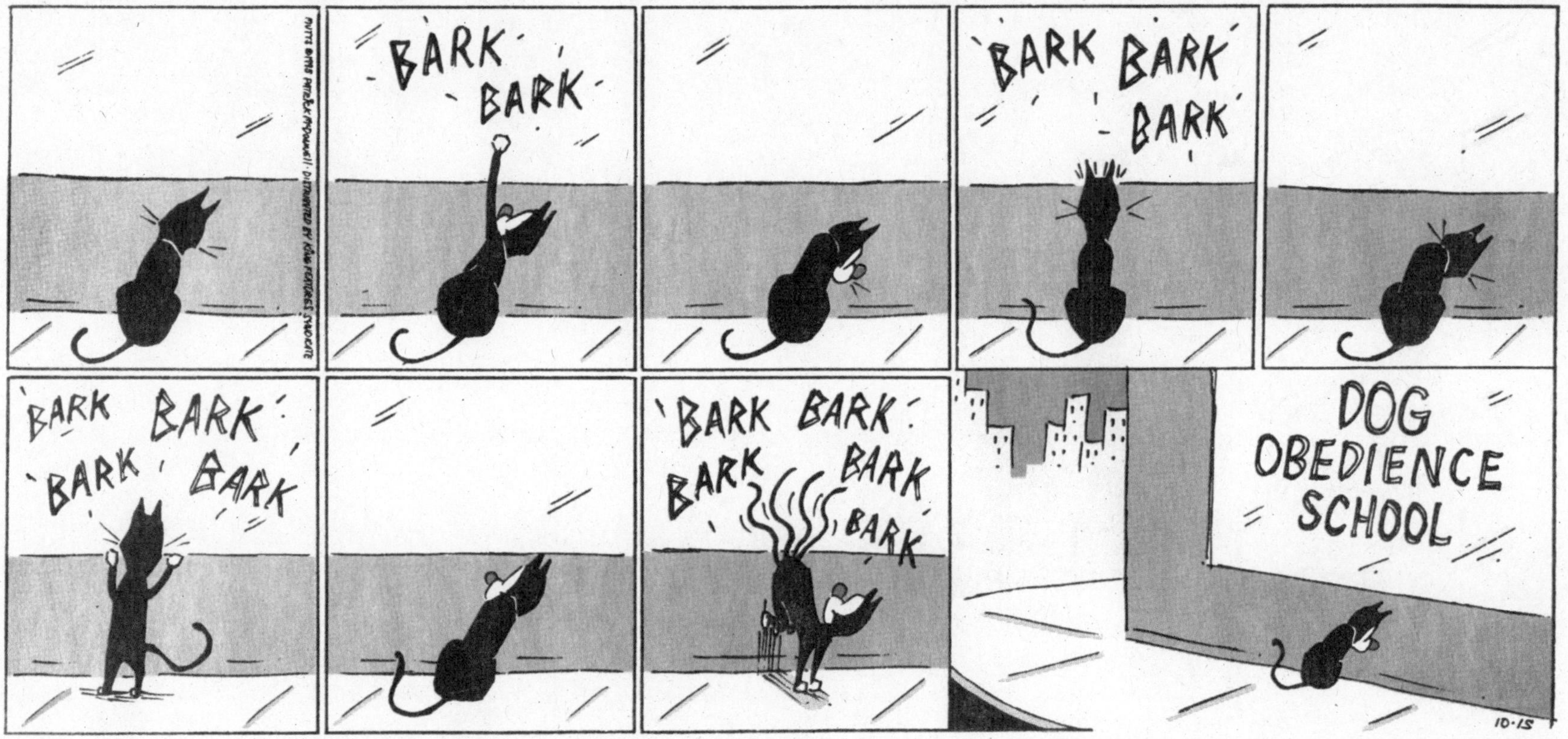
BARK
BARK
BARK BARK
BARK
BARK BARK
BARK BARK
BARK BARK
BARK BARK
BARK
DOG OBEDIENCE SCHOOL
10-15

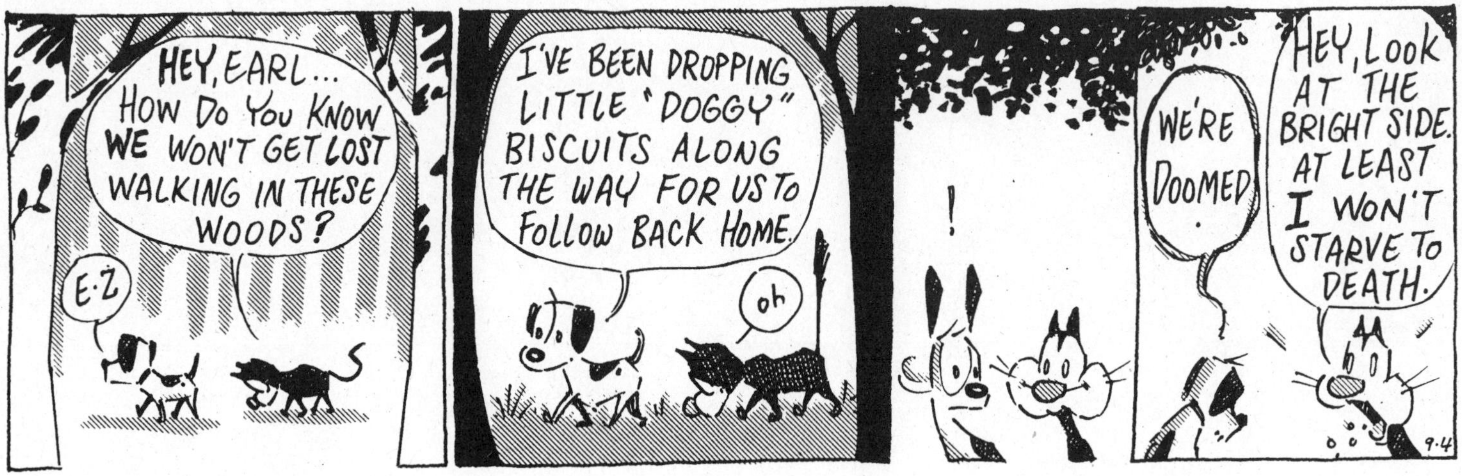
HEY, EARL... HOW DO YOU KNOW WE WON'T GET LOST WALKING IN THESE WOODS?
E·Z
I'VE BEEN DROPPING LITTLE "DOGGY" BISCUITS ALONG THE WAY FOR US TO FOLLOW BACK HOME.
oh
!
WE'RE DOOMED.
HEY, LOOK AT THE BRIGHT SIDE. AT LEAST I WON'T STARVE TO DEATH.
9·4

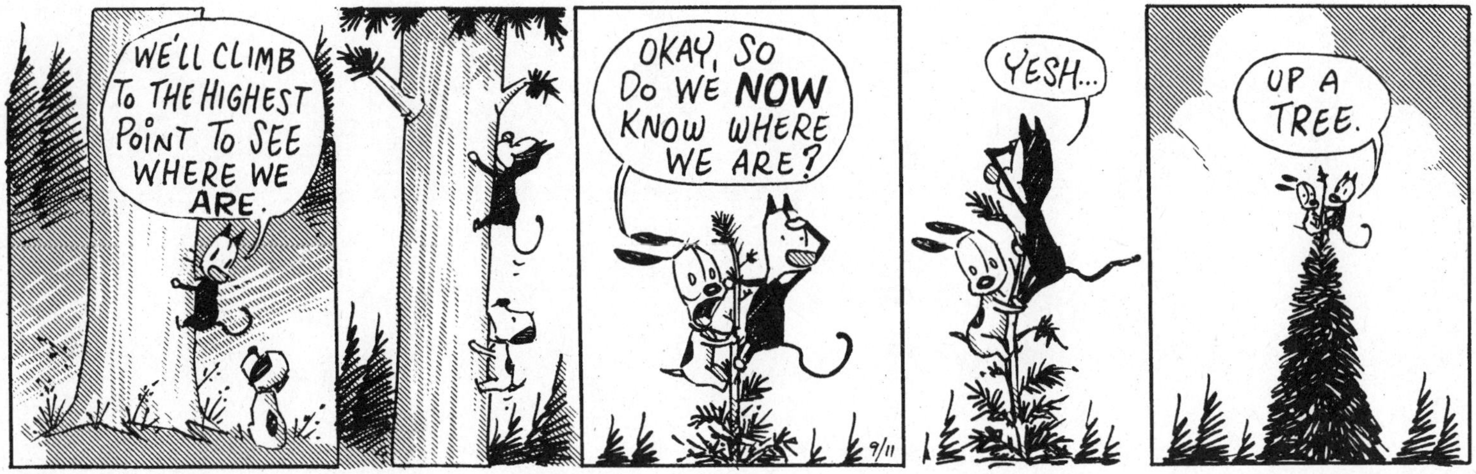
WE'LL CLIMB TO THE HIGHEST POINT TO SEE WHERE WE ARE.
OKAY, SO DO WE NOW KNOW WHERE WE ARE?
9/11
YESH...
UP A TREE.

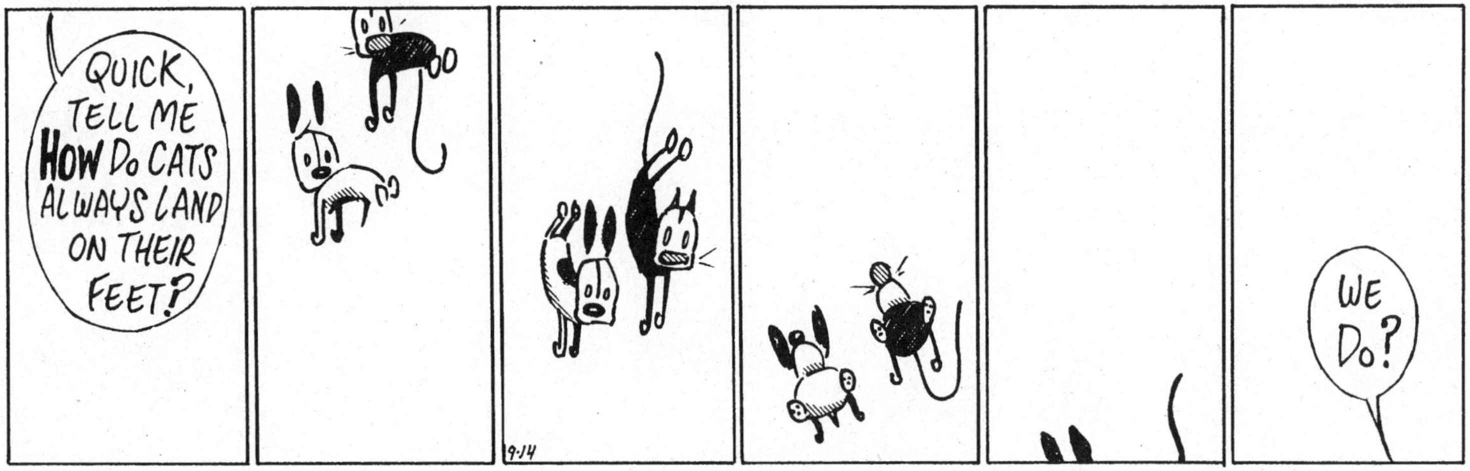
QUICK, TELL ME HOW DO CATS ALWAYS LAND ON THEIR FEET?
9·14
WE DO?

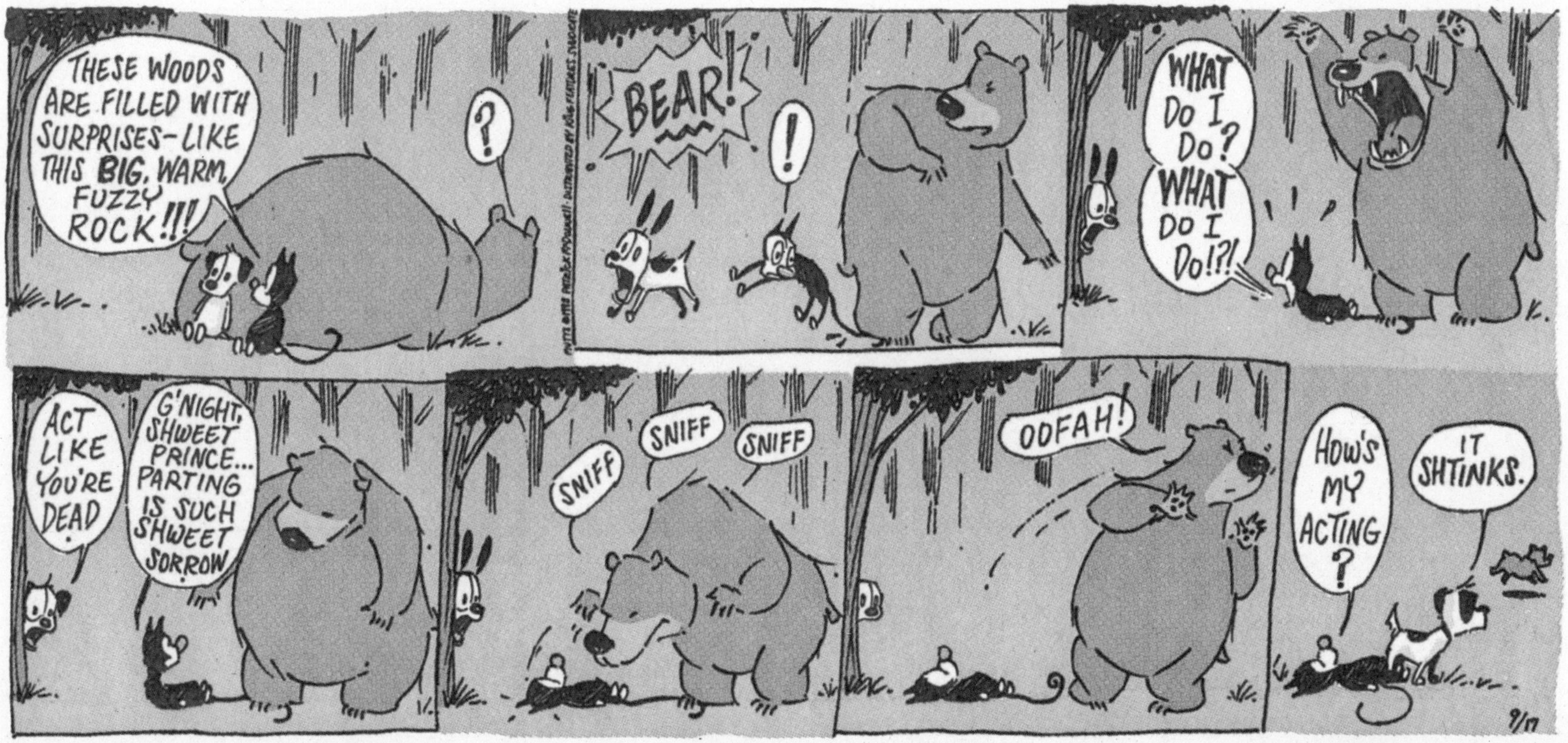
THESE WOODS ARE FILLED WITH SURPRISES–LIKE THIS BIG, WARM, FUZZY ROCK!!!
?
BEAR!
!
WHAT DO I DO? WHAT DO I DO!?!
ACT LIKE YOU'RE DEAD
G'NIGHT, SHWEET PRINCE... PARTING IS SUCH SHWEET SORROW
SNIFF
SNIFF
SNIFF
OOFAH!
HOW'S MY ACTING?
IT SHTINKS.
9/17

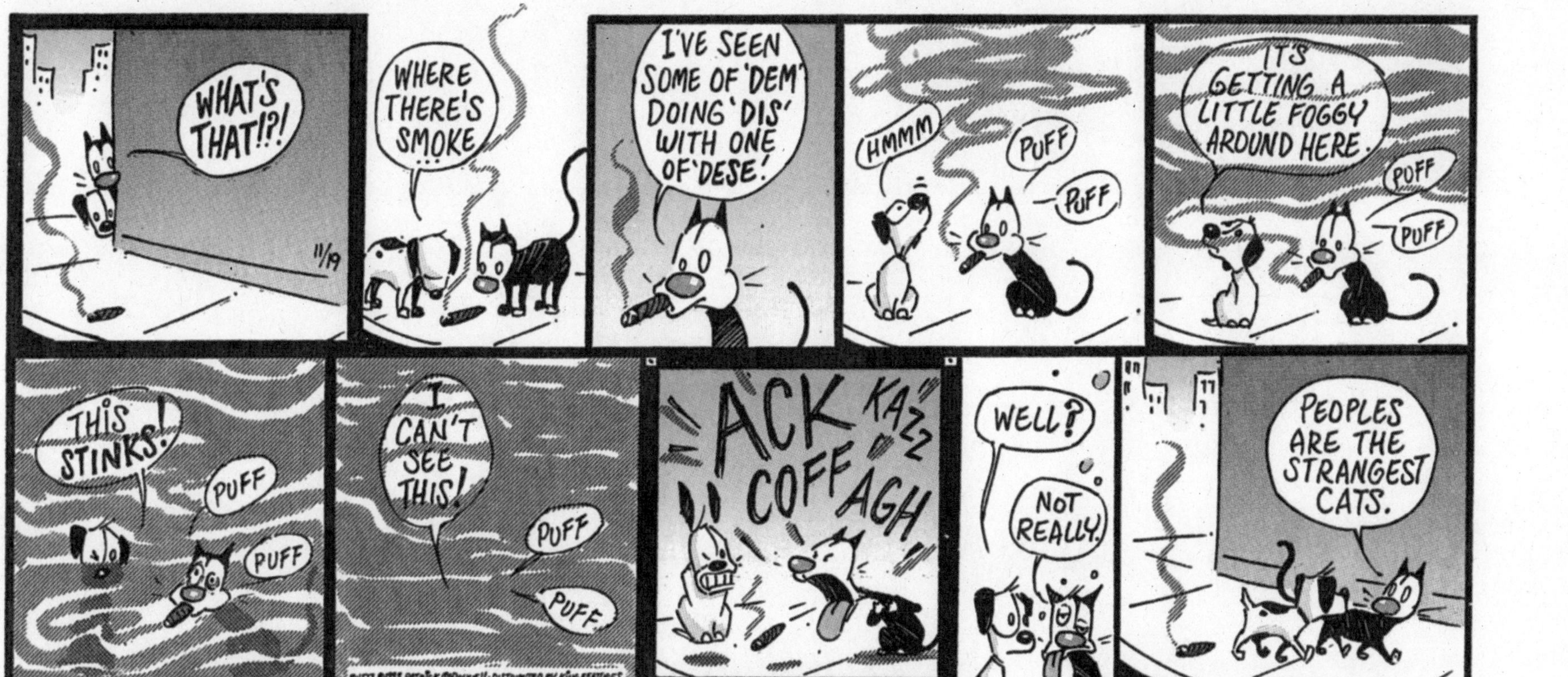
WHAT'S THAT!?!
11/19
WHERE THERE'S SMOKE...
I'VE SEEN SOME OF 'DEM' DOING 'DIS' WITH ONE OF 'DESE'
HMMM
PUFF
PUFF
IT'S GETTING A LITTLE FOGGY AROUND HERE.
PUFF
PUFF
THIS STINKS!
PUFF
PUFF
I CAN'T SEE THIS!
PUFF
PUFF
ACK
KAZZ
COFF
AGH
WELL?
NOT REALLY.
PEOPLES ARE THE STRANGEST CATS.

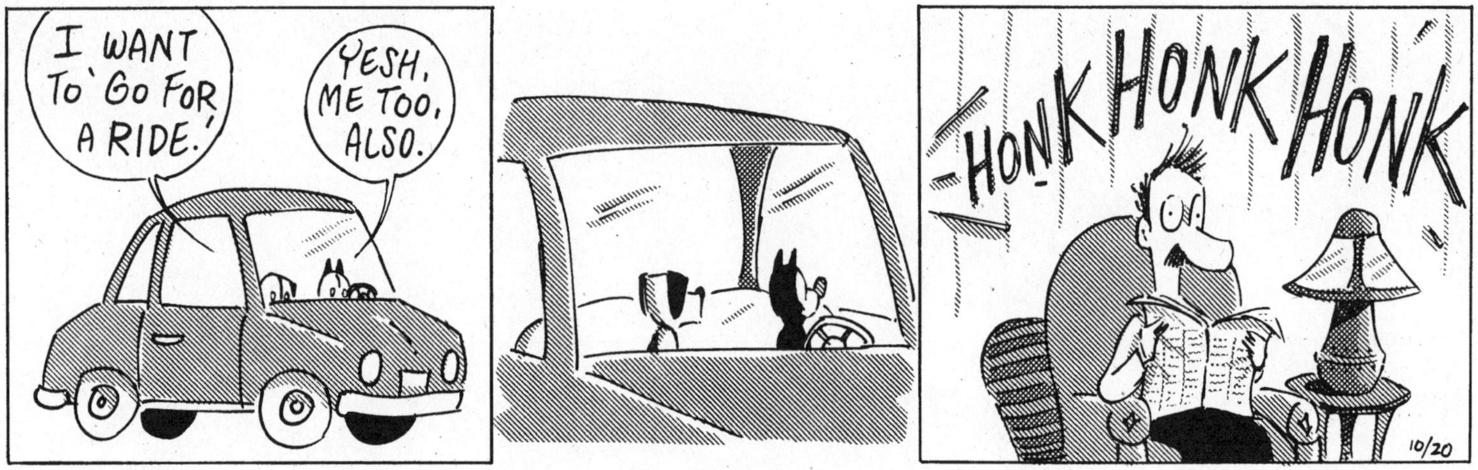
I WANT TO 'GO FOR A RIDE.'
YESH, ME TOO, ALSO.
HONK HONK HONK HONK
10/20

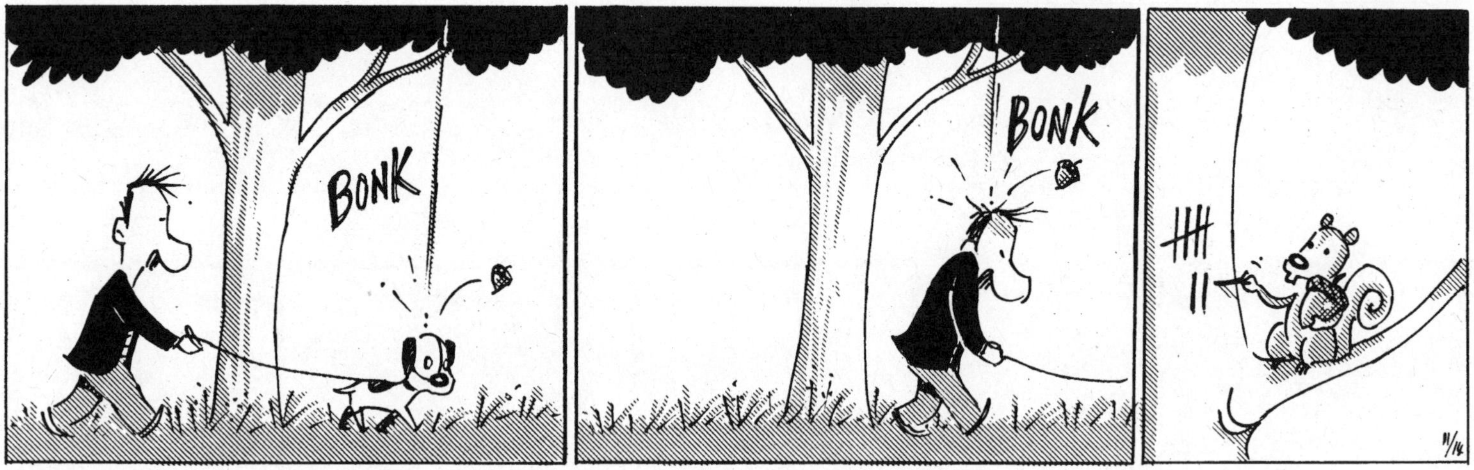
BONK
BONK
11/14

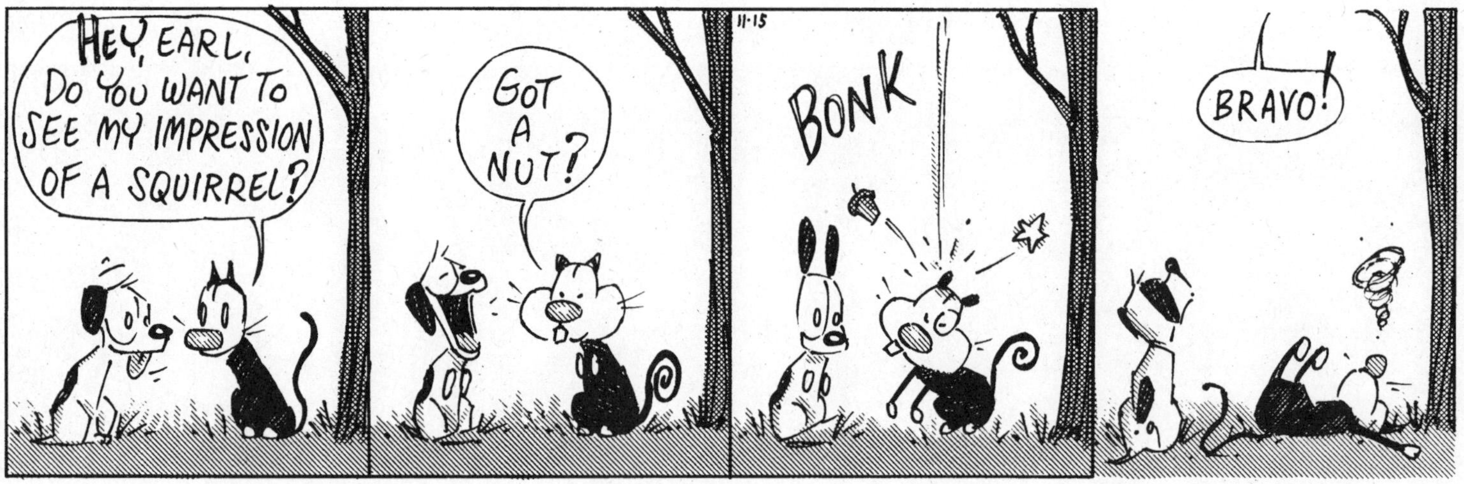
HEY, EARL, DO YOU WANT TO SEE MY IMPRESSION OF A SQUIRREL?
GOT A NUT?
11-15
BONK
BRAVO!

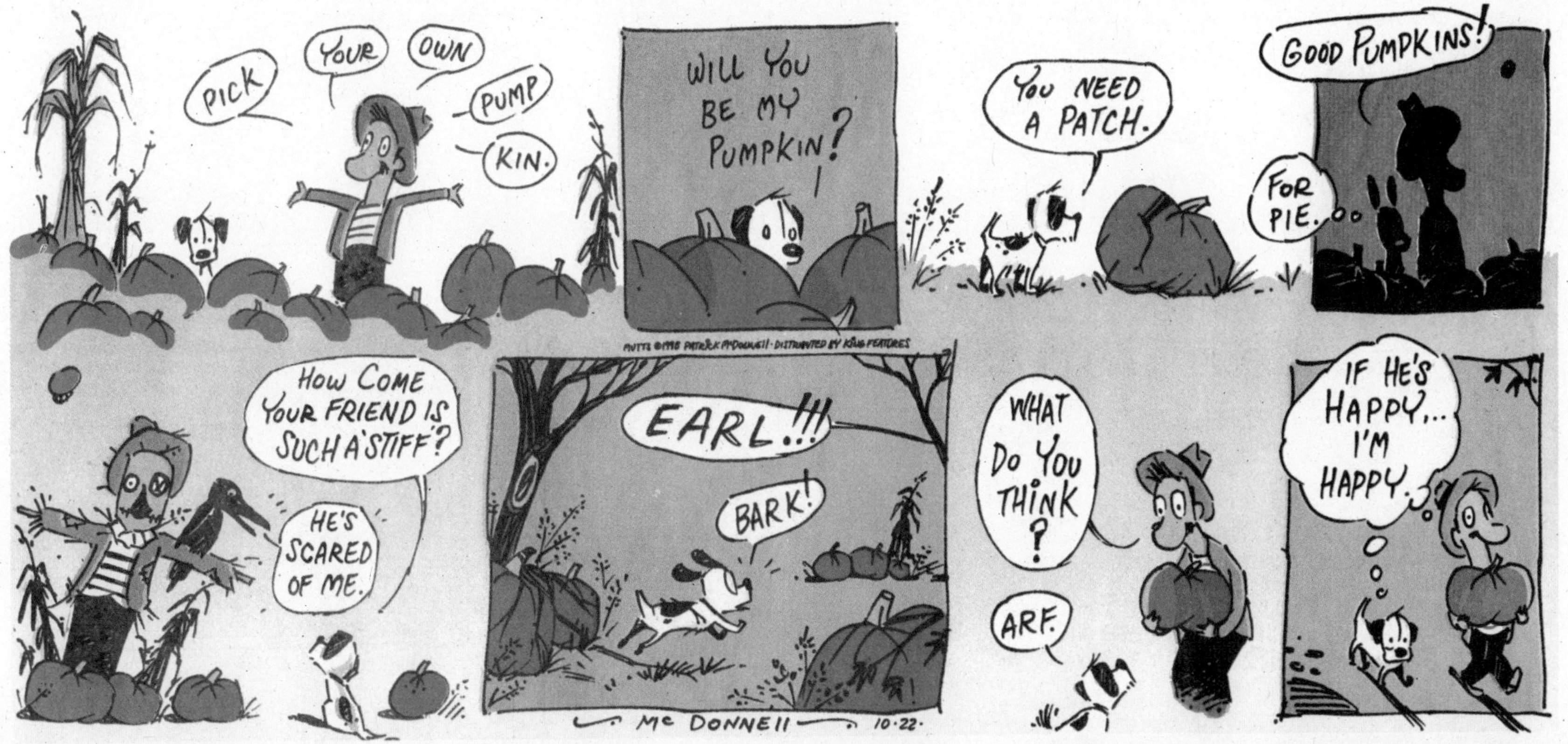
PICK
YOUR
OWN
PUMP
KIN.
WILL YOU BE MY PUMPKIN?
YOU NEED A PATCH.
GOOD PUMPKINS!
FOR PIE...
HOW COME YOUR FRIEND IS SUCH A "STIFF"?
HE'S SCARED OF ME.
EARL!!!
BARK!
WHAT DO YOU THINK?
ARF.
IF HE'S HAPPY,... I'M HAPPY.
MC DONNELL 10·22·

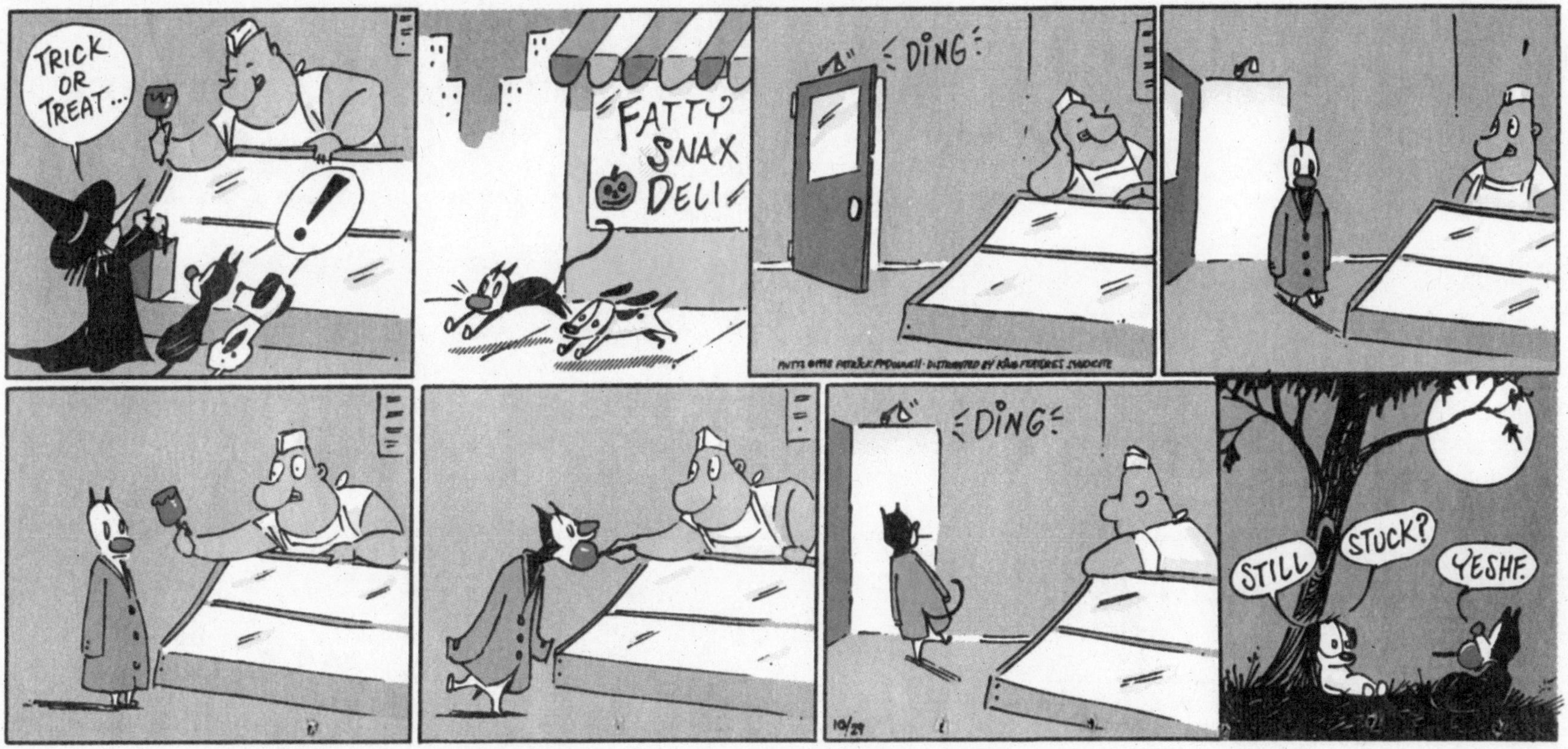
TRICK OR TREAT...
!
FATTY SNAX DELI
DING
DING
STILL
STUCK?
YESHF.

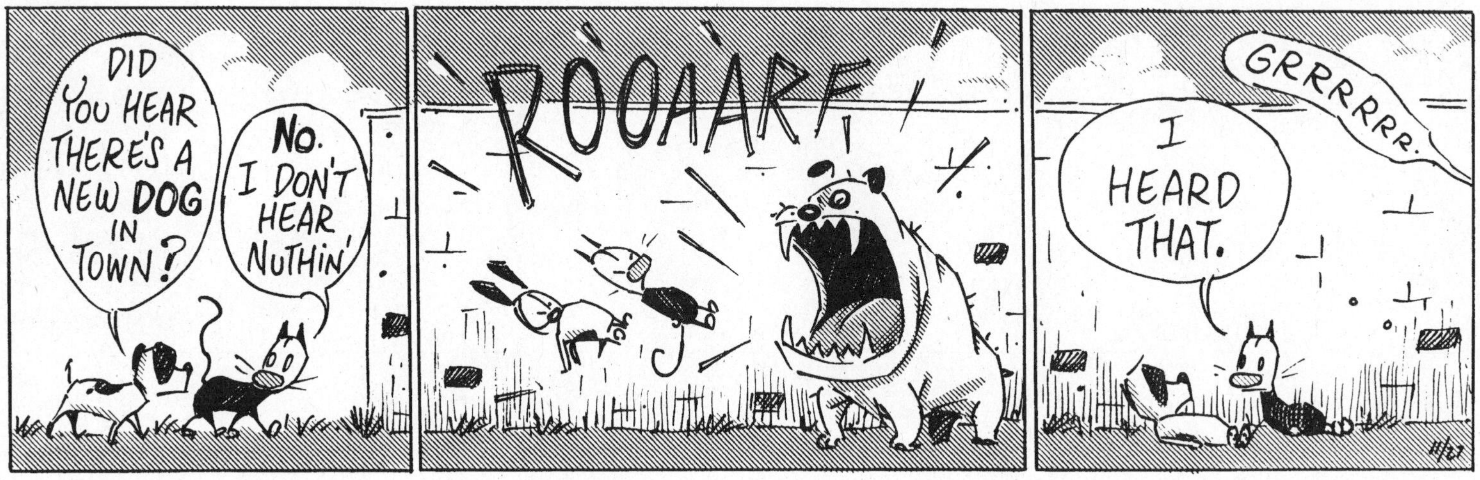
DID YOU HEAR THERE'S A NEW DOG IN TOWN?
NO. I DON'T HEAR NUTHIN'
ROOAARF
GRRRRRRR.
I HEARD THAT.
11/27

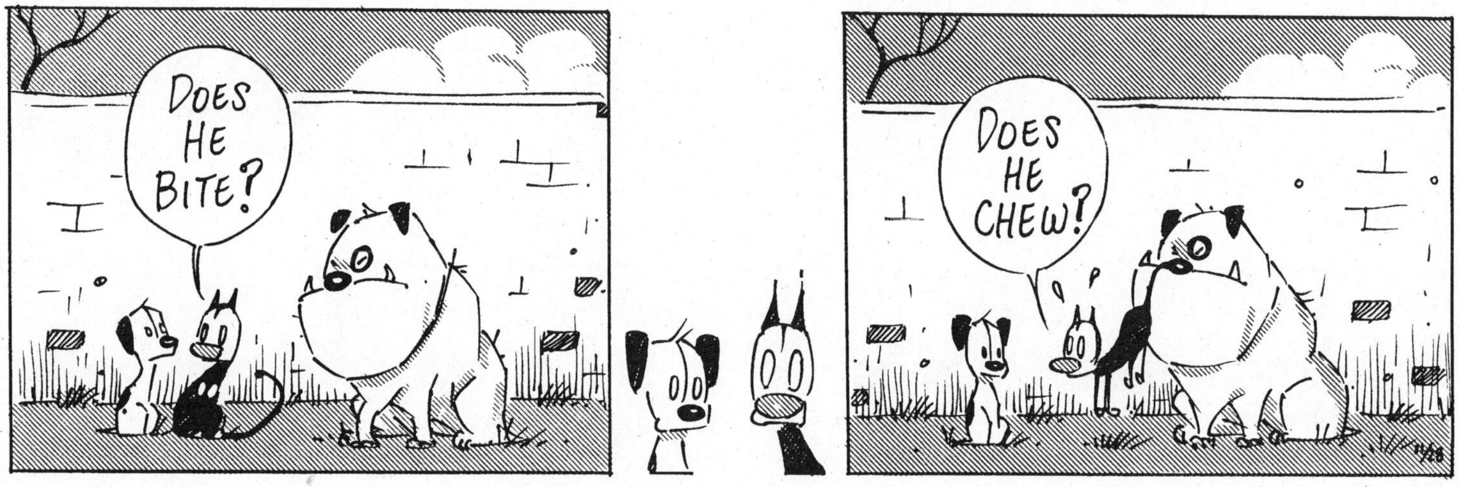
DOES HE BITE?
DOES HE CHEW?
11/28

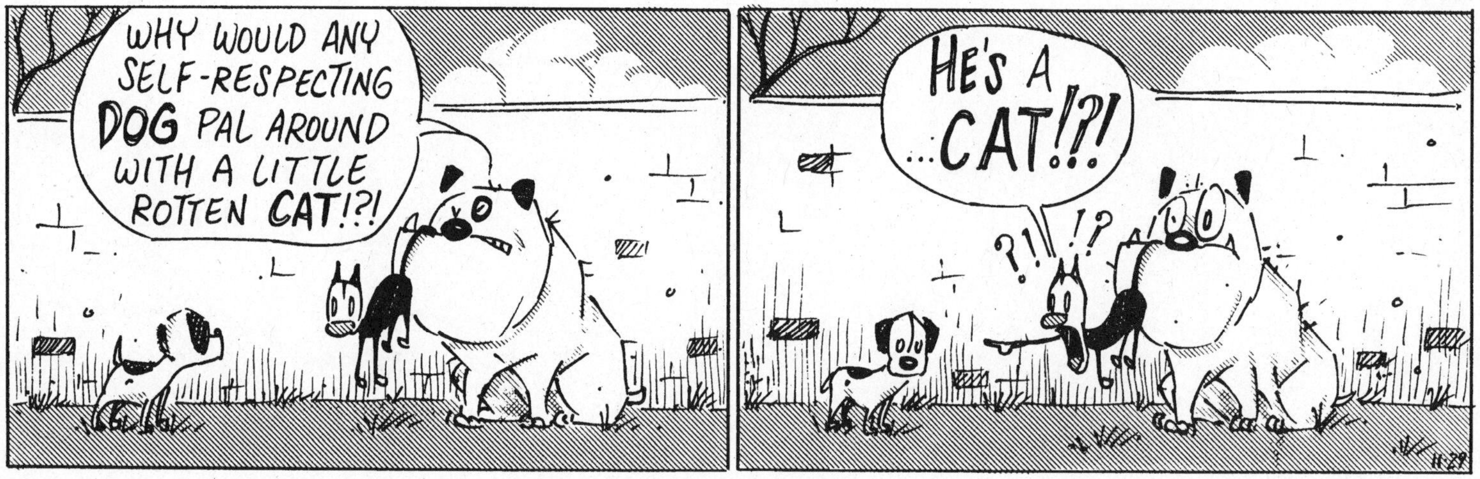
WHY WOULD ANY SELF-RESPECTING DOG PAL AROUND WITH A LITTLE ROTTEN CAT!?!
HE'S A ...CAT!?!
?!
!?
11-29

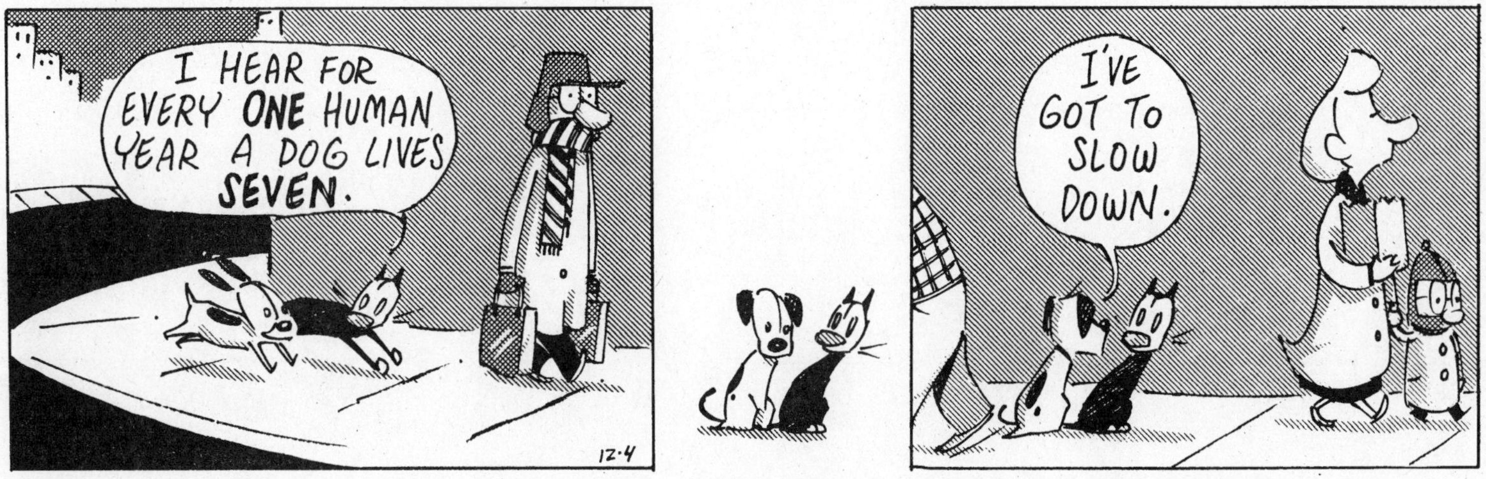
I HEAR FOR EVERY **ONE** HUMAN YEAR A DOG LIVES **SEVEN**.
I'VE GOT TO SLOW DOWN.
12·4

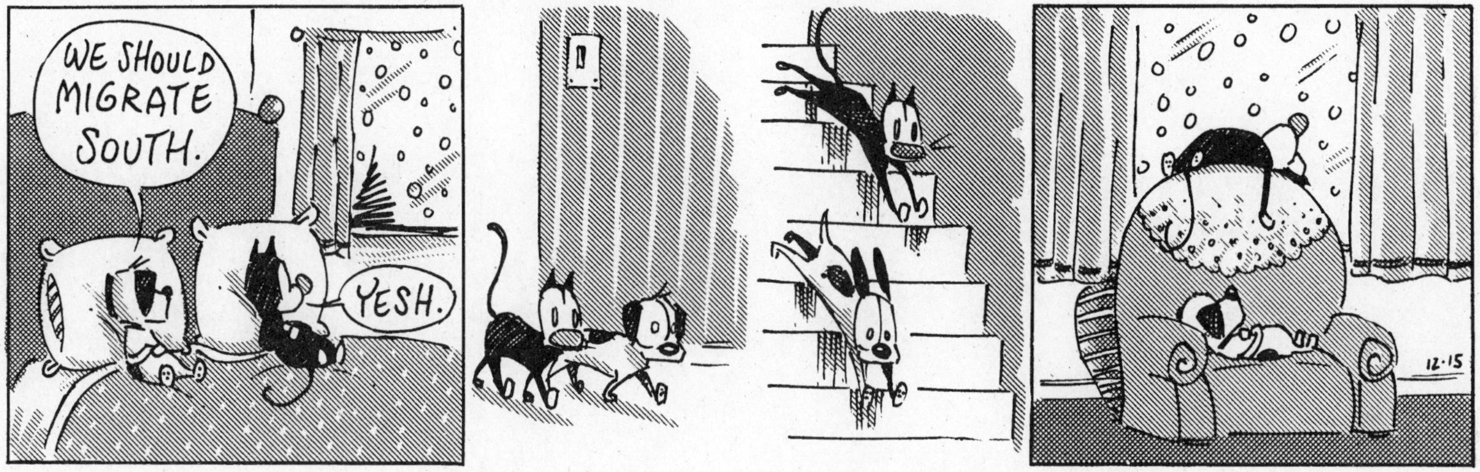
WE SHOULD MIGRATE SOUTH.
YESH.
12·15

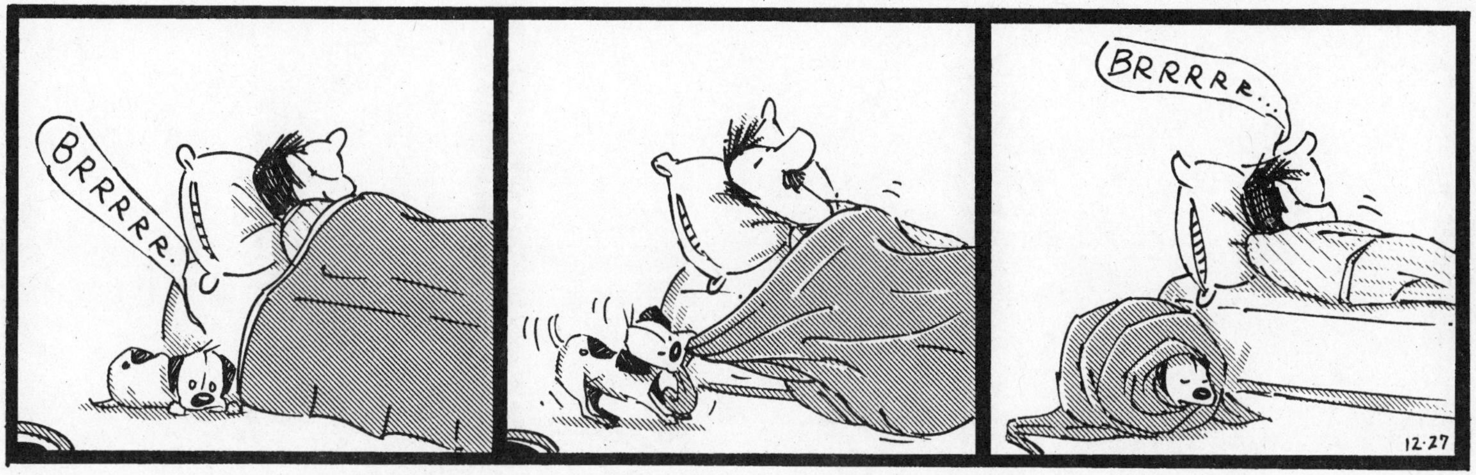
BRRRRR.
BRRRRR...
12·27

PEOPLES SURE DO ACT STRANGE THIS TIME OF SEASON.

HO HO

THEY SURE DO.

!?!

DO YOU REALLY UNDERSTAND US?

HO HO

NOW, LITTLE EARL, WHAT'S TO UNDERSTAND? YOU JUST WANT TO LOVE AND BE LOVED!

WHAT ABOUT ME?

AHH, MOOCH, MY FELINE FRIEND, YOU ARE TRULY BLESSED, FOR YOU WANT NOTHING.

EXCEPT MAYBE LUNCH.

HE DOES UNDERSTAND!

HO HO

NOW LET ME SEE... I THINK I HAVE A LITTLE GIFT FOR YOU IN MY POCKET...

HO! HO! A NICE BIG TREAT BONE AND A BOWL OF CREAM!!!

! ?

AHH, THE ALWAYS-CURIOUS CAT, IT LOOKS LIKE YOU HAVE A QUESTION...

YESH. WHAT'S IN THE OTHER POCKET?

HO HO

WHO ARE YOU!?!

I AM.

WHO?

HE AM.

HO HO

AM WHAT?

I DIDN'T GET HIS LAST NAME.

SO, LITTLE EARL AND MOOCHIE, GO AND REMIND YOUR "MASTERS" EVERY DAY OF THE SPIRIT OF GIVING AND LOVING!

THAT'S YOUR JOB!

HO HO HO

JOB!?! I THOUGHT THIS WAS A HOLIDAY!

WELL, BOYS, I'D LOVE TO STAY AND CHAT... BUT I REALLY MUST

FLY.

HO! HO!... AND TO ALL A GOOD NIGHT!

FLY!?!

AND I BET'CHA HE'S JUST THE GUY TO DO IT!

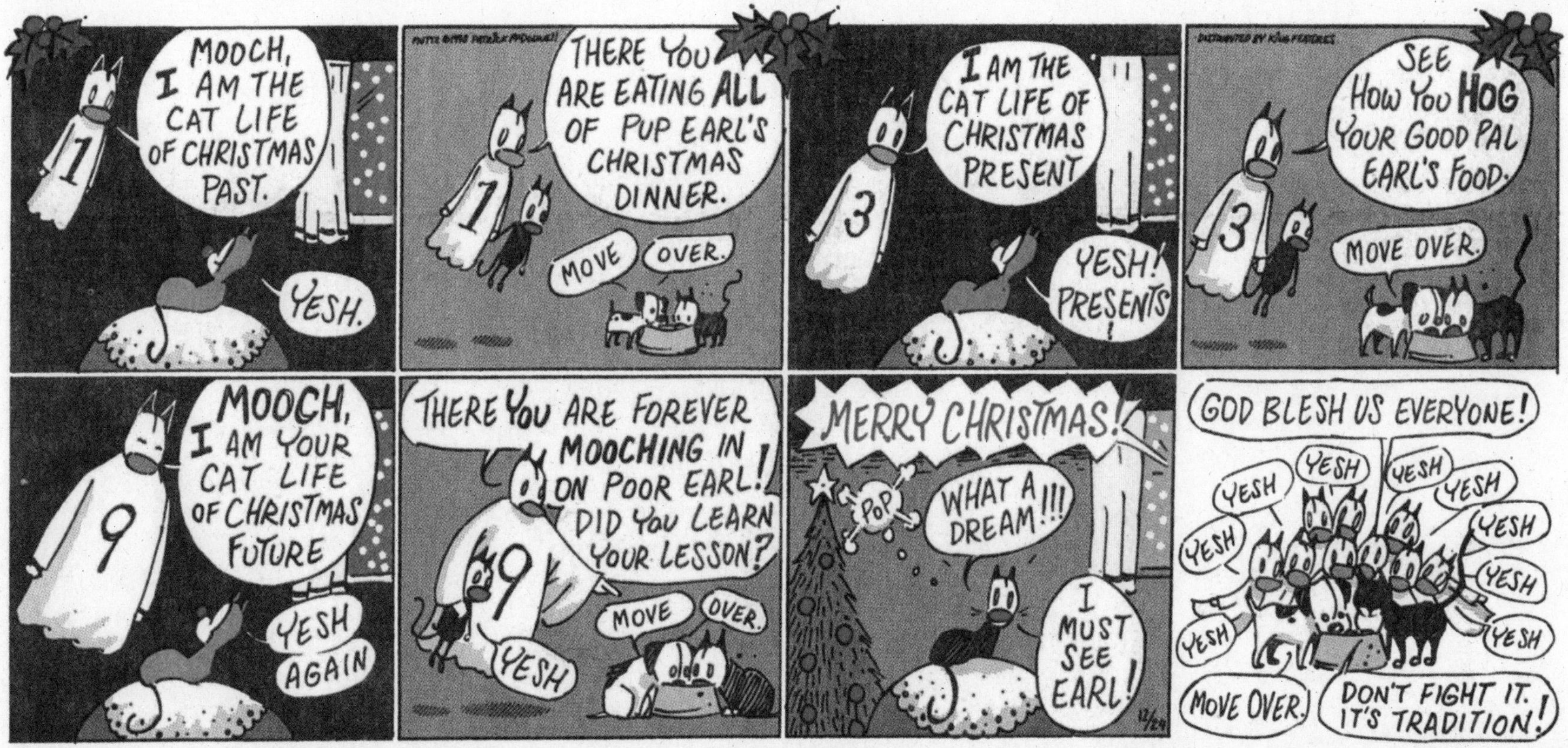
MOOCH, I AM THE CAT LIFE OF CHRISTMAS PAST.
YESH.
THERE YOU ARE EATING ALL OF PUP EARL'S CHRISTMAS DINNER.
MOVE
OVER.
I AM THE CAT LIFE OF CHRISTMAS PRESENT
YESH! PRESENTS!
SEE HOW YOU HOG YOUR GOOD PAL EARL'S FOOD.
MOVE OVER.
MOOCH, I AM YOUR CAT LIFE OF CHRISTMAS FUTURE
YESH AGAIN
THERE YOU ARE FOREVER MOOCHING IN ON POOR EARL! DID YOU LEARN YOUR LESSON?
YESH
MOVE
OVER.
MERRY CHRISTMAS!
POP
WHAT A DREAM!!!
I MUST SEE EARL!
12/24
GOD BLESH US EVERYONE!
YESH
YESH
YESH
YESH
YESH
YESH
YESH
YESH
YESH
MOVE OVER.
DON'T FIGHT IT. IT'S TRADITION!

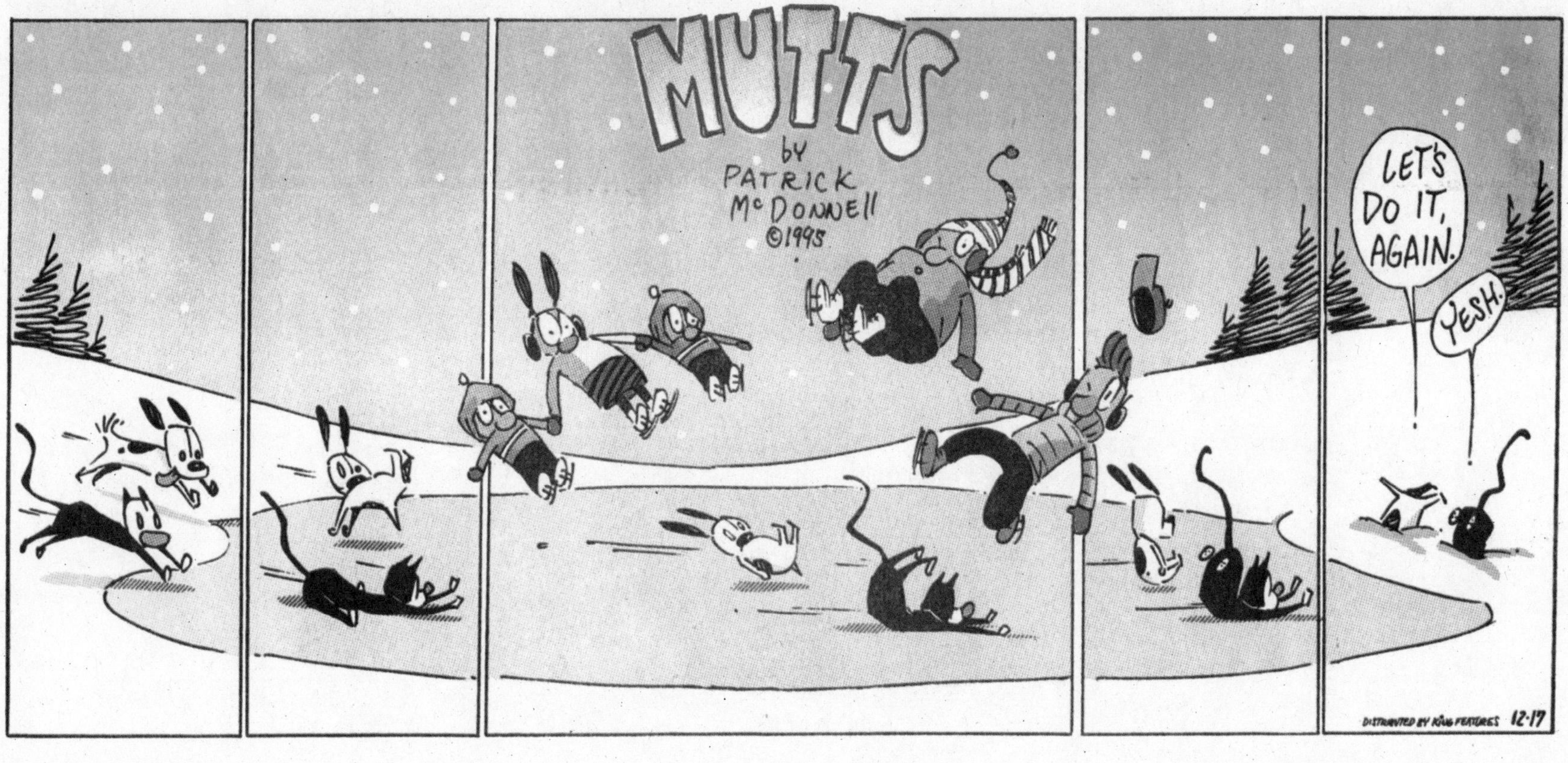
MUTTS
by PATRICK McDONNELL ©1995
LET'S DO IT, AGAIN.
YESH.
DISTRIBUTED BY KING FEATURES 12-17

**Looking back,** I think 1996 was the year I really started to get the hang of doing the strip. Everything was starting to gel.

My Sunday comics have a separate title panel. I first designed my own concepts for these panels, but late in 1995 I started playing with the idea of basing them on works by other artists. I did homages to many of my favorite painters and illustrators, along with tributes to book, album and magazine covers. It was fun and educational to attempt my own versions of the works of Vermeer, van Gogh, Gauguin, Donald Baechler, and Ernest Shepard. I always tried to pick images that would add something to that day's story. I especially enjoyed mimicking the great Japanese woodcuts by artists like Hiroshige. Their style and mood were a perfect fit for *Mutts*.

The Sunday story lines of July 21 (page 59) and December 8 (page 63, top) are two of my favorites. Both were silly ideas that I watched write themselves.

Trying to see the world through the eyes of animals made me more aware and empathetic to them and their situation. Stories about animal issues started to naturally fit into the *Mutts* world. In February I did a two-week episode about people wearing fur (as you may have guessed, Earl and Mooch were against it).

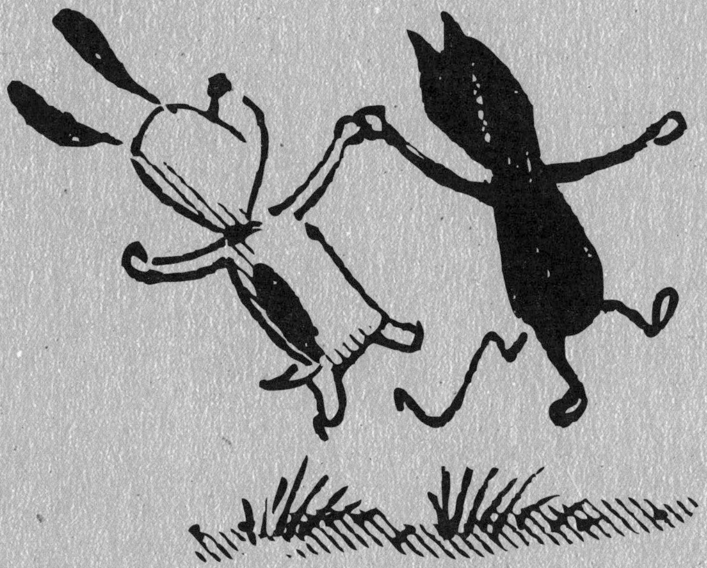

In May, we were introduced to Mooch's girlfriend, Shnelly. Shnelly is a house cat and is depicted as two ears behind a window, an enticing mystery for a curious cat.

*Mutts* is played out in the New Jersey of my mind. So this year I started the tradition of the cast going "down the shore" for the summer. It opened the strip up to a whole new locale with associated characters to explore, starting with the lovable crab Crabby. Crabby has a colorful way of speaking, using the cartoon "cursive" @*#!!. At times, when Crabby appears in the strip, I get letters complaining "How dare Crabby say that in a family newspaper!" @*#!!????

The year ended with a four-week-long holiday fable featuring a little lost tabby kitten whom Earl and Mooch named Shtinky Puddin'. A touch of little orphan Annie with whiskers.

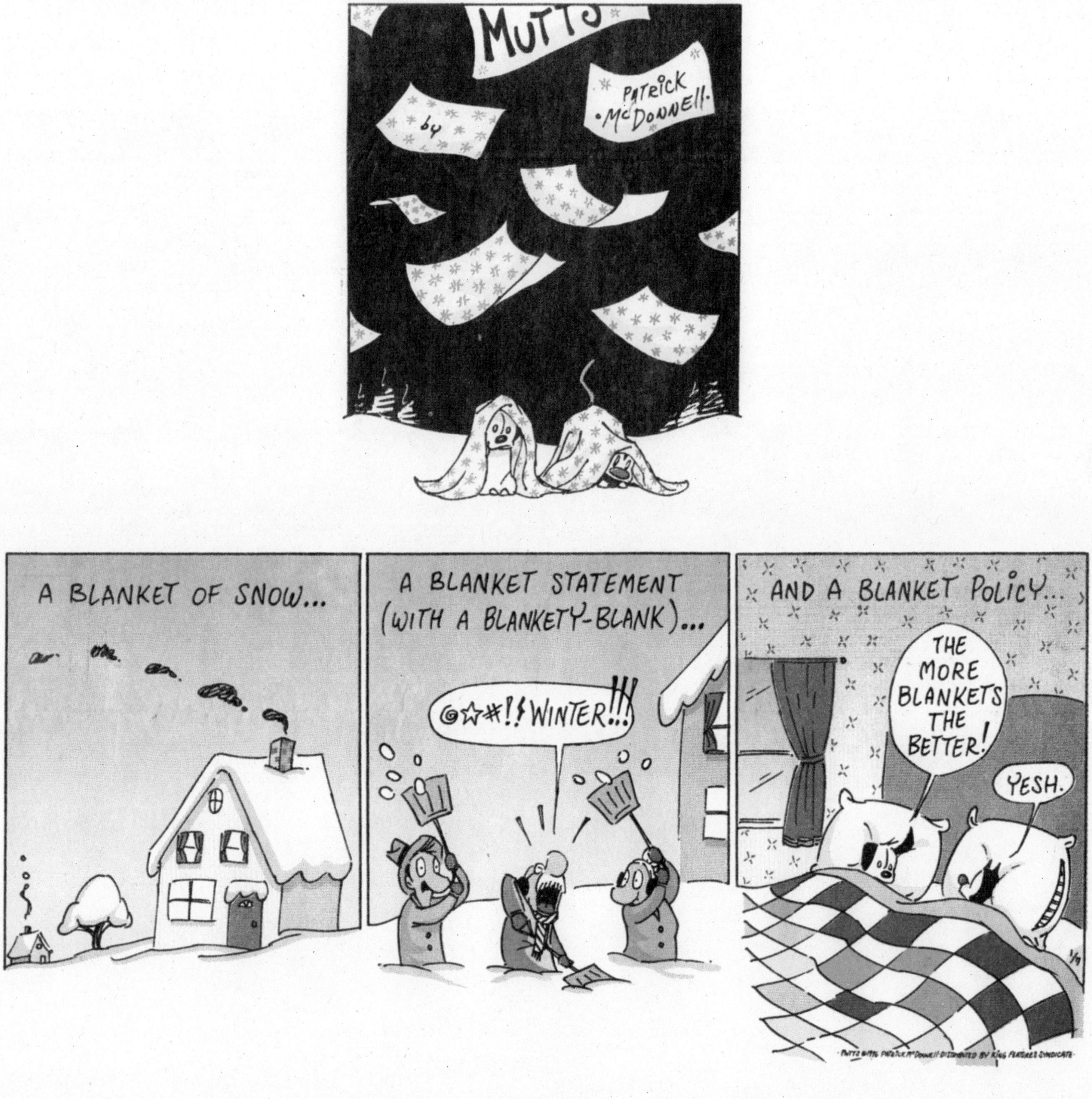
MUTTS
by
PATRICK McDONNELL
A BLANKET OF SNOW...
A BLANKET STATEMENT (WITH A BLANKETY-BLANK)...
@☆#!$ WINTER!!!
AND A BLANKET POLICY...
THE MORE BLANKETS THE BETTER!
YESH.

I'M TELLING YOU, MOOCH- BEARS SLEEP ALL WINTER!!!
HA!
WELL, IF YOU DON'T BELIEVE ME, WHO WILL YOU BELIEVE?
1·8

MOOCH, IF YOU WANT TO ASK THE BEAR IF HE SLEEPS ALL WINTER, YOU'RE GOING TO HAVE TO SOFTLY WAKE HIM...BUT BE GENTLE. DO NOT SCARE HIM!
Do I LOOK SHTUPID?
1/9

HOW ARE WE GOING TO ASK THIS BEAR IF HE SLEEPS ALL WINTER IF WE CAN'T WAKE HIM?
1/10
I HEAR BEARS LIKE TO BE COAXED WITH HONEY.
YESH
HONEY!
I'M HOME!
HONEY.
HONEY.

HOW ARE WE GOING TO WAKE THAT BEAR?
HEY, I KNOW-LET'S POKE HIM WITH A STICK...
1·11
POKE
POKE
POKE
ISN'T THAT DANGER-OUS?
NO.
I CHECKED FOR SPLINTERS.

WELL, MOOCH, WE TRIED HONEY AND POKING HIM WITH A STICK, BUT NOTHING WILL WAKE THIS BEAR UP!
1·12
I GUESSH WE'LL NEVER KNOW WHAT HE IS THINKING
NEXT YEAR, I GET A CAVE WITH A DOOR.

I'M GOING TO BE LIKE A BEAR AND SLEEP ALL WINTER!
HA
1/12
Z-Z-Z-Z
THIS I GOT TO SEE.
Z-Z-Z-Z
MOOCH! DIN-DIN TIME!
Z-Z-Z-Z
Z-Z-Z-N-N-N

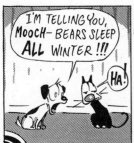

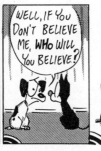

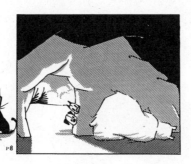

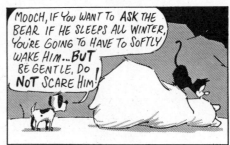

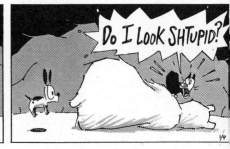

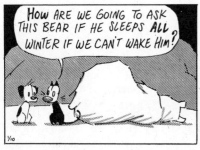

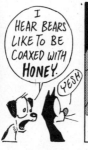

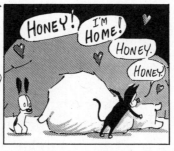

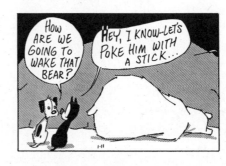

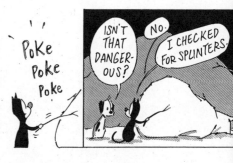

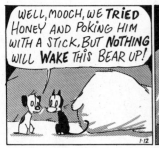

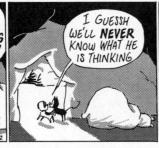

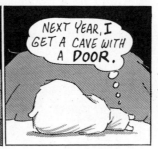

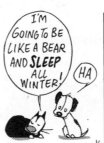

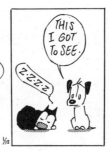

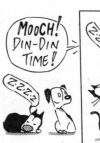

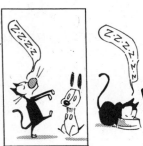

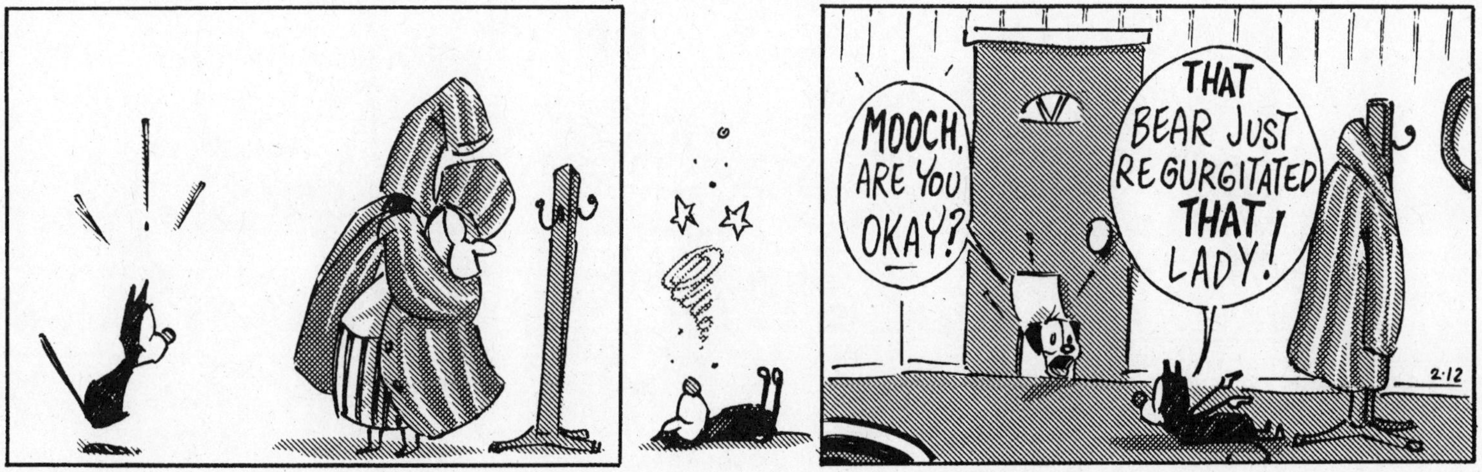
MOOCH, ARE YOU OKAY?
THAT BEAR JUST REGURGITATED THAT LADY!
2·12

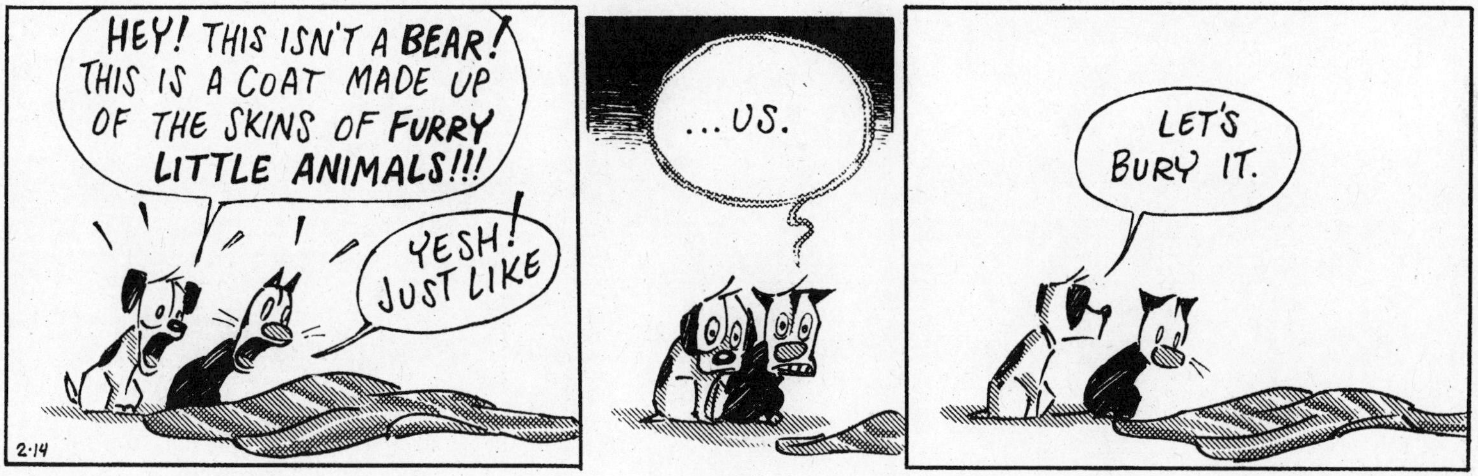
HEY! THIS ISN'T A BEAR! THIS IS A COAT MADE UP OF THE SKINS OF FURRY LITTLE ANIMALS!!!
YESH! JUST LIKE
...US.
LET'S BURY IT.
2·14

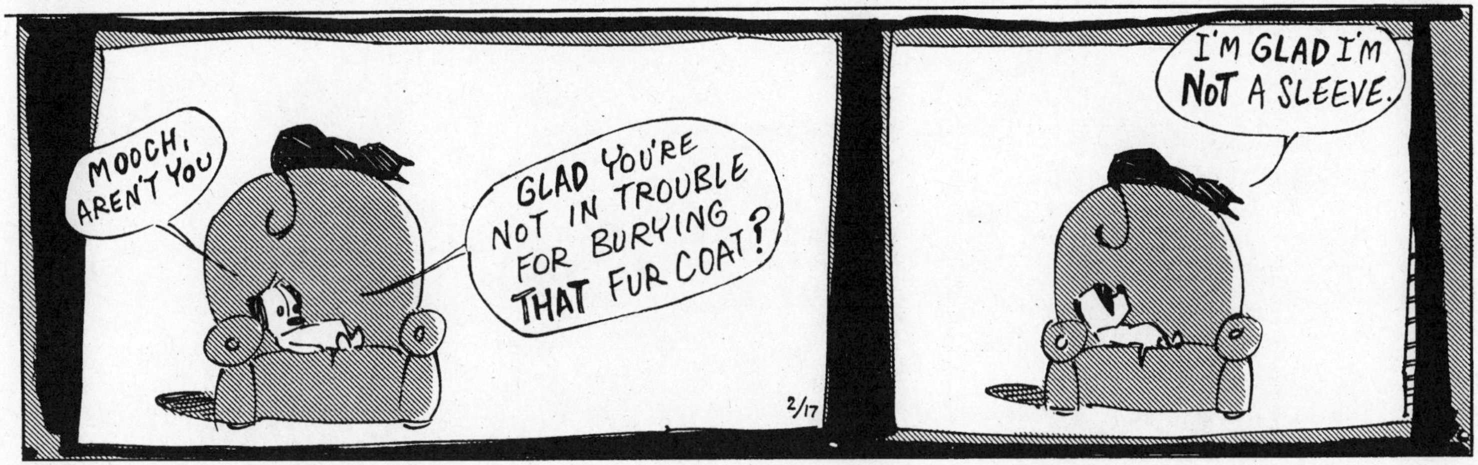
MOOCH, AREN'T YOU
GLAD YOU'RE NOT IN TROUBLE FOR BURYING THAT FUR COAT?
I'M GLAD I'M NOT A SLEEVE.
2/17

TWO O'CLOCK IN THE A.M., BUT NO WORRY, GUARD DOG IS ON DUTY.
BARK
BARK
BARK
2.22
THE CITY CAN SLEEP A LITTLE EASIER TONIGHT.

HEY, GUARD DOG, DO YOU EVER LET YOUR GUARD DOWN?
"HOLD FAST THE TIME! GUARD IT, WATCH OVER IT, EVERY HOUR, EVERY MINUTE! UNREGARDED IT SLIPS AWAY— HOLD EVERY MOMENT SACRED. GIVE EACH CLARITY AND MEANING, EACH THE WEIGHT OF THINE AWARENESS, EACH ITS TRUE AND DUE FULFILLMENT."
MAN-N,
THAT'S SOME GUARD DOG.
YESH.
2/23

SO, MOOCH HERE IS GOING TO TEACH ME HOW TO RELAX?
YESH.
3.6
US CATS HAVE LONG MASTERED THE ANCIENT ARTS OF MEDITATION. ... FIRST YOU MUST CLEAR THE MIND OF ALL THOUGHT.
THUSLY...
YEH
YEH
WHAT'S NEXT!?!
I CAN'T THINK.

NOW REMAIN IN YOUR "SIT" POSITION AND BREATHE DEEPLY, FOCUSING IN ON ONE NOTE...
LIKE SO...
PURRRP.
3.7
GRRRRRRRR..
WOW.
MEDITATION IS RELAXING!
FOR YOU!

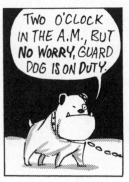

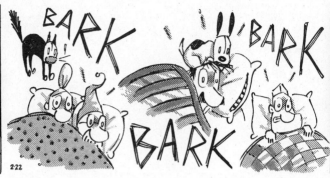

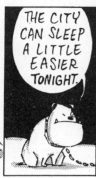

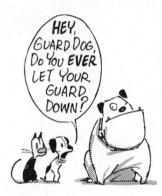

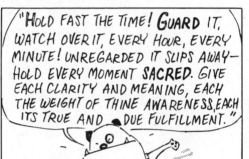

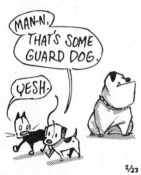

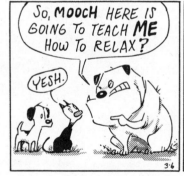

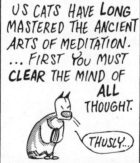

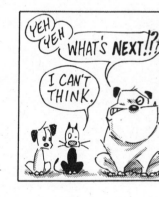

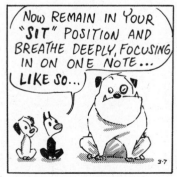

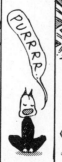

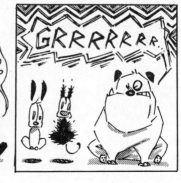

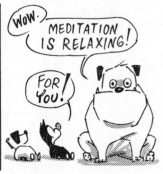

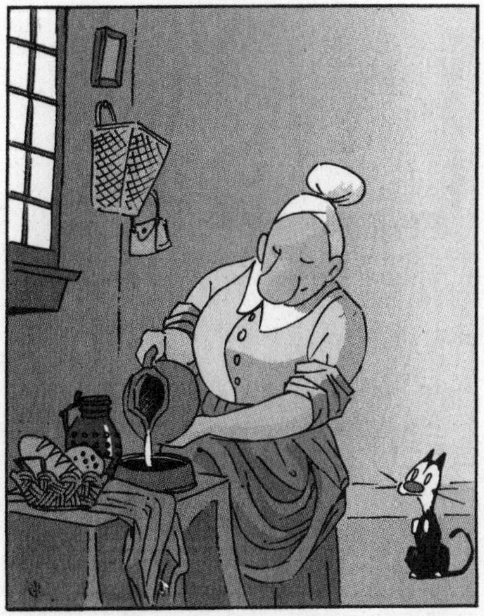

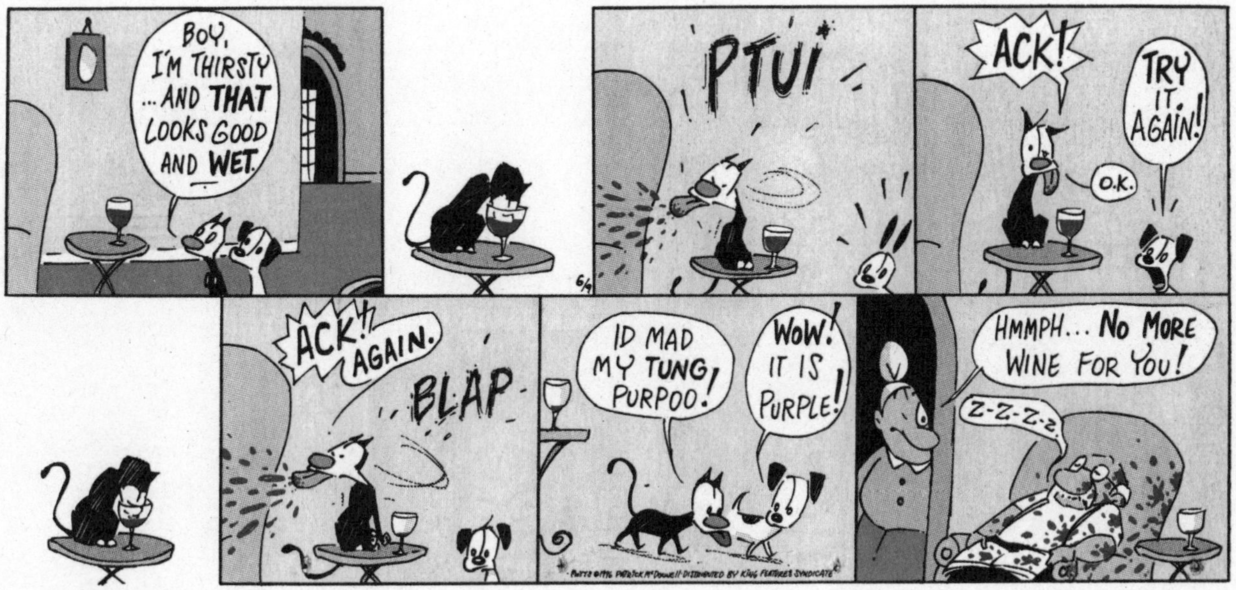
BOY, I'M THIRSTY ...AND THAT LOOKS GOOD AND WET.
PTUI
ACK!
TRY IT AGAIN!
O.K.
ACK!! AGAIN.
BLAP
ID MAD MY TUNG PURPOO!
WOW! IT IS PURPLE!
HMMPH... NO MORE WINE FOR YOU!
Z-Z-Z-z

THE PHILADELPHIA INQUIRER

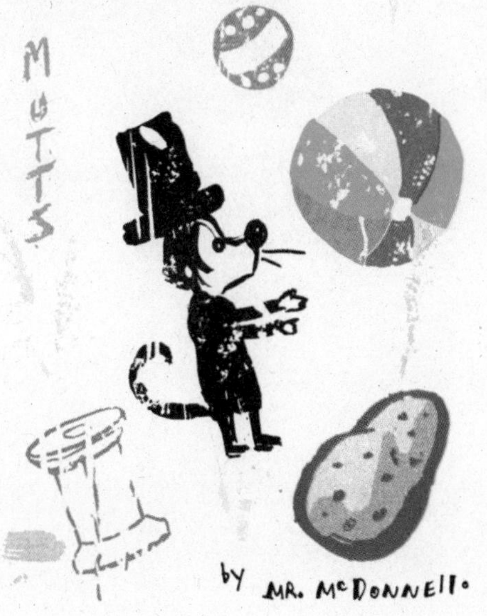
MUTTS
by MR. McDONNELL

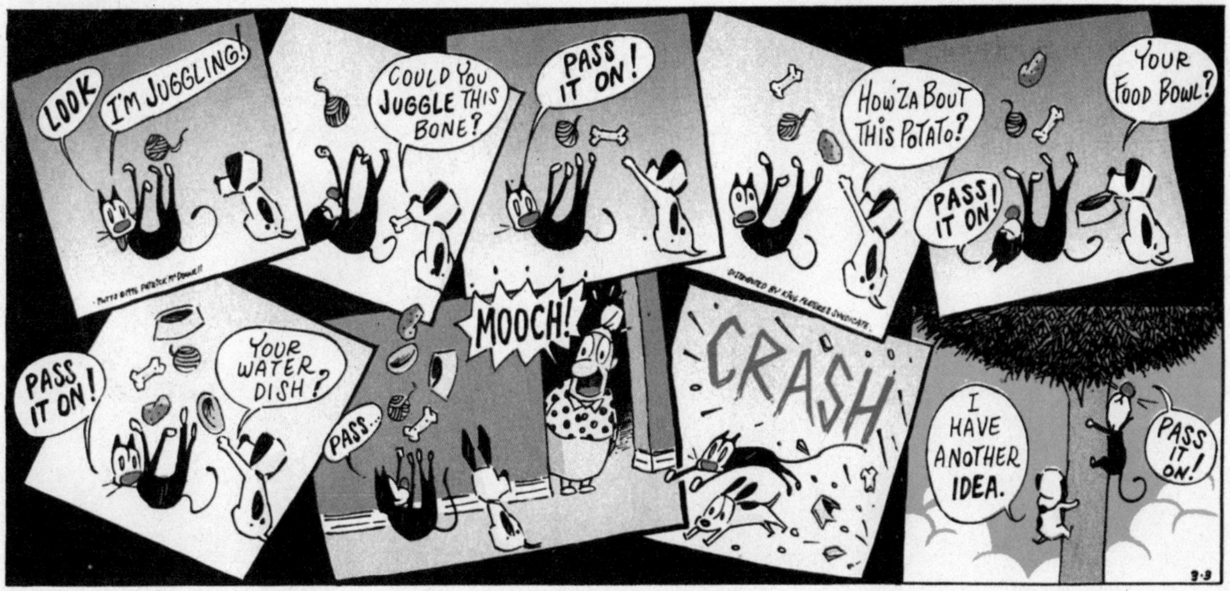
LOOK
I'M JUGGLING!
COULD YOU JUGGLE THIS BONE?
PASS IT ON!
HOW'ZA BOUT THIS POTATO?
YOUR FOOD BOWL?
PASS IT ON!
PASS IT ON!
YOUR WATER DISH?
PASS...
MOOCH!
CRASH
I HAVE ANOTHER IDEA.
PASS IT ON!

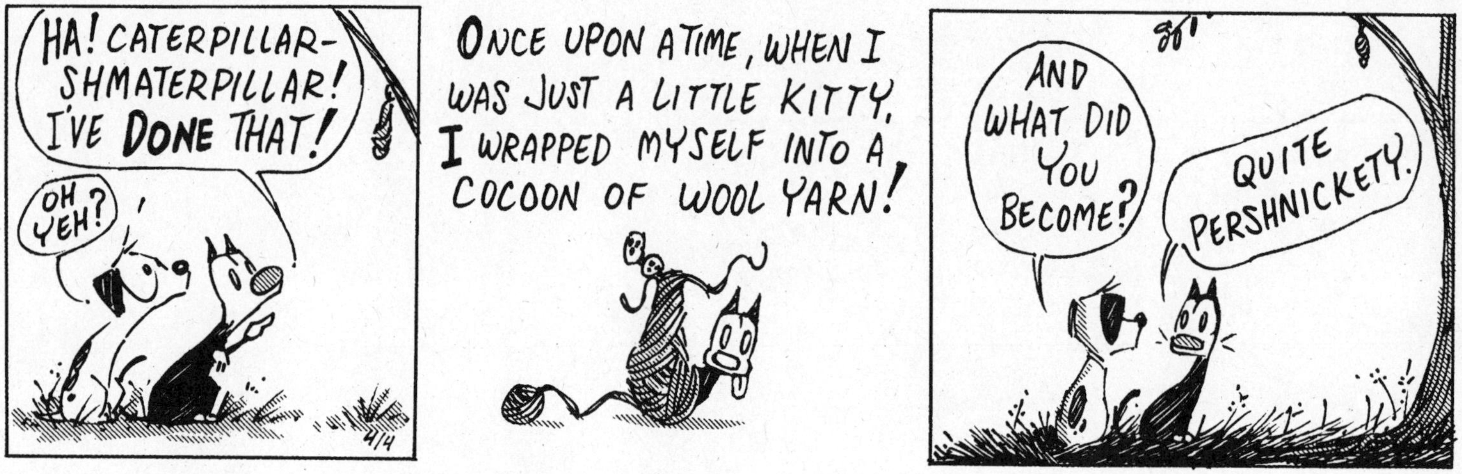
HA! CATERPILLAR-SHMATERPILLAR! I'VE **DONE** THAT!
OH YEH?
4/4
ONCE UPON A TIME, WHEN I WAS JUST A LITTLE KITTY, I WRAPPED MYSELF INTO A COCOON OF WOOL YARN!
AND WHAT DID YOU BECOME?
QUITE PERSHNICKETY.

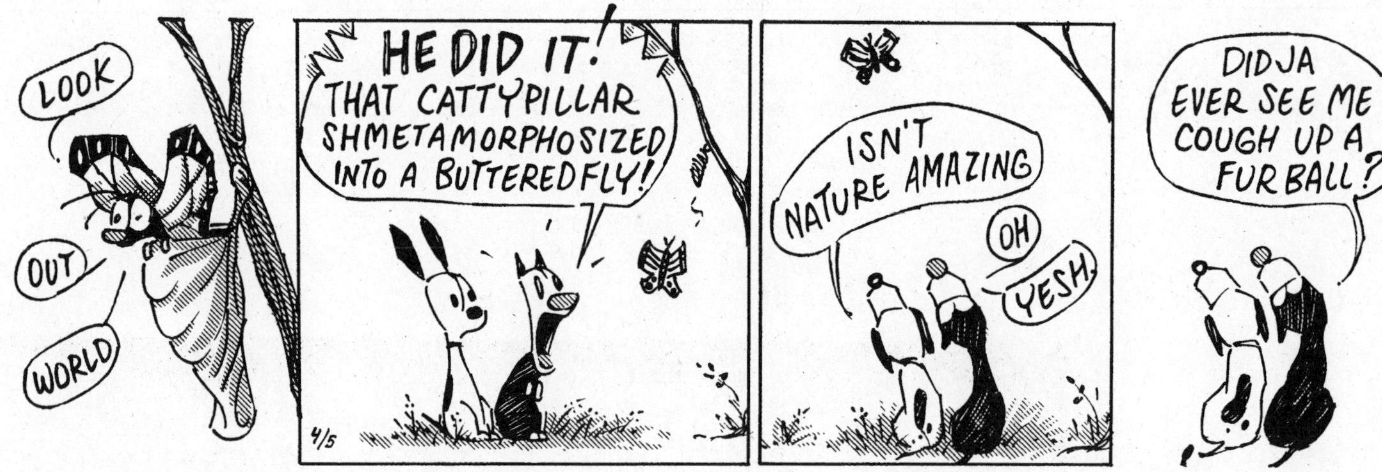
LOOK
OUT
WORLD
HE DID IT! THAT CATTYPILLAR SHMETAMORPHOSIZED INTO A BUTTEREDFLY!
4/5
ISN'T NATURE AMAZING
OH YESH.
DIDJA EVER SEE ME COUGH UP A FUR BALL?

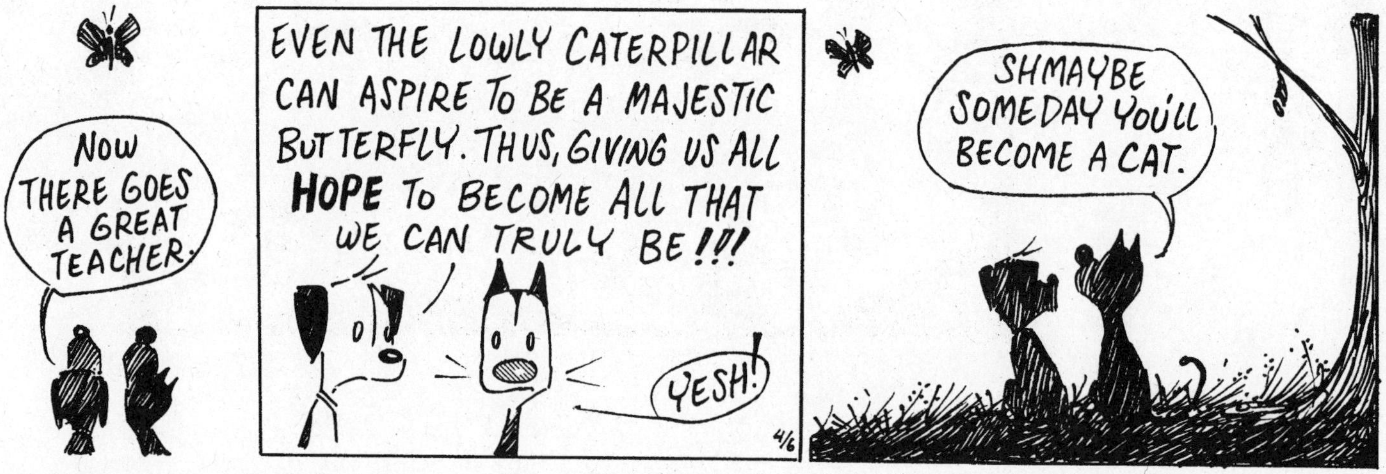
NOW THERE GOES A GREAT TEACHER.
EVEN THE LOWLY CATERPILLAR CAN ASPIRE TO BE A MAJESTIC BUTTERFLY. THUS, GIVING US ALL **HOPE** TO BECOME ALL THAT WE CAN TRULY BE!!!
YESH!
4/6
SHMAYBE SOMEDAY YOU'LL BECOME A CAT.

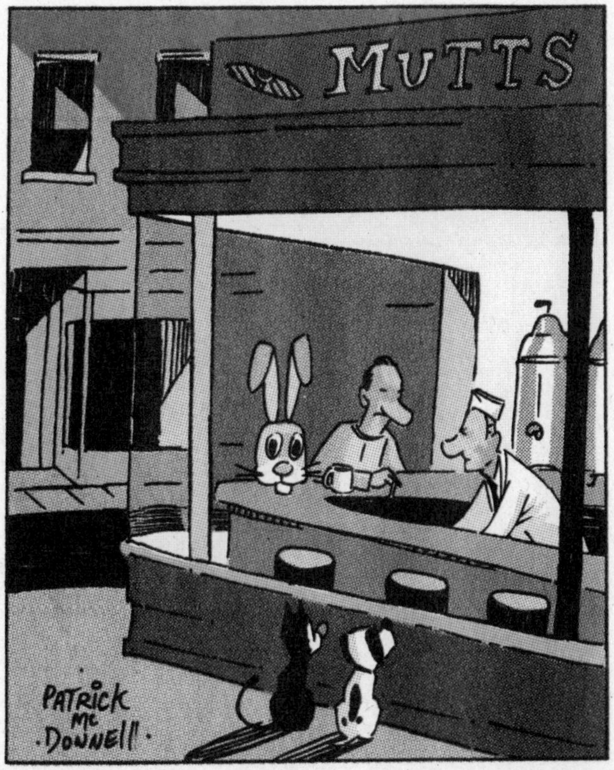
MUTTS
PATRICK Mc DONNELL

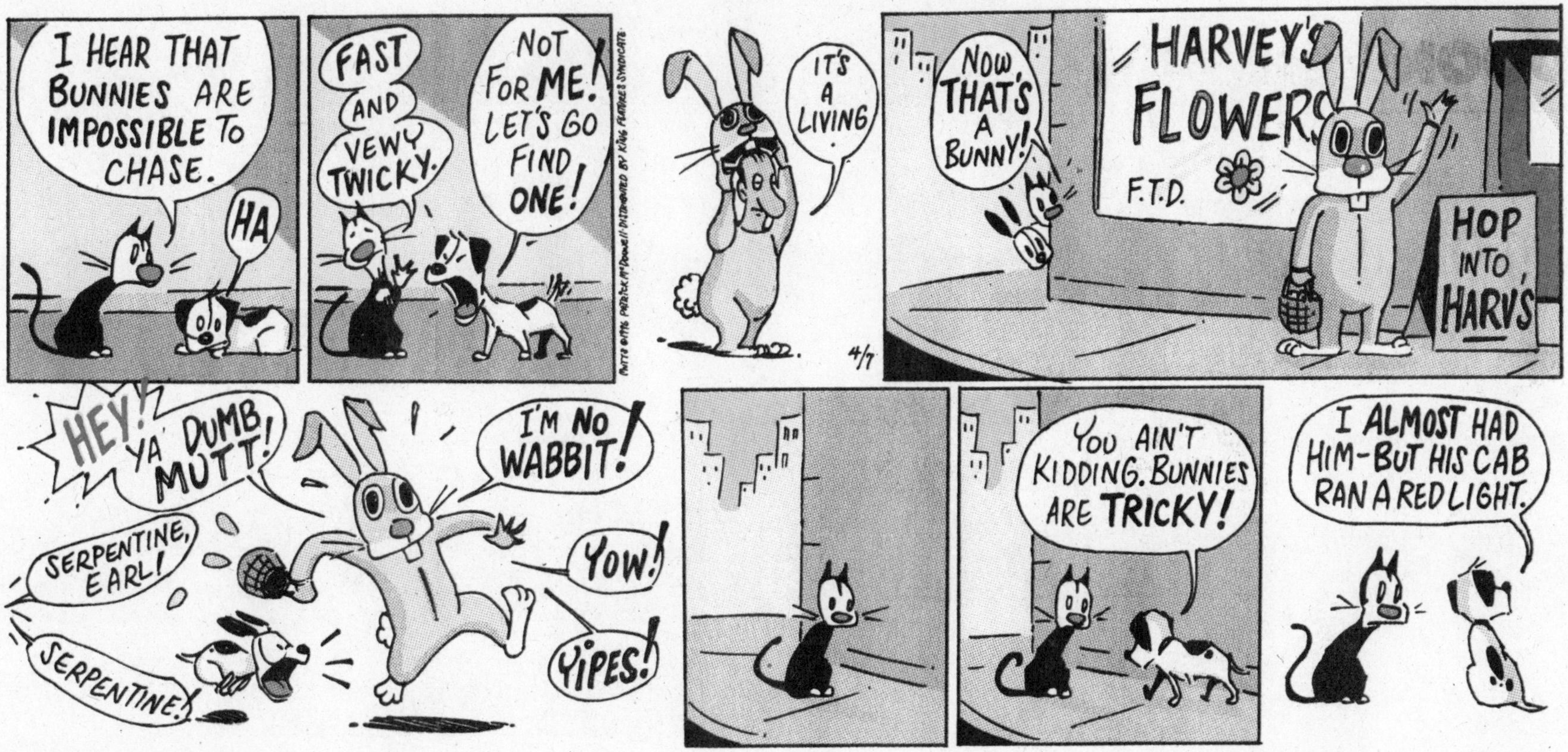
I HEAR THAT BUNNIES ARE IMPOSSIBLE TO CHASE.
HA
FAST
AND
VEWY TWICKY.
NOT FOR ME! LET'S GO FIND ONE!
MUTTS ©1996 PATRICK McDONNELL · DISTRIBUTED BY KING FEATURES SYNDICATE
IT'S A LIVING.
4/7
NOW THAT'S A BUNNY!
HARVEY'S FLOWERS
F.T.D.
HOP INTO HARV'S
HEY!
YA DUMB MUTT!
I'M NO WABBIT!
SERPENTINE, EARL!
SERPENTINE!
YOW!
YIPES!
YOU AIN'T KIDDING. BUNNIES ARE TRICKY!
I ALMOST HAD HIM-BUT HIS CAB RAN A RED LIGHT.

EARL, I'M TELLIN' YA–I'M IN LOVE! YESH, LOVE!!!
WITH A SHWELL HOUSE CAT NAMED SHNELLY... SHWEET, SHWEET, SHWEET SHNELLY!
AHHHHHHH
THERE GOES ONE SHMITTEN KITTEN
5/21

AHH, SHNELLY!
IF ONLY...
I COULD GET A GLIMPSE OF YOUR LOVELINESS...
HOTCHA!
5/24

FOR MY GIRLFRIEND I SHOULD PRACTICE MY KISHING!!!
ON WHO?
Z Z Z Z Z Z Z
SHMIK SHMAK SHMIK SHMAK SHMIK SHMAK
5/29
...YOU MINX...

SHE LOVES ME.
SHE LOVES ME
NOT.
SHE LOVES ME!
LET'S DO IT AGAIN!
THERE AREN'T ANY THREE-LEAF CLOVERS LEFT.
5/27

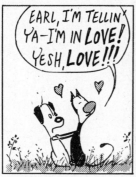

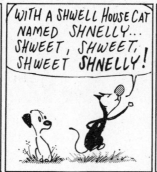

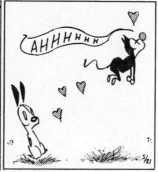

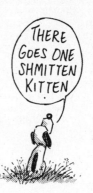

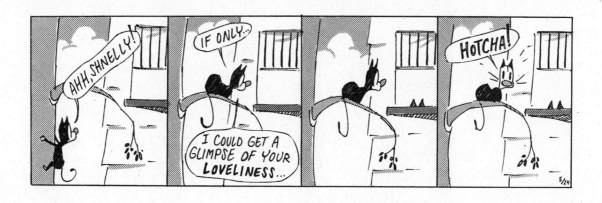

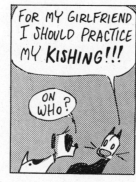

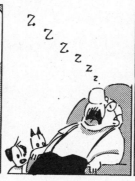

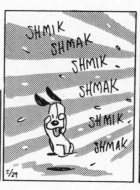

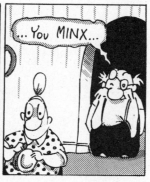

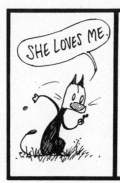

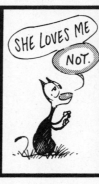

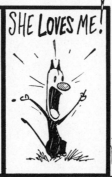

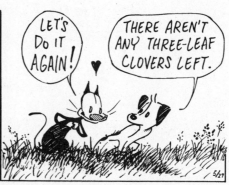

AHH, SHNELLY, LET'S SEAL OUR LOVE WITH A KISH...
LOOK OUT, NELLY—I HAVE TO SHAKE OUT THE DUST BROOM...
MMMMF
SO HOW WAS IT?
FILTHY.

PLEASE FLY TO MY SHNELLY AND GIVE HER MY LOVE.
FLY, MY FRIEND, FLY TO MY SHNELLY!
I WISH I HAD WINGS
... AND TWO DRUMSTICKS WITH GRAVY.
6.4

SO HOW'S NELLY?
WHO?
WHO?!? YOUR WHOLE WORLD REVOLVED AROUND THAT GIRL JUST YESTERDAY, AND NOW YOU CAN'T EVEN REMEMBER HER NAME!?!
AIN'T LOVE GRAND?
6/7

MY HEART IS STILL BROKEN
DON'T WORRY. "TIME HEALS ALL WOUNDS"
WOW! THAT'S PROFOUND—WHEN DID YOU THINK OF THAT?
WAITING ON LINE AT THE VET.
6/8

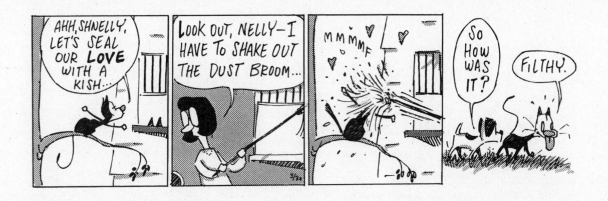

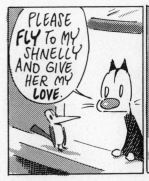

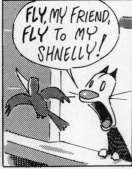

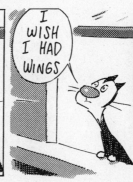

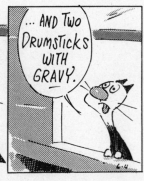

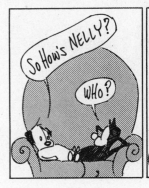

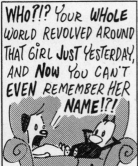

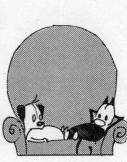

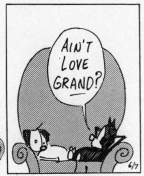

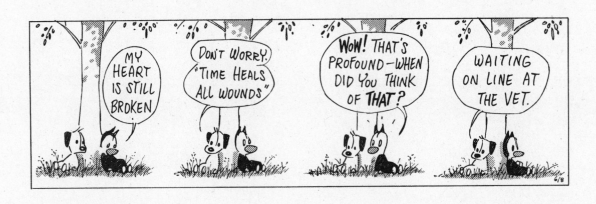

MY OZZIE LEFT ME HOME ALONE! WHAT DOES HE EXPECT ME TO DO?
JUST SIT HERE ALL DAY AND WAIT FOR HIS RETURN!?!
HA!
6/10

WHAT WAS WITH ALL THAT HOWLING YESTERDAY!?!
OH, I WAS HOWLING FOR MY OZZIE TO COME BACK HOME.
WOULDN'T HE COME BACK HOME IF YOU DIDN'T HOWL!?!
I WOULDN'T KNOW.
6/15

OOOOH, JUST LOOK AT THESE TWO!!!
OOOO DEE PUPPEE POO
WEE WEE KEE TEE
"PAT" "PAT"
"POKE" "POKE"
THE "CUTIE" CURSE.
1/29

HEY, MOOCH, WHAT'S NEW?
NOTHIN'
SAME OL' GARBAGE
7/19

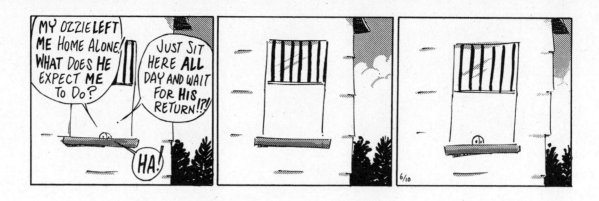

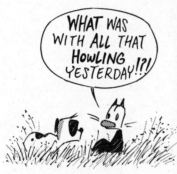

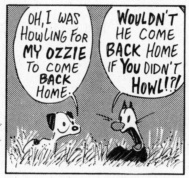

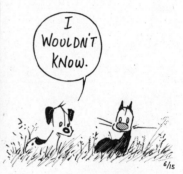

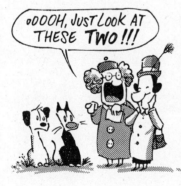

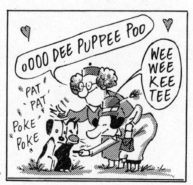

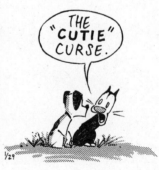

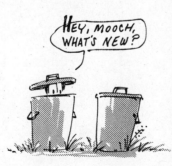

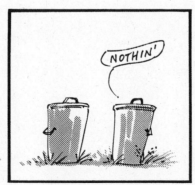

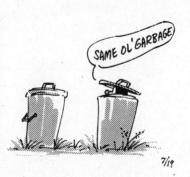

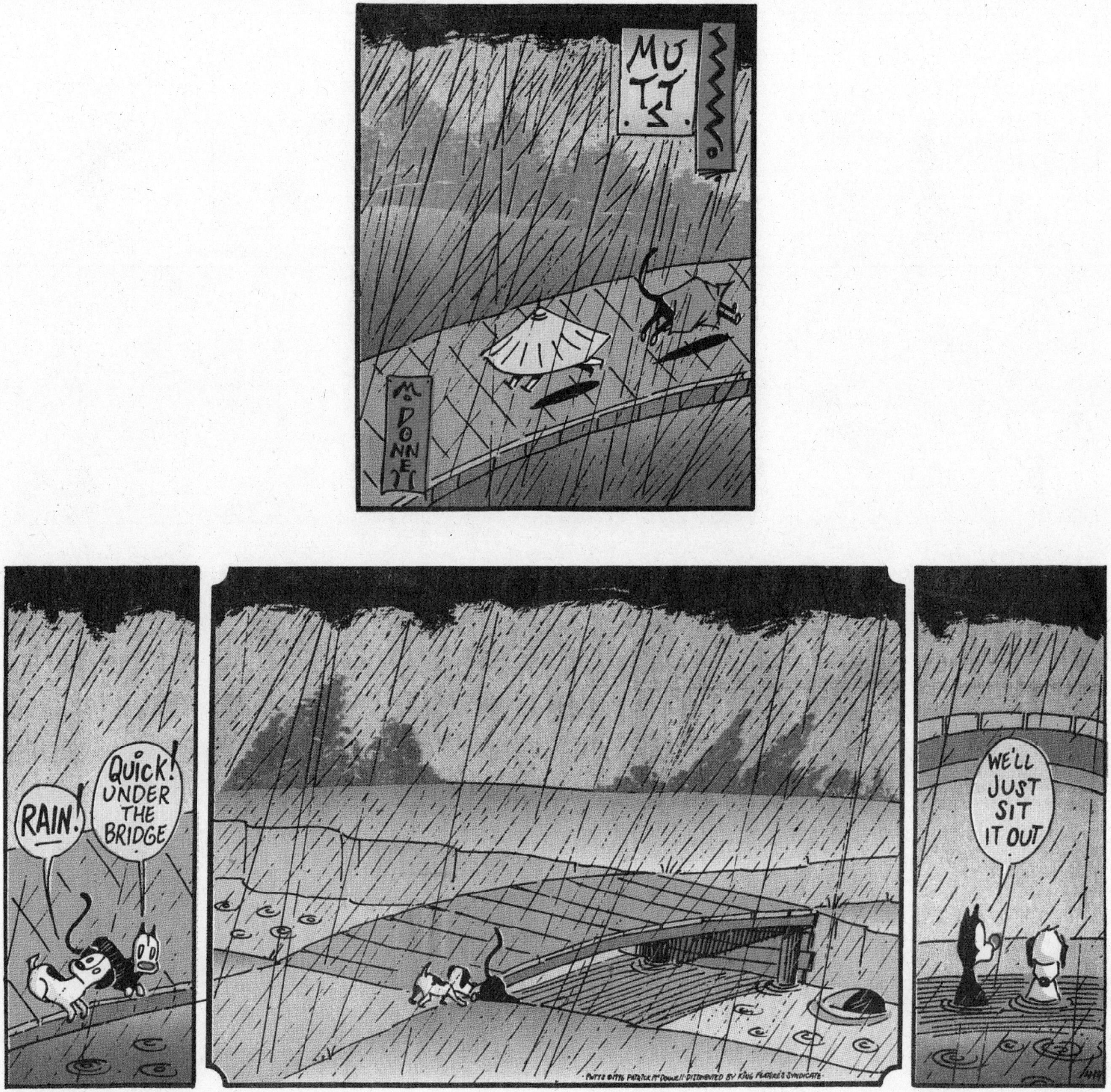
MUTTS
M. DONNELL
RAIN!
QUICK! UNDER THE BRIDGE
WE'LL JUST SIT IT OUT

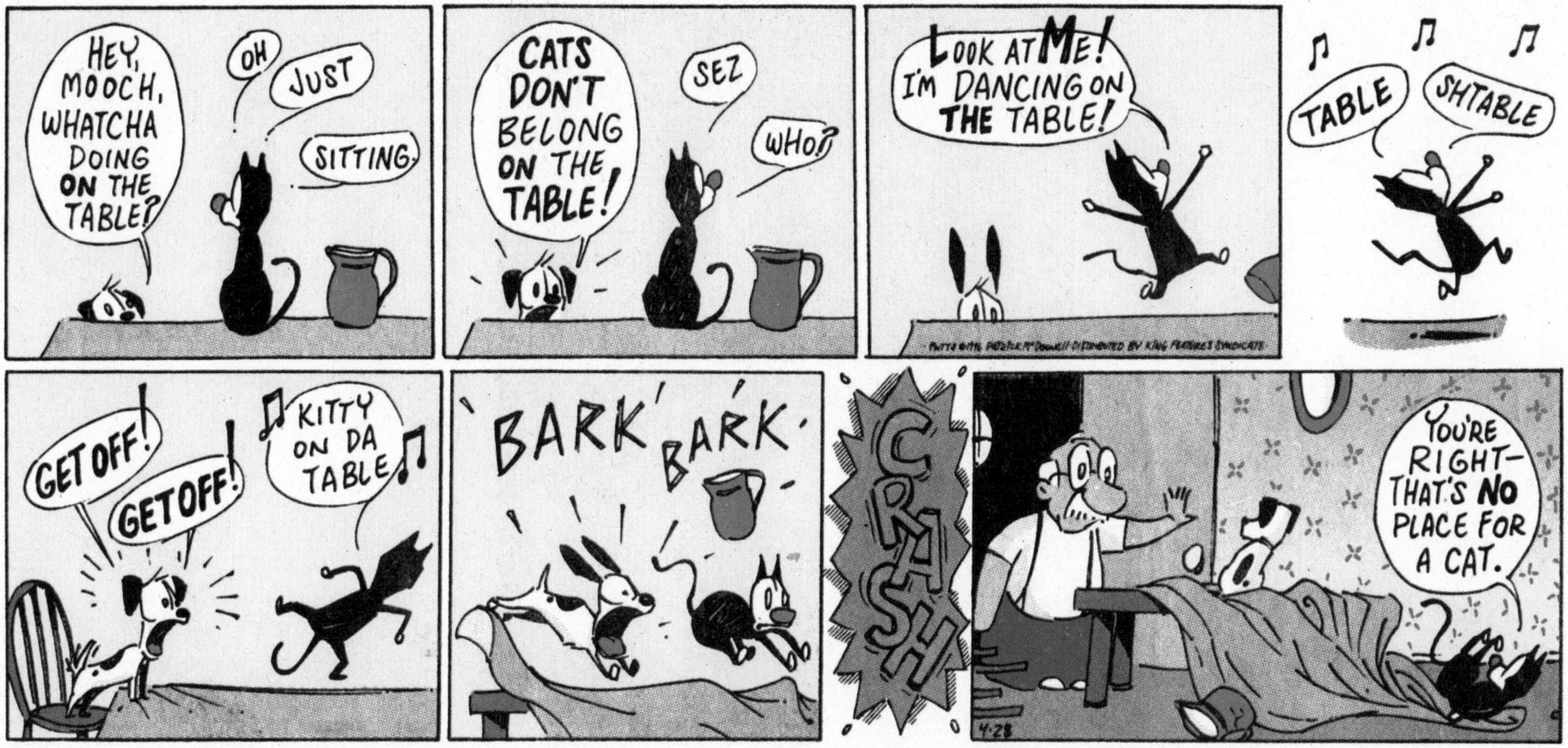
HEY, MOOCH, WHATCHA DOING ON THE TABLE?
OH
JUST
SITTING.
CATS DON'T BELONG ON THE TABLE!
SEZ
WHO?
LOOK AT ME! I'M DANCING ON THE TABLE!
TABLE
SHTABLE
GET OFF!
GET OFF!
KITTY ON DA TABLE
BARK
BARK
CRASH
4-28
YOU'RE RIGHT- THAT'S NO PLACE FOR A CAT.


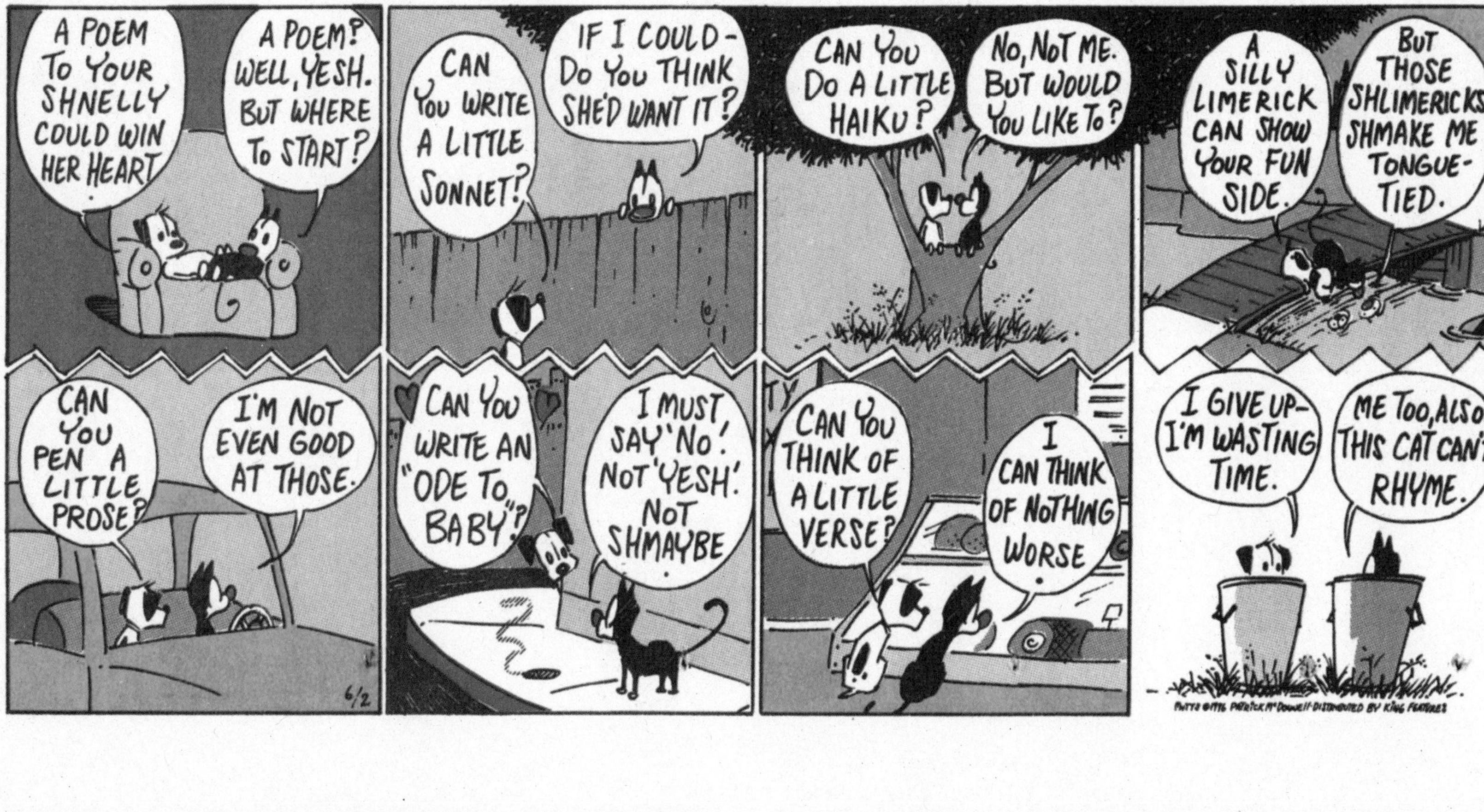
A POEM TO YOUR SHNELLY COULD WIN HER HEART.
A POEM? WELL, YESH. BUT WHERE TO START?
CAN YOU WRITE A LITTLE SONNET?
IF I COULD- DO YOU THINK SHE'D WANT IT?
CAN YOU DO A LITTLE HAIKU?
NO, NOT ME. BUT WOULD YOU LIKE TO?
A SILLY LIMERICK CAN SHOW YOUR FUN SIDE.
BUT THOSE SHLIMERICKS SHMAKE ME TONGUE-TIED.
CAN YOU PEN A LITTLE PROSE?
I'M NOT EVEN GOOD AT THOSE.
6/2
CAN YOU WRITE AN "ODE TO BABY"?
I MUST SAY 'NO.' NOT 'YESH.' NOT SHMAYBE.
CAN YOU THINK OF A LITTLE VERSE?
I CAN THINK OF NOTHING WORSE.
I GIVE UP- I'M WASTING TIME.
ME TOO, ALSO. THIS CAT CAN'T RHYME.

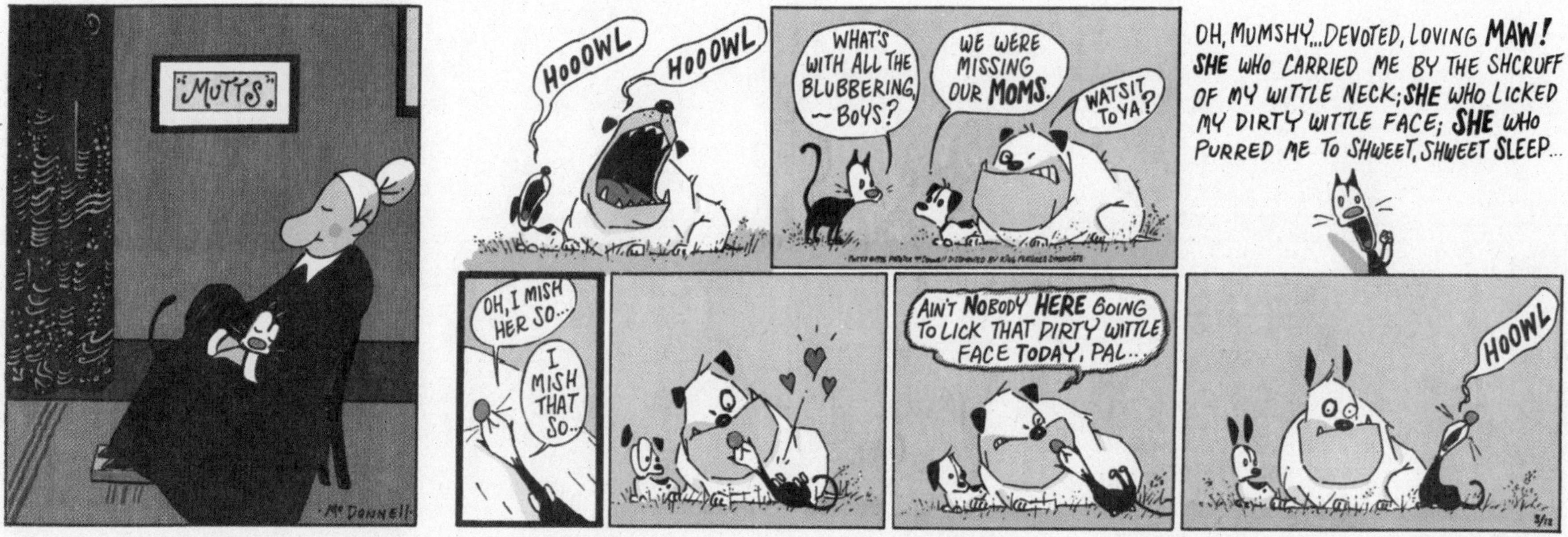
"MUTTS"
McDONNELL
HOOOWL
HOOOWL
WHAT'S WITH ALL THE BLUBBERING, ~BOYS?
WE WERE MISSING OUR MOMS.
WATSIT TO YA?
OH, MUMSHY... DEVOTED, LOVING MAW! SHE WHO CARRIED ME BY THE SHCRUFF OF MY WITTLE NECK; SHE WHO LICKED MY DIRTY WITTLE FACE; SHE WHO PURRED ME TO SHWEET, SHWEET SLEEP...
OH, I MISH HER SO...
I MISH THAT SO...
AIN'T NOBODY HERE GOING TO LICK THAT DIRTY WITTLE FACE TODAY, PAL...
HOOWL
3/12

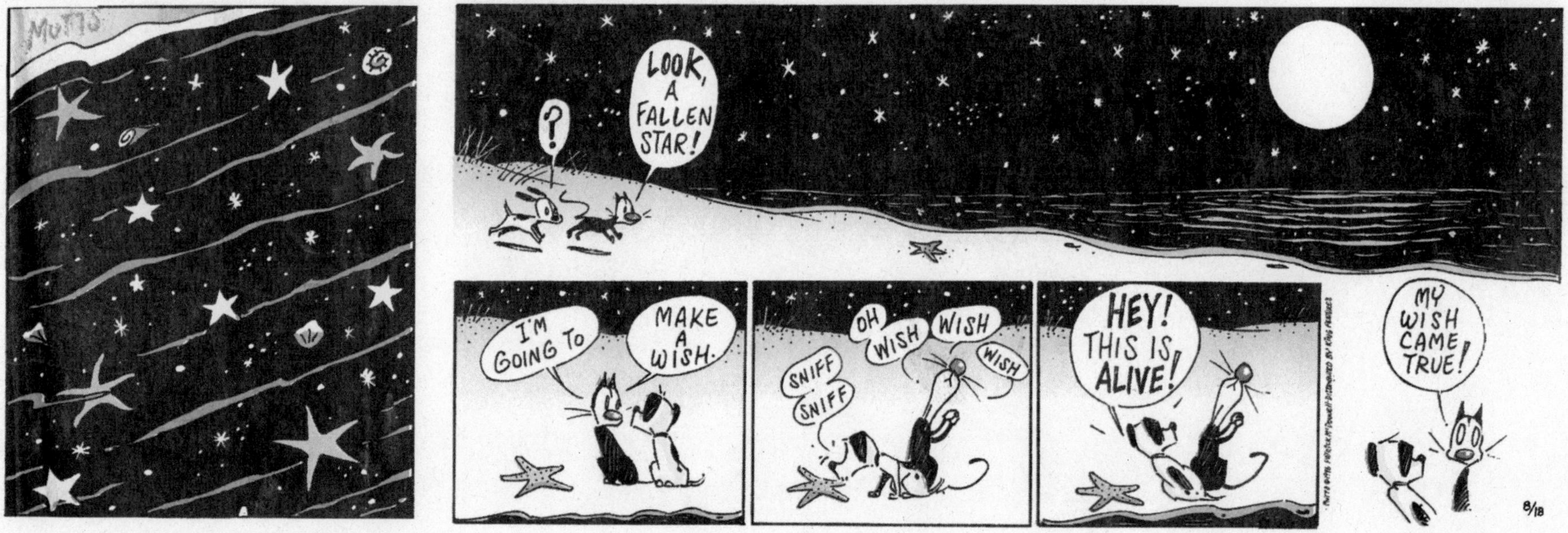
MUTTS
?
LOOK, A FALLEN STAR!
I'M GOING TO
MAKE A WISH.
OH
WISH
WISH
WISH
SNIFF
SNIFF
HEY! THIS IS ALIVE!
MY WISH CAME TRUE!
8/18

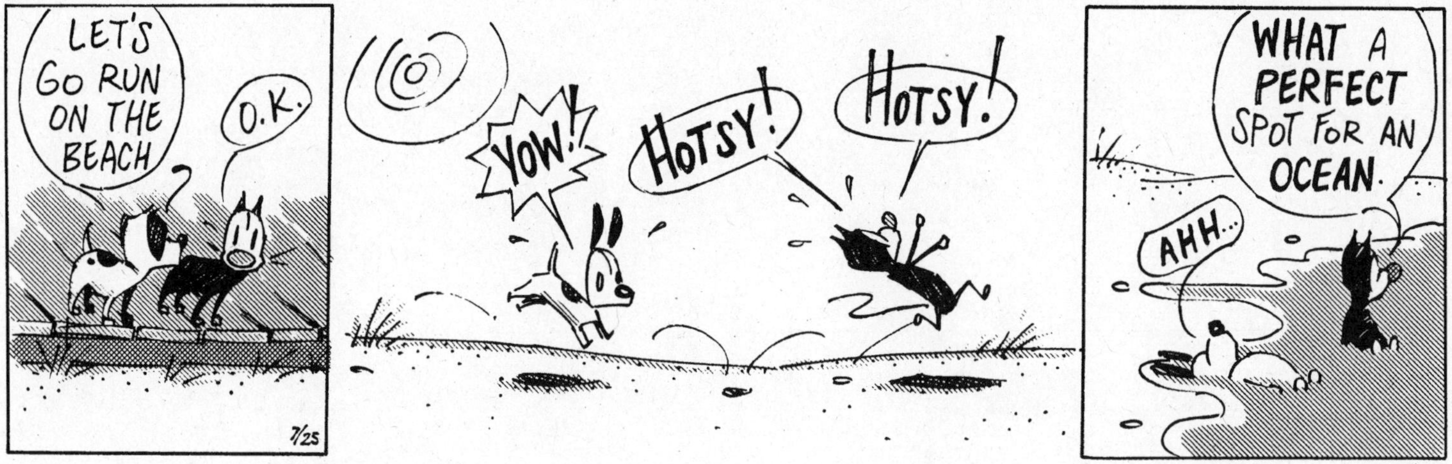
LET'S GO RUN ON THE BEACH
O.K.
7/25
YOW!
HOTSY!
HOTSY!
WHAT A PERFECT SPOT FOR AN OCEAN.
AHH..

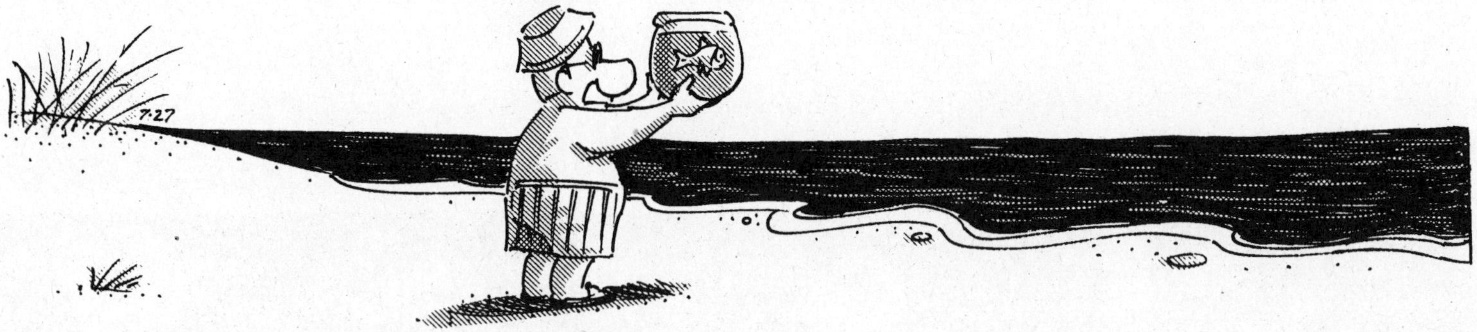
7-27

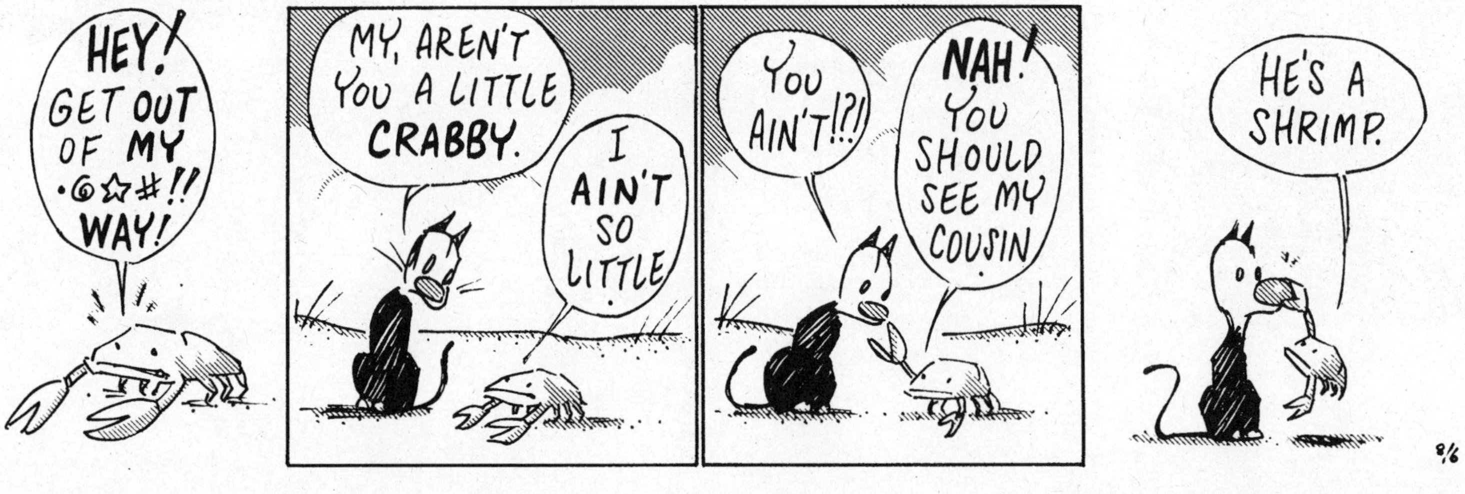
HEY! GET OUT OF MY •@☆#!! WAY!
MY, AREN'T YOU A LITTLE CRABBY.
I AIN'T SO LITTLE.
YOU AIN'T!?!
NAH! YOU SHOULD SEE MY COUSIN.
HE'S A SHRIMP.
8/6

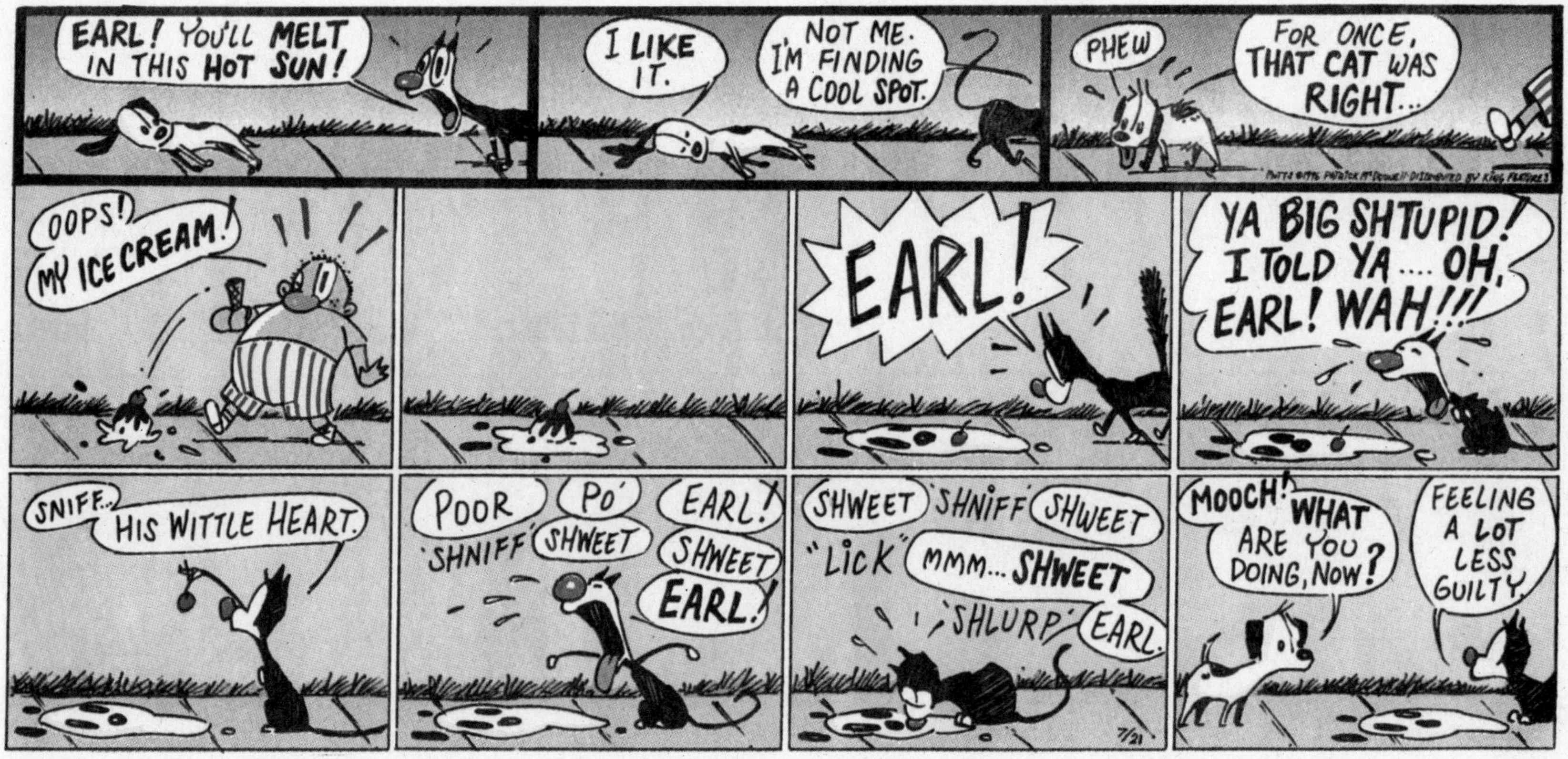
EARL! YOU'LL MELT IN THIS HOT SUN!
I LIKE IT.
NOT ME. I'M FINDING A COOL SPOT.
PHEW
FOR ONCE, THAT CAT WAS RIGHT...
OOPS!
MY ICE CREAM!
EARL!
YA BIG SHTUPID! I TOLD YA.... OH, EARL! WAH!!!
SNIFF..
HIS WITTLE HEART.
POOR
PO'
EARL!
'SHNIFF'
SHWEET
SHWEET
EARL!
SHWEET
'SHNIFF'
SHWEET
"LICK"
MMM... SHWEET
'SHLURP'
EARL.
7/21
MOOCH!
WHAT ARE YOU DOING, NOW?
FEELING A LOT LESS GUILTY.

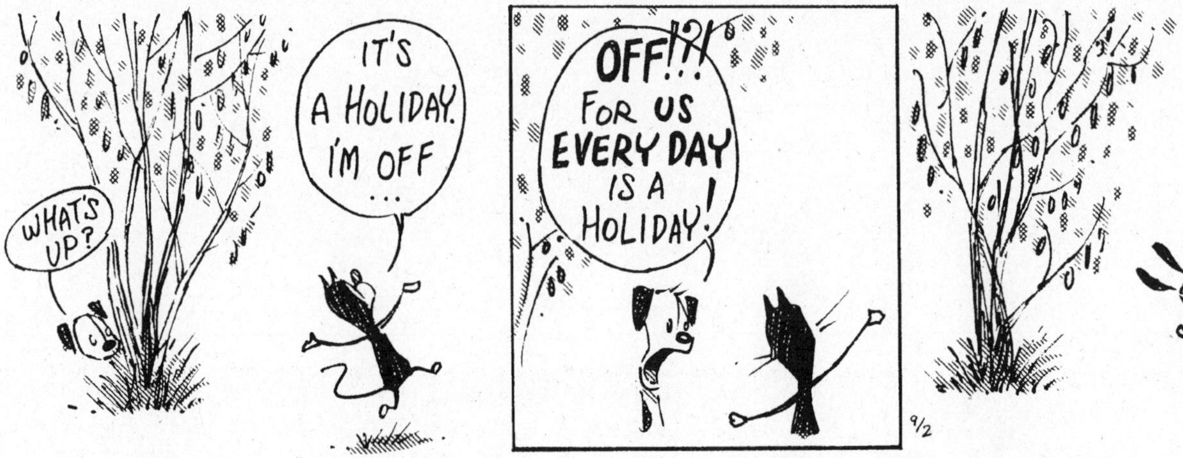
WHAT'S UP?
IT'S A HOLIDAY. I'M OFF ...
OFF!?! FOR US EVERY DAY IS A HOLIDAY!
9/2

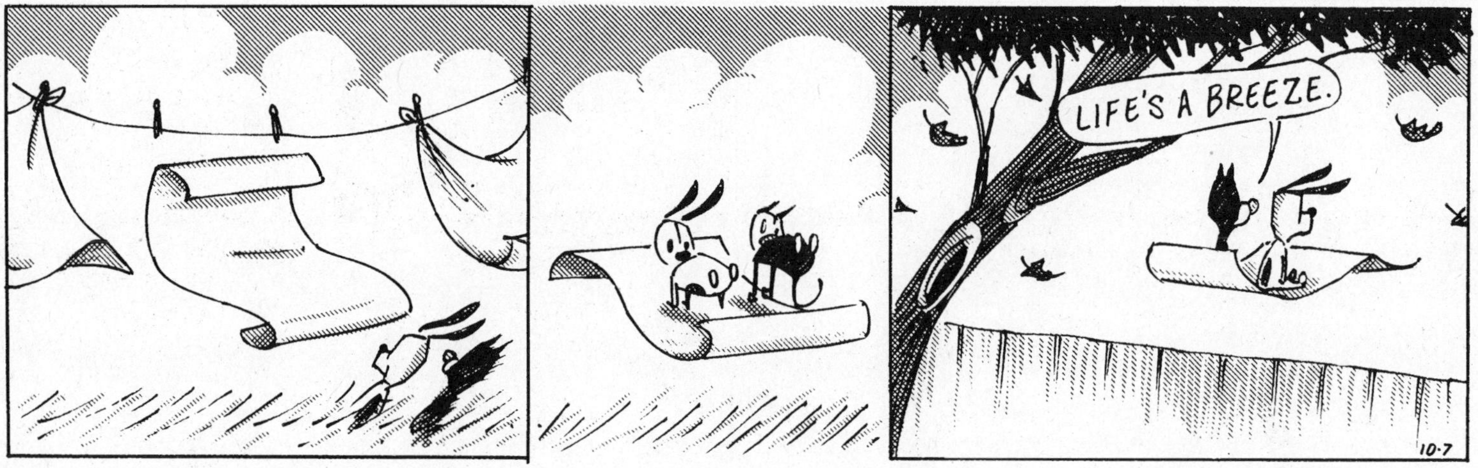
LIFE'S A BREEZE.
10·7

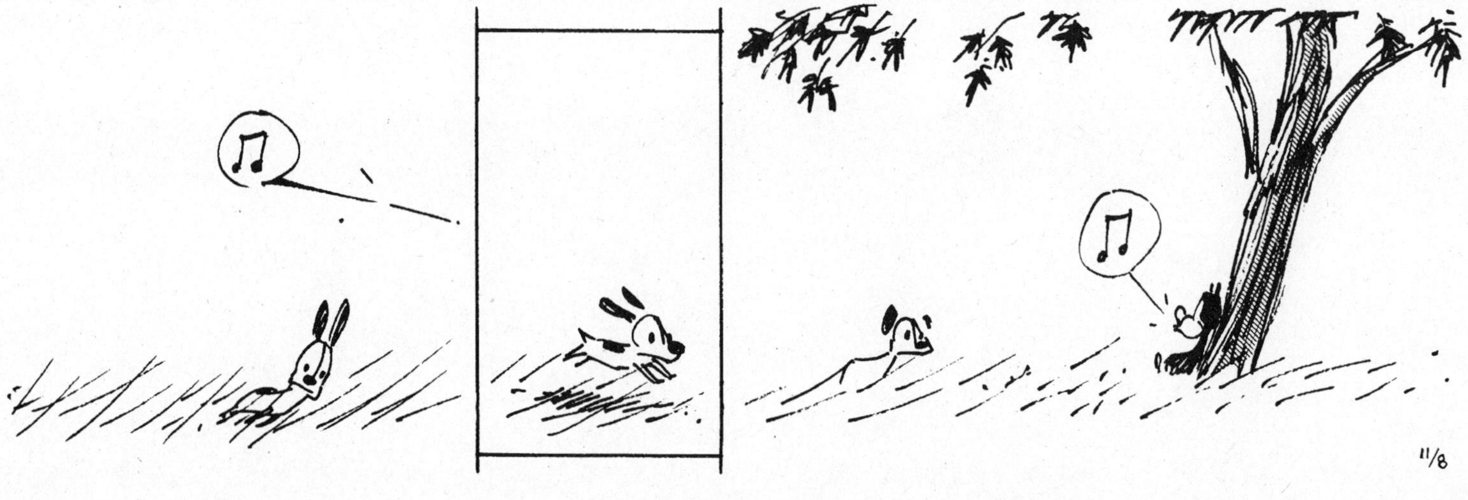
11/8

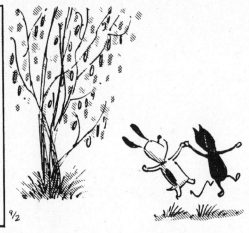

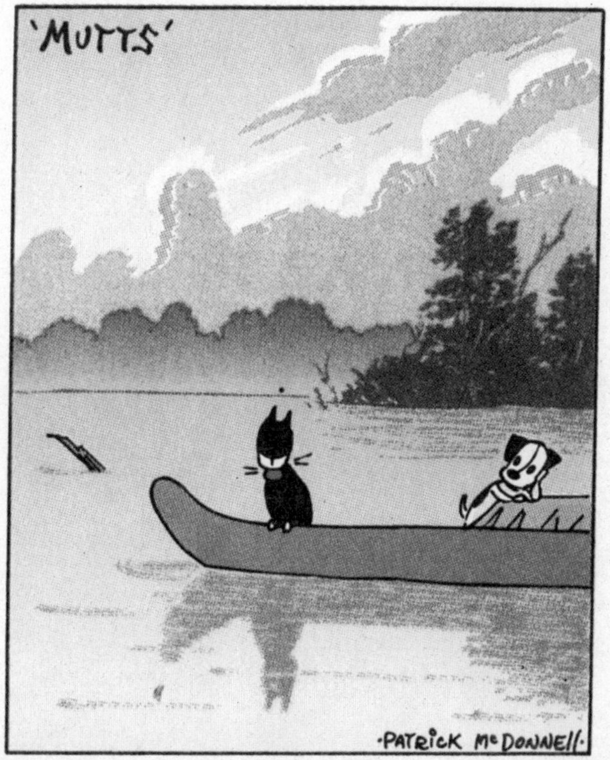
'MUTTS'
·PATRICK McDONNELL·

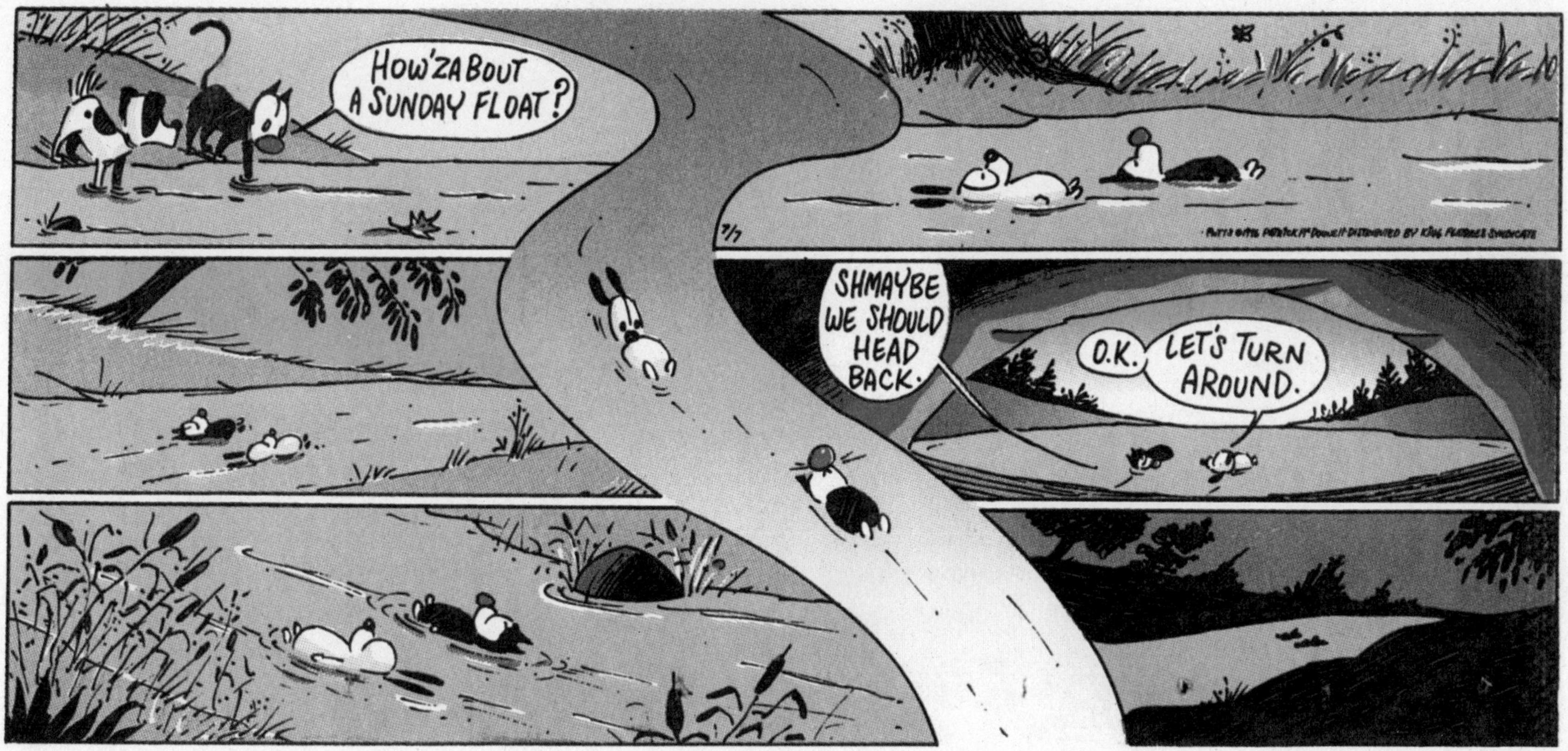
HOW'ZA BOUT A SUNDAY FLOAT?
7/7
SHMAYBE WE SHOULD HEAD BACK.
O.K.
LET'S TURN AROUND.

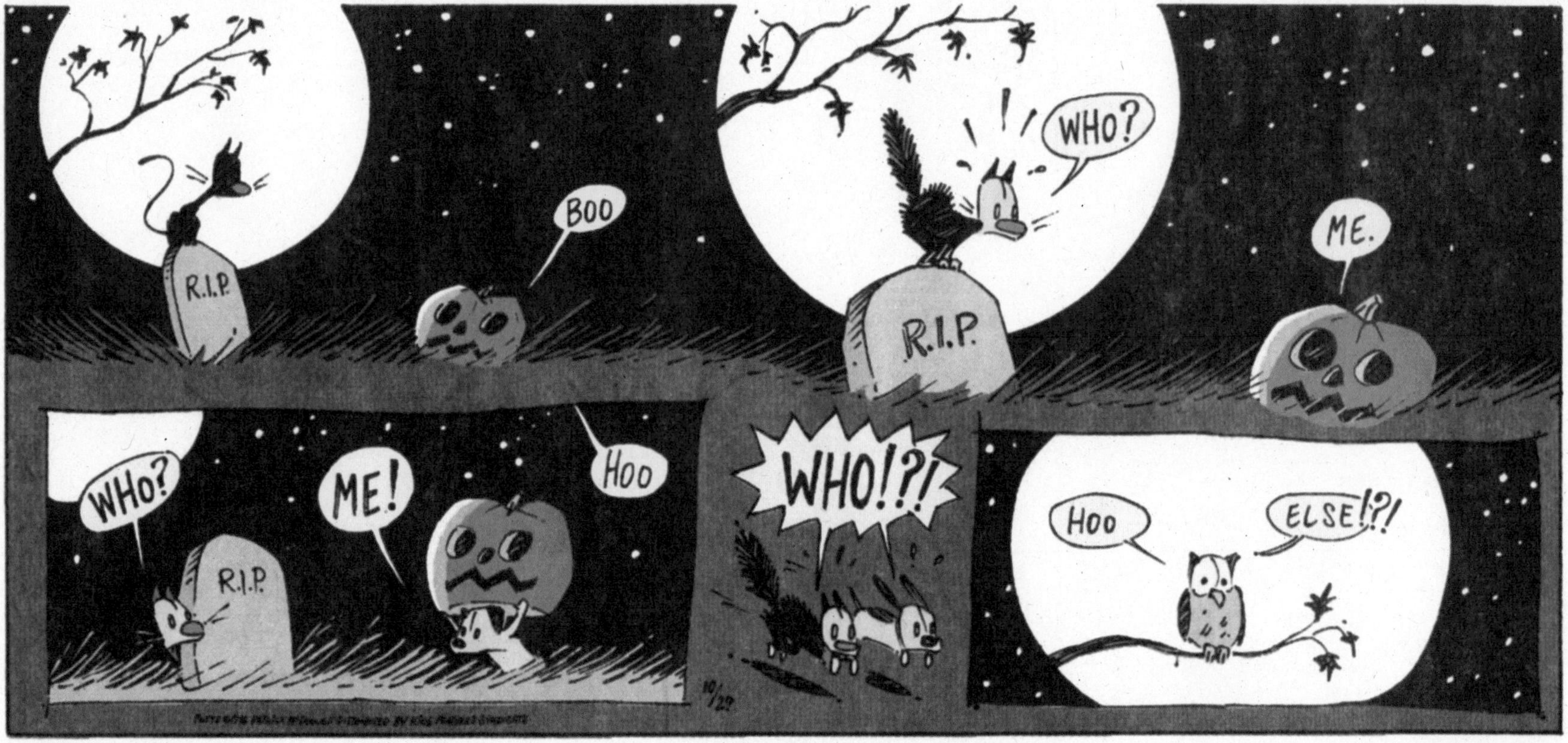
R.I.P.
BOO
WHO?
R.I.P.
ME.
WHo?
R.I.P.
ME!
Hoo
WHO!?!
Hoo
ELSE!?!

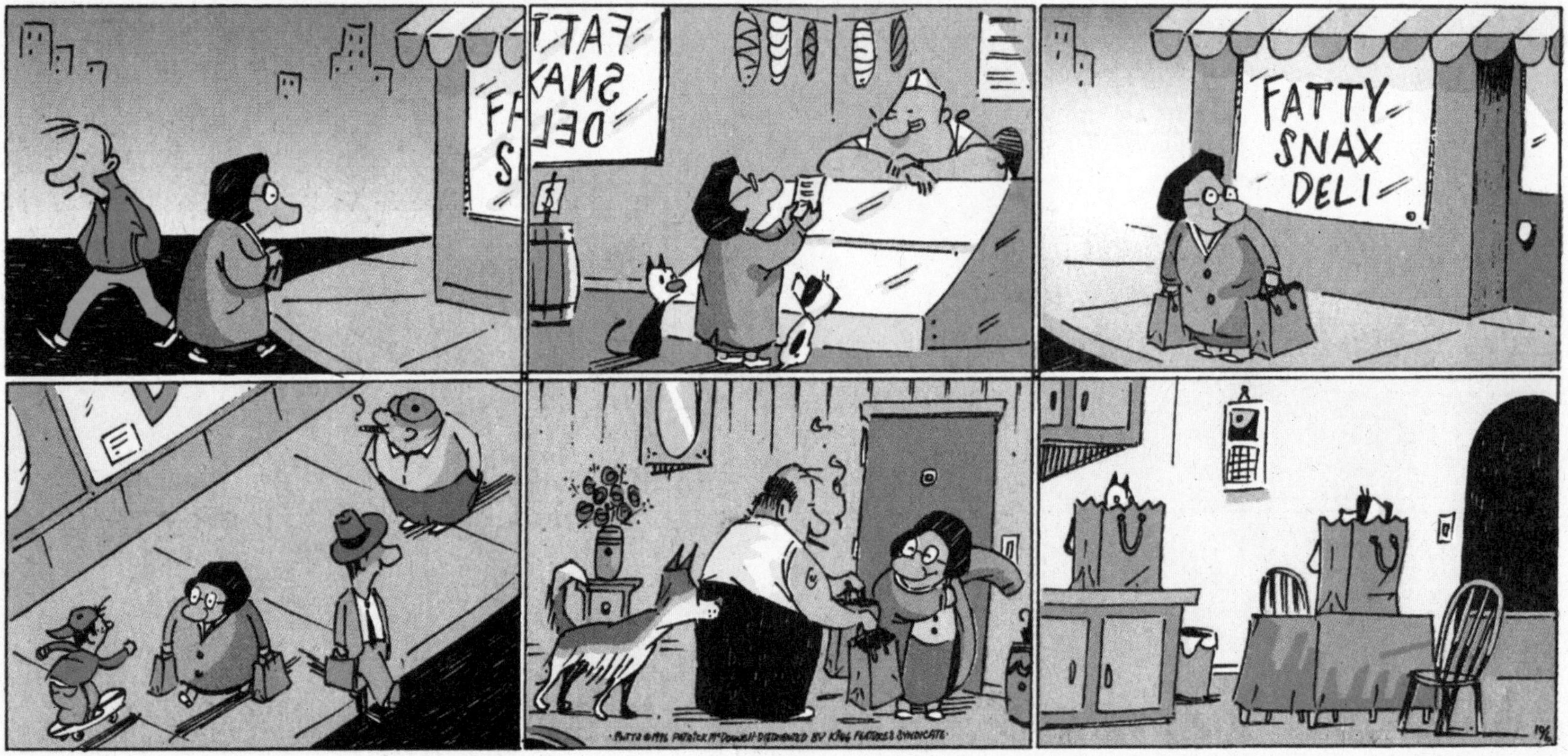
FATTY SNAX DELI

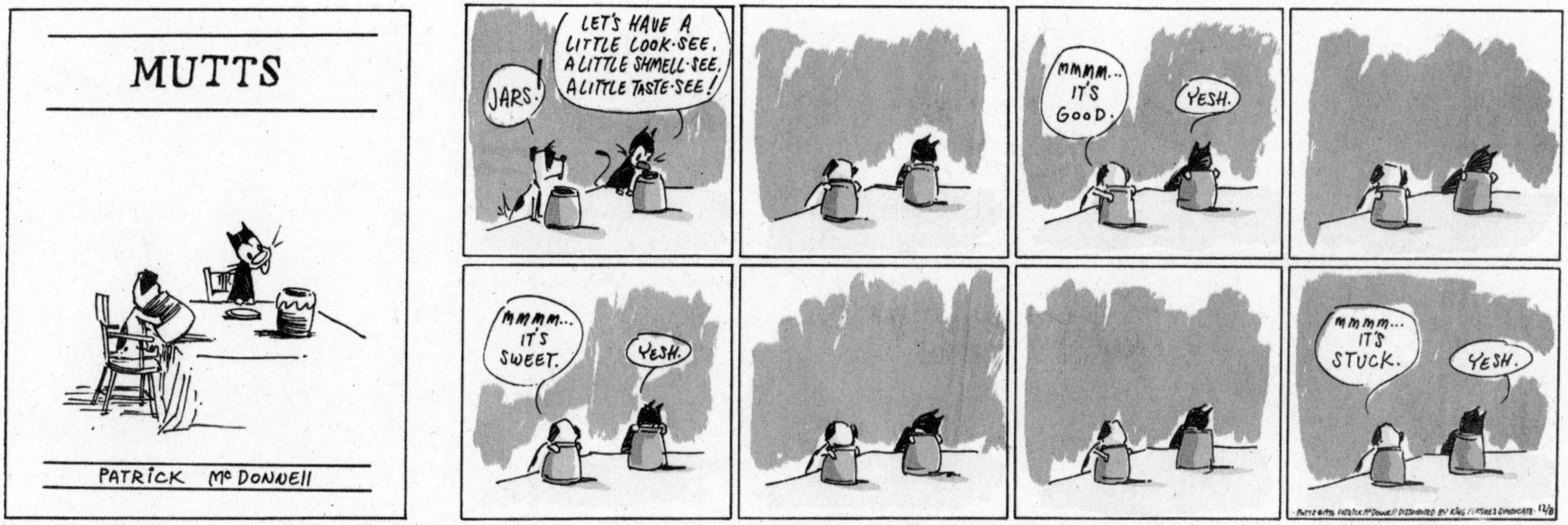

MUTTS
PATRICK McDONNELL
JARS!
LET'S HAVE A LITTLE LOOK·SEE, A LITTLE SHMELL·SEE, A LITTLE TASTE·SEE!
MMMM... IT'S GOOD.
YESH.
MMMM... IT'S SWEET.
YESH.
MMMM... IT'S STUCK.
YESH.


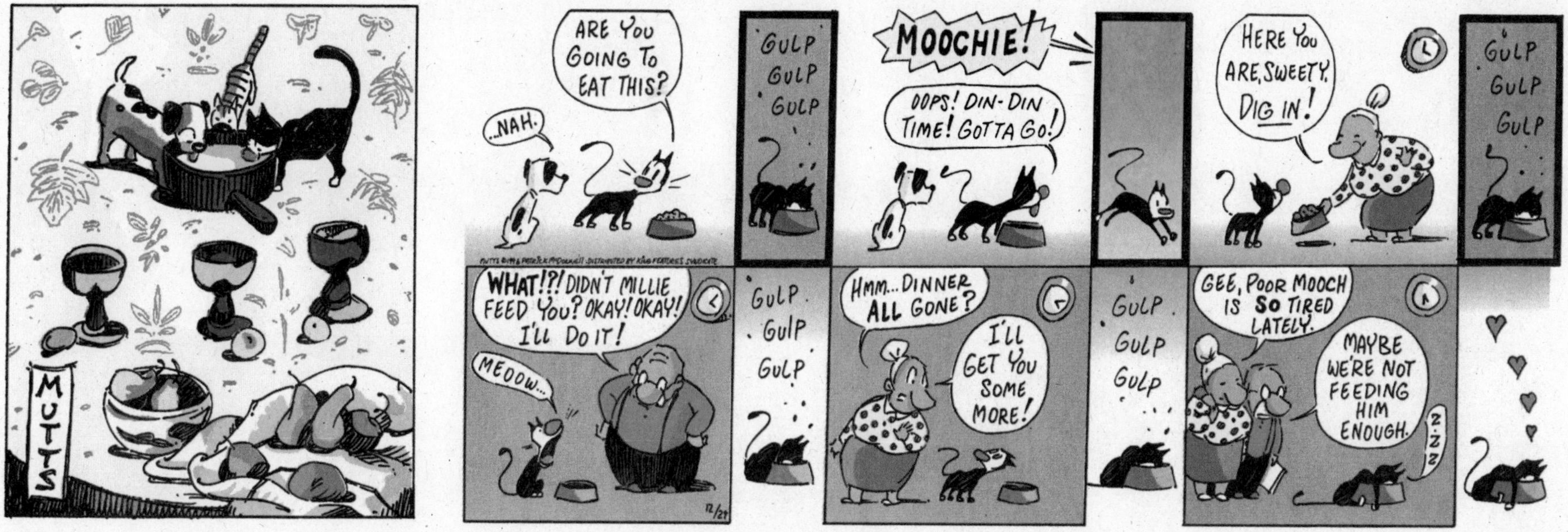

MUTTS
ARE YOU GOING TO EAT THIS?
..NAH.
GULP GULP GULP
MOOCHIE!
OOPS! DIN-DIN TIME! GOTTA GO!
HERE YOU ARE, SWEETY. DIG IN!
GULP GULP GULP
WHAT!?! DIDN'T MILLIE FEED YOU? OKAY! OKAY! I'LL DO IT!
MEOOW...
GULP GULP GULP
HMM... DINNER ALL GONE?
I'LL GET YOU SOME MORE!
GULP GULP GULP
GEE, POOR MOOCH IS SO TIRED LATELY.
MAYBE WE'RE NOT FEEDING HIM ENOUGH.
Z Z Z

HEY, EARL, I FOUND SOME-THING!
SOMETHING GOOD?
YESH.
A NEW FRIEND.
12/2

WELL, IT LOOKS LIKE WE FOUND A LITTLE ORPHAN KITTY IN THE GARBAGE.
YESH.
WHAT SHOULD WE CALL HIM?
SHTINKY.
YELLO!
12/4

WE CAN'T CALL OUR ORPHAN KITTY "SHTINKY."
PURR
12/5
LET'S NAME HIM SOMETHING SWEET, LIKE...
"PUDDING"
PURRR
I LIKE THAT!
PURR
"SHTINKY PUDDIN'."
YELLO!

EXCUSE ME
PARDON...
DID ANYONE LOSE A LITTLE KITTY?
SIR..
MADAM...
ANYONE?
GEE...
WHAT Do YOU HAVE To Do AROUND HERE...
LOST
REWARD
To GET NOTICED?
12·6

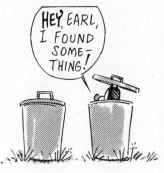

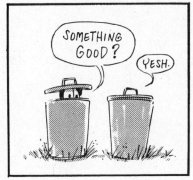

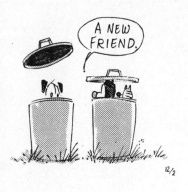

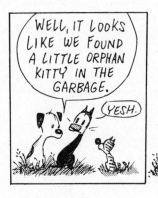

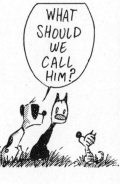

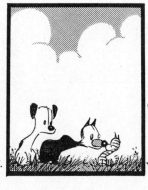

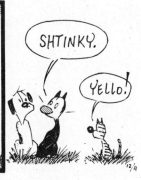

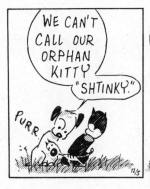

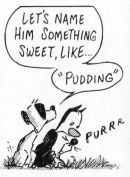

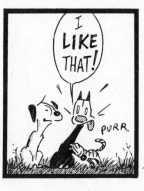

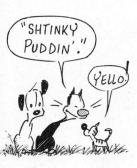

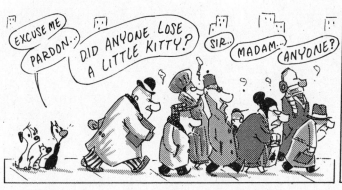

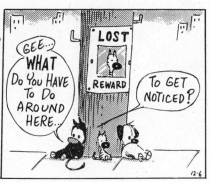

WHO SAYS I CAN'T BRING IN A FRIEND? THIS IS MY HOUSE, TOO, YA KNOW!
I KNOW.
YOW! THAT'S HIM! THAT'S THE LITTLE LOST KITTY!!! YAHOO!
QUICK, MILLIE, CALL UP FOR THE REWARD!
AND THIS IS MY GARAGE!
I KNOW.

Z-Z-Z-Z
AHH, MOOCH, HE'S SO KIND AND GENEROUS... I'M NOT GOING TO MAKE HIM A LOT OF TROUBLE— I'M NOT...
Z-Z-Z-Z
PAT
PAT

HEY, MISTER! HOWZABOUT TAKING HOME A LITTLE KITTY?
I'M REALLY NOT ALL THAT MUCH TROUBLE...
PURRR
PURRR
IT'S A COLD, COLD WORLD.

SHTINKY!!
WOOF!
WE WERE WORRIED SICK ABOUT YOU!
YOU COULD CATCH A DEATH OF COLD!
YOU WERE SAFE WITH US!
I KNOW.
I KNOW.
I KNOW.
WHAT WERE YOU THINKING!?!
I DUNNO.

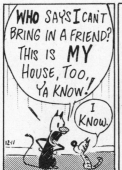

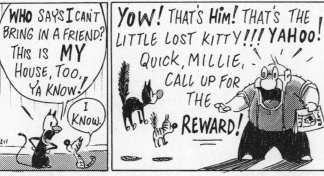

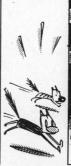

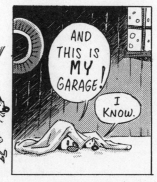

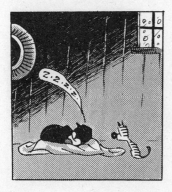

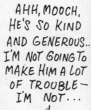

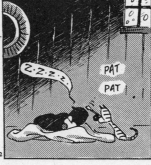

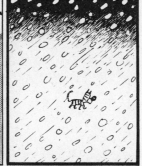

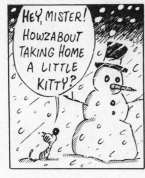

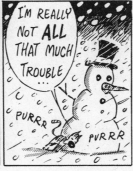

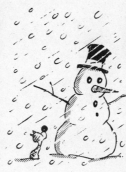

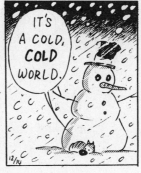

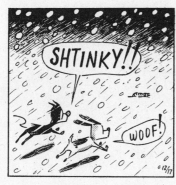

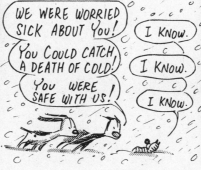

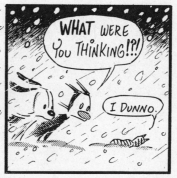

SHMAYBE SOMEONE WILL SAVE US...
HUH!?! WHAT OTHER NUT WOULD BE OUT ON A NIGHT LIKE THIS!?!
HELLO, BOYS...
YELLO.
12/20

I DO HOPE IT'S MY KITTY YOU FOUND. DESPITE ALL MY WEALTH, IT IS THE ONLY GIFT MY PRECIOUS DAUGHTER PRAYS FOR.
12/21
WELL, I'M SURE YOU KNOW, MR. GREY—"MONEY CAN'T BUY LOVE."
ON THE CONTRARY...
ONE CAN PURCHASE "UNCONDITIONAL" LOVE AT ANY ANIMAL SHELTER FOR A SMALL FEE!

HURRY, BOYS, INTO MY BAG—THERE YOU'LL BE NICE AND WARM—AND THERE'S PLENTY OF MILK AND COOKIES!
HO
HO
HO
COOKIES!
YESH!
12/23
DON'T WORRY—I'LL HAVE YOU HOME IN NO TIME.
CHOMP.
NO RUSH.
PURR

I'M SURE WE'LL FIND YOUR KITTEN, MR. GREY, BUT... WHAT'S THAT AT THE DOOR...
?
EARL!
$
MOOCH!
JULES!
MERRY CHRISTMAS
JULES!?!
YELLO.
12/25

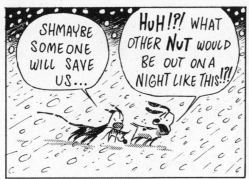

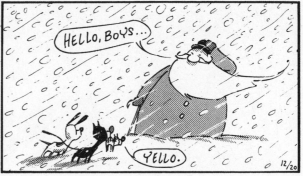

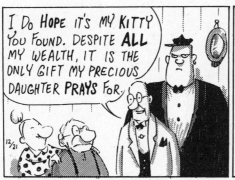

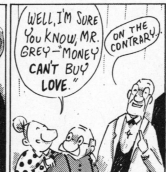

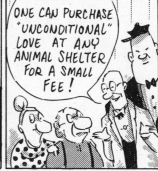

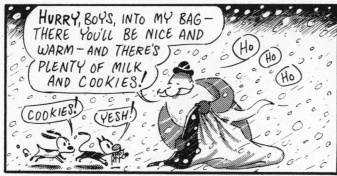

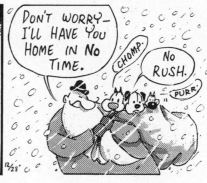

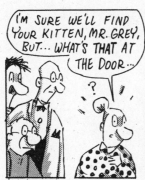

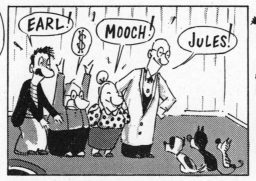

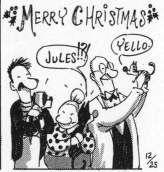

**97**

**Woofie wuvs wuv!** Much to Mooch's chagrin, Woofie, a big golden retriever–Irish setter type of dog, jumped up into the strip and proceeded to give it sloppy kisses. Some dogs just can't contain all the joy and happiness bursting inside them. Nothing can stop their enthusiasm. You just have to wuv them.

Throughout the years, birds fly in and out of *Mutts*. I'm fascinated by birds; I watch them all day outside my studio windows. I call that "working."

My brother Robert is an avid bird watcher and hawk bander. He has deepened my appreciation of our feathered friends. Some of my most blissful moments are when I am on top of a mountain with Robert, enjoying the autumn flight of majestic hawks.

In September I told the story of Phillipe and Phoebe, the tragic love between a free bird and a caged parakeet during migrating season. Shakespeare for the birds.

At the end of the year I did two stories in a row that would later play a major part in the world of *Mutts*. The first was about Mooch falling asleep in a fog and waking up thinking he must be in heaven. The second was about Mooch's quest to find the perfect gift for the dog (Earl) who has everything. Eight years later these two tales became inspirations for the first two *Mutts* children's books, *Just Like Heaven* and *The Gift of Nothing*.

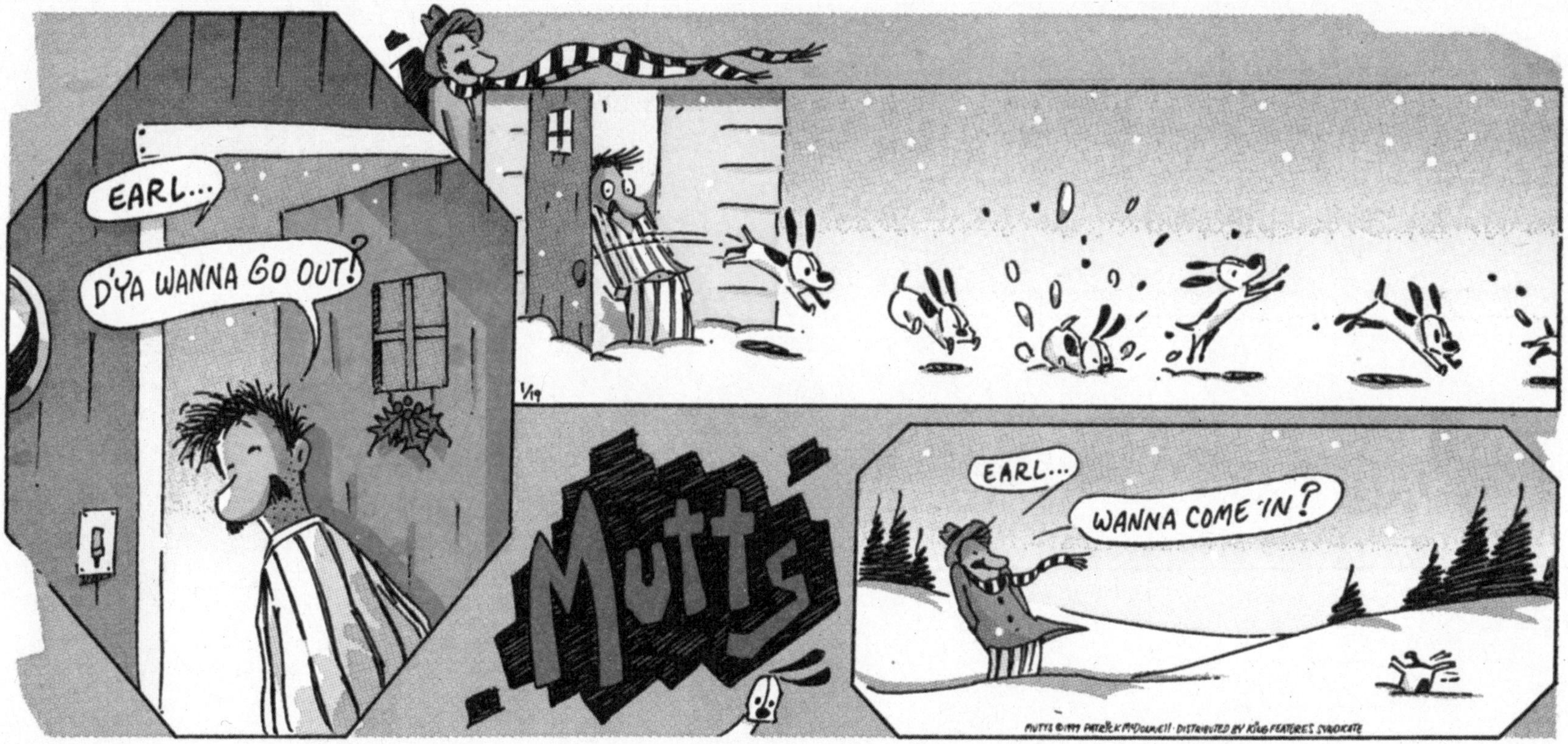
EARL...
D'YA WANNA GO OUT?
1/19
MUTTS
EARL...
WANNA COME IN?
MUTTS ©1997 PATRICK McDONNELL · DISTRIBUTED BY KING FEATURES SYNDICATE

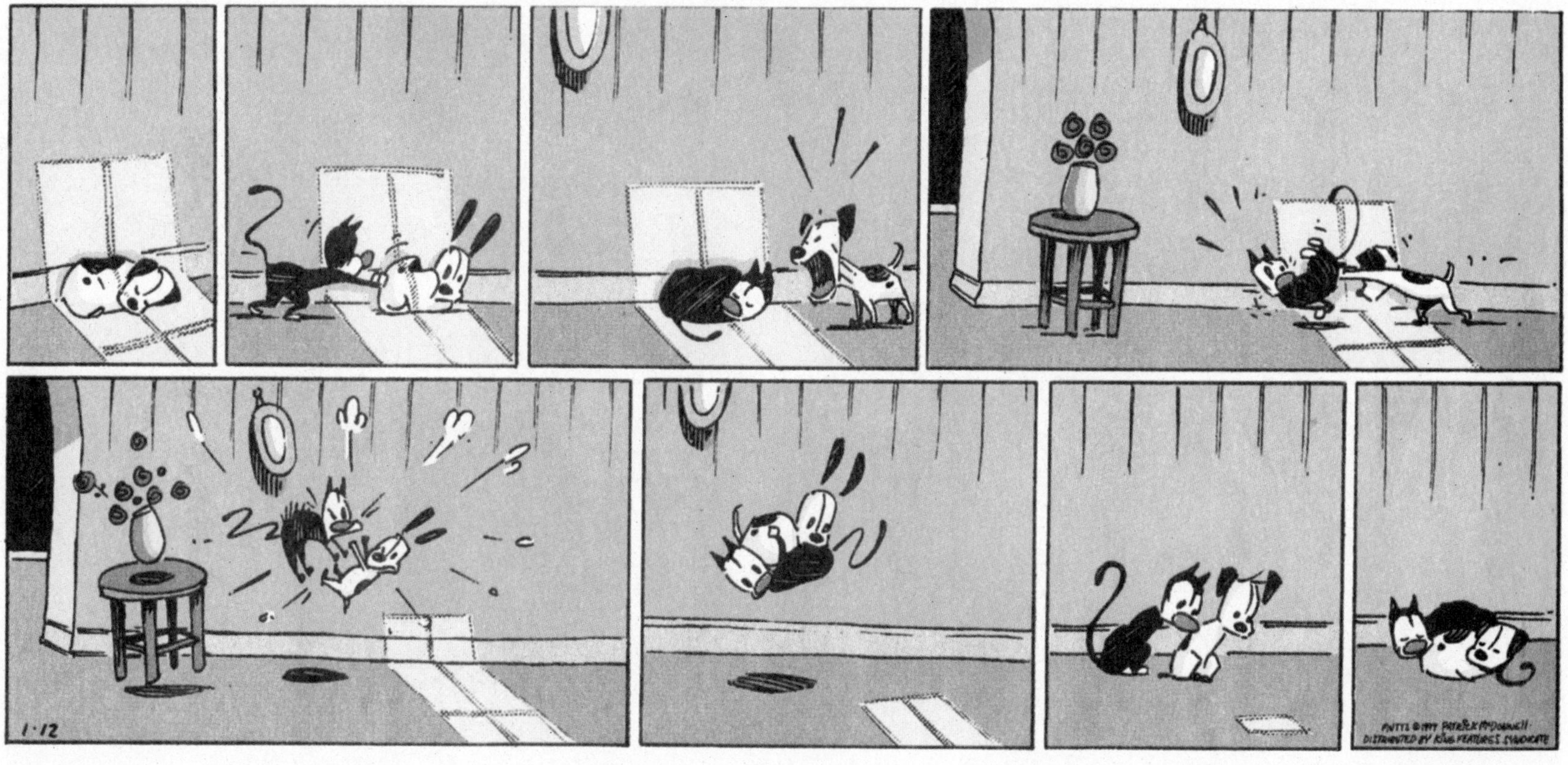
1·12
MUTTS ©1997 PATRICK McDONNELL · DISTRIBUTED BY KING FEATURES SYNDICATE

HEY! THAT'S MY DOG FOOD!
So.
SO!?! YOU'RE A CAT!
So.
SO WHAT DO YOU HAVE TO SAY FOR YOURSELF?
WOOF
WOOF
1/6

ACK!!! I ATE DOG FOOD!!! PTUi - PTUi
OH
NO.
I'M TURNING
INTO
A
POOCH.
HA HA HA
HOOWL
BOW
WOW
WOW
HIDE ALL THE HOUSE SLIPPERS.
1/7

EATING DOG FOOD HAS CHANGED ME —I FEEL LIKE ...CHASING A SHTICK!
HECK! I FEEL LIKE CHASING ME!
WOOF WOOF WOOF
I GOT AWAY.
DARN, THAT CAT IS TOO SHMART FOR ME!
1/9

ARF
HA! TWO CAN PLAY AT THIS GAME! I'M GONNA EAT YOUR CAT FOOD!
GULP
GULP
GULP.
OOOH... I FEEL ALL FLUFFY IN THE HEAD—LIKE A WITTLE PUSSY!
AUGH!!! YOU'RE GETTING CAT FUR ALL OVER ME!!!
PURRRRR.
1/13

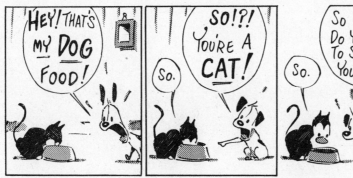

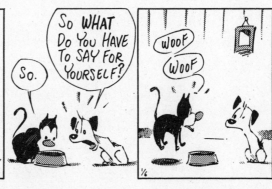

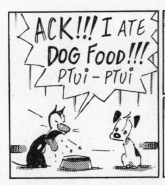

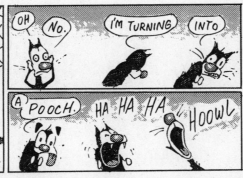

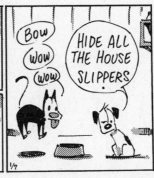

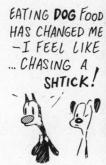

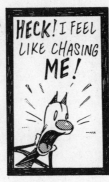

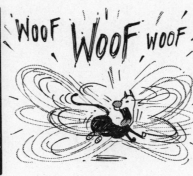

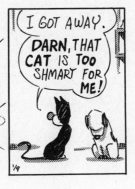

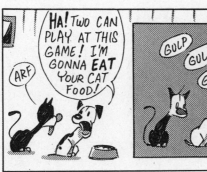

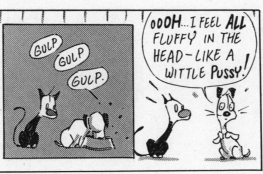

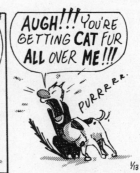

BARK
BARK
BARK
MEOW!
THOSE TWO HAVE BEEN TOGETHER TOO LONG.
1/14

SAY...
WHAT WOULD HAPPEN IF WE ATE PEOPLES FOOD?
HA HA
IT'S MINE! ALL MINE!
MINE TOO, ALSO!
1/15

GOOD BEASTIE!
BUT REMEMBER, DON'T SIT ON THE FURNITURE.
HAR HAR
!
JOLLY GOOD.
RATHER.
1/16

EARL, I'M TIRED OF BEING SHOMETHING I'M NOT.
IT'S HARD ENOUGH TO BE SHOMETHING I AM.
FROM NOW ON —I'M A CAT!
SURE, YOU'RE GOOD AT THAT.
1/17
YESH.
I'VE HAD A LOT OF PRACTICE.

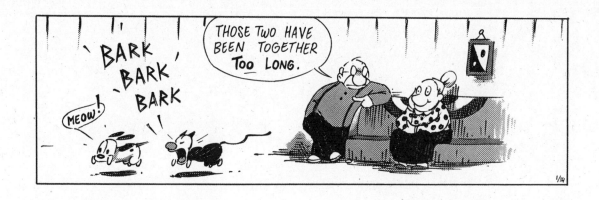

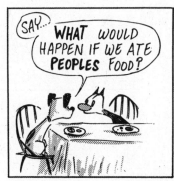

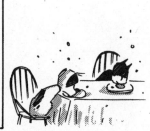

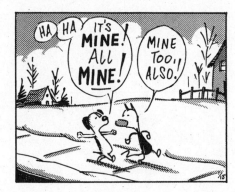

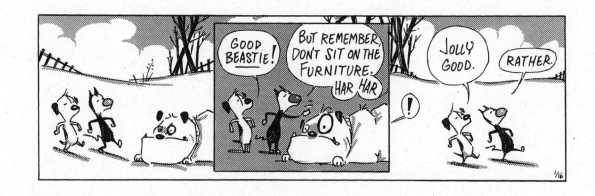

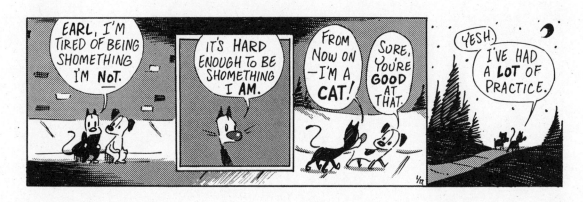

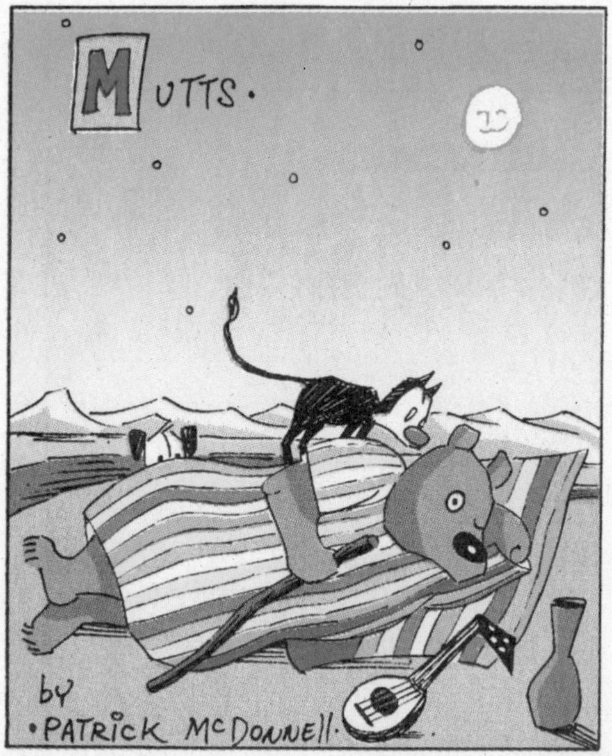
MUTTS.
by
PATRICK McDONNELL

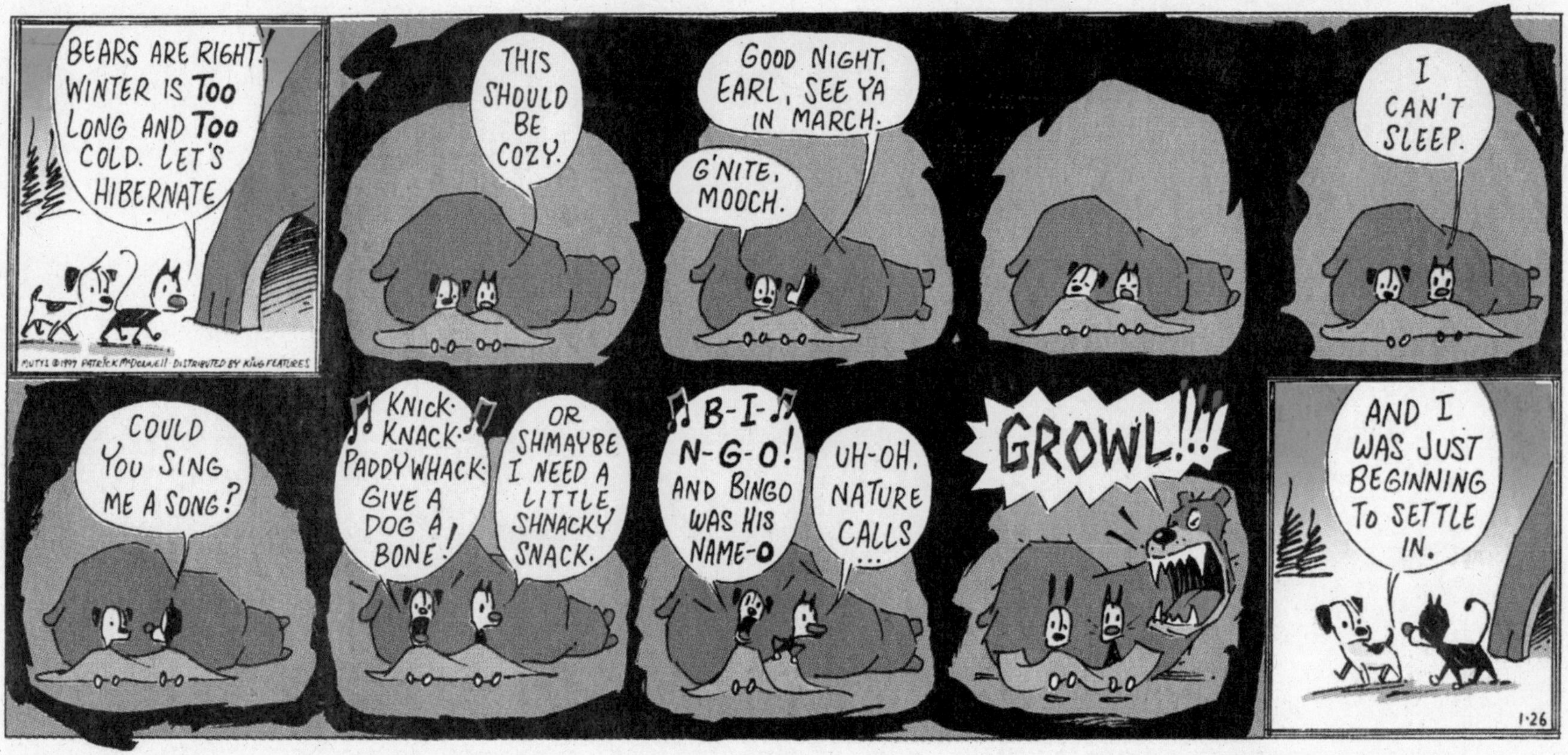
BEARS ARE RIGHT! WINTER IS TOO LONG AND TOO COLD. LET'S HIBERNATE.
MUTTS ©1997 PATRICK McDONNELL DISTRIBUTED BY KING FEATURES
THIS SHOULD BE COZY.
GOOD NIGHT, EARL, SEE YA IN MARCH.
G'NITE, MOOCH.
I CAN'T SLEEP.
COULD YOU SING ME A SONG?
KNICK-KNACK-PADDYWHACK-GIVE A DOG A BONE!
OR SHMAYBE I NEED A LITTLE SHNACKY SNACK.
B-I-N-G-O! AND BINGO WAS HIS NAME-O
UH-OH. NATURE CALLS...
GROWL!!!
AND I WAS JUST BEGINNING TO SETTLE IN.
1-26

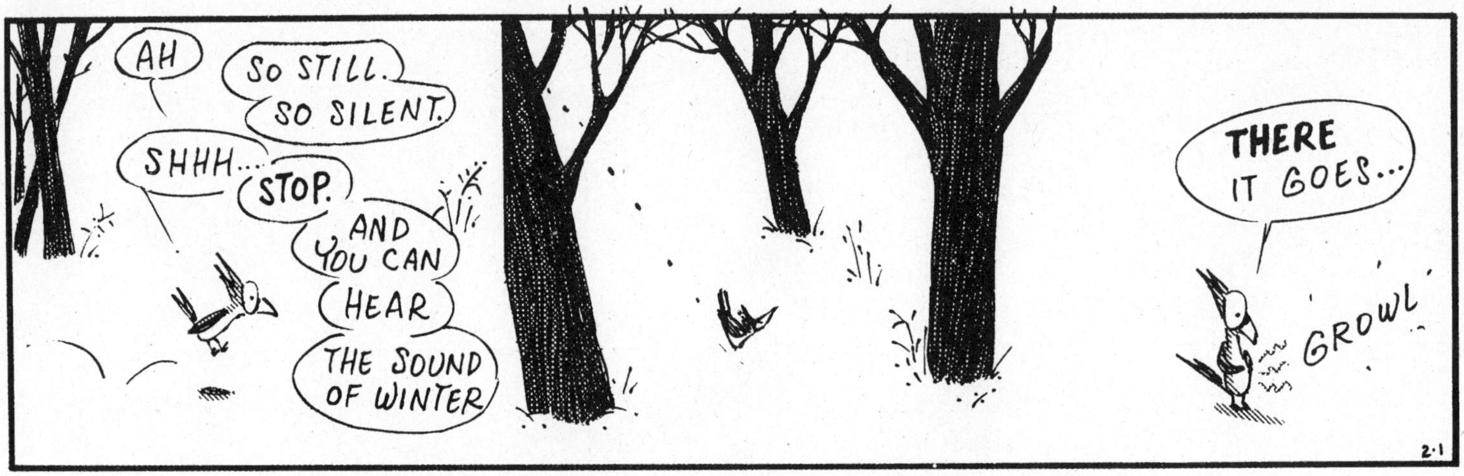
AH
SO STILL.
SO SILENT.
SHHH....
STOP.
AND YOU CAN
HEAR
THE SOUND OF WINTER
THERE IT GOES...
GROWL
2·1

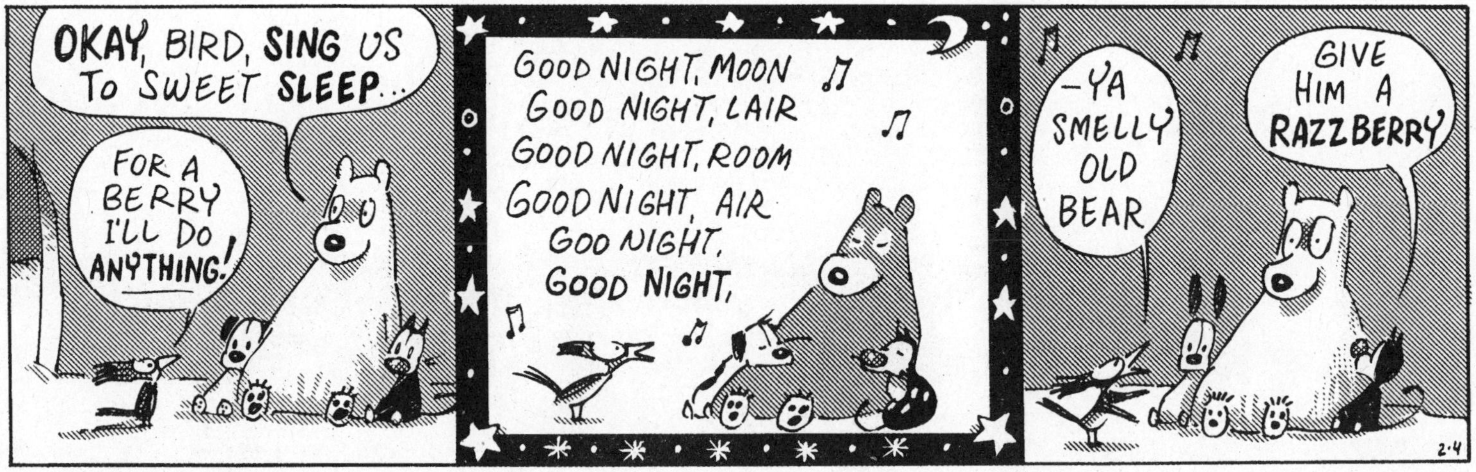
OKAY, BIRD, SING US TO SWEET SLEEP...
FOR A BERRY I'LL DO ANYTHING!
GOOD NIGHT, MOON
GOOD NIGHT, LAIR
GOOD NIGHT, ROOM
GOOD NIGHT, AIR
GOO NIGHT,
GOOD NIGHT,
—YA SMELLY OLD BEAR
GIVE HIM A RAZZBERRY
2·4

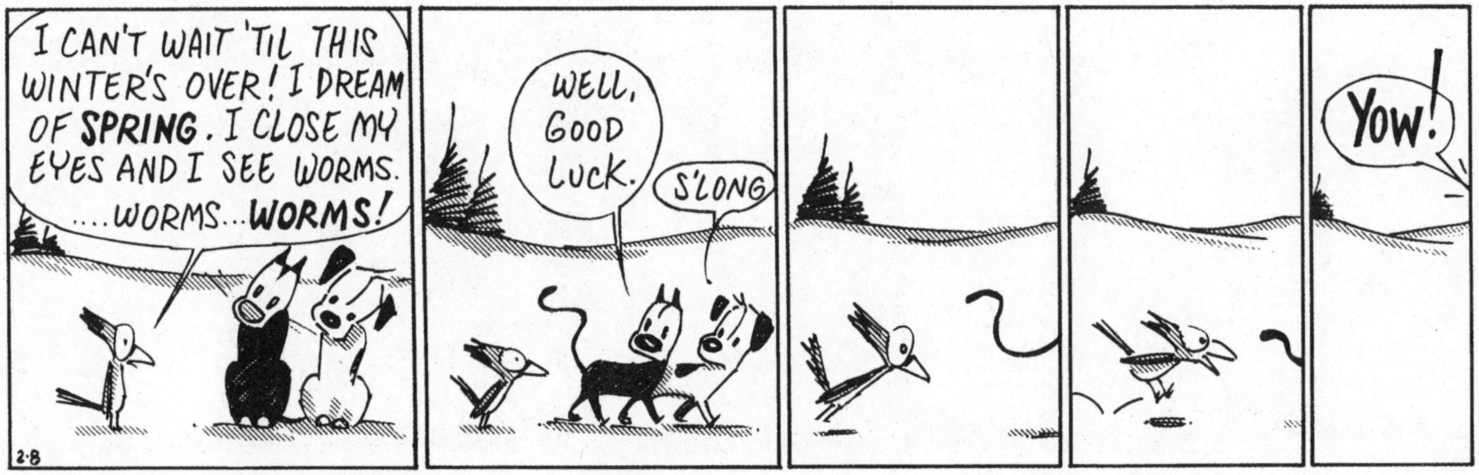
I CAN'T WAIT 'TIL THIS WINTER'S OVER! I DREAM OF SPRING. I CLOSE MY EYES AND I SEE WORMS. ....WORMS...WORMS!
2·8
WELL, GOOD LUCK.
S'LONG
YOW!

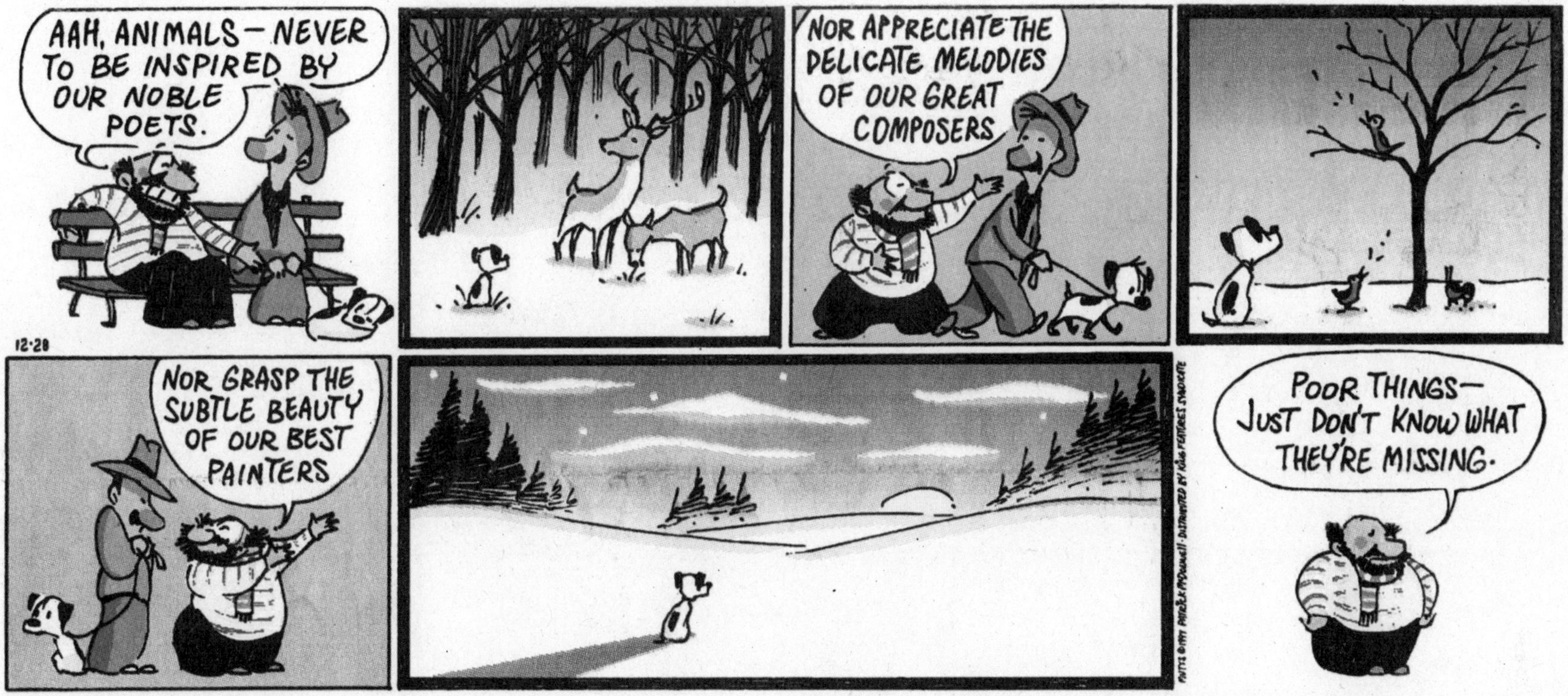
AAH, ANIMALS — NEVER TO BE INSPIRED BY OUR NOBLE POETS.
12·28
NOR APPRECIATE THE DELICATE MELODIES OF OUR GREAT COMPOSERS
NOR GRASP THE SUBTLE BEAUTY OF OUR BEST PAINTERS
POOR THINGS — JUST DON'T KNOW WHAT THEY'RE MISSING.

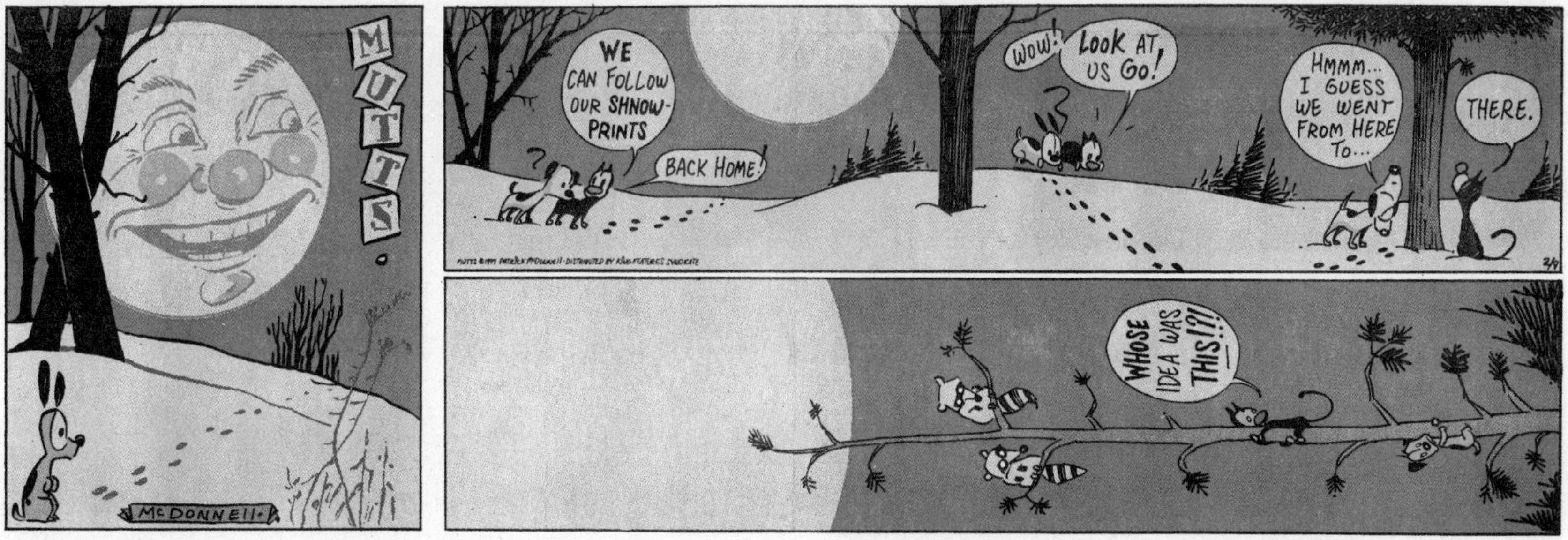
MUTTS.
McDONNELL
WE CAN FOLLOW OUR SHNOW-PRINTS
BACK HOME!
WOW!
LOOK AT US GO!
HMMM... I GUESS WE WENT FROM HERE TO...
THERE.
2/7
WHOSE IDEA WAS THIS!?!

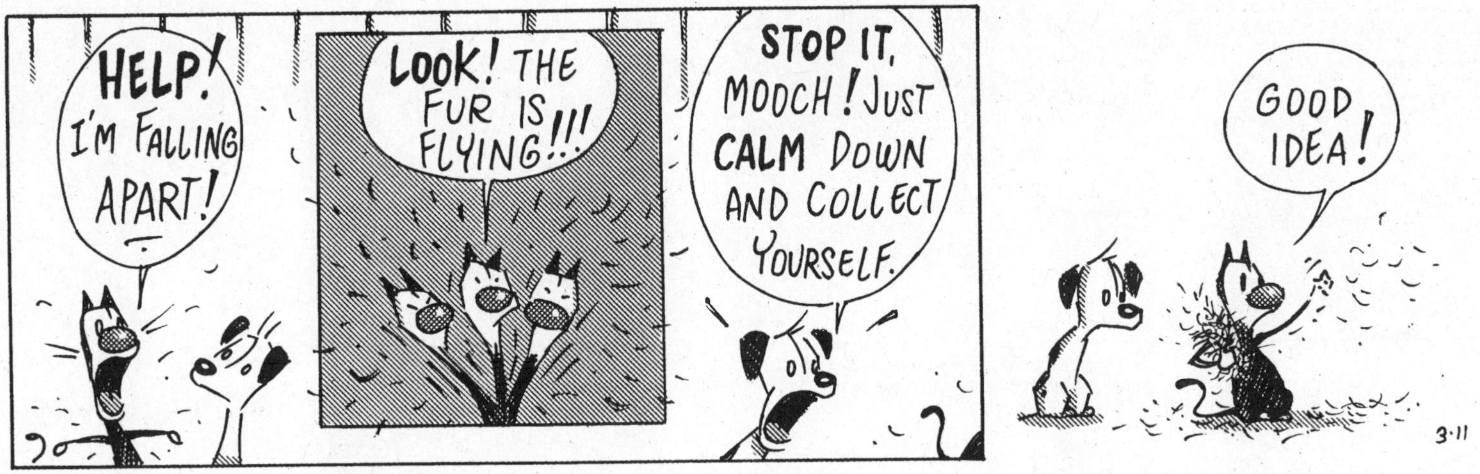
HELP! I'M FALLING APART!
LOOK! THE FUR IS FLYING!!!
STOP IT, MOOCH! JUST CALM DOWN AND COLLECT YOURSELF.
GOOD IDEA!
3·11

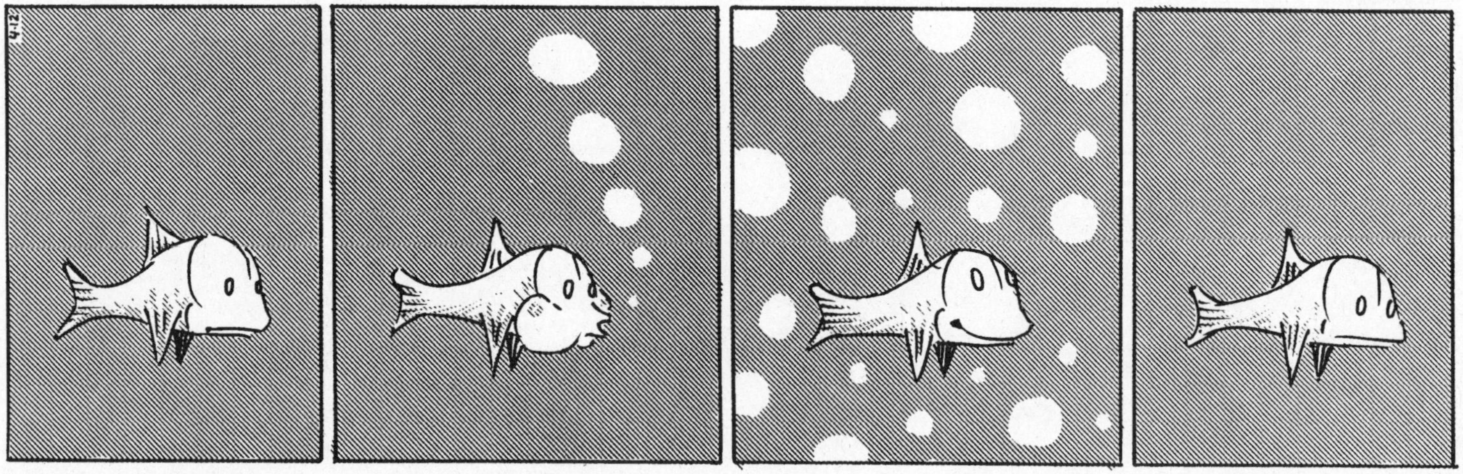
4·12

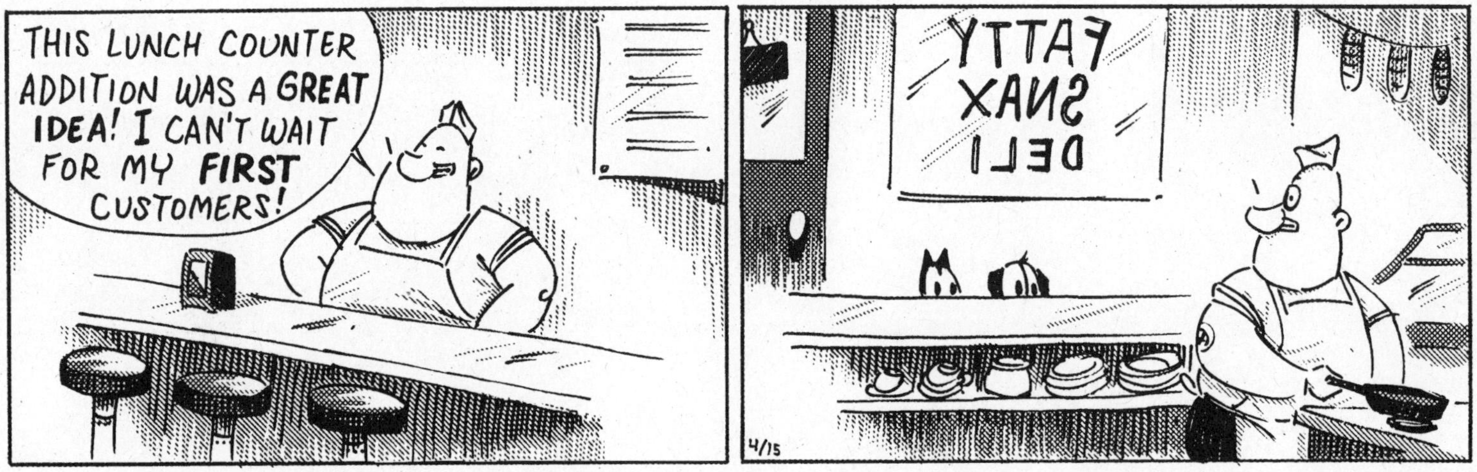
THIS LUNCH COUNTER ADDITION WAS A GREAT IDEA! I CAN'T WAIT FOR MY FIRST CUSTOMERS!
FATTY SNAX DELI
4/15

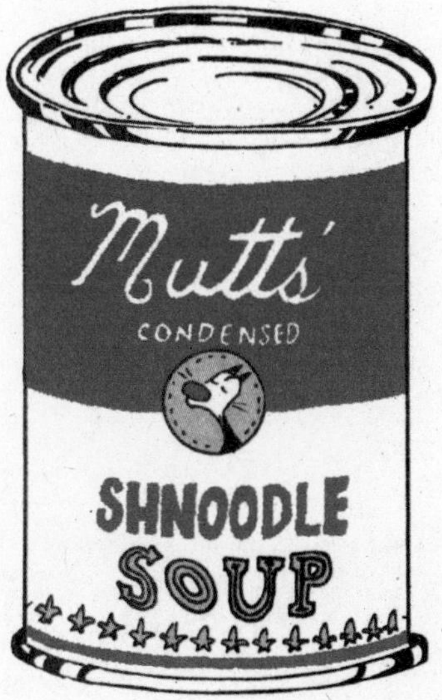
Mutts'
CONDENSED
SHNOODLE
SOUP

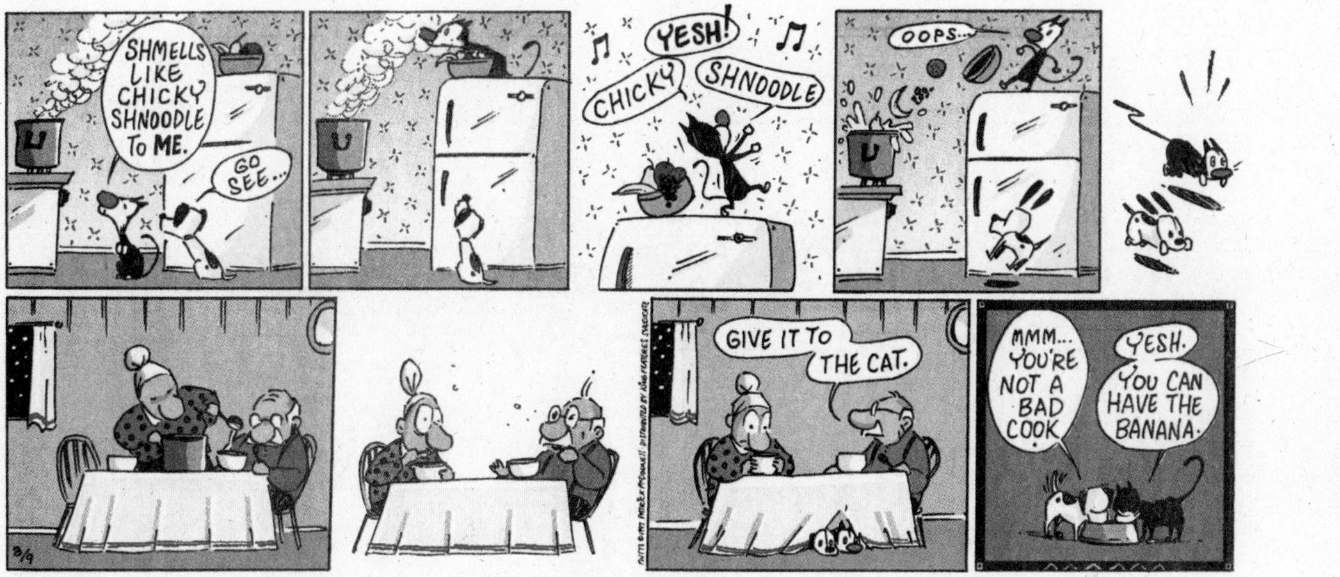
SHMELLS LIKE CHICKY SHNOODLE TO ME.
GO SEE...
YESH!
CHICKY
SHNOODLE
OOPS...
3/9
GIVE IT TO THE CAT.
MMM... YOU'RE NOT A BAD COOK.
YESH. YOU CAN HAVE THE BANANA.

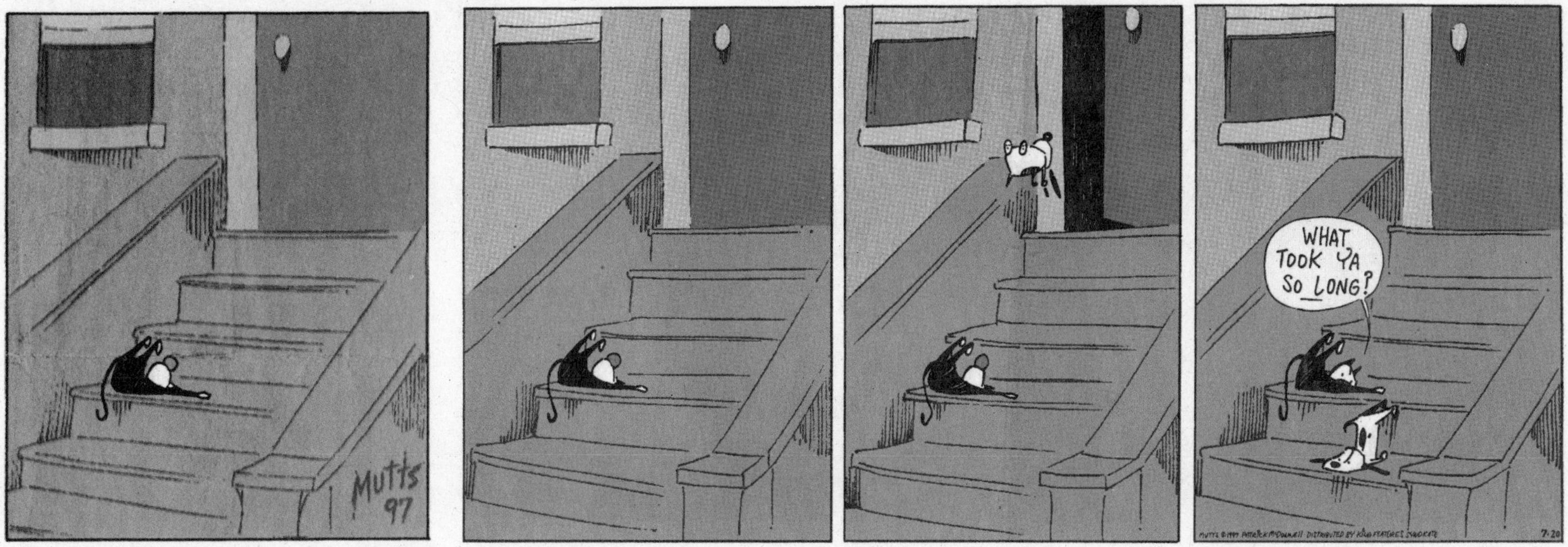
MUTTS 97
WHAT TOOK YA SO LONG?
7·20

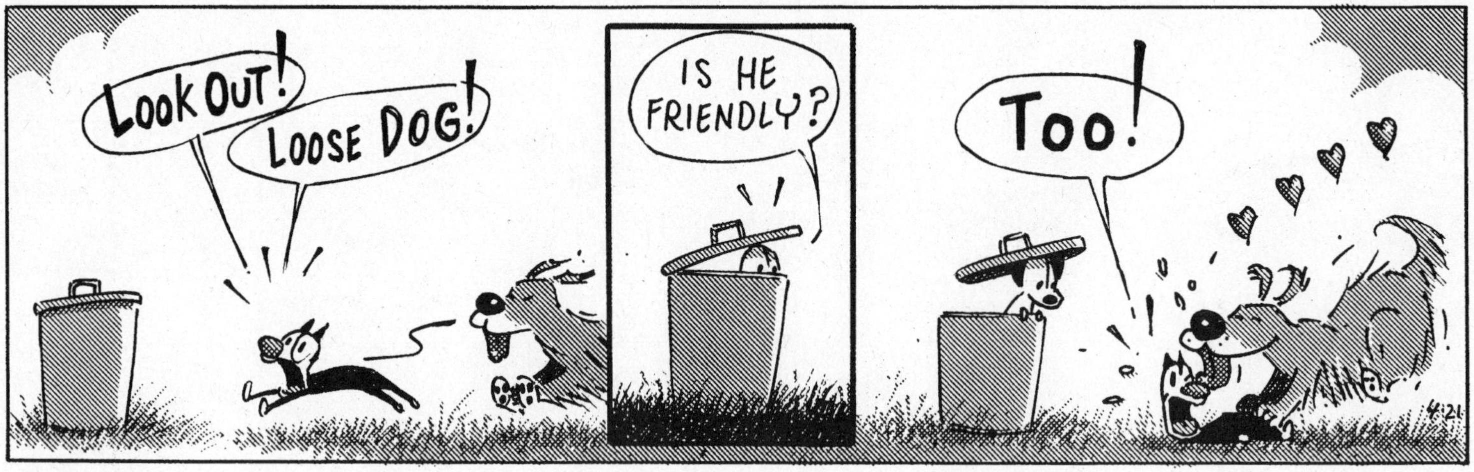
LOOK OUT!
LOOSE DOG!
IS HE FRIENDLY?
TOO!
4·21

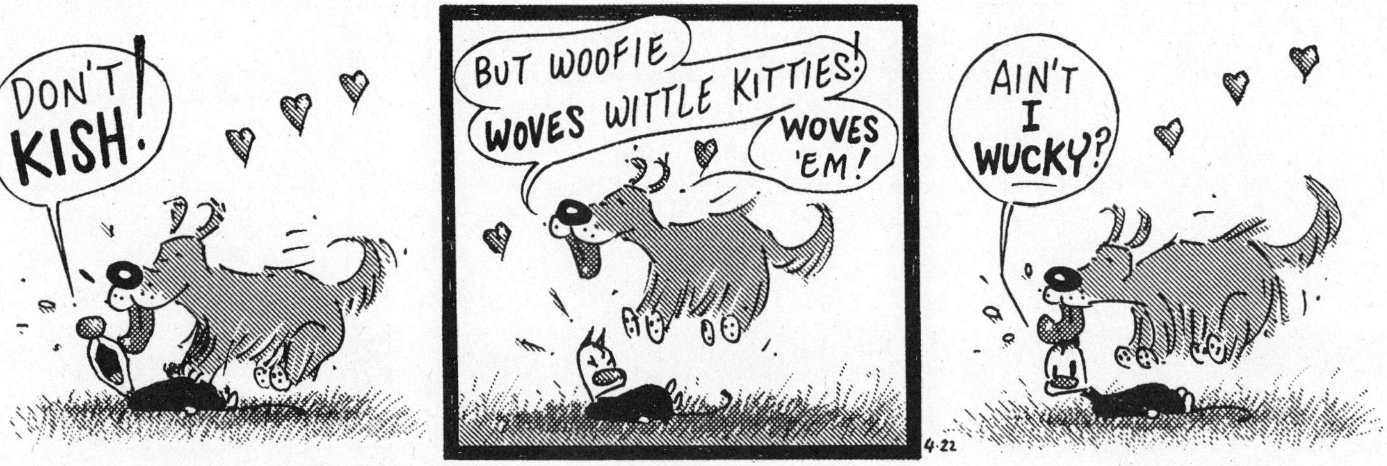
DON'T KISH!
BUT WOOFIE
WOVES WITTLE KITTIES!
WOVES 'EM!
AIN'T I WUCKY?
4·22

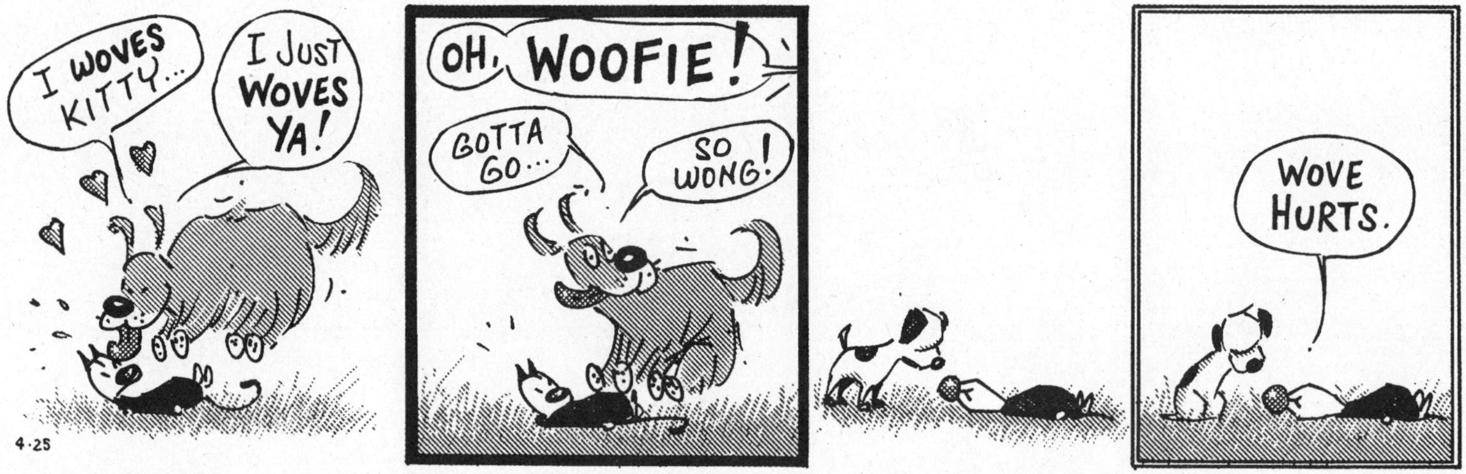
I WOVES KITTY...
I JUST WOVES YA!
4·25
OH, WOOFIE!
GOTTA GO...
SO WONG!
WOVE HURTS.

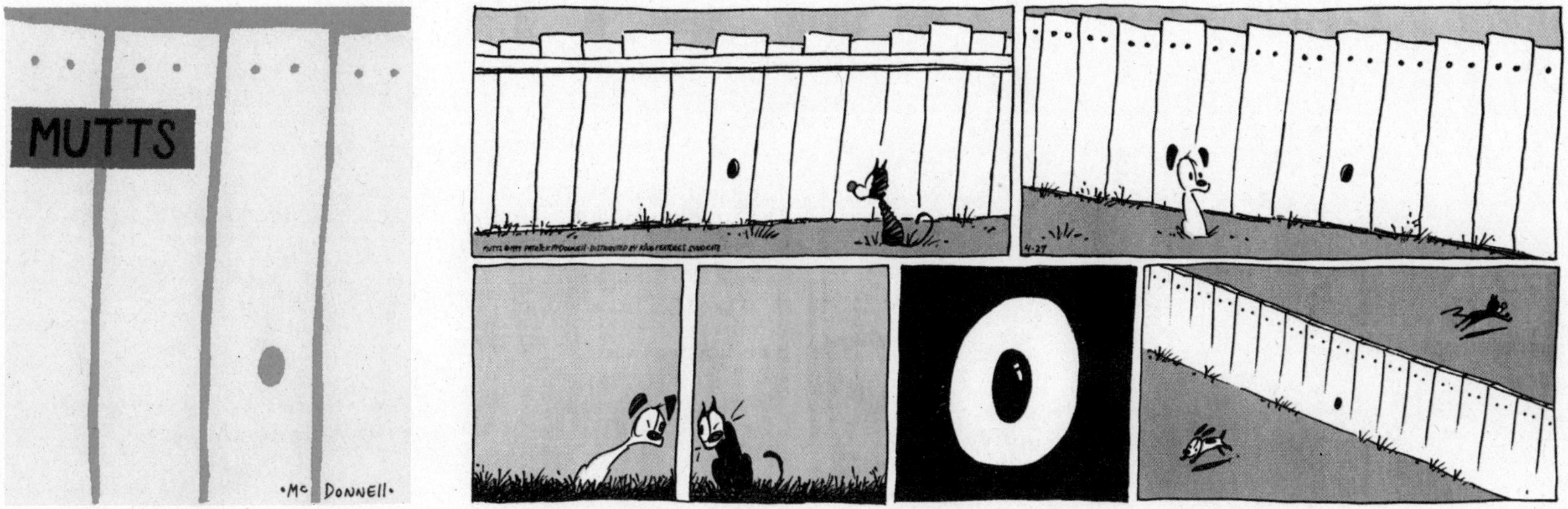
MUTTS
McDONNELL
4-27

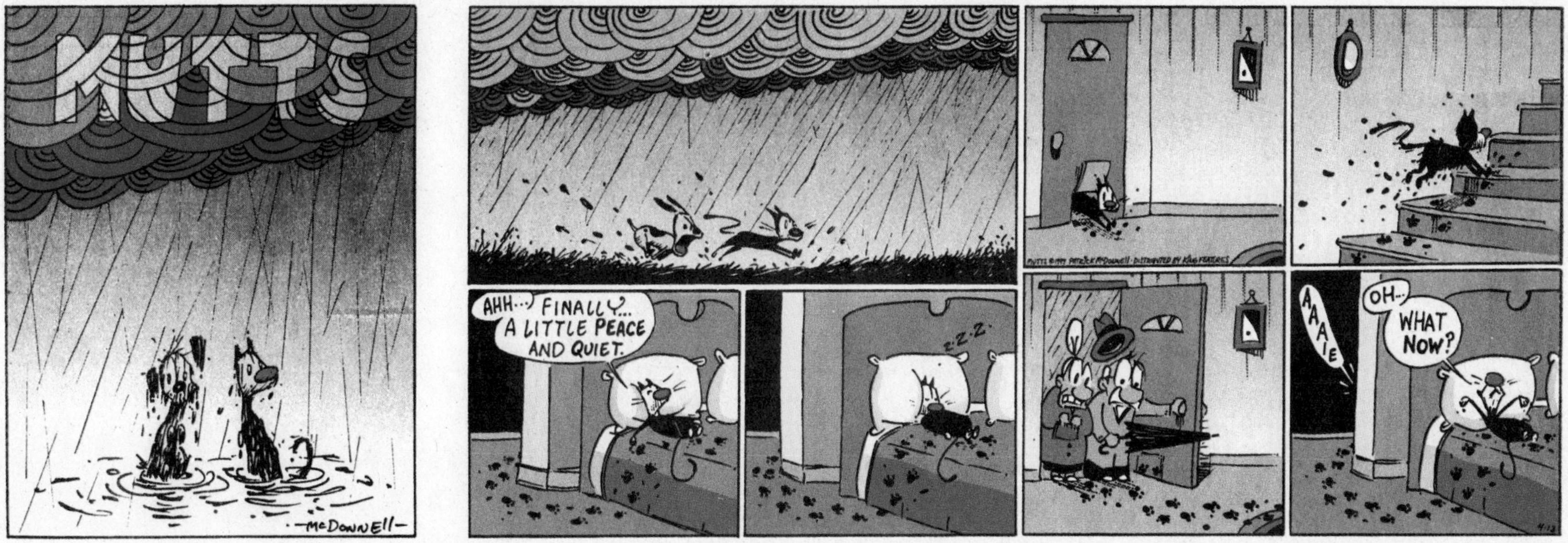
MUTTS
McDONNELL
AHH... FINALLY... A LITTLE PEACE AND QUIET.
Z-Z-Z
AAAIE
OH... WHAT NOW?

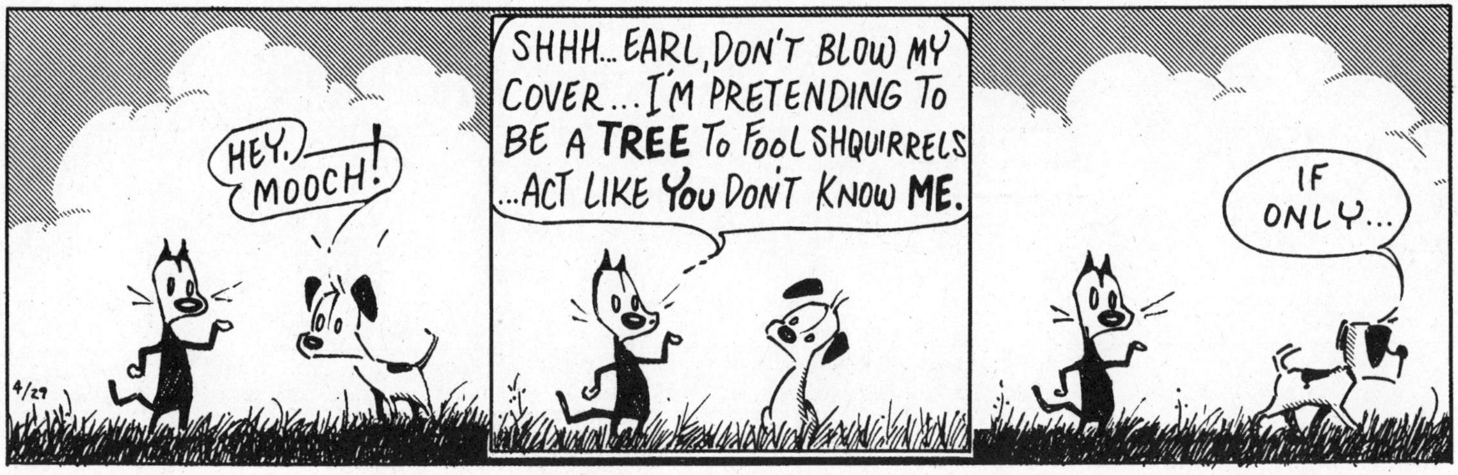
HEY, MOOCH!
SHHH... EARL, DON'T BLOW MY COVER... I'M PRETENDING TO BE A TREE TO FOOL SHQUIRRELS ...ACT LIKE YOU DON'T KNOW ME.
IF ONLY...
4/29

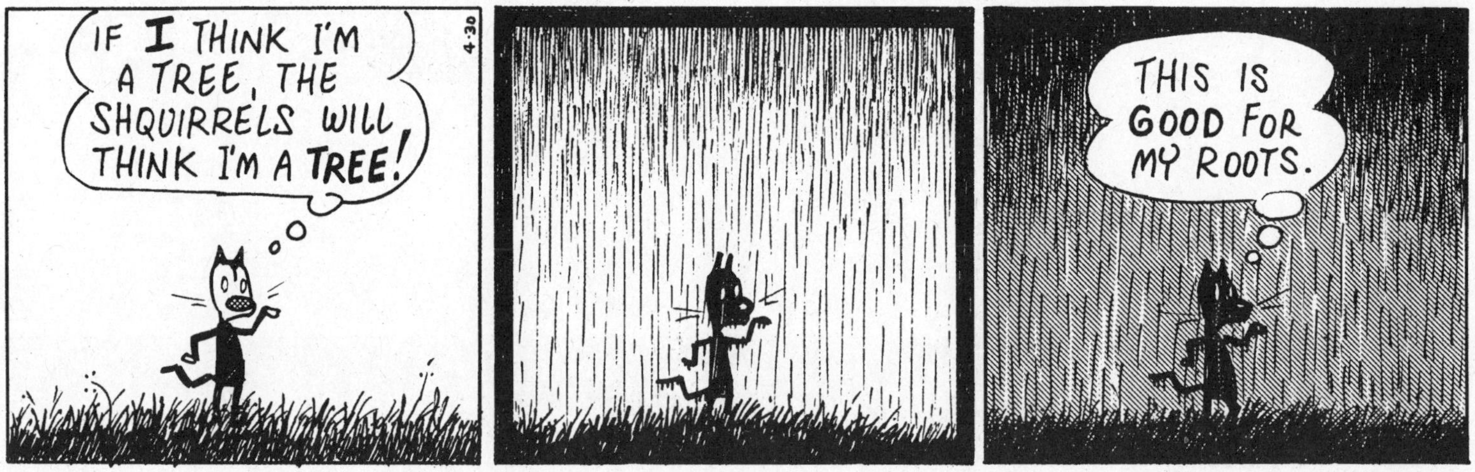
IF I THINK I'M A TREE, THE SHQUIRRELS WILL THINK I'M A TREE!
4·30
THIS IS GOOD FOR MY ROOTS.

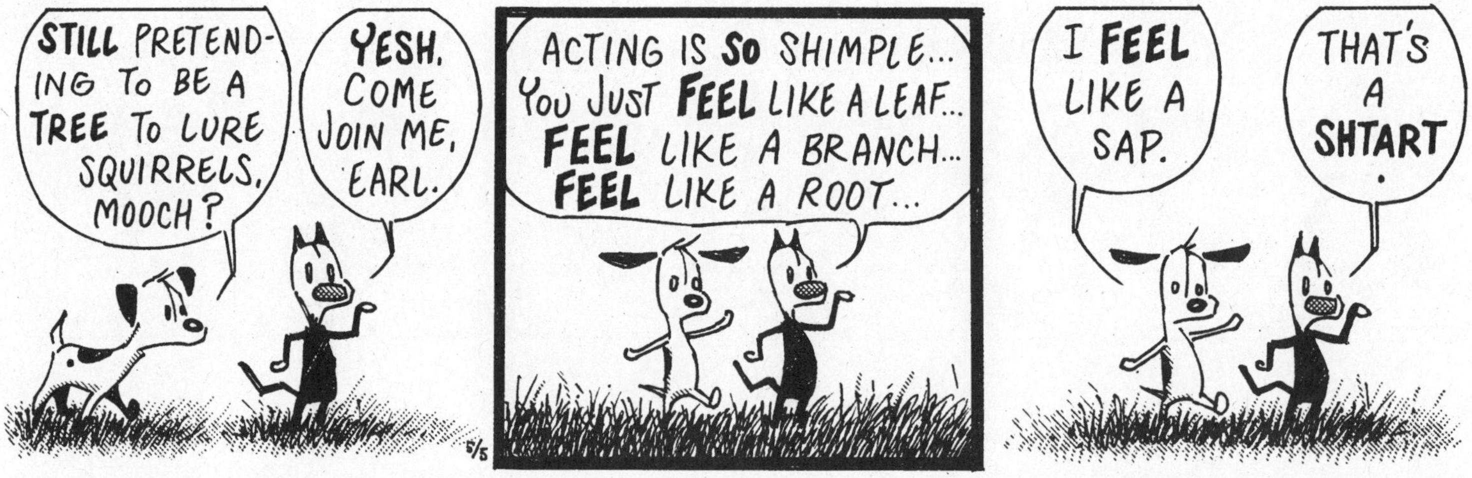
STILL PRETENDING TO BE A TREE TO LURE SQUIRRELS, MOOCH?
YESH. COME JOIN ME, EARL.
ACTING IS SO SHIMPLE... YOU JUST FEEL LIKE A LEAF... FEEL LIKE A BRANCH... FEEL LIKE A ROOT...
I FEEL LIKE A SAP.
THAT'S A SHTART.
5/5

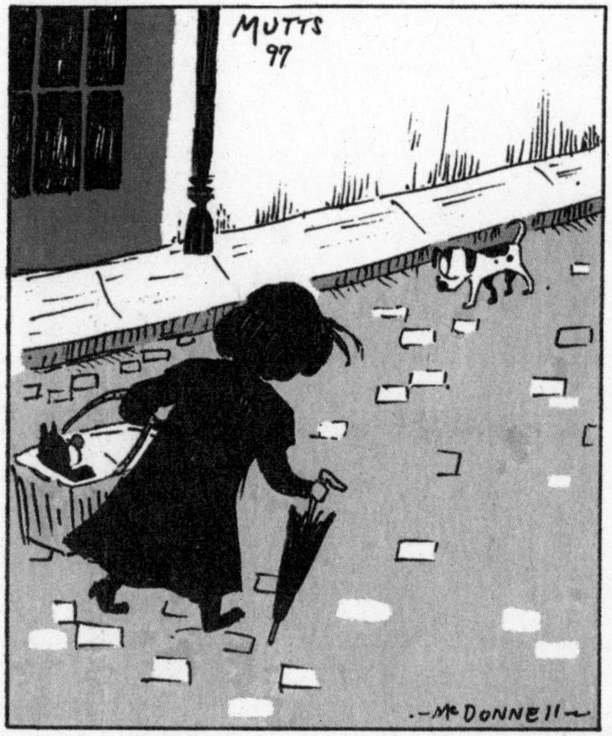
MUTTS
97
-McDONNELL-

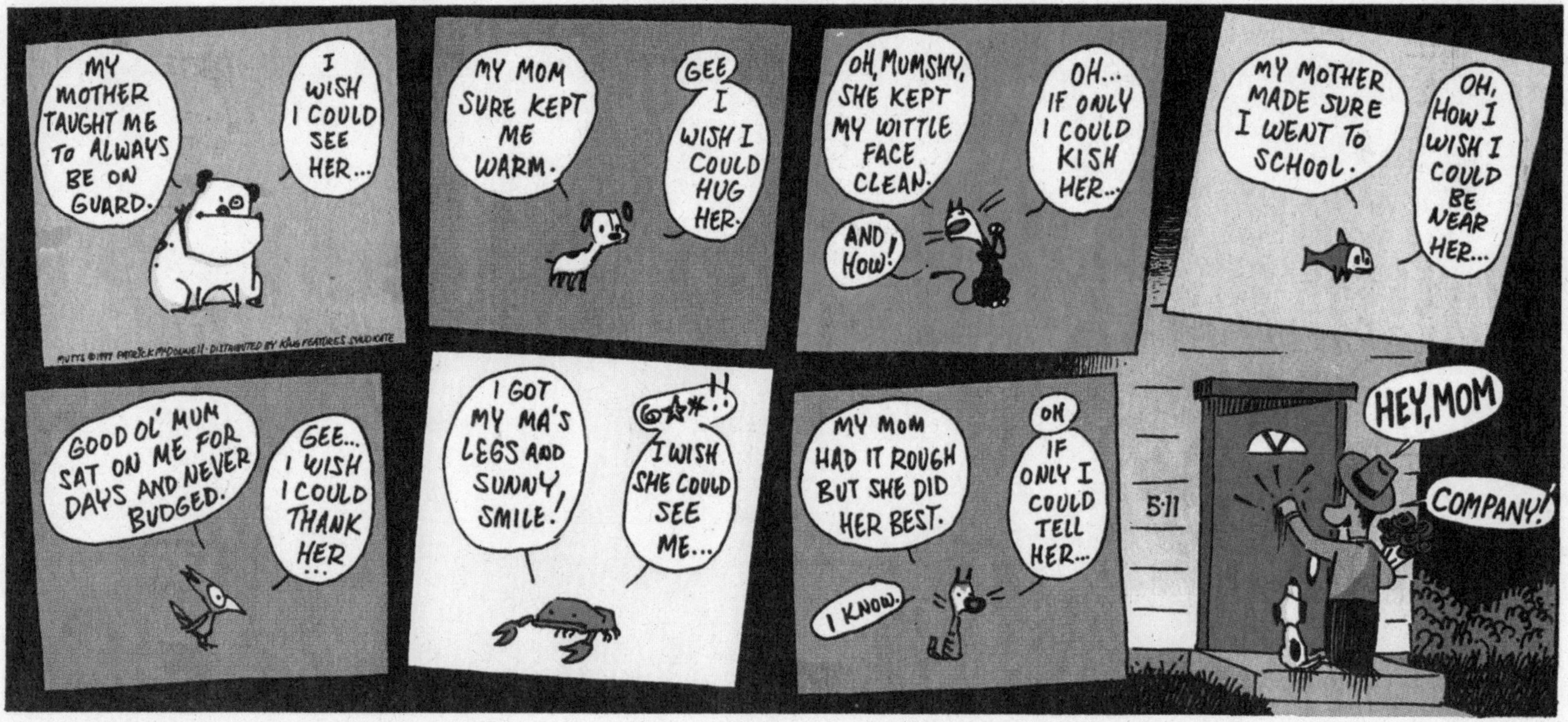
MY MOTHER TAUGHT ME TO ALWAYS BE ON GUARD.
I WISH I COULD SEE HER...
MUTTS © 1997 PATRICK McDONNELL · DISTRIBUTED BY KING FEATURES SYNDICATE
MY MOM SURE KEPT ME WARM.
GEE I WISH I COULD HUG HER.
OH, MUMSHY, SHE KEPT MY WITTLE FACE CLEAN.
AND HOW!
OH... IF ONLY I COULD KISH HER...
MY MOTHER MADE SURE I WENT TO SCHOOL.
OH, HOW I WISH I COULD BE NEAR HER...
GOOD OL' MUM SAT ON ME FOR DAYS AND NEVER BUDGED.
GEE... I WISH I COULD THANK HER...
I GOT MY MA'S LEGS AND SUNNY SMILE!
@☆*!!
I WISH SHE COULD SEE ME...
MY MOM HAD IT ROUGH BUT SHE DID HER BEST.
OH IF ONLY I COULD TELL HER...
I KNOW.
5·11
HEY, MOM
COMPANY!

LET'S TRY AN ECHO DOWN THIS WELL...
YESH!
HELLO!
YELLO.

GEE... I THOUGHT I HEARD OUR KITTY PAL "SHTINKY PUDDIN'" DOWN THIS WELL!
SHTINKY, IS THAT YOU?
I DUNNO...
IT'S DARK DOWN HERE.

OH NO! SHTINKY PUDDIN' COULD DROWN...
CALM DOWN! THIS WELL SHMAY BE DRY.
SHTINKY... IS THE WELL EMPTY?
NO.
I'M IN IT.

HEY, SHTINKY! THAT WAS PRETTY SHTUPID TO FALL DOWN A WELL.
I KNOW I KNOW I KNOW I KNOW I KNOW
I KNOW.
HE "KNOWS" TOO MUCH.
I KNOW.

MOOCH... I'M SCARED... IT'S DARK DOWN HERE... AND I'M ALL ALONE...
SHTINKY, YOU MUST ALWAYS REMEMBER NO MATTER WHERE YOU ARE, YOU'RE NEVER ALONE.
I KNOW...
FLEAS.

WELL, JULES, YOU SILLY THING!
STUCK DOWN A DECORATIVE WELL...
...THAT YOU COULD HAVE CLIMBED OUT OF ANY OLD TIME.
WELL?
WHAT D'YA KNOW.

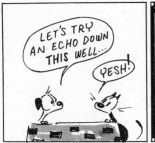

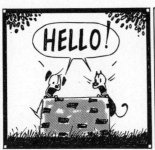

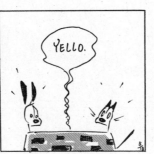

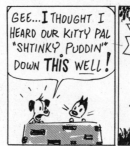

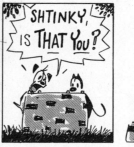

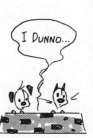

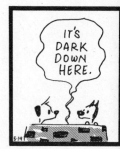

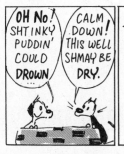

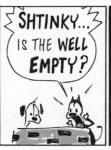

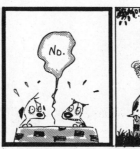

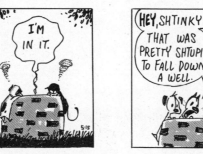

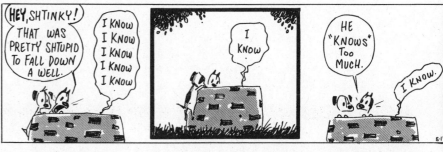

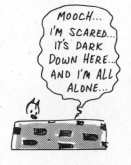

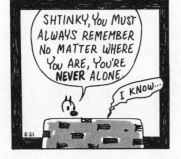

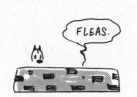

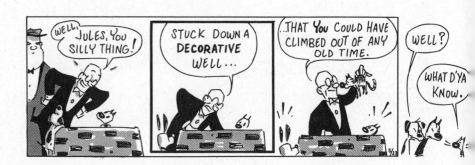

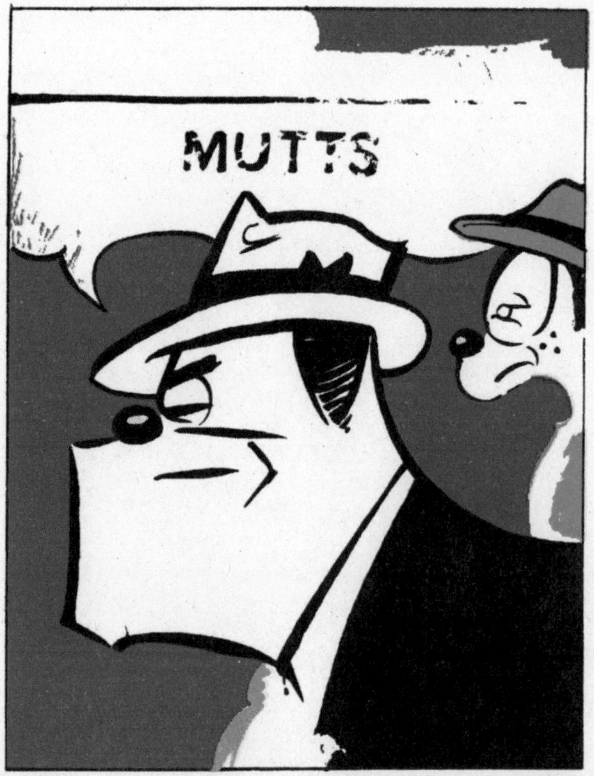
MUTTS

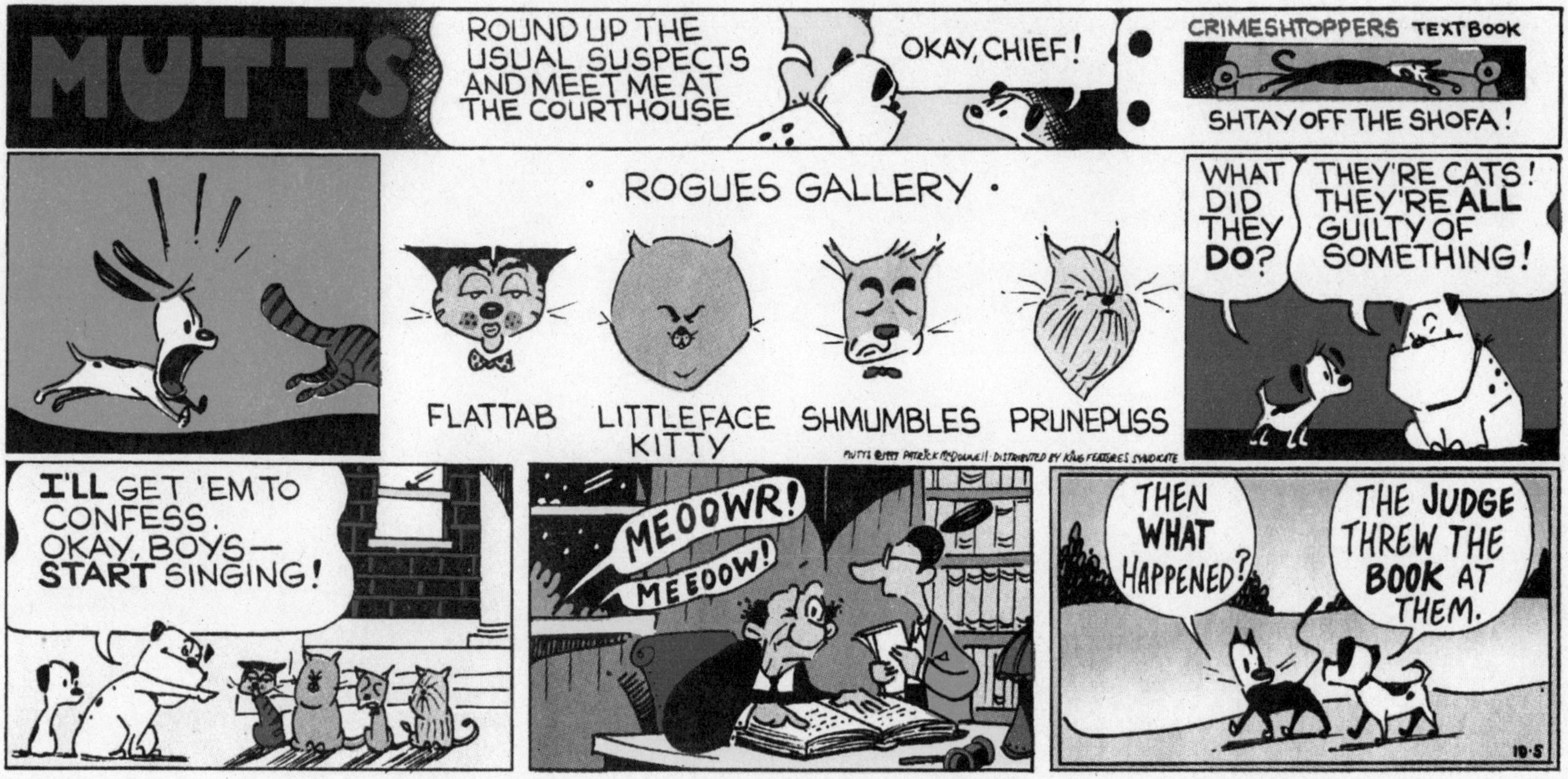
MUTTS
ROUND UP THE USUAL SUSPECTS AND MEET ME AT THE COURTHOUSE
OKAY, CHIEF!
CRIMESHTOPPERS TEXTBOOK
SHTAY OFF THE SHOFA!
• ROGUES GALLERY •
FLATTAB
LITTLEFACE KITTY
SHMUMBLES
PRUNEPUSS
WHAT DID THEY DO?
THEY'RE CATS! THEY'RE ALL GUILTY OF SOMETHING!
I'LL GET 'EM TO CONFESS. OKAY, BOYS— START SINGING!
MEOOWR!
MEEOOW!
THEN WHAT HAPPENED?
THE JUDGE THREW THE BOOK AT THEM.

HEY, EARL, REMEMBER THESE?
CHEW CHEW CHEW CHEW CHEW
CHEW CHEW CHEW CHEW CHEW
CHEW CHEW CHEW CHEW
CHEW CHEW CHEW
PTUI
I GUESS SO.
7·1

OUT HERE–YOU MEET **ALL** KINDS.
YESH.
**WHO** ARE YOU?
I'M COUGH DROP.
COUGH-DROP!?!
I'M A LITTLE "HOARSE."
8/11

BACK TO WORK.
BACK TO SCHOOL.
BACK TO NORMAL.
9·1

10·10

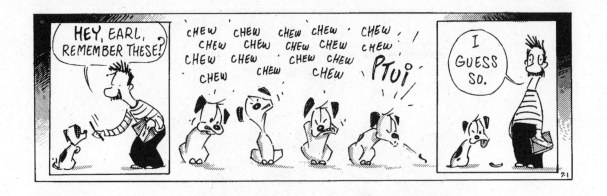

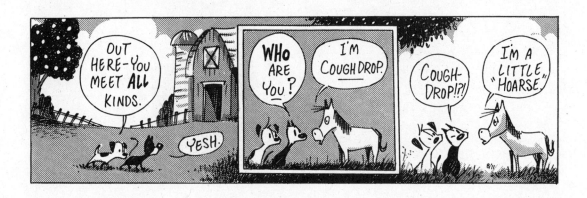

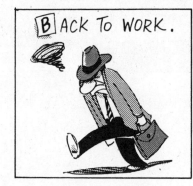

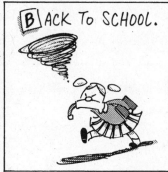

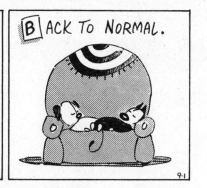

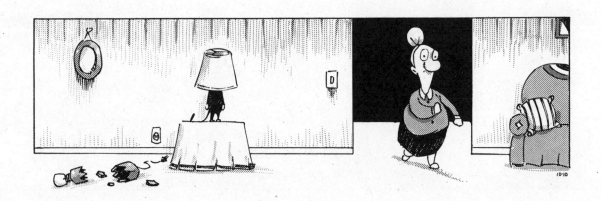

EARL, MOOCH- I'M IN LOVE!
SHE'S JUST THE SWEETEST TWEETY I'VE EVER MET!
SHE SOUNDS SWELL.
YESH. DON'T LET THIS ONE GET AWAY.
WELL...

A MIRROR!?!
-INSTEAD OF A MATE!
WHAT!?! Do I LOOK LIKE AN IDIOT!?!

PRETTY BIRD— PRETTY BIRD.
OOH
PHOEBE, MY LOVE, YOU SPEAK "PEOPLE"?
I DABBLE
WHAT DID YOU SAY?
I'M NOT SURE...
... BUT I HOPE IT'S— "GET ME OUTTA THIS CAGE!!!"

GOLLY, PHOEBE, HOW LONG HAVE YOU BEEN IN THERE?
FOURTEEN MONTHS.

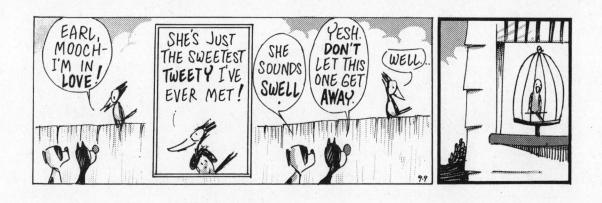

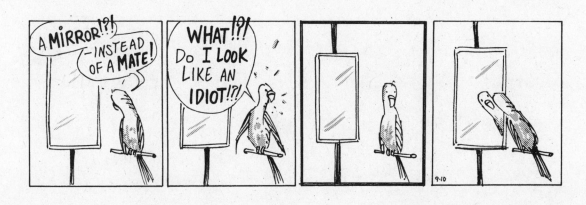

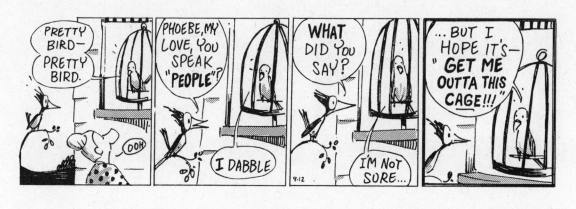

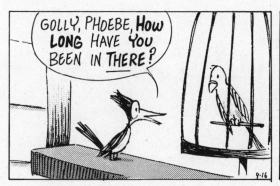

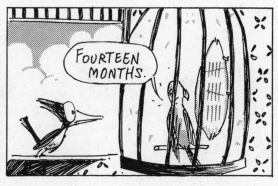

OH, PHILIPPE, I WOULD LOVE TO MIGRATE WITH YOU, BUT LOOK AT ME–I'M A CAGED BIRD–WITH NO WAY OUT.
DID YOU EVER TRY THIS LITTLE DOOR?
9·17

PHOEBE, YOU'RE FREE! FREE TO FLY AWAY WITH ME!
I CAN'T
...YOU CAN'T...
MY WINGS ARE CLIPPED ...
9·18

OH, PHILIPPE, YOU CAN'T STAY IN THIS CAGE WITH ME.
9·19
YOU MUST BE FREE! FREE TO FLY OVER THE MOUNTAINS, THE OCEANS, THE TREES– GO! DO IT FOR... US.
FAREWELL, MY PHOEBE, I SHALL RETURN WITH THE FIRST HINT OF SPRING.
PRETTY BIRD.
PRETTY BIRD.

"THE SWEETEST SONGS ARE THOSE THAT TELL OF SAD-DEST THOUGHT."
YESH.
9·20

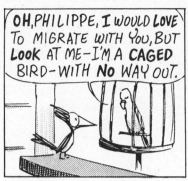

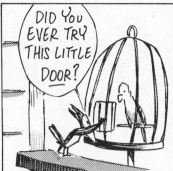

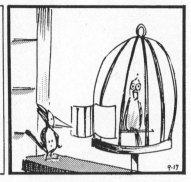

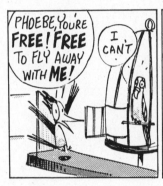

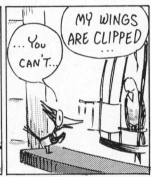

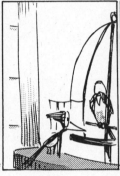

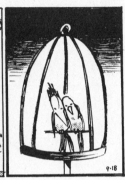

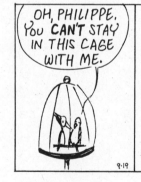

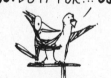

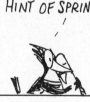

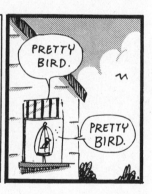

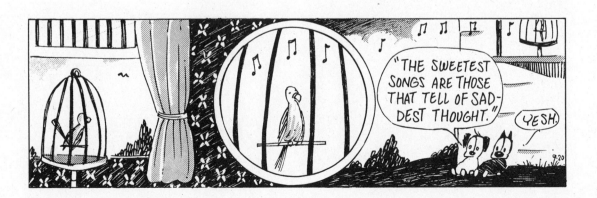

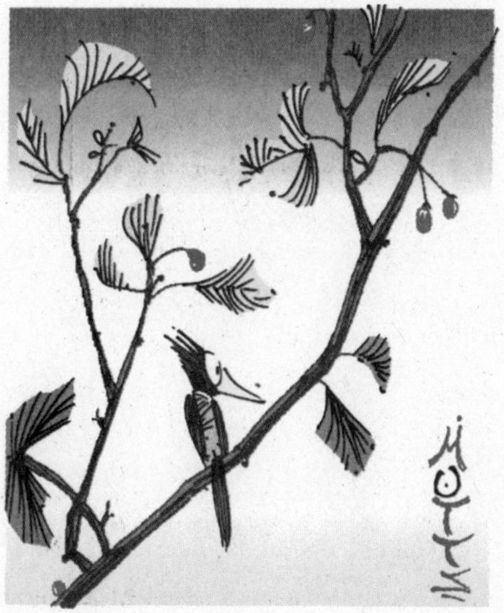

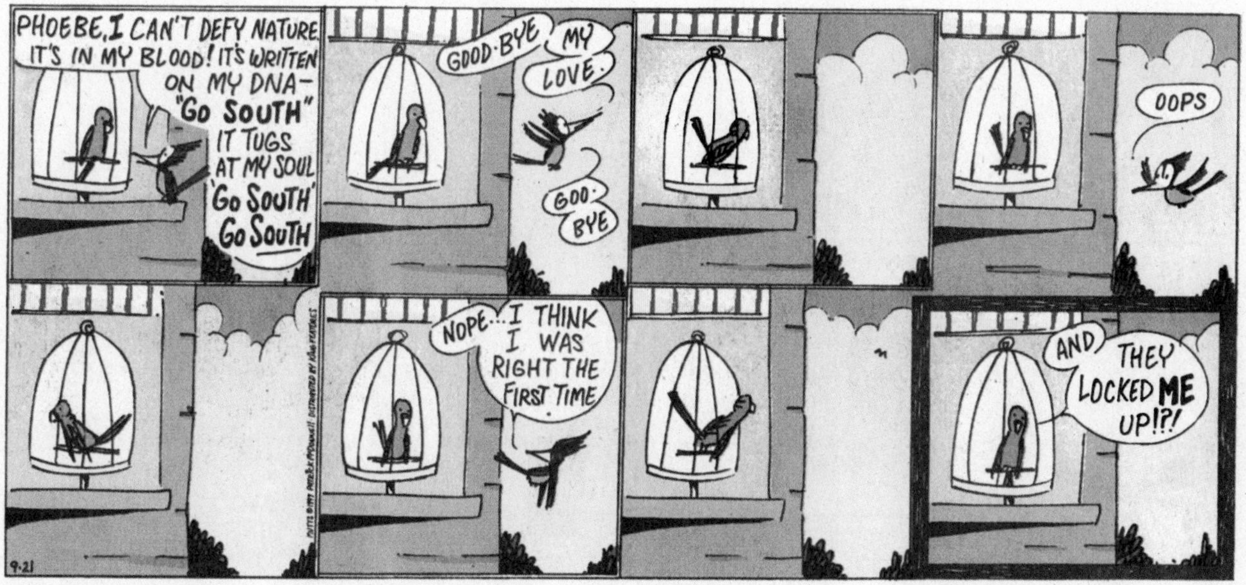
PHOEBE, I CAN'T DEFY NATURE. IT'S IN MY BLOOD! IT'S WRITTEN ON MY DNA– "GO SOUTH" IT TUGS AT MY SOUL 'GO SOUTH' GO SOUTH
GOOD-BYE
MY LOVE.
GOO-BYE
OOPS
NOPE... I THINK I WAS RIGHT THE FIRST TIME
AND
THEY LOCKED ME UP!?!
9-21

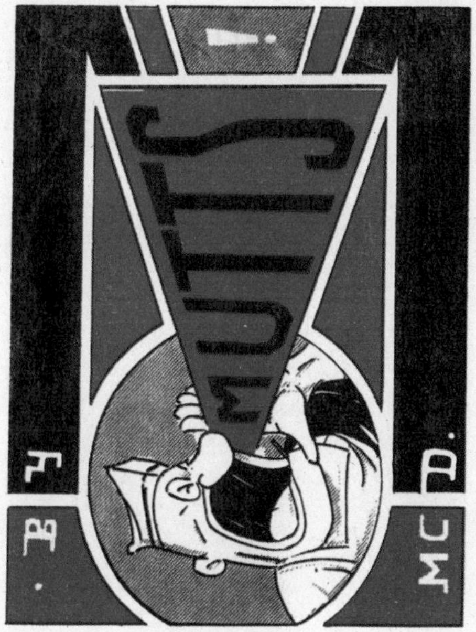
MUTTS

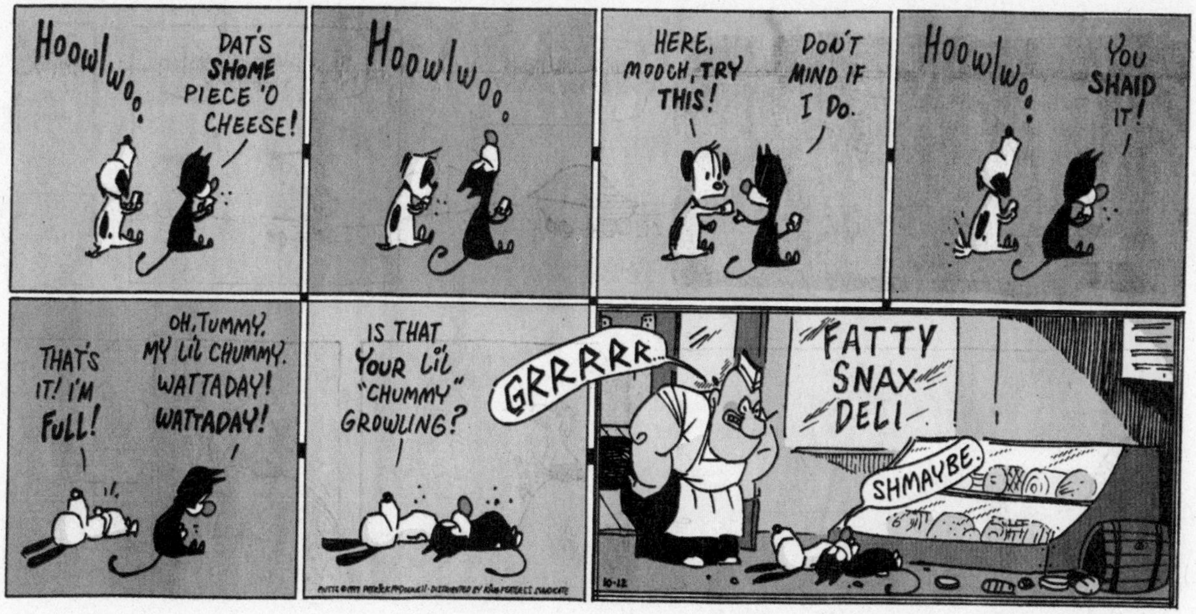
Hoowlwoo.
DAT'S SHOME PIECE 'O CHEESE!
Hoowlwoo.
HERE, MOOCH, TRY THIS!
DON'T MIND IF I DO.
Hoowlwoo.
YOU SHAID IT!
THAT'S IT! I'M FULL!
OH, TUMMY, MY LIL CHUMMY. WATTADAY! WATTADAY!
IS THAT YOUR LIL "CHUMMY" GROWLING?
GRRRRR...
FATTY SNAX DELI
SHMAYBE.
10-12

UMPF.
ARG.
THERE GOES MY DAY.
10·13

C'MON, EARL
HELP ME SHAKE THEM SHQUIRRELS OUT OF THIS TREE!
11·5
NGOGN...
NGOGNOG
DID ANYTHING DROP?
JUST TWO NUTS.

AHH...
...NATURE.
THE WILD KINGDOM.
THE UNTAMED JUNGLE.
CHOMP
11·8
THE GREAT INDOORS!

WOOOAH!
DOG BREATH!
...WHAT'S YOUR EXCUSE?
10·9

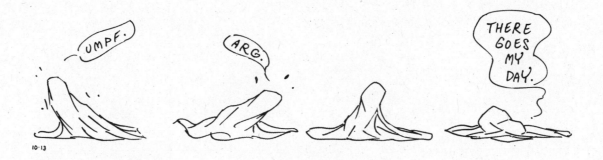

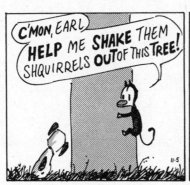

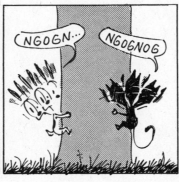

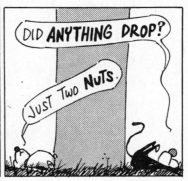

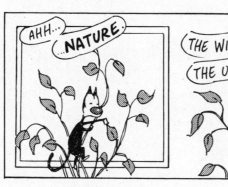

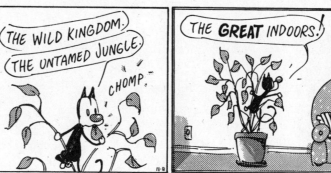

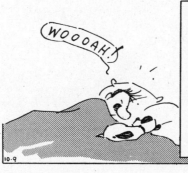

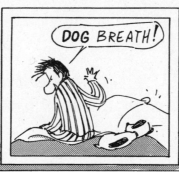

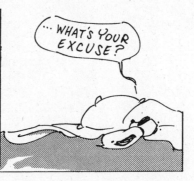

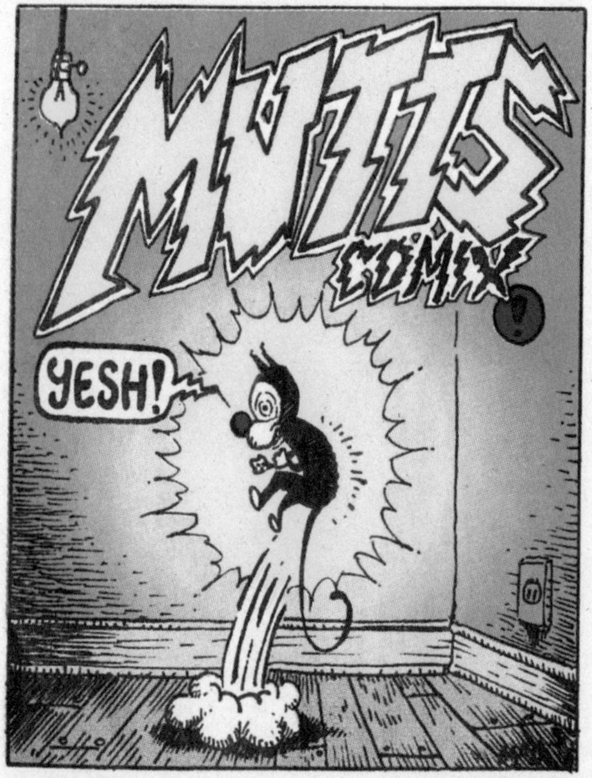
MUTTS
COMIX
YESH!

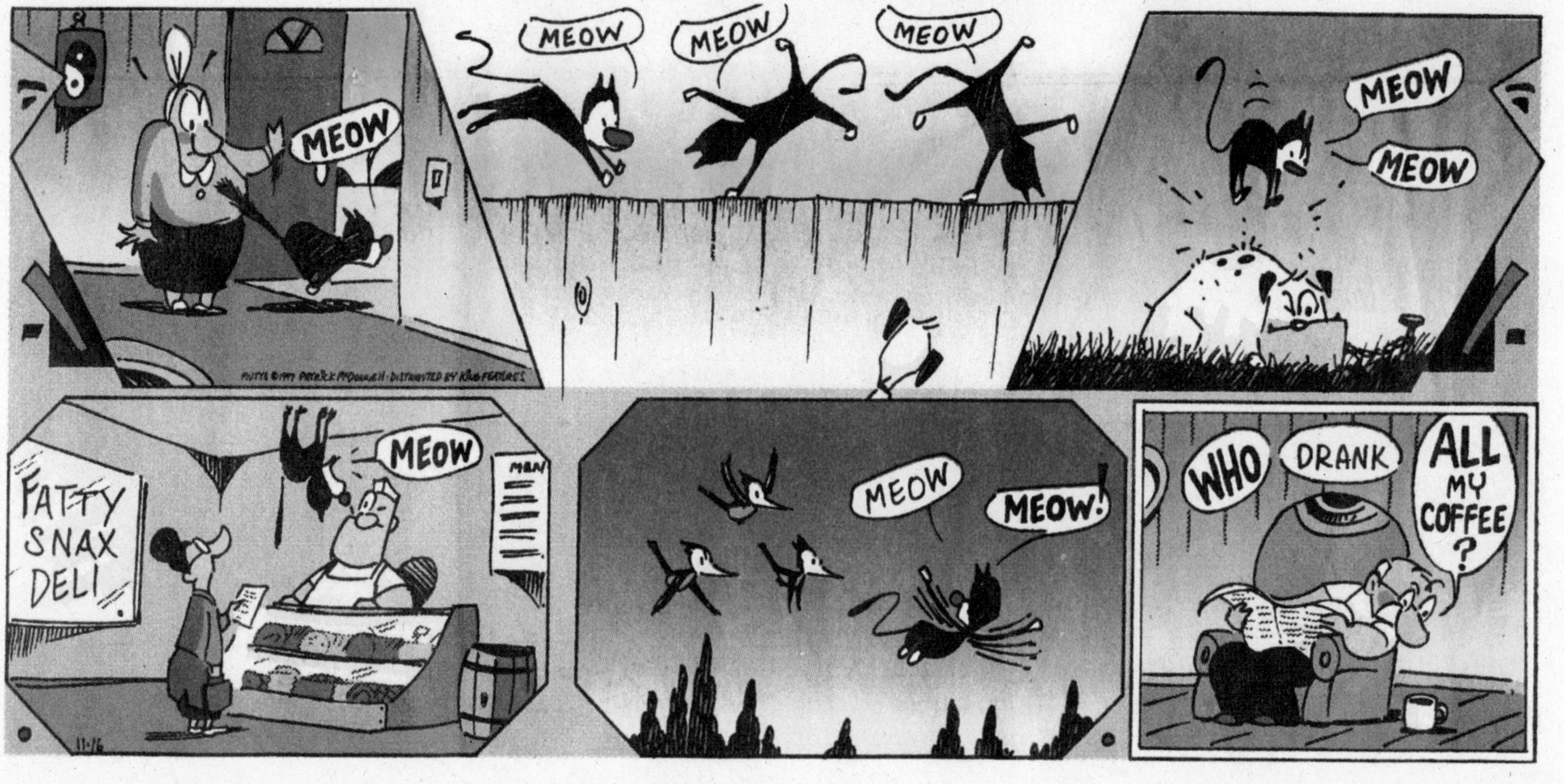
MEOW
MEOW
MEOW
MEOW
MEOW
MEOW
FATTY SNAX DELI
MEOW
MEOW
MEOW!
WHO
DRANK
ALL MY COFFEE ?
11-16

NAPPY TIME.
"THE FOG COMES ON LITTLE CAT FEET..."
WHAT FEET?

MOOCH WAKES UP IN A FOG...
YOW!
I MUST HAVE DIED AND GONE TO HEAVEN.
A DEEP FOG...
GEE...
NINE WEREN'T ENUFF.

SO...
THIS IS...
HEAVEN.

THE MORNING FOG...
WHERE'S MY CHEWY BONE!?!
WHERE'S MY HOUSE!?!
WHERE'S MY CAR!?!
WHERE'S MY COFFEE!?!

GUESSH WHAT!?!
I'M AN ANGEL!
OH YEH... WHERE'S YOUR 'HALO'?
...OH
EXCUSE
ME.
'HELLO!'
GUESSH WHAT?
YOU'RE A DOPEY ANGEL.

YOU SAY I AWOKE IN A FOG!
YUP, THAT'S YOU.
SO THEN- THIS AIN'T HEAVEN?
IT IS- IF YOU WANT IT TO BE.
EVERY-ONE SHOULD HAVE A DOG.

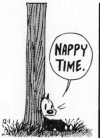

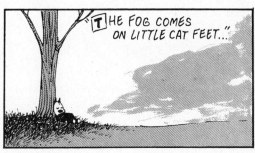

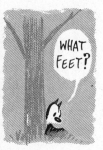

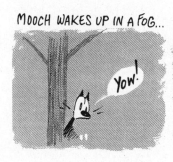

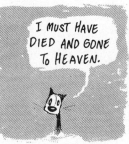

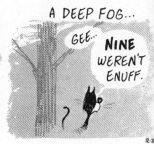

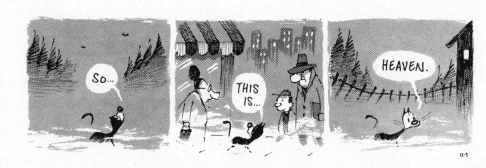

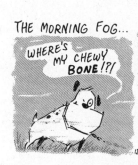

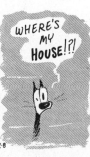

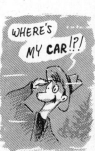

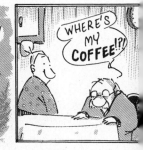

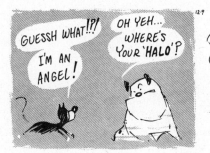

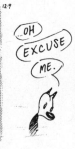

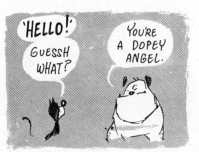

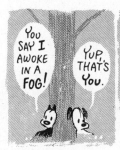

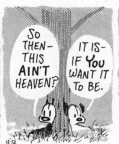

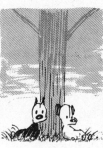

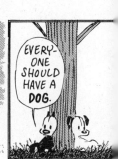

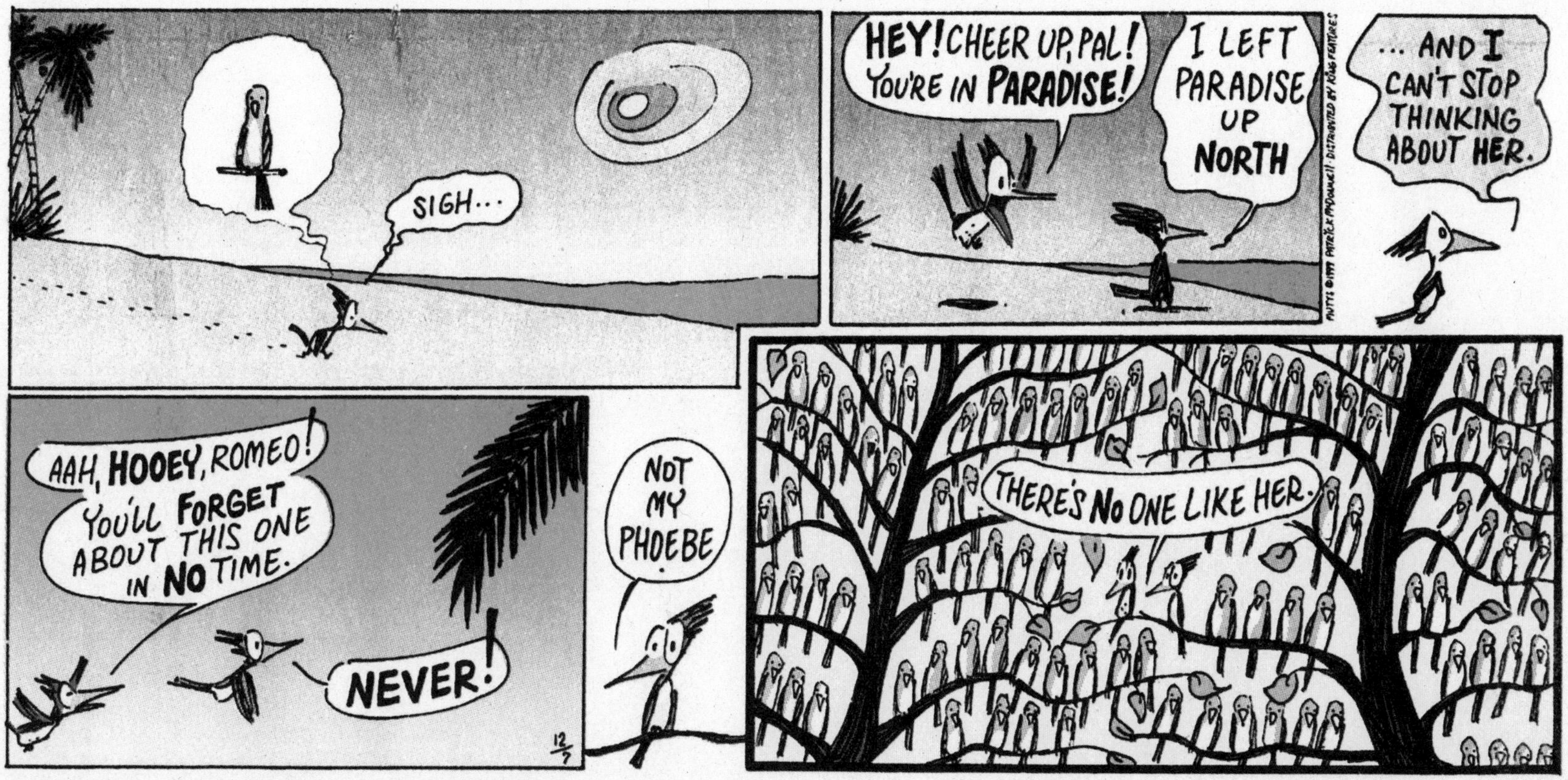

SIGH...
HEY! CHEER UP, PAL! YOU'RE IN PARADISE!
I LEFT PARADISE UP NORTH
... AND I CAN'T STOP THINKING ABOUT HER.
AAH, HOOEY, ROMEO! YOU'LL FORGET ABOUT THIS ONE IN NO TIME.
NEVER!
NOT MY PHOEBE
THERE'S NO ONE LIKE HER.


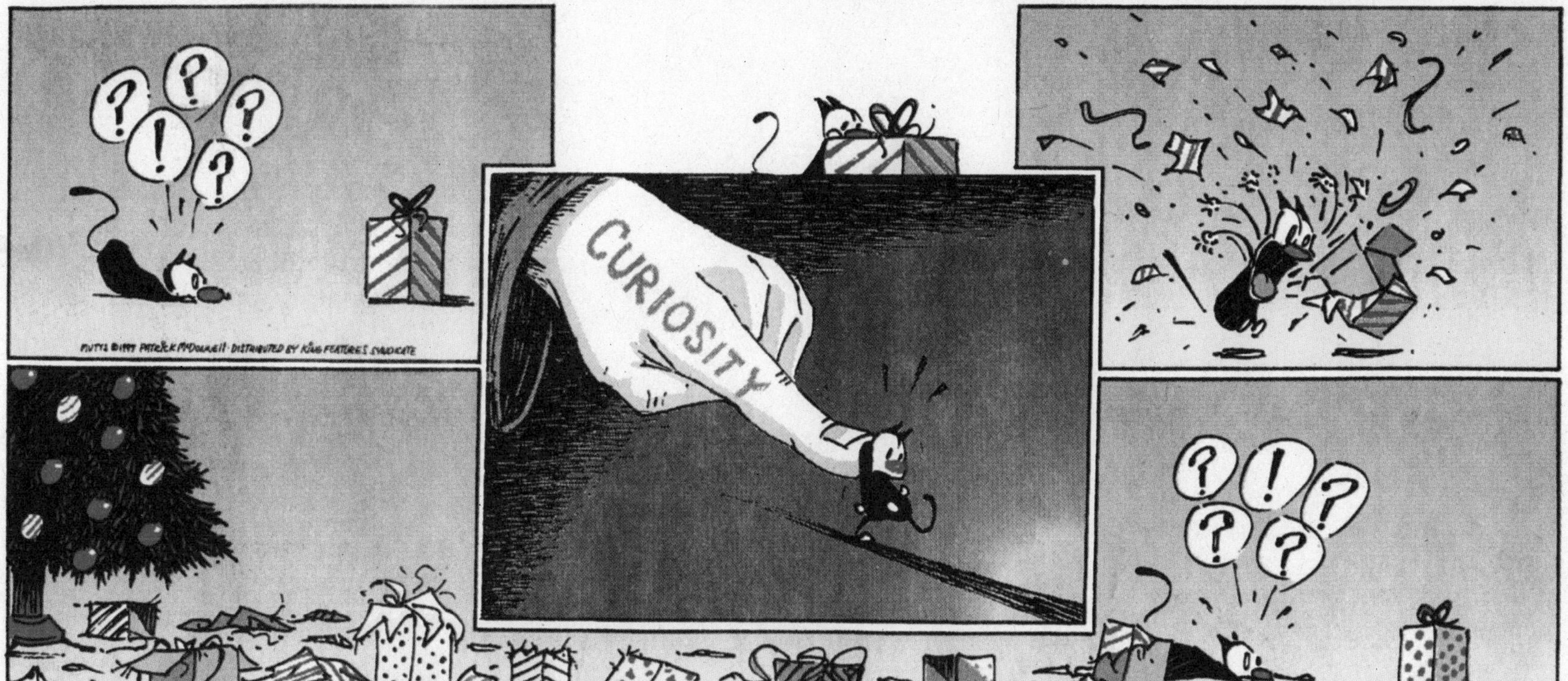

?
!
?
?
?
MUTTS ©1999 PATRICK McDONNELL · DISTRIBUTED BY KING FEATURES SYNDICATE
CURIOSITY
?
!
?
?
?
12·21

WHAT
DO I GET EARL FOR CHRIST-MAS?
HE HAS
A FOOD BOWL.
A WATER DISH.
A DOG BED...
12-15
ARG!
WHAT DO YOU GET A GUY WHO HAS EVERYTHING?

WHAT DO YOU GET A GUY WHO HAS EVERYTHING!?! WHAT? WHAT? WHAT?
LET ME THINK... IF YOU HAD EVERY-THING... WHAT WOULD YOU WANT?...
...NOTHING!
YESH!
SHOPPING IS SO MUCH EASIER WHEN YOU MAKE A LIST.

I KNOW WHAT TO GET EARL-ABSHOLUTELY "NOTHING."
12-20
SALE
BUY
MORE MORE!
ALTHOUGH AT THIS TIME OF YEAR IT SHMAY BE HARD TO FIND.
BUY

NOW
HOW DO YOU GIVE A GUY 'NOTHING'?
HMMMM....
I'LL JUST PUT 'NOTHING' IN THIS BOX.
GEE...I DUNNO... SHMAYBE MY OL' PAL EARL DESHERVES MORE THAN THIS...

FOR ME? YOU SHOULDN'T HAVE.
I DIDN'T.
12-23
WOW
GO ON...
OPEN IT.
OH, MOOCH, YOU DIDN'T HAVE TO GET ME ANY-THING.
WHO TOLD YA!?!

WELL, MOOCH, THANKS FOR 'NOTHING'.
ANYTIME.
SO DID YOU GET GUARD DOG THE SAME THING?
NO!
'NOTHING' IS TOO GOOD FOR HIM.

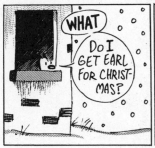

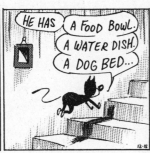

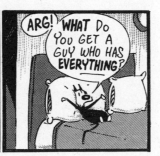

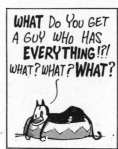

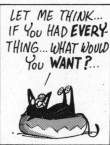

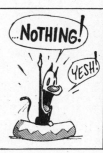

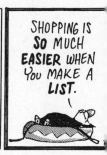

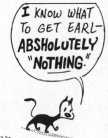

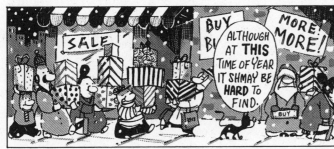

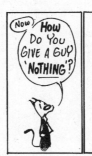

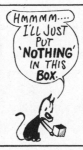

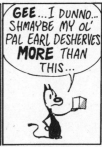

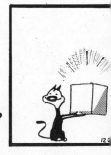

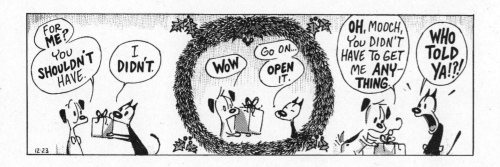

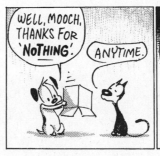

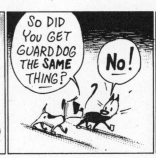

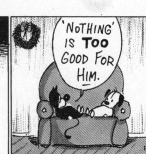

# 98

**With the help of** a common dish towel, Mooch channeled the link to his ancient Egyptian feline past and became the all-knowing Shphinx. The Shphinx is master of the inshcrutable wise riddle and the unbearable bad pun. Sphinx shtick.

While we're discussing ridiculous characters, we now have Crabby's cohort, Mussels Marinara, the world's toughest mussel. Unlike a novel, there's no master outline for a daily comic strip. The cartoonist is basically along for the ride, generally not much farther ahead of the reading public. Believe me, I had no idea when I started *Mutts* that one of my favorite characters would be a mollusk with an attitude problem.

As companion animals, Earl and Mooch have loving homes, but I also wanted to tell the stories of all the dogs and cats on the streets and in the shelters who are waiting for the same. Inspired by the Humane Society of the United States' National Animal Shelter Awareness Week, I launched *Mutts* Shelter Stories on November 2. Over the years I've received many letters from people who said they were moved to adopt or to volunteer as a result of these strips. It's the part of *Mutts* of which I am most proud.

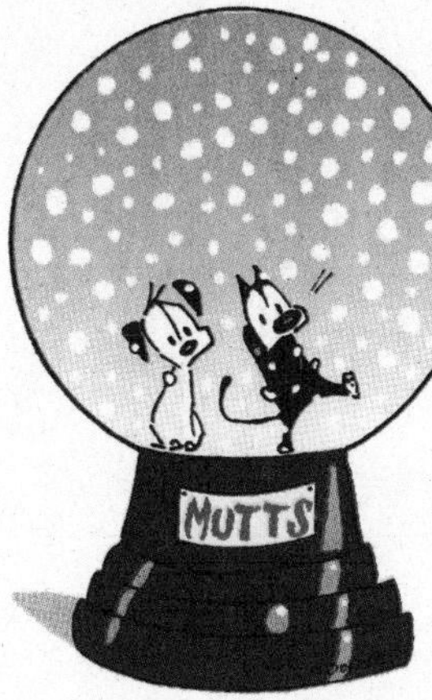
MUTTS

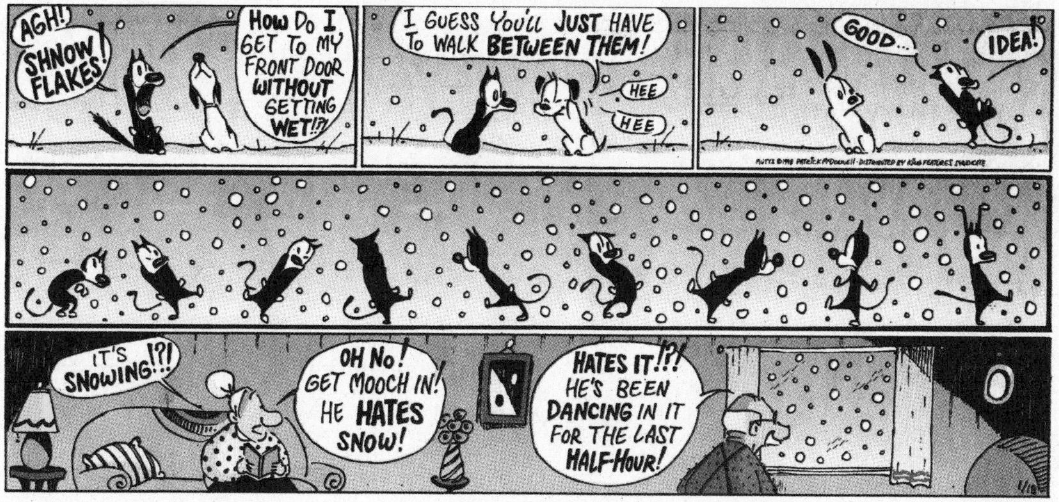
AGH! SHNOW! FLAKES!
HOW DO I GET TO MY FRONT DOOR WITHOUT GETTING WET!?!
I GUESS YOU'LL JUST HAVE TO WALK BETWEEN THEM!
HEE
HEE
GOOD...
IDEA!
IT'S SNOWING!?!
OH NO! GET MOOCH IN! HE HATES SNOW!
HATES IT!?! HE'S BEEN DANCING IN IT FOR THE LAST HALF-HOUR!

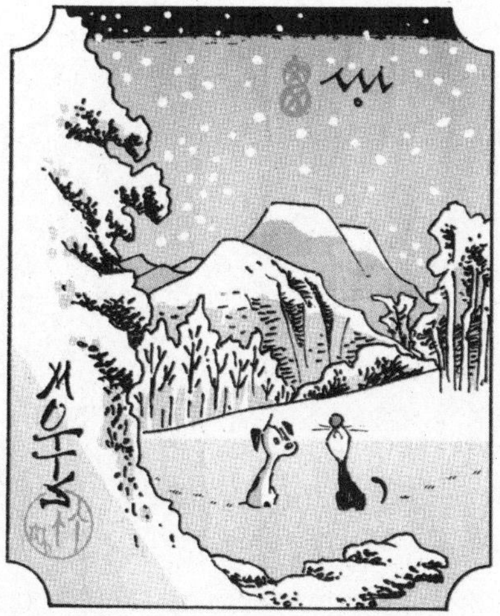

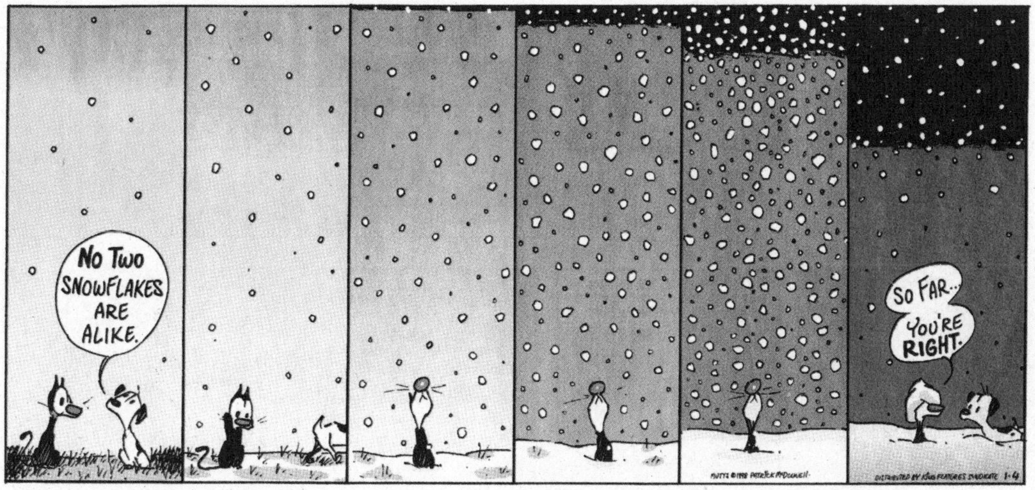
NO TWO SNOWFLAKES ARE ALIKE.
SO FAR... YOU'RE RIGHT.

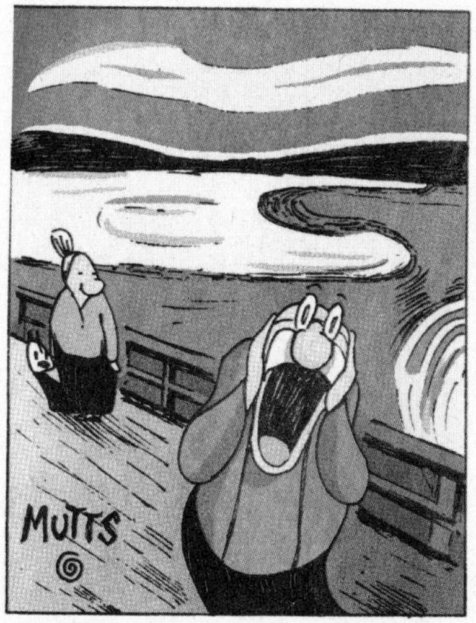
MUTTS

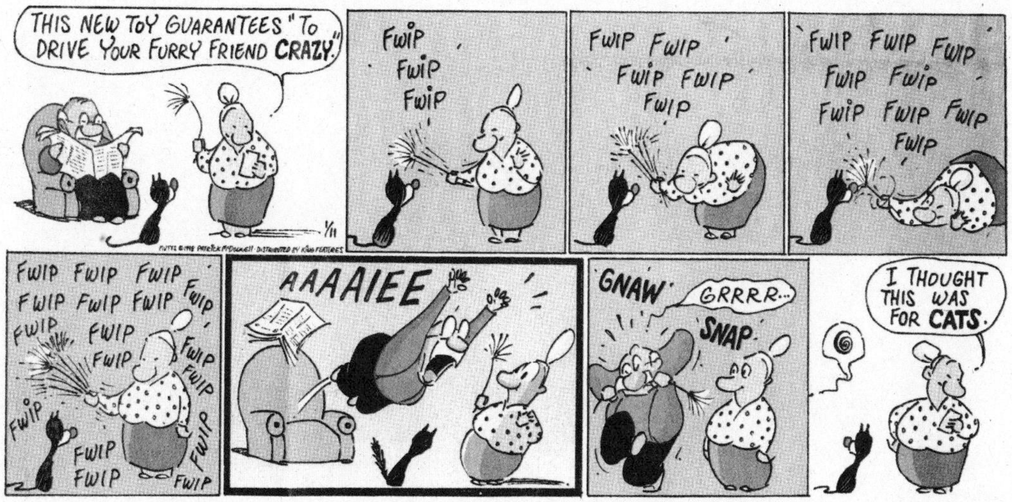
THIS NEW TOY GUARANTEES "TO DRIVE YOUR FURRY FRIEND CRAZY."
FWIP FWIP FWIP
FWIP FWIP FWIP FWIP FWIP
FWIP FWIP FWIP FWIP FWIP FWIP FWIP FWIP FWIP
FWIP FWIP FWIP FWIP FWIP FWIP FWIP FWIP FWIP FWIP FWIP FWIP FWIP FWIP FWIP
AAAAIEE
GNAW
GRRRR...
SNAP
I THOUGHT THIS WAS FOR CATS.

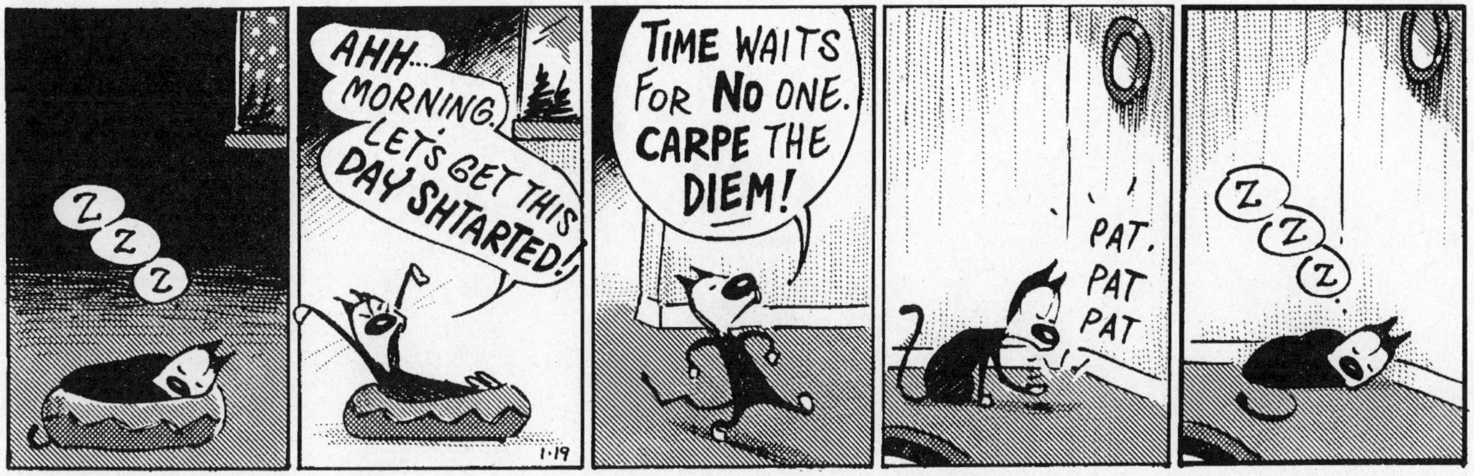
Z Z Z
AHH... MORNING.
LET'S GET THIS DAY SHTARTED!
1·19
TIME WAITS FOR NO ONE. CARPE THE DIEM!
PAT, PAT PAT
Z Z Z

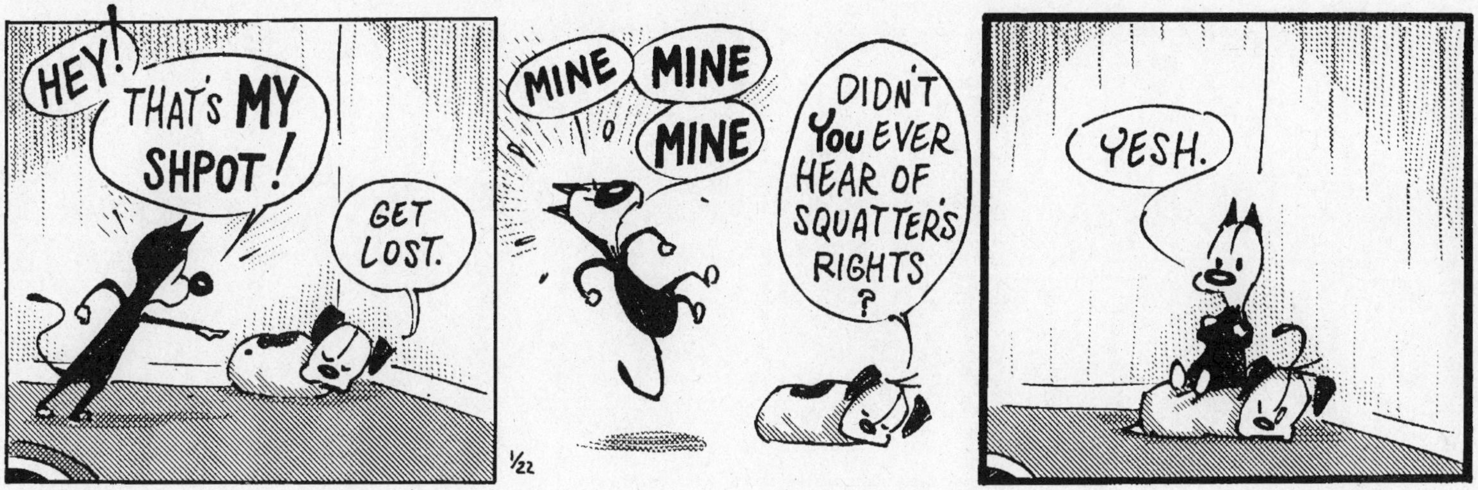
HEY!
THAT'S MY SHPOT!
GET LOST.
1/22
MINE
MINE
MINE
DIDN'T YOU EVER HEAR OF SQUATTER'S RIGHTS ?
YESH.

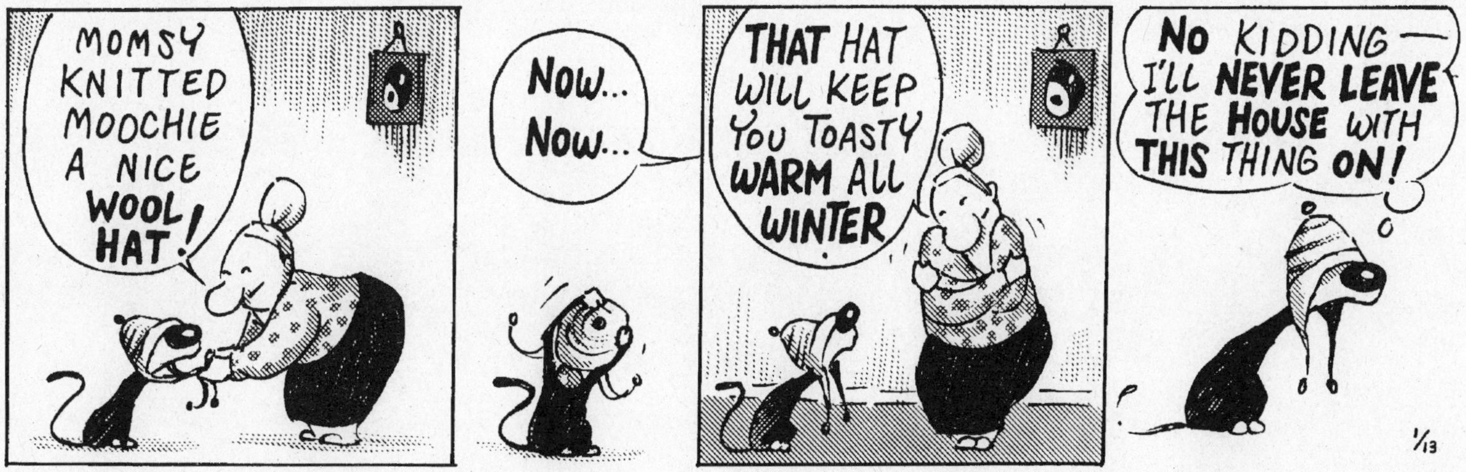
MOMSY KNITTED MOOCHIE A NICE WOOL HAT!
NOW... NOW...
THAT HAT WILL KEEP YOU TOASTY WARM ALL WINTER
NO KIDDING — I'LL NEVER LEAVE THE HOUSE WITH THIS THING ON!
1/13

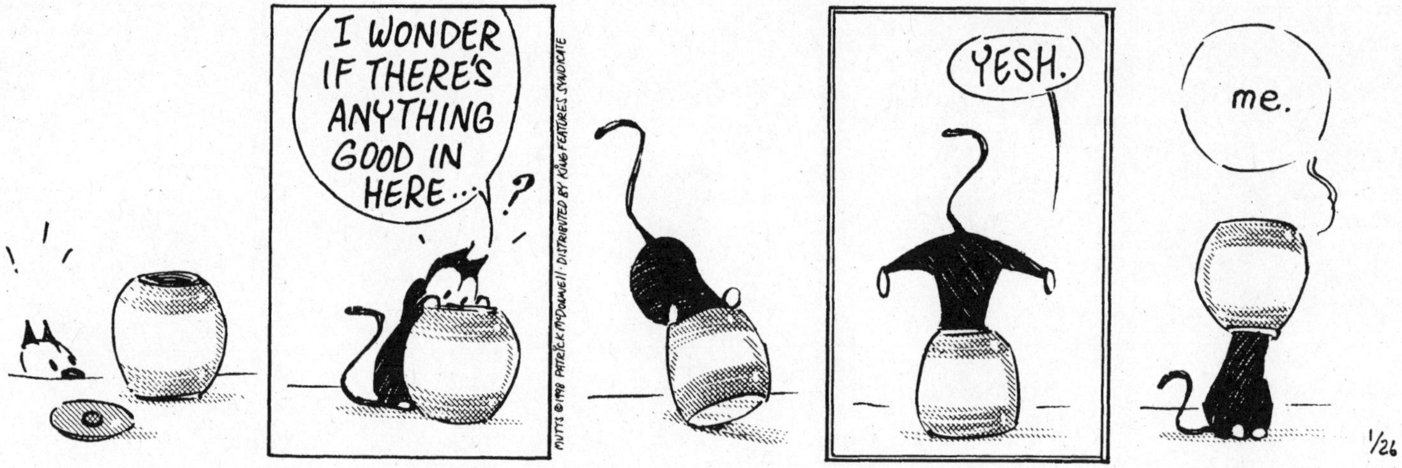
I WONDER IF THERE'S ANYTHING GOOD IN HERE...?
MUTTS ©1998 PATRICK McDONNELL. DISTRIBUTED BY KING FEATURES SYNDICATE
YESH.
me.
1/26

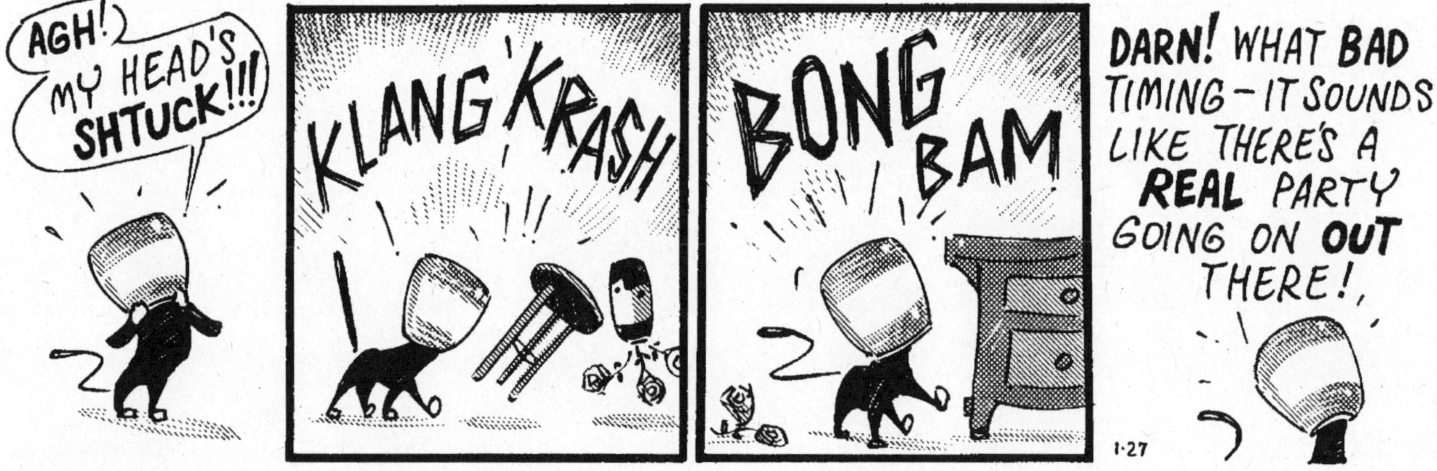
AGH! MY HEAD'S SHTUCK!!!
KLANG KRASH
BONG BAM
DARN! WHAT BAD TIMING – IT SOUNDS LIKE THERE'S A REAL PARTY GOING ON OUT THERE!
1·27

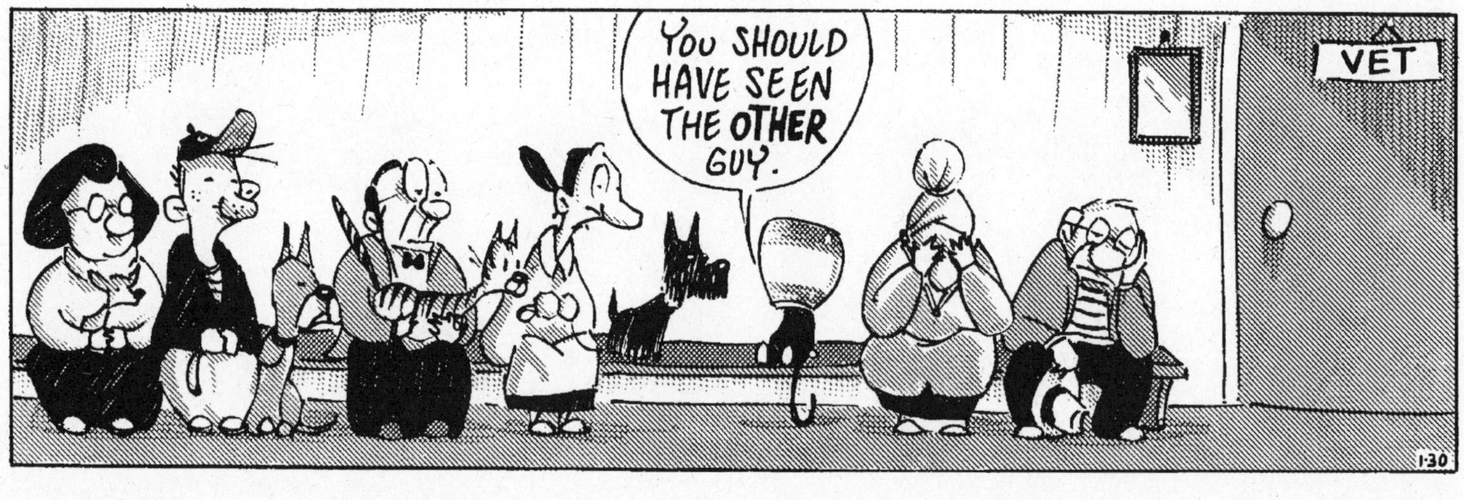
YOU SHOULD HAVE SEEN THE OTHER GUY.
VET
1·30

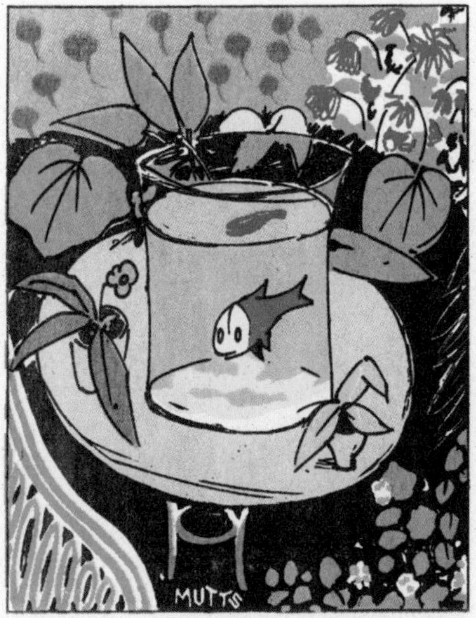
MUTTS

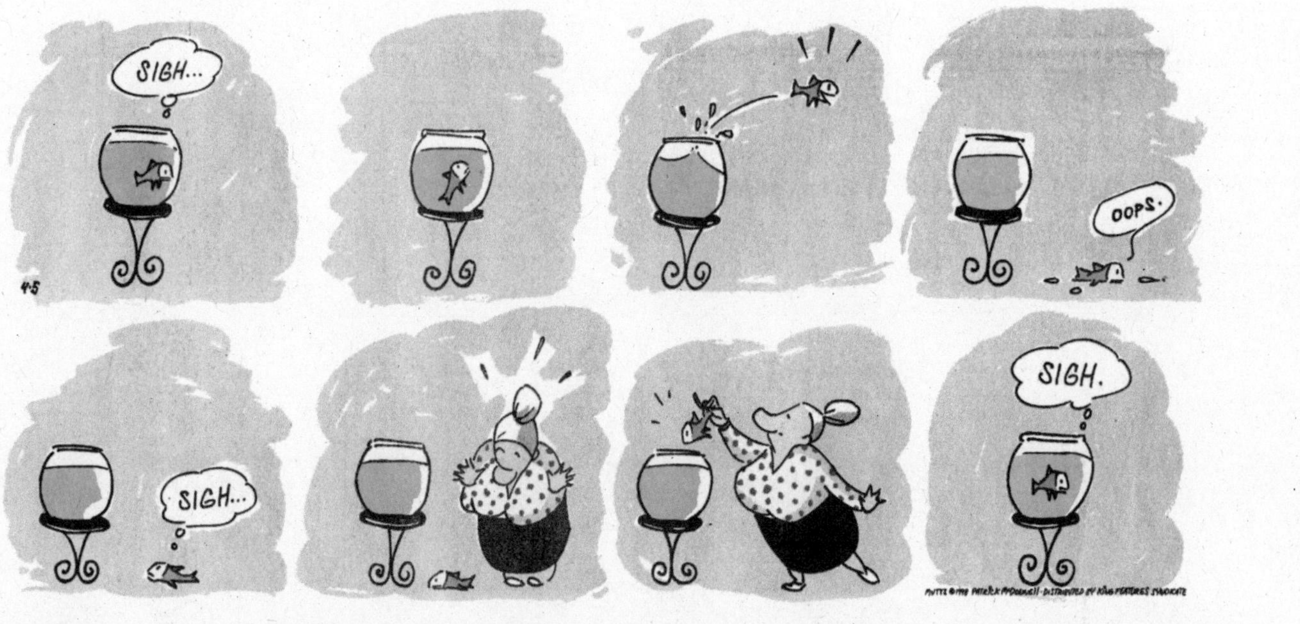
SIGH...
OOPS.
SIGH...
SIGH.

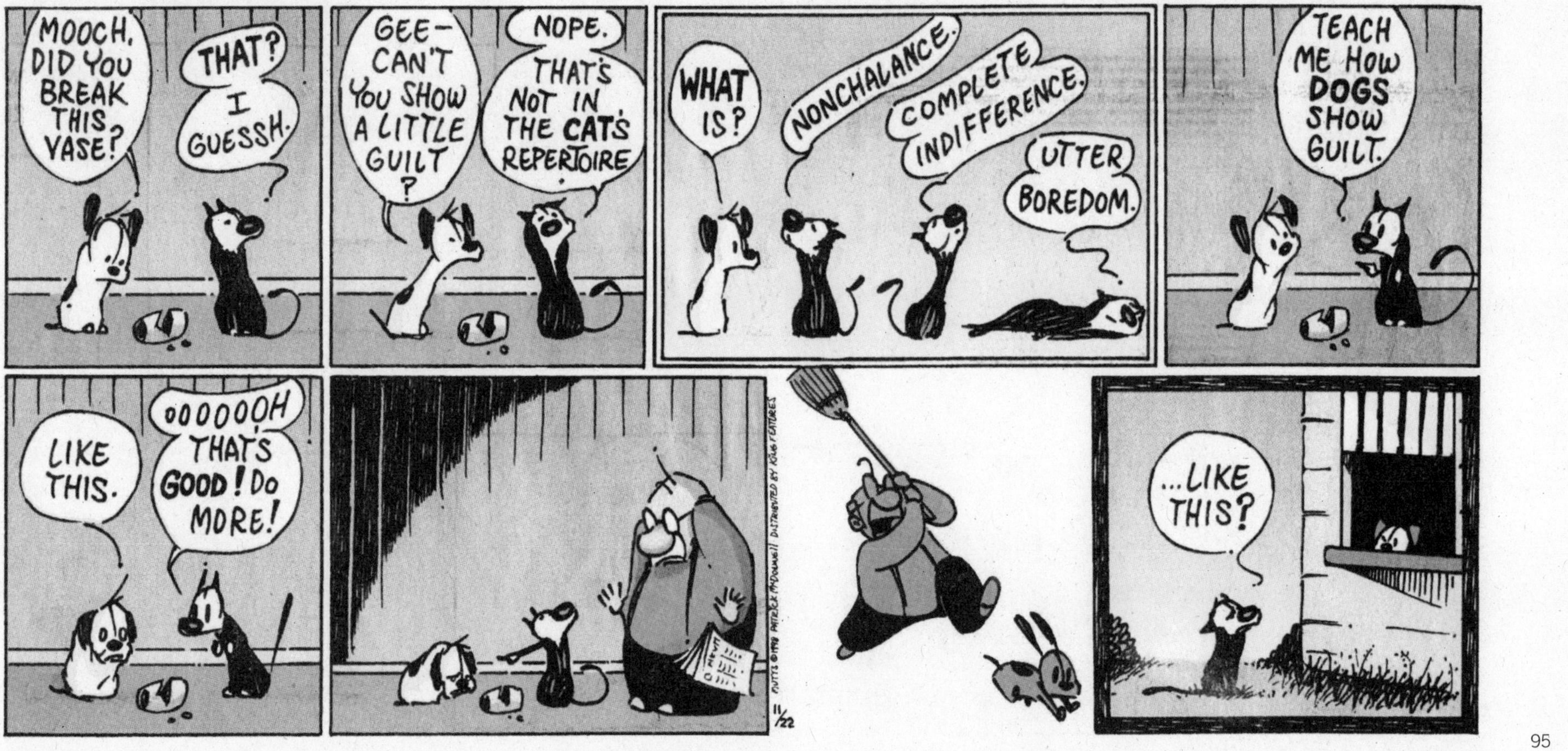
MOOCH, DID YOU BREAK THIS VASE?
THAT? I GUESSH.
GEE—CAN'T YOU SHOW A LITTLE GUILT?
NOPE. THAT'S NOT IN THE CAT'S REPERTOIRE.
WHAT IS?
NONCHALANCE.
COMPLETE INDIFFERENCE.
UTTER BOREDOM.
TEACH ME HOW DOGS SHOW GUILT.
LIKE THIS.
OOOOOOH THAT'S GOOD! DO MORE!
...LIKE THIS?

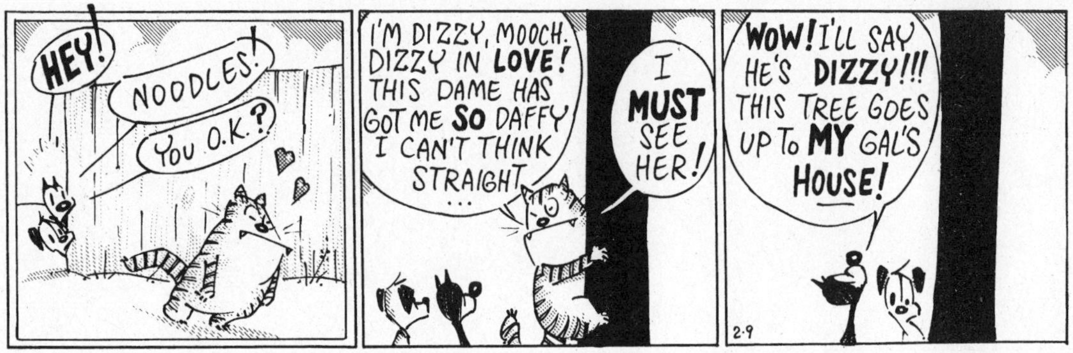
HEY!
NOODLES!
YOU O.K.?
I'M DIZZY, MOOCH. DIZZY IN LOVE! THIS DAME HAS GOT ME SO DAFFY I CAN'T THINK STRAIGHT...
I MUST SEE HER!
WOW! I'LL SAY HE'S DIZZY!!! THIS TREE GOES UP TO MY GAL'S HOUSE!
2·9

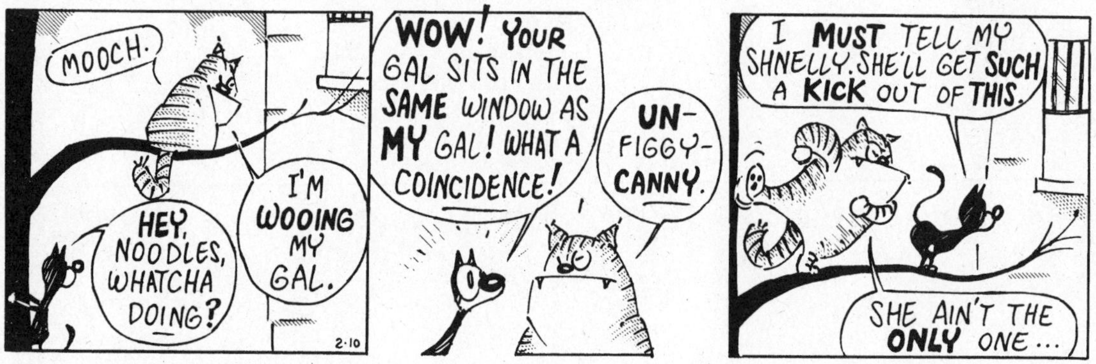
MOOCH.
HEY, NOODLES, WHATCHA DOING?
I'M WOOING MY GAL.
2·10
WOW! YOUR GAL SITS IN THE SAME WINDOW AS MY GAL! WHAT A COINCIDENCE!
UN-FIGGY-CANNY.
I MUST TELL MY SHNELLY. SHE'LL GET SUCH A KICK OUT OF THIS.
SHE AIN'T THE ONLY ONE...

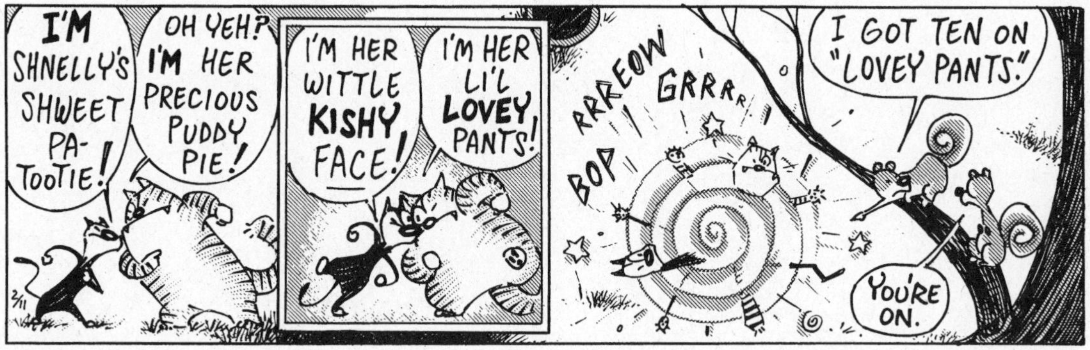
I'M SHNELLY'S SHWEET PA-TOOTIE!
OH YEH? I'M HER PRECIOUS PUDDY PIE!
2/11
I'M HER WITTLE KISHY FACE!
I'M HER LI'L LOVEY PANTS!
RRREOW
GRRRR
BOP
I GOT TEN ON "LOVEY PANTS."
YOU'RE ON.

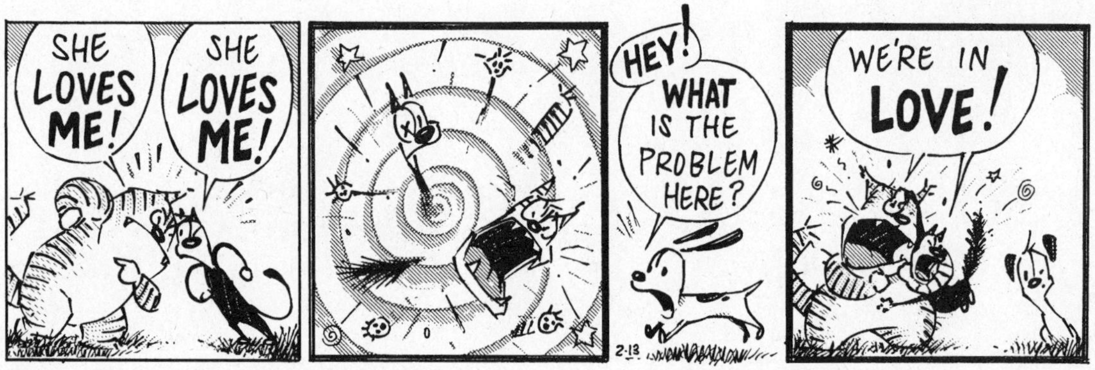
SHE LOVES ME!
SHE LOVES ME!
HEY! WHAT IS THE PROBLEM HERE?
2·13
WE'RE IN LOVE!

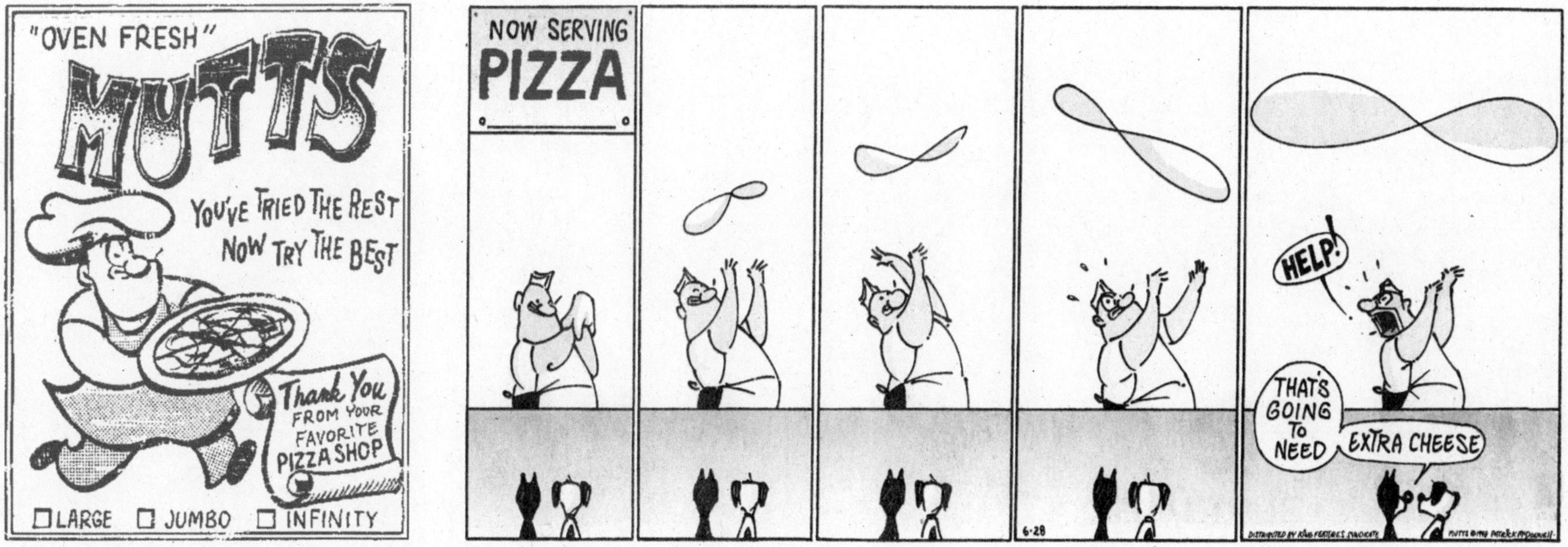
"OVEN FRESH"
MUTTS
YOU'VE TRIED THE REST NOW TRY THE BEST
Thank You FROM YOUR FAVORITE PIZZA SHOP
LARGE JUMBO INFINITY
NOW SERVING PIZZA
6-28
HELP!
THAT'S GOING TO NEED
EXTRA CHEESE

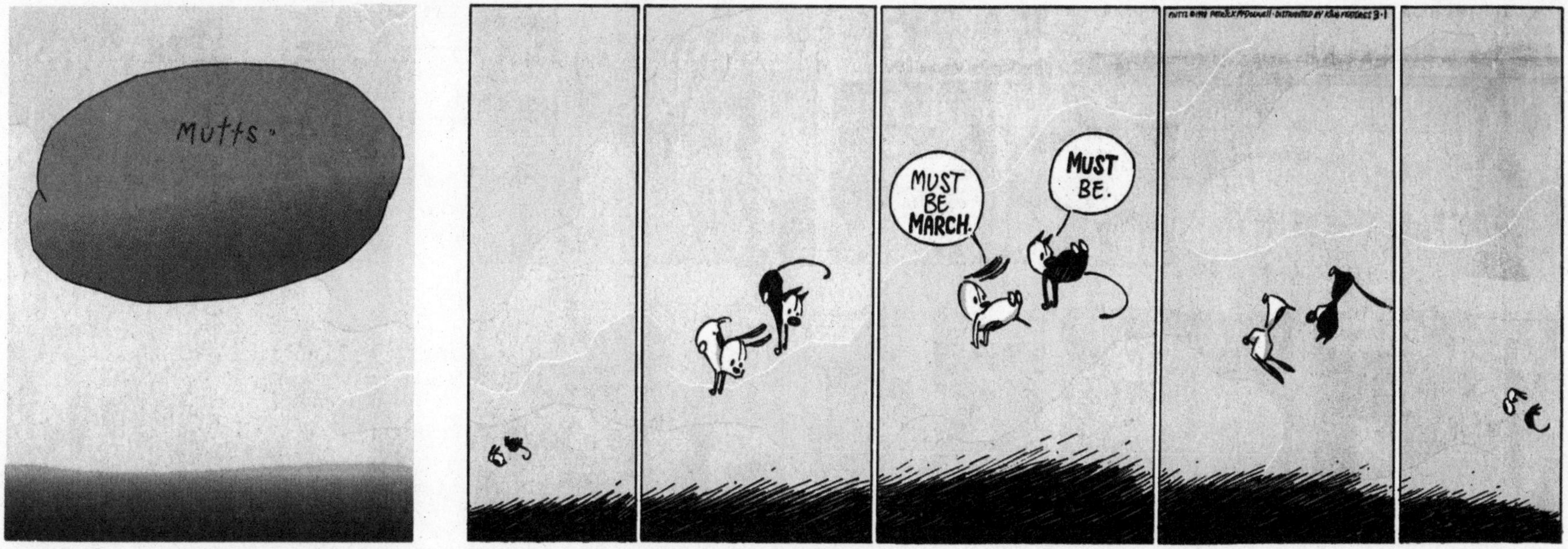
mutts
MUST BE MARCH.
MUST BE.

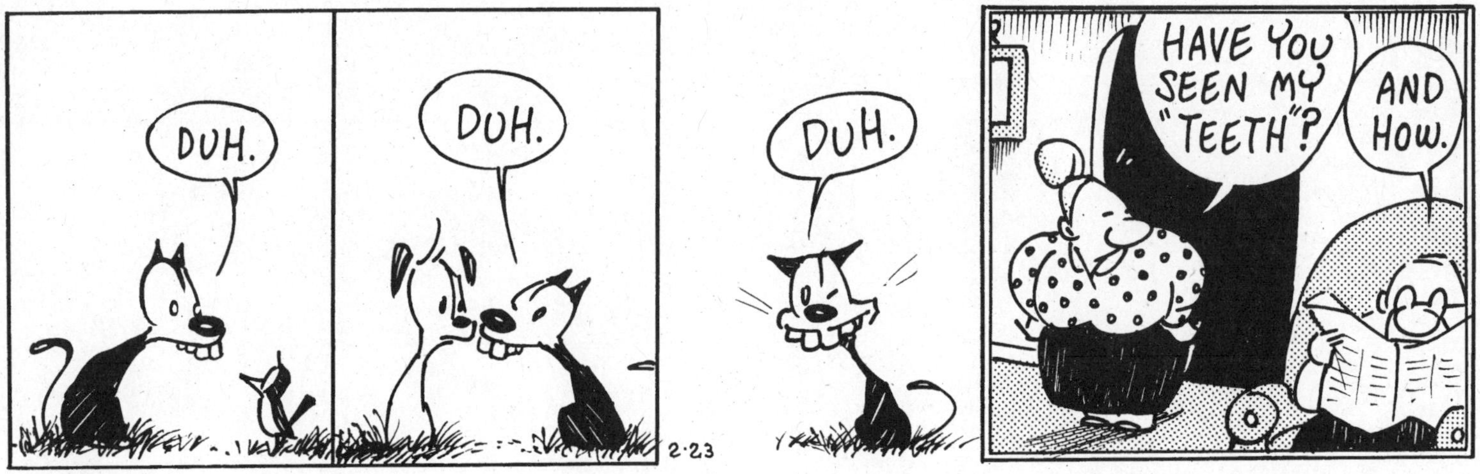
DUH.
DUH.
2·23
DUH.
HAVE YOU SEEN MY "TEETH"?
AND HOW.

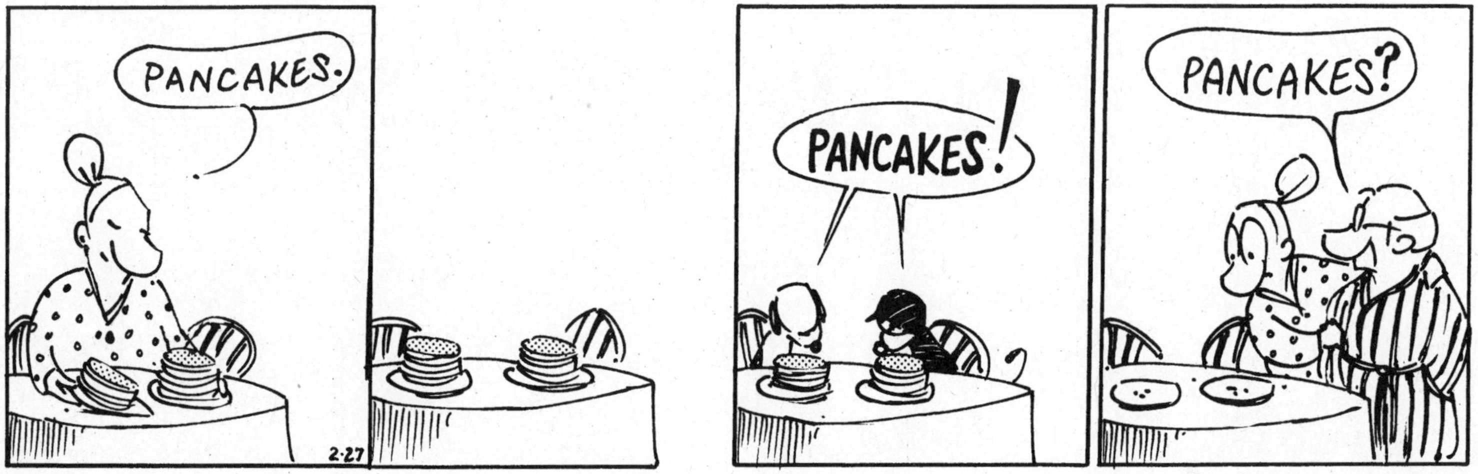
PANCAKES.
2·27
PANCAKES!
PANCAKES?

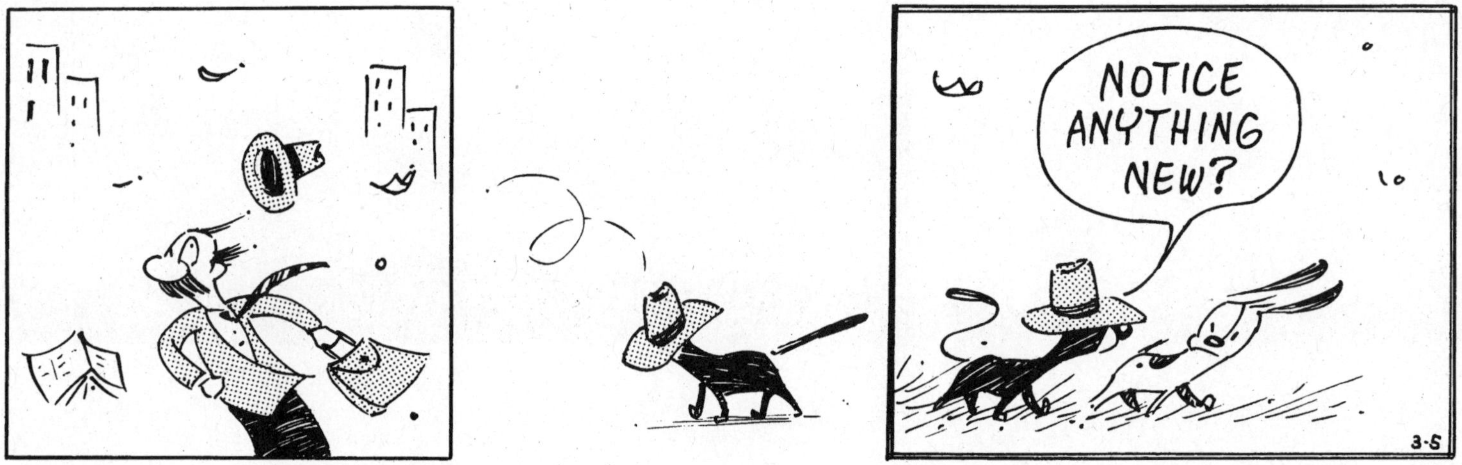
NOTICE ANYTHING NEW?
3·5

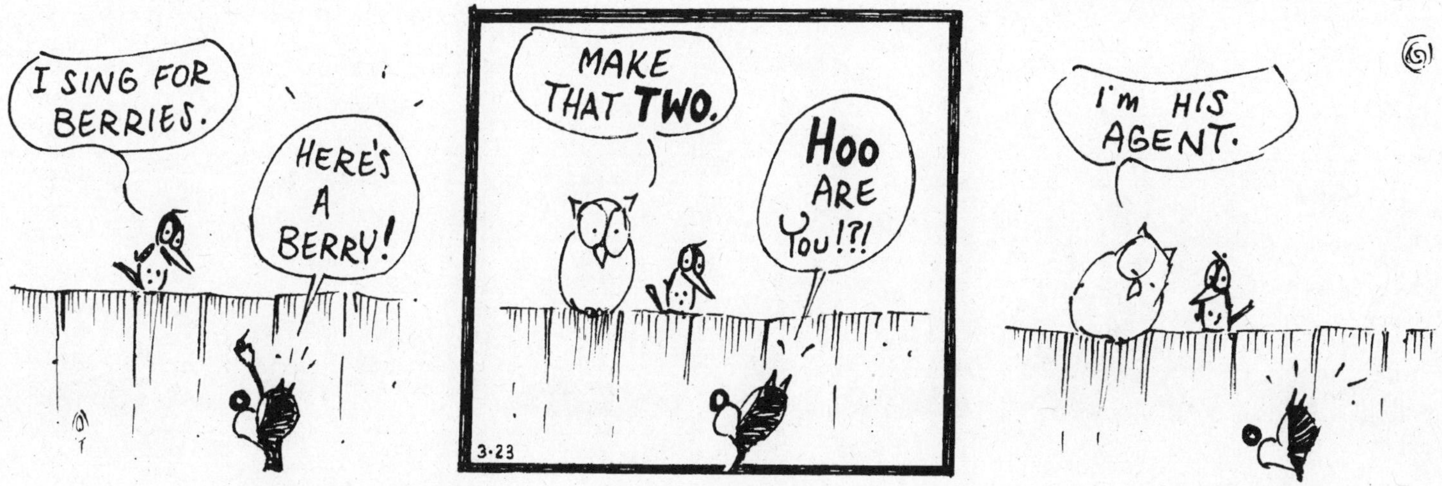
I SING FOR BERRIES.
HERE'S A BERRY!
MAKE THAT TWO.
HOO ARE YOU!?!
3·23
I'M HIS AGENT.

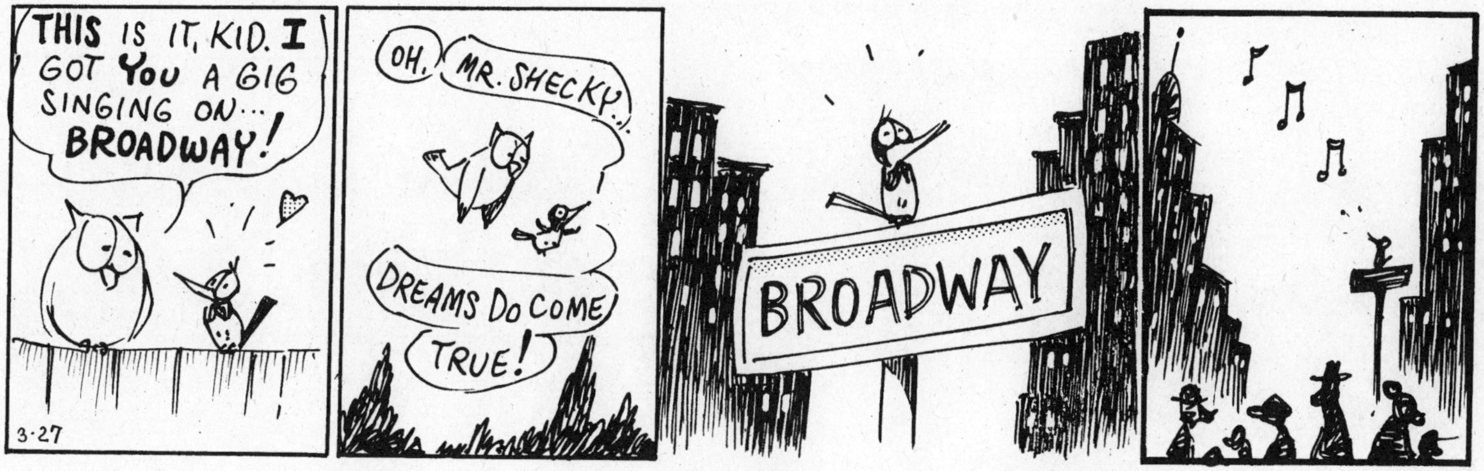
THIS IS IT, KID. I GOT YOU A GIG SINGING ON... BROADWAY!
3·27
OH,
MR. SHECKY...
DREAMS DO COME TRUE!
BROADWAY

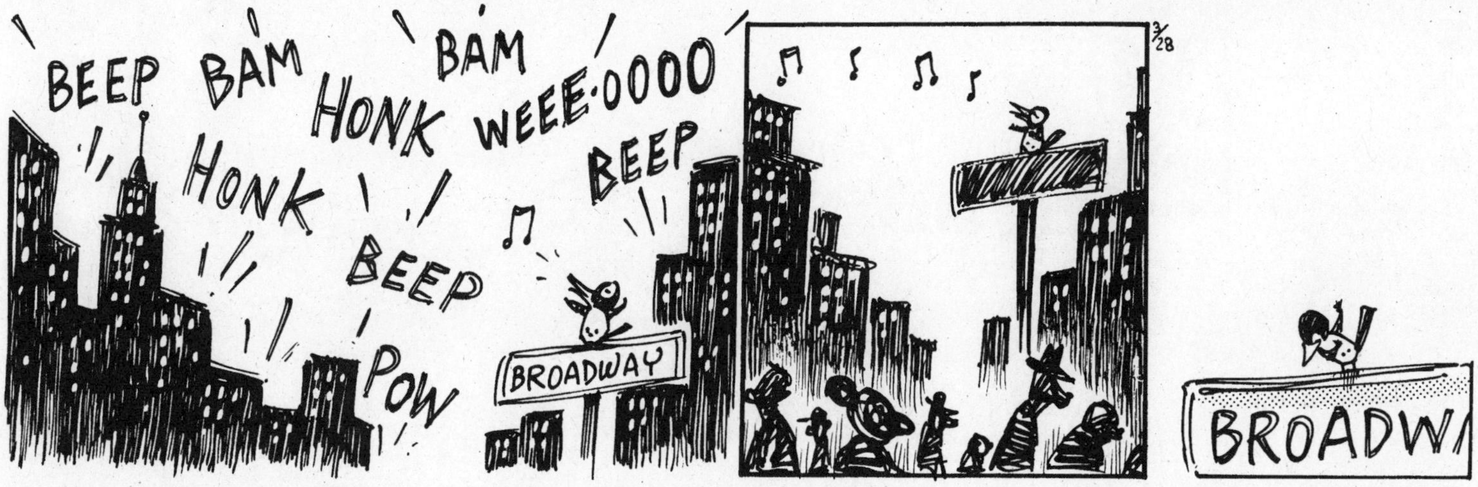
BEEP BAM
BAM
HONK WEEE·OOOO
HONK
BEEP
BEEP
POW
BROADWAY
3/28
BROADW

MUDDAY.

TWOSDAY.

WETSDAY.

TURNSDAY.

FLYDAY.

SPLATTERDAY.

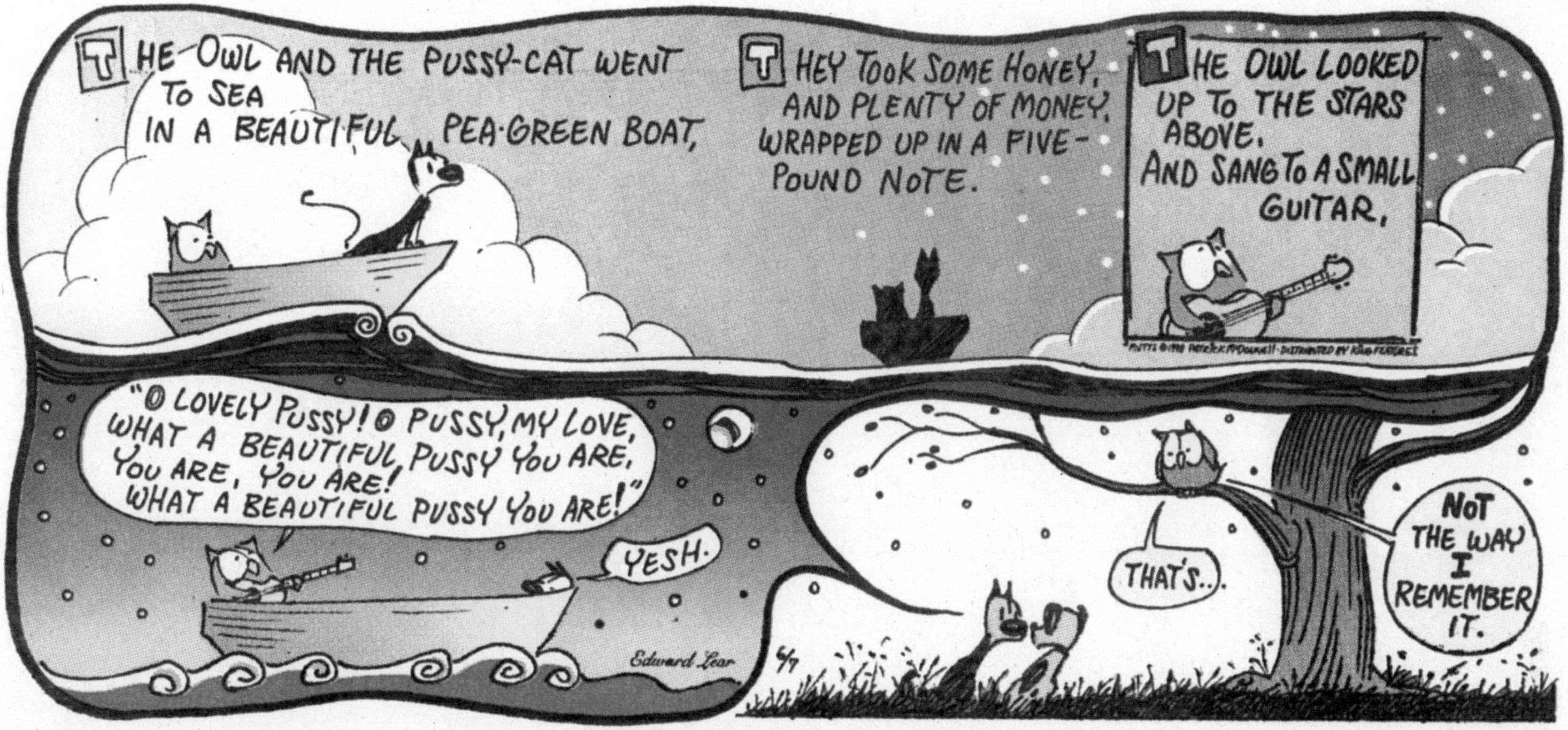
THE OWL AND THE PUSSY-CAT WENT TO SEA
IN A BEAUTIFUL PEA-GREEN BOAT,
THEY TOOK SOME HONEY, AND PLENTY OF MONEY, WRAPPED UP IN A FIVE-POUND NOTE.
THE OWL LOOKED UP TO THE STARS ABOVE, AND SANG TO A SMALL GUITAR,
"O LOVELY PUSSY! O PUSSY, MY LOVE, WHAT A BEAUTIFUL PUSSY YOU ARE, YOU ARE, YOU ARE! WHAT A BEAUTIFUL PUSSY YOU ARE!"
YESH.
Edward Lear
THAT'S..
NOT THE WAY I REMEMBER IT.

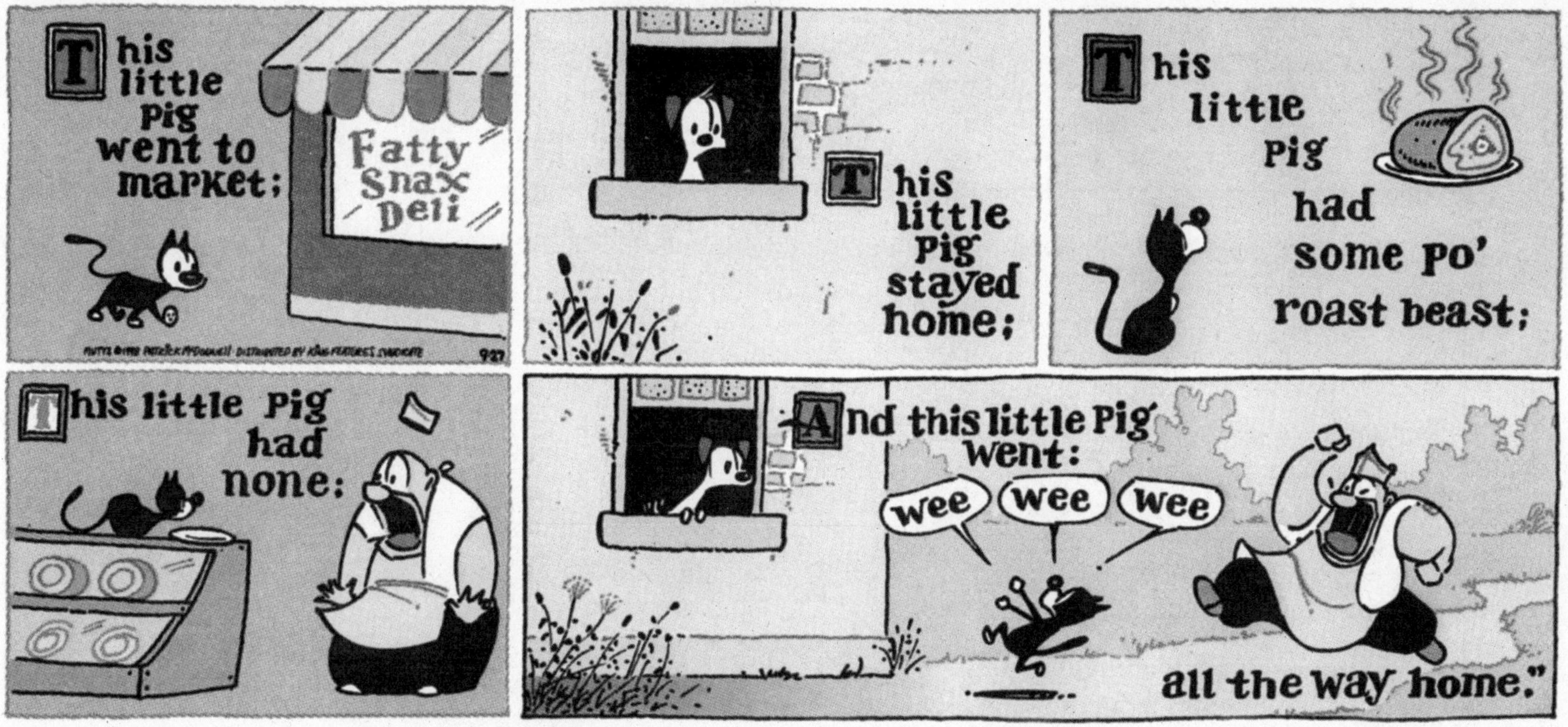
This little Pig went to market;
Fatty Snax Deli
This little Pig stayed home;
This little Pig had some po' roast beast;
This little Pig had none;
And this little Pig went:
wee
wee
wee
all the way home."

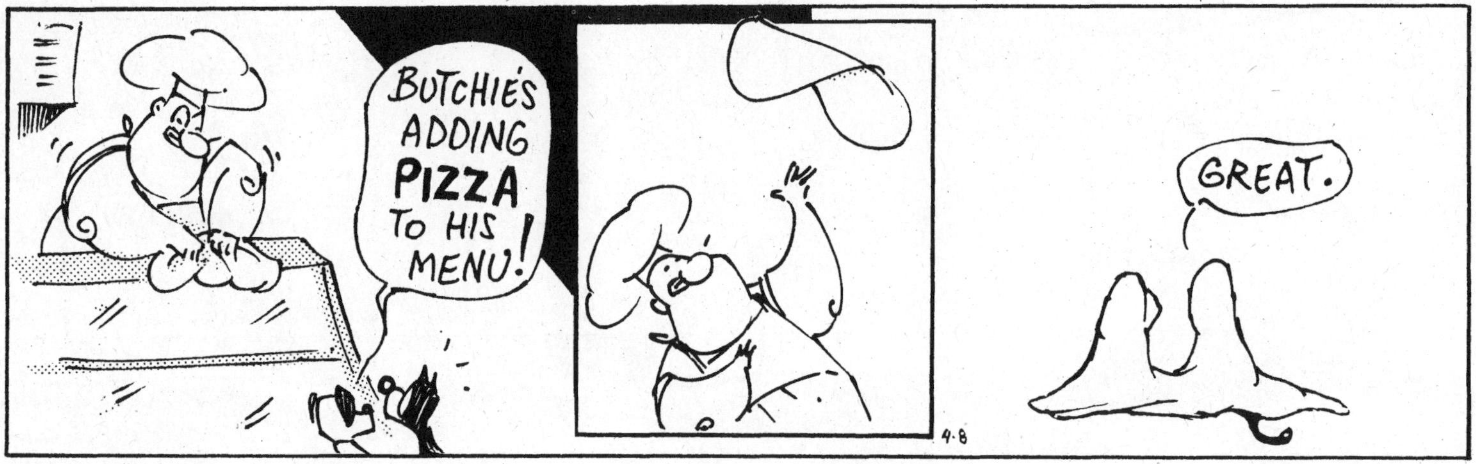
BUTCHIE'S ADDING PIZZA TO HIS MENU!
GREAT.
4·8

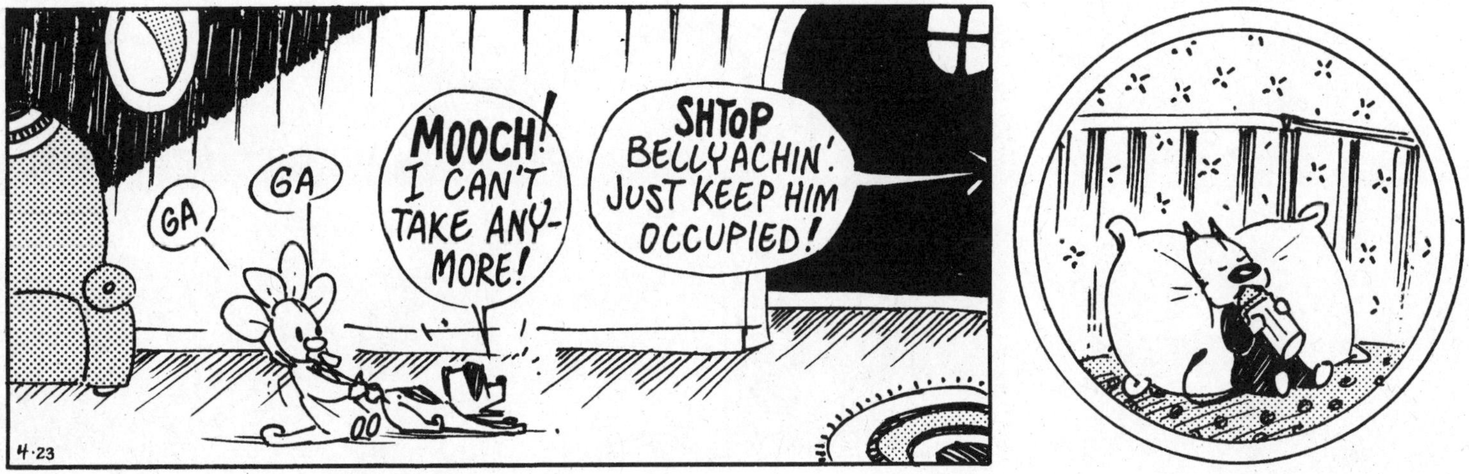
GA
GA
MOOCH! I CAN'T TAKE ANY-MORE!
SHTOP BELLYACHIN'. JUST KEEP HIM OCCUPIED!
4·23

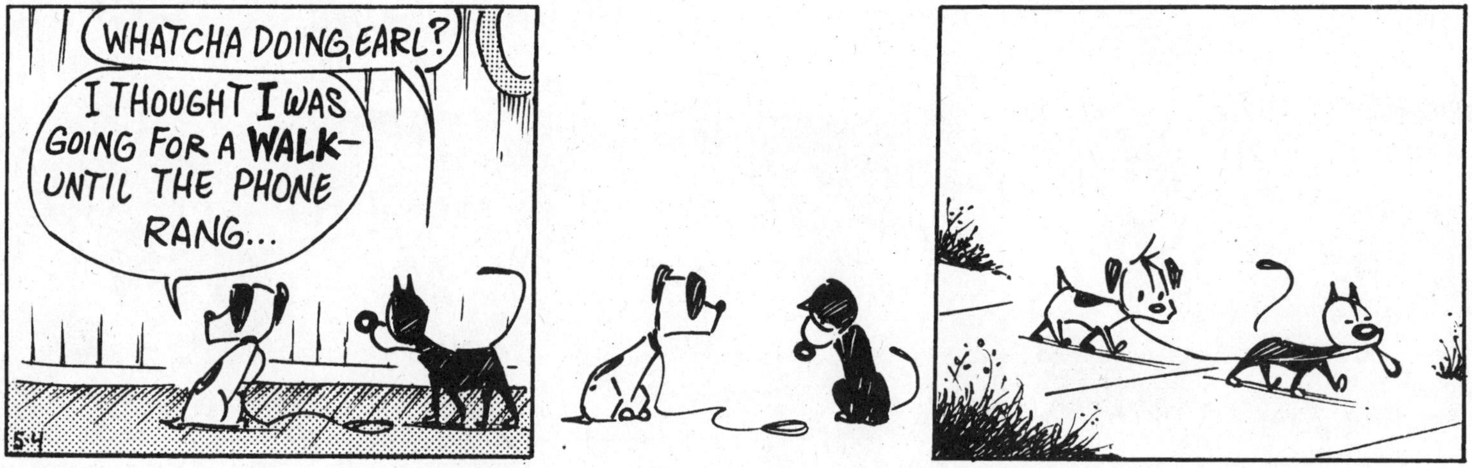
WHATCHA DOING, EARL?
I THOUGHT I WAS GOING FOR A WALK- UNTIL THE PHONE RANG...
5·4

DO YOU KNOW THE LEGEND OF YOUR EGYPTIAN ANCESTOR-THE SPHINX?
5·25
THE ALL-KNOWING SPHINX WOULD ASK A RIDDLE, AND IF YOU GOT IT WRONG HE'D DEVOUR YOU.
THE LEGEND SAYS YOU MUST ANSWER THE RIDDLE OF THE SHPHINX CORRECTLY —OR BE DEVOURED!
OH YEH?
5·26
WHAT'S IN IT FOR ME?
HEY!
I ASK THE RIDDLES AROUND HERE.
LEGEND SAYS YOU MUST ANSWER THE RIDDLE OF THE SHPHINX OR BE DEVOURED.
5·27
WHAT WEIGHS MORE- A TON OF LEAD OR A TON OF FEATHERS?
YOUR MOTHER?
I AM THE ALL-KNOWING SHPHINX. I SEE ALL.
YOU DO?
I CAN SEE INTO SPACE AND BEYOND! I CAN SEE CLEAR 'ROUND THE WORLD!
WHAT DO YOU SEE?
I SEE THE BACK OF A BLACK CAT WITH A DISH TOWEL ON HIS HEAD
YOW!
HE'S GOOD!
6·2

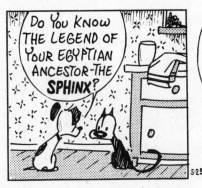

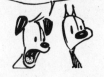

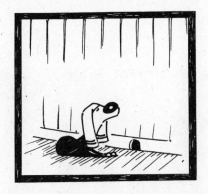

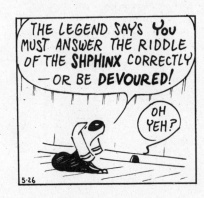

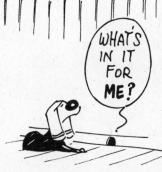

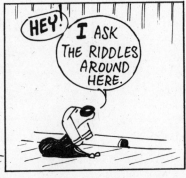

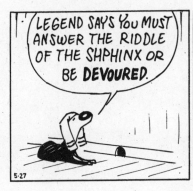

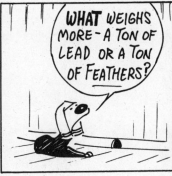

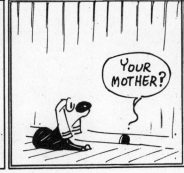

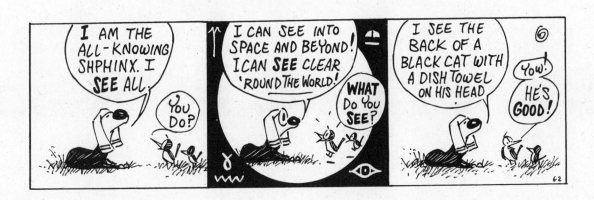

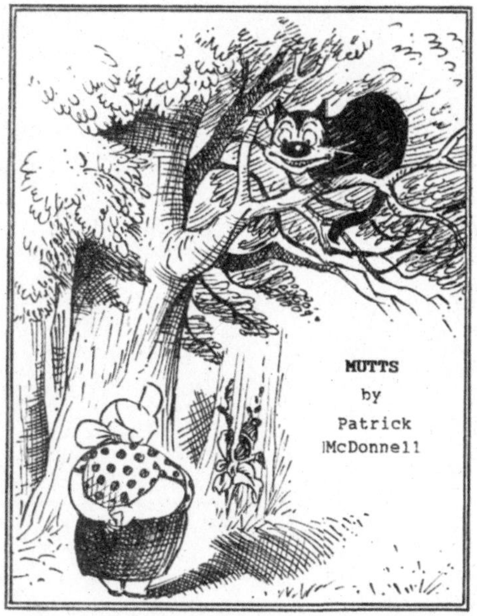
MUTTS
by
Patrick
McDonnell

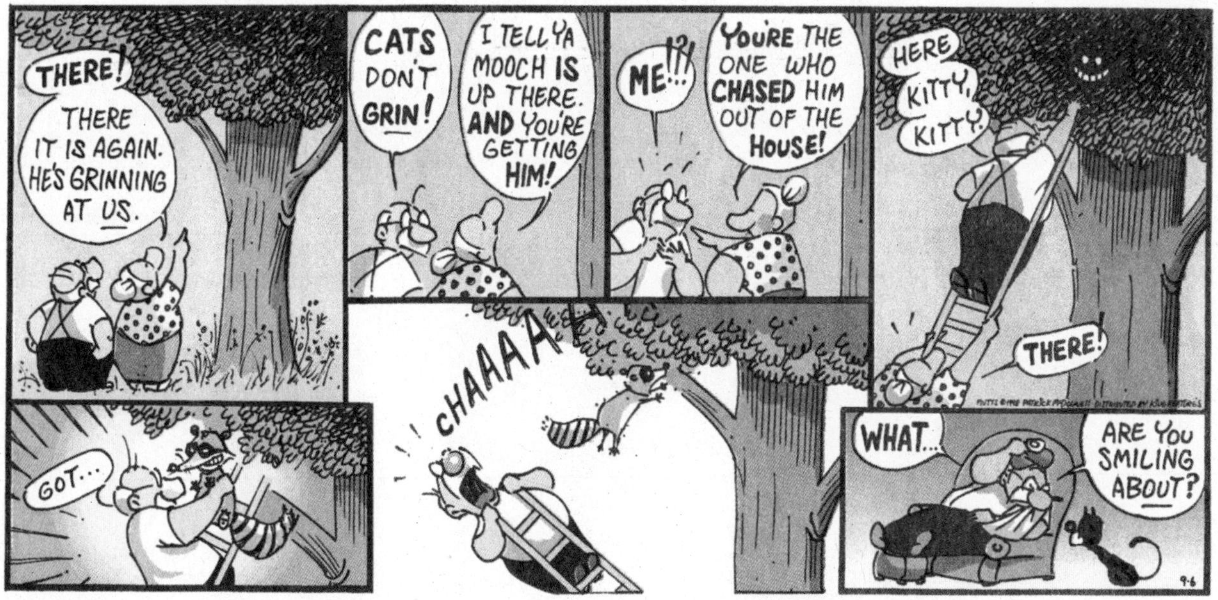
THERE!
THERE IT IS AGAIN. HE'S GRINNING AT US.
CATS DON'T GRIN!
I TELL YA MOOCH IS UP THERE. AND YOU'RE GETTING HIM!
ME!?!...
YOU'RE THE ONE WHO CHASED HIM OUT OF THE HOUSE!
HERE KITTY, KITTY.
THERE!
GOT...
CHAAAAA
WHAT...
ARE YOU SMILING ABOUT?
9-6

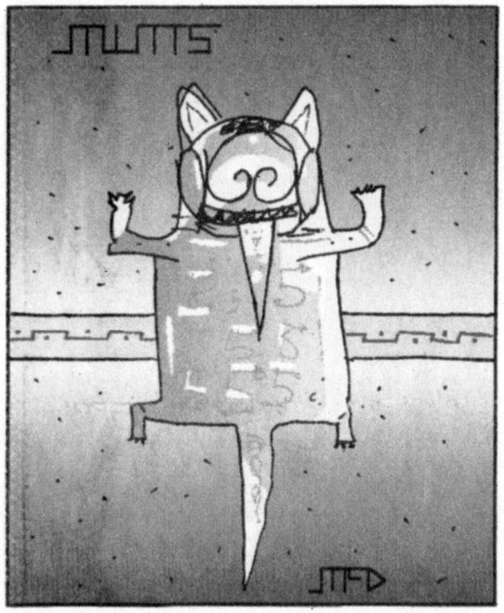

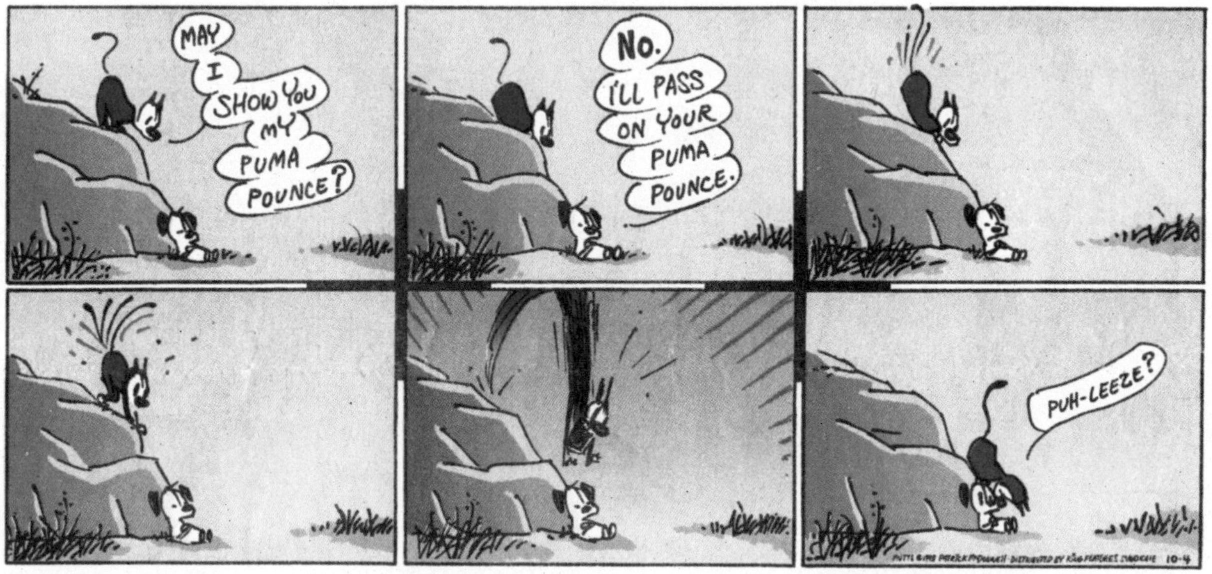
MAY I SHOW YOU MY PUMA POUNCE?
NO.
I'LL PASS ON YOUR PUMA POUNCE.
PUH-LEEZE?
10-4

FROM THIS BOAT THE FISH LOOK SO CLOSE.
YOU FEEL LIKE YOU CAN ALMOST REACH OUT AND TOUCH 'EM.
ALMOST.
7/23

IF YA HAD A STRING YA COULD GO FISHIN'.
LIKE THIS?
WHERE DID YOU GET THAT?
OVER THERE.
7/24

WHAT A STRANGE FEELING. WANDERING AIMLESSLY... WITHOUT ANY DIRECTION... WITHOUT ANY PURPOSE...
STRANGE FOR ME, THAT IS.
YESH.
7·27

THIS IS GETTING MONOTONOUS.
WHAT?
THIS.
THIS WHAT?
THIS MONOTONY.
WHAT ABOUT IT?
7·31

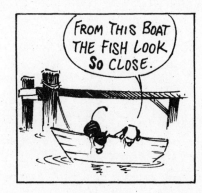

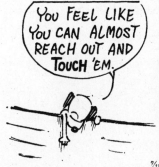

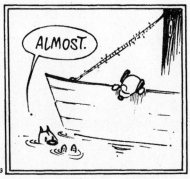

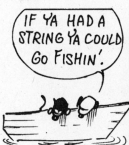

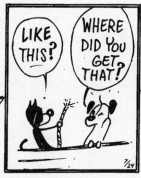

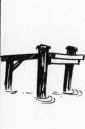

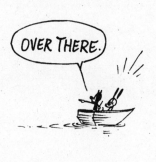

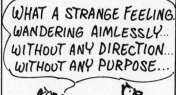

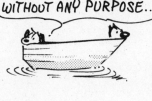

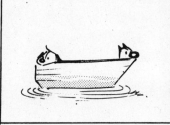

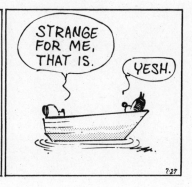

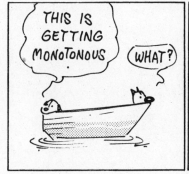

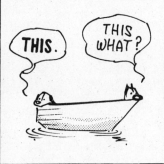

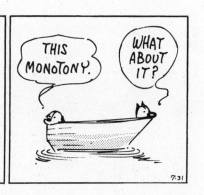

LOOK!
A MERMAID!
A SHIREN OF THE...
SEA!
SHING! SHING YOUR SHWEET LOVE SHONGS! I'M OBLIVIOUS TO YOUR SHEDUCTIVE MERMAID CHARMS!
YOU'RE OBLIVIOUS TO A LOT.
DON'T TRY TO SHWEET-TALK THIS SHAILOR!
8·10

I'M NOT A MERMAID. I'M A MANATEE.
WHAT'S THE DIFF?
WELL...
MERMAIDS DON'T EXIST. THEY ARE JUST PART OF OUR OCEAN'S FOLKLORE.
AND MAN-A-TEES?
...MIGHT BE NEXT.
8·11

WHOA!
HOW DID YOU GET ALL THESE SCARS?
FROM
SPEED BOATS
SPEED JETS
SPEED SKIS
YOW!
IS THERE SOME KIND OF CRAZY RACE 'ROUND HERE?
YEH...
HUMAN.
8·12

MERMAID... MANATEE... ...WHATEVER!!!... MOOCH BELIEVES IN YOU!
THE WORLD COULD USE A LI'L... "COMPASSION."
TALK ABOUT "ENDANGERED"...
8·13

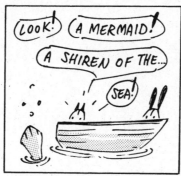

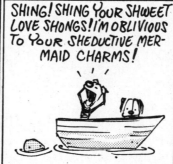

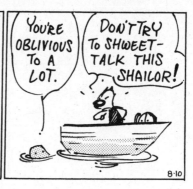

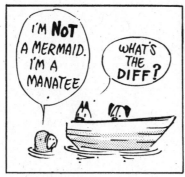

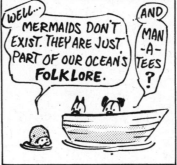

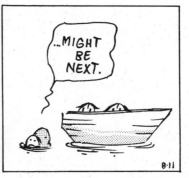

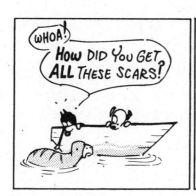

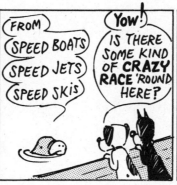

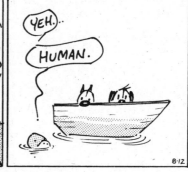

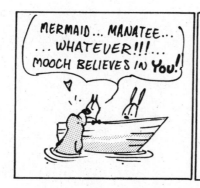

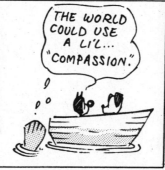

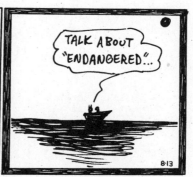

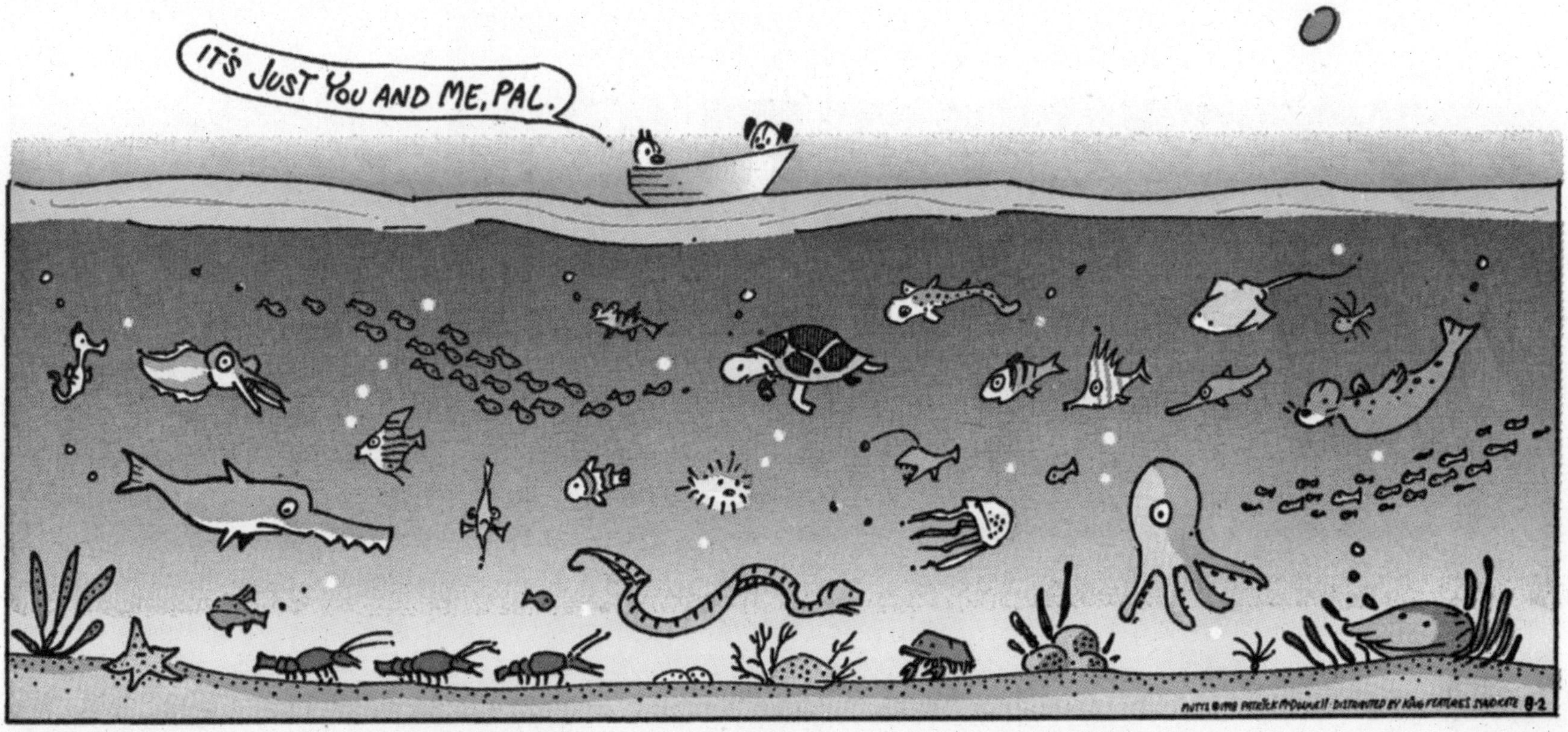
IT'S JUST YOU AND ME, PAL.

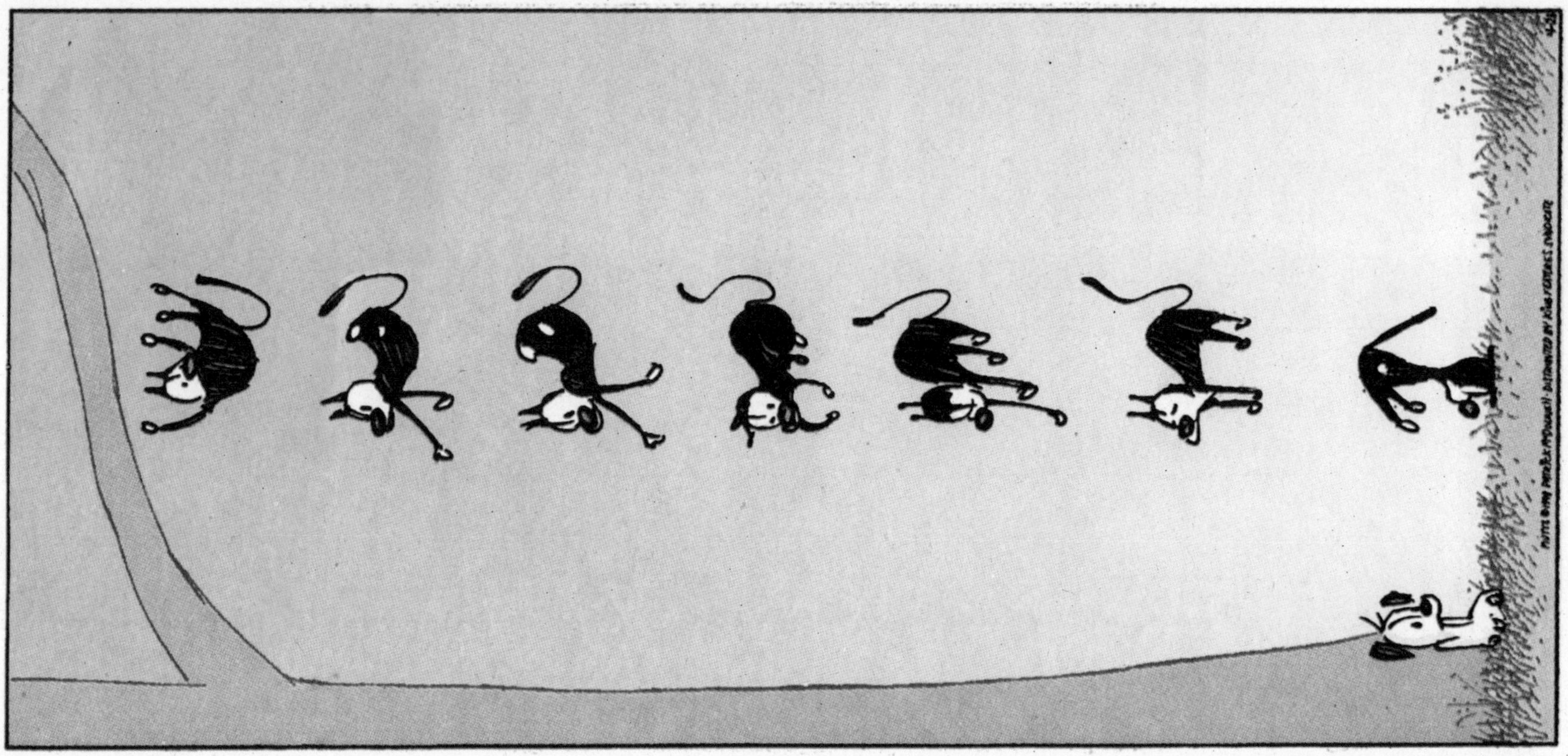

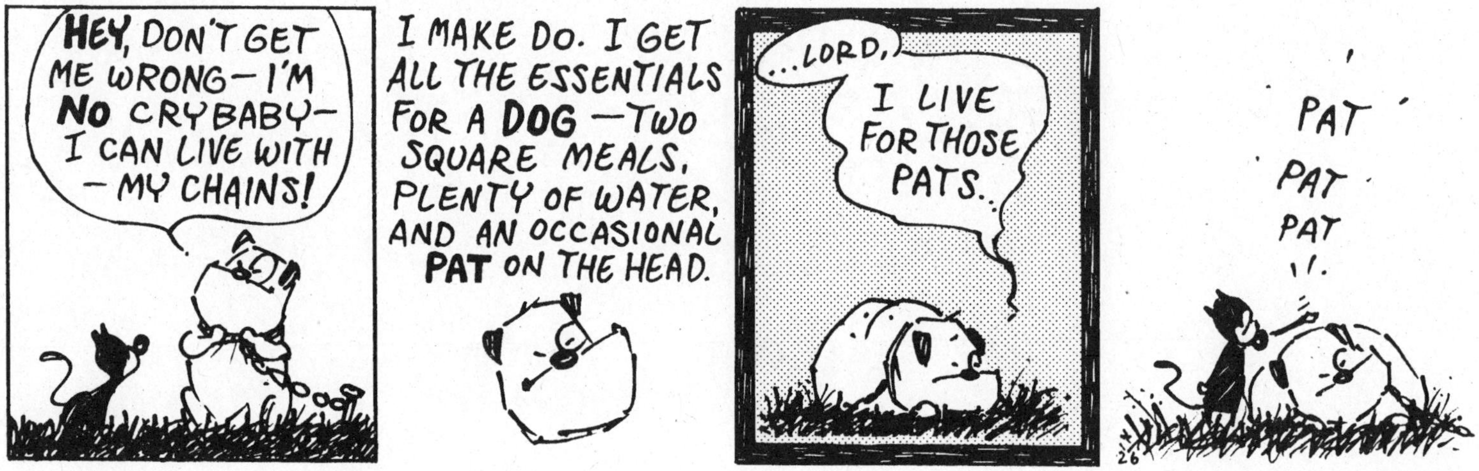
HEY, DON'T GET ME WRONG— I'M NO CRYBABY— I CAN LIVE WITH — MY CHAINS!
I MAKE DO. I GET ALL THE ESSENTIALS FOR A DOG —TWO SQUARE MEALS, PLENTY OF WATER, AND AN OCCASIONAL PAT ON THE HEAD.
...LORD,
I LIVE FOR THOSE PATS..
PAT
PAT
PAT
26

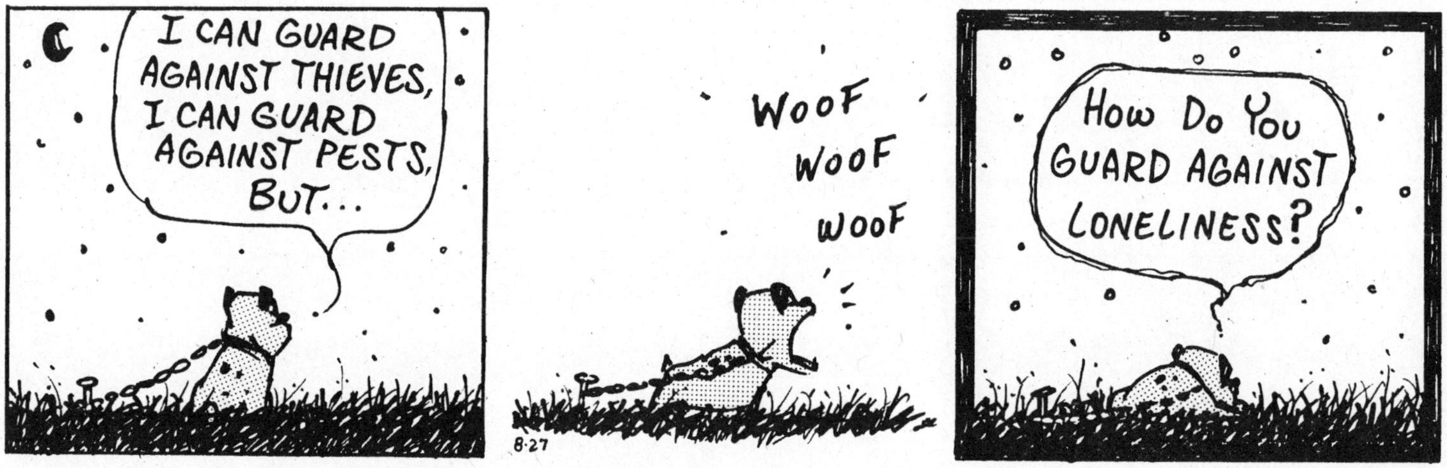
I CAN GUARD AGAINST THIEVES, I CAN GUARD AGAINST PESTS, BUT...
WOOF
WOOF
WOOF
8·27
HOW DO YOU GUARD AGAINST LONELINESS?

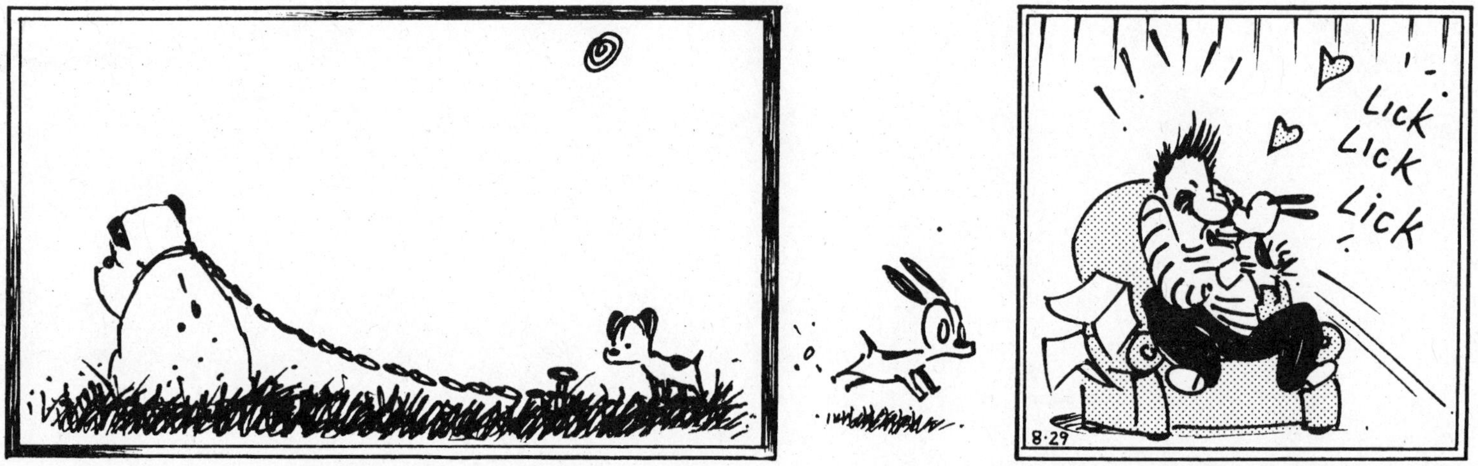
LICK
LICK
LICK
8·29

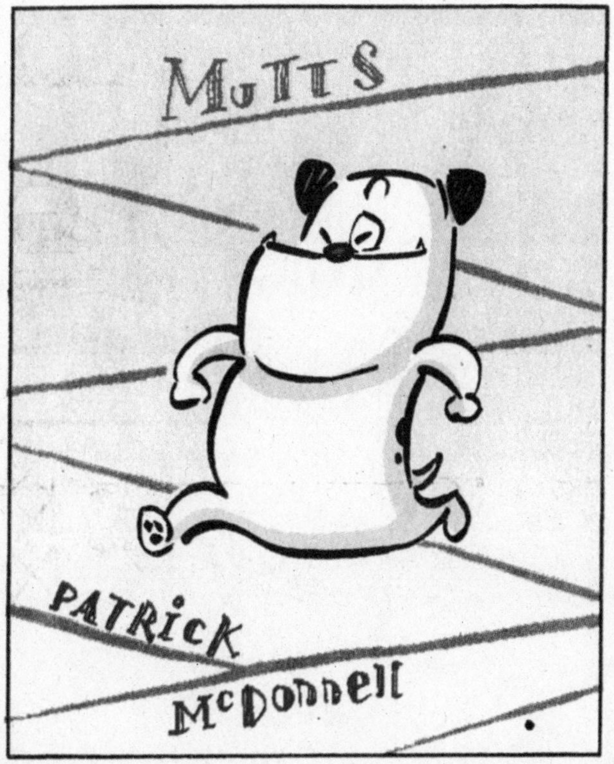
MUTTS
PATRICK
McDONNELL

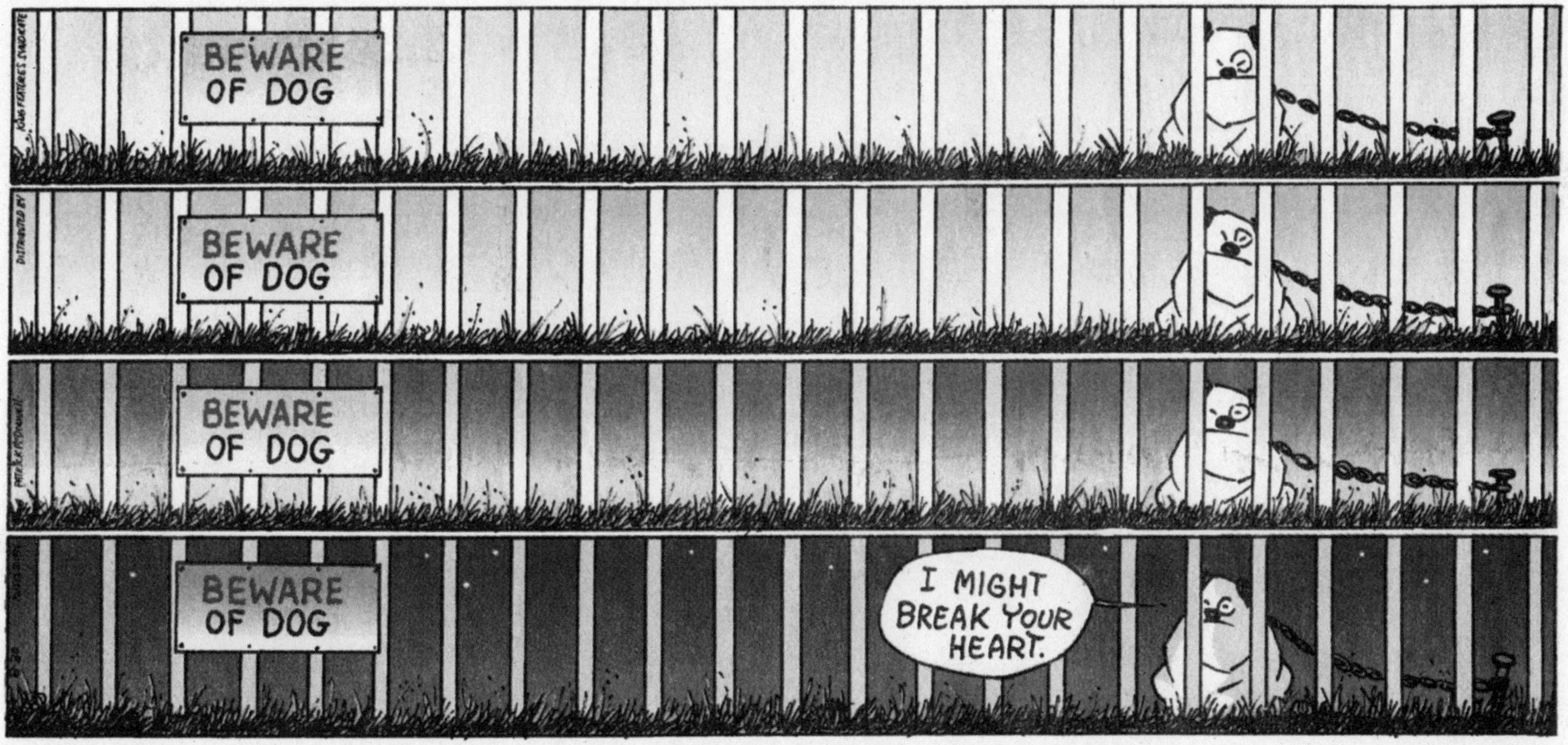
BEWARE
OF DOG
BEWARE
OF DOG
BEWARE
OF DOG
BEWARE
OF DOG
I MIGHT BREAK YOUR HEART.

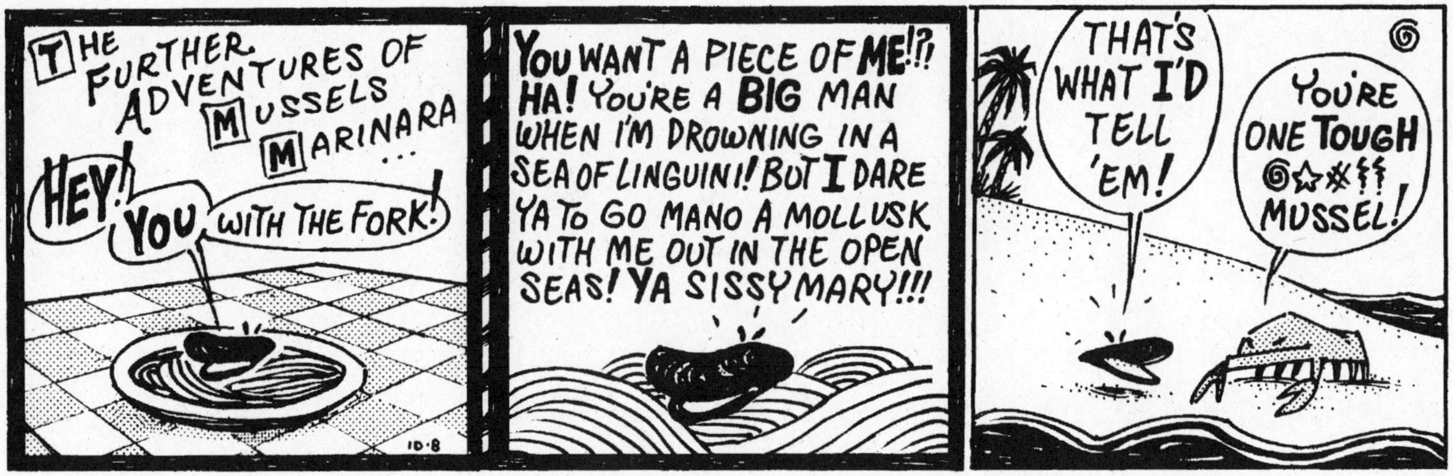
THE FURTHER ADVENTURES OF MUSSELS MARINARA...
HEY!
YOU, WITH THE FORK!
YOU WANT A PIECE OF ME!?! HA! YOU'RE A BIG MAN WHEN I'M DROWNING IN A SEA OF LINGUINI! BUT I DARE YA TO GO MANO A MOLLUSK WITH ME OUT IN THE OPEN SEAS! YA SISSYMARY!!!
THAT'S WHAT I'D TELL 'EM!
YOU'RE ONE TOUGH
MUSSEL!

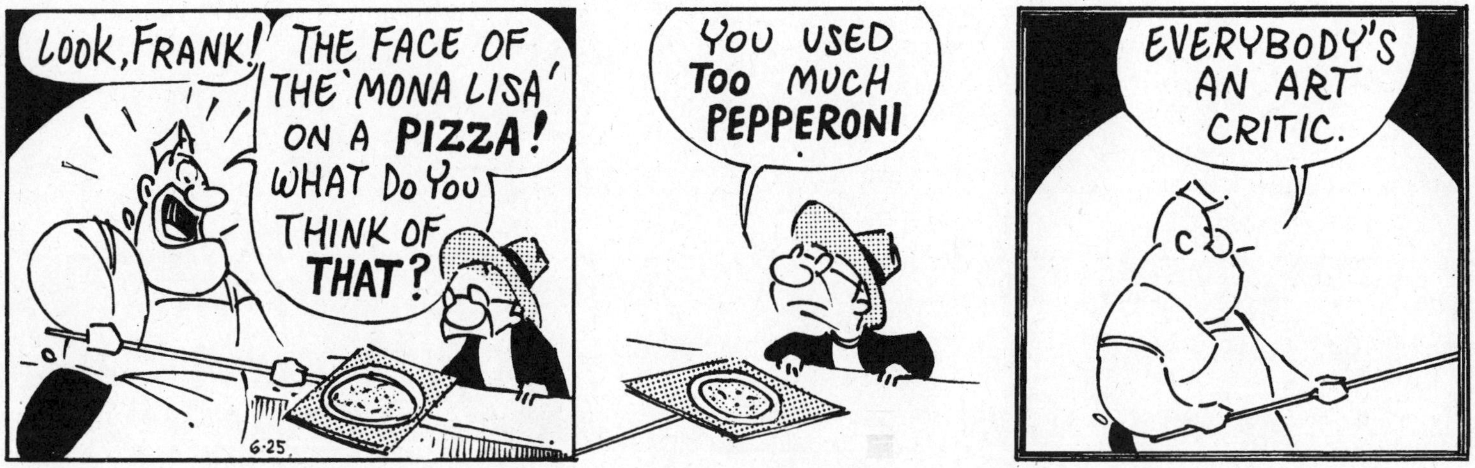
LOOK, FRANK!
THE FACE OF THE 'MONA LISA' ON A PIZZA! WHAT DO YOU THINK OF THAT?
YOU USED TOO MUCH PEPPERONI
EVERYBODY'S AN ART CRITIC.

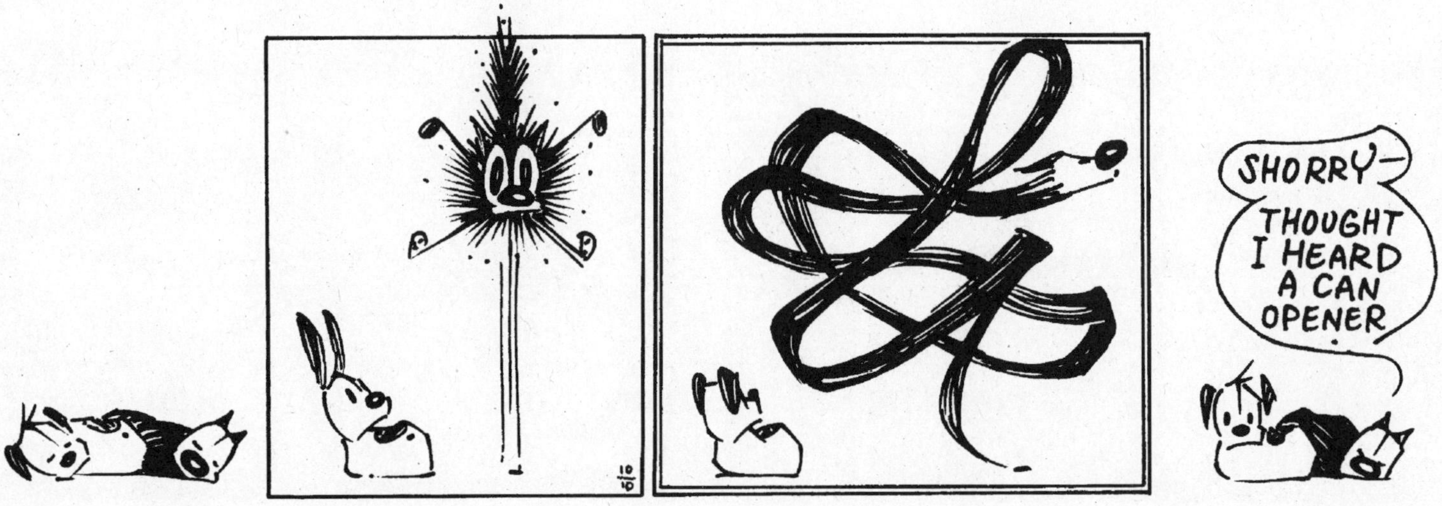
SHORRY—
THOUGHT I HEARD A CAN OPENER

D'YA KNOW WHAT I LIKE BEST ABOUT CLIMBING TREES?
WHAT?
9·14
THE CHALLENGE!
I LIKE WHEN THE FIRE TRUCK COMES.

FROM MY WINDOW THE WHOLE WORLD'S A STAGE
10·16
THERE GOES THE STAR.

I HEAR THAT BLACK CATS CAN BE MAGICAL AND FLY ON BROOMS!
SURE. I'VE DONE THAT!
10·26
FATTY SNAX DELI

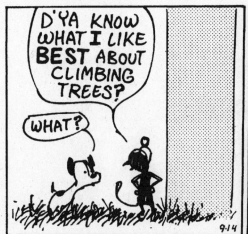

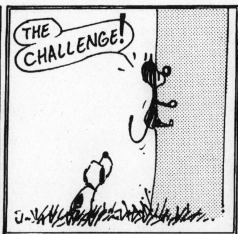

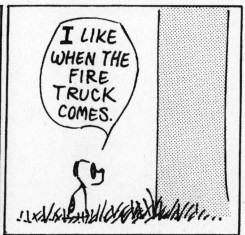

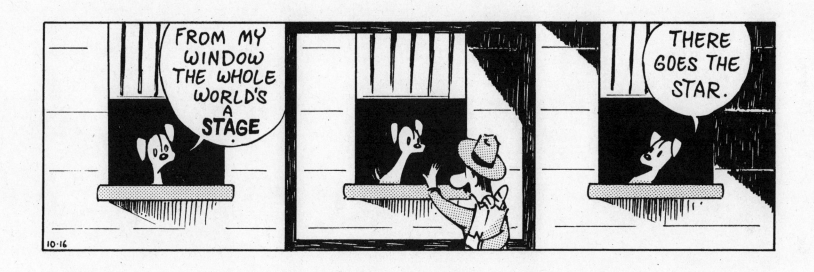

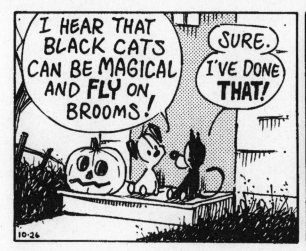

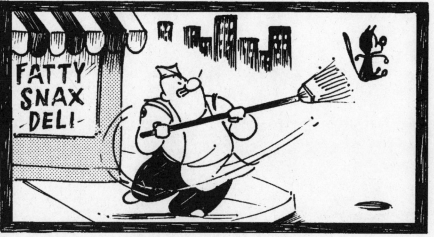

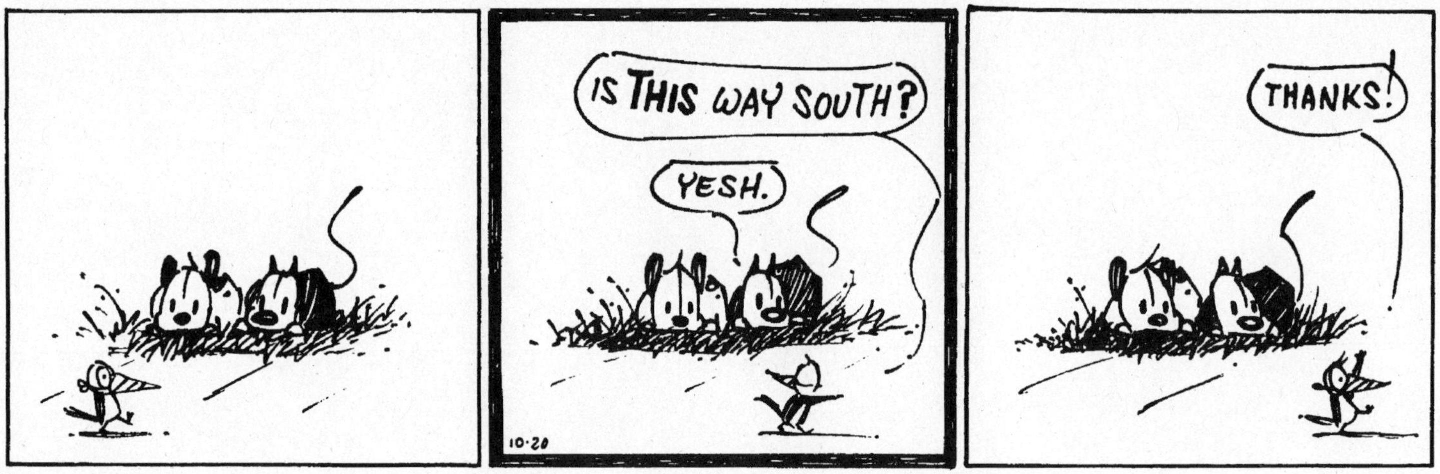
IS THIS WAY SOUTH?
YESH.
10·20
THANKS!

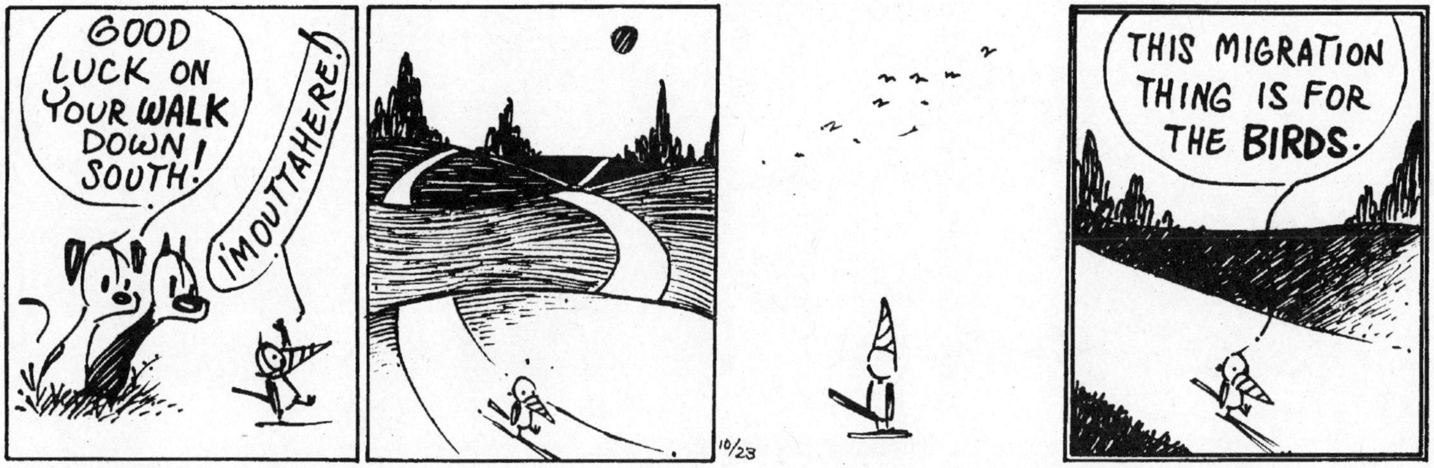
GOOD LUCK ON YOUR WALK DOWN SOUTH!
I'MOUTTAHERE!
10/23
THIS MIGRATION THING IS FOR THE BIRDS.

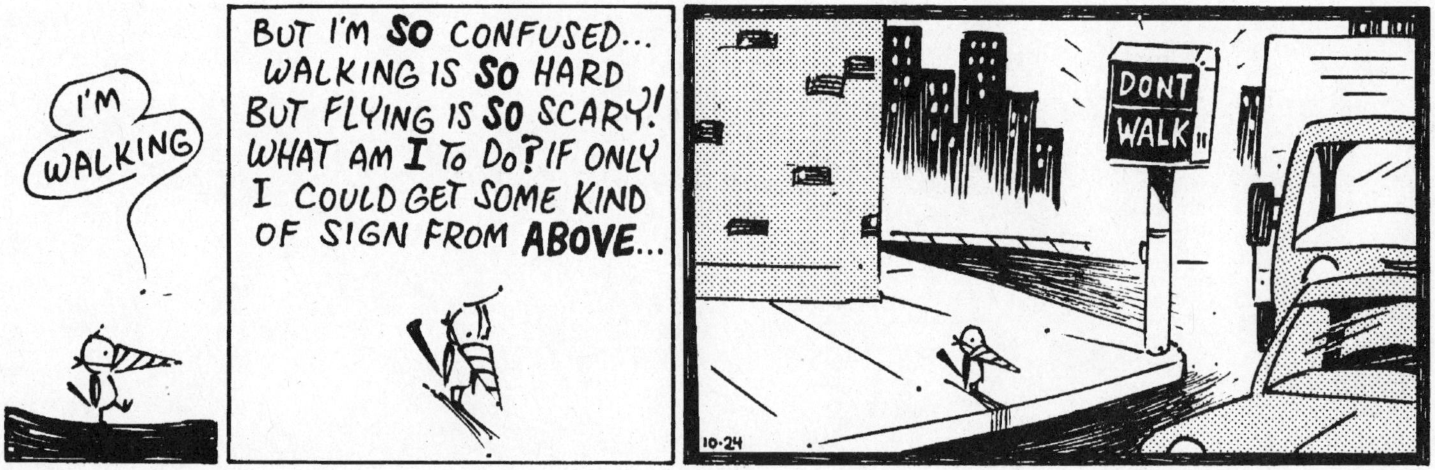
I'M WALKING
BUT I'M SO CONFUSED... WALKING IS SO HARD BUT FLYING IS SO SCARY! WHAT AM I TO DO? IF ONLY I COULD GET SOME KIND OF SIGN FROM ABOVE...
DONT WALK
10·24

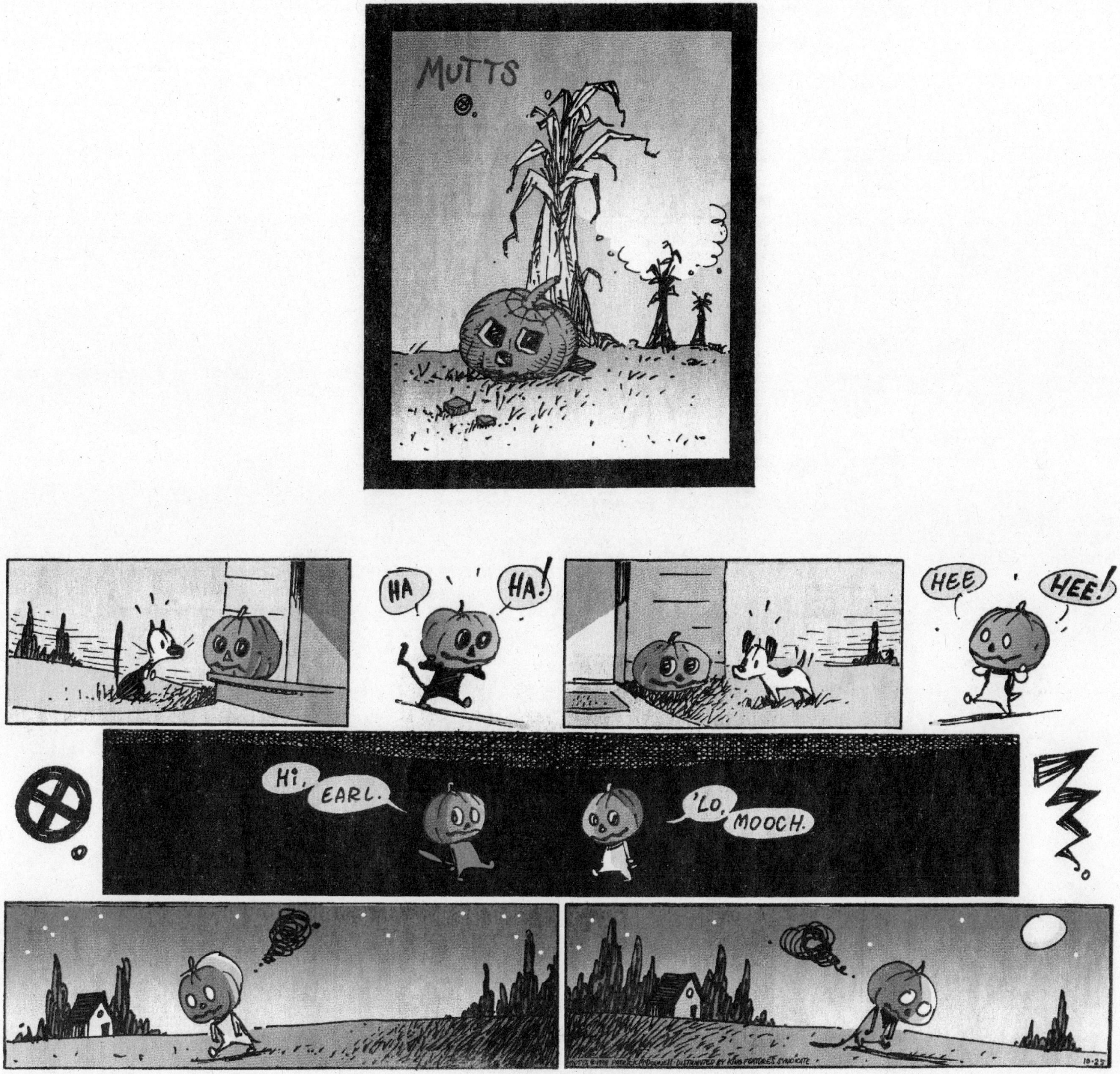
MUTTS
HA
HA!
HEE
HEE!
HI,
EARL.
'LO,
MOOCH.

A-HA! TRACKS! LET'S FOLLOW 'EM!
11-17
FOR WHAT?
FOR THE ADVENTURE! WHO KNOWS WHAT THEY MIGHT LEAD TO!
MY GUESSH IS... FEET.

YOU'RE RIGHT, EARL- TRACKING IS FUN...
11-19
BONK
HEY, YA BIG GALOOT!
GET OUT'A THE WAY! YOU'RE STANDING IN OUR TRACKS!

SO, ARE YOU THE PALOOKA WE'VE BEEN TRACKING?
11-20
C'MON- LET ME SEE YOUR FOOT PRINTS!
YEH...
THAT'S HIM.

I'M A GOOD TRACKER-BUT EVEN I CAN'T FOLLOW THOSE STEPS!
YESH!
11/21

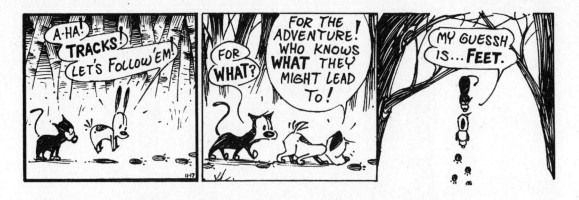

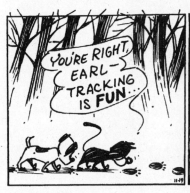

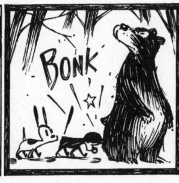

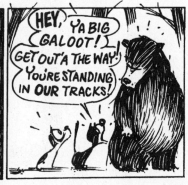

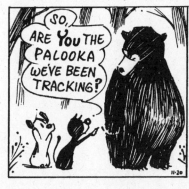

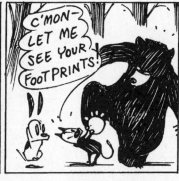

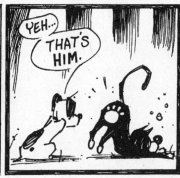

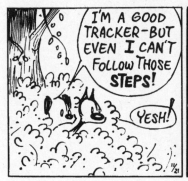

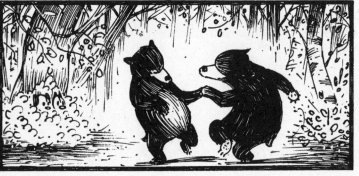

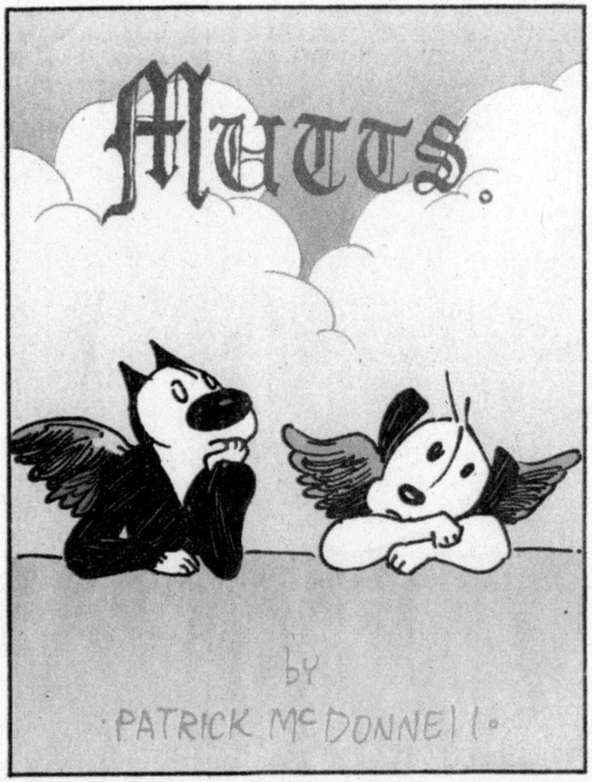
MUTTS.
by
PATRICK McDONNELL.

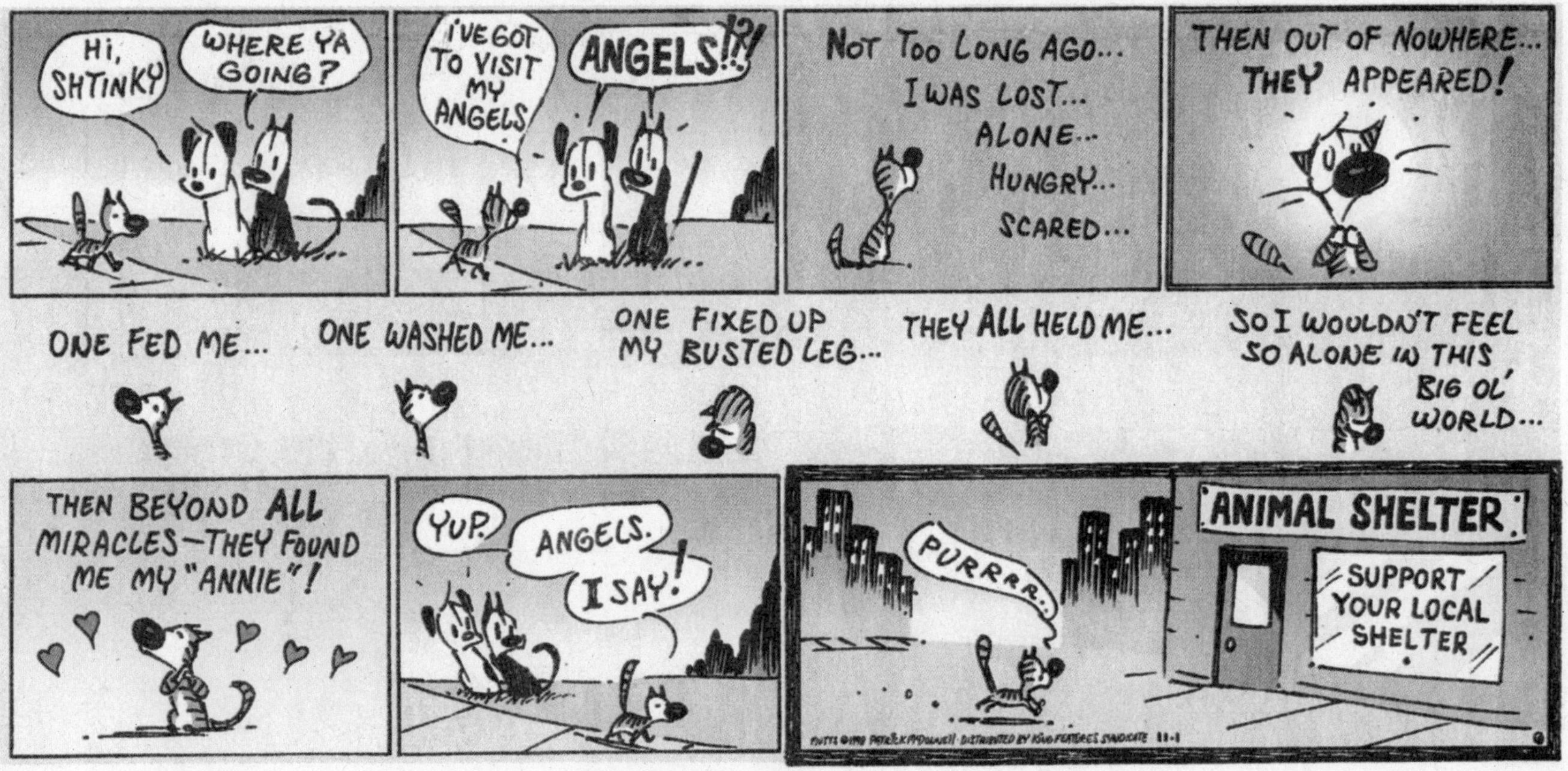
Hi, SHTINKY
WHERE YA GOING?
I'VE GOT TO VISIT MY ANGELS
ANGELS!?!
NOT TOO LONG AGO... I WAS LOST... ALONE... HUNGRY... SCARED...
THEN OUT OF NOWHERE... THEY APPEARED!
ONE FED ME...
ONE WASHED ME...
ONE FIXED UP MY BUSTED LEG...
THEY ALL HELD ME...
SO I WOULDN'T FEEL SO ALONE IN THIS BIG OL' WORLD...
THEN BEYOND ALL MIRACLES—THEY FOUND ME MY "ANNIE"!
YUP.
ANGELS.
I SAY!
PURRRRR...
ANIMAL SHELTER
SUPPORT YOUR LOCAL SHELTER

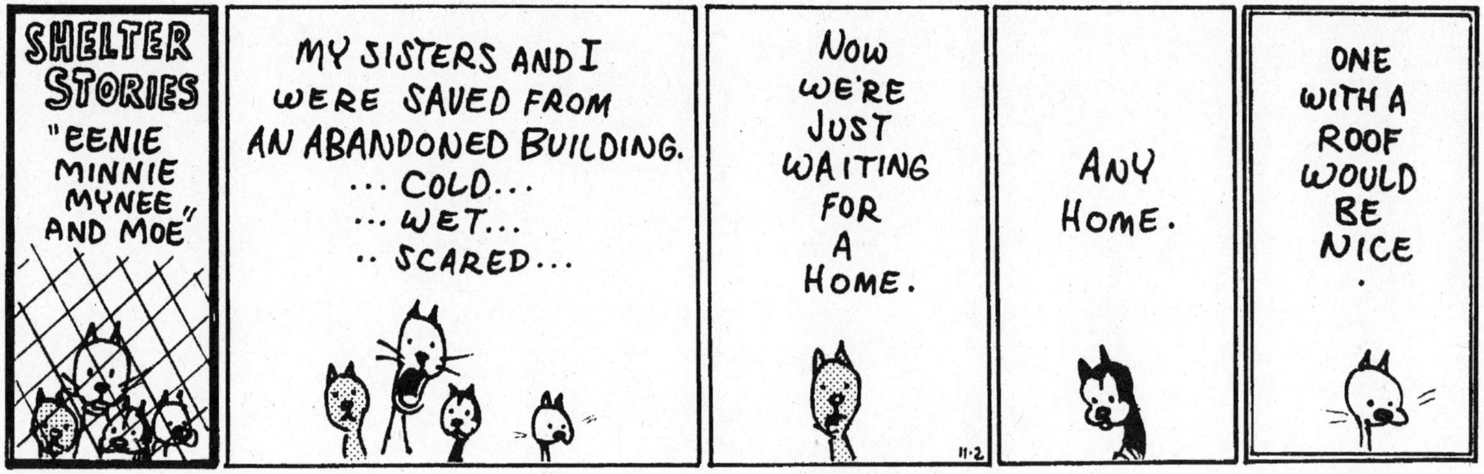
SHELTER STORIES
"EENIE MINNIE MYNEE AND MOE"
MY SISTERS AND I WERE SAVED FROM AN ABANDONED BUILDING. ... COLD... ... WET... .. SCARED...
NOW WE'RE JUST WAITING FOR A HOME.
ANY HOME.
ONE WITH A ROOF WOULD BE NICE.

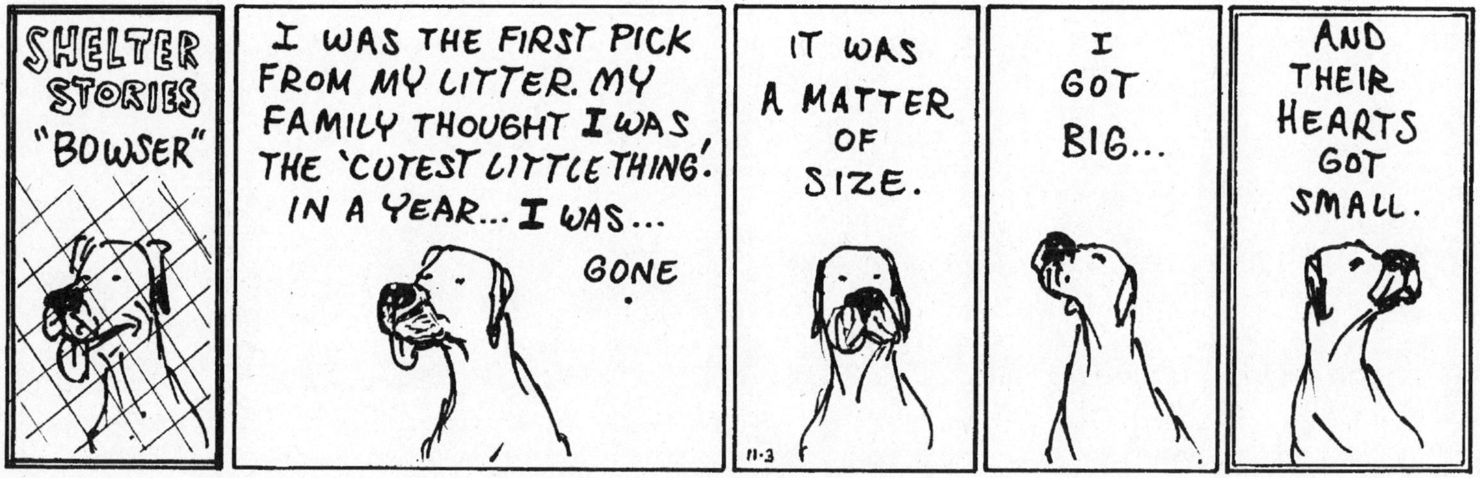
SHELTER STORIES
"BOWSER"
I WAS THE FIRST PICK FROM MY LITTER. MY FAMILY THOUGHT I WAS THE 'CUTEST LITTLE THING'. IN A YEAR... I WAS...
GONE.
IT WAS A MATTER OF SIZE.
I GOT BIG...
AND THEIR HEARTS GOT SMALL.

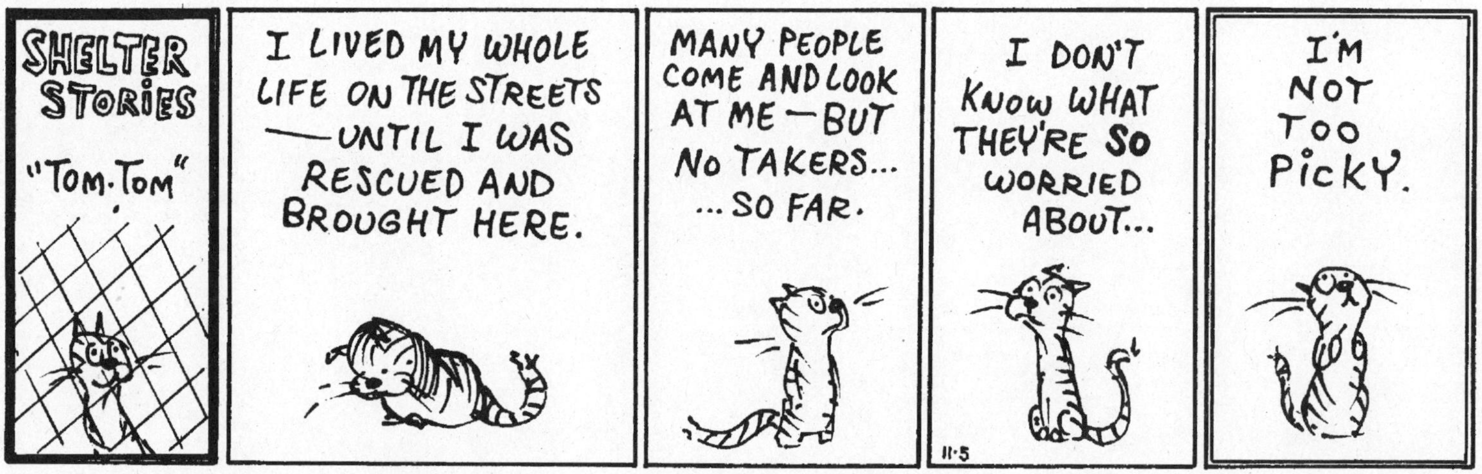
SHELTER STORIES
"TOM-TOM".
I LIVED MY WHOLE LIFE ON THE STREETS —UNTIL I WAS RESCUED AND BROUGHT HERE.
MANY PEOPLE COME AND LOOK AT ME—BUT NO TAKERS... ...SO FAR.
I DON'T KNOW WHAT THEY'RE SO WORRIED ABOUT...
I'M NOT TOO PICKY.

## Shtinky Puddin', aka Jules,

a little kitten with a big heart, is *Mutts*' voice for animal advocacy. Like any caring being, Shtinky is concerned about the plight of endangered animals. Motivated by the thought that the beautiful diversity of this planet is disappearing, Shtinky has made saving animals his personal crusade. Being an orange tabby, Shtinky identifies most with the wild tiger. At this writing, there are only about five thousand free tigers left on this earth, and, unless the situation changes, they can disappear in our lifetime. The noble, elegant tiger—gone—to become a mythological beast found only in tales of old is unthinkable. These story lines featuring Shtinky try to remind us of the bigger picture.

Sourpuss, on the other hand, represents the cat who wants to be left alone, and on rare occasion, may grace us with his or her presence. He is also my comic archetype for the negativity we find in today's entertainment.

I'm naturally attracted to the brevity and directness of comic strips. They live in the less-is-more state of mind. A few simple panels can get to the heart of the matter rather quickly, like a Zen koan or a parable.

At the close of 1990, we have my personal favorite *Mutts* story. The ever-curious Mooch falls down a hole and has a near-death experience, meeting his "first life," a little Mooch with angel wings. It's a spiritual journey with a little cat spirit.

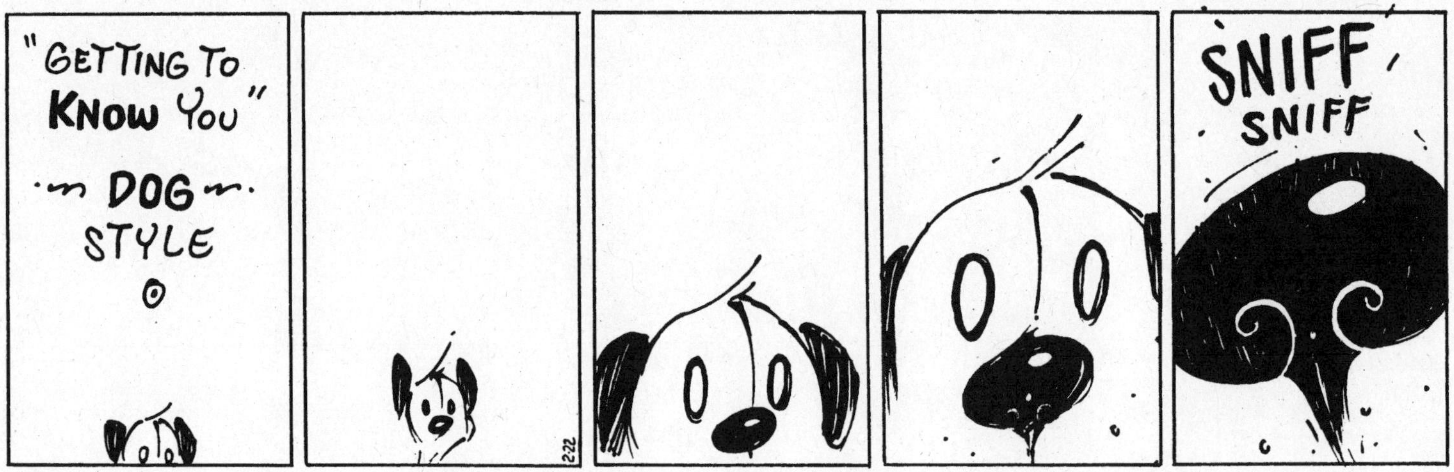
"GETTING TO KNOW YOU"
DOG STYLE
2·22
SNIFF
SNIFF

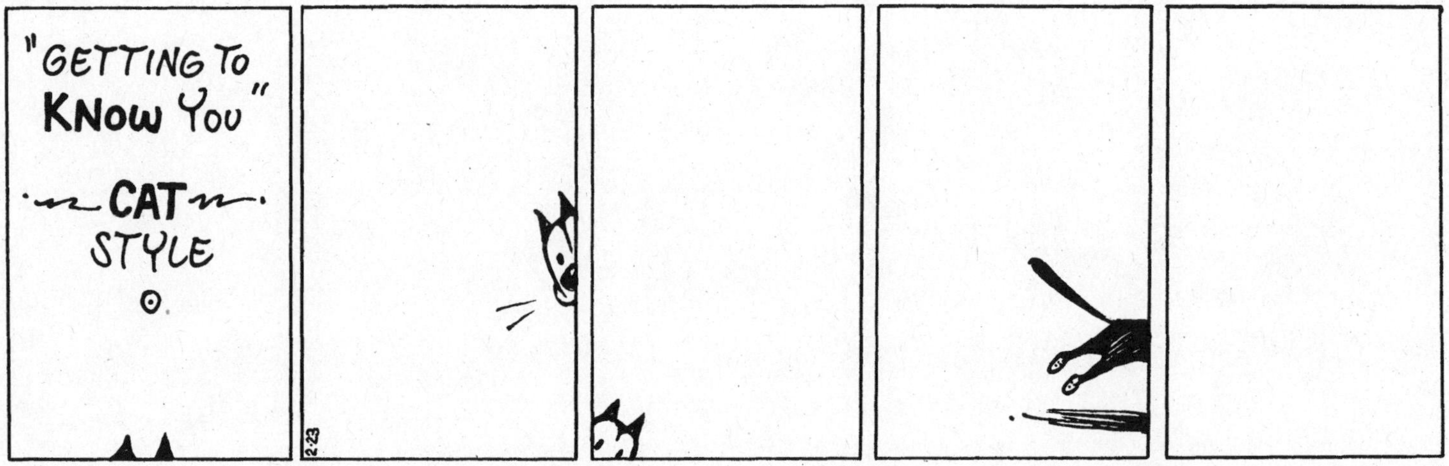
"GETTING TO KNOW YOU"
CAT STYLE
2·23

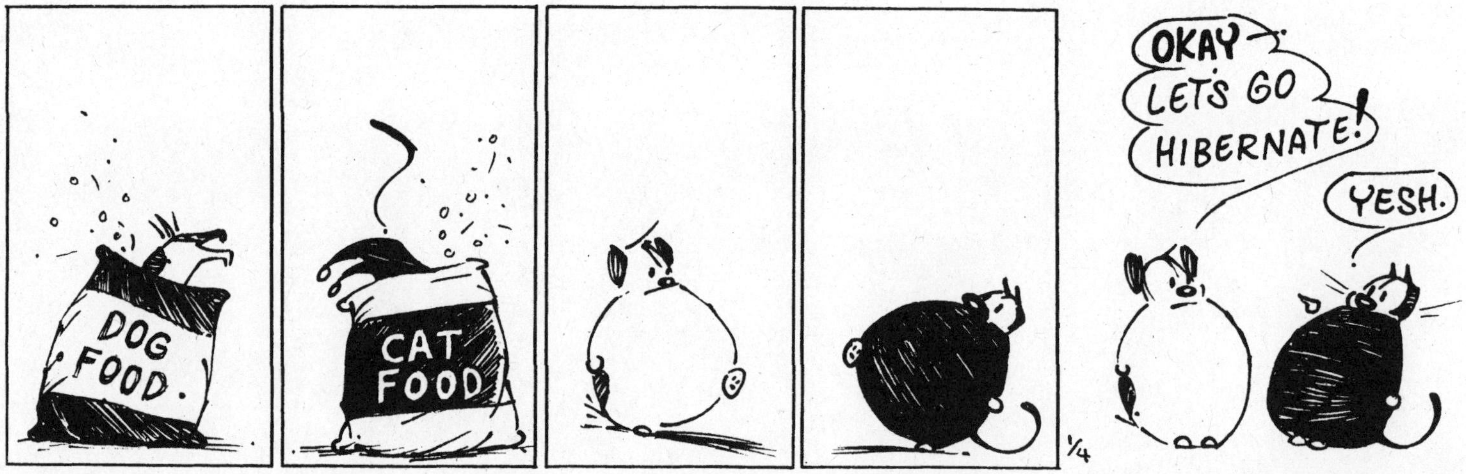
DOG FOOD.
CAT FOOD
1/4
OKAY LET'S GO HIBERNATE!
YESH.

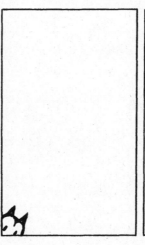

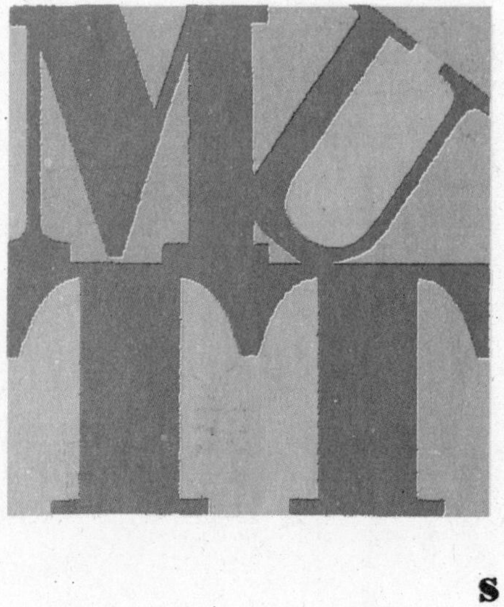

s

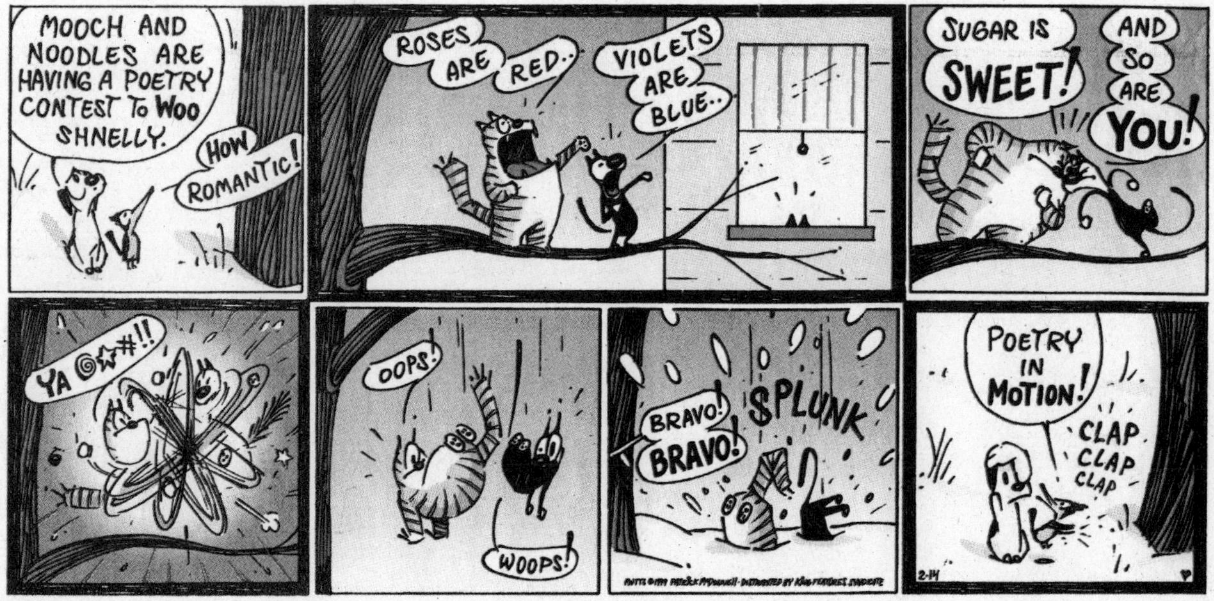

MOOCH AND NOODLES ARE HAVING A POETRY CONTEST TO WOO SHNELLY.
HOW ROMANTIC!
ROSES ARE RED..
VIOLETS ARE BLUE..
SUGAR IS SWEET!
AND SO ARE YOU!
YA @✿#!!
OOPS!
WOOPS!
BRAVO! BRAVO!
SPLUNK
POETRY IN MOTION!
CLAP CLAP CLAP
2-14

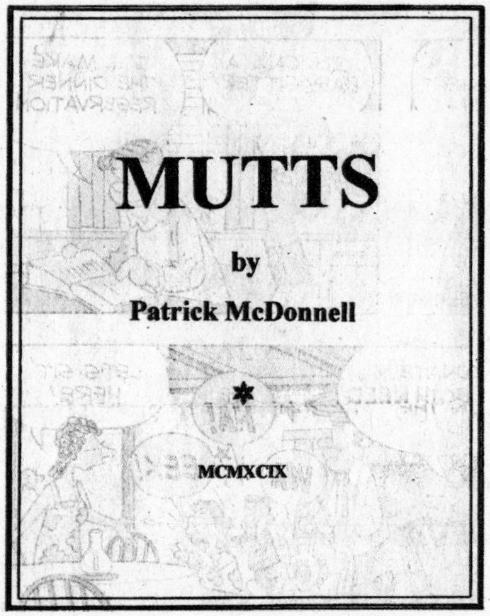

MUTTS
by
Patrick McDonnell
*
MCMXCIX

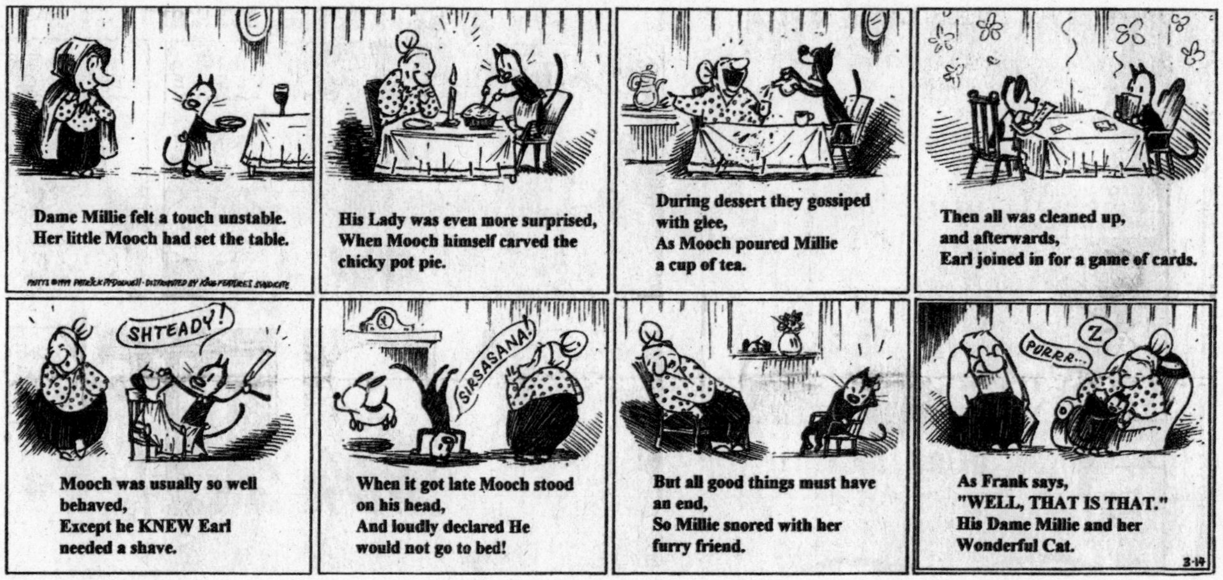

Dame Millie felt a touch unstable.
Her little Mooch had set the table.
His Lady was even more surprised,
When Mooch himself carved the chicky pot pie.
During dessert they gossiped with glee,
As Mooch poured Millie a cup of tea.
Then all was cleaned up, and afterwards,
Earl joined in for a game of cards.
SHTEADY!
Mooch was usually so well behaved,
Except he KNEW Earl needed a shave.
SIRSASANA!
When it got late Mooch stood on his head,
And loudly declared He would not go to bed!
But all good things must have an end,
So Millie snored with her furry friend.
PURRR...
Z
As Frank says,
"WELL, THAT IS THAT."
His Dame Millie and her Wonderful Cat.
2-14

HI, EARL. I'M DR. WOO. ...THERE, THERE... ARE YOU A LITTLE **NERVOUS**?
A LITTLE.

EARL'S TEETH CLEANING WILL BE A SAFE, ROUTINE PROCEDURE.
THE ONLY PROBLEM I FORESEE IS WE MIGHT HAVE TO DO **ONE** EXTRACTION.
OH?
DOG FROM OWNER.

HOWLWOOOO...

EARL'S TEETH CLEANING WENT **FINE**, BUT HE STILL MIGHT ACT A BIT **WOOZY** FROM THE ANESTHESIA.

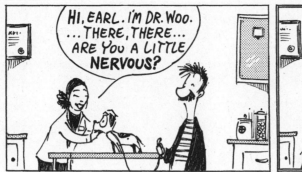

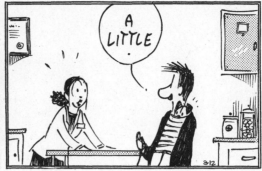

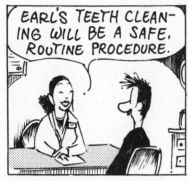

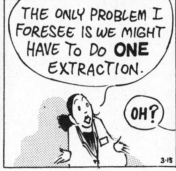

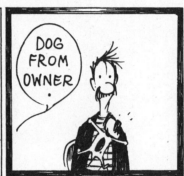

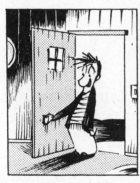

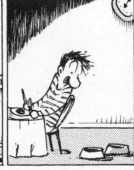

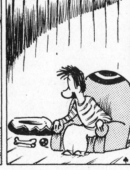

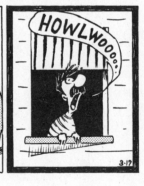

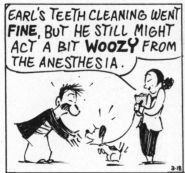

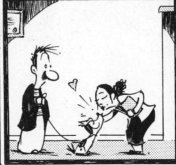

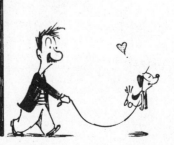

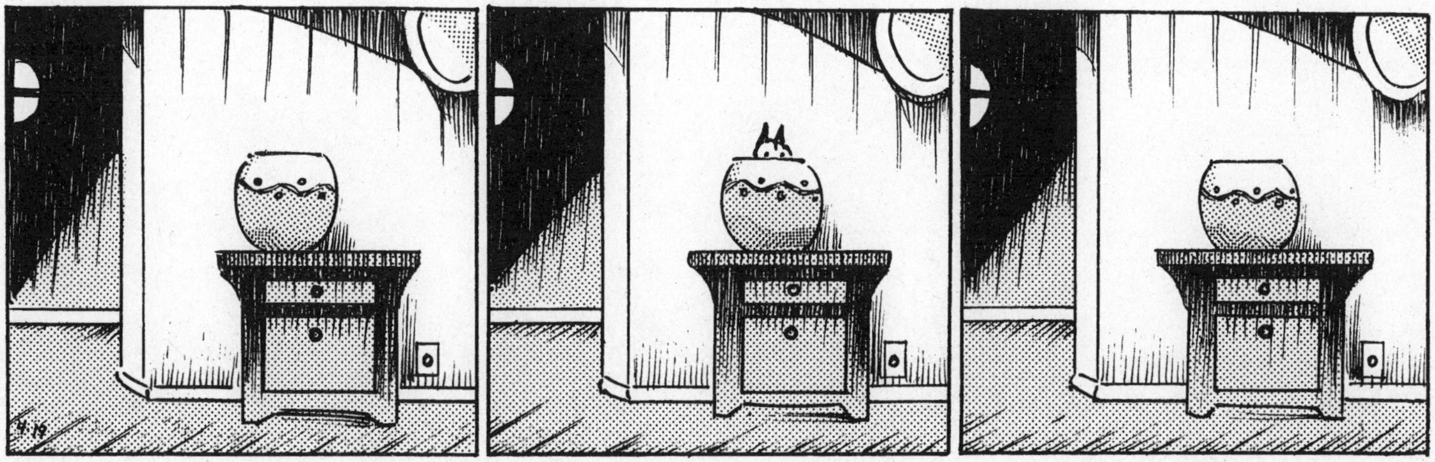
4.19

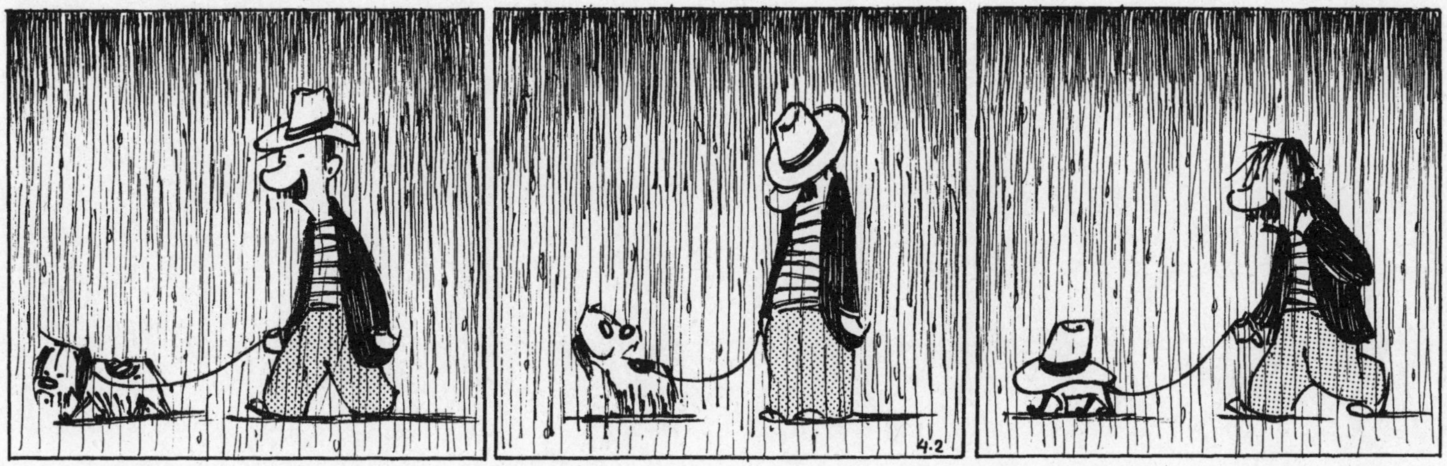
4.2

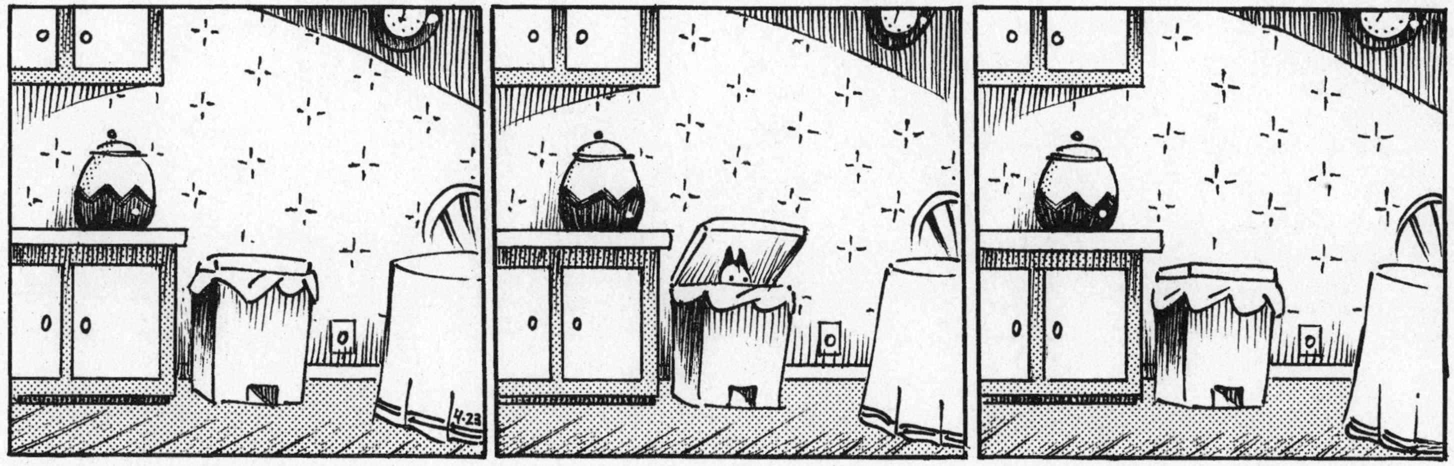
4.23

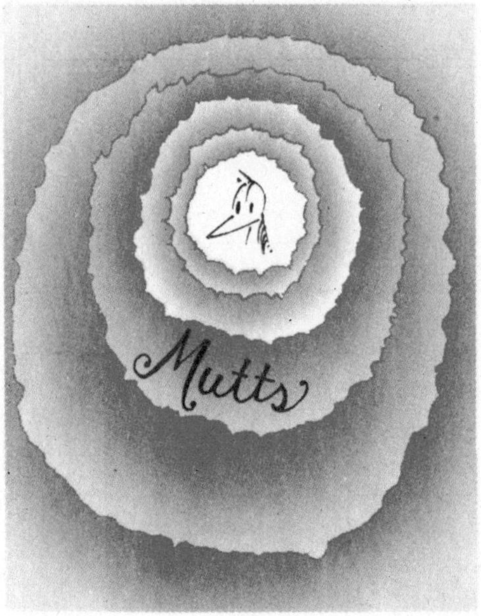
Mutts

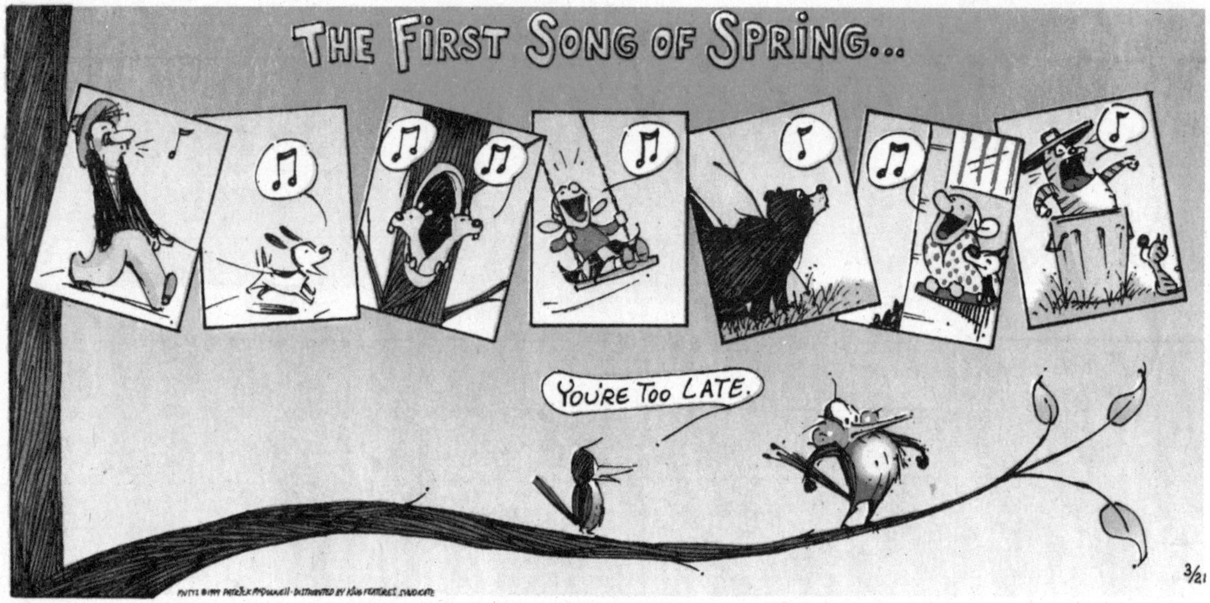
THE FIRST SONG OF SPRING...
YOU'RE TOO LATE.
3/21

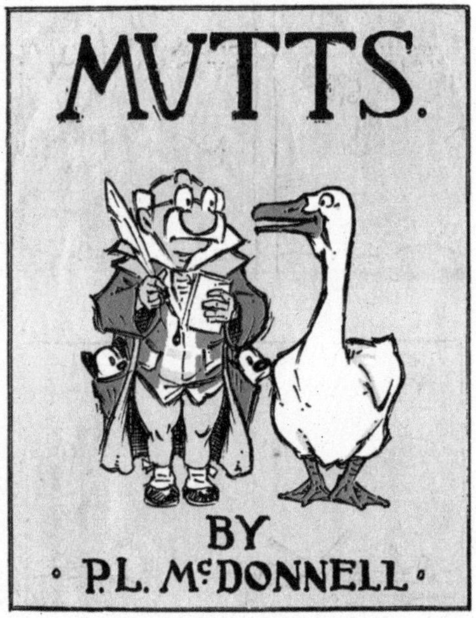
MUTTS.
BY
• P.L. McDONNELL •

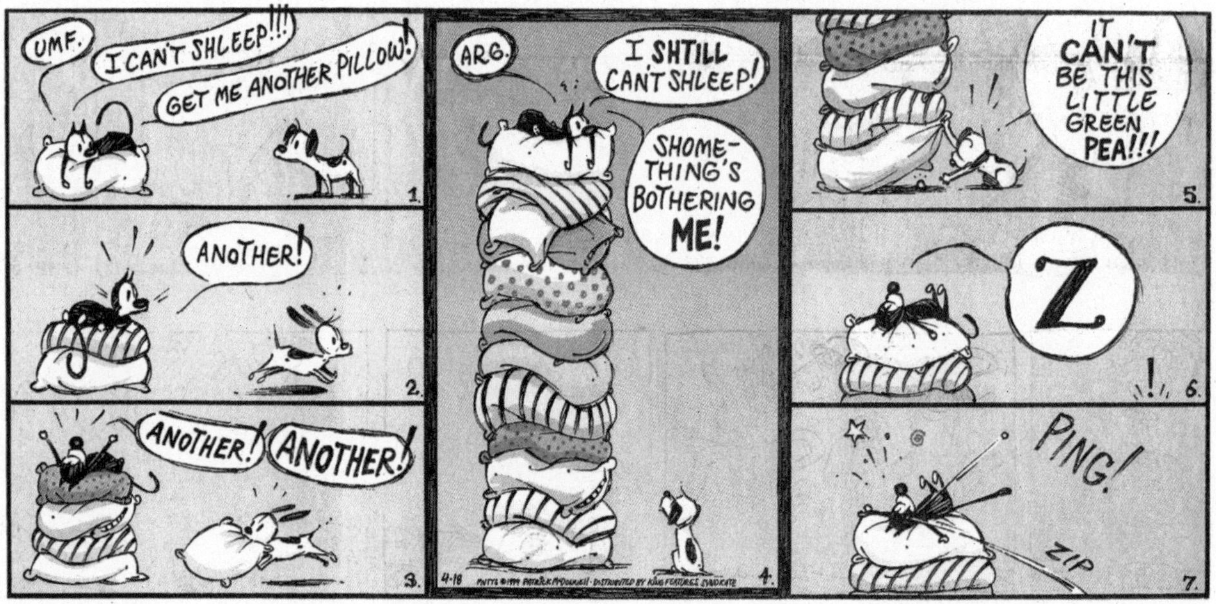
UMF.
I CAN'T SHLEEP!!!
GET ME ANOTHER PILLOW!
1.
ANOTHER!
2.
ANOTHER!
ANOTHER!
3.
ARG.
I SHTILL CAN'T SHLEEP!
SHOME-THING'S BOTHERING ME!
4-18
4.
IT CAN'T BE THIS LITTLE GREEN PEA!!!
5.
Z
6.
PING!
ZIP
7.

MUTTS

WHAT ARE THOSE TWO DOING!?!
OH, THAT'S THEIR "CATS ARE BETTER THAN DOGS" RAIN DANCE.

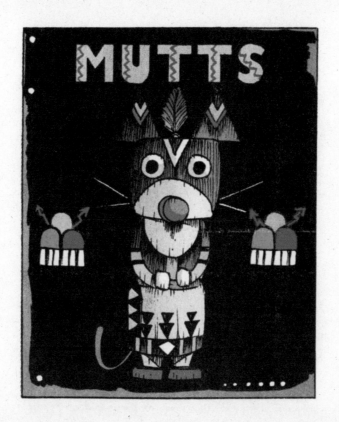

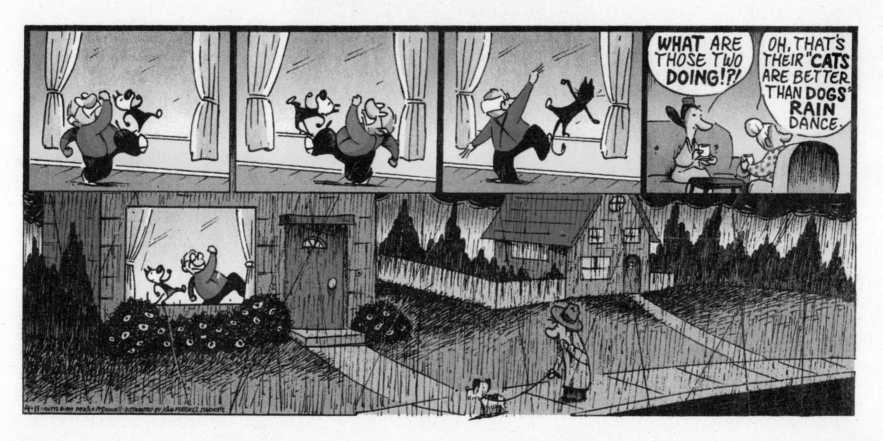

I HATE...
MONDAYS.

I HATE MONDAYS.
TODAY IS TUESDAY.
TUESDAYS ARE THE WORST KIND OF MONDAYS.
MUTTS ©1999 PATRICK McDONNELL · DISTRIBUTED BY KING FEATURES SYNDICATE

HEY, SOURPUSS, TELL US A JOKE!
I HATE WEDNESDAYS.
THAT'S TOPICAL HUMOR.

I HATE SATURDAYS.
HA! HA!
I DON'T GET IT.
I LOVE SATURDAYS, I LOVE SUNDAYS, FRIDAYS, THURSDAYS, WEDNESDAYS, AND TUESDAYS, AND I LOVE MONDAYS
!
WHO'S THIS PILL!?!

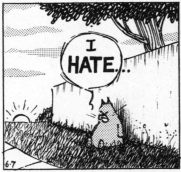

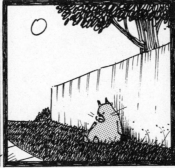

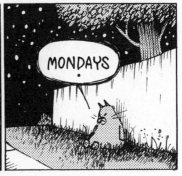

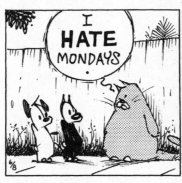

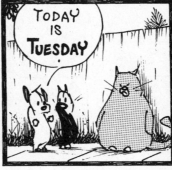

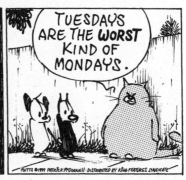

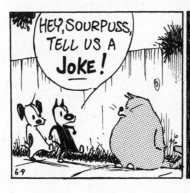

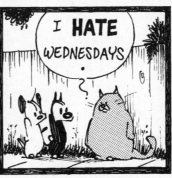

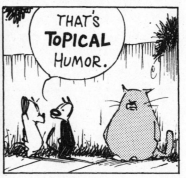

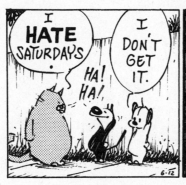

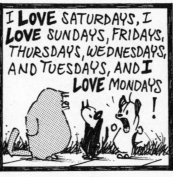

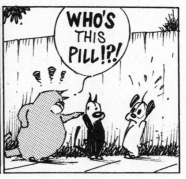

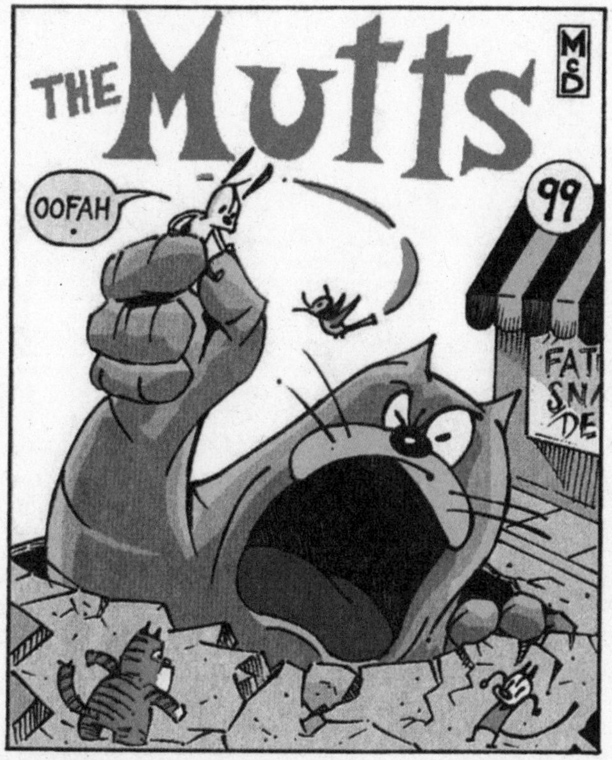
THE Mutts
McD
OOFAH
99

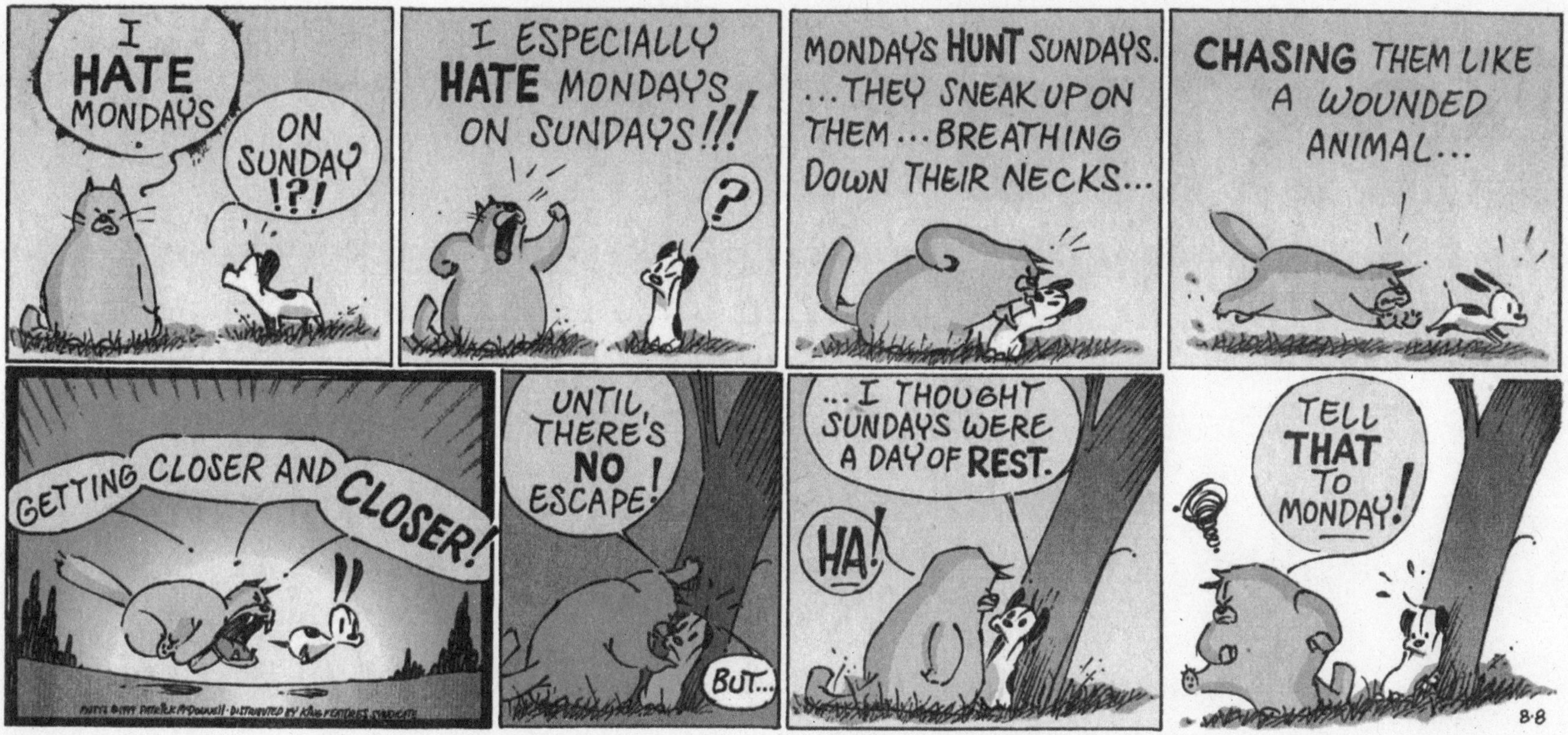
I HATE MONDAYS.
ON SUNDAY !?!
I ESPECIALLY HATE MONDAYS ON SUNDAYS!!!
?
MONDAYS HUNT SUNDAYS. ...THEY SNEAK UP ON THEM...BREATHING DOWN THEIR NECKS...
CHASING THEM LIKE A WOUNDED ANIMAL...
GETTING CLOSER AND CLOSER!
UNTIL, THERE'S NO ESCAPE!
BUT...
...I THOUGHT SUNDAYS WERE A DAY OF REST.
HA!
TELL THAT TO MONDAY!
8.8

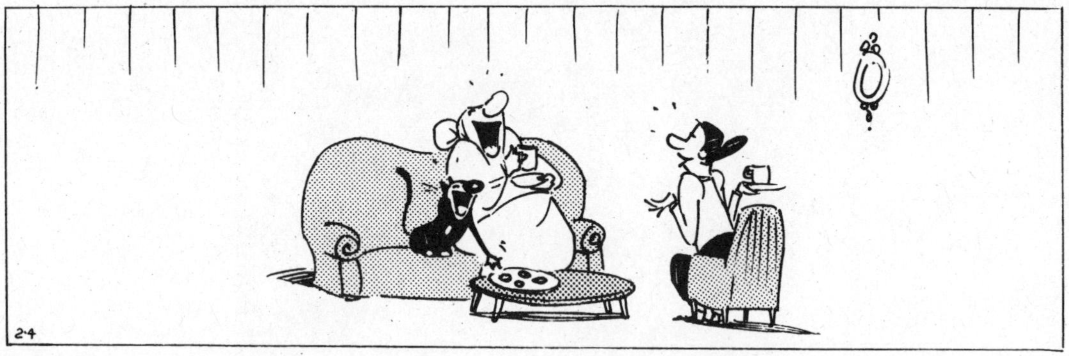
2·4

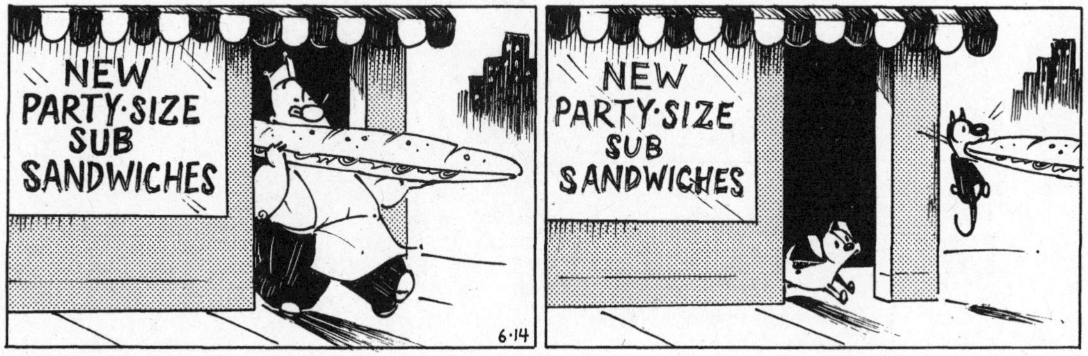
NEW PARTY·SIZE SUB SANDWICHES
6·14
NEW PARTY·SIZE SUB SANDWICHES

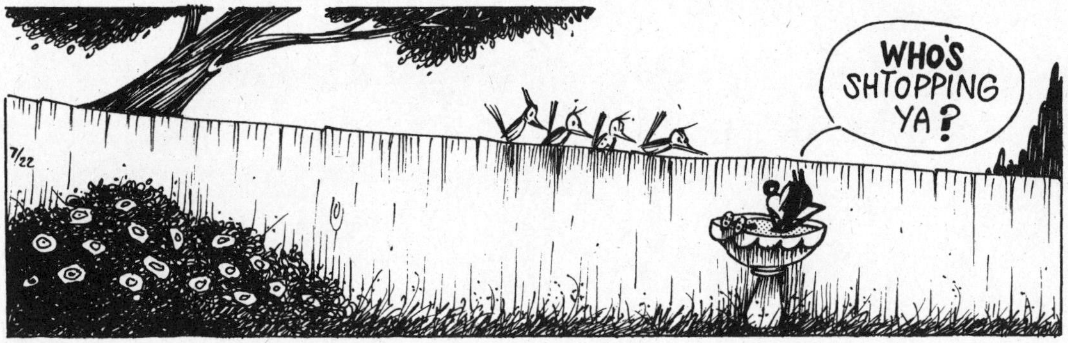
7/22
WHO'S SHTOPPING YA?

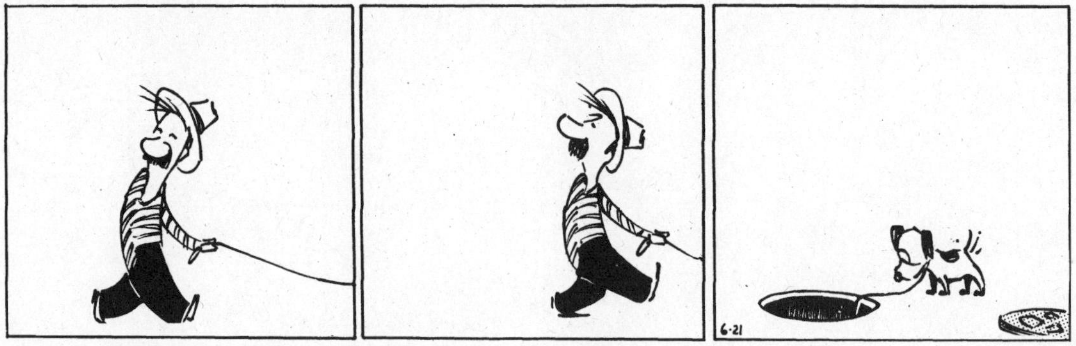
6·21

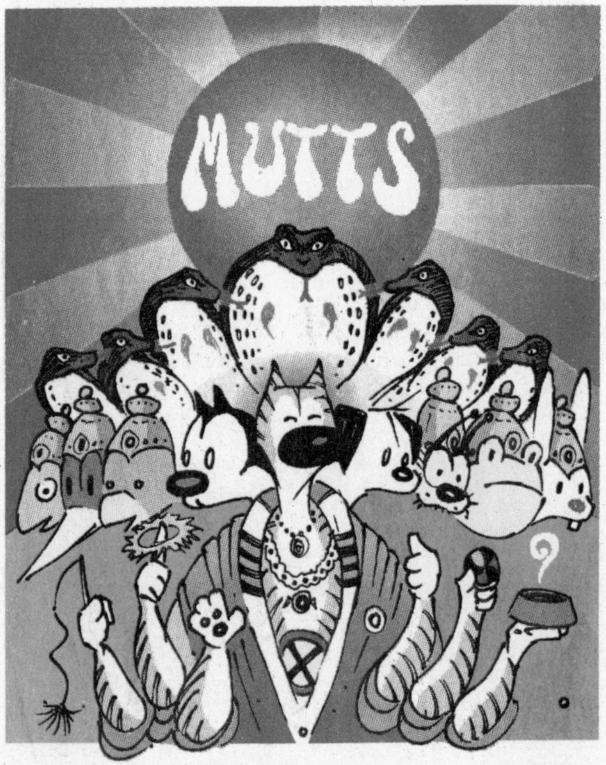
MUTTS

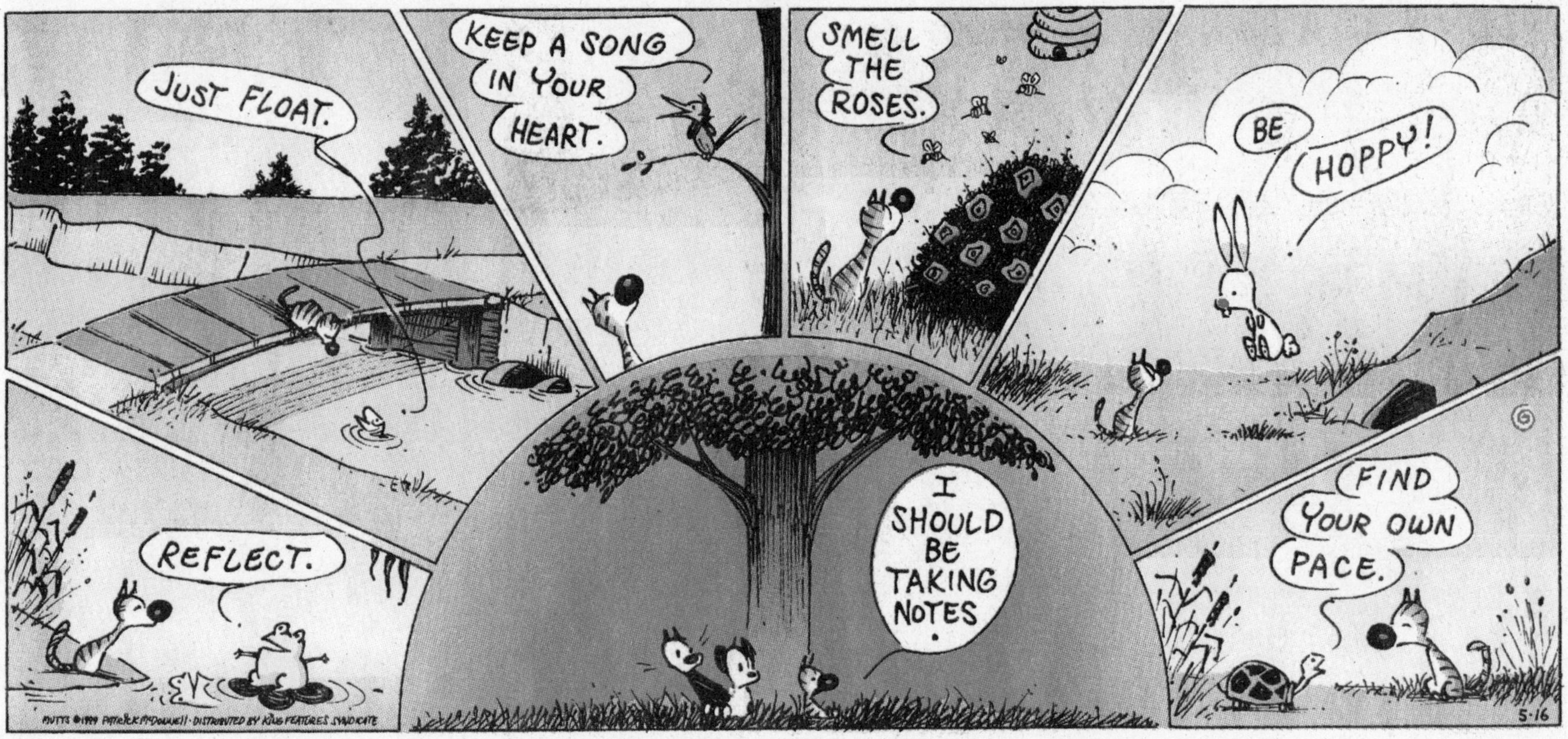
JUST FLOAT.
KEEP A SONG IN YOUR HEART.
SMELL THE ROSES.
BE
HOPPY!
REFLECT.
I SHOULD BE TAKING NOTES.
FIND YOUR OWN PACE.
MUTTS ©1999 PATRICK McDONNELL · DISTRIBUTED BY KING FEATURES SYNDICATE
5·16

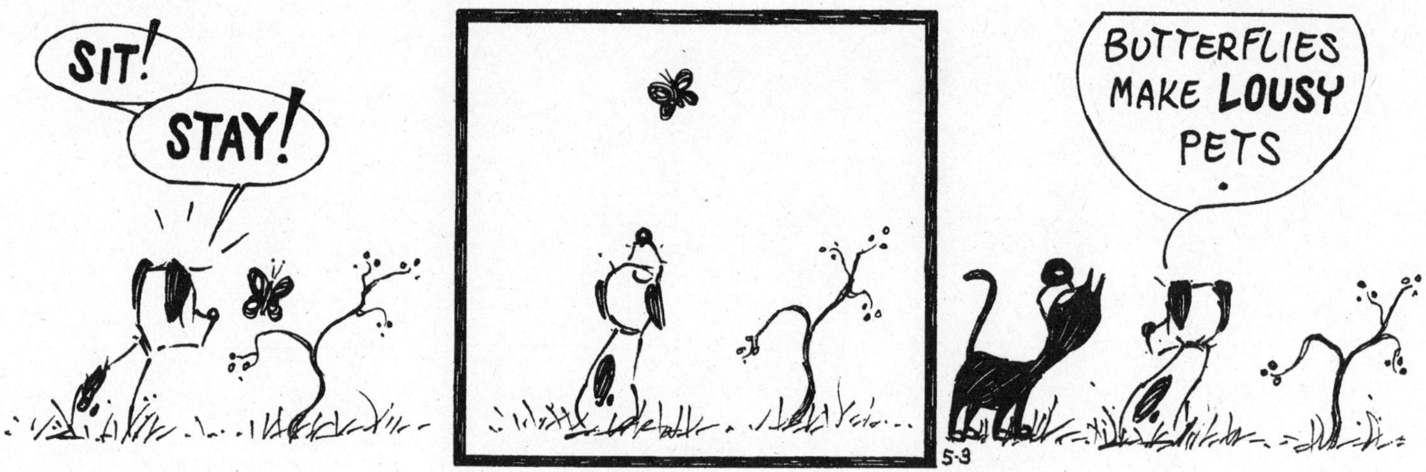
SIT!
STAY!
BUTTERFLIES MAKE LOUSY PETS
5-3

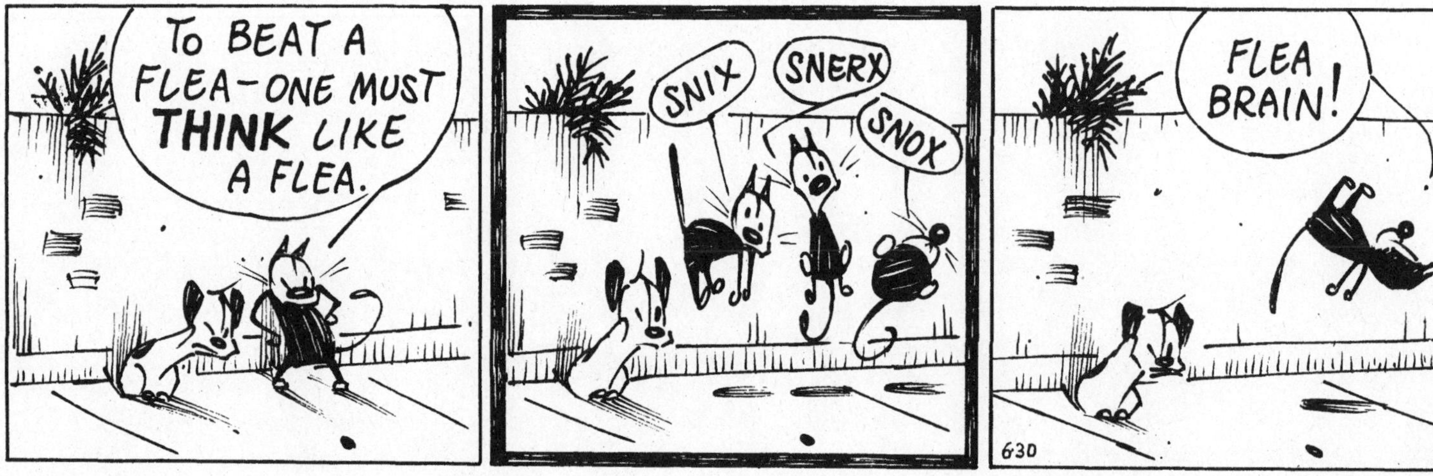
TO BEAT A FLEA—ONE MUST THINK LIKE A FLEA.
SNIX
SNERX
SNOX
FLEA BRAIN!
630

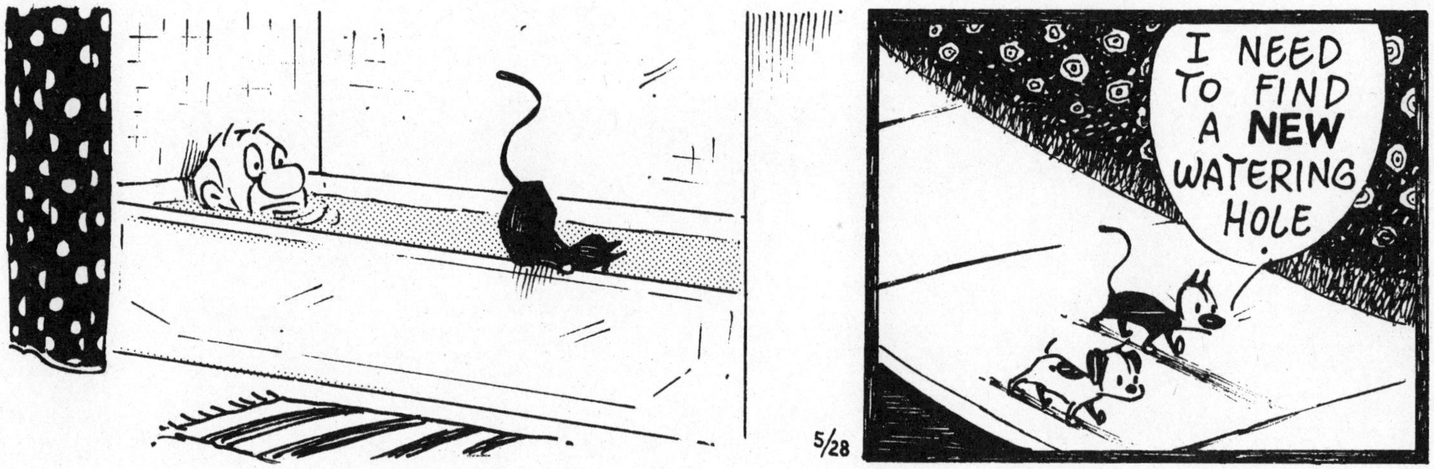
I NEED TO FIND A NEW WATERING HOLE
5/28

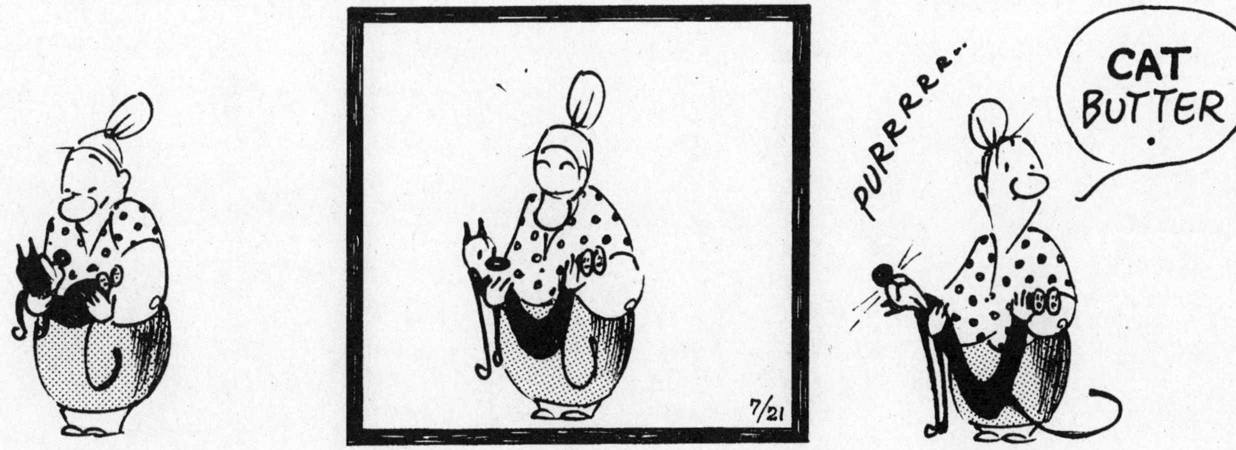
7/21
PURRRRR...
CAT BUTTER.

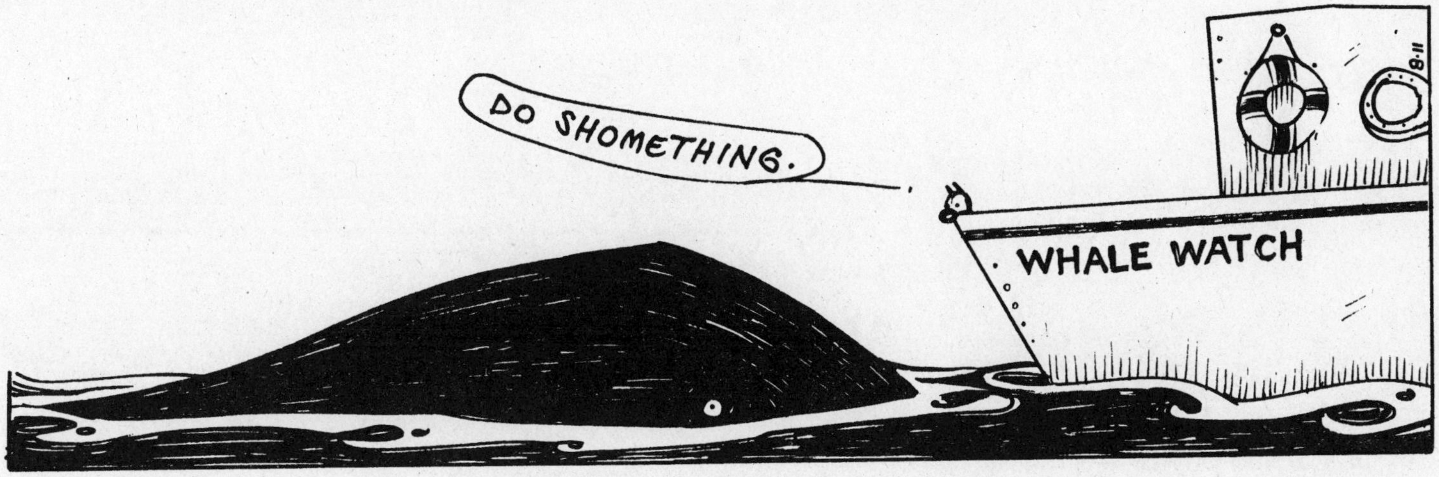
DO SHOMETHING.
WHALE WATCH

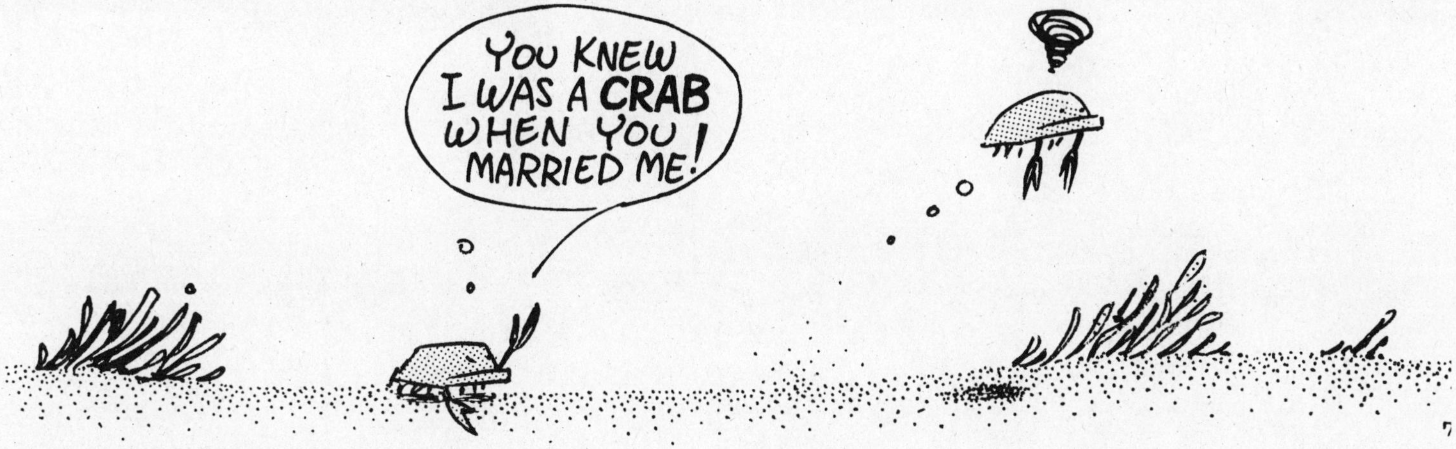
YOU KNEW I WAS A CRAB WHEN YOU MARRIED ME!

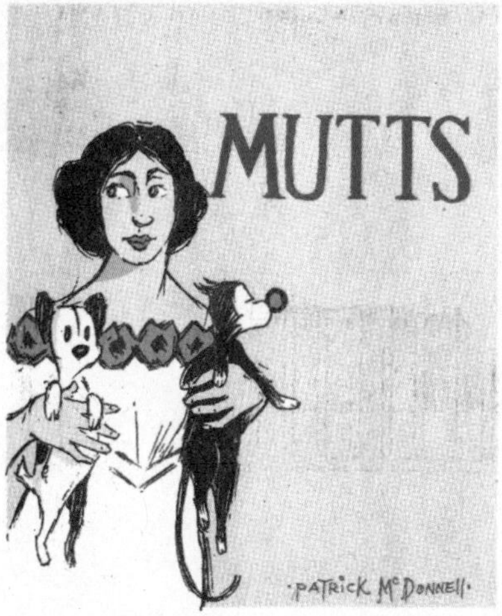
MUTTS
·PATRICK McDONNELL·

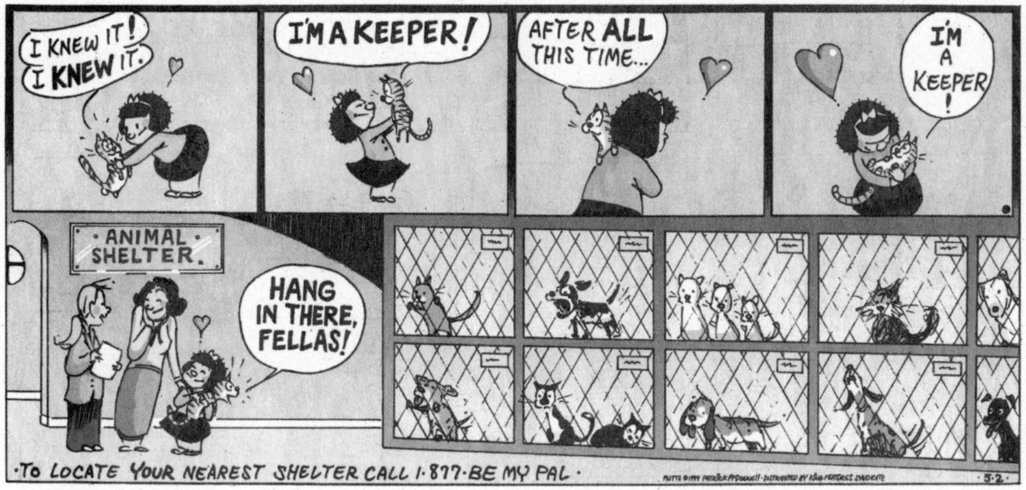
I KNEW IT! I KNEW IT.
I'M A KEEPER!
AFTER ALL THIS TIME...
I'M A KEEPER!
·ANIMAL· SHELTER.
HANG IN THERE, FELLAS!
·TO LOCATE YOUR NEAREST SHELTER CALL 1·877·BE MY PAL·
5·2·

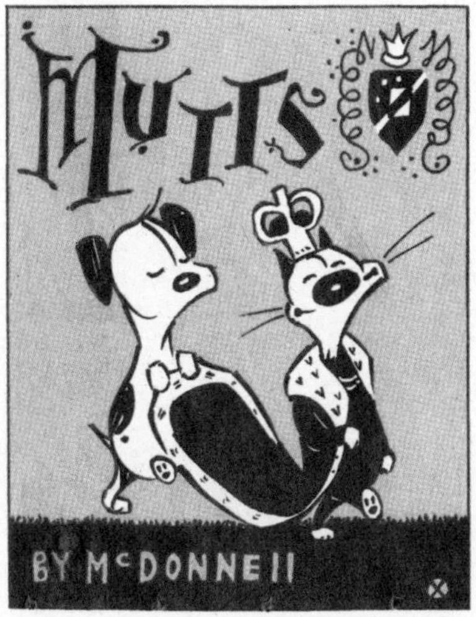
MUTTS
BY McDONNELL

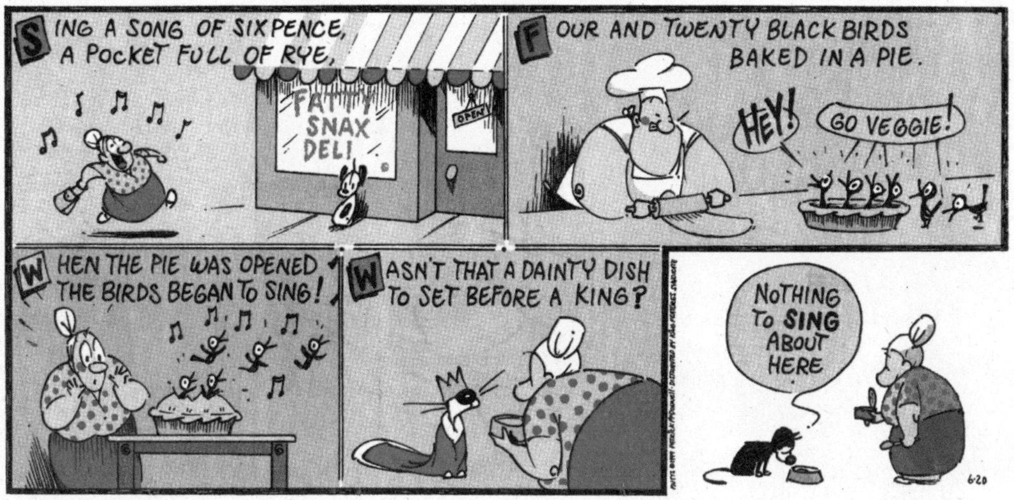
SING A SONG OF SIXPENCE, A POCKET FULL OF RYE,
FAT SNAX DELI
OPEN
FOUR AND TWENTY BLACK BIRDS BAKED IN A PIE.
HEY!
GO VEGGIE!
WHEN THE PIE WAS OPENED THE BIRDS BEGAN TO SING!
WASN'T THAT A DAINTY DISH TO SET BEFORE A KING?
NOTHING TO SING ABOUT HERE
6·20

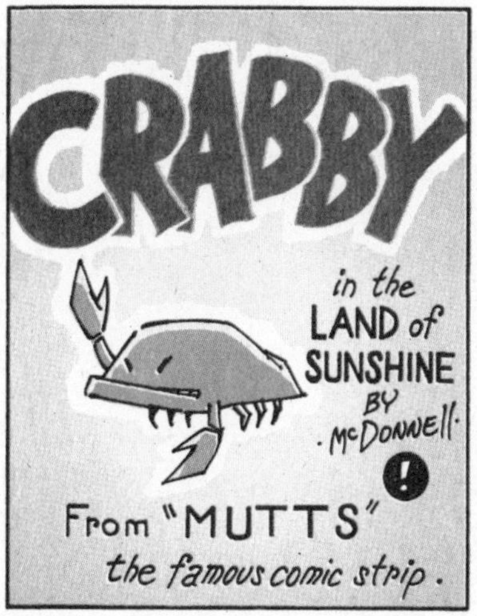
CRABBY
in the LAND of SUNSHINE
BY ·McDONNELL·
!
From "MUTTS" the famous comic strip.

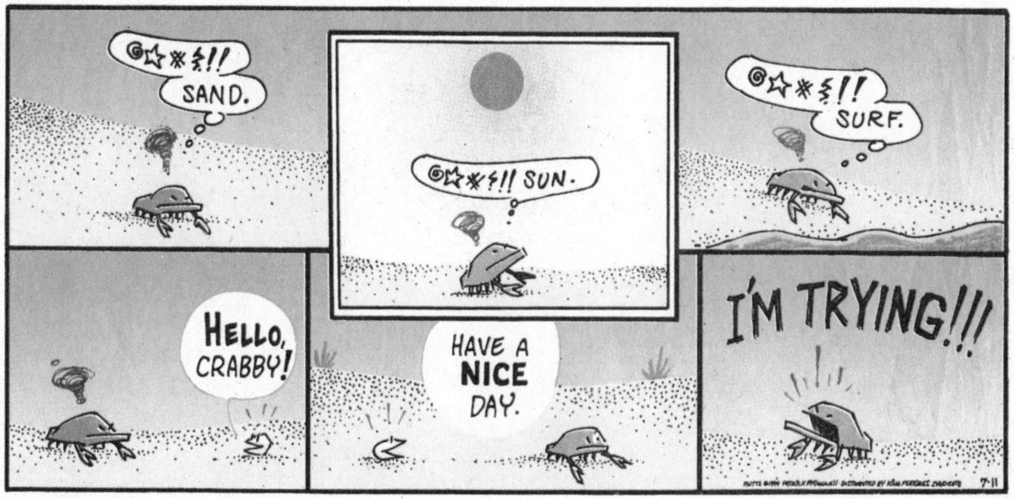
@☆✻⚡!! SAND.
@☆✻⚡!! SUN.
@☆✻⚡!! SURF.
HELLO, CRABBY!
HAVE A NICE DAY.
I'M TRYING!!!
7·11

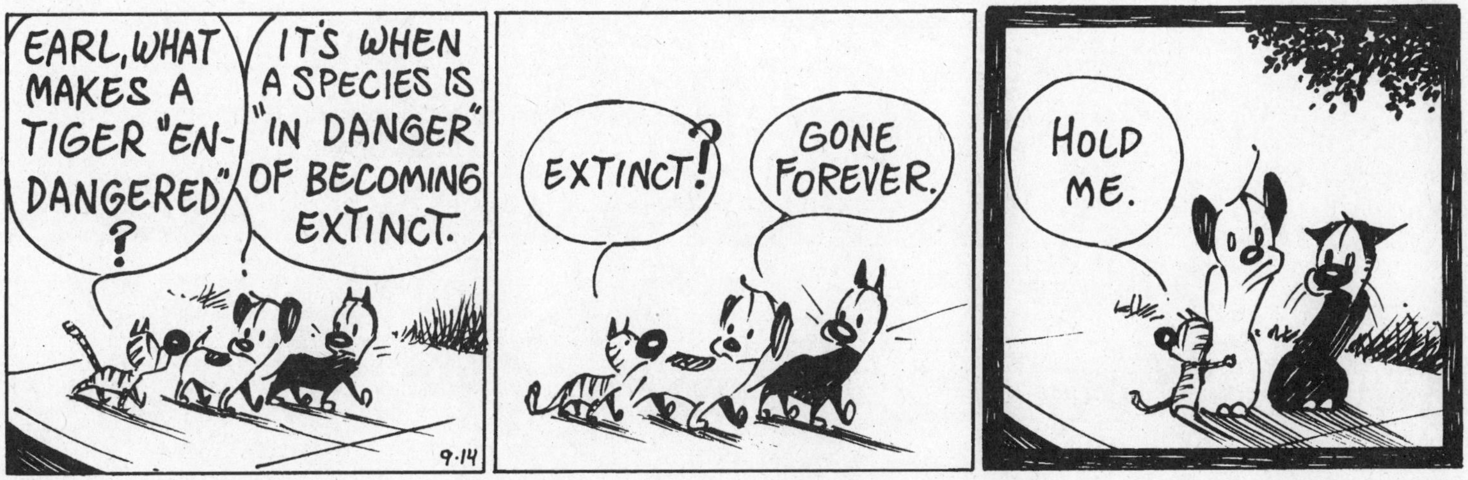
EARL, WHAT MAKES A TIGER "EN-DANGERED"?
IT'S WHEN A SPECIES IS "IN DANGER" OF BECOMING EXTINCT.
9·14
EXTINCT?!
GONE FOREVER.
HOLD ME.

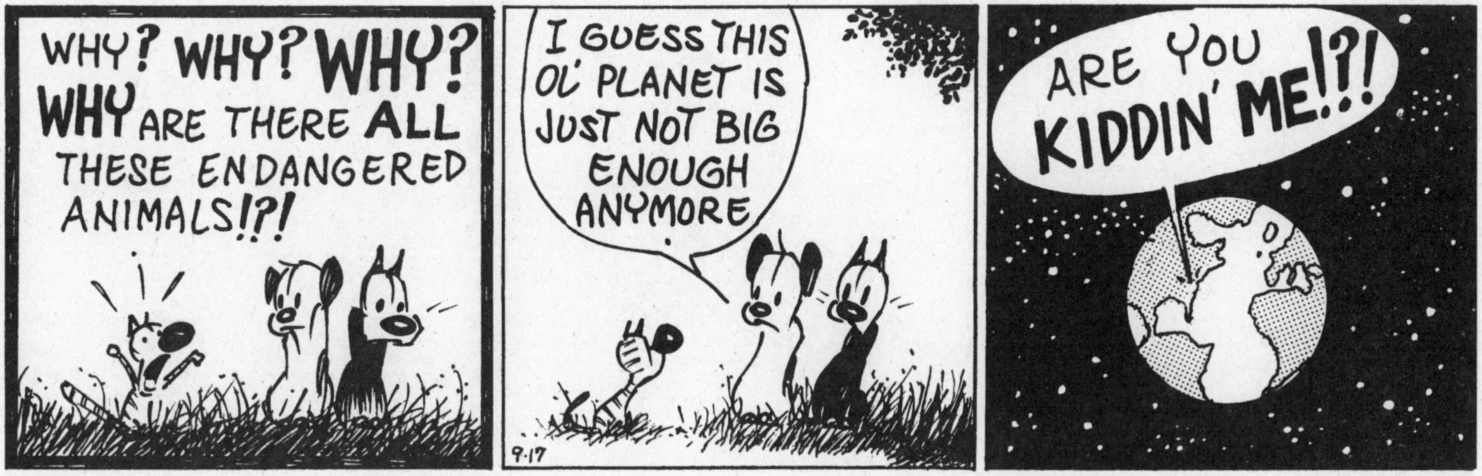
WHY? WHY? WHY? WHY ARE THERE ALL THESE ENDANGERED ANIMALS!?!
I GUESS THIS OL' PLANET IS JUST NOT BIG ENOUGH ANYMORE.
9·17
ARE YOU KIDDIN' ME!?!

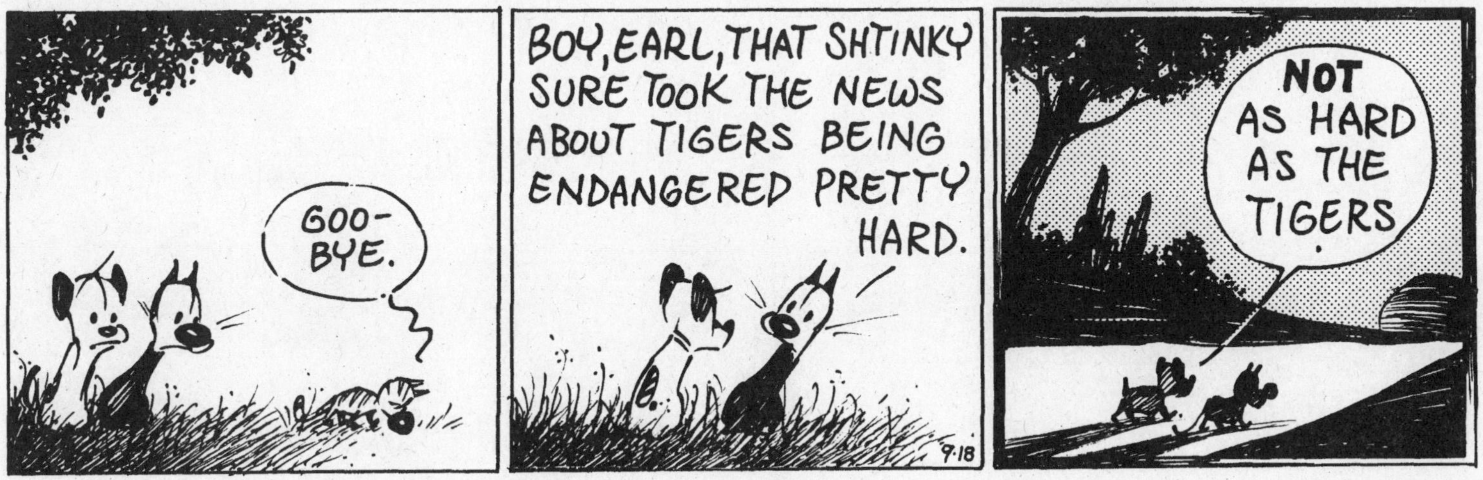
GOO-BYE.
BOY, EARL, THAT SHTINKY SURE TOOK THE NEWS ABOUT TIGERS BEING ENDANGERED PRETTY HARD.
9·18
NOT AS HARD AS THE TIGERS.

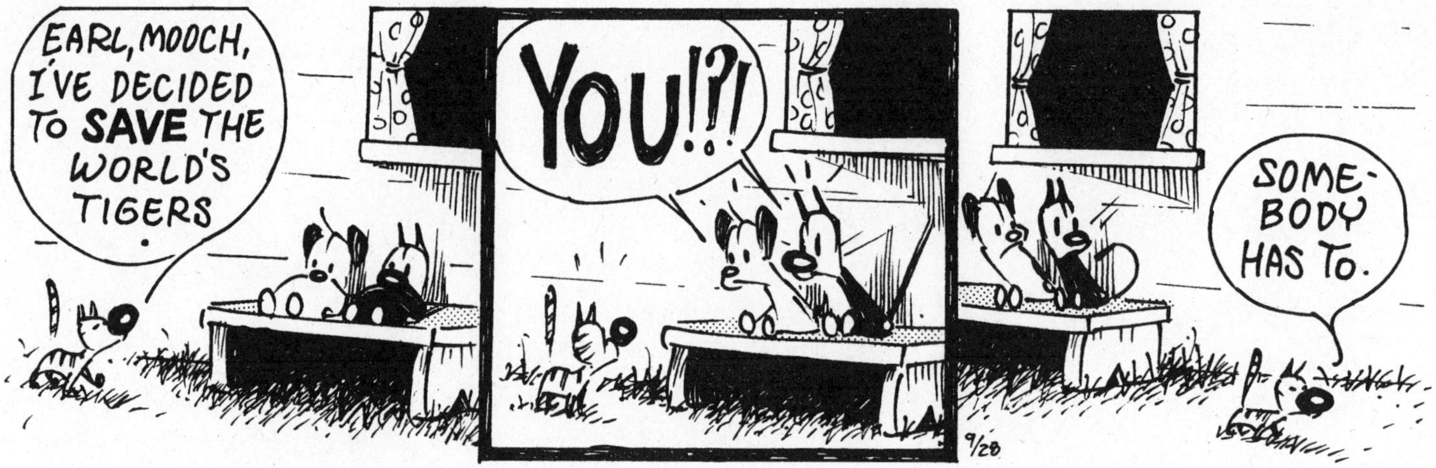
EARL, MOOCH, I'VE DECIDED TO SAVE THE WORLD'S TIGERS.
YOU!?!
SOME-BODY HAS TO.
9/28

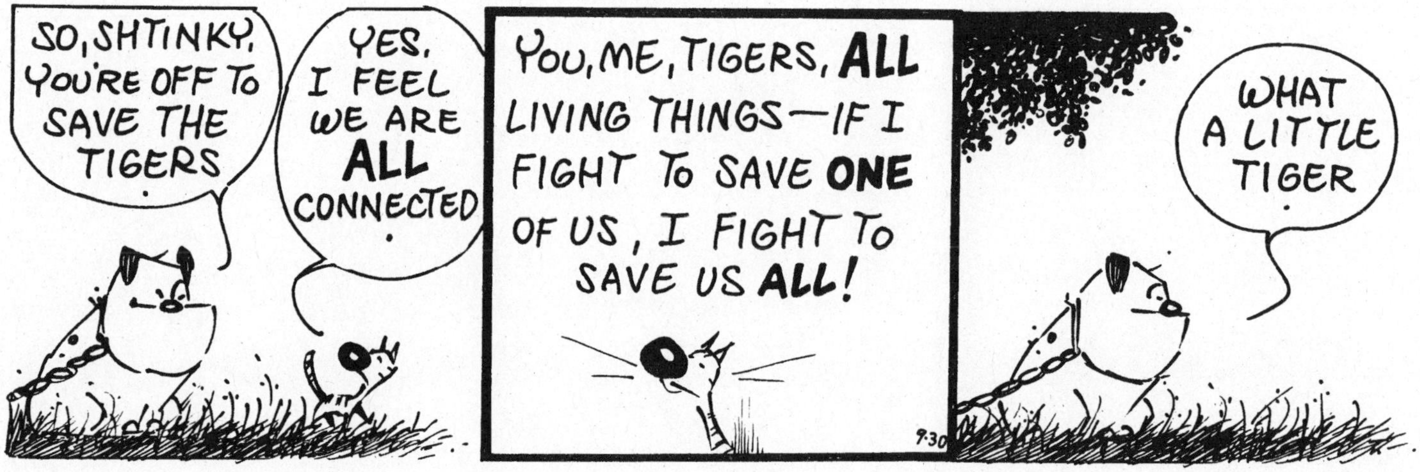
SO, SHTINKY, YOU'RE OFF TO SAVE THE TIGERS.
YES. I FEEL WE ARE ALL CONNECTED.
YOU, ME, TIGERS, ALL LIVING THINGS—IF I FIGHT TO SAVE ONE OF US, I FIGHT TO SAVE US ALL!
WHAT A LITTLE TIGER.
9·30

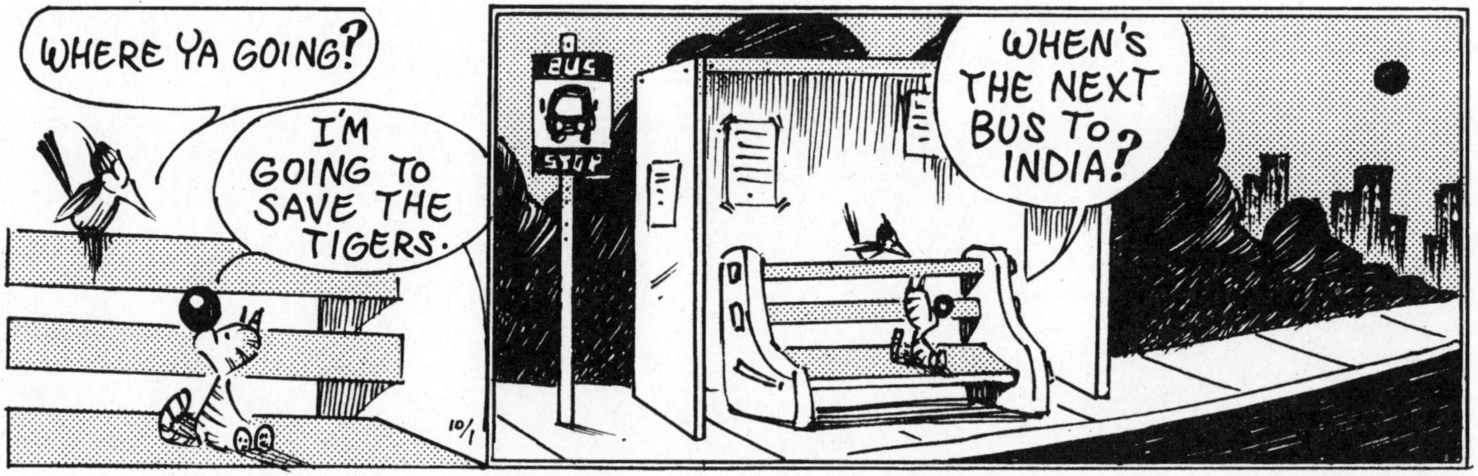
WHERE YA GOING?
I'M GOING TO SAVE THE TIGERS.
10/1
BUS
STOP
WHEN'S THE NEXT BUS TO INDIA?

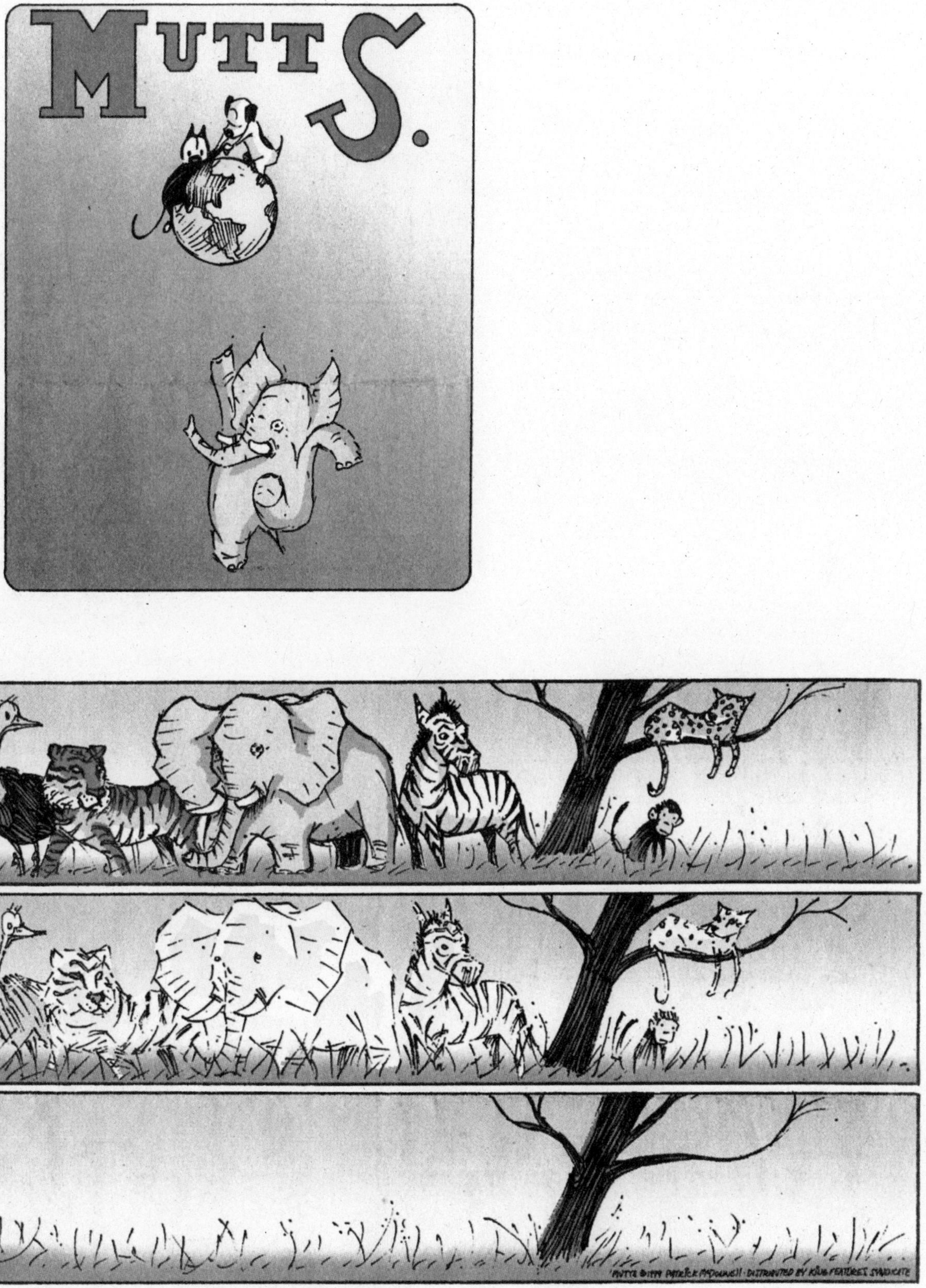
MUTTS.
9-19
MUTTS ©1999 PATRICK McDONNELL · DISTRIBUTED BY KING FEATURES SYNDICATE

... RIGHT BEFORE OUR EYES...

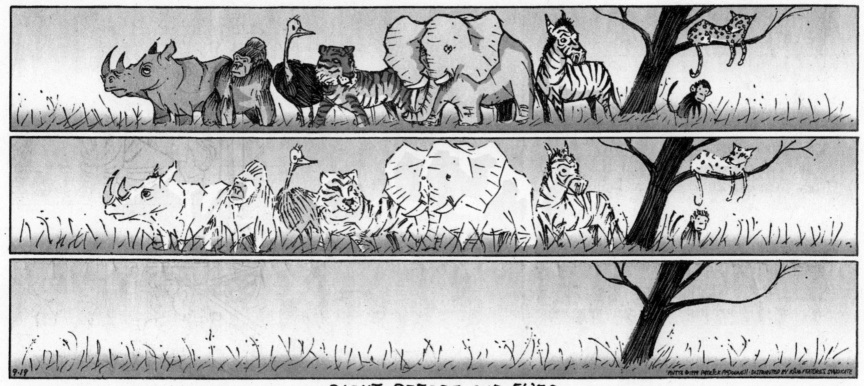

CAFETERIA
9.9

LICK LICK LICK LICK LICK LICK
LICK LICK LICK LICK LICK
LICK LICK LICK LICK LICK
LICK LICK LICK LICK
LICK LICK LICK LICK
HE'S MY FAVORITE FLAVOR.
10/2

BRRRRR
SWEATER WEATHER.
I'LL SAY.
10.4

BOOPSY— WILL YOU MARRY ME?
10.13
BONK
SOME DAY— SHE'LL THANK ME.

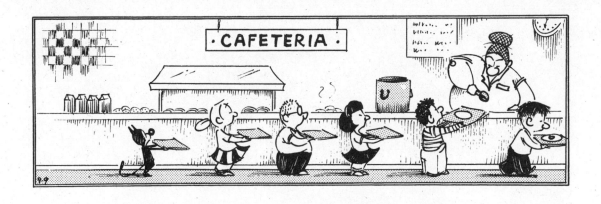

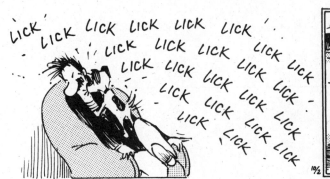

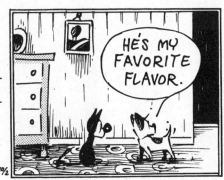

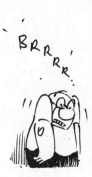

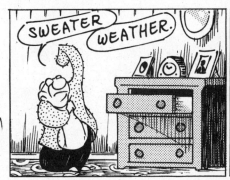

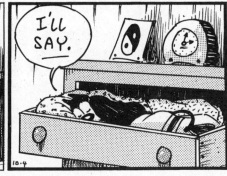

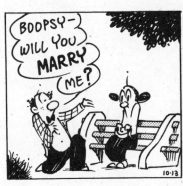

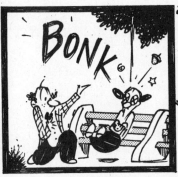

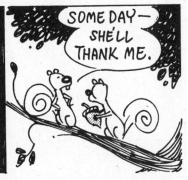

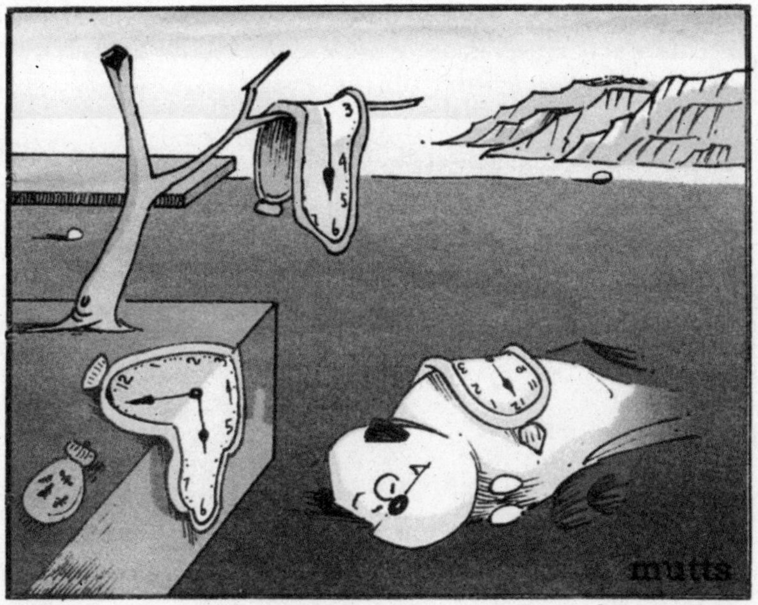
mutts

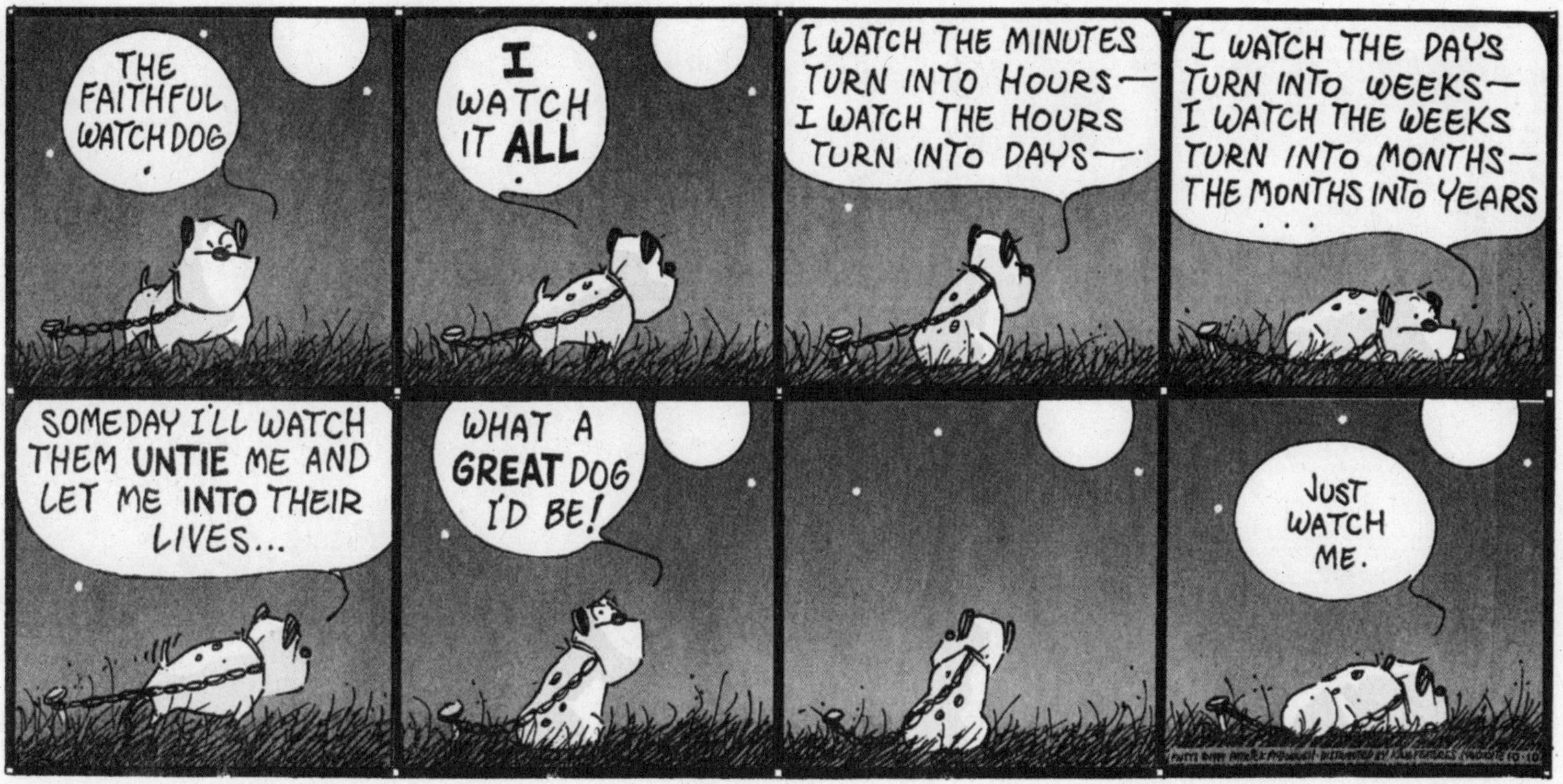
THE FAITHFUL WATCHDOG.
I WATCH IT ALL.
I WATCH THE MINUTES TURN INTO HOURS— I WATCH THE HOURS TURN INTO DAYS—.
I WATCH THE DAYS TURN INTO WEEKS— I WATCH THE WEEKS TURN INTO MONTHS— THE MONTHS INTO YEARS . . .
SOMEDAY I'LL WATCH THEM UNTIE ME AND LET ME INTO THEIR LIVES...
WHAT A GREAT DOG I'D BE!
JUST WATCH ME.

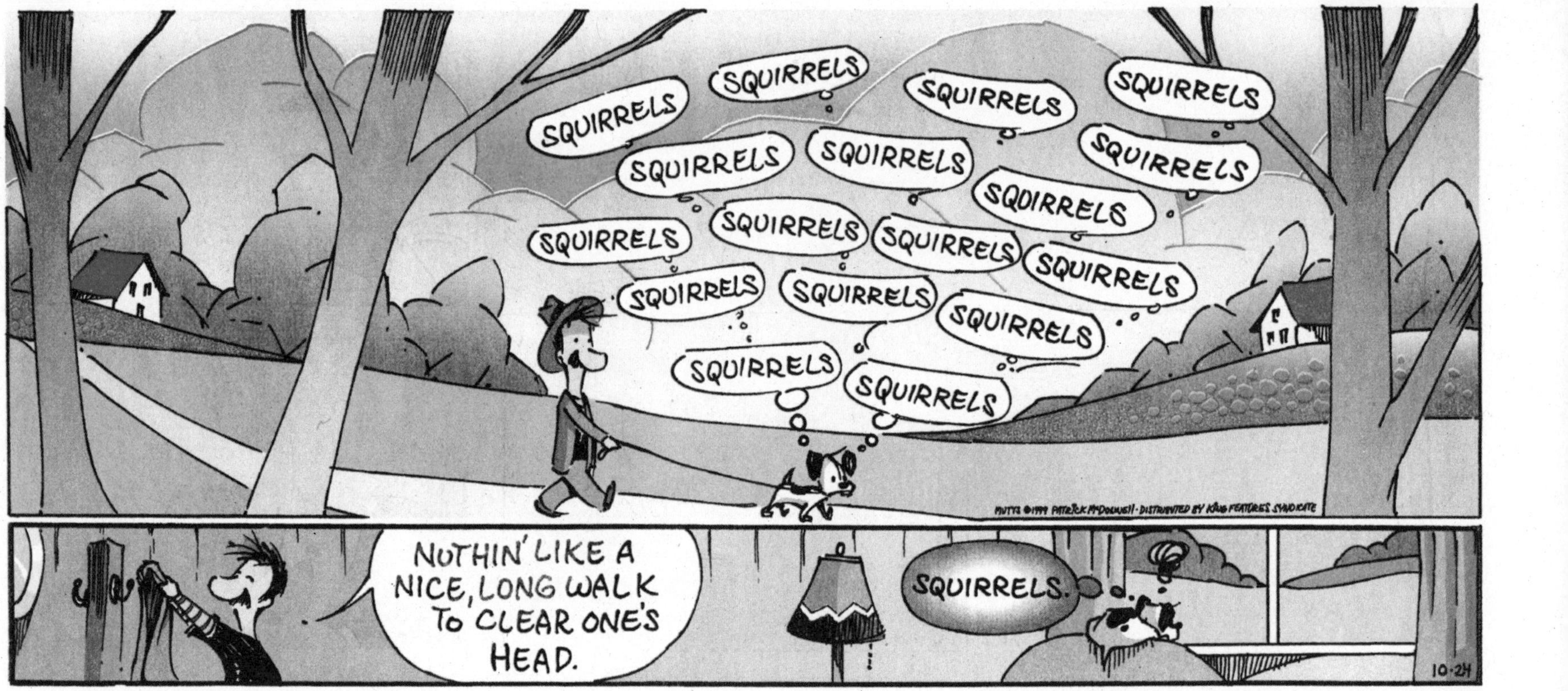
SQUIRRELS
SQUIRRELS
SQUIRRELS
SQUIRRELS
SQUIRRELS
SQUIRRELS
SQUIRRELS
SQUIRRELS
SQUIRRELS
SQUIRRELS
SQUIRRELS
SQUIRRELS
SQUIRRELS
SQUIRRELS
SQUIRRELS
SQUIRRELS
SQUIRRELS
MUTTS ©1999 PATRICK McDONNELL · DISTRIBUTED BY KING FEATURES SYNDICATE
NUTHIN' LIKE A NICE, LONG WALK TO CLEAR ONE'S HEAD.
SQUIRRELS.
10·24

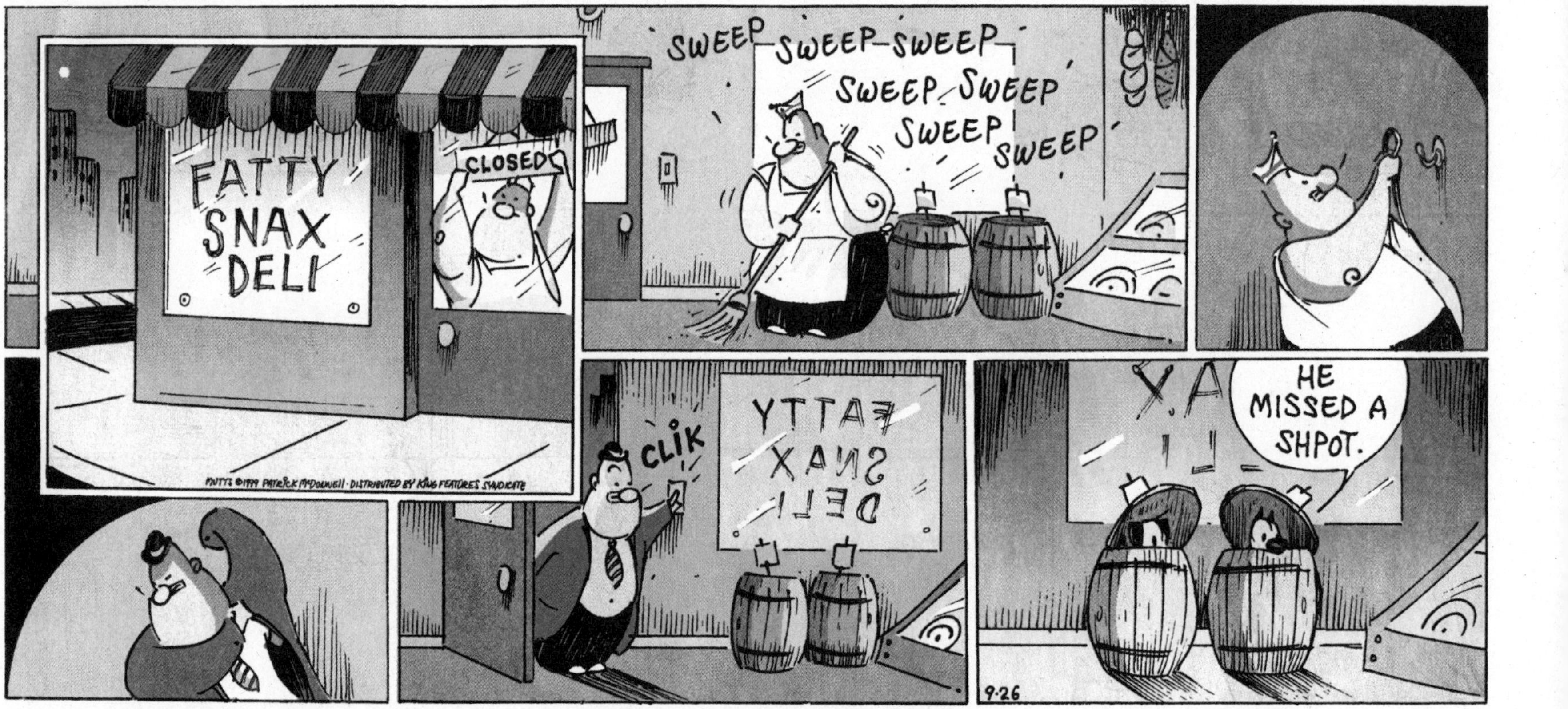
FATTY SNAX DELI
CLOSED
MUTTS ©1999 PATRICK McDONNELL · DISTRIBUTED BY KING FEATURES SYNDICATE
SWEEP SWEEP SWEEP SWEEP SWEEP SWEEP SWEEP
CLIK
HE MISSED A SHPOT.
9·26

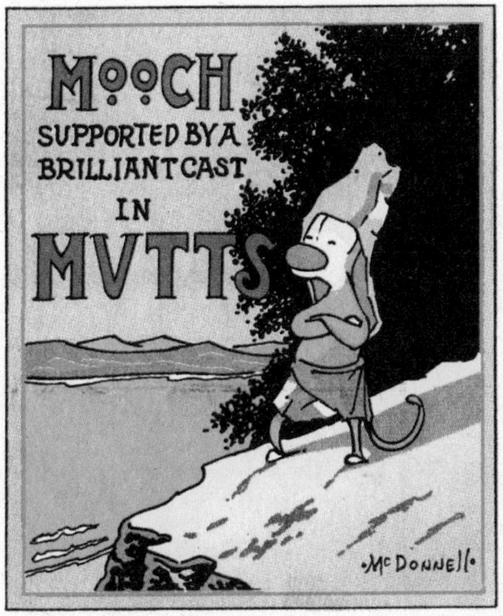
MOOCH
SUPPORTED BY A BRILLIANT CAST
IN
MUTTS
•McDONNELL•

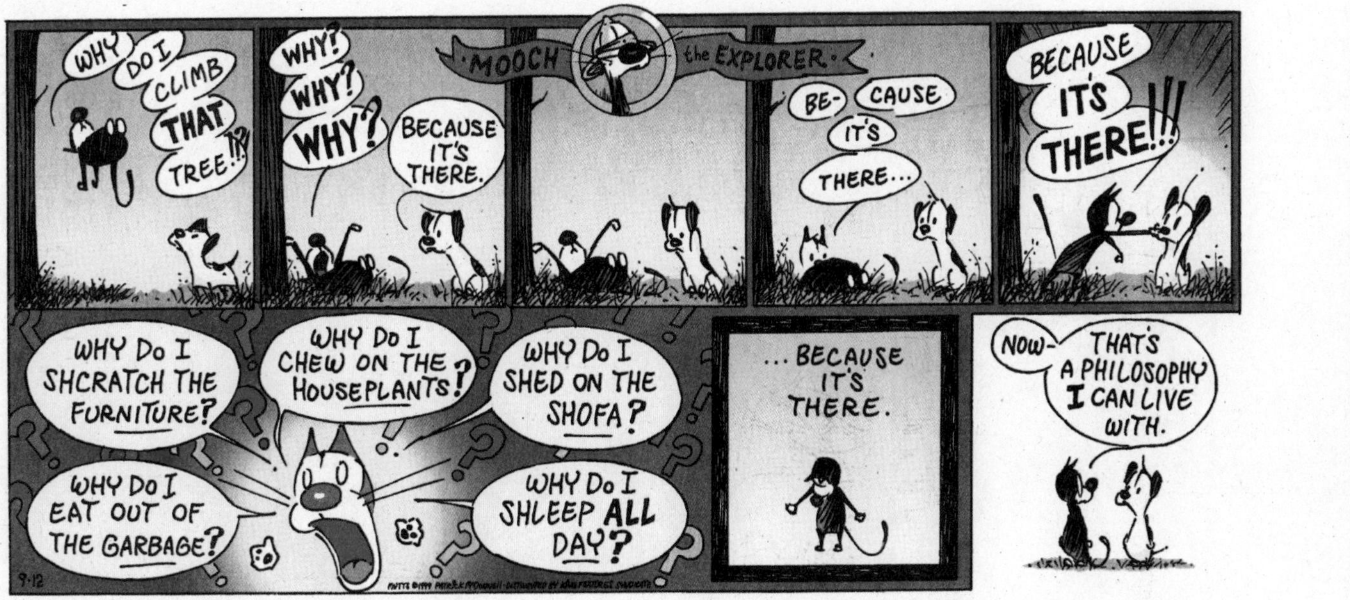
WHY DO I CLIMB THAT TREE!?
WHY? WHY? WHY?
BECAUSE IT'S THERE.
MOOCH the EXPLORER
BE- CAUSE IT'S THERE...
BECAUSE IT'S THERE!!!
WHY DO I SHCRATCH THE FURNITURE?
WHY DO I CHEW ON THE HOUSEPLANTS?
WHY DO I SHED ON THE SHOFA?
WHY DO I EAT OUT OF THE GARBAGE?
WHY DO I SHLEEP ALL DAY?
9-12
... BECAUSE IT'S THERE.
NOW-
THAT'S A PHILOSOPHY I CAN LIVE WITH.

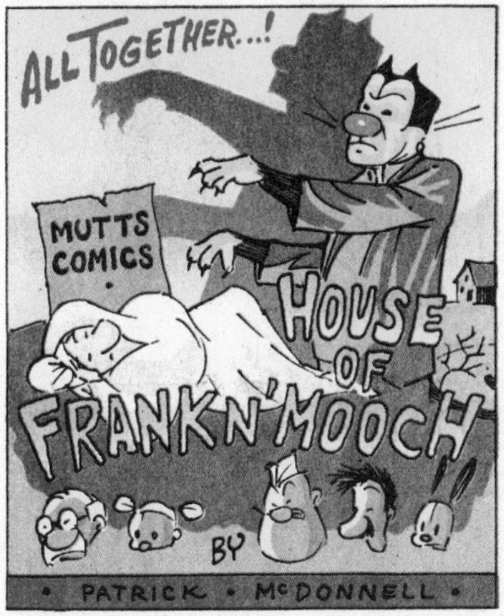
ALL TOGETHER...!
MUTTS COMICS
HOUSE OF FRANK N' MOOCH
BY
• PATRICK • McDONNELL •

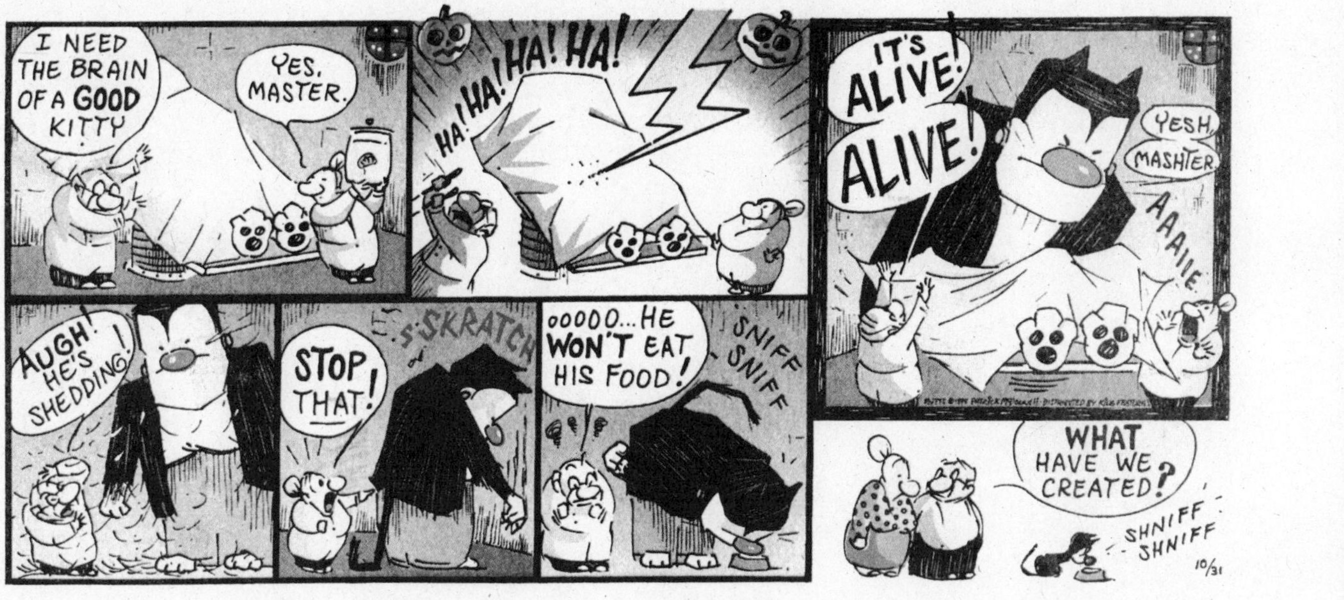
I NEED THE BRAIN OF A GOOD KITTY
YES, MASTER.
HA! HA! HA! HA!
IT'S ALIVE! ALIVE!
YESH, MASHTER.
AAAIIIE.
AUGH! HE'S SHEDDING!
S-SKRATCH
STOP THAT!
OOOOO... HE WON'T EAT HIS FOOD!
SNIFF SNIFF
WHAT HAVE WE CREATED?
SHNIFF SHNIFF
10/31

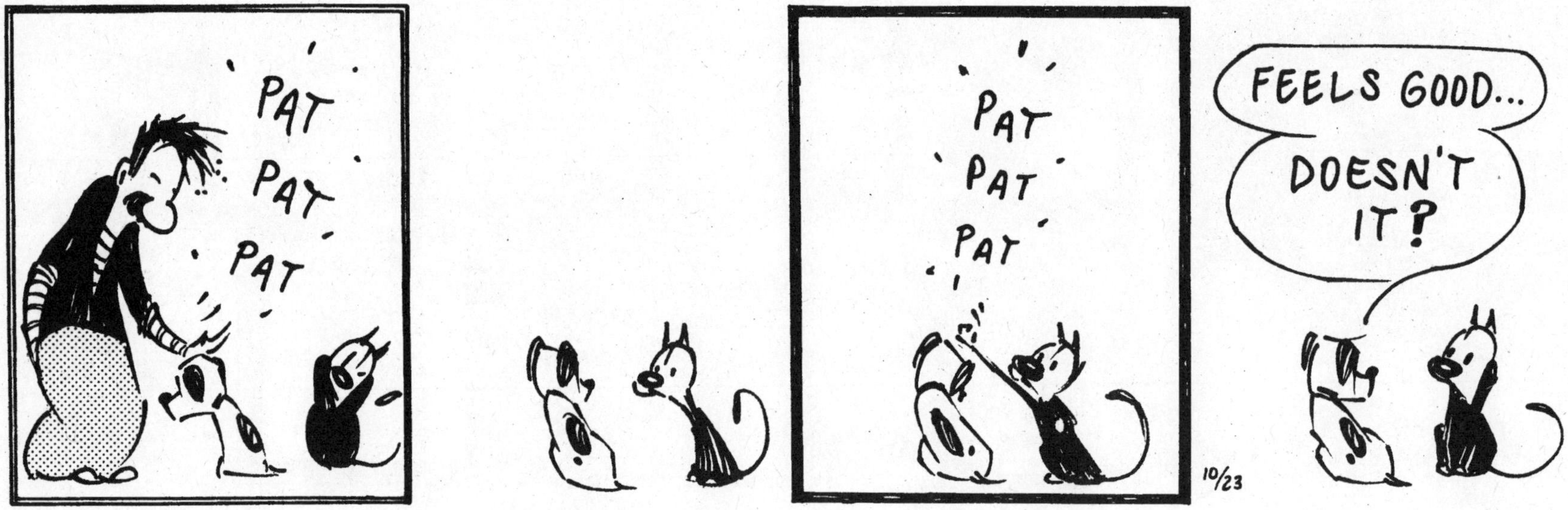
PAT
PAT
PAT
PAT
PAT
PAT
FEELS GOOD...
DOESN'T IT?
10/23

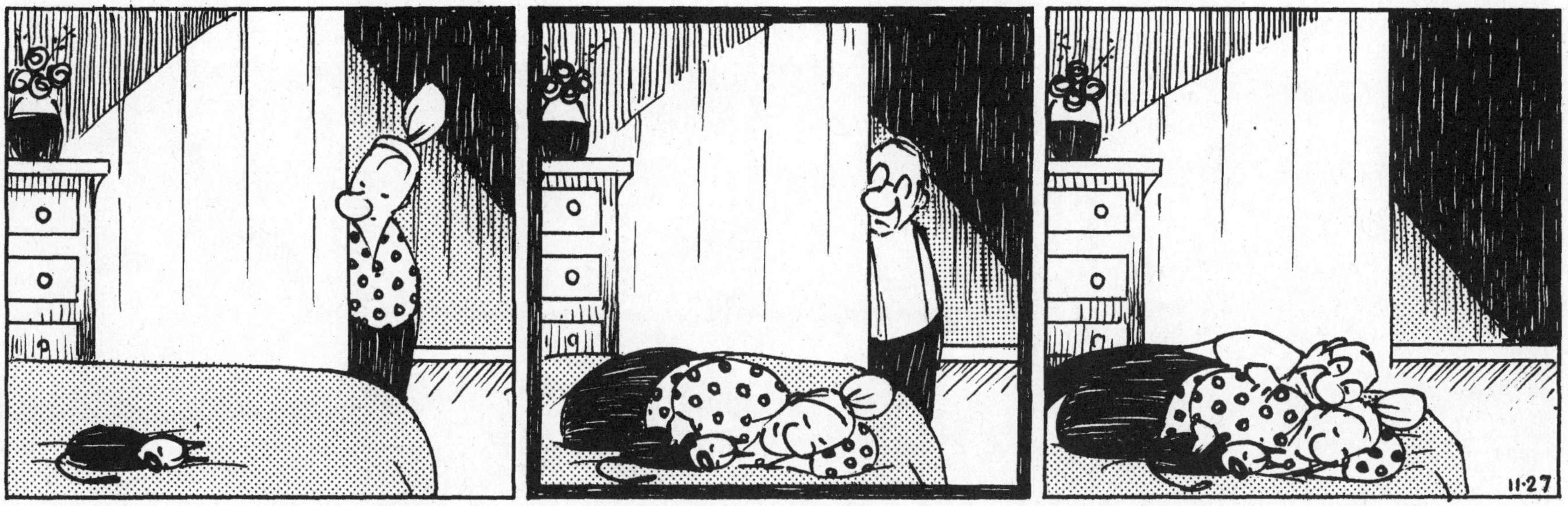
11·27

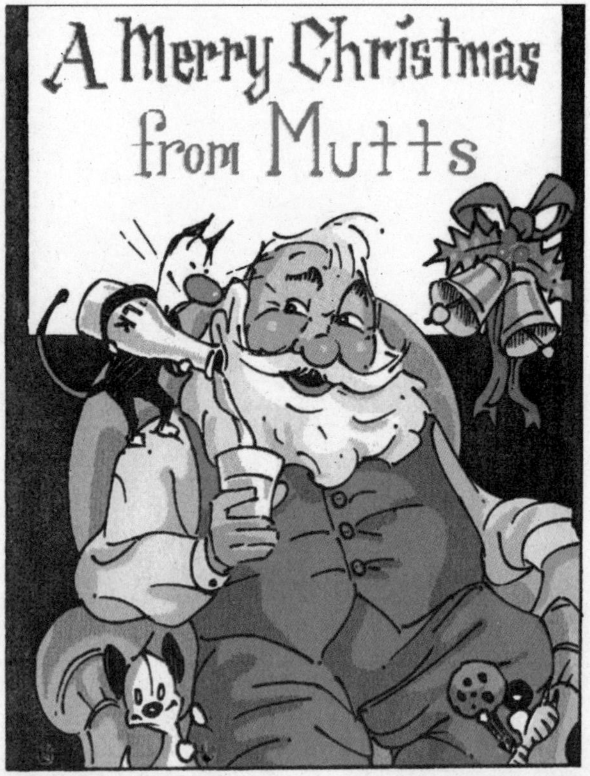
A Merry Christmas
from Mutts

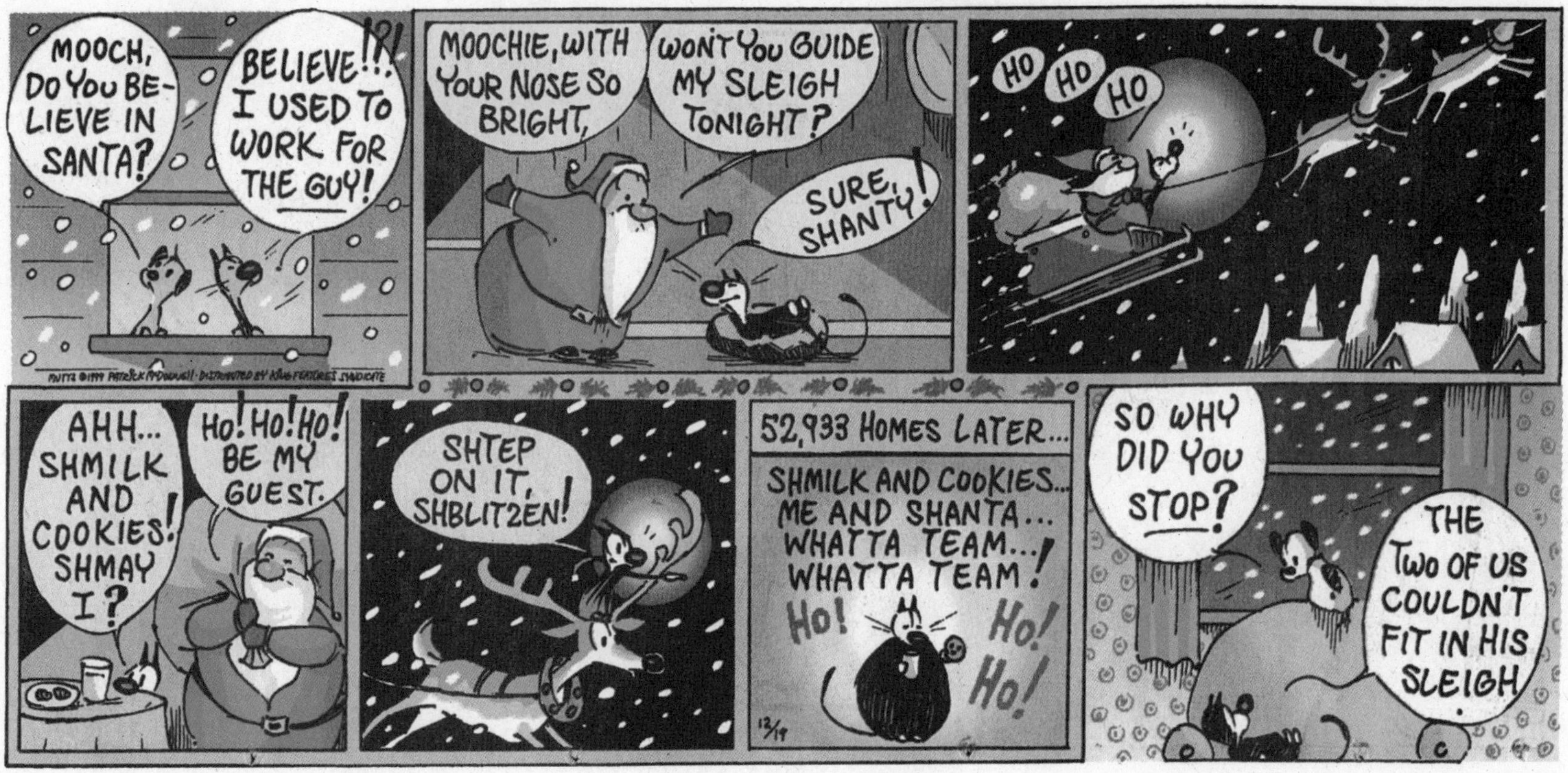
MOOCH, DO YOU BELIEVE IN SANTA?
BELIEVE!?! I USED TO WORK FOR THE GUY!
MOOCHIE, WITH YOUR NOSE SO BRIGHT,
WON'T YOU GUIDE MY SLEIGH TONIGHT?
SURE, SHANTY!
HO HO HO
AHH... SHMILK AND COOKIES! SHMAY I?
HO! HO! HO! BE MY GUEST.
SHTEP ON IT, SHBLITZEN!
52,933 HOMES LATER...
SHMILK AND COOKIES... ME AND SHANTA... WHATTA TEAM...! WHATTA TEAM!
HO! HO! HO!
12/19
SO WHY DID YOU STOP?
THE TWO OF US COULDN'T FIT IN HIS SLEIGH.

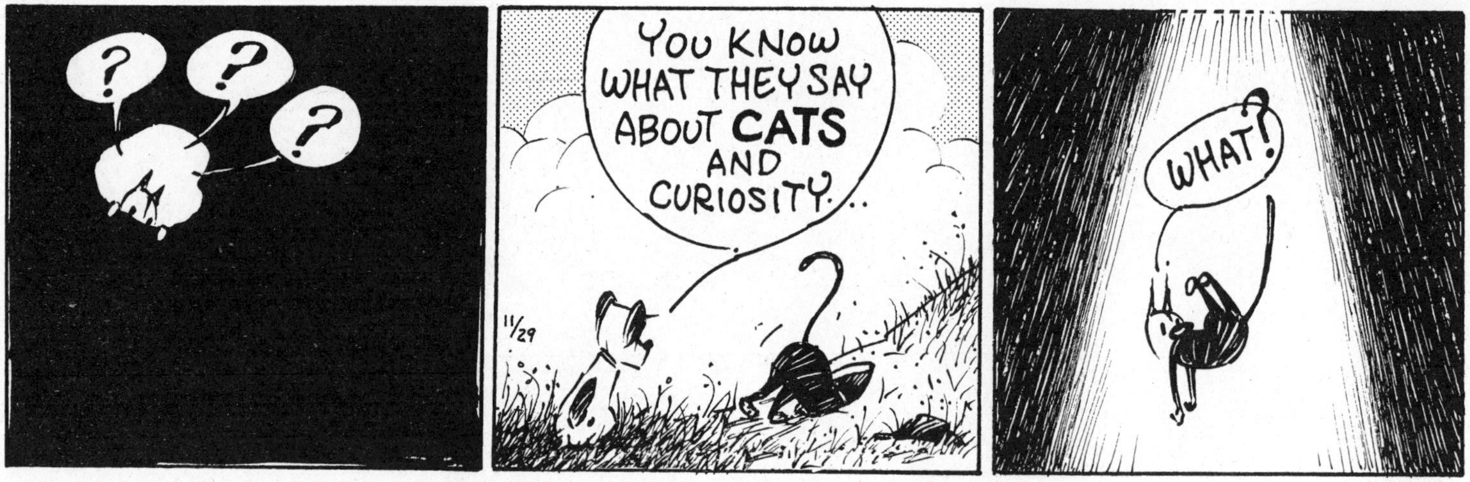
?
?
?
YOU KNOW WHAT THEY SAY ABOUT CATS AND CURIOSITY...
11/29
WHAT!

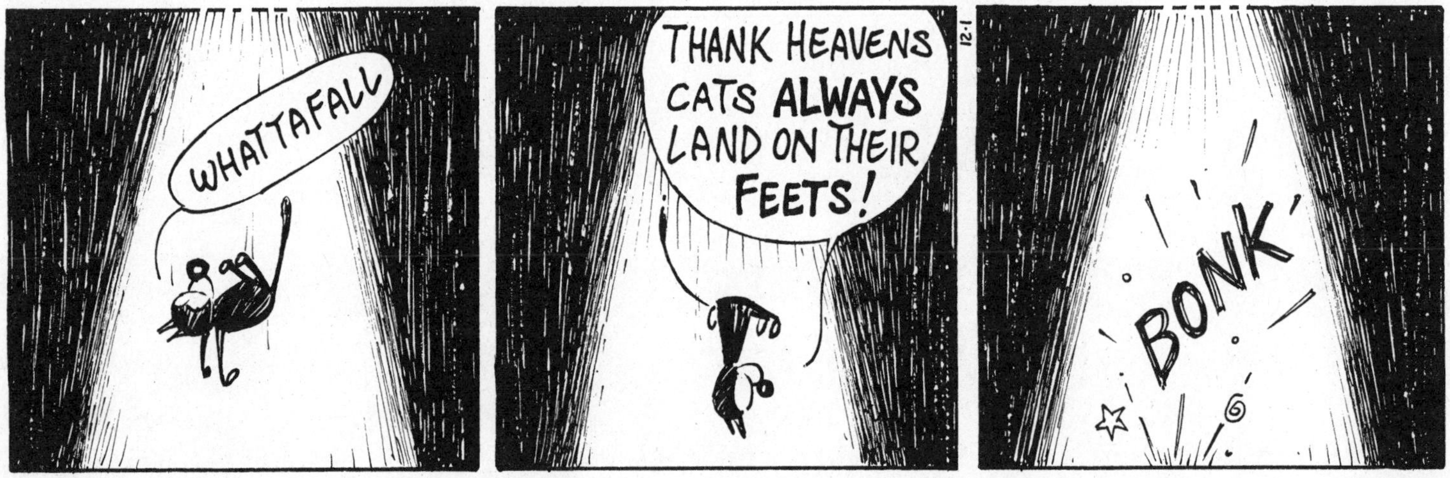
WHATTAFALL
THANK HEAVENS CATS ALWAYS LAND ON THEIR FEETS!
12·1
BONK

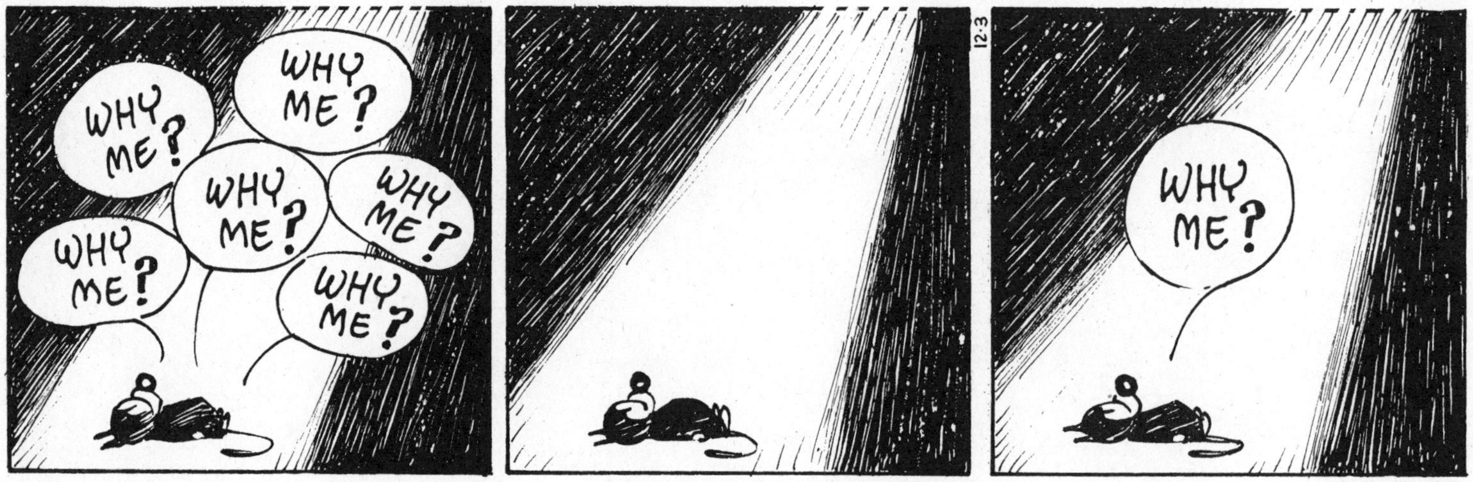
WHY ME?
WHY ME?
WHY ME?
WHY ME?
WHY ME?
WHY ME?
12·3
WHY ME?

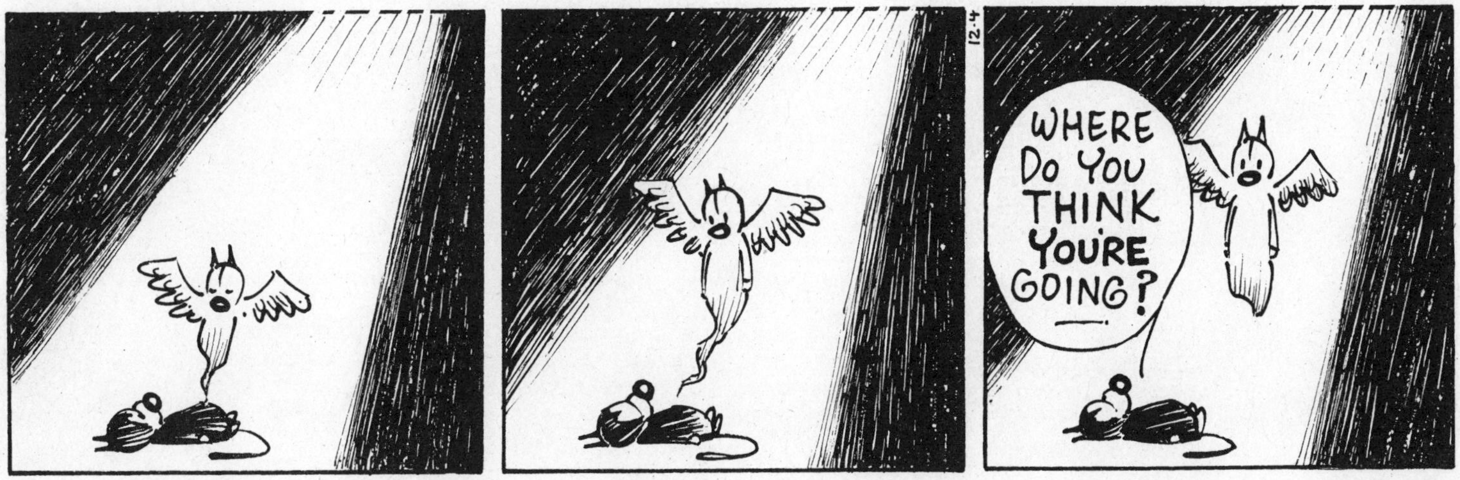
12-4
WHERE DO YOU THINK YOU'RE GOING?

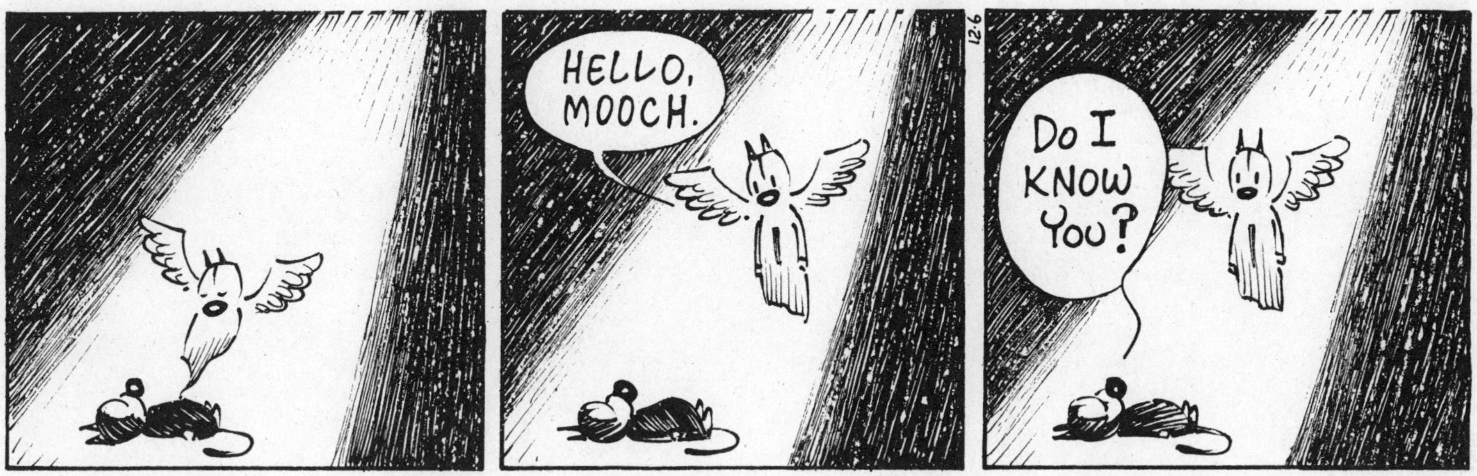
HELLO, MOOCH.
12-6
DO I KNOW YOU?

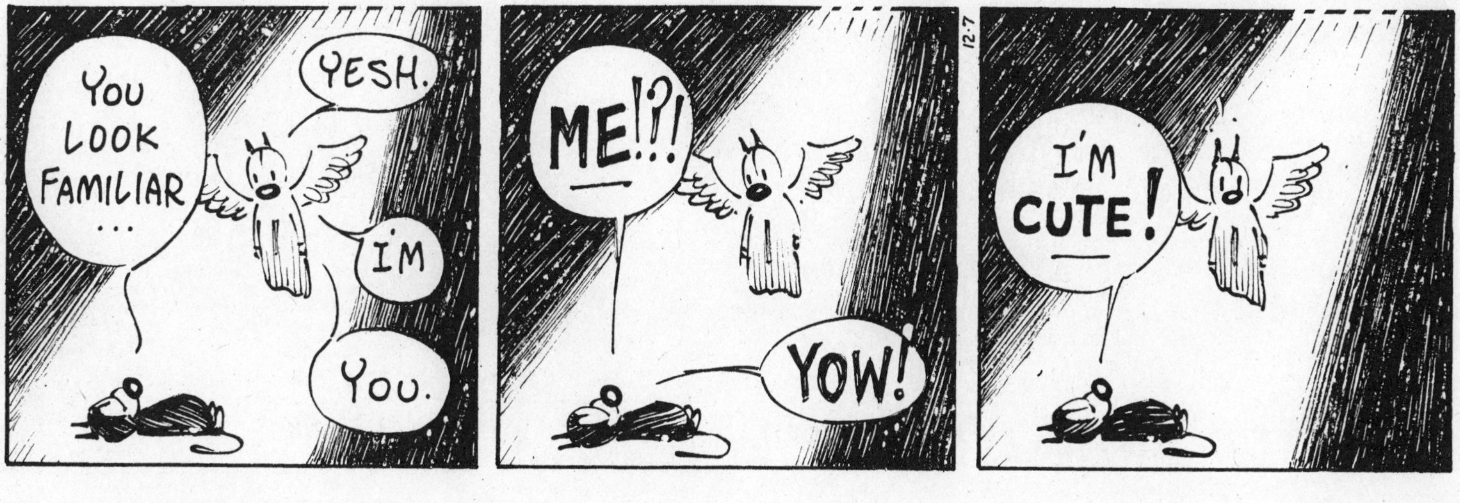
YOU LOOK FAMILIAR . . .
YESH.
I'M
YOU.
ME!?!
YOW!
12-7
I'M CUTE!

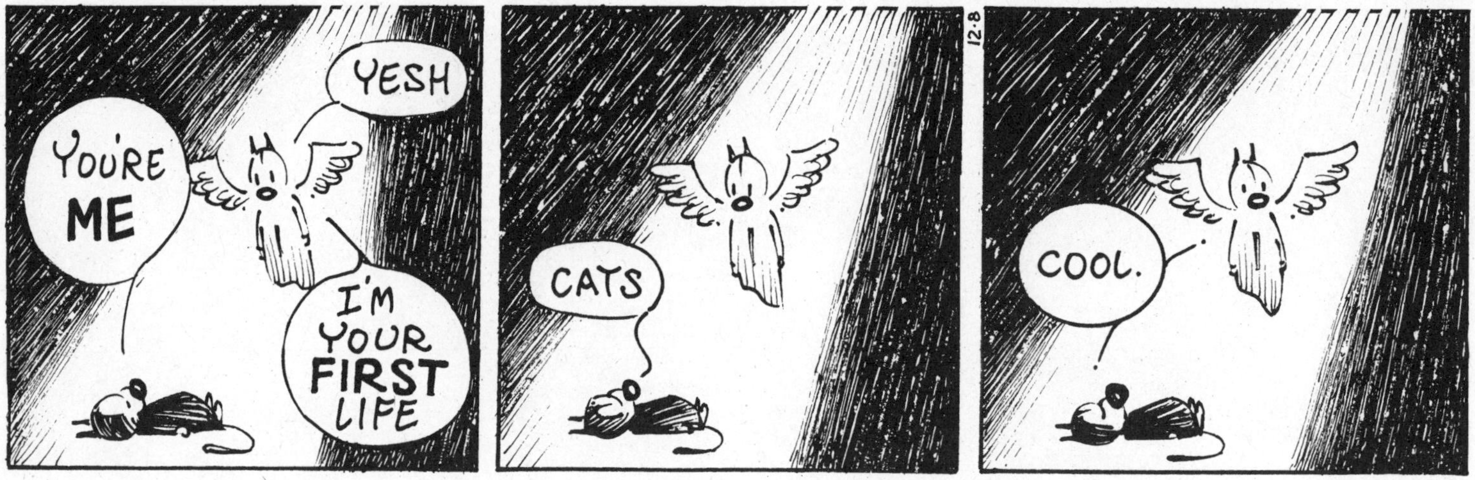
YOU'RE ME
YESH
I'M YOUR FIRST LIFE
12-8
CATS
COOL.

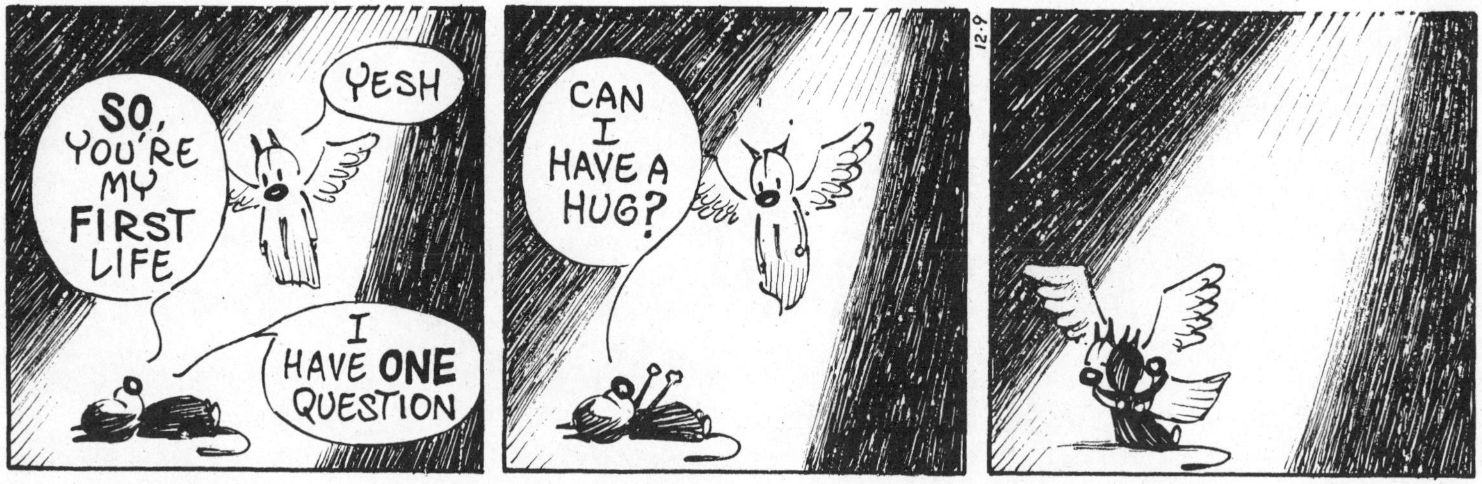
SO, YOU'RE MY FIRST LIFE
YESH
I HAVE ONE QUESTION
12-9
CAN I HAVE A HUG?

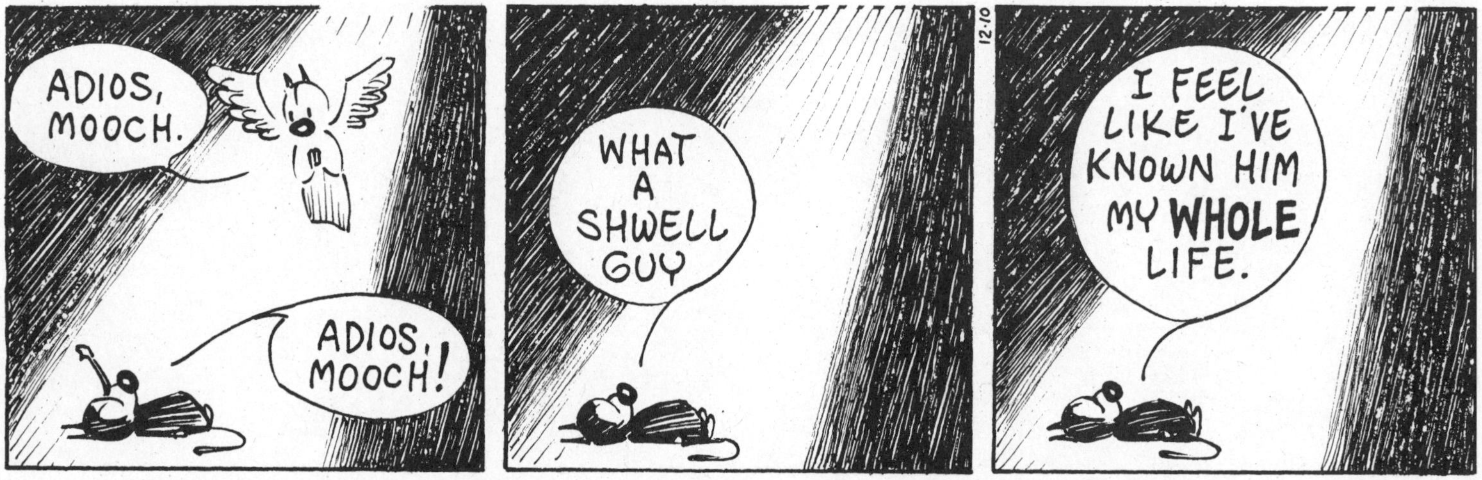
ADIOS, MOOCH.
ADIOS, MOOCH!
12-10
WHAT A SHWELL GUY
I FEEL LIKE I'VE KNOWN HIM MY WHOLE LIFE.

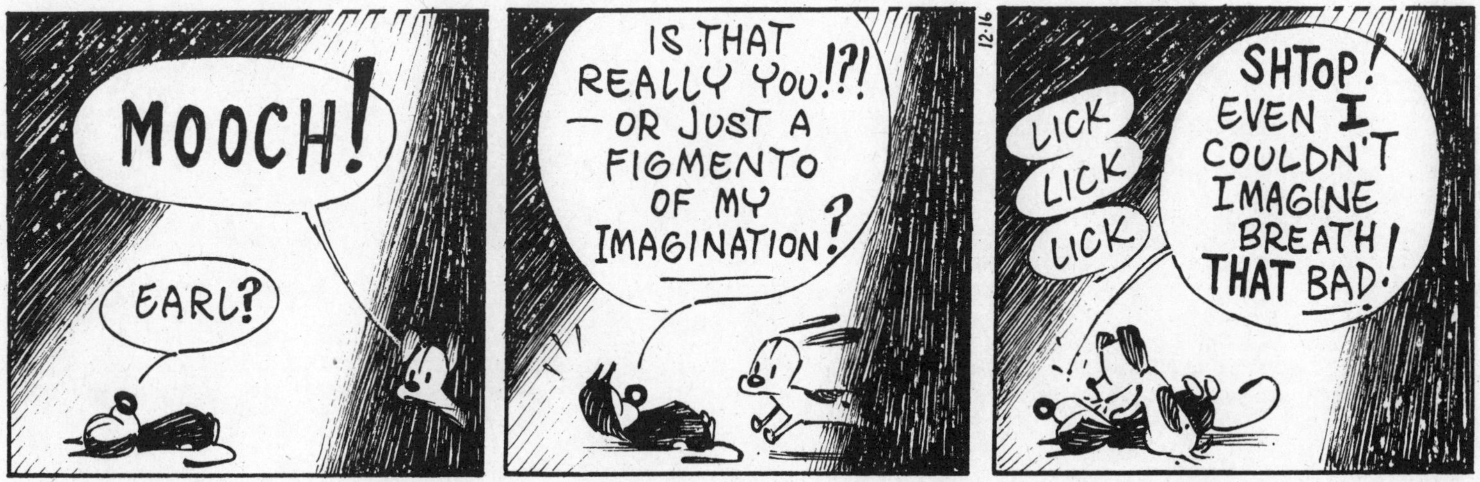
MOOCH!
EARL?
IS THAT REALLY YOU!?! —OR JUST A FIGMENTO OF MY IMAGINATION?
LICK
LICK
LICK
SHTOP! EVEN I COULDN'T IMAGINE BREATH THAT BAD!
12·16

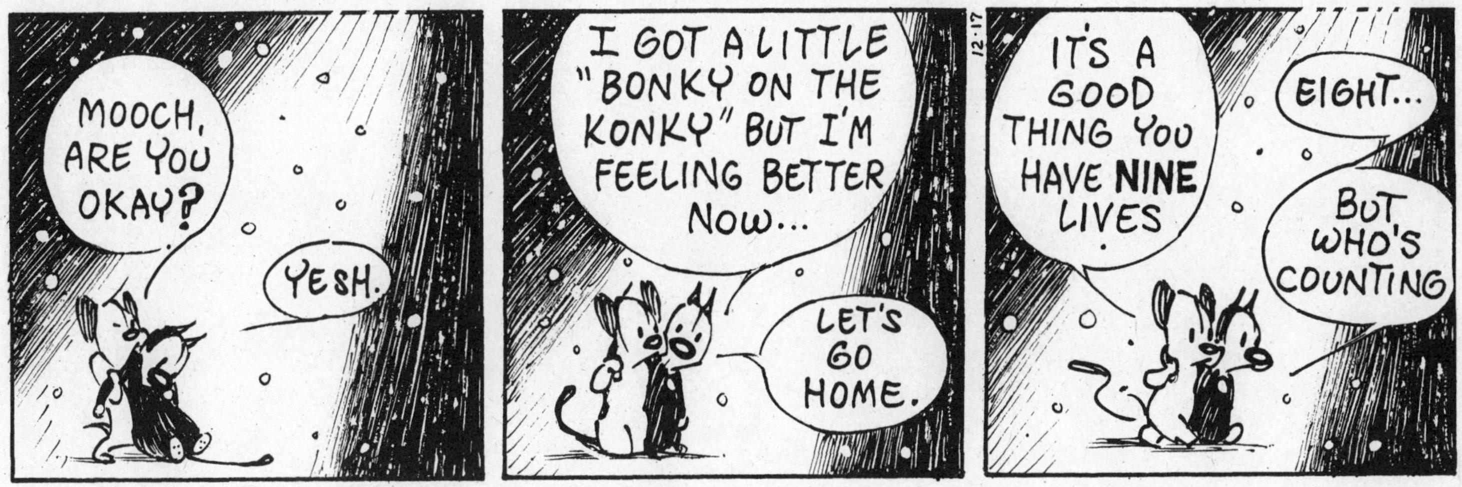
MOOCH, ARE YOU OKAY?
YESH.
I GOT A LITTLE "BONKY ON THE KONKY" BUT I'M FEELING BETTER NOW...
LET'S GO HOME.
IT'S A GOOD THING YOU HAVE NINE LIVES
EIGHT...
BUT WHO'S COUNTING
12·17

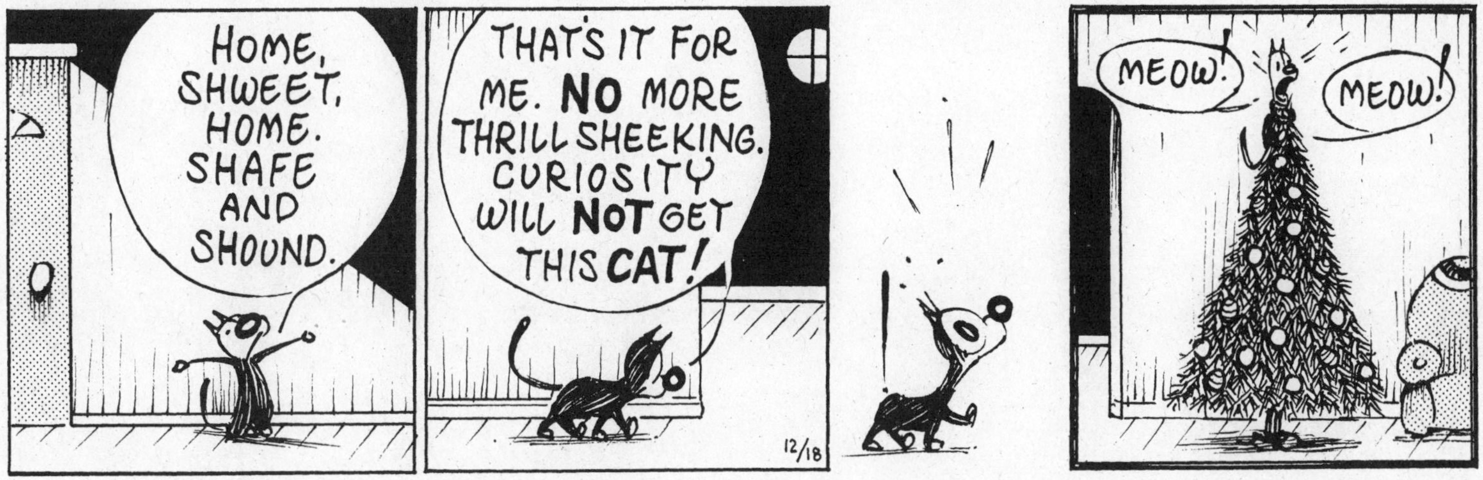
HOME, SHWEET, HOME. SHAFE AND SHOUND.
THAT'S IT FOR ME. NO MORE THRILL SHEEKING. CURIOSITY WILL NOT GET THIS CAT!
12/18
MEOW!
MEOW!

**The year 2000 was notable** for the strip and for me personally. In May, I received the National Cartoonists Society's highest honor—the Reuben Award. As a fan and student of this art form, I was proud to be part of such a rich heritage. Cartooning is a unique and wonderful profession. You will never meet a nicer, funnier, more generous, friendlier group of professional shut-ins anywhere.

Also in 2000, I was asked to join the board of directors of the Humane Society of the United States. The HSUS is the nation's largest and most powerful animal protection organization, working in the United States and abroad to defend the interests of animals. I am honored to be part of this dynamic group. It has changed my life, giving me a stronger awareness of and empathy for all animals, and has added a depth to *Mutts*.

That summer, my wife, Karen, surprised me with an opportunity to visit Africa. Weeks before I even knew I was going, I drew a Sunday page with Doozy dressing up Earl and Mooch as a lion and a zebra. She named Earl "Zambezi" (a name I randomly chose from a map of Africa). Eight weeks later, when that strip appeared in the newspaper, I was staring back at a hippopotamus while I was floating in a canoe down the mighty Zambezi River.

Karen and I were captivated by South Africa, Botswana, Zimbabwe, and Zambia. During that trip we saw elephants, lions, rhinoceroses, giraffes, zebras, water buffaloes, fish eagles, a serval, and many monkeys. I even petted a cheetah while visiting a South African sanctuary.

The whole experience was so primal and so real that it felt a bit unreal. I was at the sacred birthplace of our wonderful world. It was all so beautiful and sad. Our planet is so fragile; we must learn how to cherish and protect it all. Like Mooch, I still dream of Africa.

My wife is a student of Iyengar yoga, and I occasionally take a class. When her teacher, Gopali, visited B. K. S. Iyengar in Pune, India, she presented him with a print of the September 10 strip (page 162). She tells me it hangs near the dressing room at his Institute.

Namasté.

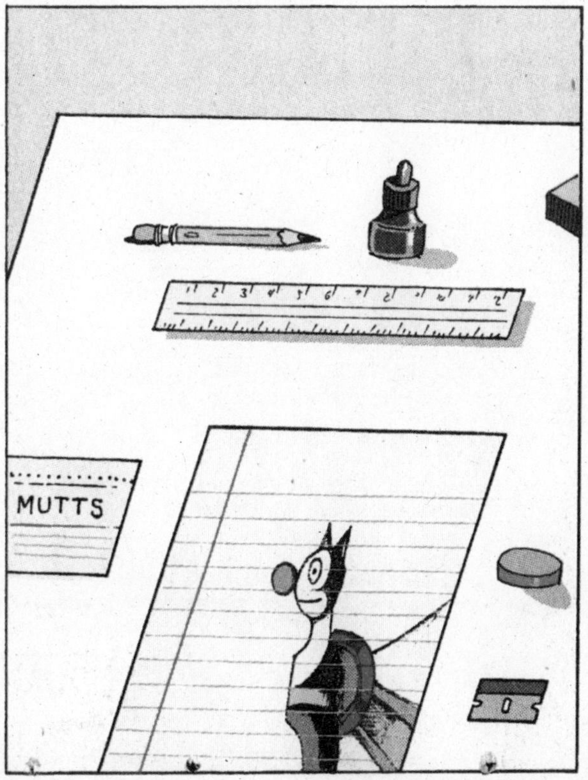
MUTTS

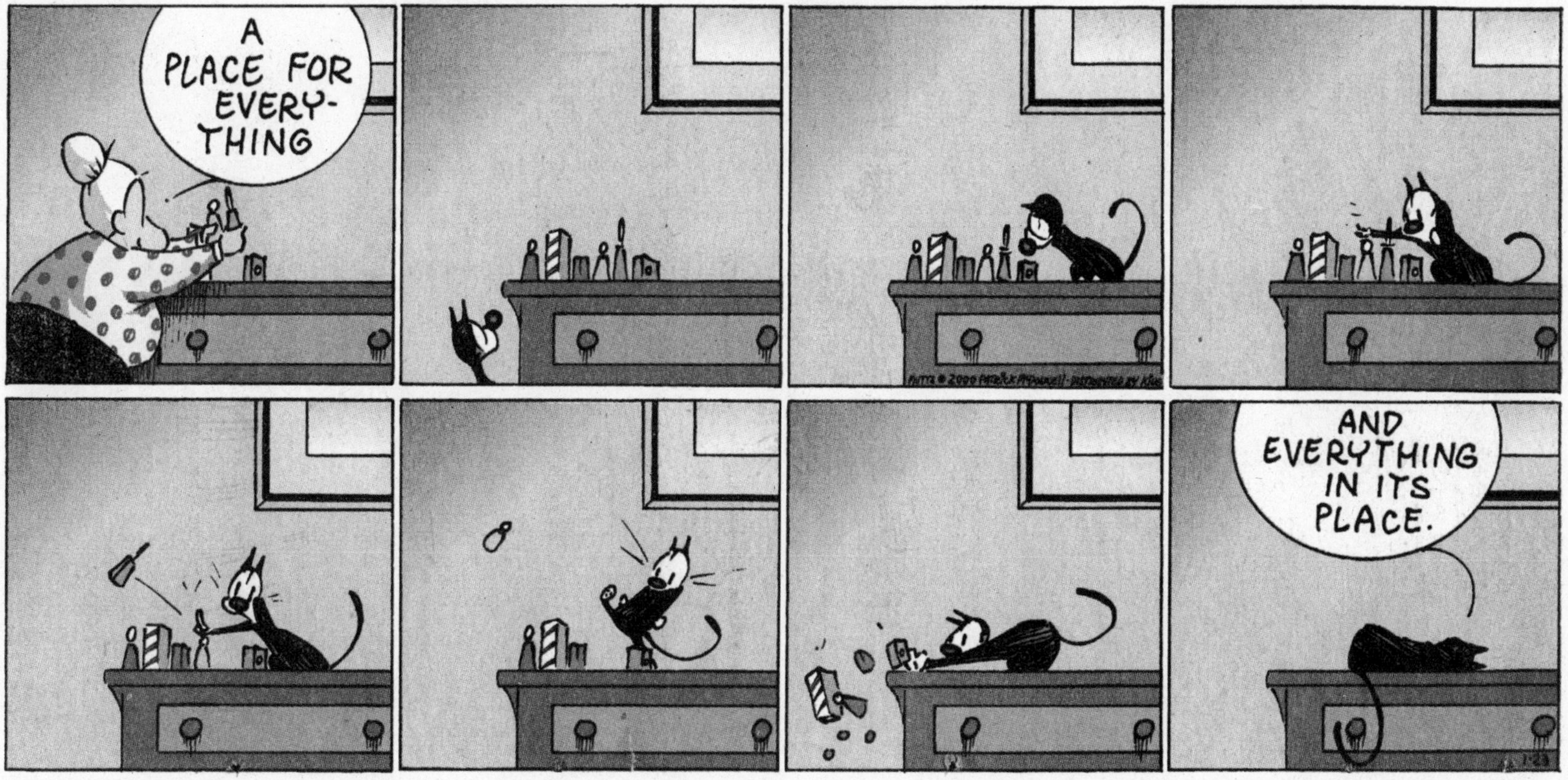
A PLACE FOR EVERY-THING
AND EVERYTHING IN ITS PLACE.

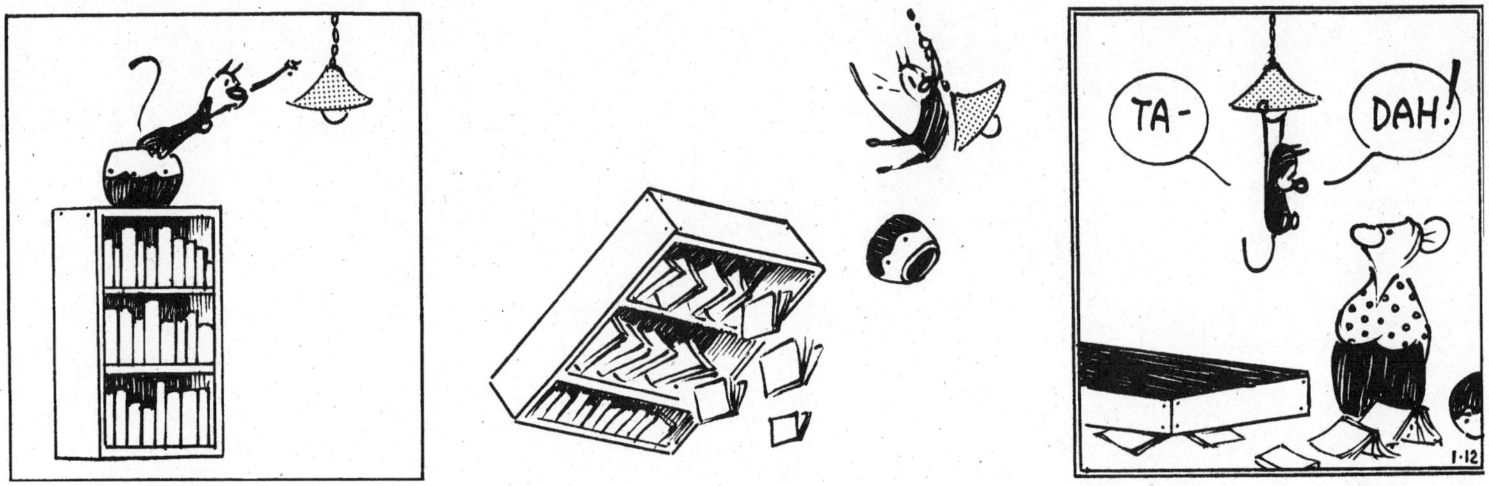
TA-
DAH!
1-12

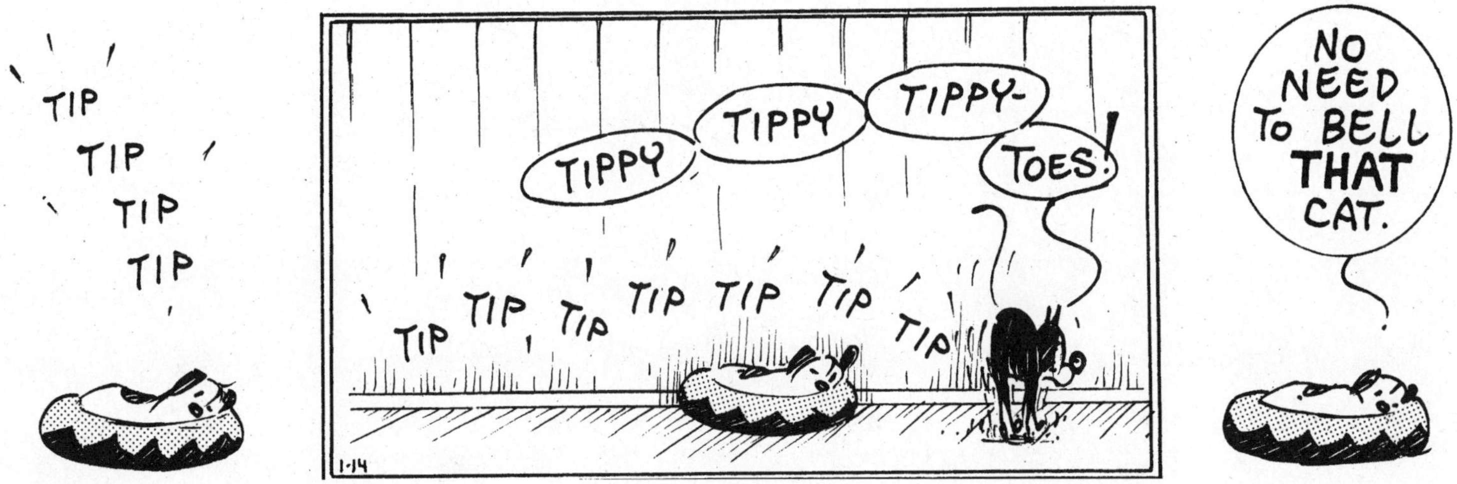
TIP
TIP
TIP
TIP
TIPPY
TIPPY
TIPPY-
TOES!
TIP TIP TIP TIP TIP TIP TIP
1-14
NO NEED TO BELL THAT CAT.

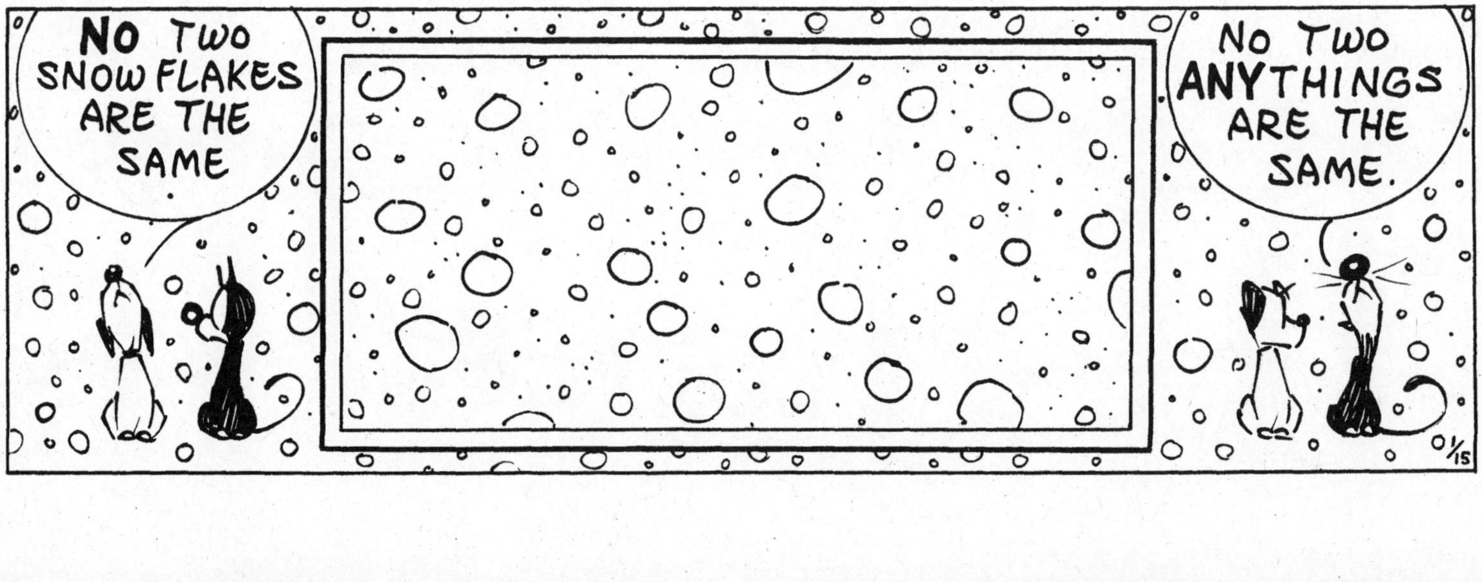
NO TWO SNOW FLAKES ARE THE SAME
NO TWO ANYTHINGS ARE THE SAME.
1/15

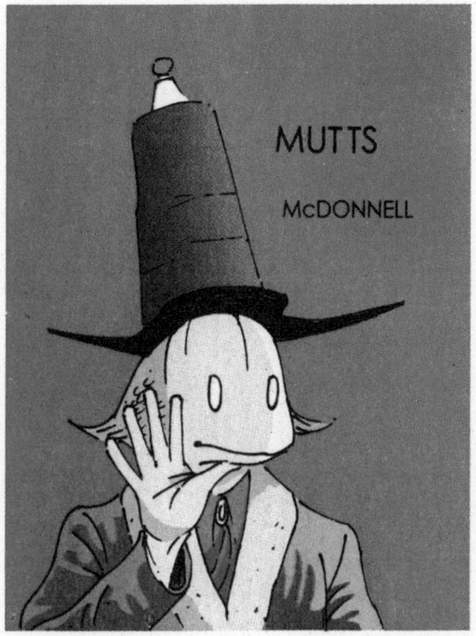
MUTTS
McDONNELL

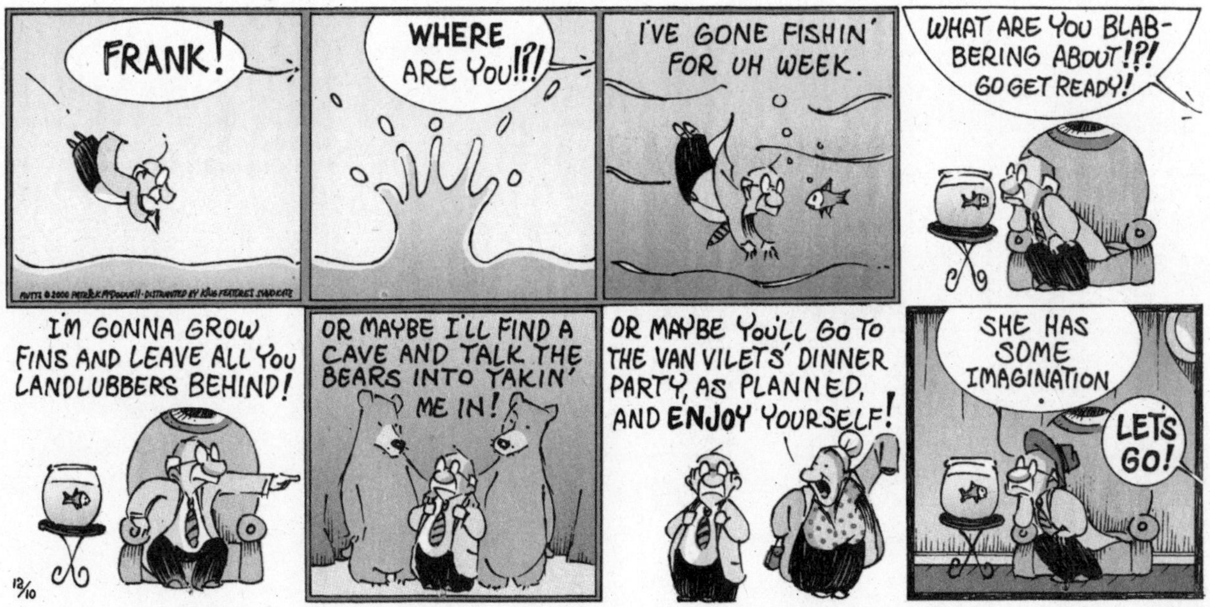
FRANK!
WHERE ARE YOU!?!
I'VE GONE FISHIN' FOR UH WEEK.
WHAT ARE YOU BLABBERING ABOUT!?! GO GET READY!
I'M GONNA GROW FINS AND LEAVE ALL YOU LANDLUBBERS BEHIND!
12/10
OR MAYBE I'LL FIND A CAVE AND TALK THE BEARS INTO TAKIN' ME IN!
OR MAYBE YOU'LL GO TO THE VAN VILETS' DINNER PARTY, AS PLANNED, AND ENJOY YOURSELF!
SHE HAS SOME IMAGINATION
LET'S GO!

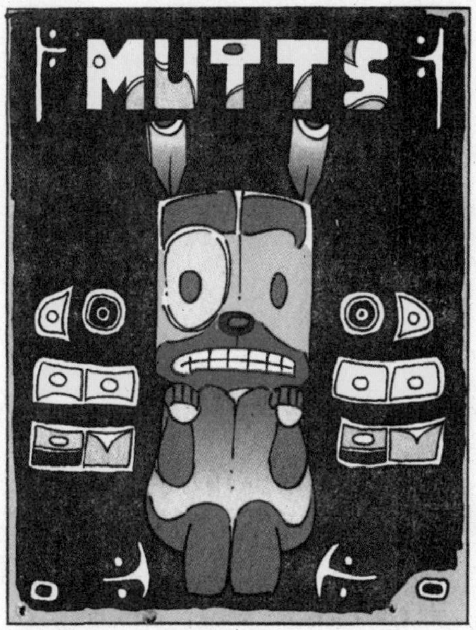
MUTTS

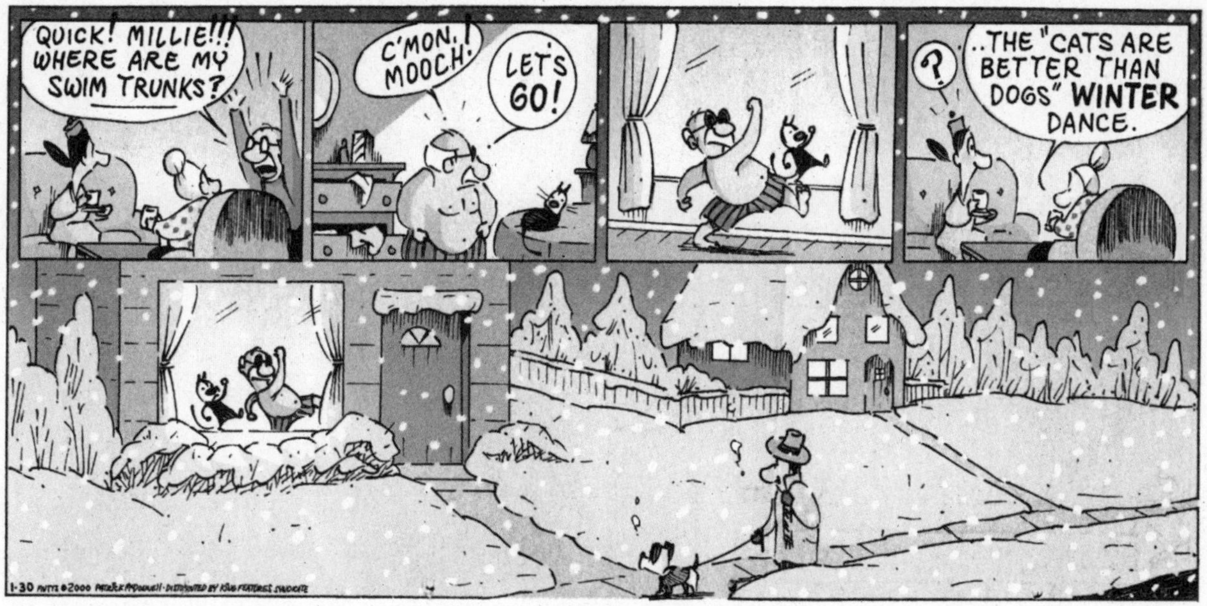
QUICK! MILLIE!!! WHERE ARE MY SWIM TRUNKS?
C'MON, MOOCH!
LET'S GO!
?
...THE "CATS ARE BETTER THAN DOGS" WINTER DANCE.
1-30

THIS IS MY "YOU NEED TO HUG A KITTY" FACE.
LIKE A CHARM.
3·13

THIS IS MY "I HAVEN'T THE FAINTEST IDEA WHAT YOU'RE TALKING ABOUT" FACE.
WHO KNOCKED OVER MY MILK SHAKE!?!
AAAARGHH...
THE SECRET IS TO KEEP FROM LAUGHING.

THIS IS MY "HE'S GOT THAT CRAZY LOOK IN HIS EYES" FACE.
WHAT YOU SEE IS WHAT YOU GET.
3·15

THIS IS MY "DON'T MESS WITH ME" FACE.
SMAK
IT NEEDS WORK.

THIS IS MY "POOR PO HUNGRY WITTLE KITTY" FACE.
THIS IS MY "I JUST FED YOU AN HOUR AGO!" FACE.
I'VE BEEN OUT-FACED.
3·17

THIS IS MY "WHAT ARE YOU- SOME KIND OF WISEGUY?" FACE.
SO WHAT.

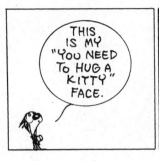

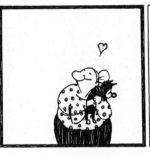

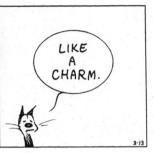

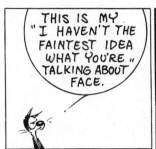

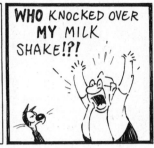

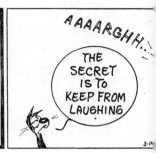

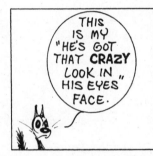

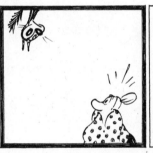

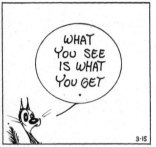

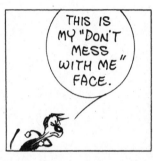

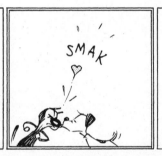

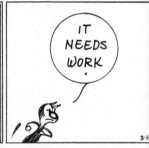

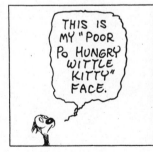

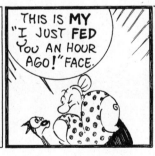

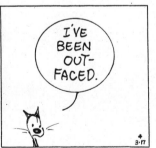

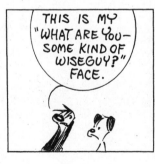

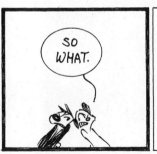

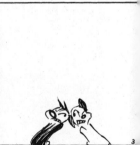

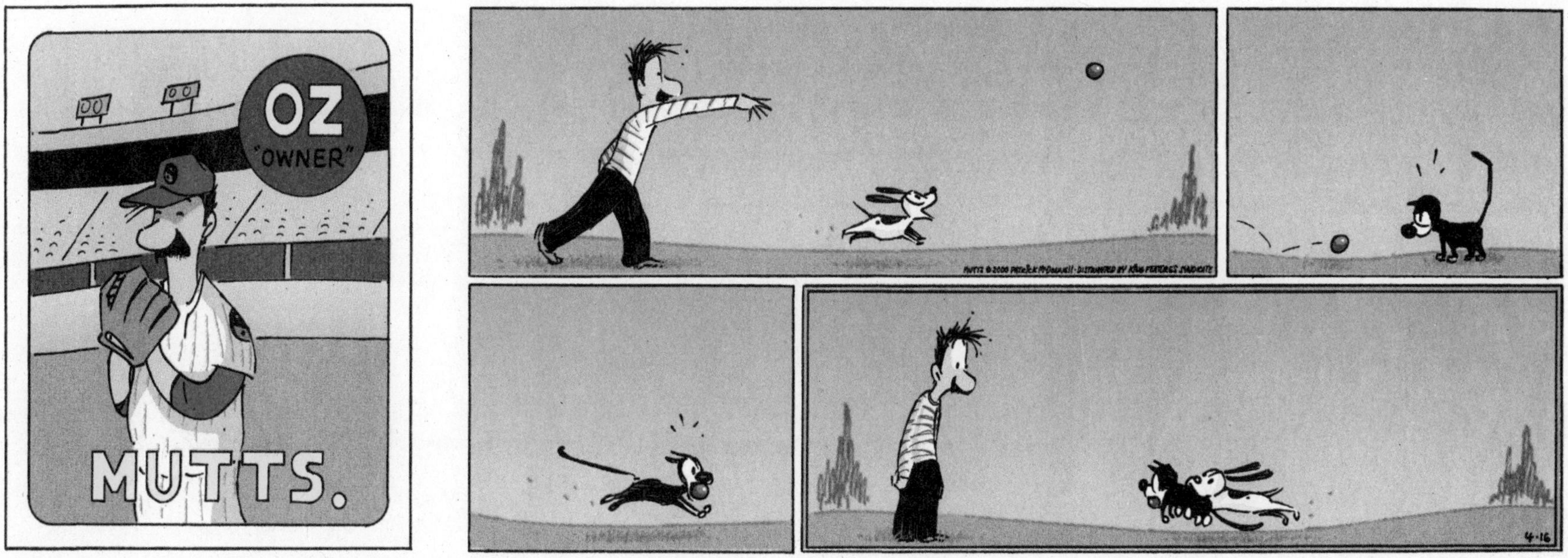
OZ
"OWNER"
MUTTS.
MUTTS © 2000 PATRICK McDONNELL · DISTRIBUTED BY KING FEATURES SYNDICATE
4·16

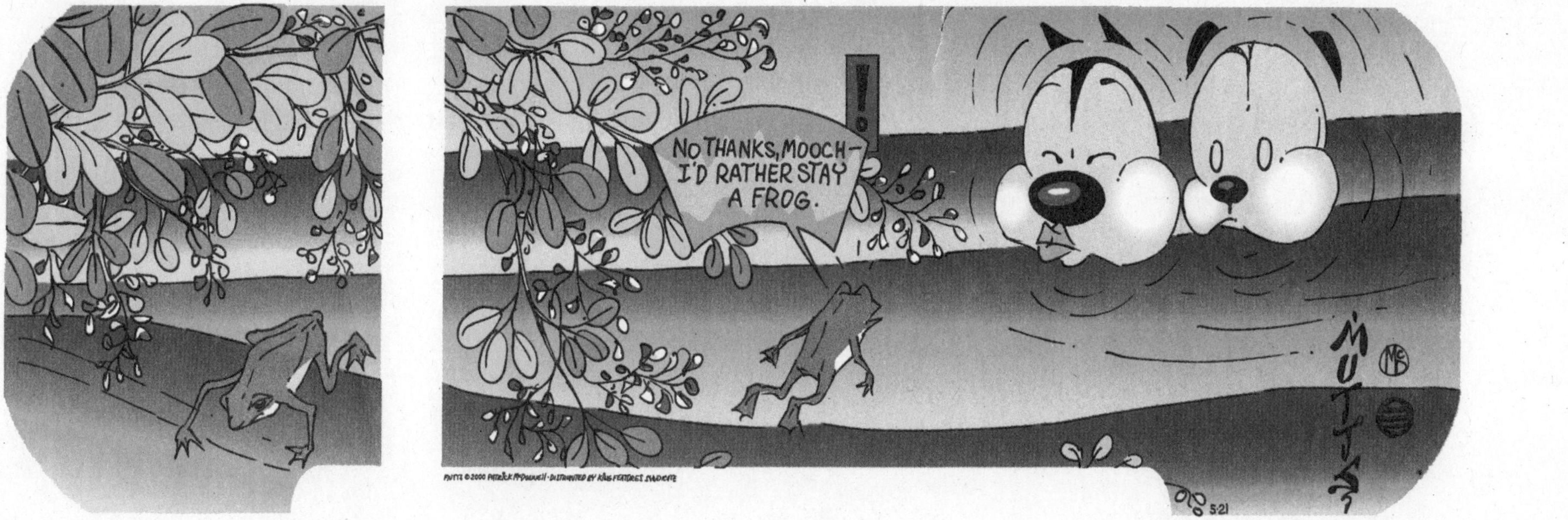
NO THANKS, MOOCH—
I'D RATHER STAY
A FROG.
!
MUTTS
MUTTS © 2000 PATRICK McDONNELL · DISTRIBUTED BY KING FEATURES SYNDICATE
5·21

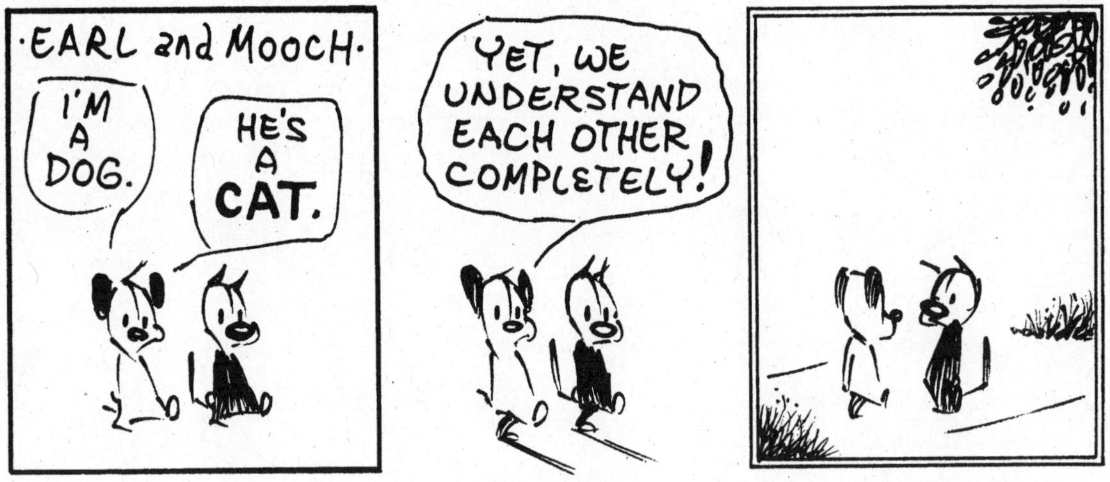
·EARL and MOOCH·
I'M A DOG.
HE'S A CAT.
YET, WE UNDERSTAND EACH OTHER COMPLETELY!
WHAT ARE YOU TALKING ABOUT!?!

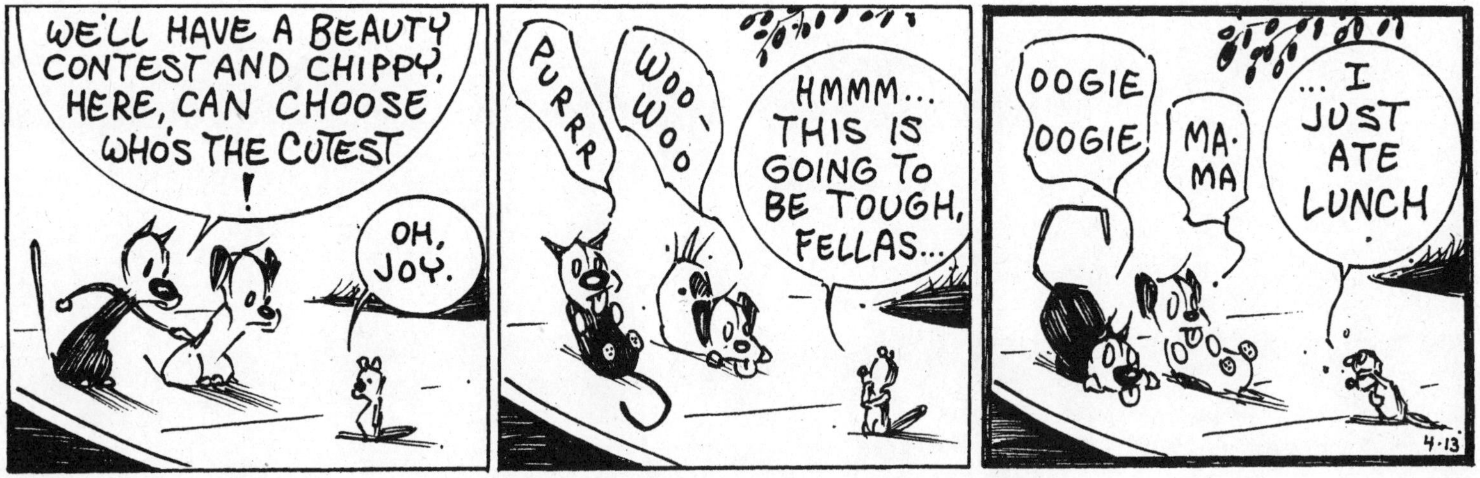
WE'LL HAVE A BEAUTY CONTEST AND CHIPPY, HERE, CAN CHOOSE WHO'S THE CUTEST!
OH, JOY.
PURRR
WOO-WOO
HMMM... THIS IS GOING TO BE TOUGH, FELLAS...
OOGIE OOGIE
MA·MA
... I JUST ATE LUNCH.
4·13

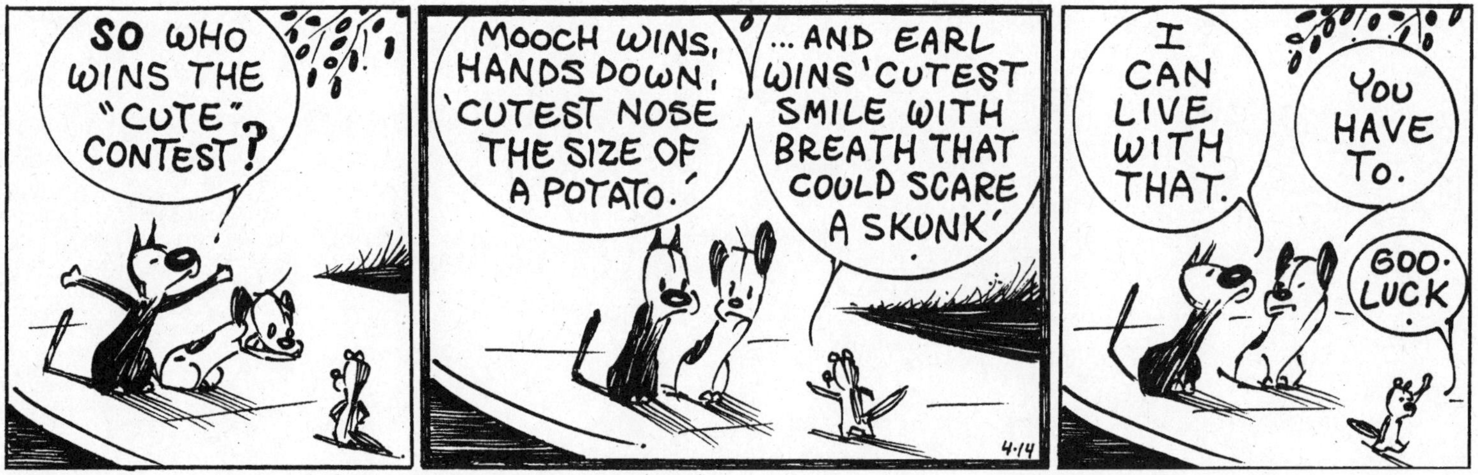
SO WHO WINS THE "CUTE" CONTEST?
MOOCH WINS, HANDS DOWN. 'CUTEST NOSE THE SIZE OF A POTATO.'
... AND EARL WINS 'CUTEST SMILE WITH BREATH THAT COULD SCARE A SKUNK'
I CAN LIVE WITH THAT.
YOU HAVE TO.
GOO·LUCK.
4·14

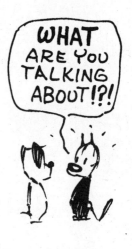

MOOCH, LET'S JUST SIT HERE AND WATCH THE WORLD GO BY.
YESH.
MY
GLOBE!!!
BONK
BONK
BONK
OKAY— NOW WHAT?
5·22

4·6

I CAN'T FIND THE KEYS!!!
HURRY!
CRACK
AAIEE! THIS IS HORRIBLE!
WHO'S GOING TO FEED THE KITTY !?!
4·4

OH, SOURPUSS, FOR ALL THE TIME WE'VE SPENT TOGETHER— I'VE NEVER HEARD YOU PURR..
SIGH..
WELL... I GUESS I'LL JUST LEAVE YOU ALONE.
8/23
PURRRRR....

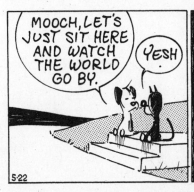

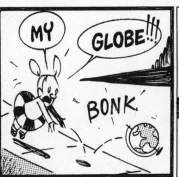

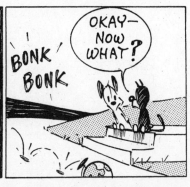

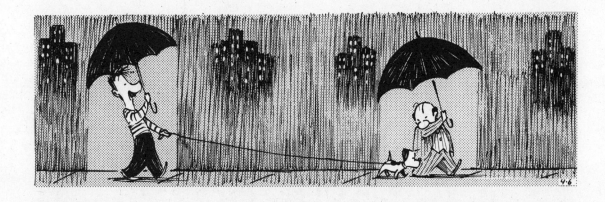

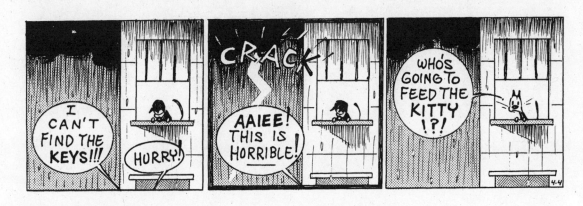

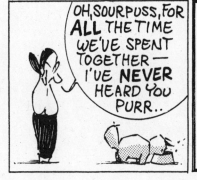

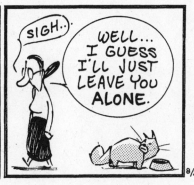

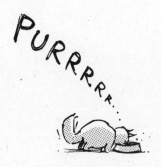

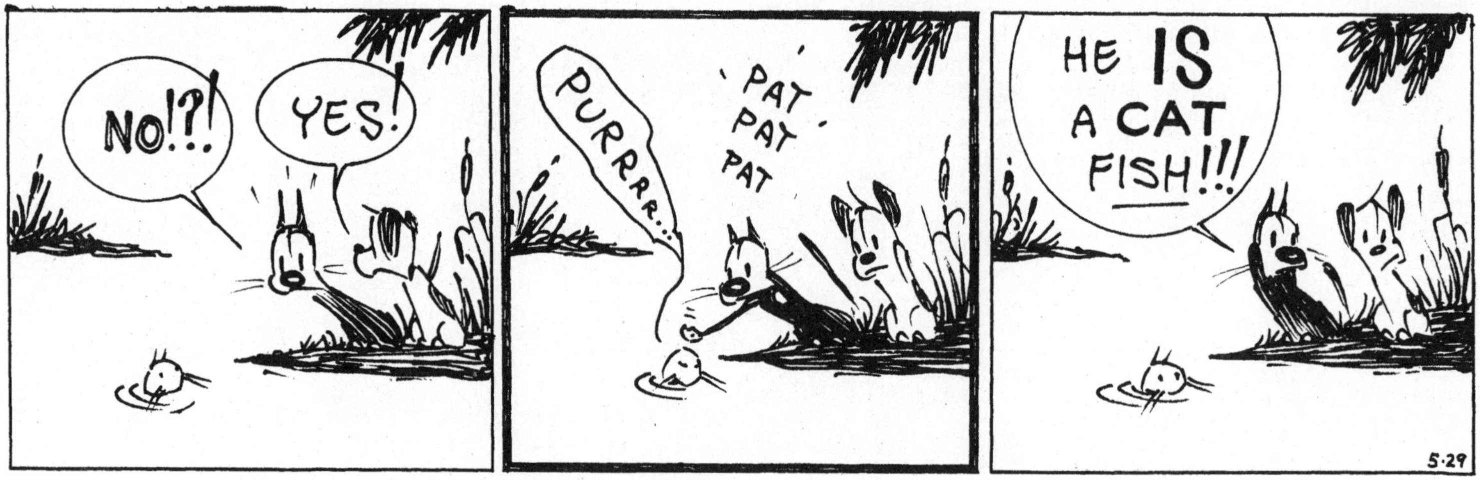
NO!?!
YES!
PURRRR...
PAT PAT PAT
HE IS A CAT FISH!!!
5·29

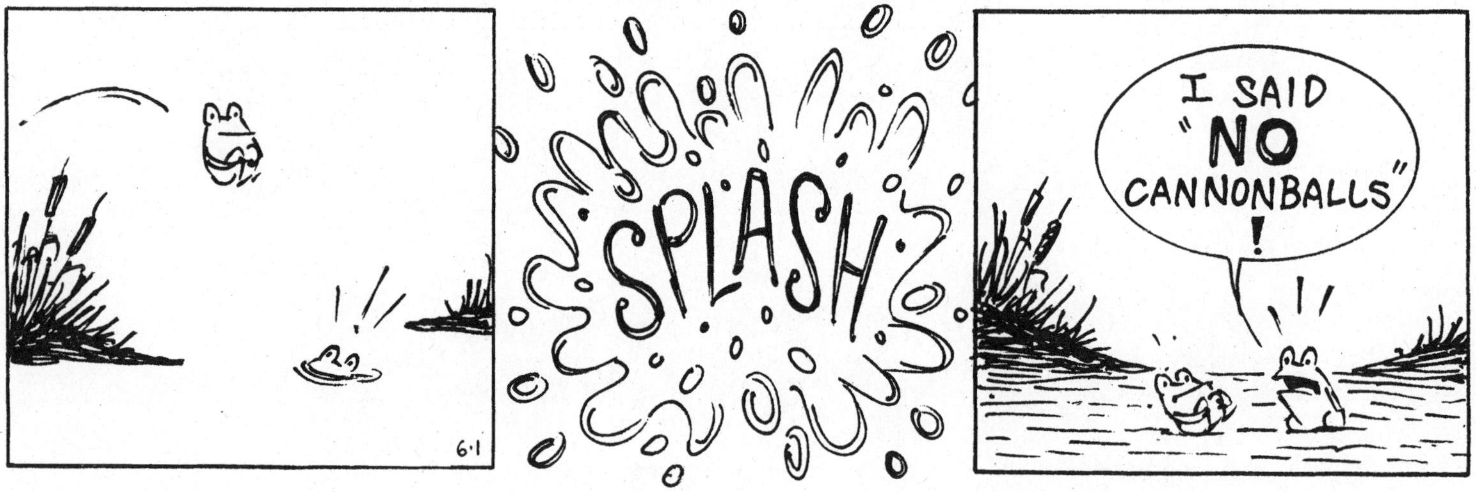
6·1
SPLASH
I SAID "NO CANNONBALLS"!

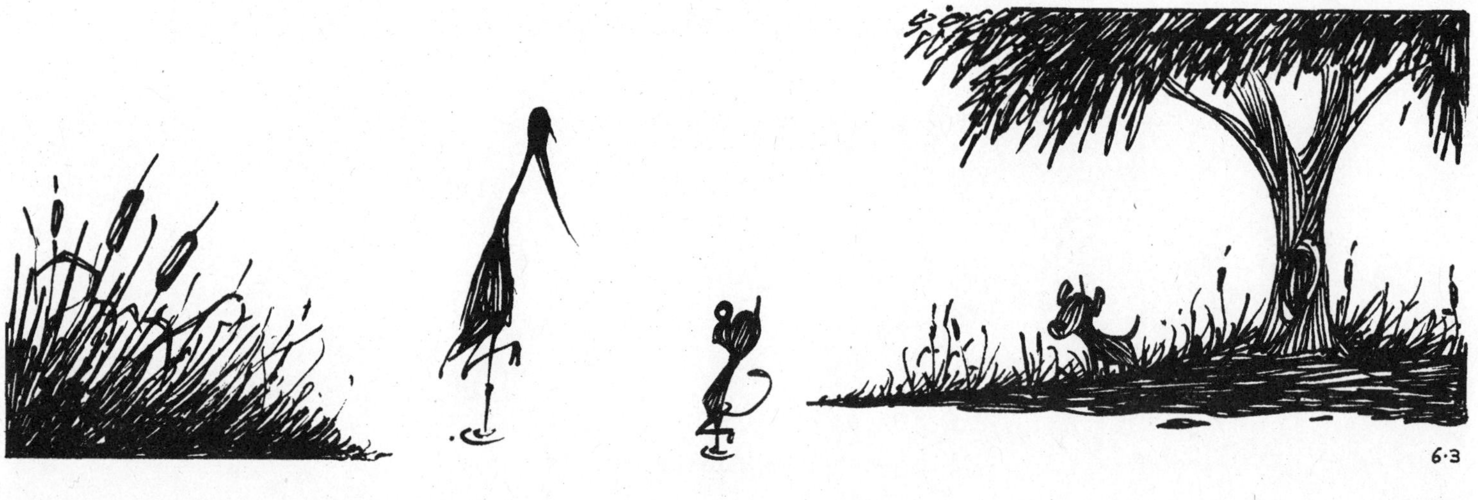
6·3

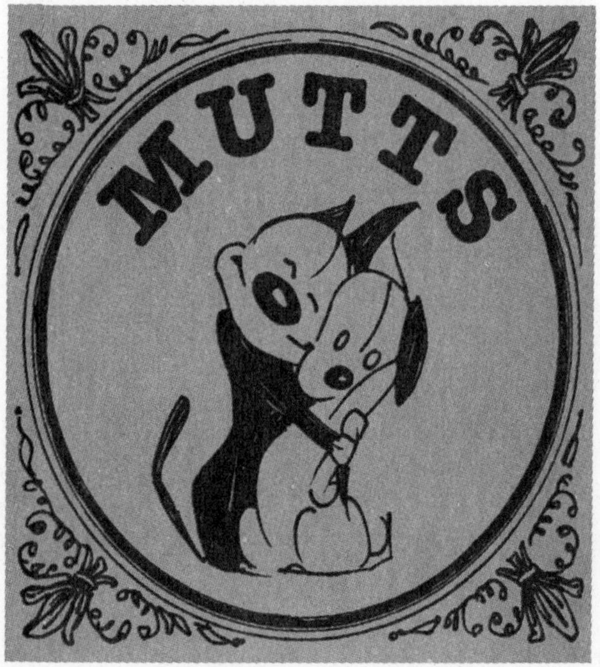
MUTTS

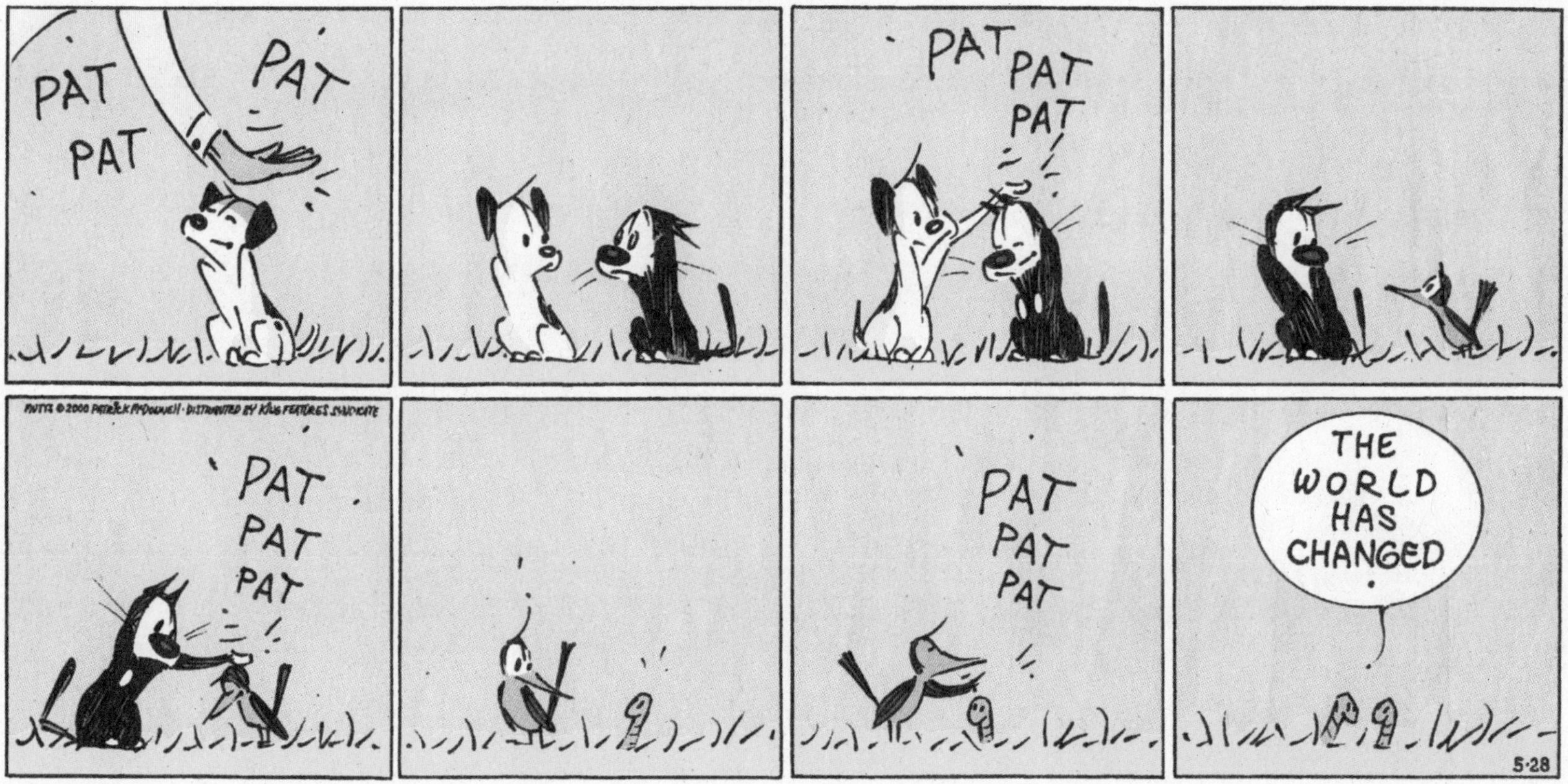
PAT
PAT
PAT
PAT
PAT
PAT
MUTTS © 2000 PATRICK McDONNELL · DISTRIBUTED BY KING FEATURES SYNDICATE
PAT
PAT
PAT
PAT
PAT
PAT
THE WORLD HAS CHANGED.
5·28

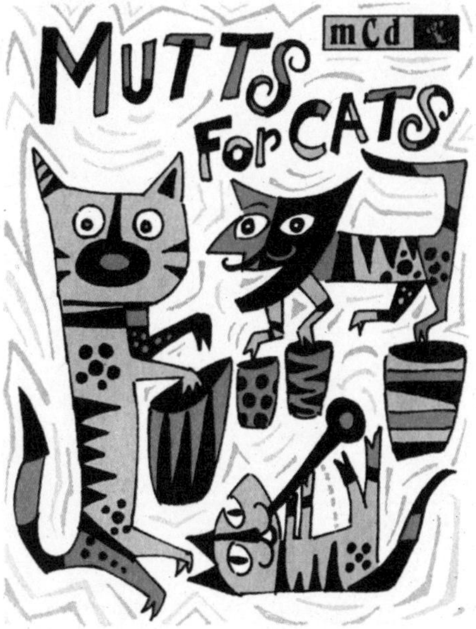
MUTTS For CATS
mCd

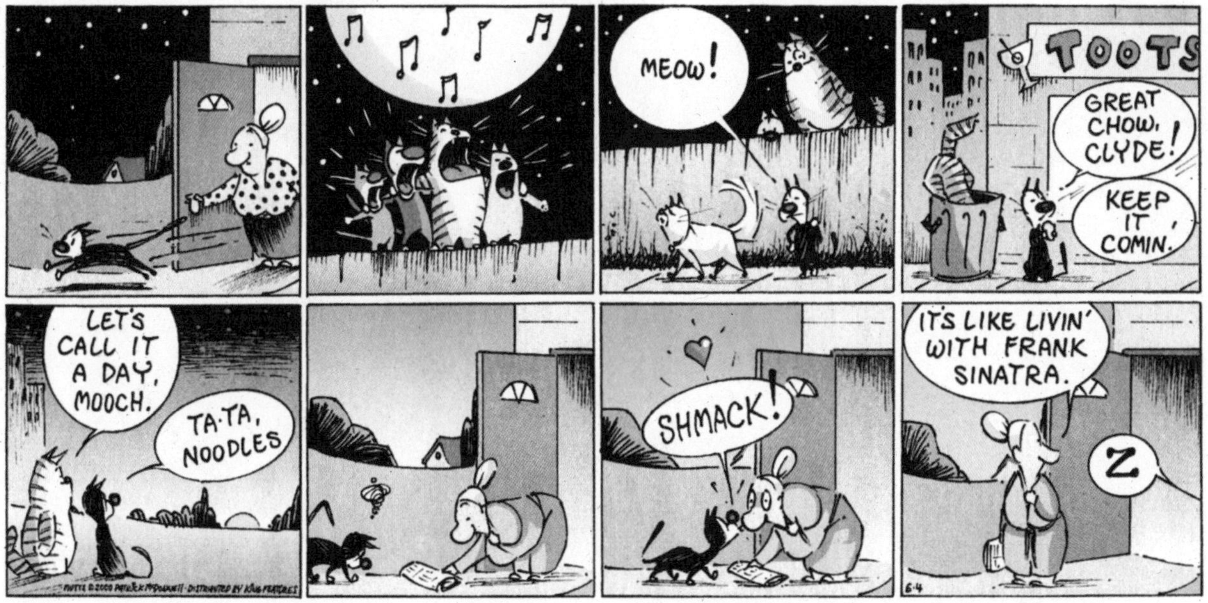
MEOW!
TOOTS
GREAT CHOW, CLYDE!
KEEP IT COMIN'.
LET'S CALL IT A DAY, MOOCH.
TA-TA, NOODLES
SHMACK!
IT'S LIKE LIVIN' WITH FRANK SINATRA.
Z
6·4

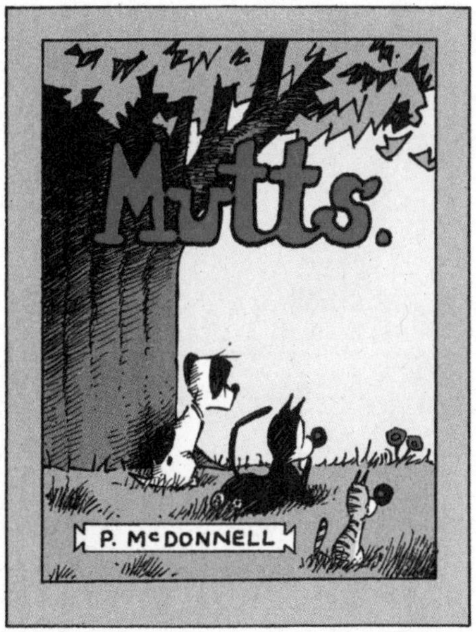
Mutts.
P. McDONNELL

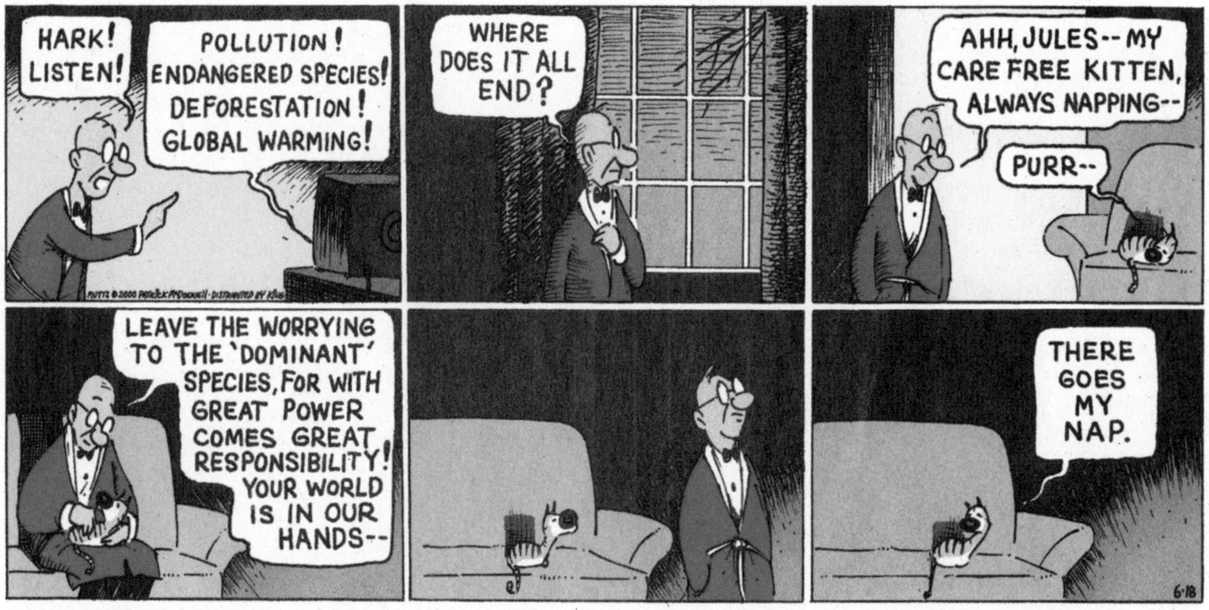
HARK! LISTEN!
POLLUTION! ENDANGERED SPECIES! DEFORESTATION! GLOBAL WARMING!
WHERE DOES IT ALL END?
AHH, JULES-- MY CARE FREE KITTEN, ALWAYS NAPPING--
PURR--
LEAVE THE WORRYING TO THE 'DOMINANT' SPECIES, FOR WITH GREAT POWER COMES GREAT RESPONSIBILITY! YOUR WORLD IS IN OUR HANDS--
THERE GOES MY NAP.
6·18

IT'S ME!

HEY, EARL- COME OVER AND MEET THIS SHNOUT.
6·13

I KEEP THINKING IT'S TUESDAY.
6·14

WOW.
A FOUR-LEAF CLOVER
6·15

OUR FIRST SHPAT.

BZZZZZ....
SO-
WE MEET AGAIN.
6·17

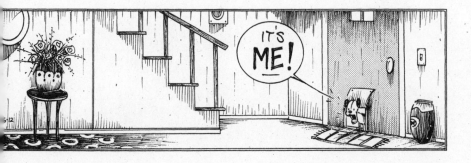

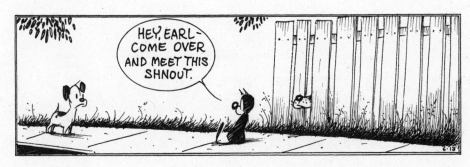

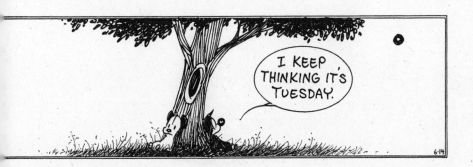

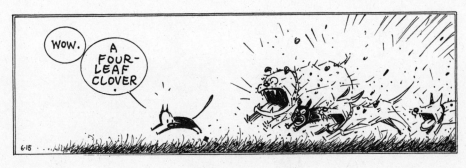

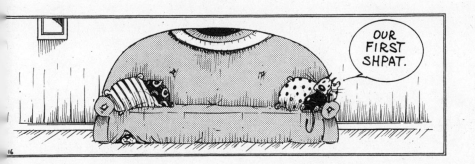

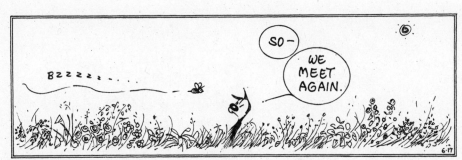

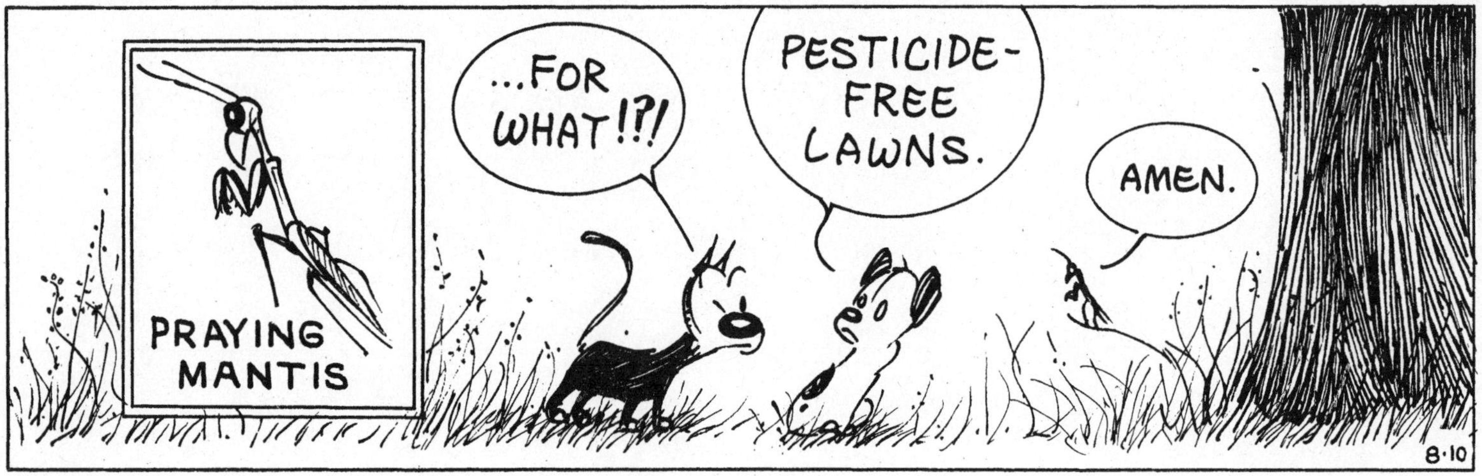
PRAYING MANTIS
...FOR WHAT!?!
PESTICIDE-FREE LAWNS.
AMEN.
8·10

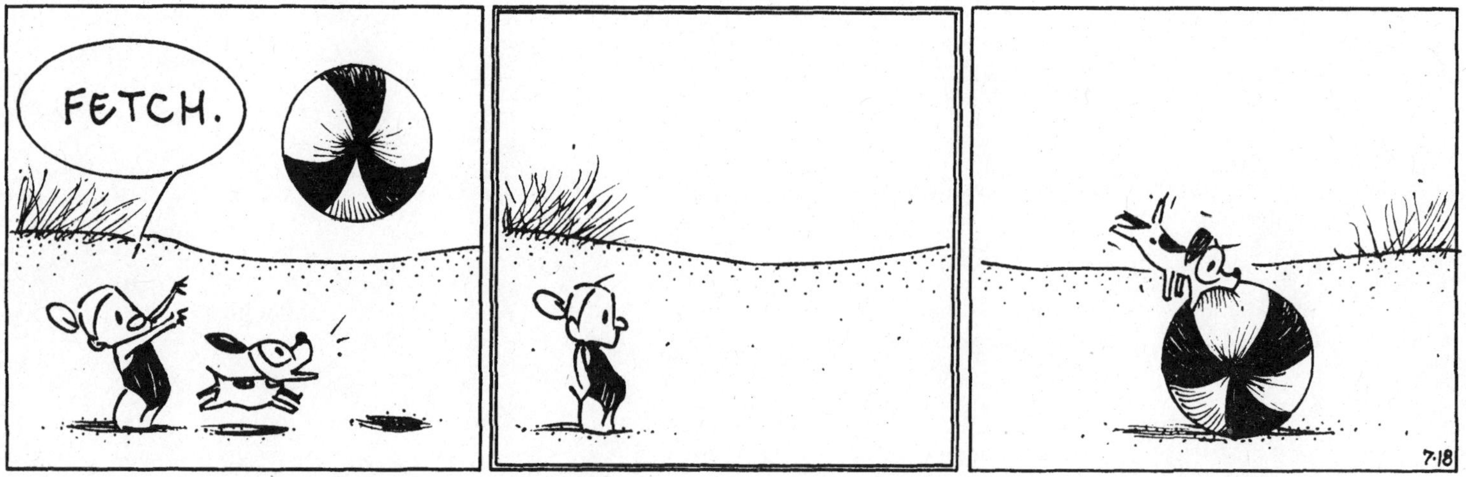
FETCH.
7·18

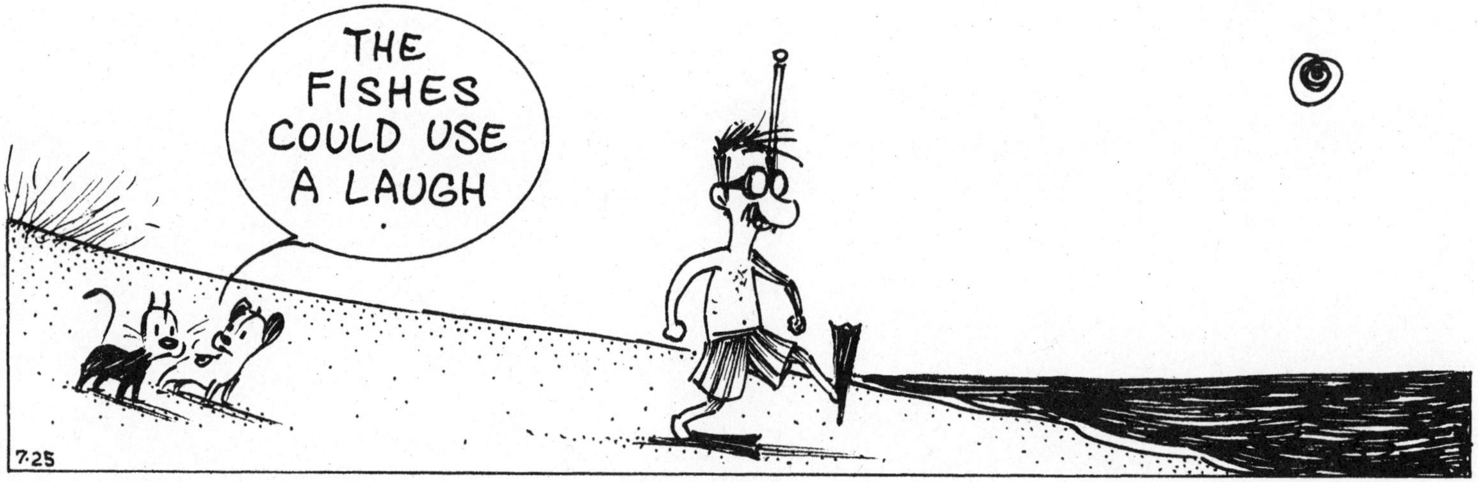
THE FISHES COULD USE A LAUGH
7·25

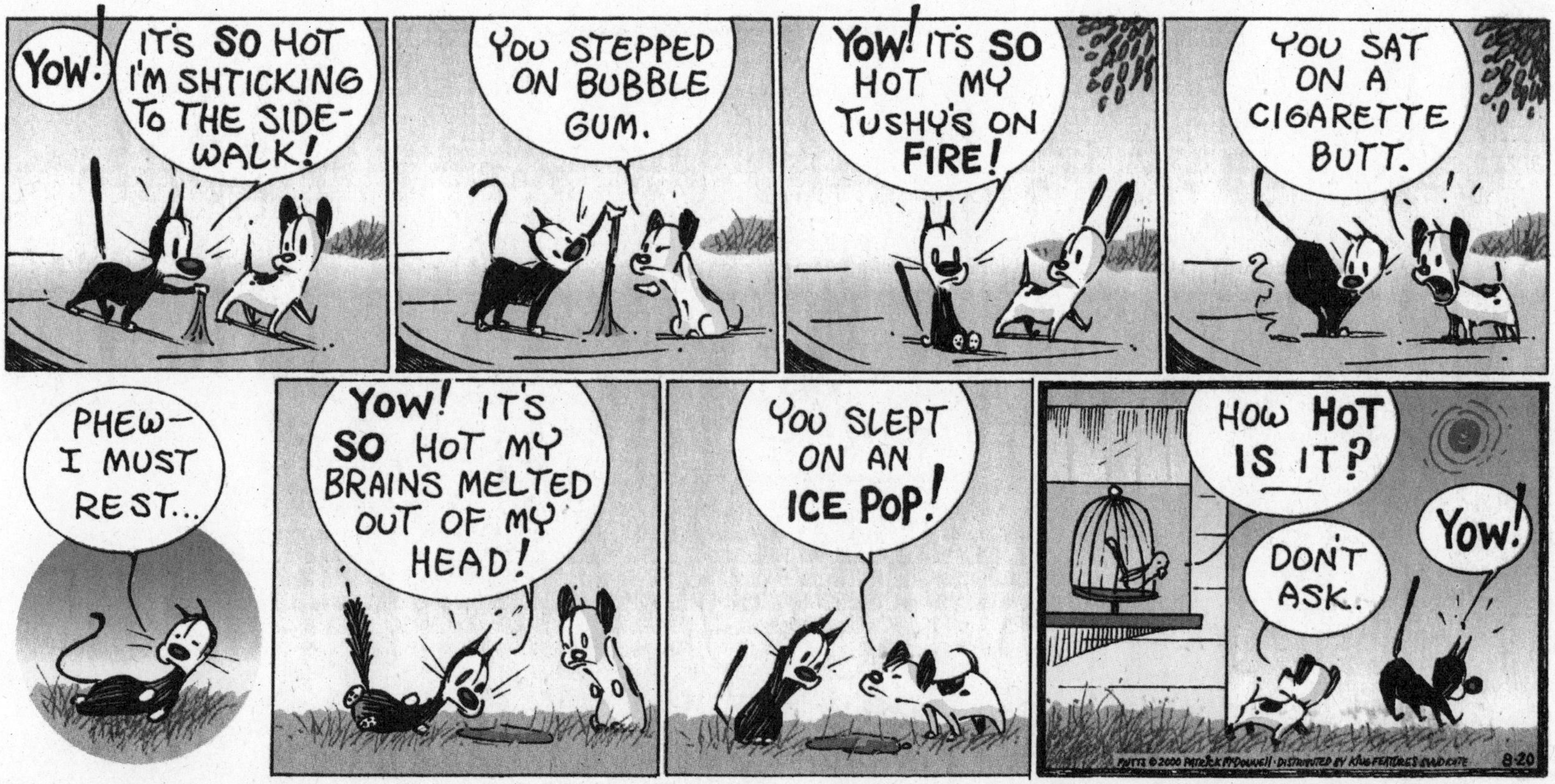
YOW!
IT'S SO HOT I'M SHTICKING TO THE SIDEWALK!
YOU STEPPED ON BUBBLE GUM.
YOW! IT'S SO HOT MY TUSHY'S ON FIRE!
YOU SAT ON A CIGARETTE BUTT.
PHEW— I MUST REST...
YOW! IT'S SO HOT MY BRAINS MELTED OUT OF MY HEAD!
YOU SLEPT ON AN ICE POP!
HOW HOT IS IT?
DON'T ASK.
YOW!
MUTTS © 2000 PATRICK McDONNELL · DISTRIBUTED BY KING FEATURES SYNDICATE
8·20

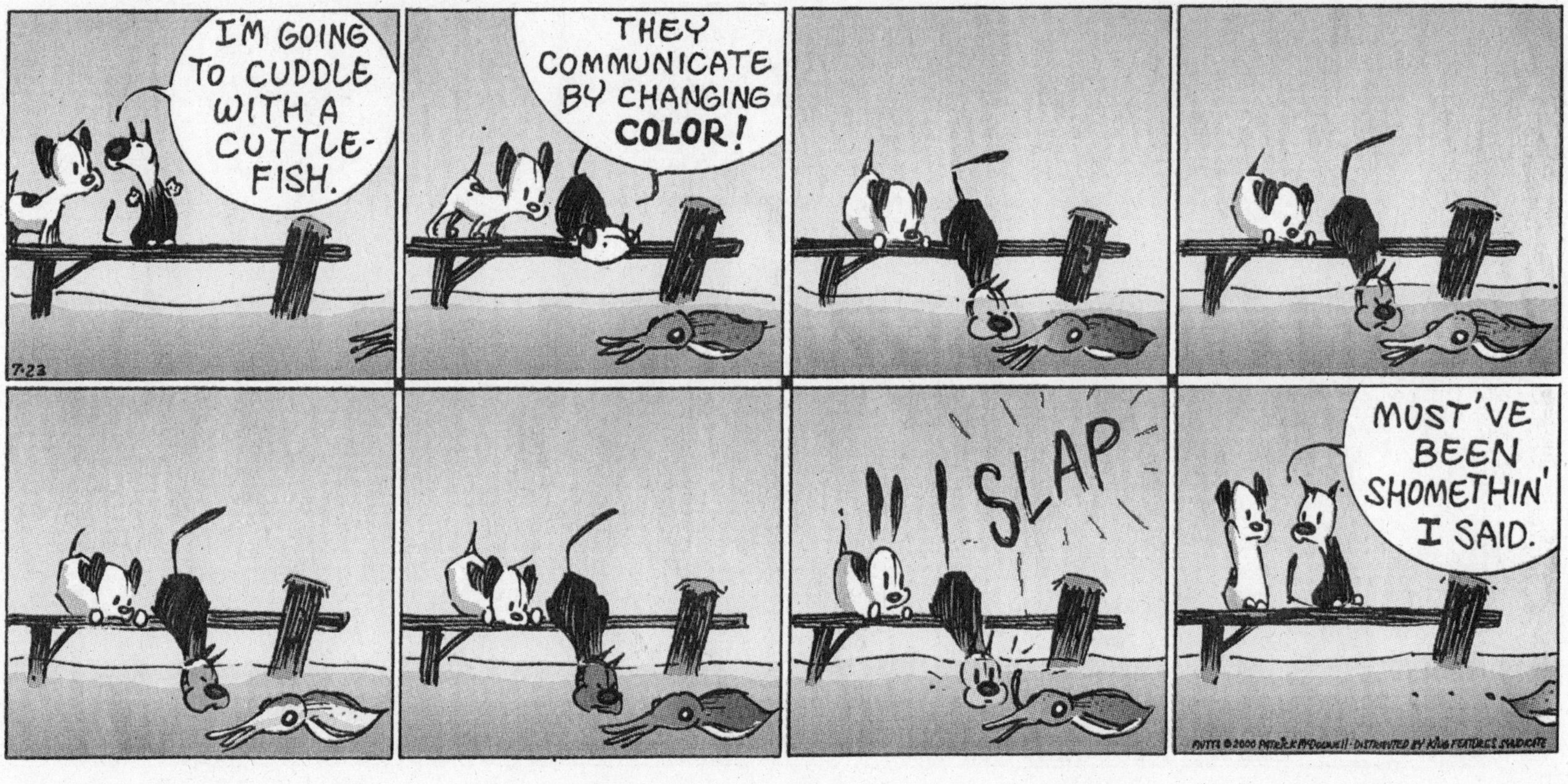
7·23
I'M GOING TO CUDDLE WITH A CUTTLEFISH.
THEY COMMUNICATE BY CHANGING COLOR!
SLAP
MUST'VE BEEN SHOMETHIN' I SAID.
MUTTS © 2000 PATRICK McDONNELL · DISTRIBUTED BY KING FEATURES SYNDICATE

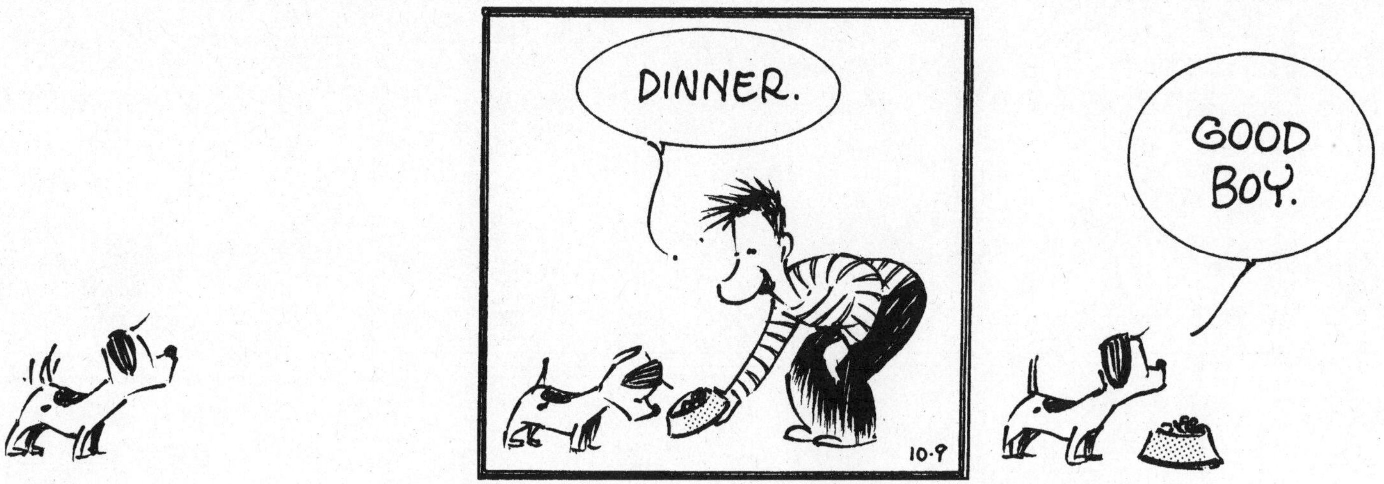
DINNER.
GOOD BOY.
10·9

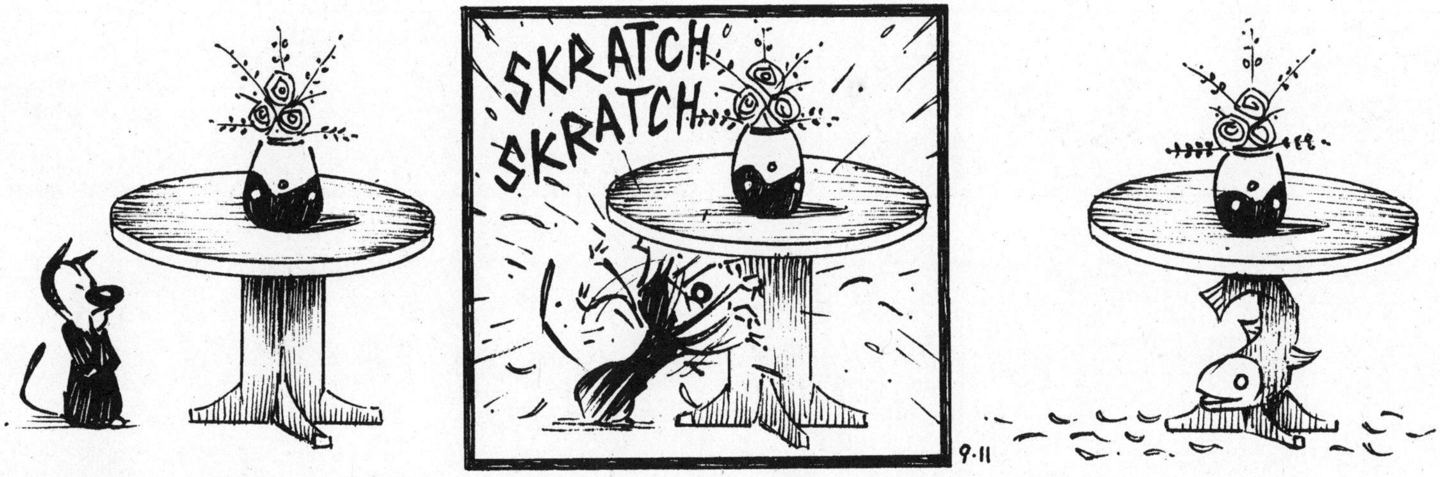
SKRATCH
SKRATCH
9·11

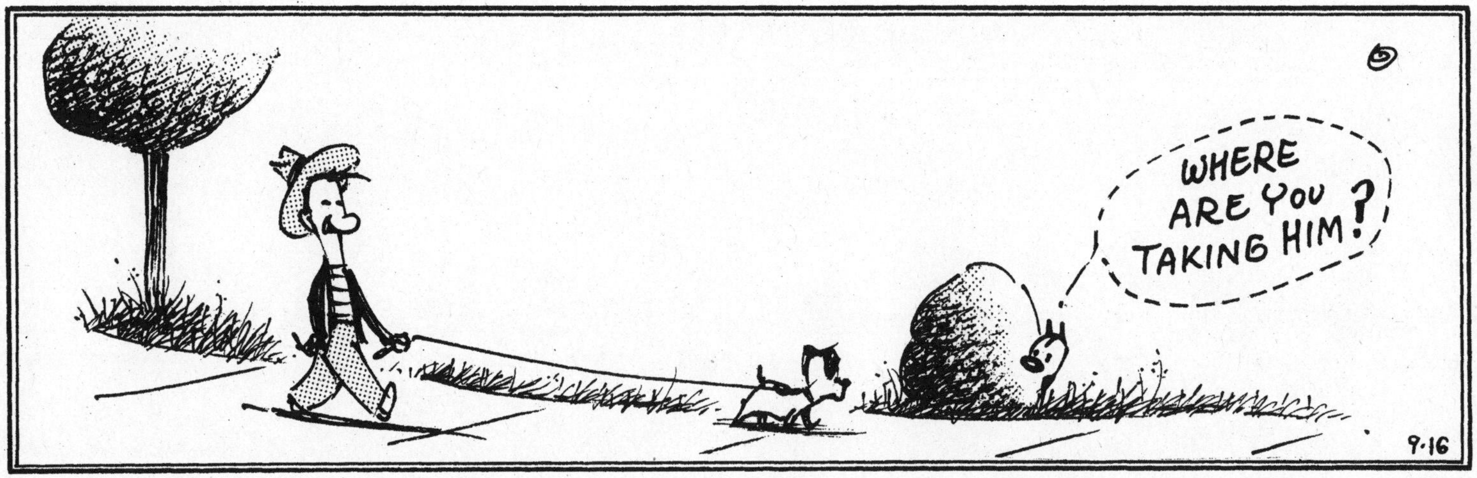
WHERE ARE YOU TAKING HIM?
9·16

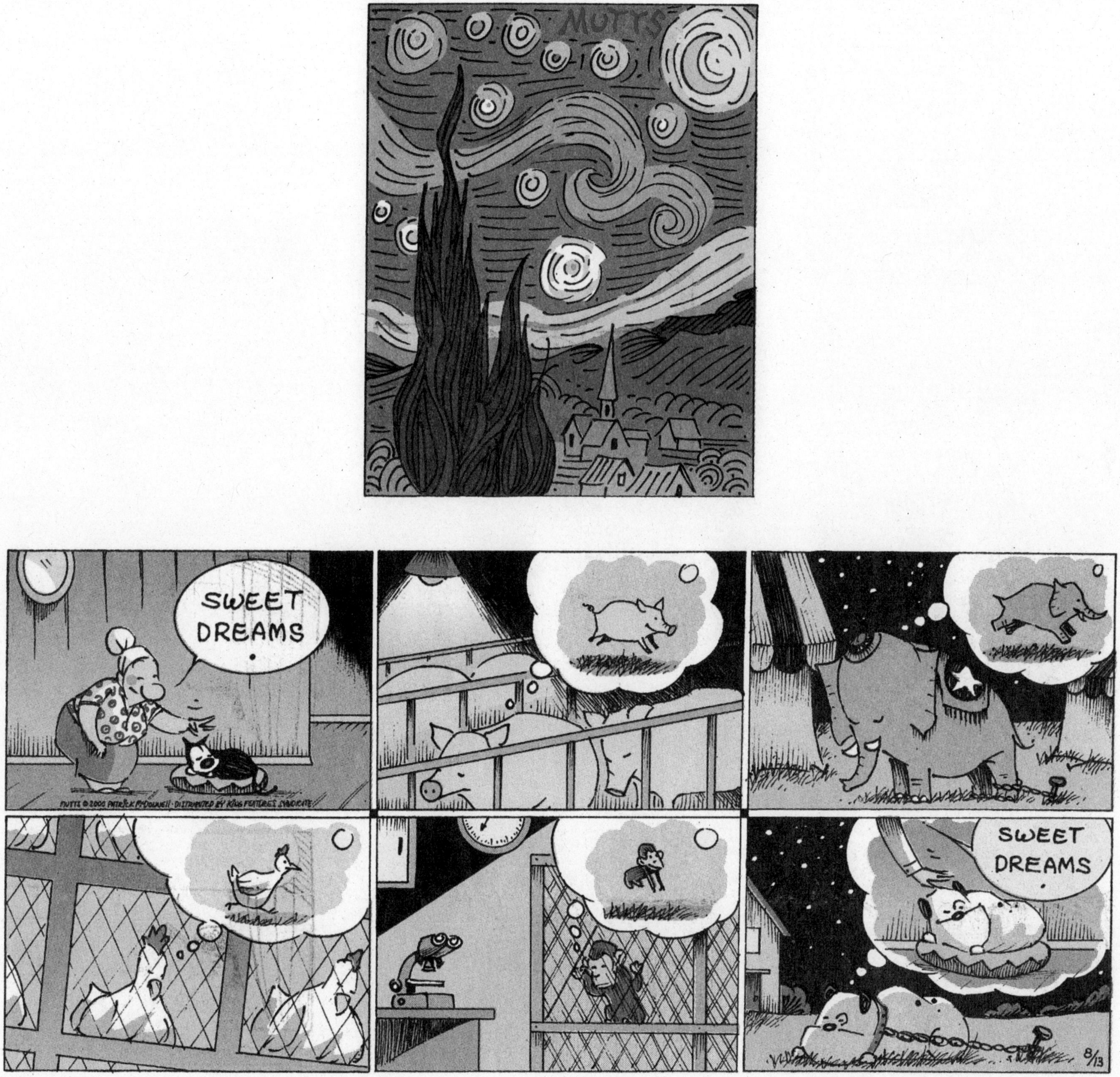
MUTTS
SWEET DREAMS.
MUTTS © 2000 PATRICK McDONNELL · DISTRIBUTED BY KING FEATURES SYNDICATE
SWEET DREAMS.
8/13

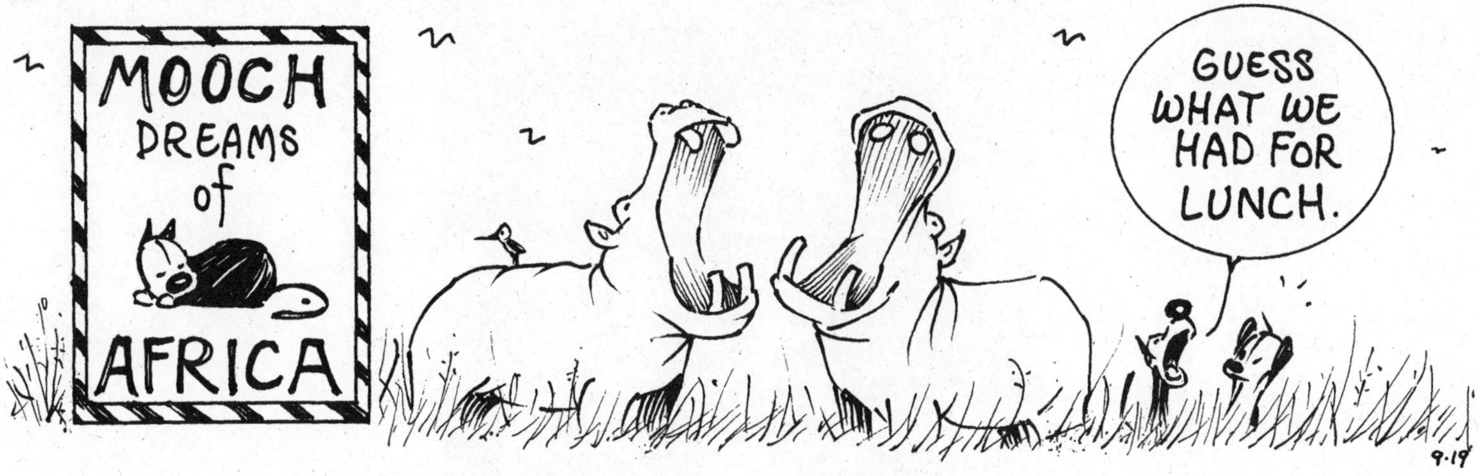
MOOCH DREAMS of AFRICA
GUESS WHAT WE HAD FOR LUNCH.
9·19

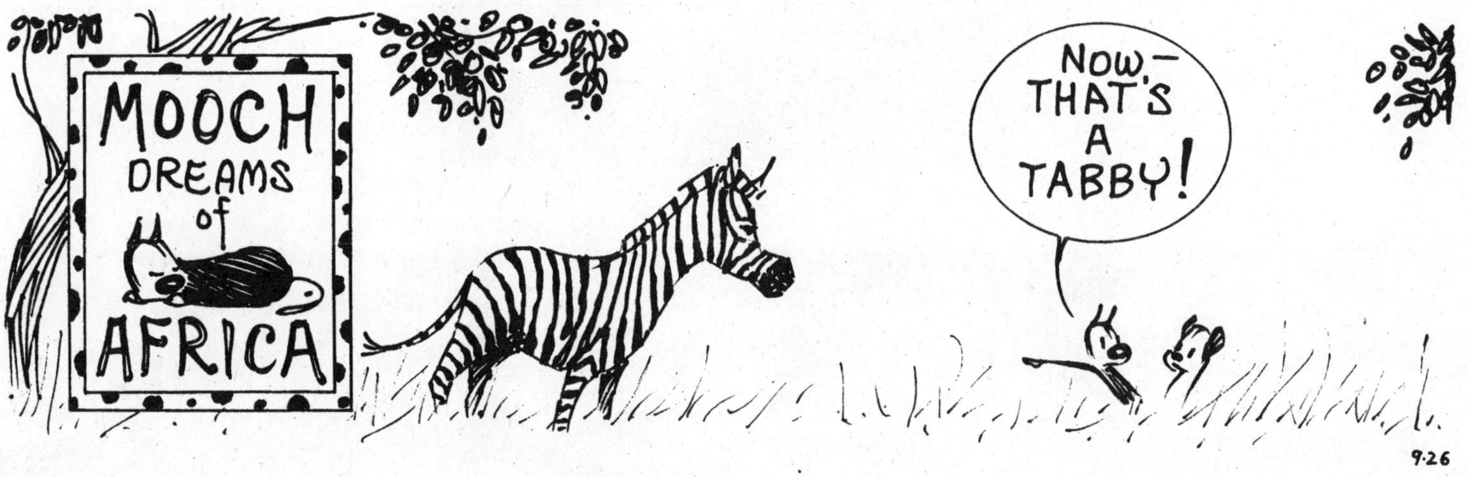
MOOCH DREAMS of AFRICA
NOW— THAT'S A TABBY!
9·26

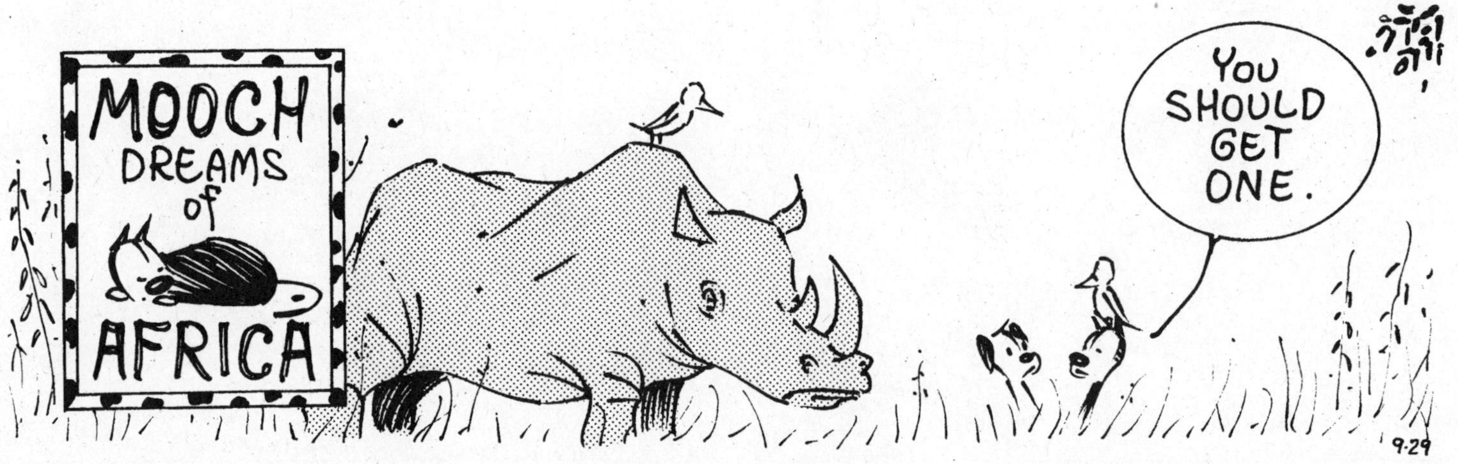
MOOCH DREAMS of AFRICA
YOU SHOULD GET ONE.
9·29

MUTTS

MOOCH DREAMS of AFRICA
WE'RE SCARED.
10·22 MUTTS © 2000 PATRICK McDONNELL · DISTRIBUTED BY KING FEATURES

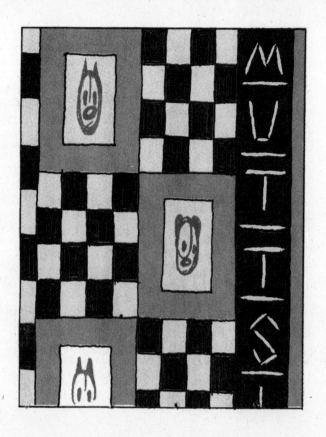

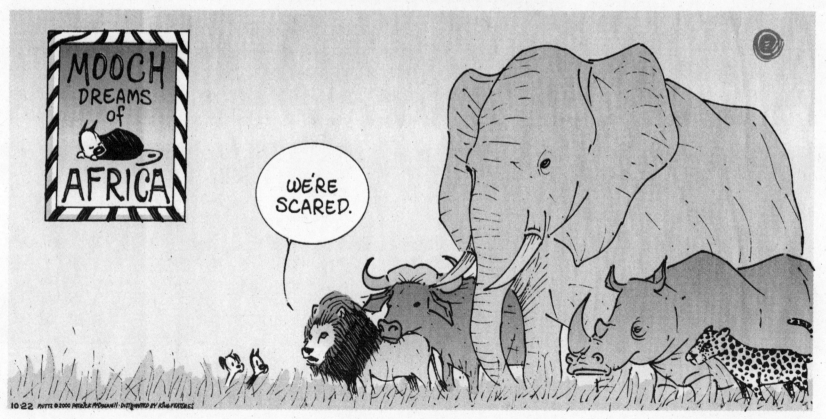

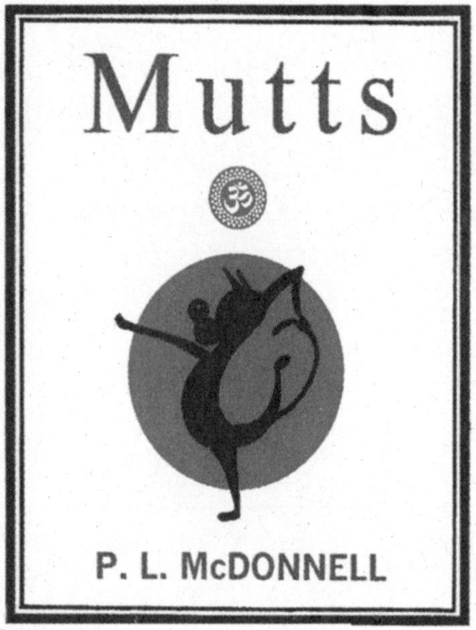
Mutts
P. L. McDONNELL

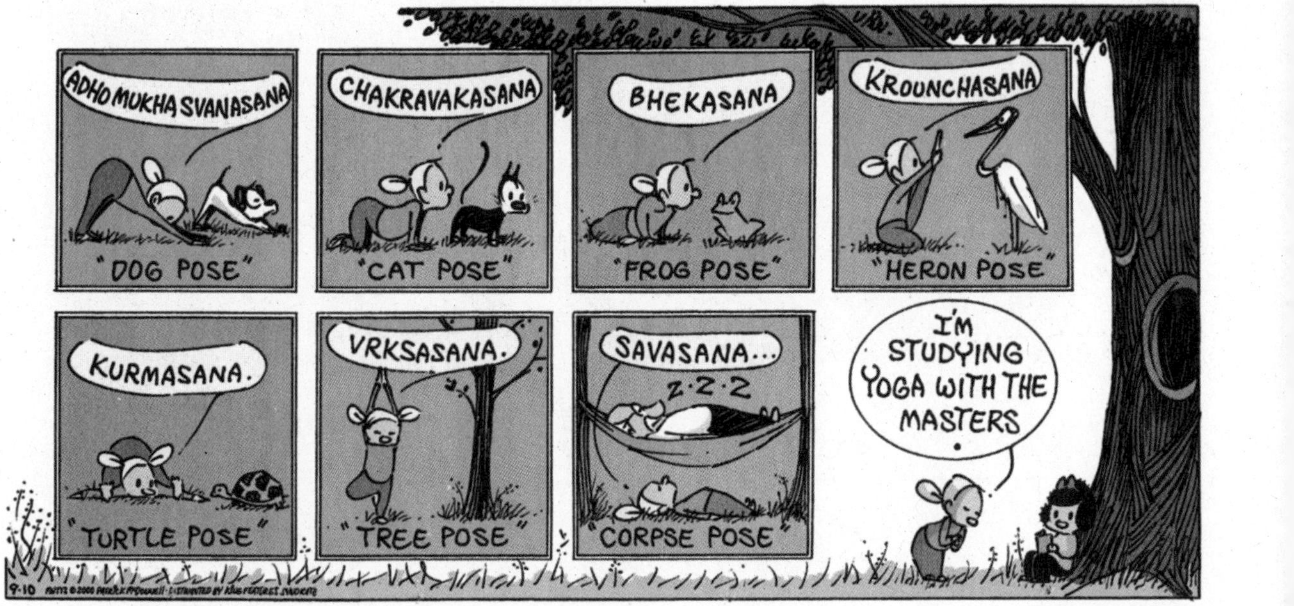
ADHO MUKHA SVANASANA
"DOG POSE"
CHAKRAVAKASANA
"CAT POSE"
BHEKASANA
"FROG POSE"
KROUNCHASANA
"HERON POSE"
KURMASANA.
"TURTLE POSE"
VRKSASANA.
"TREE POSE"
SAVASANA...
Z·Z·Z
"CORPSE POSE"
I'M STUDYING YOGA WITH THE MASTERS.

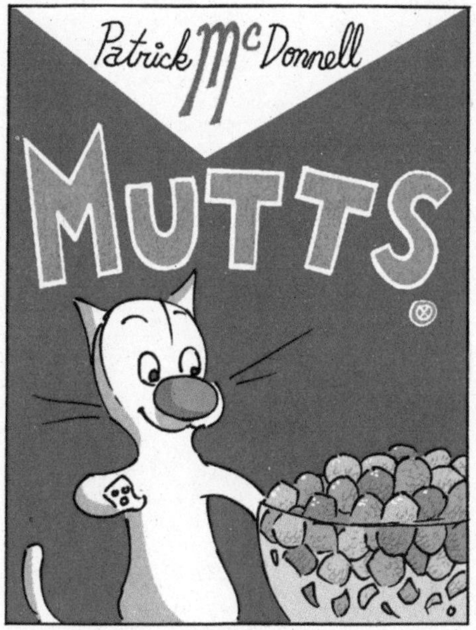
Patrick McDonnell
MUTTS

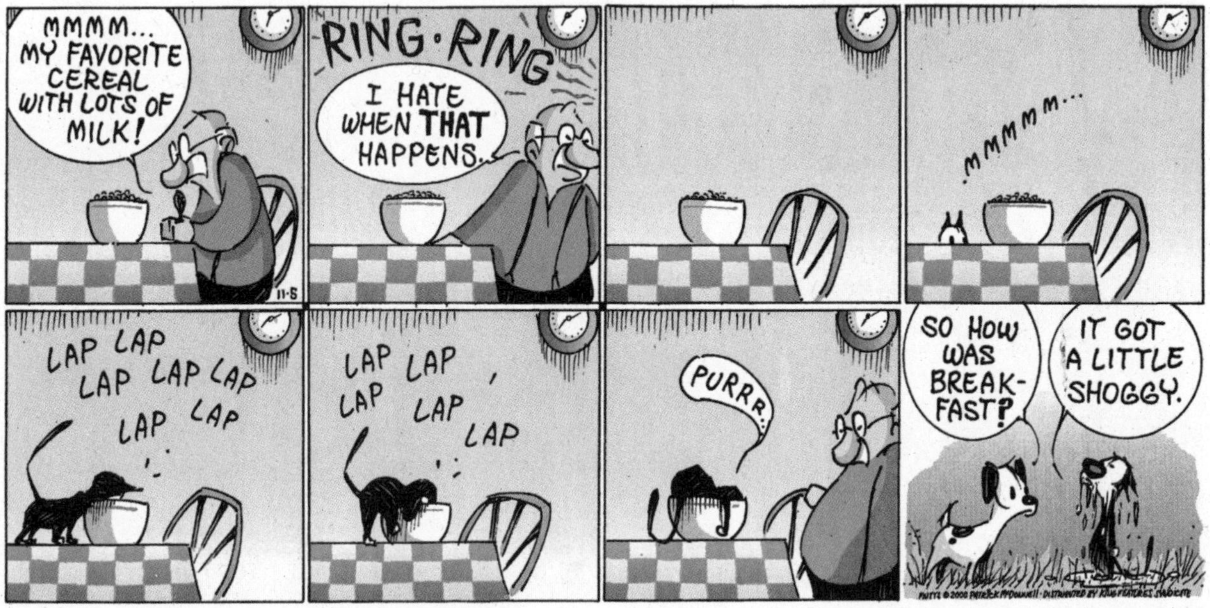
MMMM... MY FAVORITE CEREAL WITH LOTS OF MILK!
RING·RING
I HATE WHEN THAT HAPPENS.
MMMMM...
LAP LAP LAP LAP LAP LAP LAP
LAP LAP LAP LAP LAP
PURRR...
SO HOW WAS BREAK-FAST?
IT GOT A LITTLE SHOGGY.

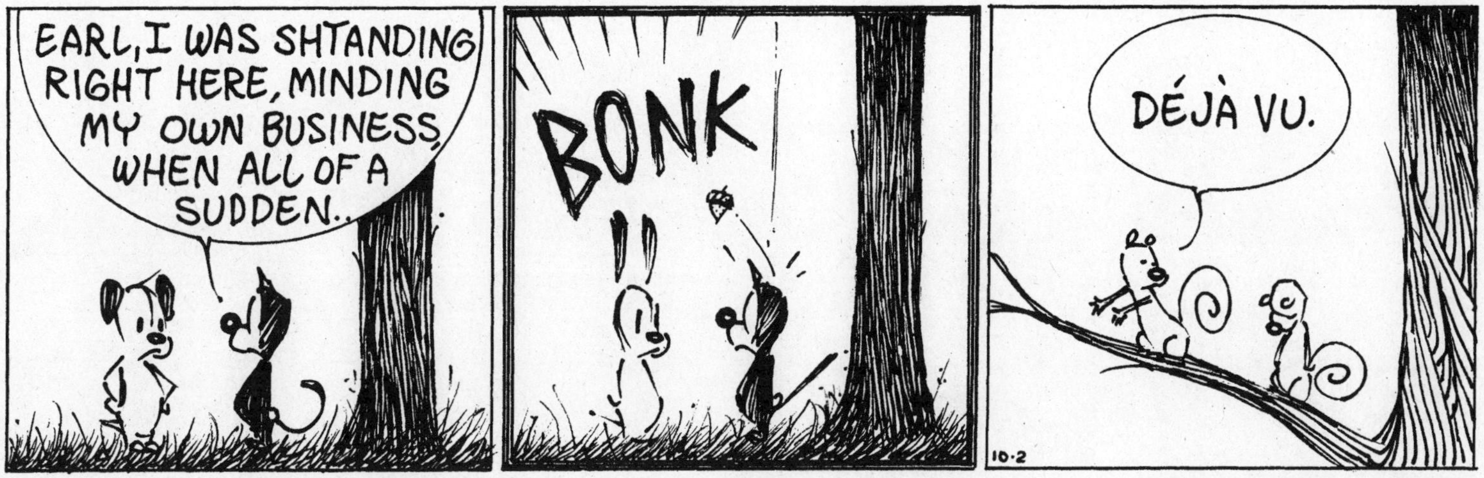
EARL, I WAS SHTANDING RIGHT HERE, MINDING MY OWN BUSINESS, WHEN ALL OF A SUDDEN...
BONK
DÉJÀ VU.
10·2

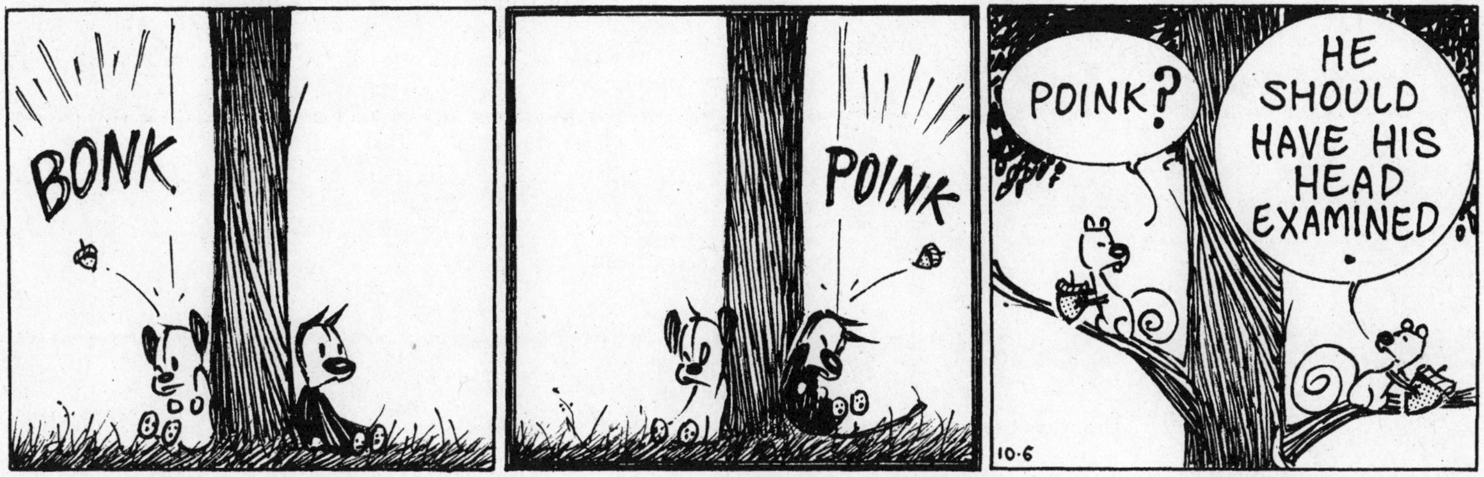
BONK
POINK
POINK?
HE SHOULD HAVE HIS HEAD EXAMINED.
10·6

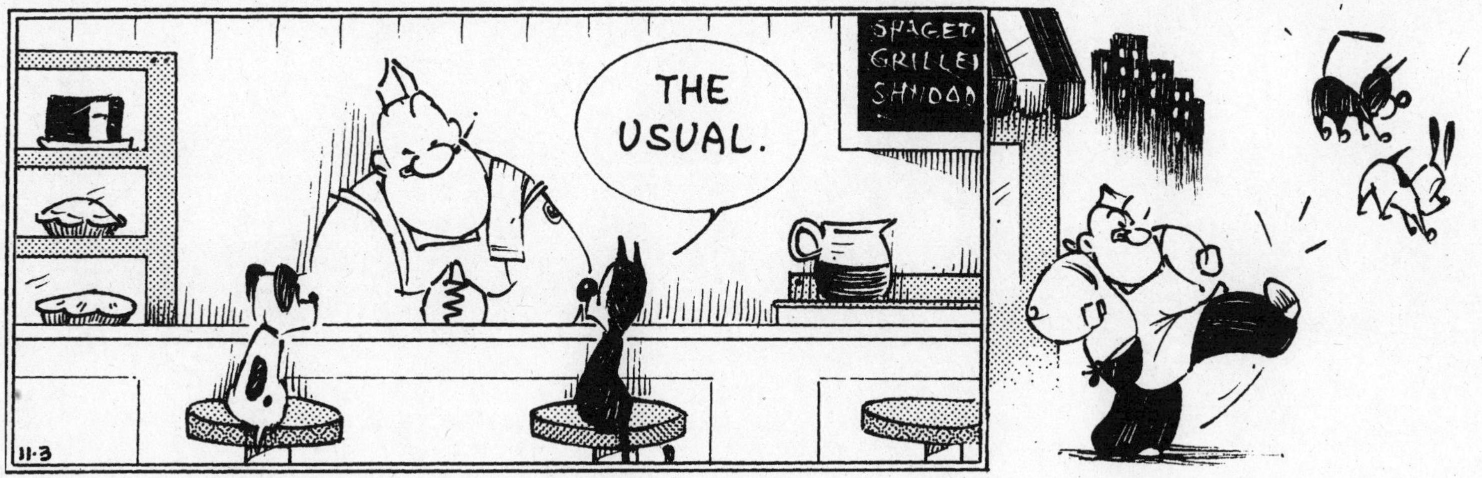
THE USUAL.
11·3

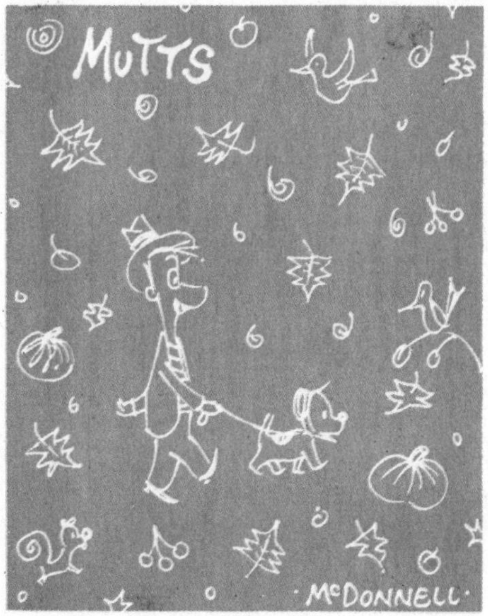
MUTTS
McDONNELL

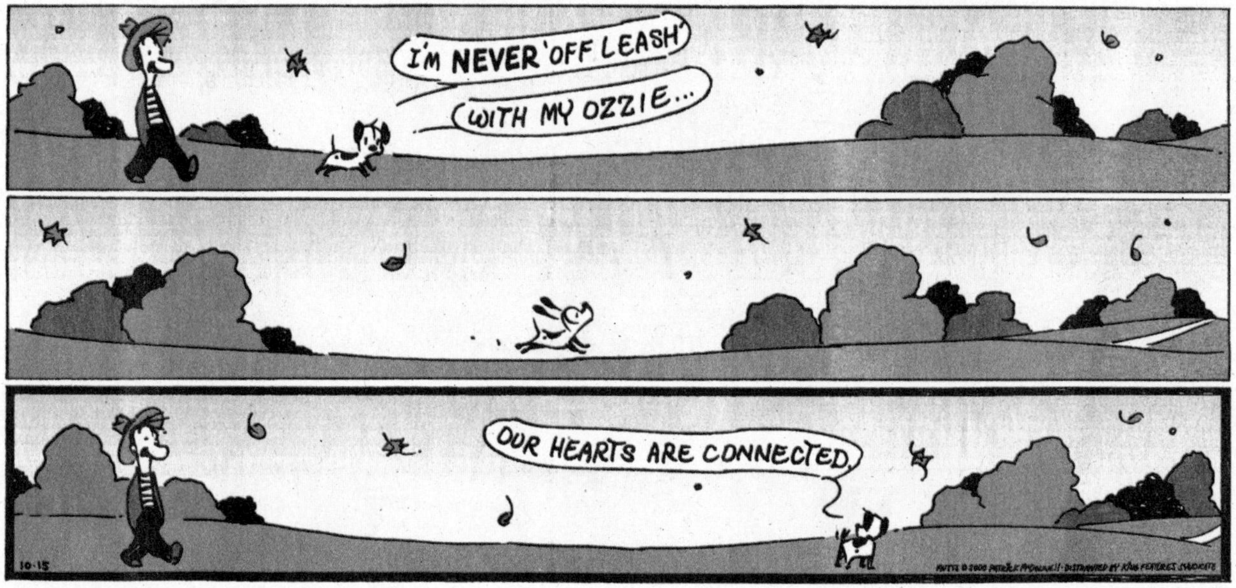
I'M NEVER 'OFF LEASH'
WITH MY OZZIE...
OUR HEARTS ARE CONNECTED.
10-15

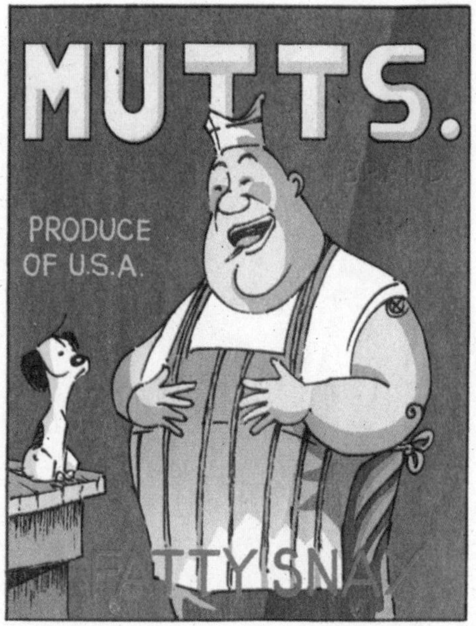
MUTTS.
PRODUCE OF U.S.A.

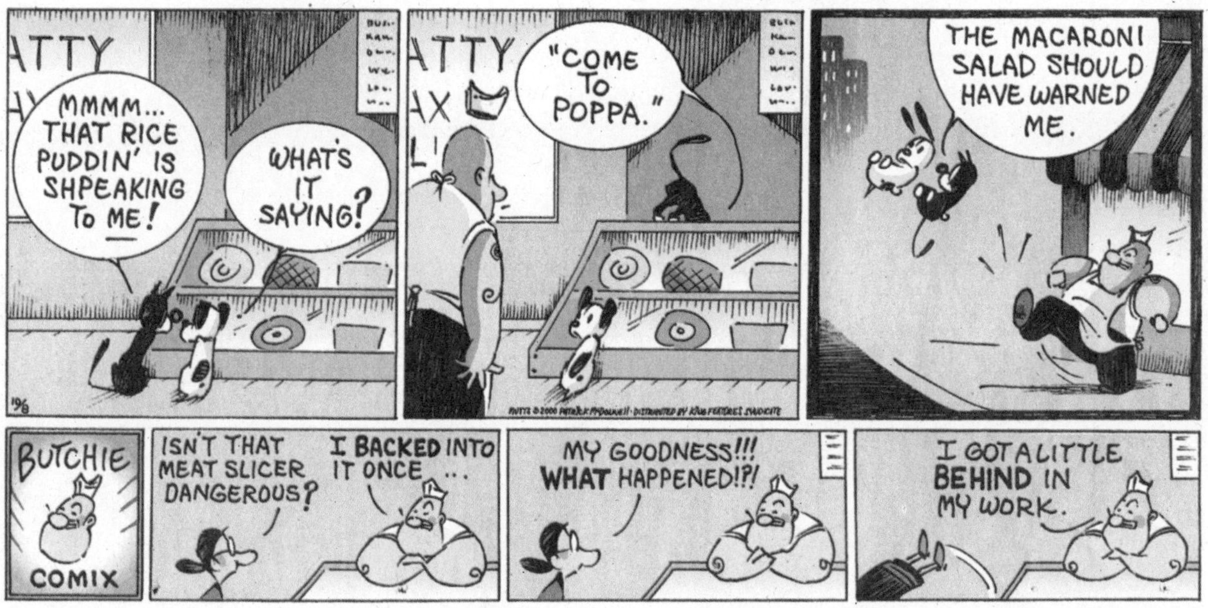
BUTCHIE COMIX
ISN'T THAT MEAT SLICER DANGEROUS?
I BACKED INTO IT ONCE ...
MY GOODNESS!!! WHAT HAPPENED!?!
I GOT A LITTLE BEHIND IN MY WORK.
MMMM... THAT RICE PUDDIN' IS SHPEAKING TO ME!
WHAT'S IT SAYING?
"COME TO POPPA."
THE MACARONI SALAD SHOULD HAVE WARNED ME.

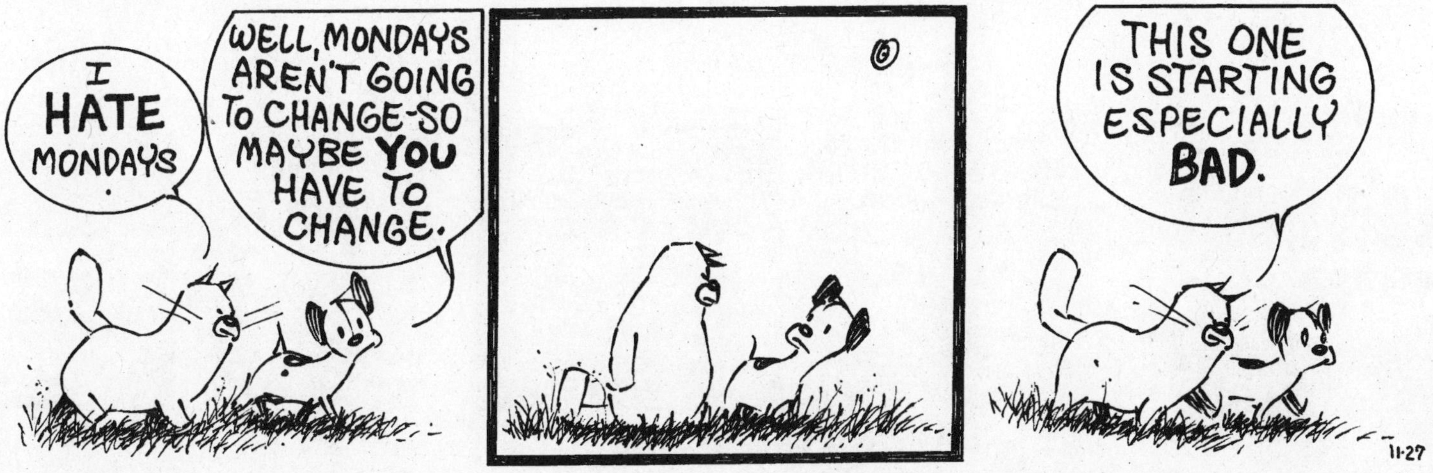
I HATE MONDAYS.
WELL, MONDAYS AREN'T GOING TO CHANGE-SO MAYBE YOU HAVE TO CHANGE.
THIS ONE IS STARTING ESPECIALLY BAD.
11-27

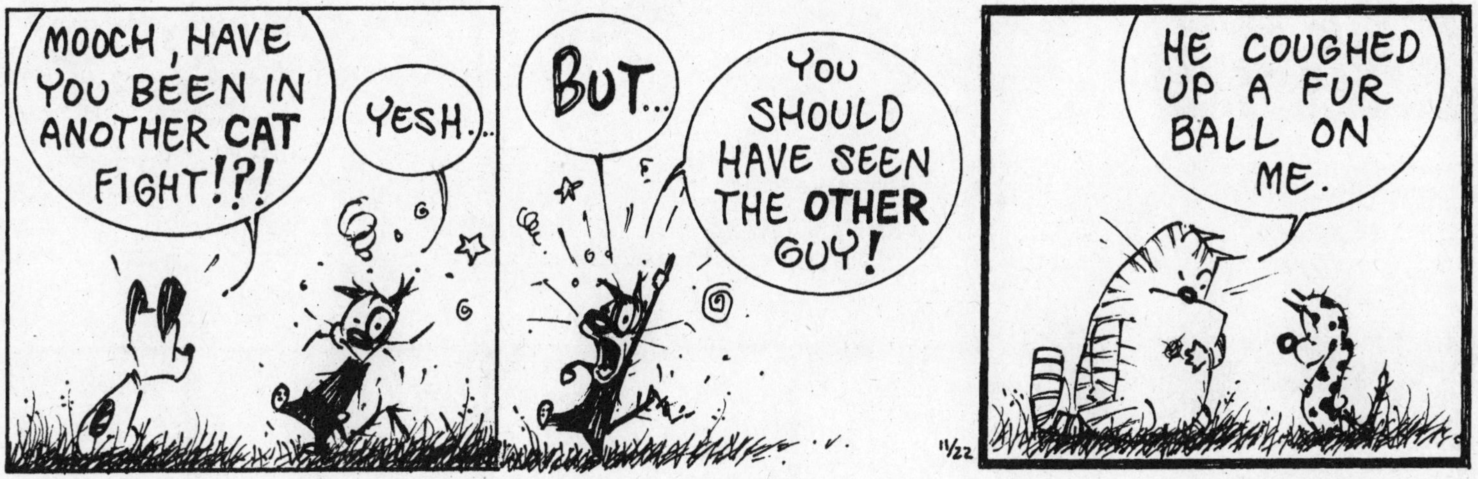
MOOCH, HAVE YOU BEEN IN ANOTHER CAT FIGHT!?!
YESH...
BUT...
YOU SHOULD HAVE SEEN THE OTHER GUY!
HE COUGHED UP A FUR BALL ON ME.
11/22

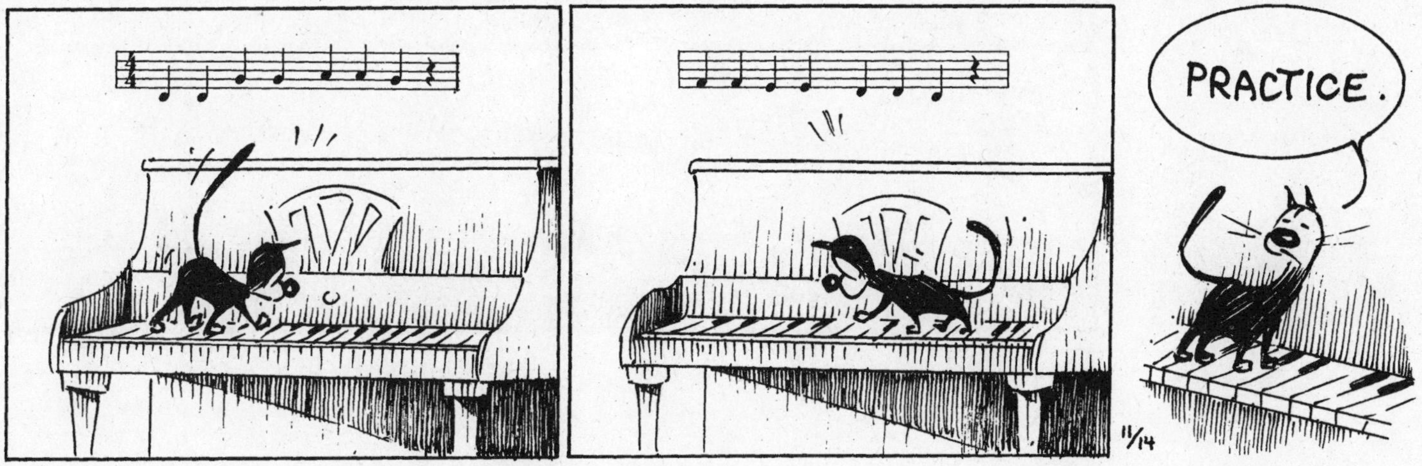
PRACTICE.
11/14

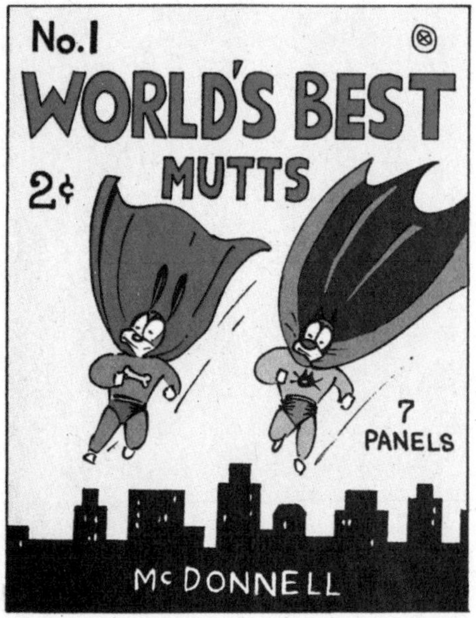
No.1
WORLD'S BEST
MUTTS
2¢
7 PANELS
McDONNELL

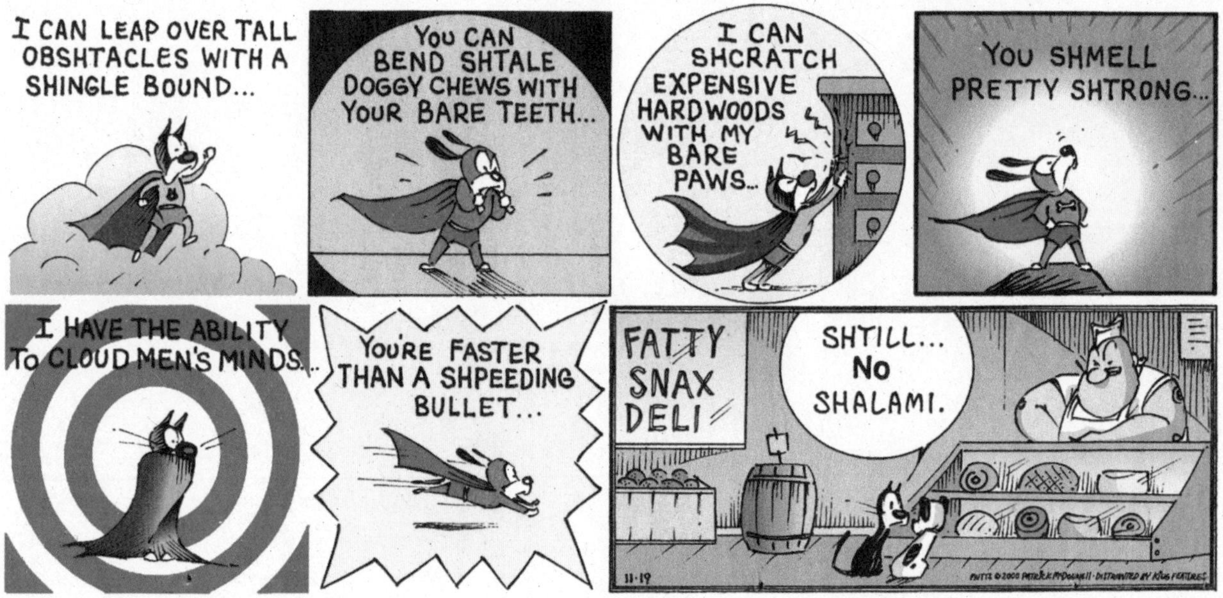
I CAN LEAP OVER TALL OBSHTACLES WITH A SHINGLE BOUND...
YOU CAN BEND SHTALE DOGGY CHEWS WITH YOUR BARE TEETH...
I CAN SHCRATCH EXPENSIVE HARDWOODS WITH MY BARE PAWS...
YOU SHMELL PRETTY SHTRONG...
I HAVE THE ABILITY TO CLOUD MEN'S MINDS...
YOU'RE FASTER THAN A SHPEEDING BULLET...
FATTY SNAX DELI
SHTILL... NO SHALAMI.
11-19

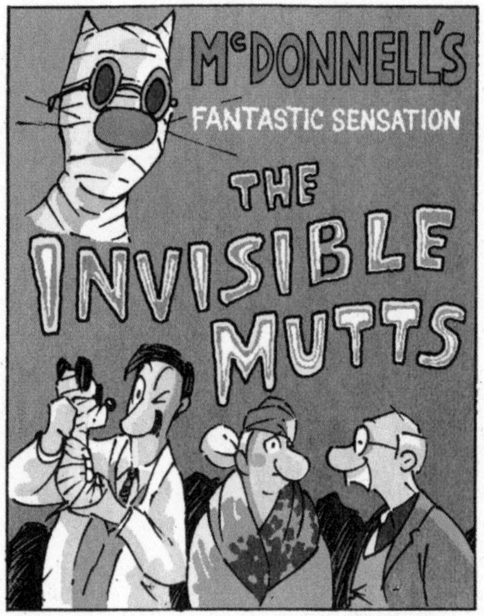
McDONNELL'S
FANTASTIC SENSATION
THE INVISIBLE MUTTS

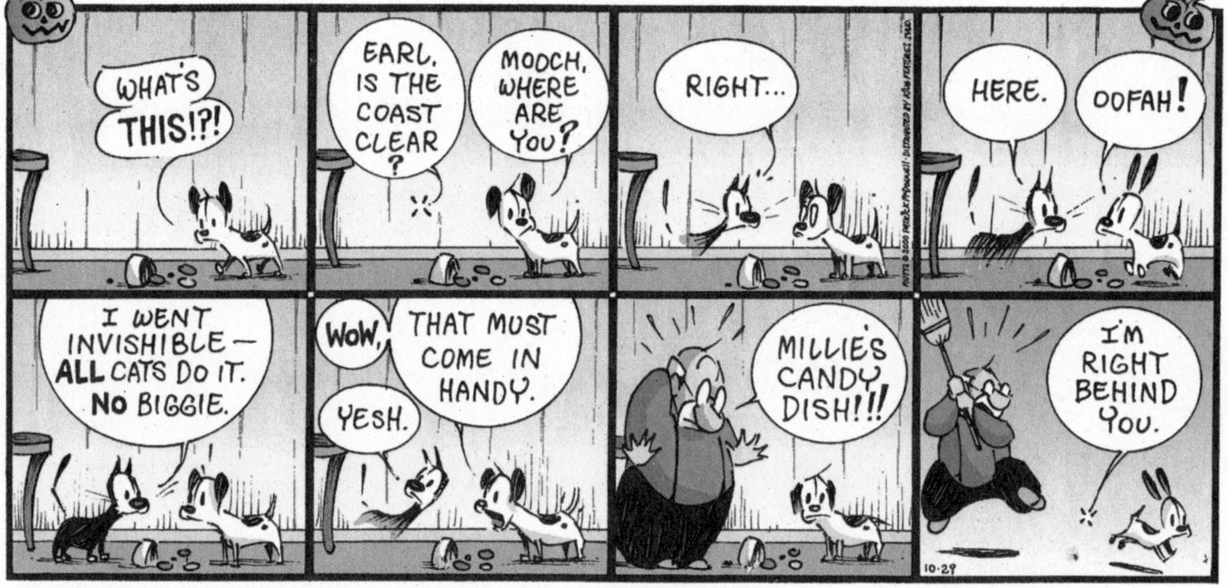
WHAT'S THIS!?!
EARL, IS THE COAST CLEAR?
MOOCH, WHERE ARE YOU?
RIGHT...
HERE.
OOFAH!
I WENT INVISHIBLE— ALL CATS DO IT. NO BIGGIE.
WOW,
THAT MUST COME IN HANDY.
YESH.
MILLIE'S CANDY DISH!!!
I'M RIGHT BEHIND YOU.
10-29

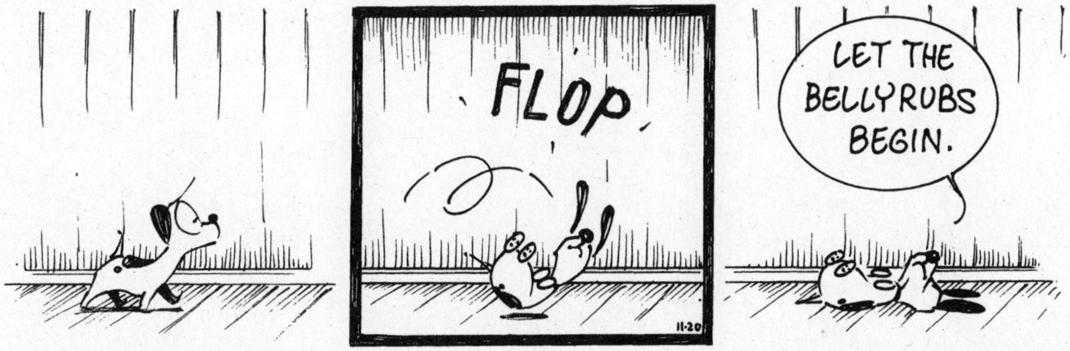
FLOP
LET THE BELLYRUBS BEGIN.

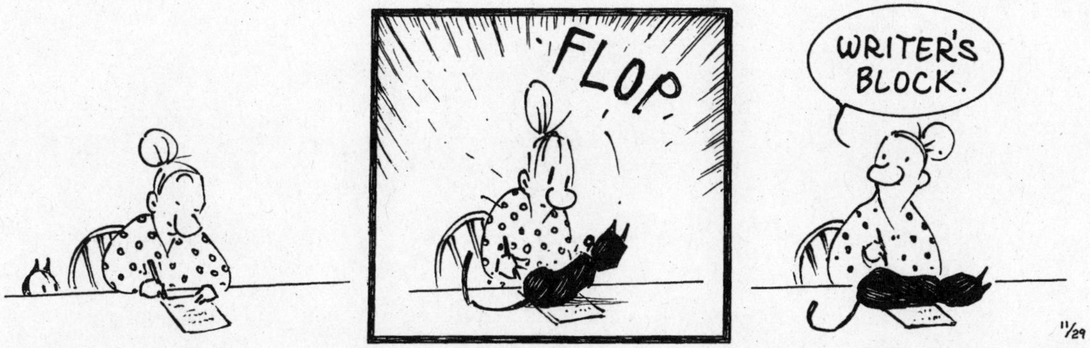
FLOP
WRITER'S BLOCK.

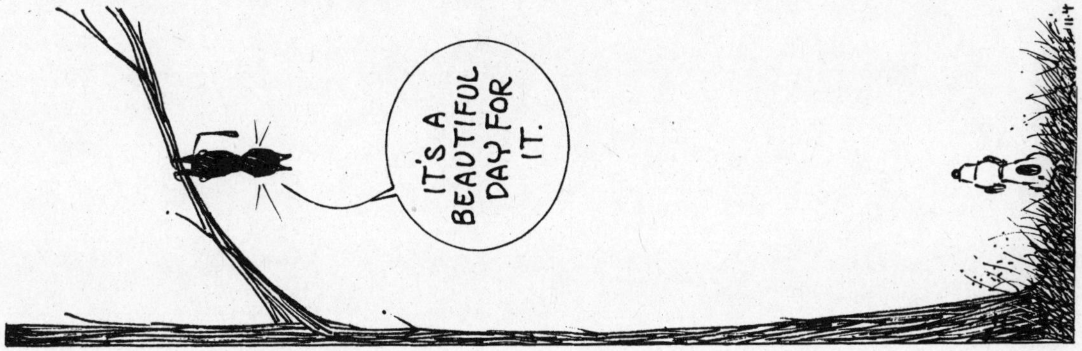
IT'S A BEAUTIFUL DAY FOR IT.

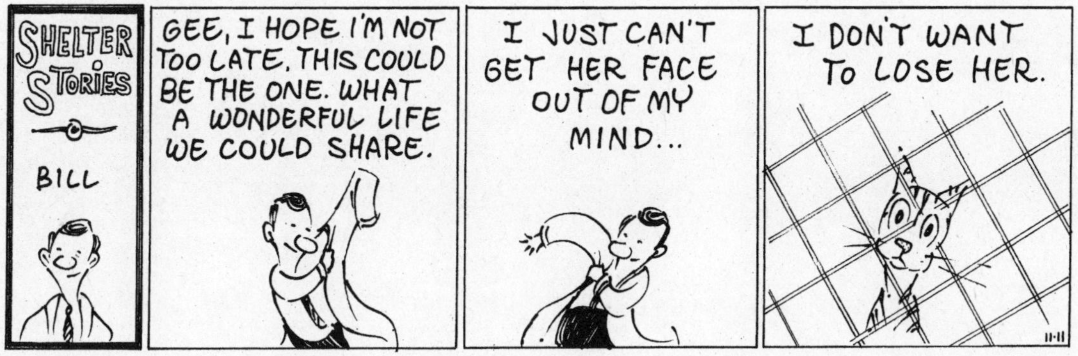
SHELTER STORIES
BILL
GEE, I HOPE I'M NOT TOO LATE. THIS COULD BE THE ONE. WHAT A WONDERFUL LIFE WE COULD SHARE.
I JUST CAN'T GET HER FACE OUT OF MY MIND...
I DON'T WANT TO LOSE HER.

## Little pink sock, little pink sock!

Mooch begins his obsession with colorful footwear. According to my mail, there are a lot of cats who believe that happiness is a warm sock.

During the two shelter story weeks I focused on a bunny (Flop), and two hamsters (Marla and Larry). I wanted to inform and remind us that there are many other lovable critters, along with the cats and dogs, waiting at our local shelters.

In November, Earl and Mooch visited a farm to help celebrate the HSUS National Farm Animals Awareness Week. Over nine billion animals are slaughtered (in this country alone) each year, and most of them are raised on factory farms that deny them any kind of normal life. That's a lot of animal suffering. I've been a vegetarian for about fifteen years now and I feel it's the single most important choice I've ever made. As Paul McCartney said, "If slaughterhouses had glass walls, everyone would be a vegetarian."

01

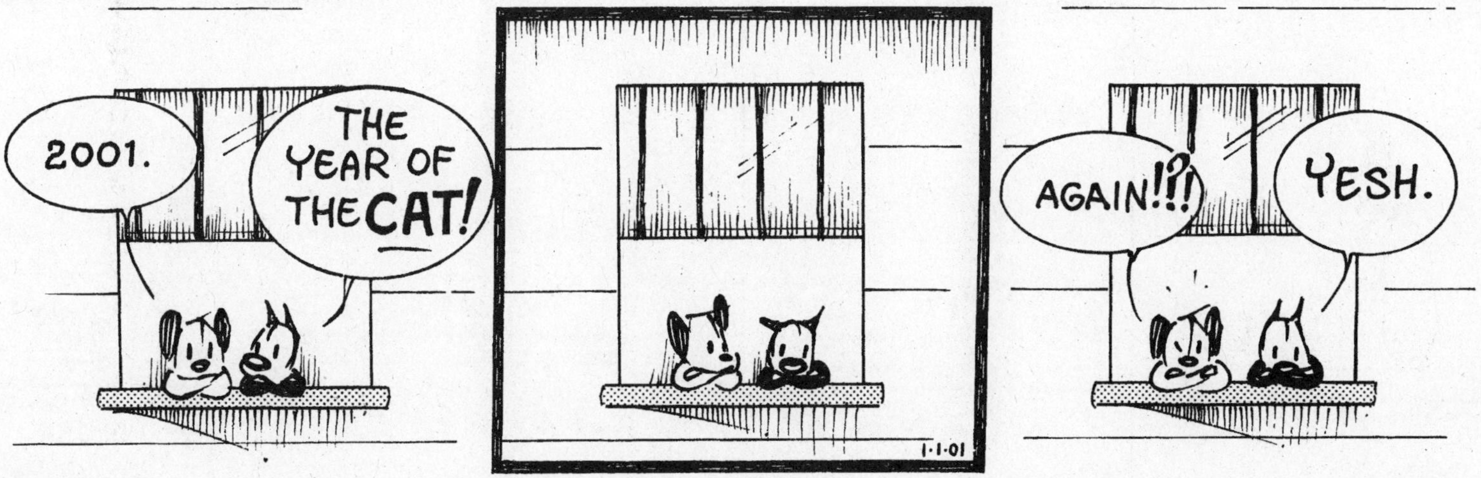
2001.
THE YEAR OF THE CAT!
AGAIN!?!!
YESH.
1·1·01

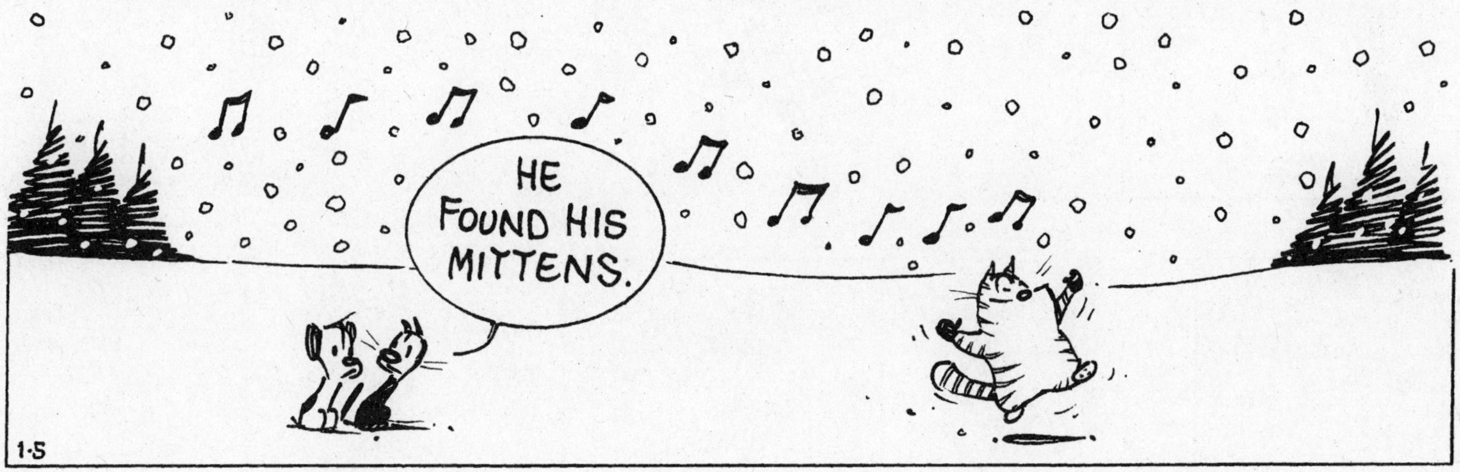
HE FOUND HIS MITTENS.
1·5

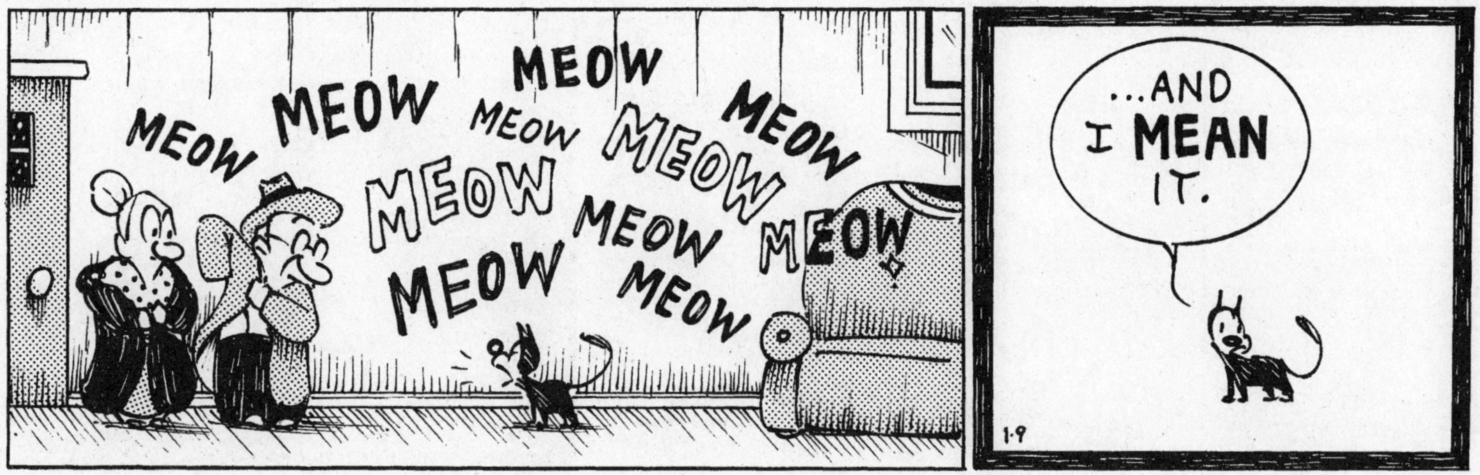
MEOW MEOW MEOW MEOW MEOW MEOW MEOW MEOW MEOW MEOW MEOW MEOW
...AND I MEAN IT.
1·9

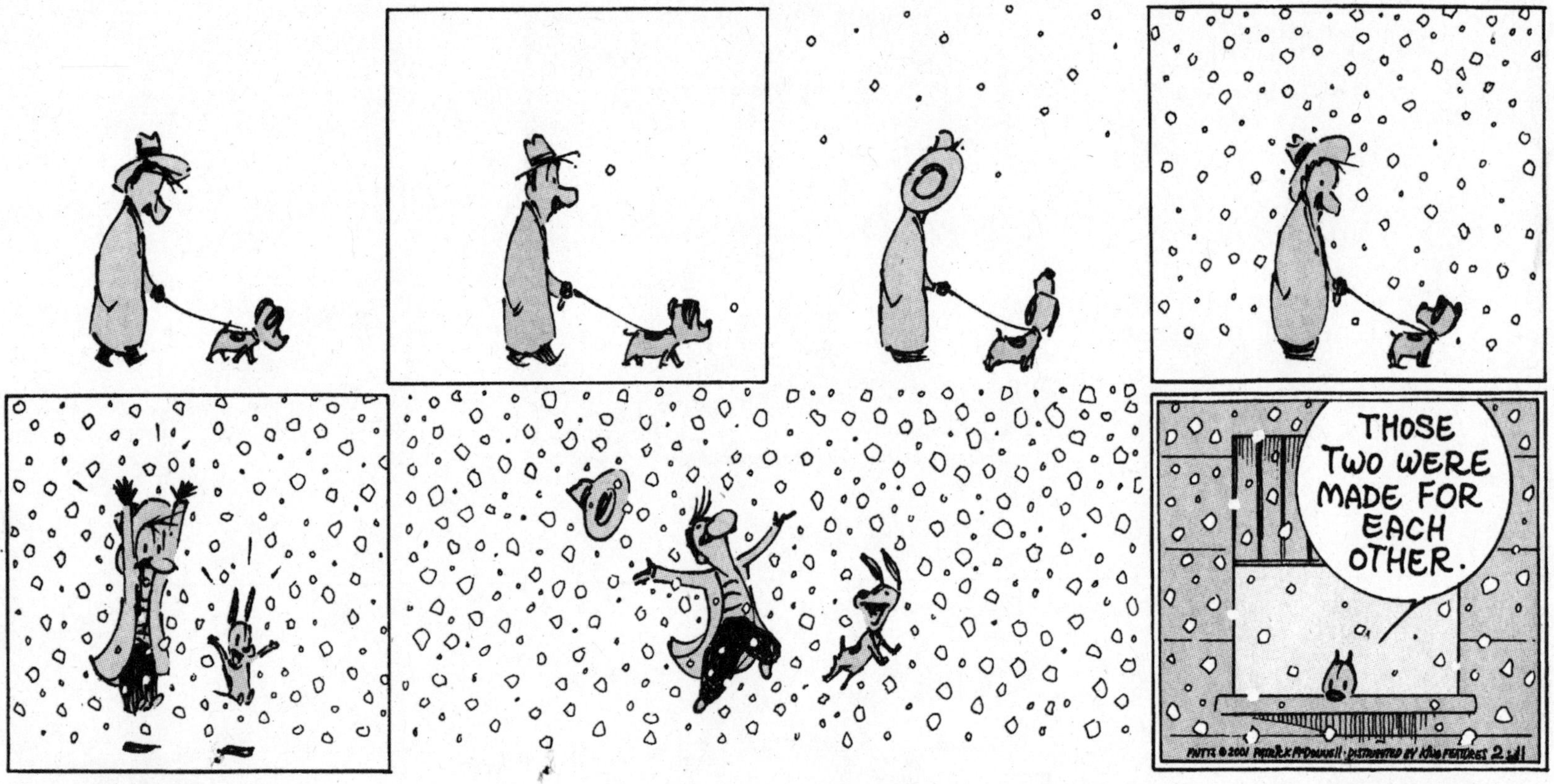
THOSE TWO WERE MADE FOR EACH OTHER.

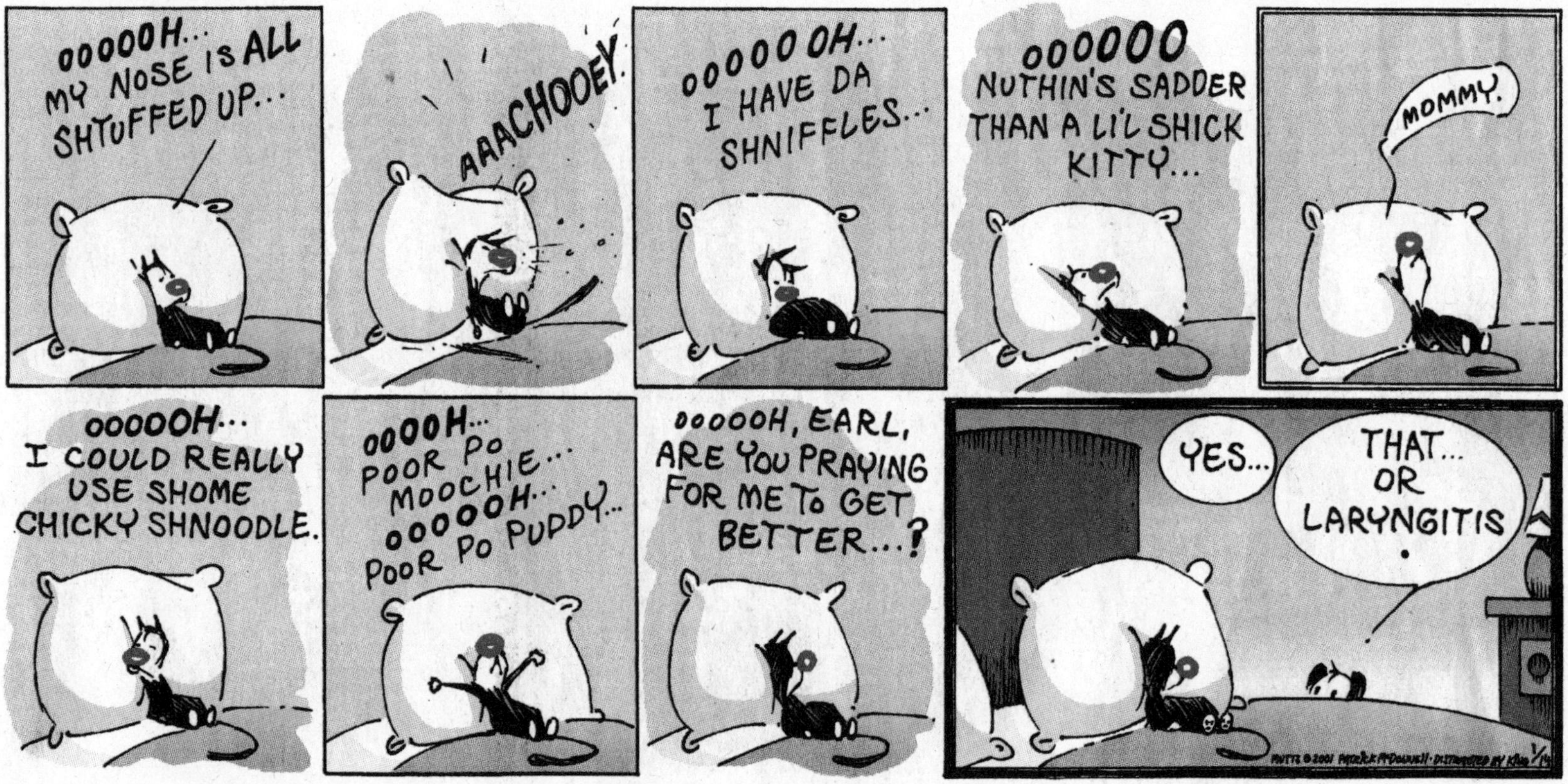
OOOOOH... MY NOSE IS ALL SHTUFFED UP...
AAACHOOEY.
OOOOOOH... I HAVE DA SHNIFFLES...
OOOOOO NUTHIN'S SADDER THAN A LI'L SHICK KITTY...
MOMMY.
OOOOOH... I COULD REALLY USE SHOME CHICKY SHNOODLE.
OOOOH... POOR PO MOOCHIE... OOOOOH... POOR PO PUDDY...
OOOOOH, EARL, ARE YOU PRAYING FOR ME TO GET BETTER...?
YES...
THAT... OR LARYNGITIS.

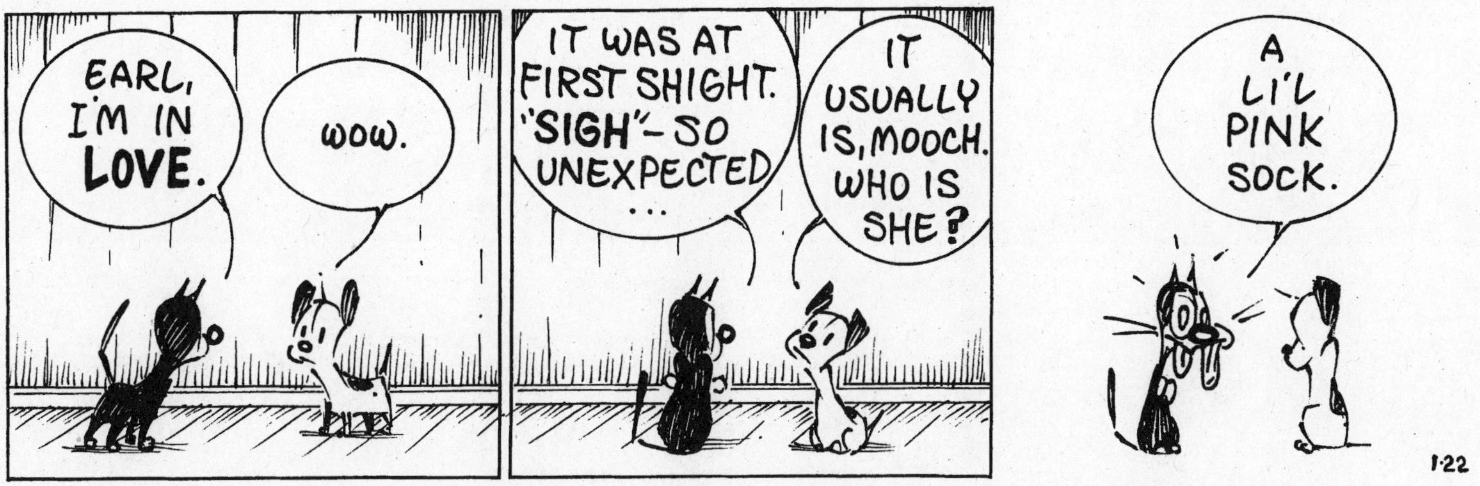
EARL, I'M IN LOVE.
WOW.
IT WAS AT FIRST SHIGHT. "SIGH"- SO UNEXPECTED ...
IT USUALLY IS, MOOCH. WHO IS SHE?
A LI'L PINK SOCK.
1·22

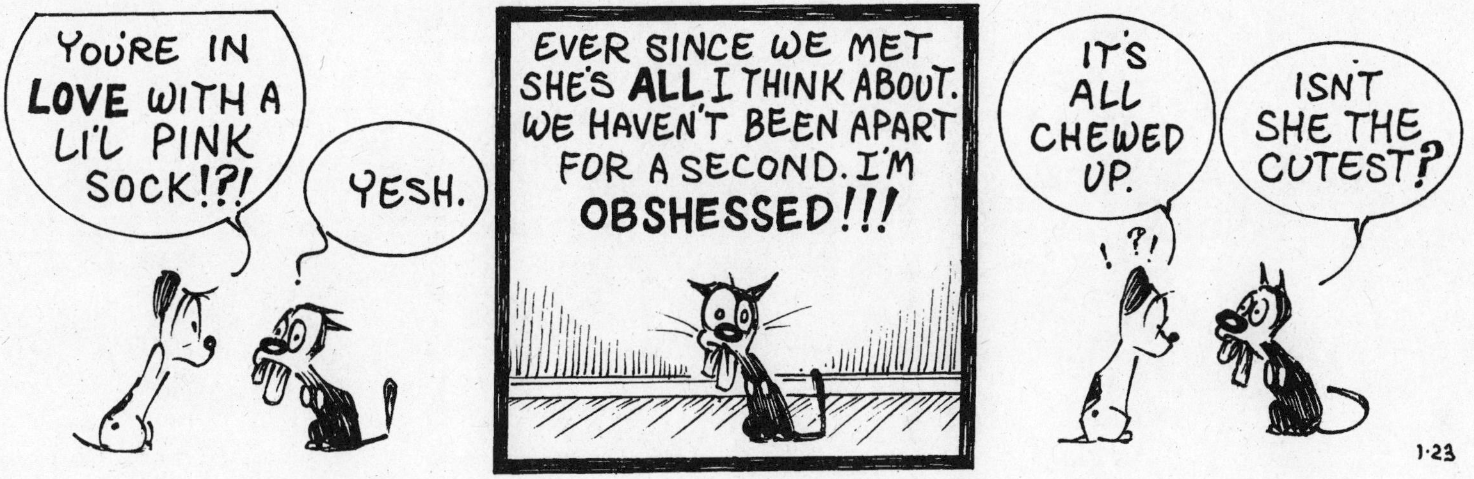
YOU'RE IN LOVE WITH A LI'L PINK SOCK!?!
YESH.
EVER SINCE WE MET SHE'S ALL I THINK ABOUT. WE HAVEN'T BEEN APART FOR A SECOND. I'M OBSHESSED!!!
IT'S ALL CHEWED UP.
! ?!
ISN'T SHE THE CUTEST?
1·23

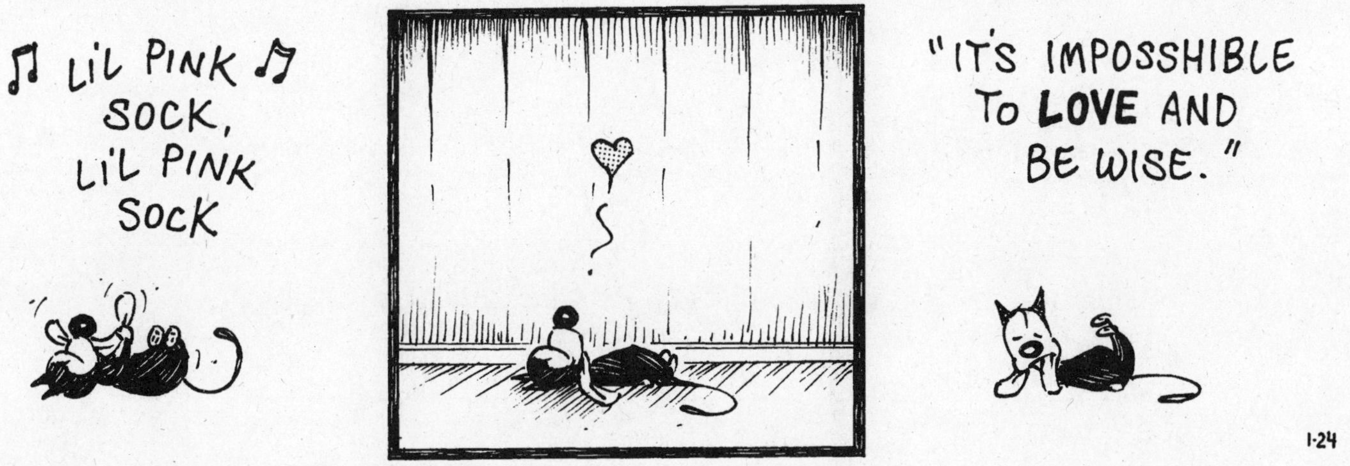
♫ LI'L PINK ♫ SOCK, LI'L PINK SOCK
"IT'S IMPOSSHIBLE TO LOVE AND BE WISE."
1·24

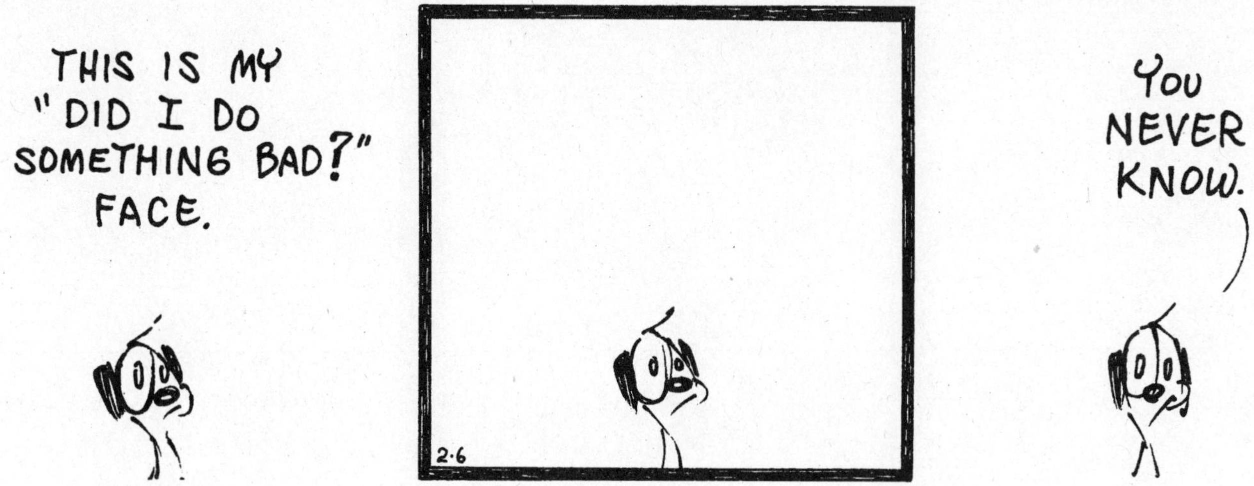
THIS IS MY "DID I DO SOMETHING BAD?" FACE.
2·6
YOU NEVER KNOW.

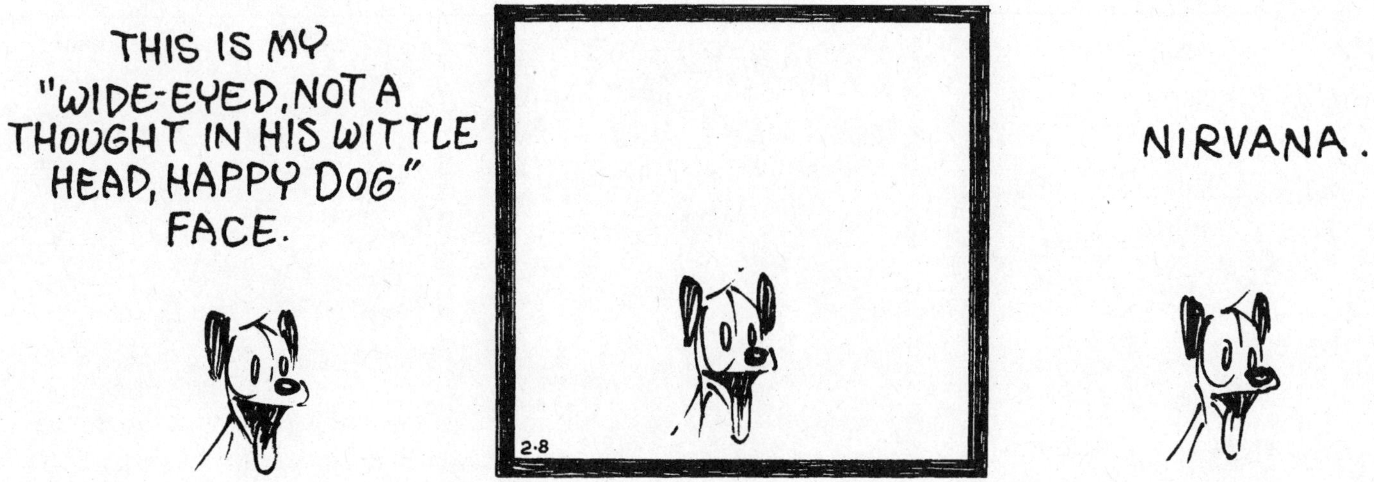
THIS IS MY "WIDE-EYED, NOT A THOUGHT IN HIS WITTLE HEAD, HAPPY DOG" FACE.
2·8
NIRVANA.

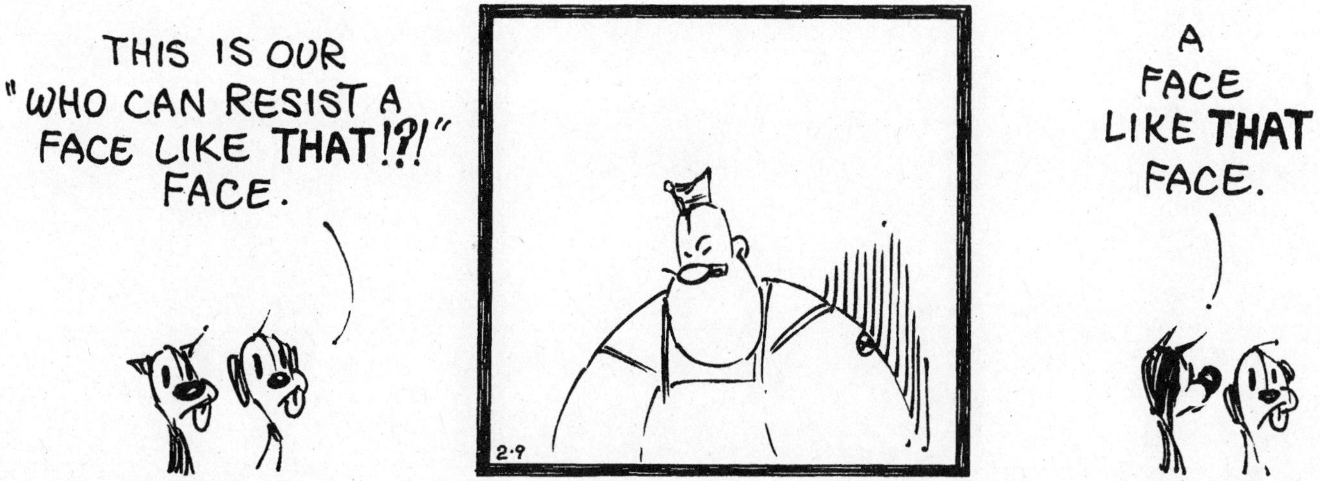
THIS IS OUR "WHO CAN RESIST A FACE LIKE THAT!?!" FACE.
2·9
A FACE LIKE THAT FACE.

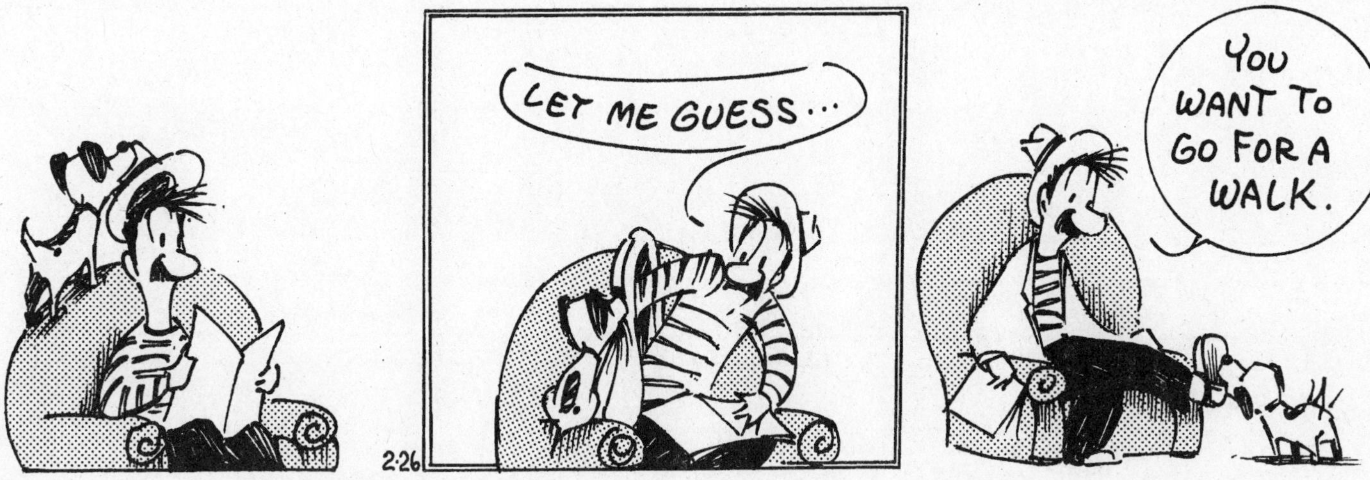
2·26
LET ME GUESS...
YOU WANT TO GO FOR A WALK.

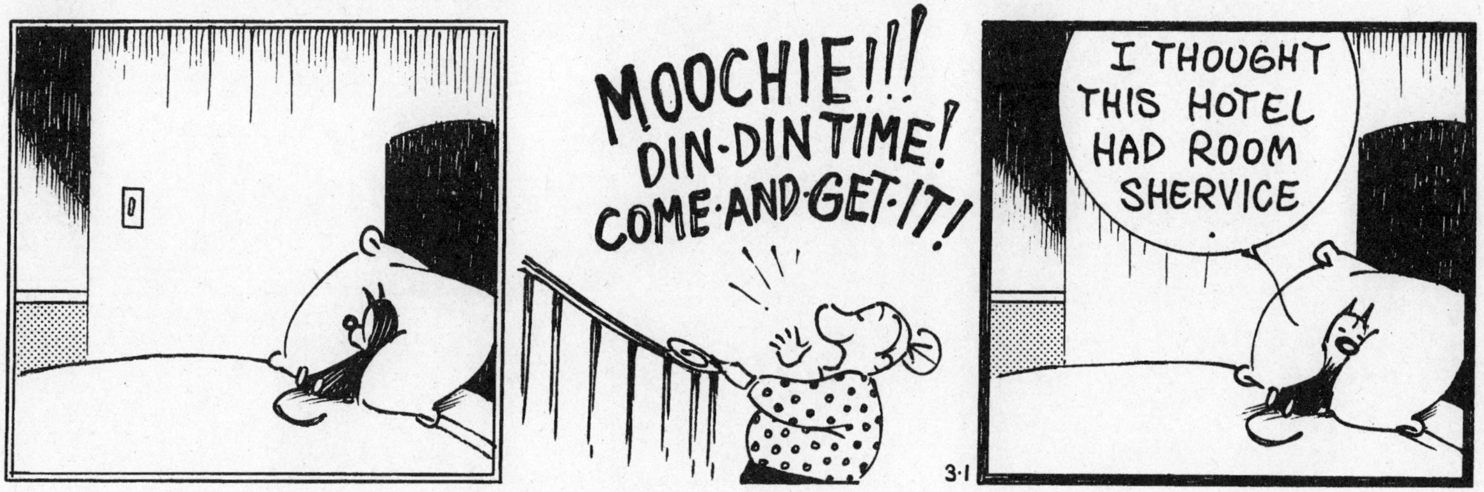
MOOCHIE!!! DIN-DIN TIME! COME-AND-GET-IT!
3·1
I THOUGHT THIS HOTEL HAD ROOM SHERVICE.

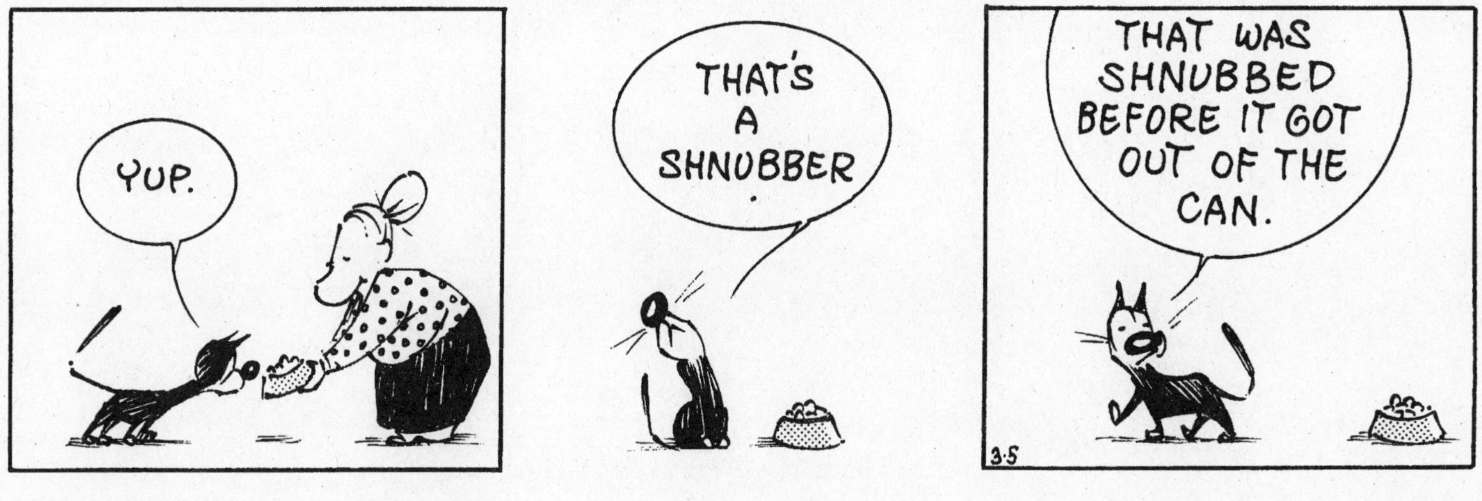
YUP.
THAT'S A SHNUBBER.
THAT WAS SHNUBBED BEFORE IT GOT OUT OF THE CAN.
3·5

BE MINE, VAWENTINE!
No.
BE MINE, VAWENTINE!
SCRAM.
THE DAY IS STILL YOUNG.
2·12

BE MINE, VAWENTINE!
NO WAY.
BE MINE, VAWENTINE!
GET LOST.
EVERYONE'S AFWAID OF A SERIOUS COMMITMENT.
2·13

BE MINE, VAWEN-TINE!
YUCK!
UGH!!
FOOEY!!!
WUV TALK.
2·14

WOOFIE WUVS KITTY!
DOES IT FEEL LIKE LOVE, MOOCH?
...IT'S MORE LIKE A 'CRUSH.'
2·16

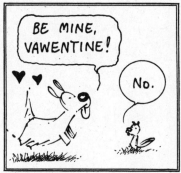

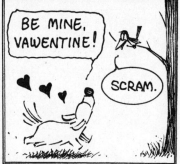

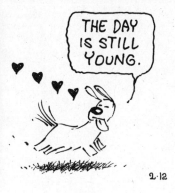

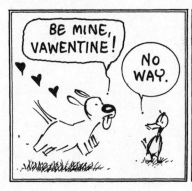

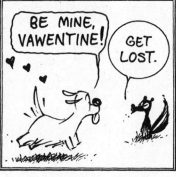

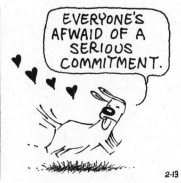

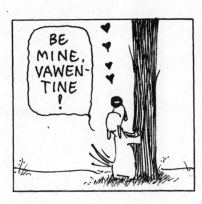

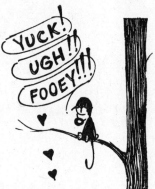

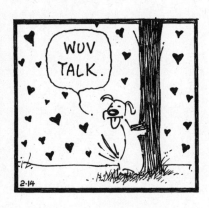

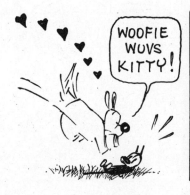

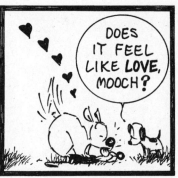

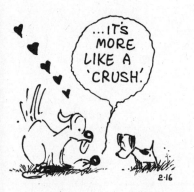

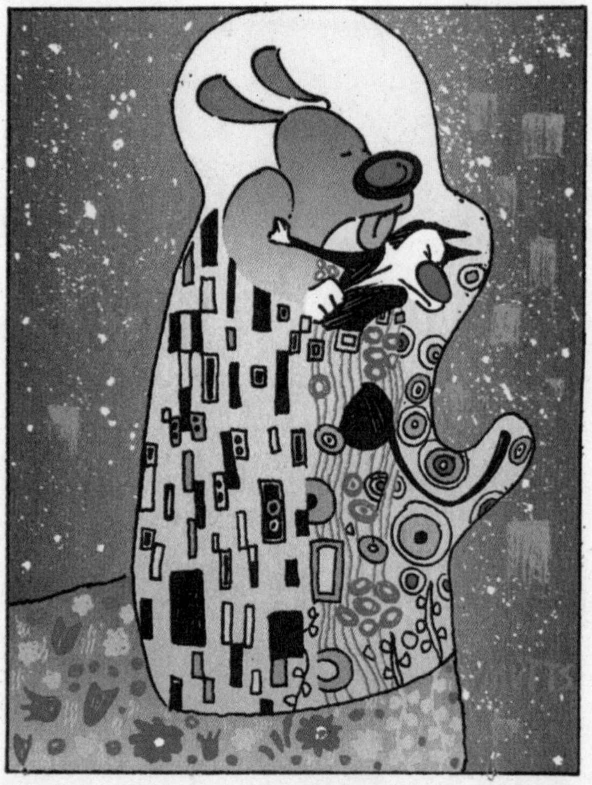

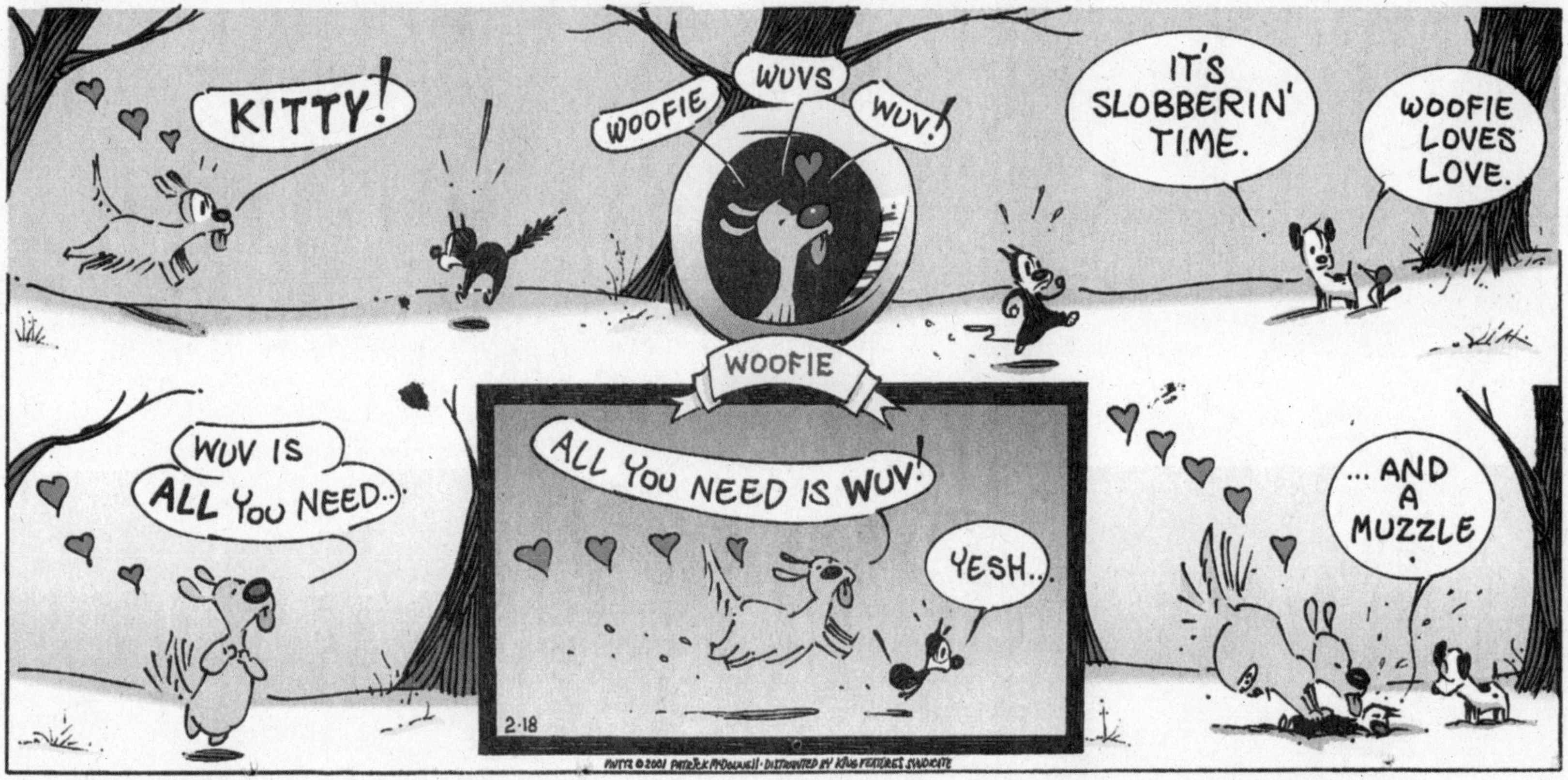
KITTY!
WOOFIE
WUVS
WUV!
WOOFIE
IT'S SLOBBERIN' TIME.
WOOFIE LOVES LOVE.
WUV IS ALL YOU NEED..
ALL YOU NEED IS WUV!
YESH..
... AND A MUZZLE
2·18

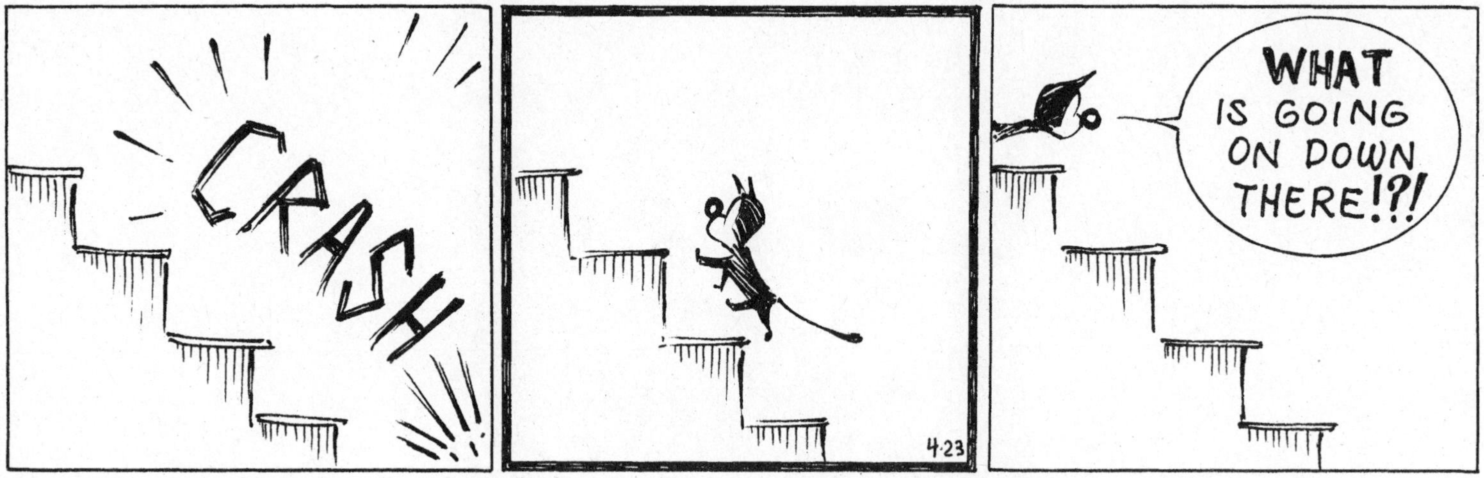
CRASH
4·23
WHAT IS GOING ON DOWN THERE!?!

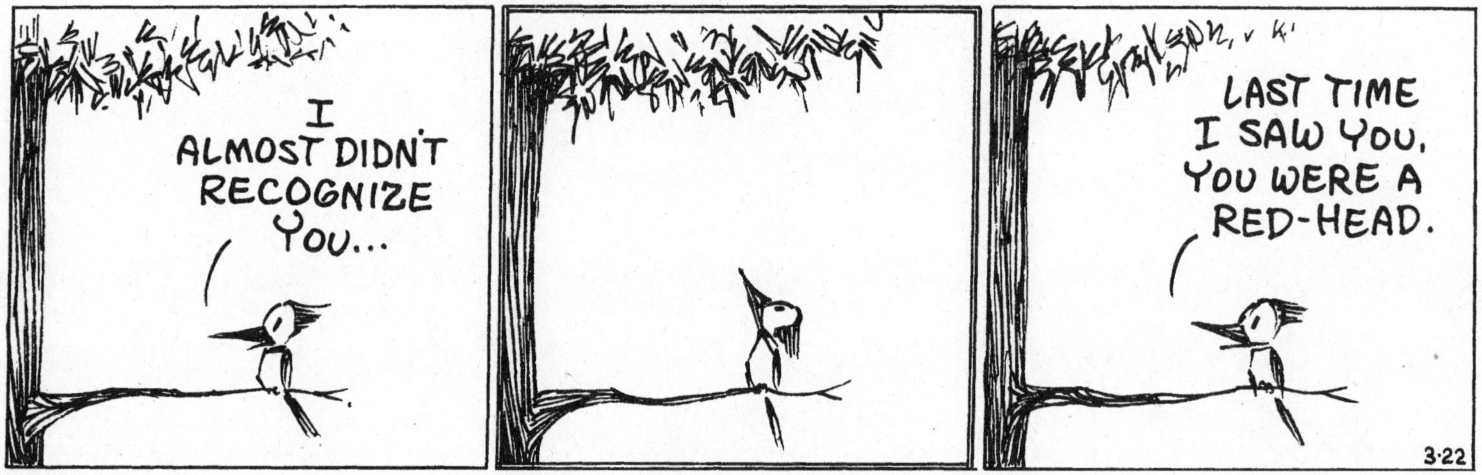
I ALMOST DIDN'T RECOGNIZE YOU...
LAST TIME I SAW YOU, YOU WERE A RED-HEAD.
3·22

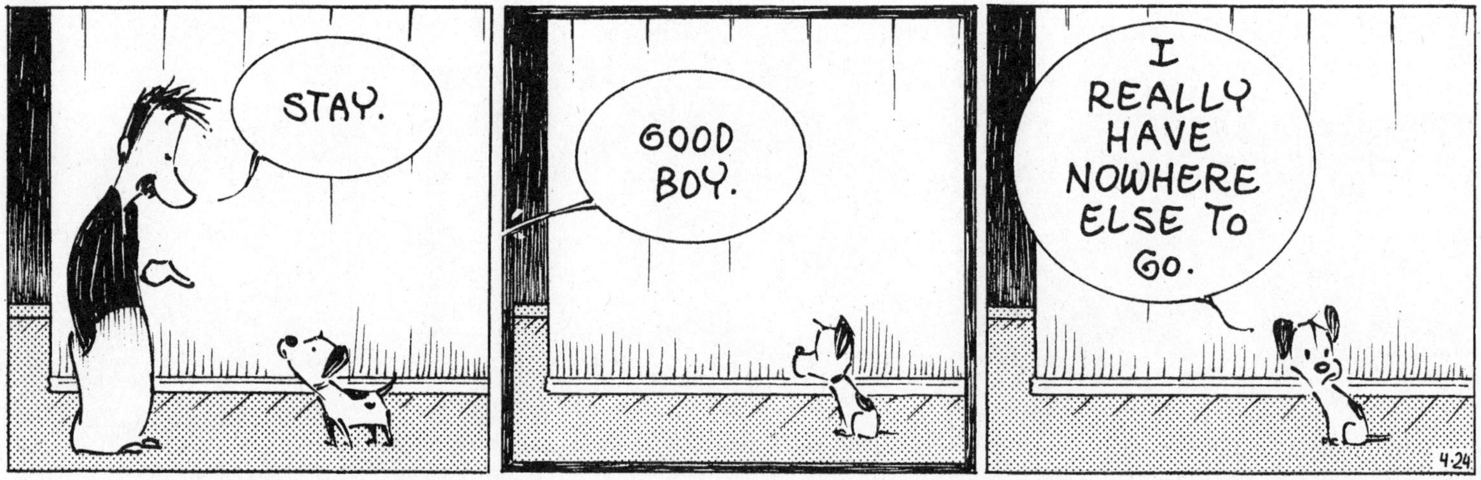
STAY.
GOOD BOY.
I REALLY HAVE NOWHERE ELSE TO GO.
4·24

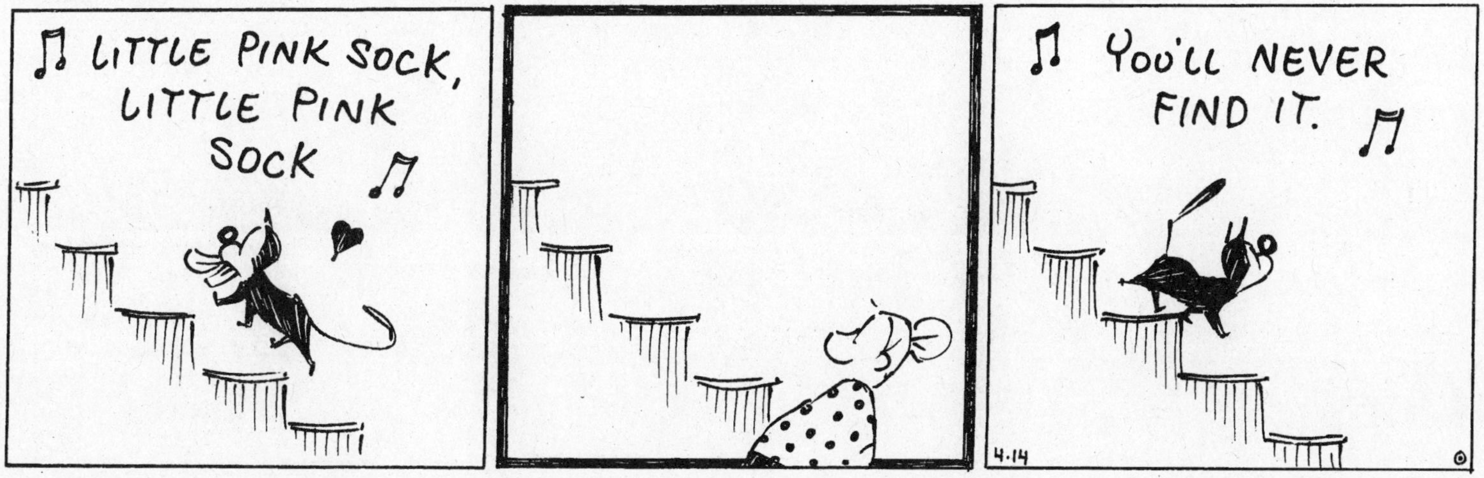
LITTLE PINK SOCK,
LITTLE PINK
SOCK
YOU'LL NEVER
FIND IT.
4.14

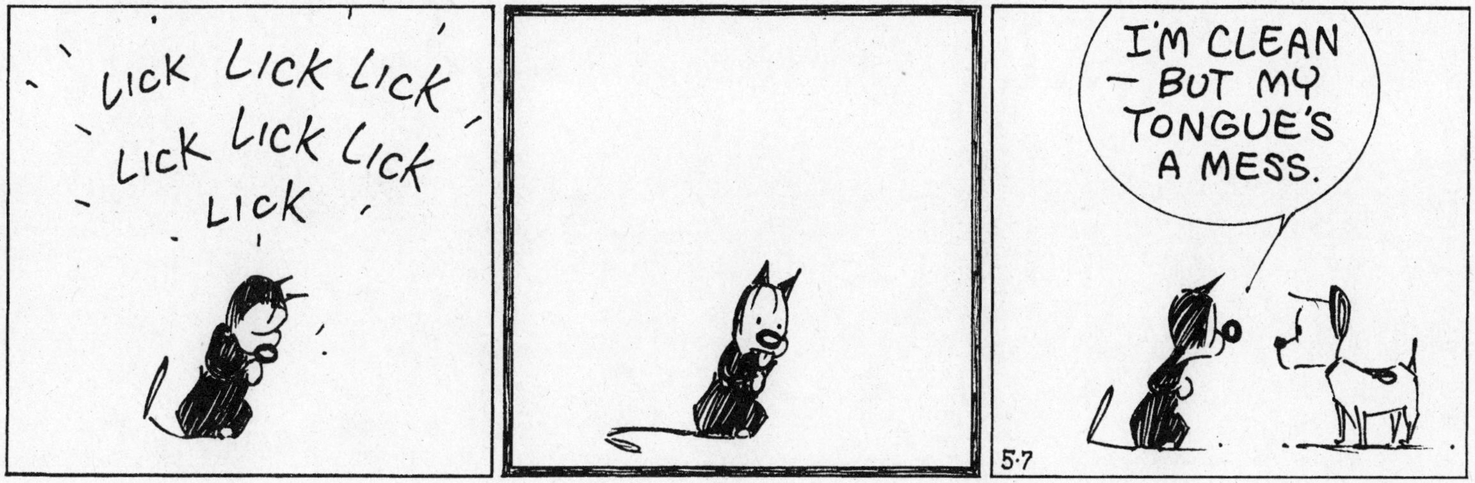
LICK LICK LICK
LICK LICK LICK
LICK
I'M CLEAN
— BUT MY
TONGUE'S
A MESS.
5.7

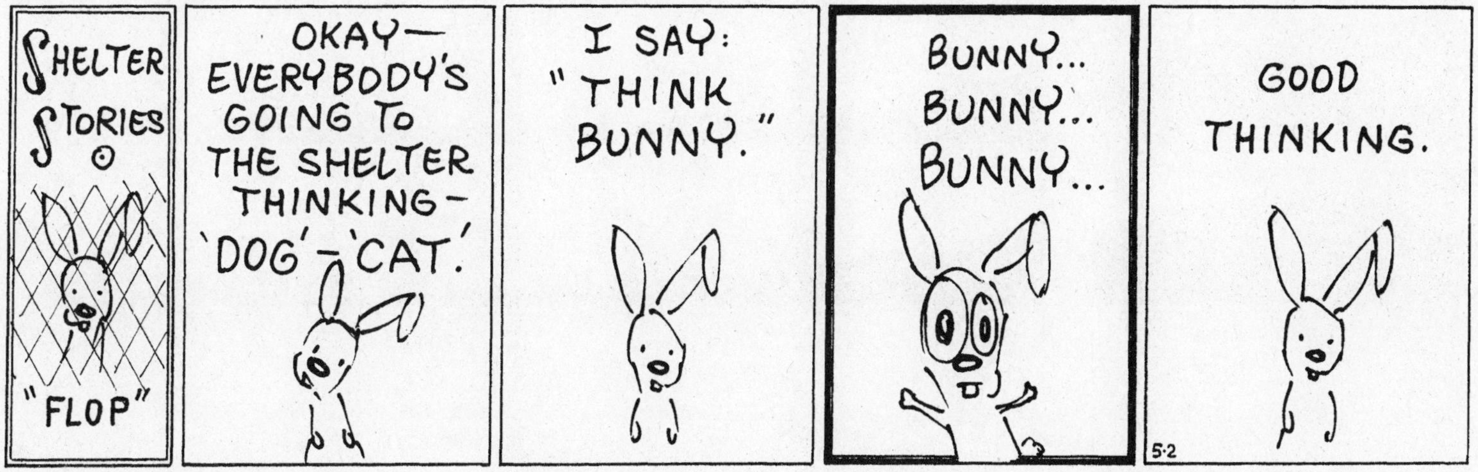
SHELTER
STORIES
"FLOP"
OKAY—
EVERYBODY'S
GOING TO
THE SHELTER
THINKING—
'DOG'—'CAT.'
I SAY:
"THINK
BUNNY."
BUNNY...
BUNNY...
BUNNY...
GOOD
THINKING.
5.2

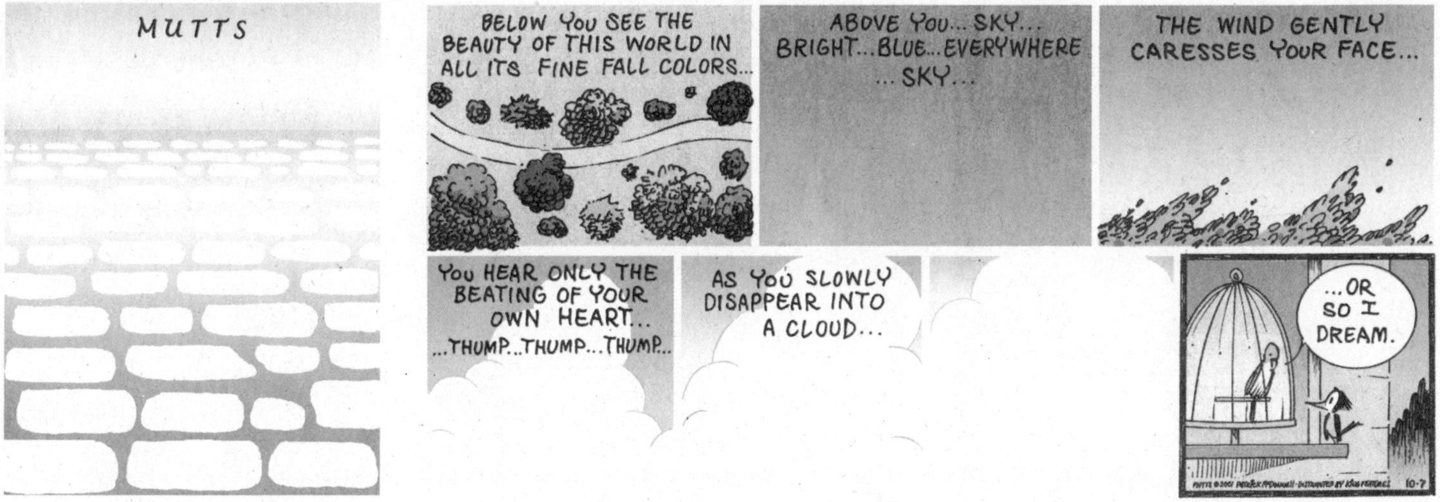
MUTTS
BELOW YOU SEE THE BEAUTY OF THIS WORLD IN ALL ITS FINE FALL COLORS...
ABOVE YOU... SKY... BRIGHT...BLUE...EVERYWHERE ...SKY...
THE WIND GENTLY CARESSES YOUR FACE...
YOU HEAR ONLY THE BEATING OF YOUR OWN HEART...
...THUMP...THUMP...THUMP...
AS YOU SLOWLY DISAPPEAR INTO A CLOUD...
...OR SO I DREAM.
10-7

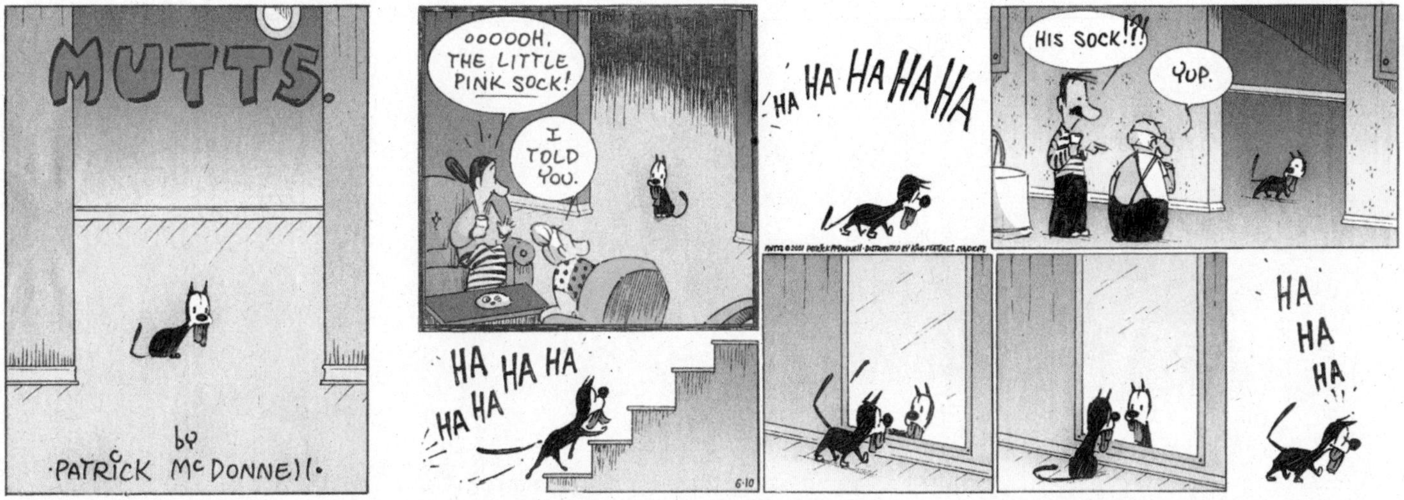
MUTTS
by PATRICK McDONNELL
OOOOOH, THE LITTLE PINK SOCK!
I TOLD YOU.
HA HA HA HA HA
HIS SOCK!?!
YUP.
HA HA HA HA HA HA
6-10
HA HA HA

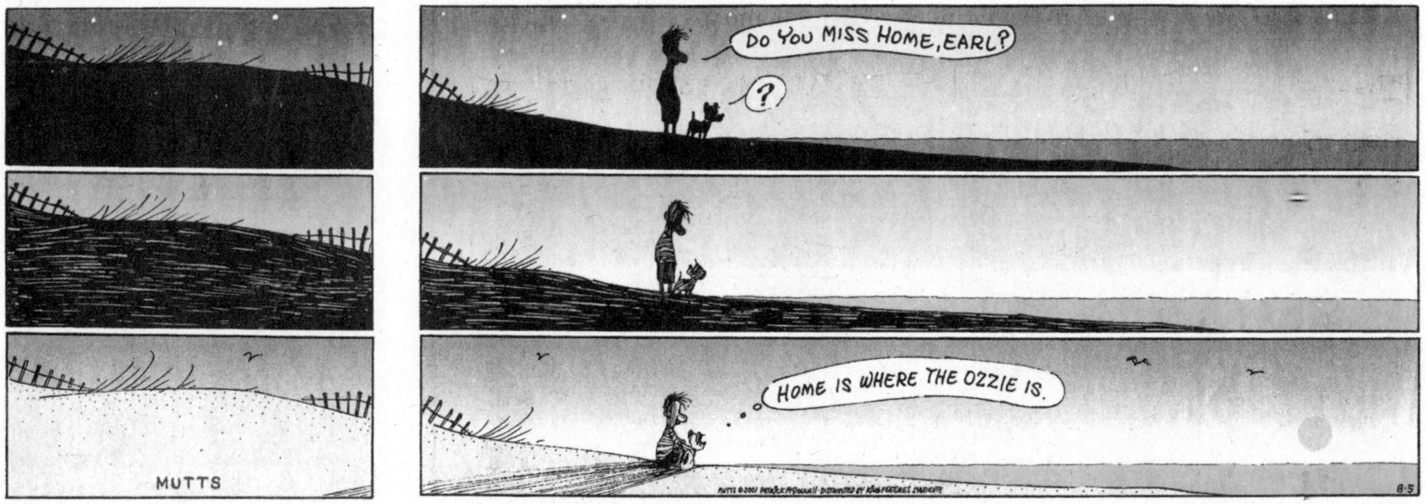
MUTTS
DO YOU MISS HOME, EARL?
?
HOME IS WHERE THE OZZIE IS.
8-5

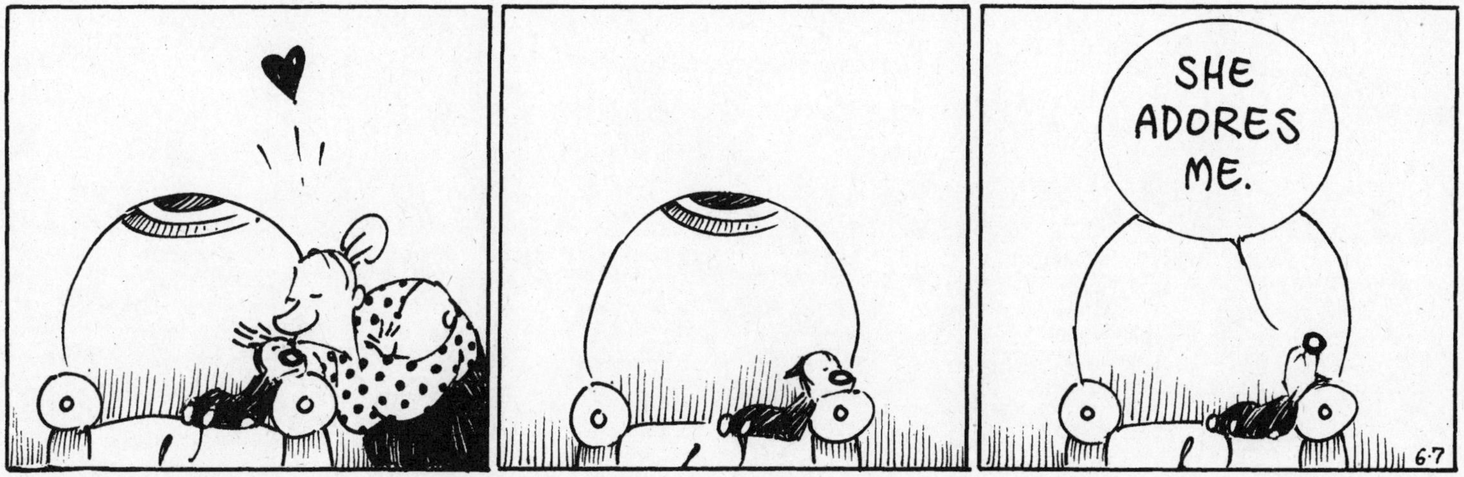
SHE ADORES ME.
6·7

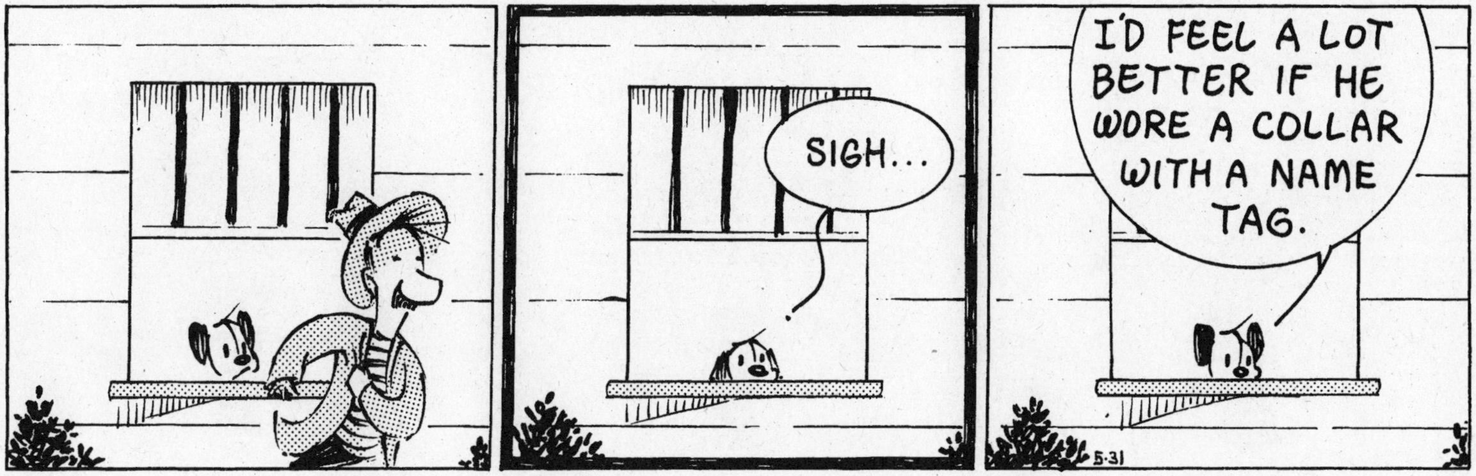
SIGH...
I'D FEEL A LOT BETTER IF HE WORE A COLLAR WITH A NAME TAG.
5·31

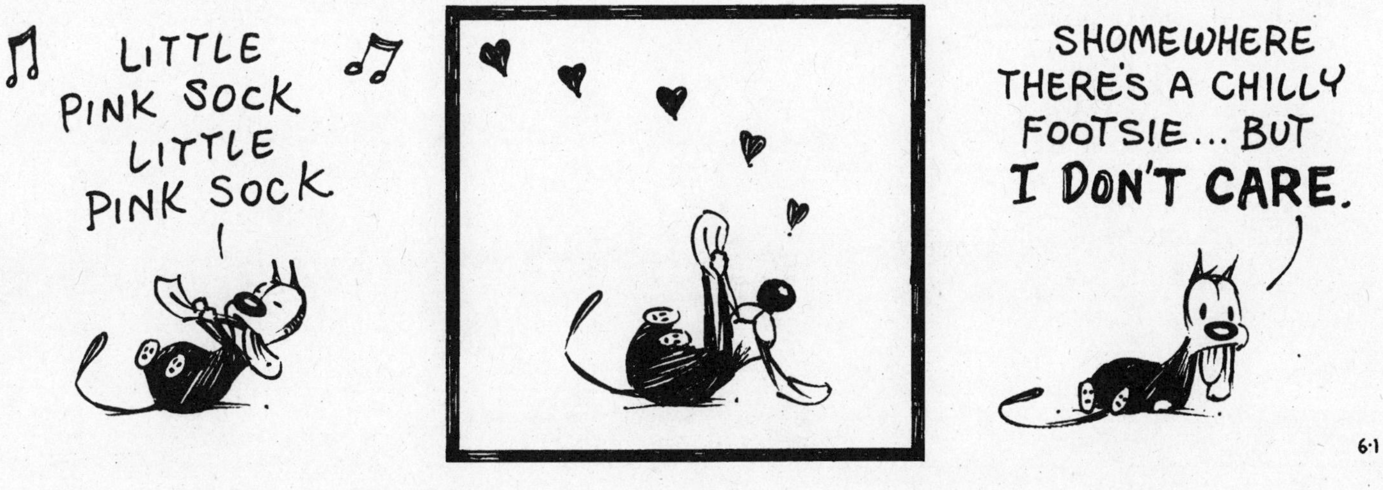
LITTLE PINK SOCK LITTLE PINK SOCK
SHOMEWHERE THERE'S A CHILLY FOOTSIE... BUT I DON'T CARE.
6·1

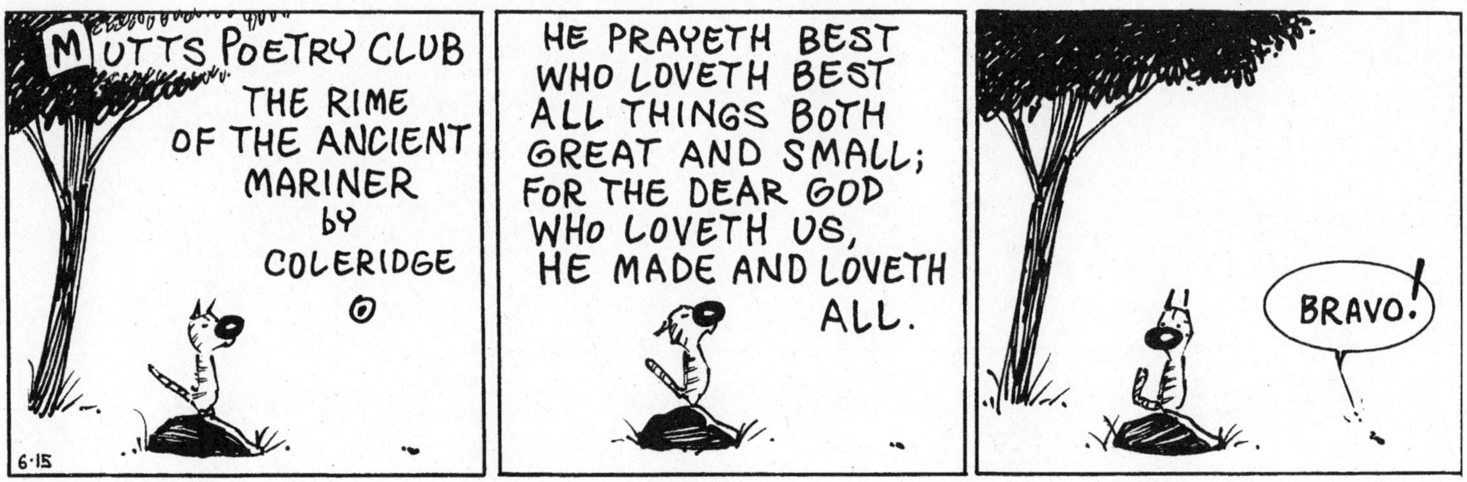
MUTTS POETRY CLUB
THE RIME OF THE ANCIENT MARINER by COLERIDGE
6·15
HE PRAYETH BEST WHO LOVETH BEST ALL THINGS BOTH GREAT AND SMALL; FOR THE DEAR GOD WHO LOVETH US, HE MADE AND LOVETH ALL.
BRAVO!

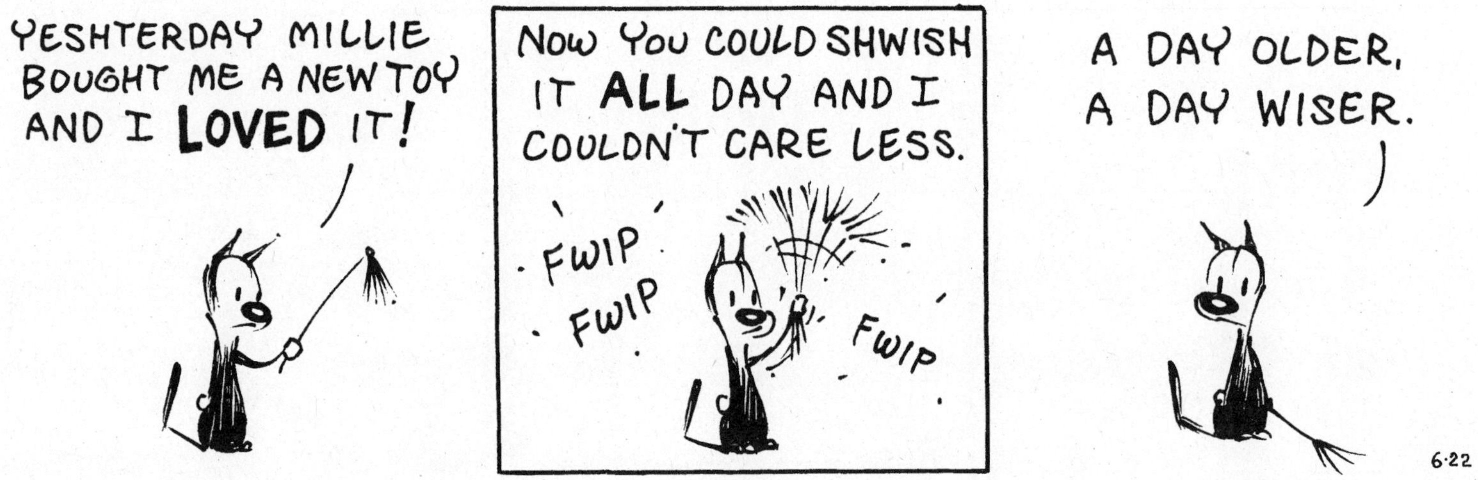
YESHTERDAY MILLIE BOUGHT ME A NEW TOY AND I **LOVED** IT!
NOW YOU COULD SHWISH IT **ALL** DAY AND I COULDN'T CARE LESS.
FWIP
FWIP
FWIP
A DAY OLDER, A DAY WISER.
6·22

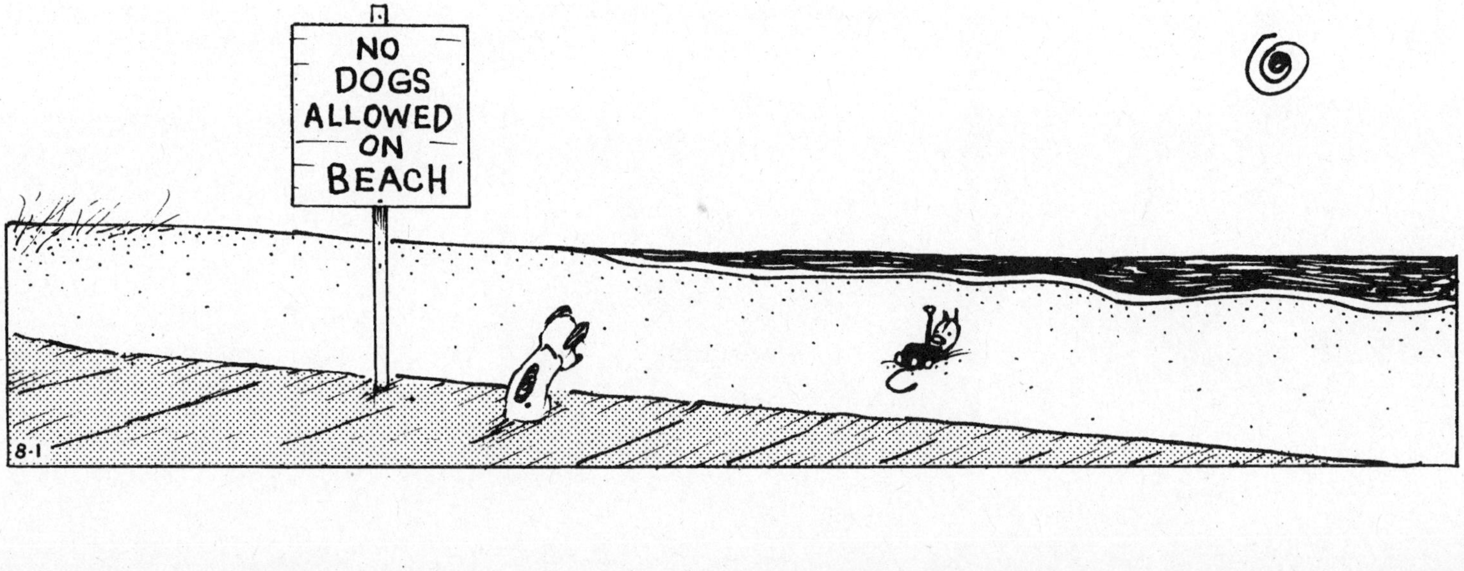
NO DOGS ALLOWED ON BEACH
8·1

MUTTS
A SALTY CRAB
YOU'RE LATE!
@☆*!
CRABBY'S TALES OF THE SEA
IT'S LIKE THIS — I WAS FLOATING ALONG MINDING MY OWN @☆*! BUSINESS, WHEN ALL OF A SUDDEN 'BIG FISHY' OPENED UP...
OOFAH!
INSIDE I RAN INTO TWO OLD SEABEE PALS O' MINE...
ARG.
GO FISH.
ARG.
...AND SOME CRAZY ITALIAN PUPPET WITH A SINGING CRICKET —
I @☆*! SWEAR!!!
DO YOU KNOW "RAVE ON"?
AFTER SOME FINAGLING I WAS ABLE TO BLOW THE JOINT. I'M TELLING YOU, LOLLIPOP, I WAS VERY LUCKY...
@☆*!
YEH — EVEN A WHALE FINDS YOU HARD TO SWALLOW.
ARG.
7·22

THE "MOONDOGS" ARE AT IT AGAIN — MONITORING ALL DOGGY TRANSMISSIONS FROM PLANET EARTH...
HOWL
HOWLWOOO
HOWL
EARL'S BEEN LEFT HOME ALONE, SIR.
WOOOOO
PETE IS STILL WAITING TO BE ADOPTED.
HOWL
AND GUARD DOG REMAINS CHAINED IN HIS YARD.
9·2
WHAT KIND OF UNCIVILIZED WORLD IS THIS!?!
HOWL
BUT NOT ALL THE NEWS IS BAD...
HOWLWOOO
WOOFIE LOVES A FULL MOON.
DON'T WE ALL, SIR.

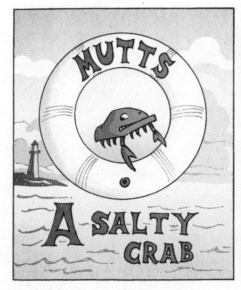

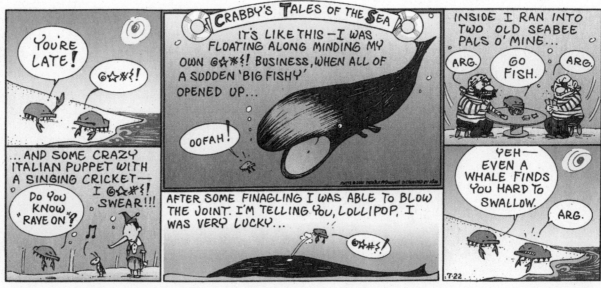

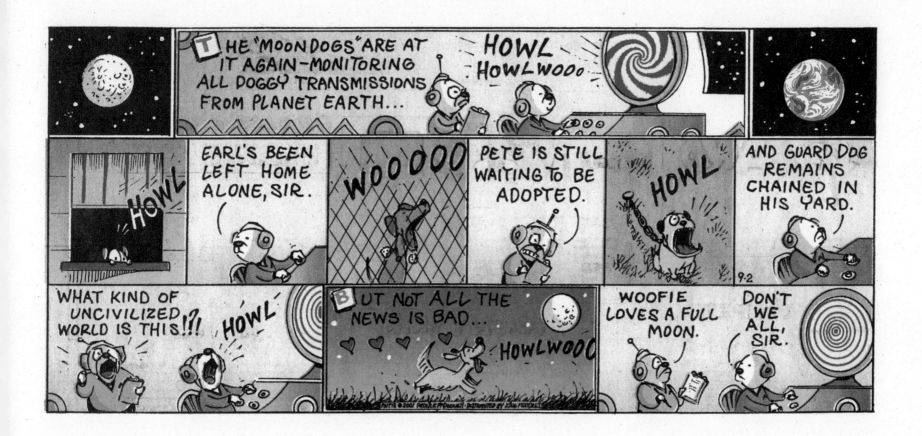

OH, KING, I'M NOT CRABBY ANYMORE! I'M... HAPPY!!! WHAT SHOULD I DO!?!
CRABBY, YOU'RE ONLY HAPPY BECAUSE YOU CHOOSE TO BE HAPPY.
8-24
THEN I CHOOSE TO BE CRABBY!
WHAT-EVER MAKES YOU @☆✱$! HAPPY.

WHERE DO YOU KEEP THE GUEST TOWELS?
8-31

MOOCH, DID YOU EVER WISH YOU WERE A LION, "KING OF THE JUNGLE"?
NO.
I'M CONTENT BEING JUST WHO I AM...
"KING OF EVERYTHING ELSE."
9-7

HAD A LITTLE TROUBLE GETTING OUT OF BED THIS MORNING.
9-8

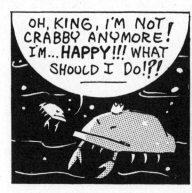

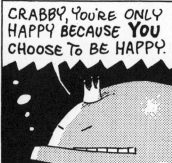

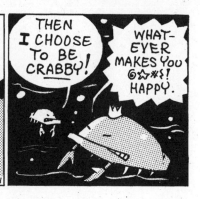

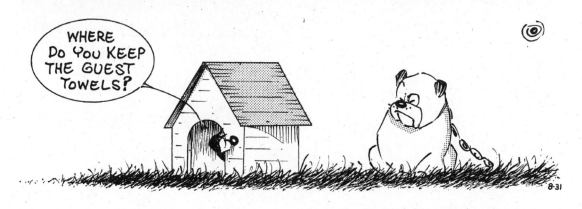

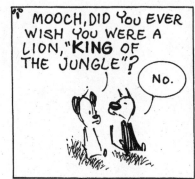

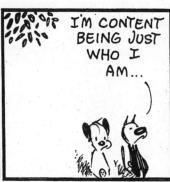

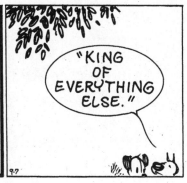

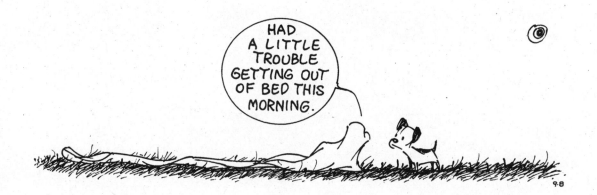

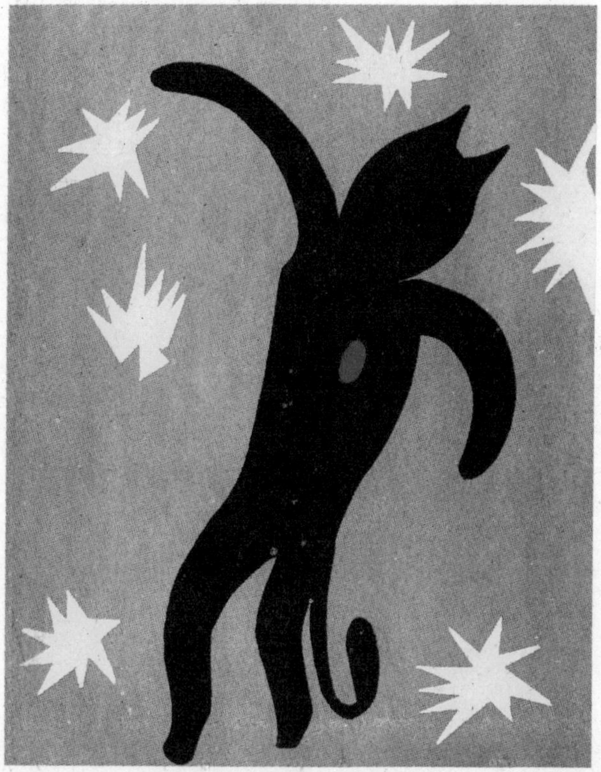

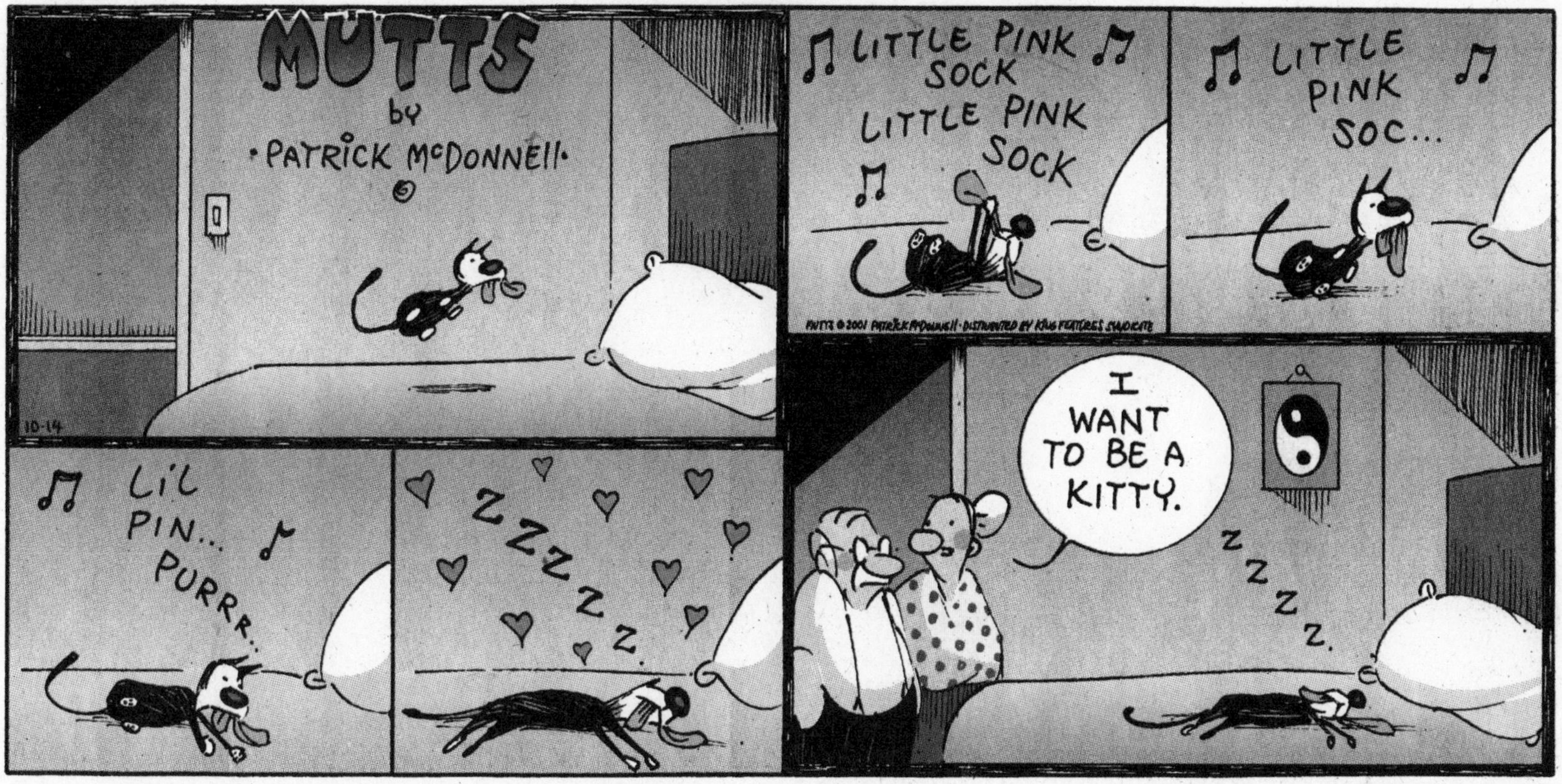
MUTTS
by
· PATRICK McDONNELL ·
©
10-14
LITTLE PINK SOCK
LITTLE PINK SOCK
MUTTS © 2001 PATRICK McDONNELL · DISTRIBUTED BY KING FEATURES SYNDICATE
LITTLE PINK SOC...
LI'L PIN... PURRR...
ZZZZZZ.
I WANT TO BE A KITTY.
ZZZZ.

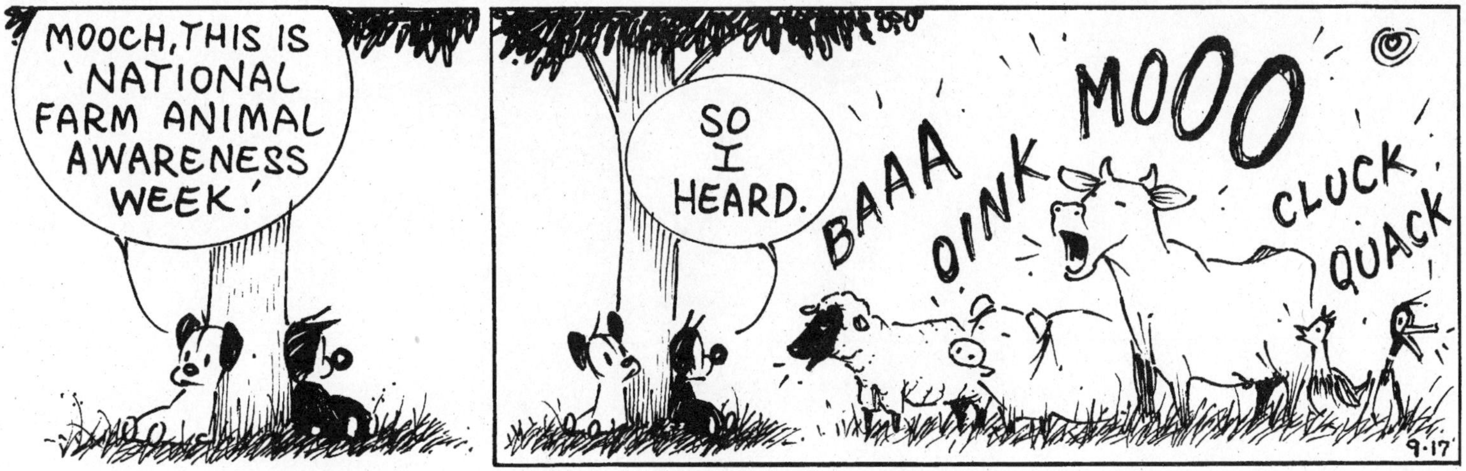
MOOCH, THIS IS 'NATIONAL FARM ANIMAL AWARENESS WEEK.'
SO I HEARD.
BAAA
OINK
MOOO
CLUCK
QUACK
9·17

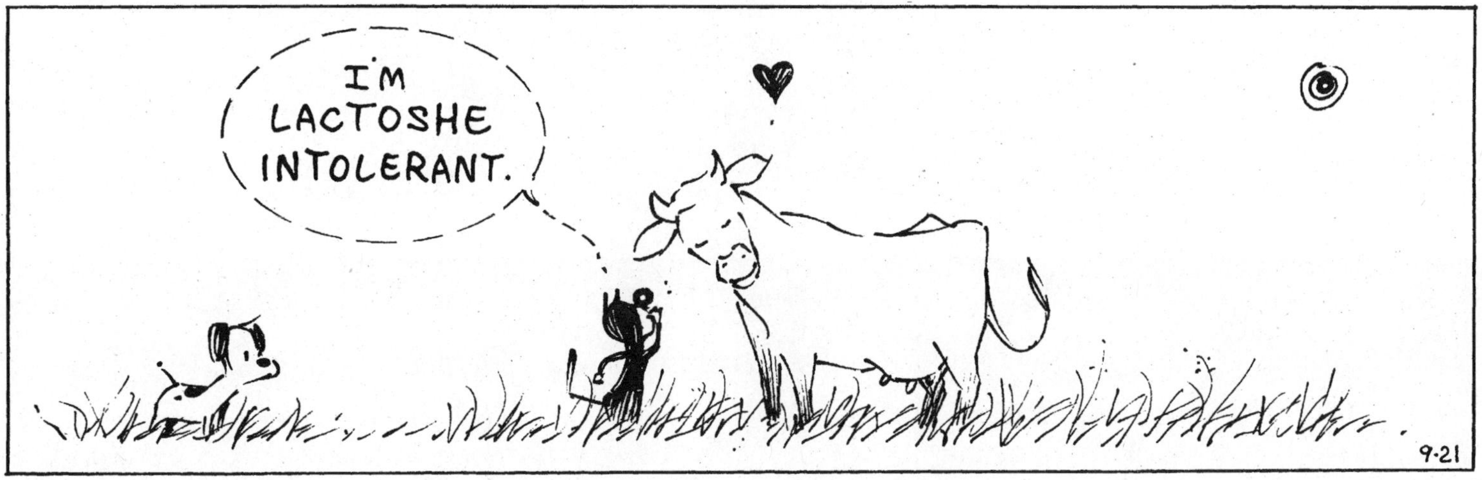
I'M LACTOSHE INTOLERANT.
9·21

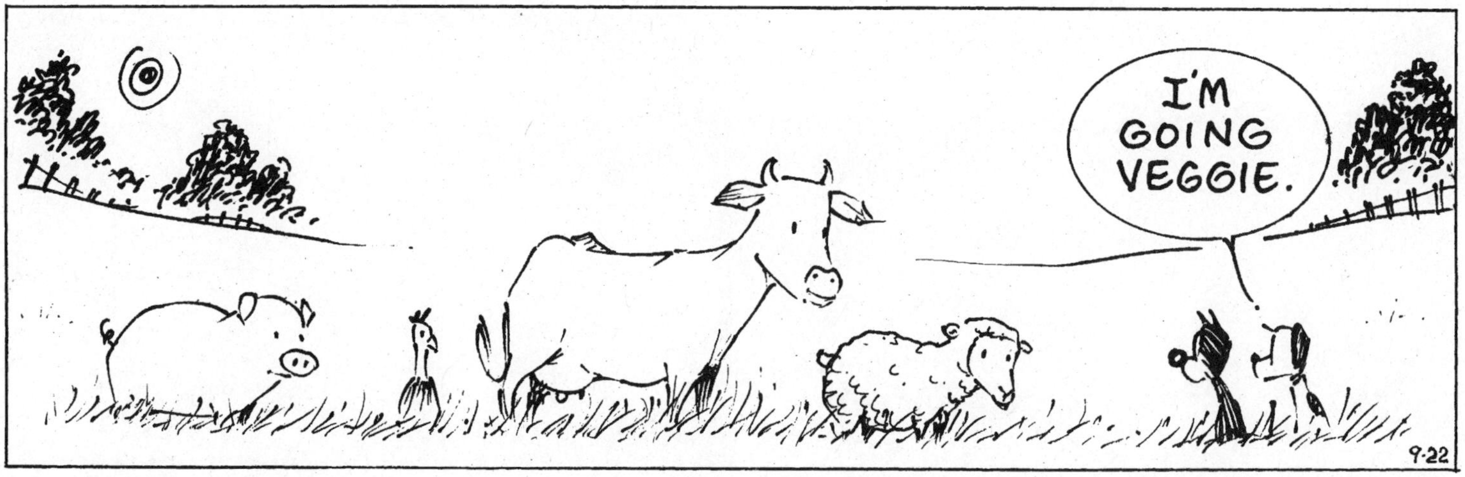
I'M GOING VEGGIE.
9·22

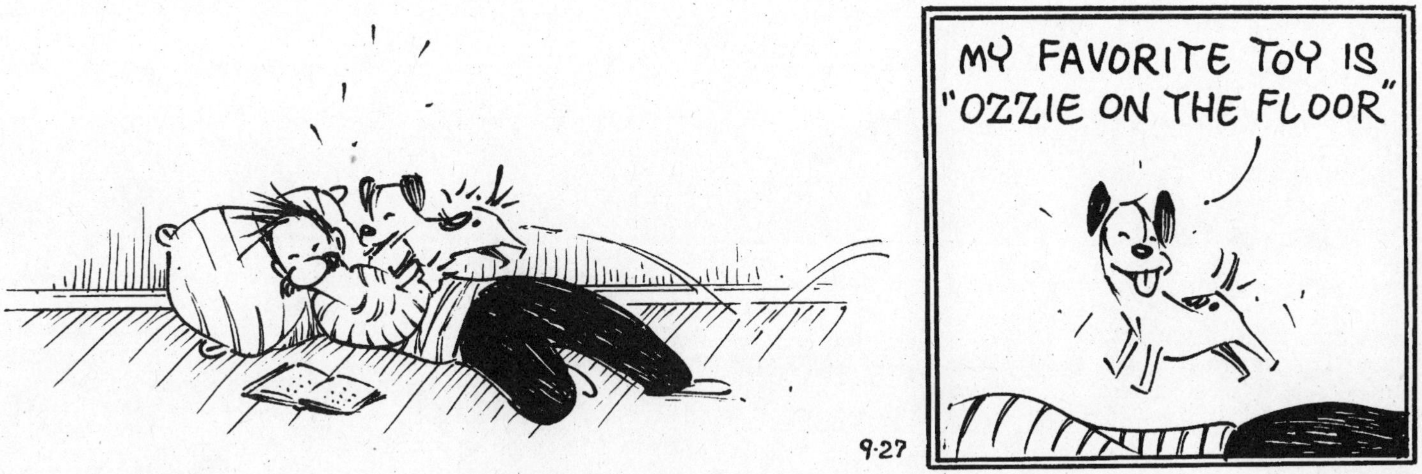
MY FAVORITE TOY IS "OZZIE ON THE FLOOR"
9·27

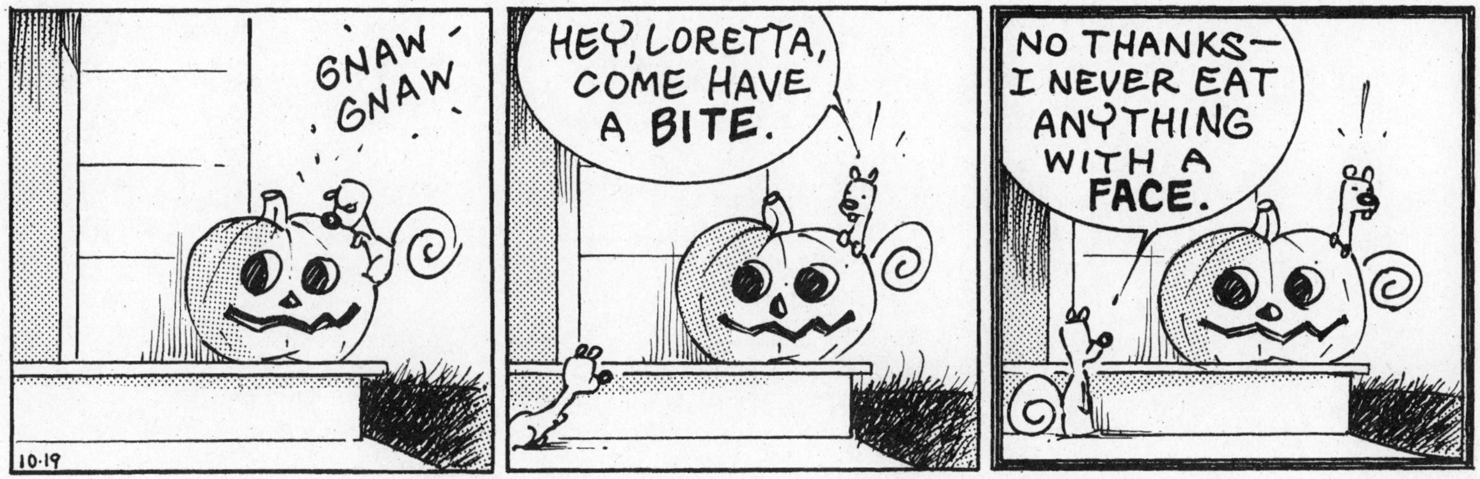
GNAW GNAW
10·19
HEY, LORETTA, COME HAVE A **BITE**.
NO THANKS— I NEVER EAT ANYTHING WITH A **FACE**.

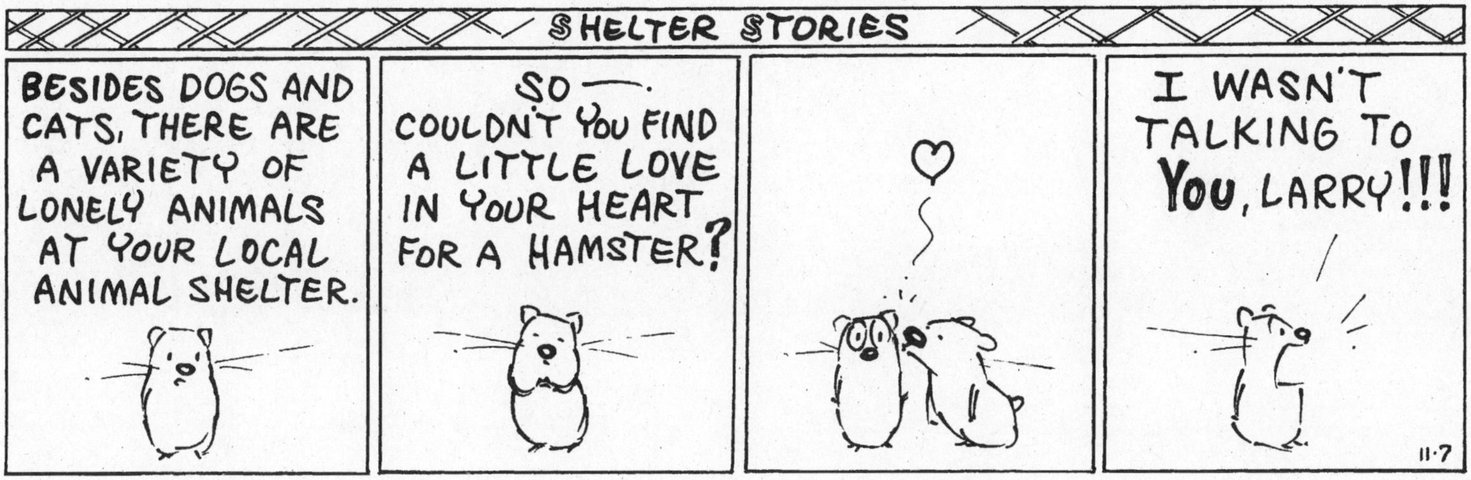
SHELTER STORIES
BESIDES DOGS AND CATS, THERE ARE A VARIETY OF LONELY ANIMALS AT YOUR LOCAL ANIMAL SHELTER.
SO— COULDN'T YOU FIND A LITTLE LOVE IN YOUR HEART FOR A HAMSTER?
I WASN'T TALKING TO **YOU**, LARRY!!!
11·7

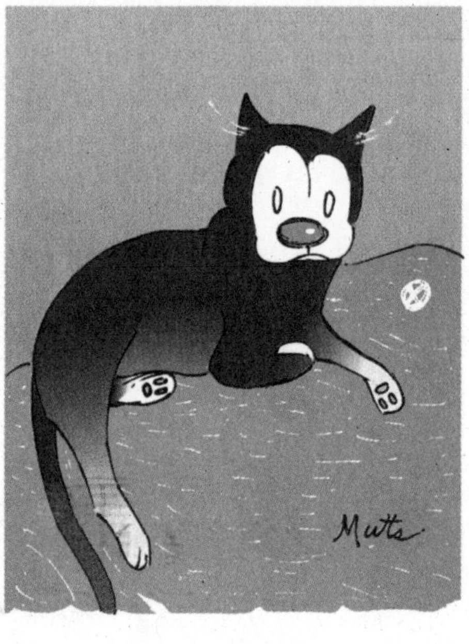

Mutts


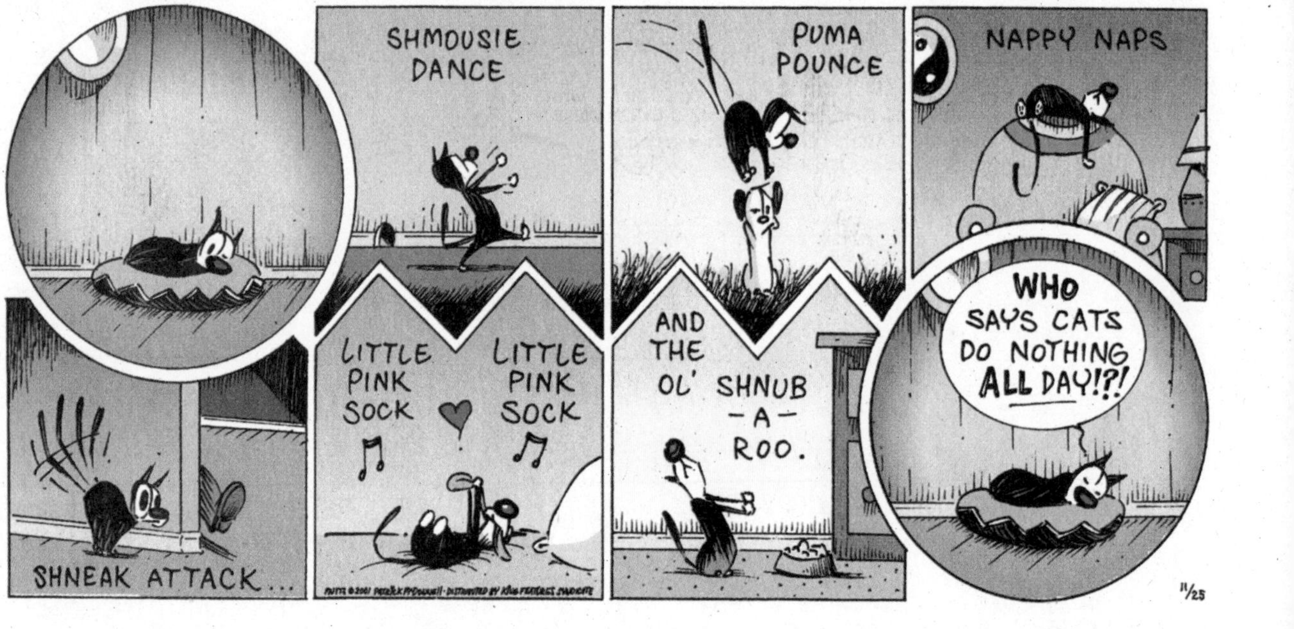

SHNEAK ATTACK...
SHMOUSIE DANCE
LITTLE PINK SOCK
LITTLE PINK SOCK
PUMA POUNCE
AND THE OL' SHNUB -A- ROO.
NAPPY NAPS
WHO SAYS CATS DO NOTHING ALL DAY!?!
11/25


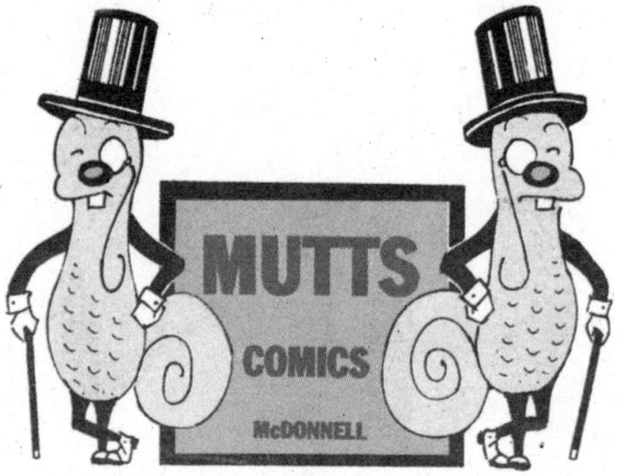

MUTTS
COMICS
McDONNELL


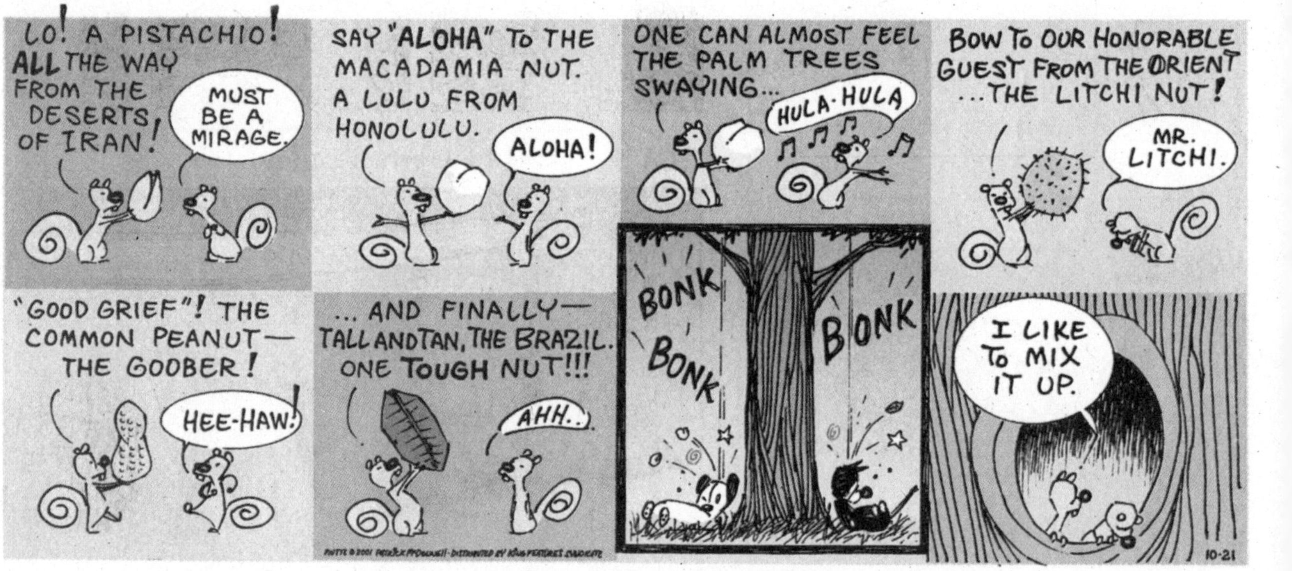

LO! A PISTACHIO! ALL THE WAY FROM THE DESERTS OF IRAN!
MUST BE A MIRAGE.
SAY "ALOHA" TO THE MACADAMIA NUT. A LULU FROM HONOLULU.
ALOHA!
ONE CAN ALMOST FEEL THE PALM TREES SWAYING...
HULA-HULA
BOW TO OUR HONORABLE GUEST FROM THE ORIENT ...THE LITCHI NUT!
MR. LITCHI.
"GOOD GRIEF"! THE COMMON PEANUT— THE GOOBER!
HEE-HAW!
... AND FINALLY— TALL AND TAN, THE BRAZIL. ONE TOUGH NUT!!!
AHH..
BONK
BONK
BONK
I LIKE TO MIX IT UP.
10-21

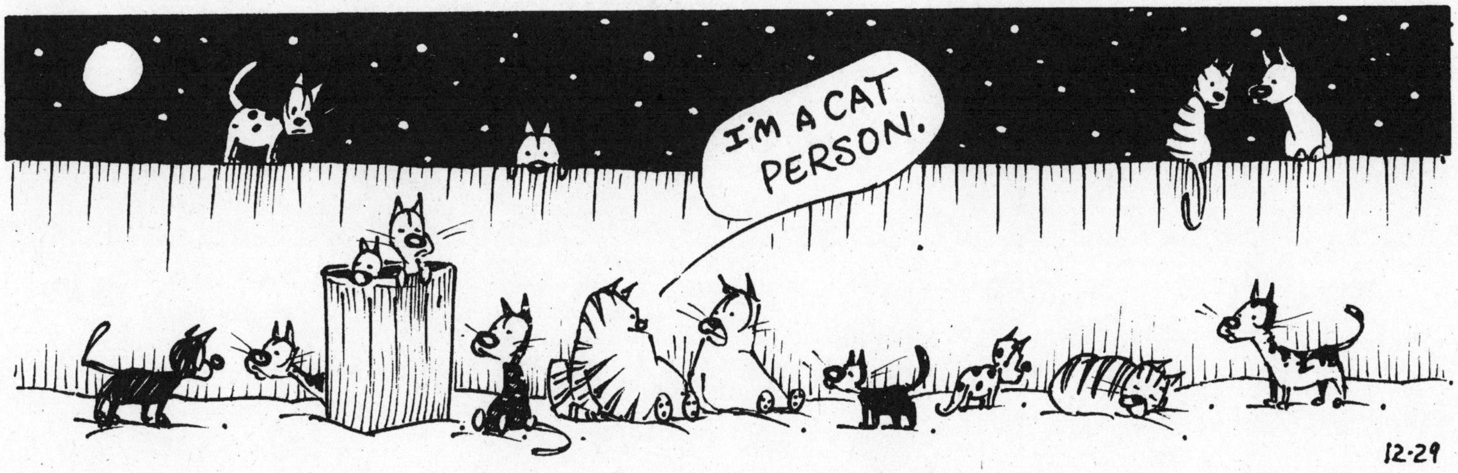
I'M A CAT PERSON.
12-29

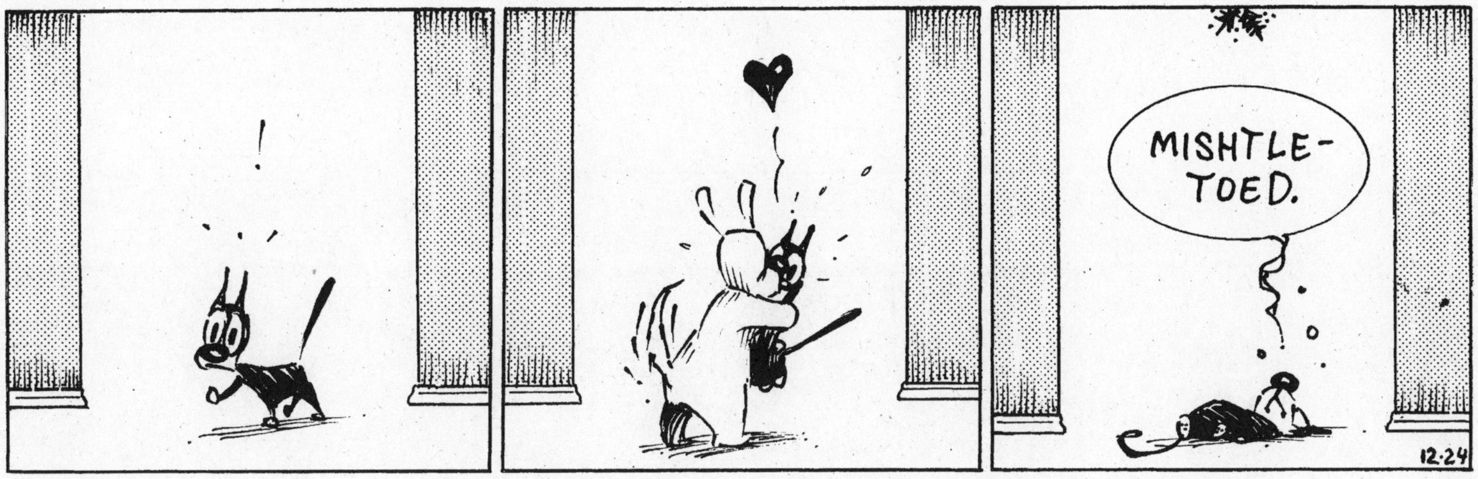
!
MISHTLE-TOED.
12-24

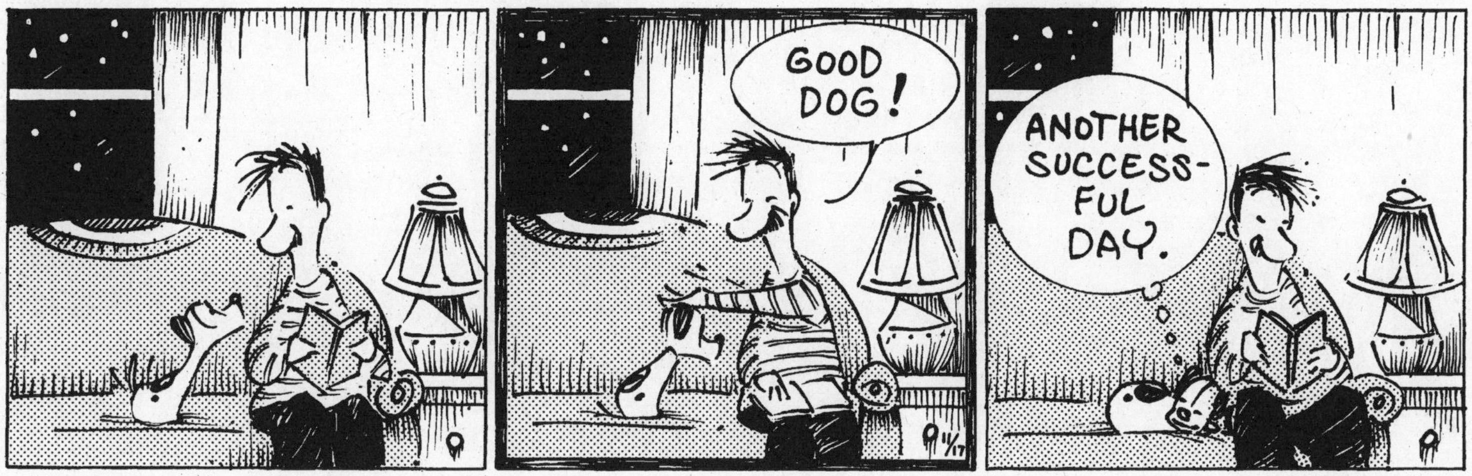
GOOD DOG!
ANOTHER SUCCESS-FUL DAY.

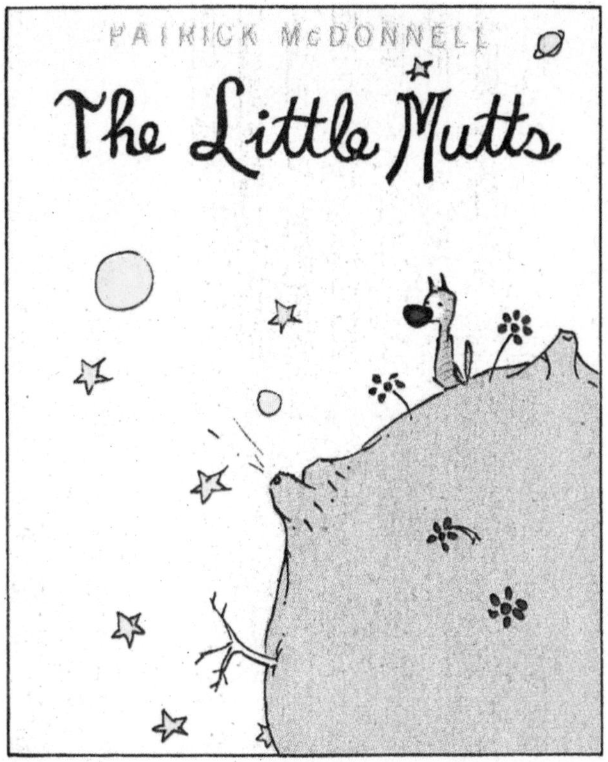
PATRICK McDONNELL
The Little Mutts

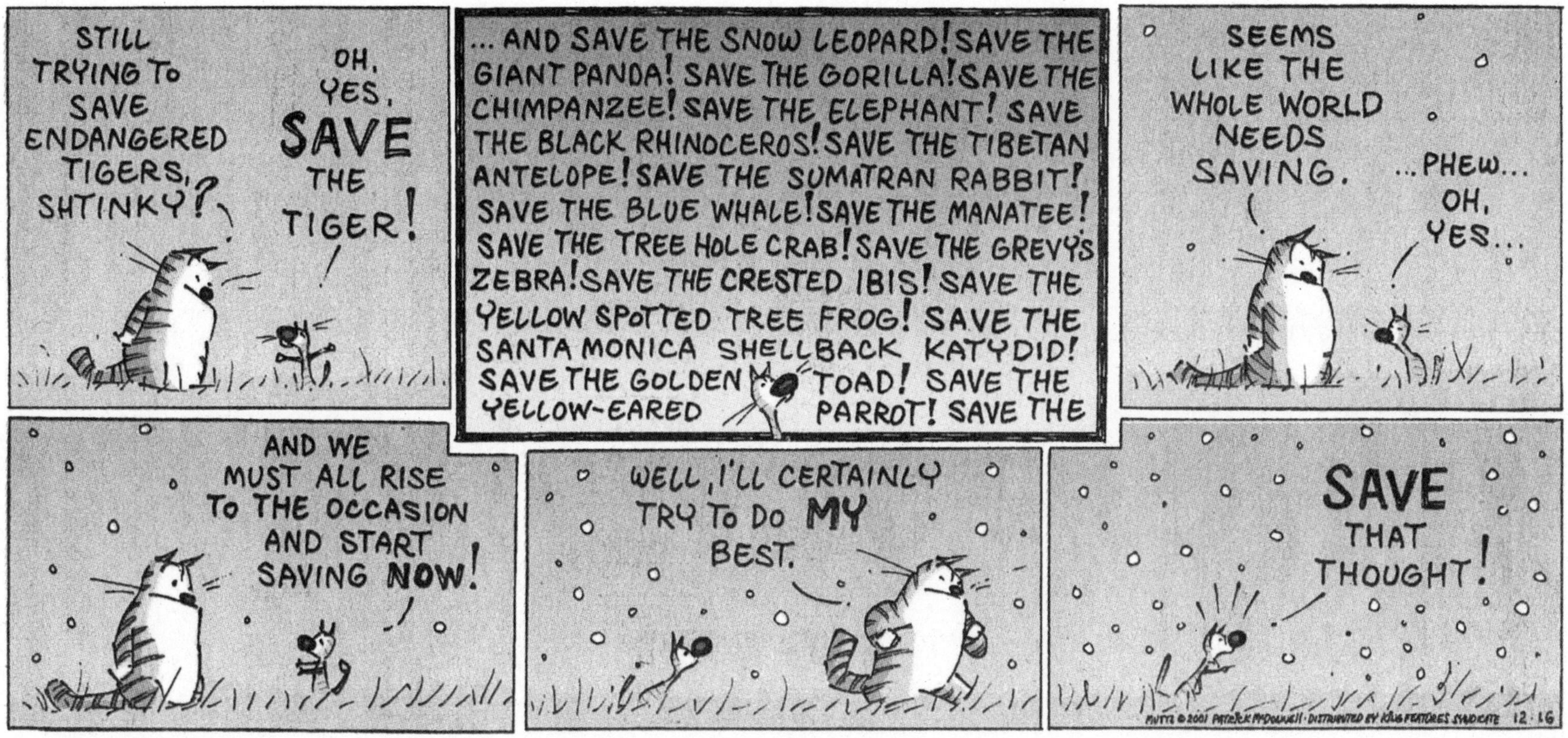
STILL TRYING TO SAVE ENDANGERED TIGERS, SHTINKY?
OH, YES. SAVE THE TIGER!
... AND SAVE THE SNOW LEOPARD! SAVE THE GIANT PANDA! SAVE THE GORILLA! SAVE THE CHIMPANZEE! SAVE THE ELEPHANT! SAVE THE BLACK RHINOCEROS! SAVE THE TIBETAN ANTELOPE! SAVE THE SUMATRAN RABBIT! SAVE THE BLUE WHALE! SAVE THE MANATEE! SAVE THE TREE HOLE CRAB! SAVE THE GREVY'S ZEBRA! SAVE THE CRESTED IBIS! SAVE THE YELLOW SPOTTED TREE FROG! SAVE THE SANTA MONICA SHELLBACK KATYDID! SAVE THE GOLDEN TOAD! SAVE THE YELLOW-EARED PARROT! SAVE THE
SEEMS LIKE THE WHOLE WORLD NEEDS SAVING.
...PHEW... OH, YES...
AND WE MUST ALL RISE TO THE OCCASION AND START SAVING NOW!
WELL, I'LL CERTAINLY TRY TO DO MY BEST.
SAVE THAT THOUGHT!

**This year started off** with Mooch in Frank and Millie's big cozy bed, preparing to hibernate through the winter. Of course, Earl, the ever-faithful canine, tags along. But in typical Mooch fashion, the one thing he doesn't do while hibernating is actually sleep.

In this fast, and getting faster, busy world I think we're all overwhelmed with obligations and hectic schedules. Most people I know have very long To Do lists. We're lucky if we are able to complete half of all we plan to do on a given day. All this craziness had me thinking about my cat MeeMow's To Do list. What would it look like? Hmmmm . . . I think I'd trade lists with her any day.

I believe I received more feedback from the May 26 Sunday page (page 199) than from any other strip. It was a takeoff of Big Brother and the Holding Company's *Cheap Thrills* album cover, which was drawn by the great cartoonist Robert Crumb. A lot of the letters were written by people who reminisced about that special time in our history. I think we all wanted to celebrate the powerful and lasting impact that that music and art had on us.

The comic strip from September 11 (page 205) was drawn to commemorate the anniversary of 9/11.

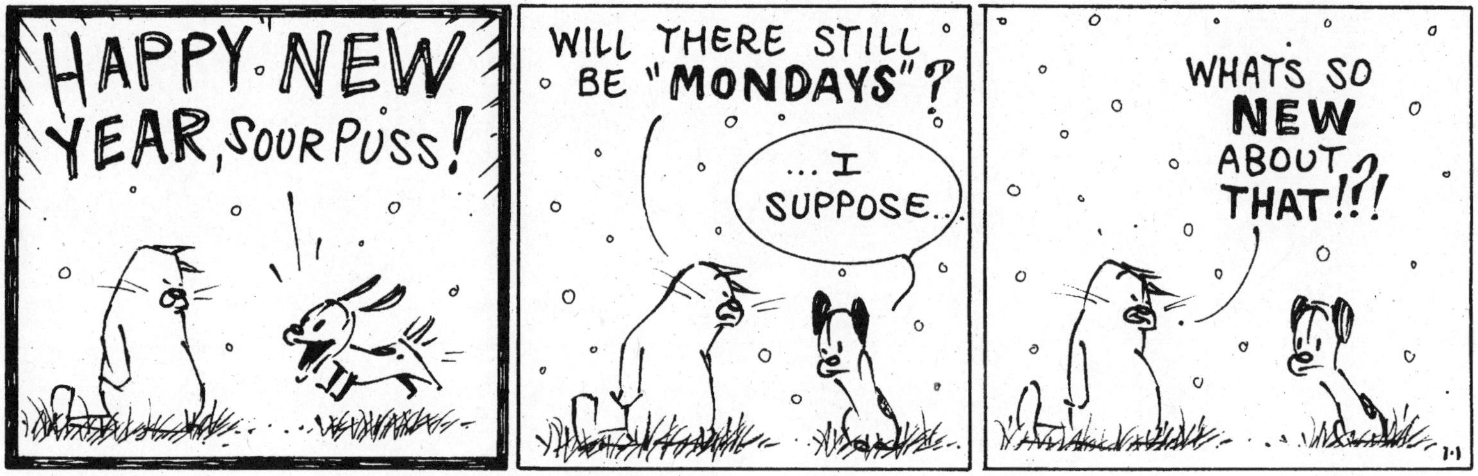
HAPPY NEW YEAR, SOUR PUSS!
WILL THERE STILL BE "MONDAYS"?
...I SUPPOSE...
WHATS SO NEW ABOUT THAT!?!

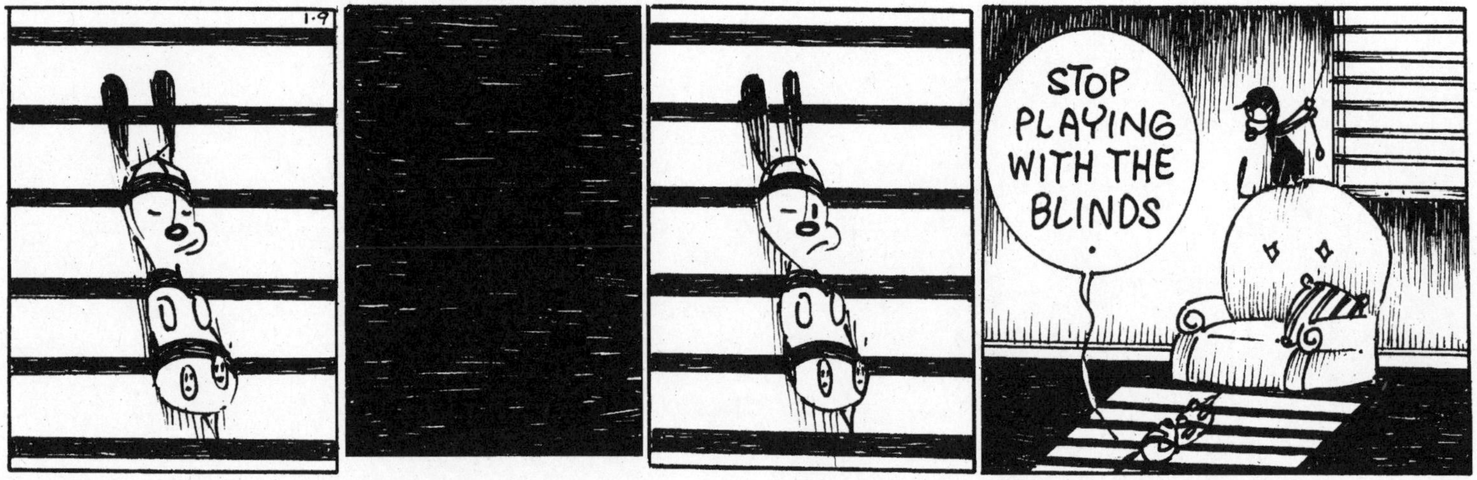
STOP PLAYING WITH THE BLINDS

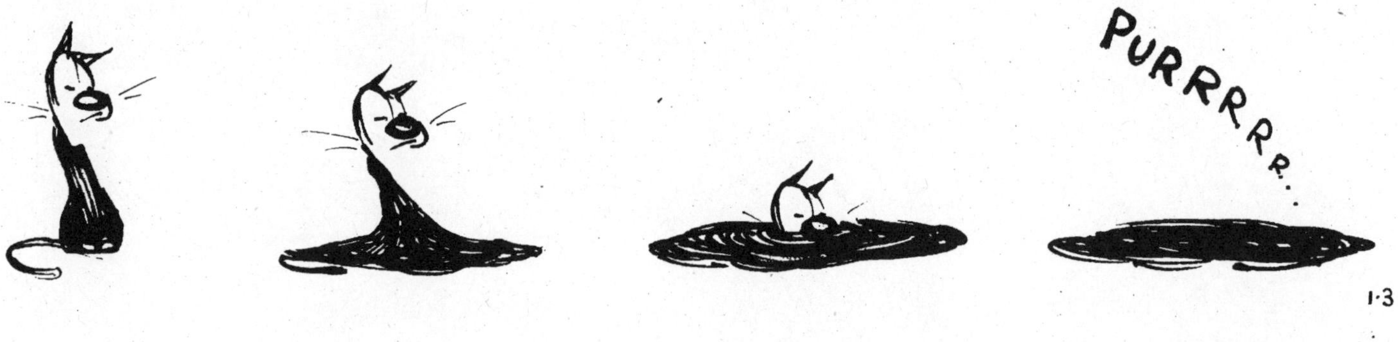
PURRRRR...

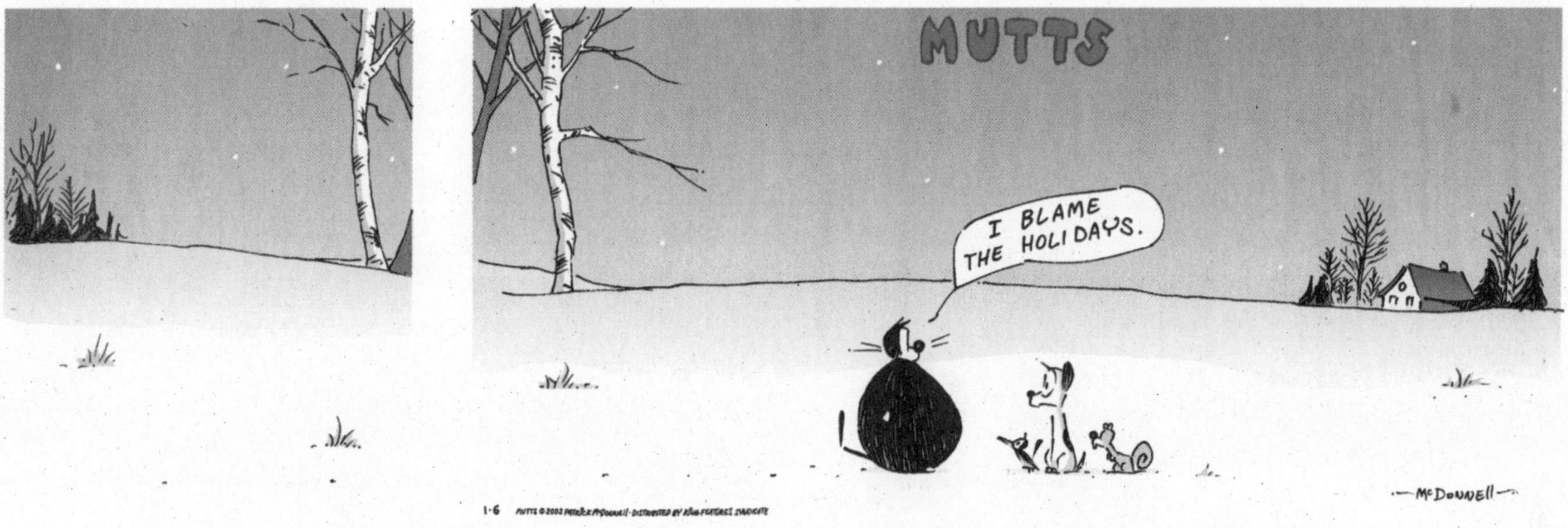
MUTTS
I BLAME THE HOLIDAYS.
1-6
McDONNELL

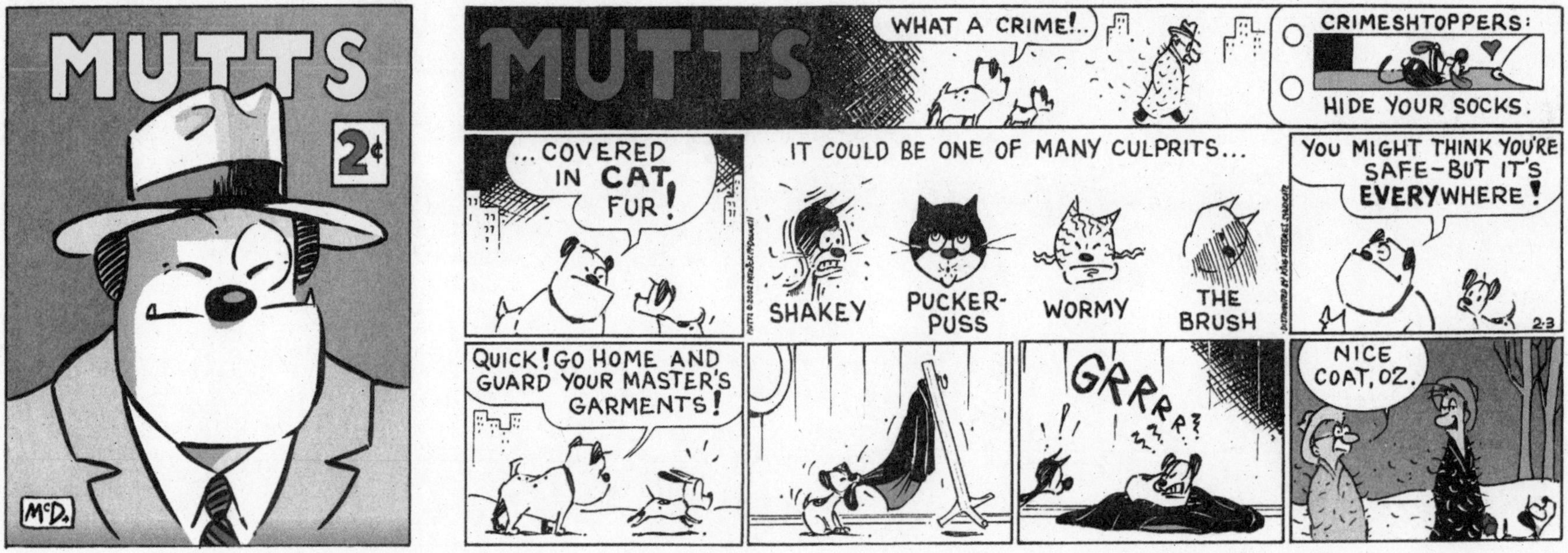
MUTTS
2¢
McD.
MUTTS
WHAT A CRIME!..
CRIMESHTOPPERS:
HIDE YOUR SOCKS.
... COVERED IN CAT FUR!
IT COULD BE ONE OF MANY CULPRITS...
SHAKEY
PUCKER-PUSS
WORMY
THE BRUSH
YOU MIGHT THINK YOU'RE SAFE–BUT IT'S EVERYWHERE!
2-3
QUICK! GO HOME AND GUARD YOUR MASTER'S GARMENTS!
GRRRRR
NICE COAT, OZ.

I THINK I'LL SHTAY IN BED ALL DAY TODAY.
mmmmm...
A MAN WITH A PLAN.
1·14

MOOCH! ARE YOU GOING TO STAY IN BED ALL WINTER!?!
I'M THINKING ABOUT IT.
THAT'S CRAZY! GET YOUR TUSHIE OUT OF THAT BED RIGHT NOW!
I CAN'T...
HE'S ASHLEEP.
1·15

MOOCH— YOU'RE CRAZY TO STAY IN BED ALL WINTER!!!
YESH...
...AND TOASHTY.
MOVE OVER.
1·16

MMMM... NOW FOR A NICE, LONG HIBERNATION.
YESH.
HEY!
KICK KICK KICK
JIMMY LEGS.
1·17

OKAY, MOOCH— THAT'S IT! NO MORE NONSENSE! LET'S HIBERNATE!
YESH.
YOUR TAIL IS ON MY SIDE OF THE BED.
YOUR BREATH KNOWS NO BOUNDARIES.
1·18

DO YOU SNORE?
HOW WOULD I KNOW?
1·19

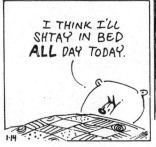

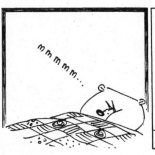

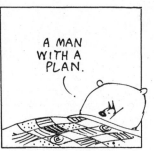

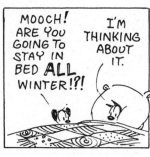

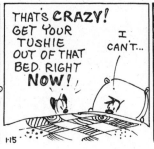

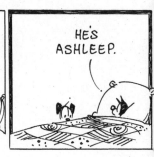

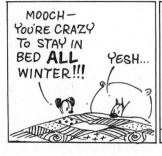

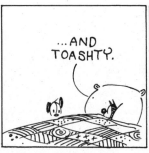

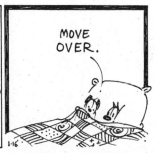

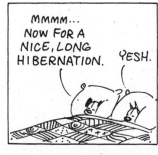

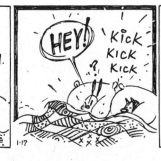

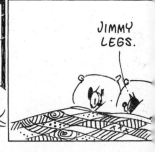

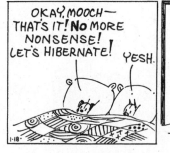

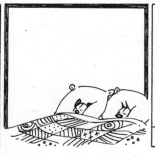

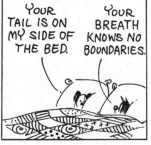

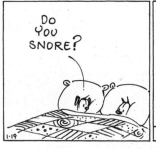

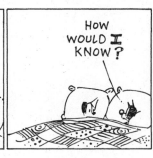

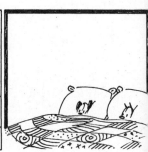

EARL, CAN YOU TELL ME A SHTORY SO I CAN HIBERNATE?
OKAY.
ONCE UPON A TIME . . .
UH...
I'VE HEARD THAT ONE.
1-21

MOOCH, CAN WE PLEASE STOP THE **NONSENSE** AND HIBERNATE!?!
YESH.
CRUNCH CRUNCH
SHPOTATO CHIP?
1-22

1-23
NOTHING'S WORKING.

AHH... MY MIND IS **FINALLY** CLEAR ... NOW I CAN SLEEP...
G'NIGHT.
DON'T LET THE BEDBUGS BITE.
Z . Z . Z
1-24

HOW LONG HAVE WE BEEN HIBERNATING, EARL?
EIGHT MINUTES.
IS THAT SHOME KIND OF RECORD?
1-25

OKAY, MOOCH, NOW LET'S DO SOME **SERIOUS** HIBERNATING! — I'LL SEE YA IN MARCH.
YESH.
1-26
DIN-DIN

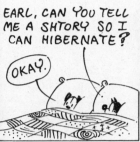

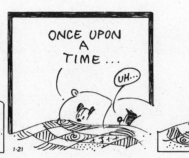

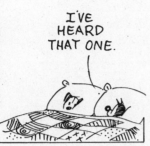

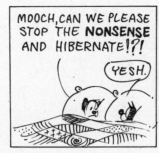

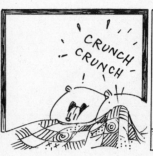

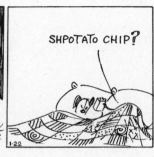

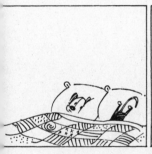

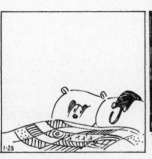

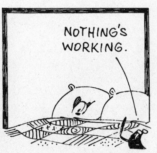

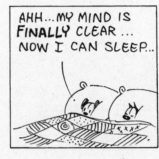

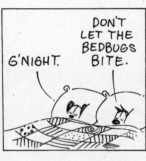

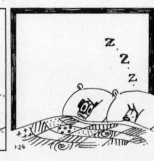

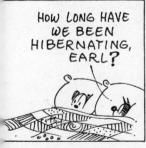

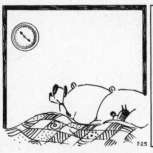

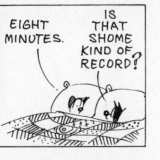

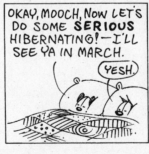

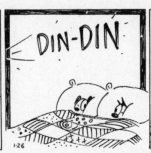

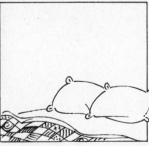

MUTTS WORLD
DRAWN BY P.L. McDONNELL

WE'RE LITTLE SNOW-FLAKES
FROM HEAVEN
WE ARE ALL UNIQUE
JUST LIKE YOU
WE'RE HERE ON EARTH
TO BECOME ONE.
IT'S DEEP.
YESH.
MUTTS © 2002 PATRICK McDONNELL

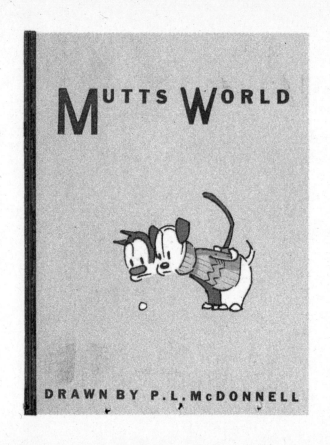

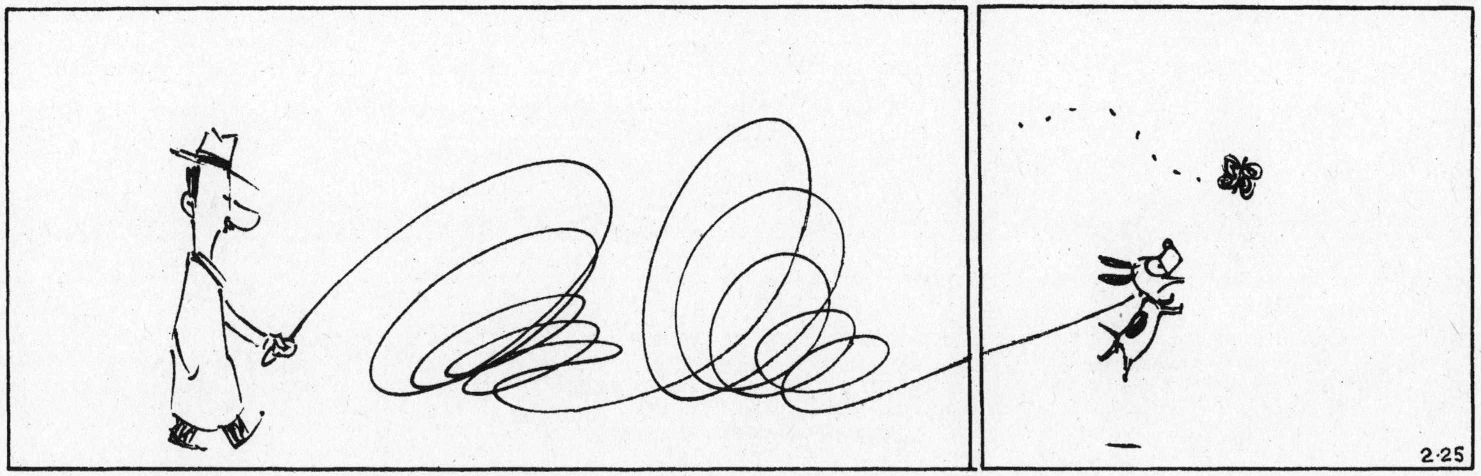
2·25

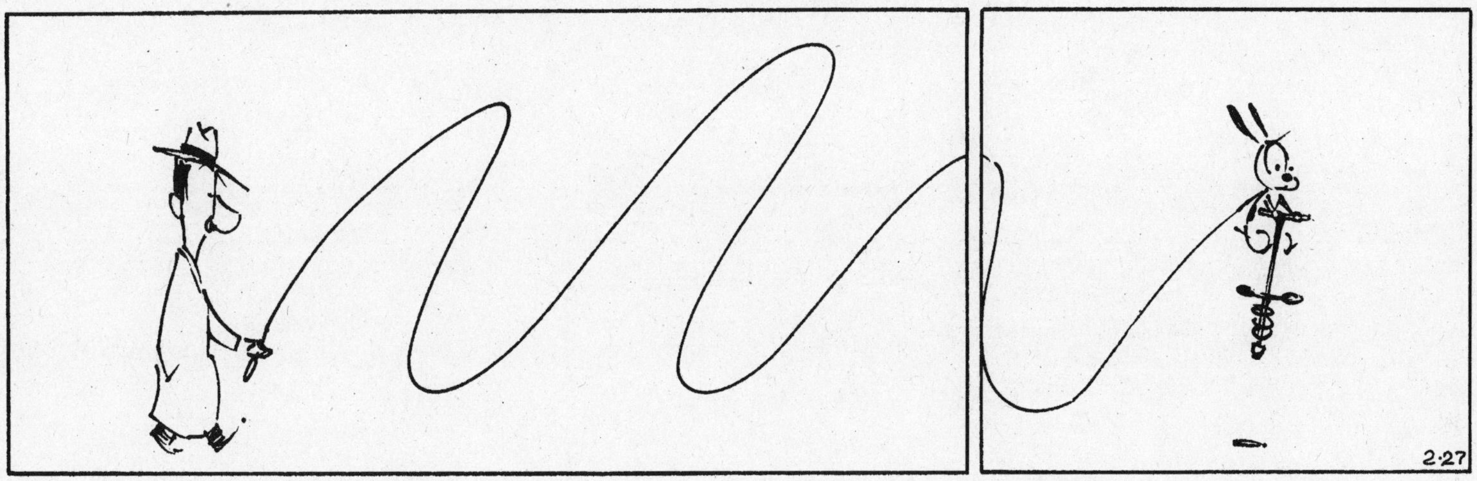
2·27

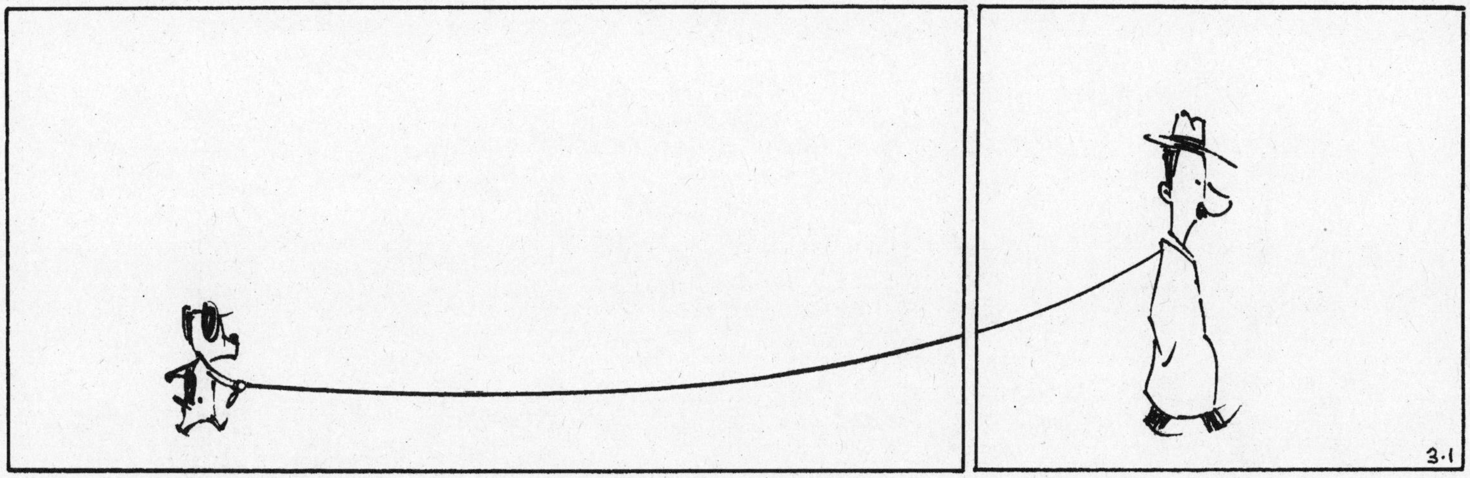
3·1

I'M IN THE MOOD FOR PISTACHIOS.
2·7

KITTY!
WHAT'S THAT, WOOFIE?
A STOMACH.
I'M IN WUV— BUT I'M ALSO A WITTLE HUNGWY.
2·15

THE SHECRET TO SHMEDITATION, EARL, IS TO CLEAR ONE'S MIND OF ALL THOUGHT.
THAT CAN'T BE TOO HARD FOR YOU, MOOCH.
No.
ONCE I GET PAST "TUNA" IT'S SHMOOTH SHAILING.
3·26

IS IT SPRING YET?
I BELIEVE IT'S THIS WEDNESDAY AT 2:16 P.M. EASTERN STANDARD TIME.
HMMM...
THAT WAS GOING TO BE MY GUESS.
3·19

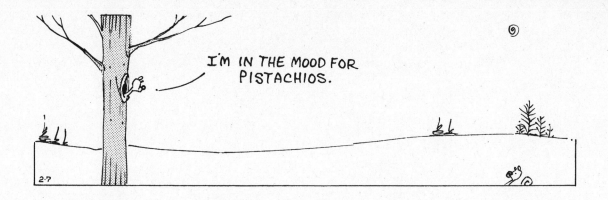

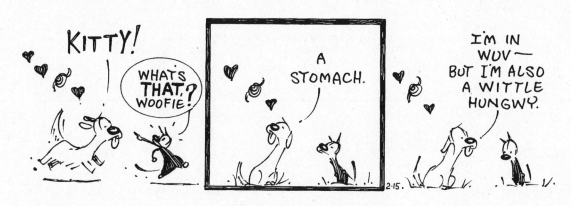

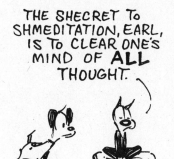

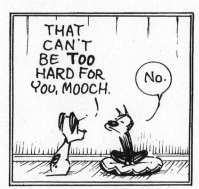

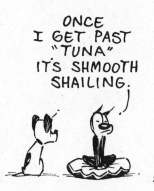

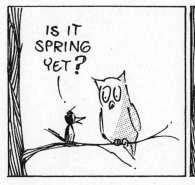

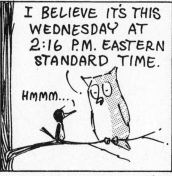

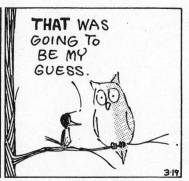

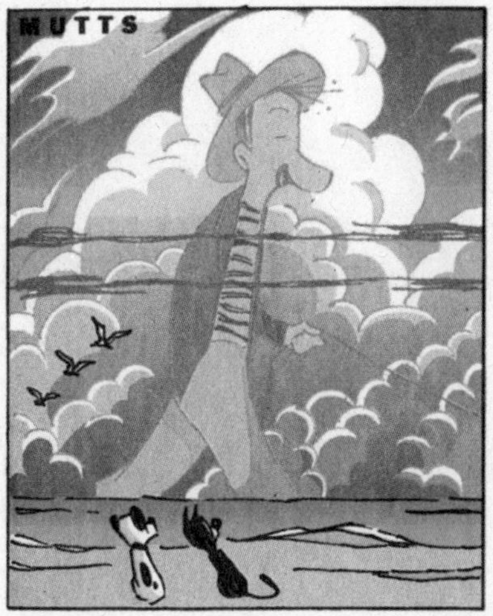
MUTTS

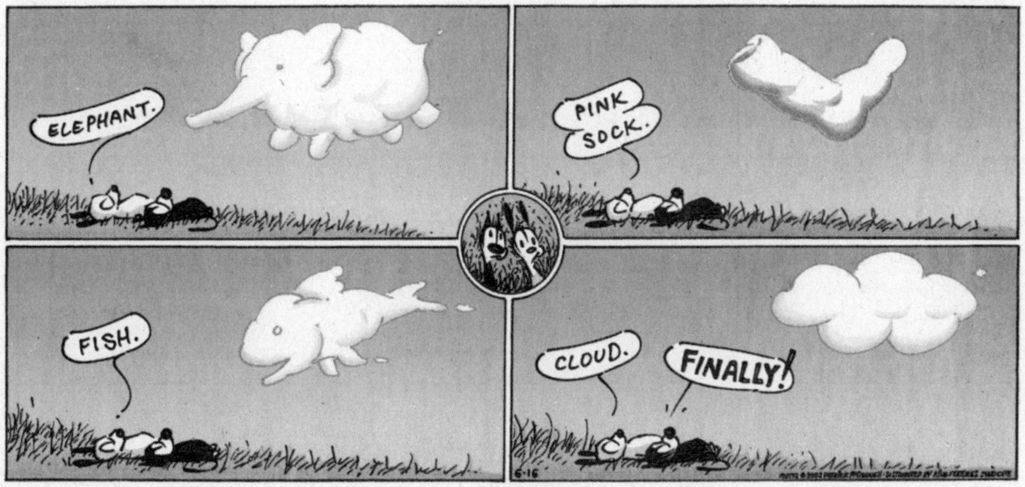
ELEPHANT.
PINK SOCK.
FISH.
CLOUD.
FINALLY!
6-16

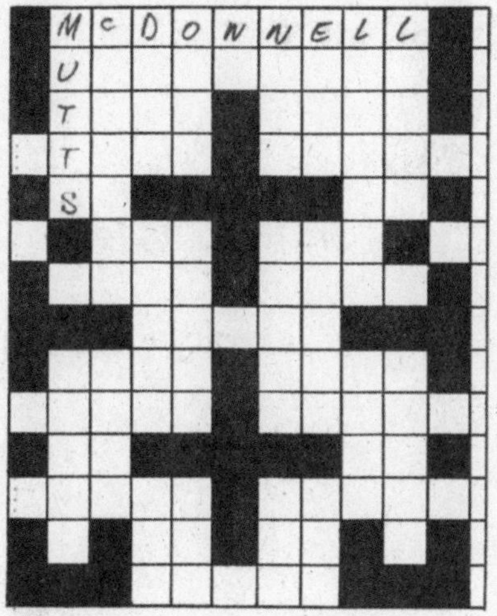
McDONNELL
MUTTS

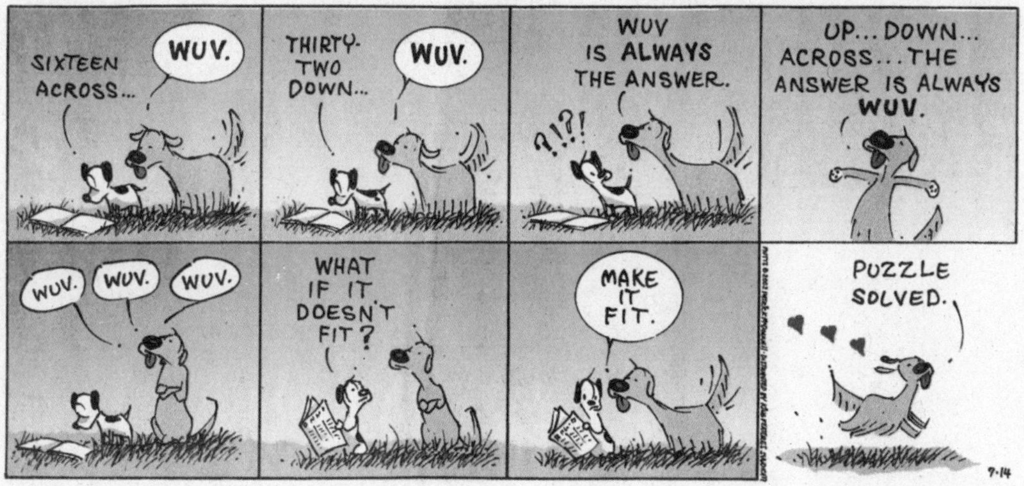
SIXTEEN ACROSS...
WUV.
THIRTY-TWO DOWN...
WUV.
WUV IS ALWAYS THE ANSWER.
?!?!
UP... DOWN... ACROSS... THE ANSWER IS ALWAYS WUV.
WUV.
WUV.
WUV.
WHAT IF IT DOESN'T FIT?
MAKE IT FIT.
PUZZLE SOLVED.
9-14

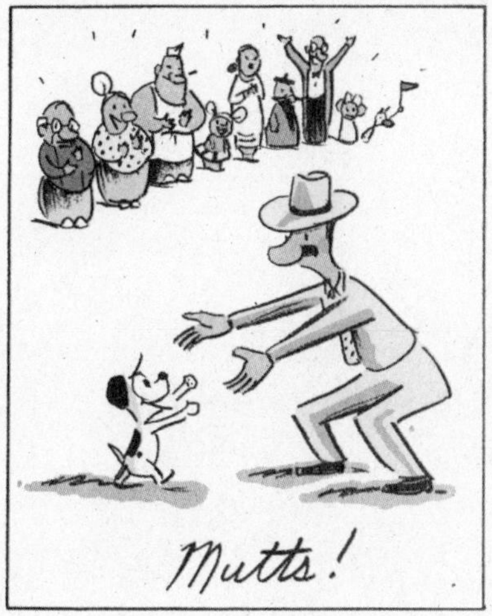
Mutts!

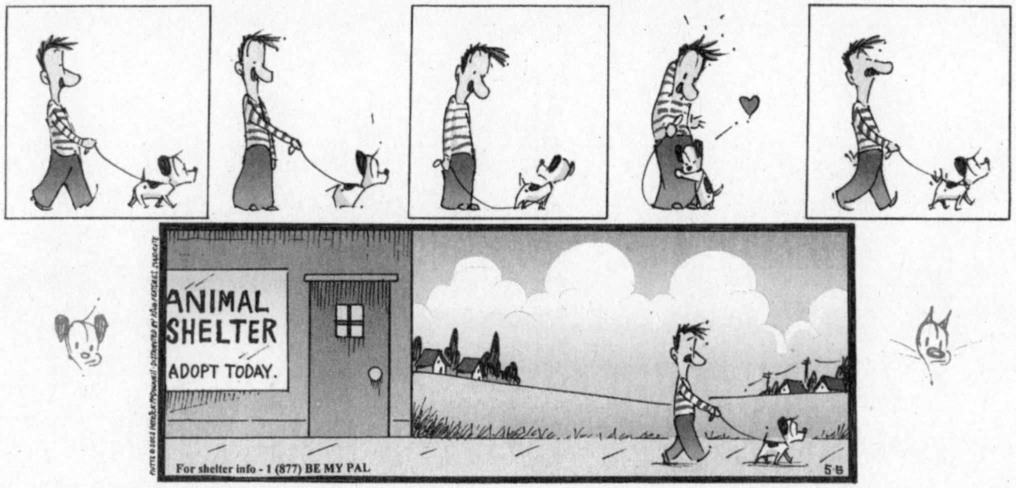
ANIMAL SHELTER
ADOPT TODAY.
For shelter info - 1 (877) BE MY PAL
5-8

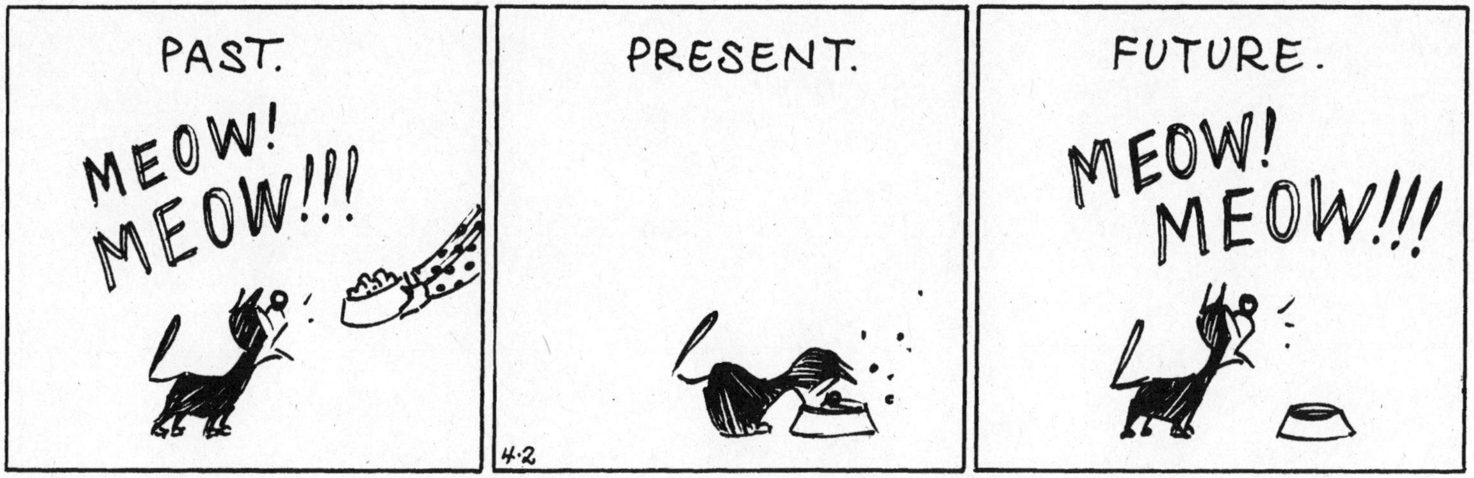
PAST.
MEOW! MEOW!!!
PRESENT.
FUTURE.
MEOW! MEOW!!!
4·2

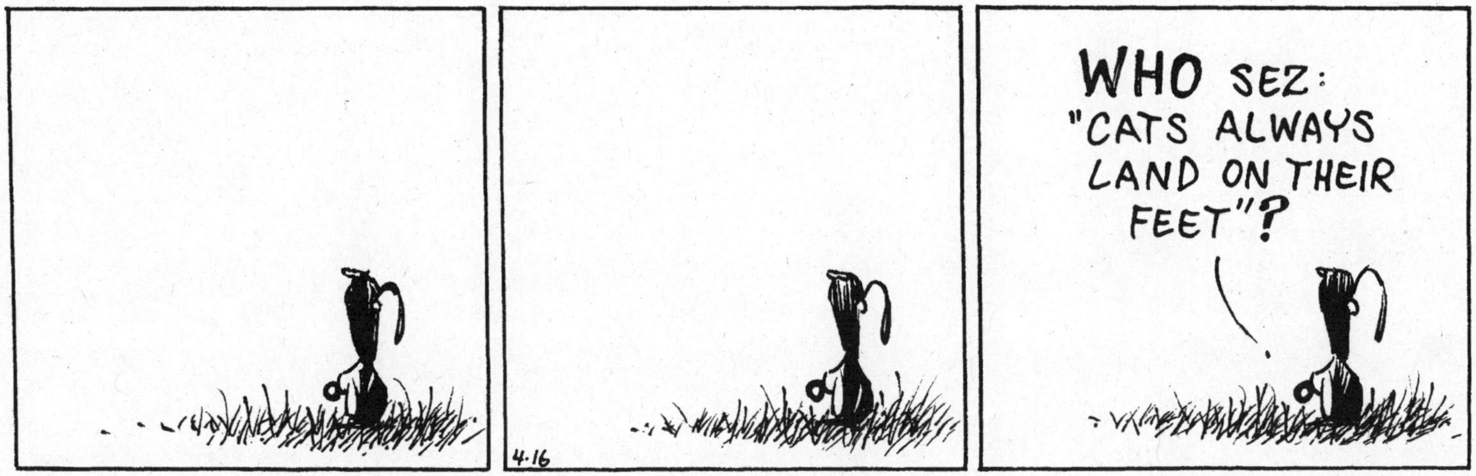
WHO SEZ: "CATS ALWAYS LAND ON THEIR FEET"?
4·16

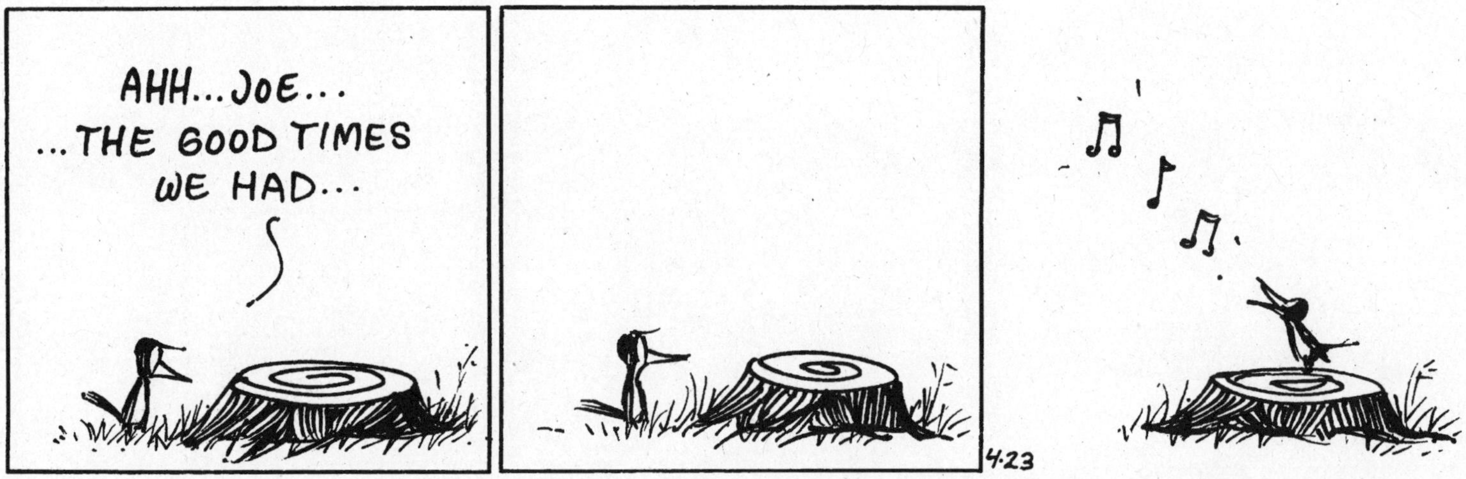
AHH...JOE... ...THE GOOD TIMES WE HAD...
4·23

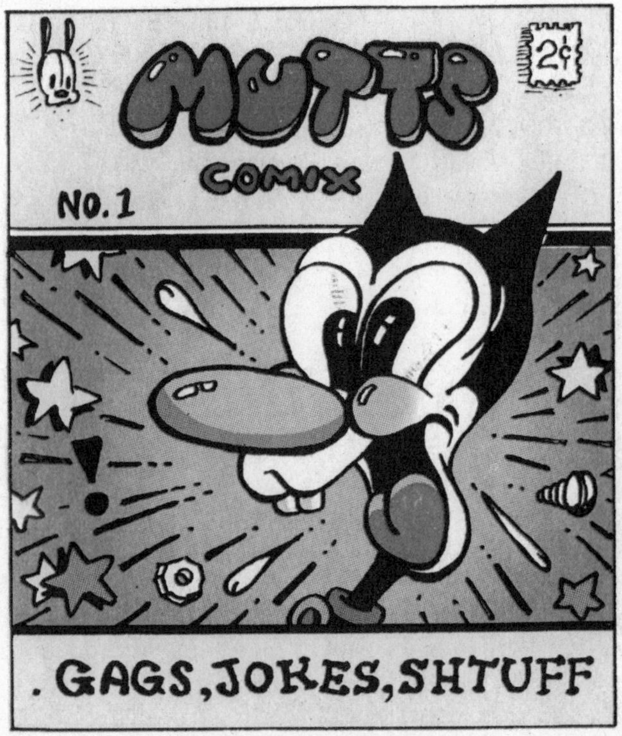
2¢
MUTTS
COMIX
NO. 1
. GAGS, JOKES, SHTUFF

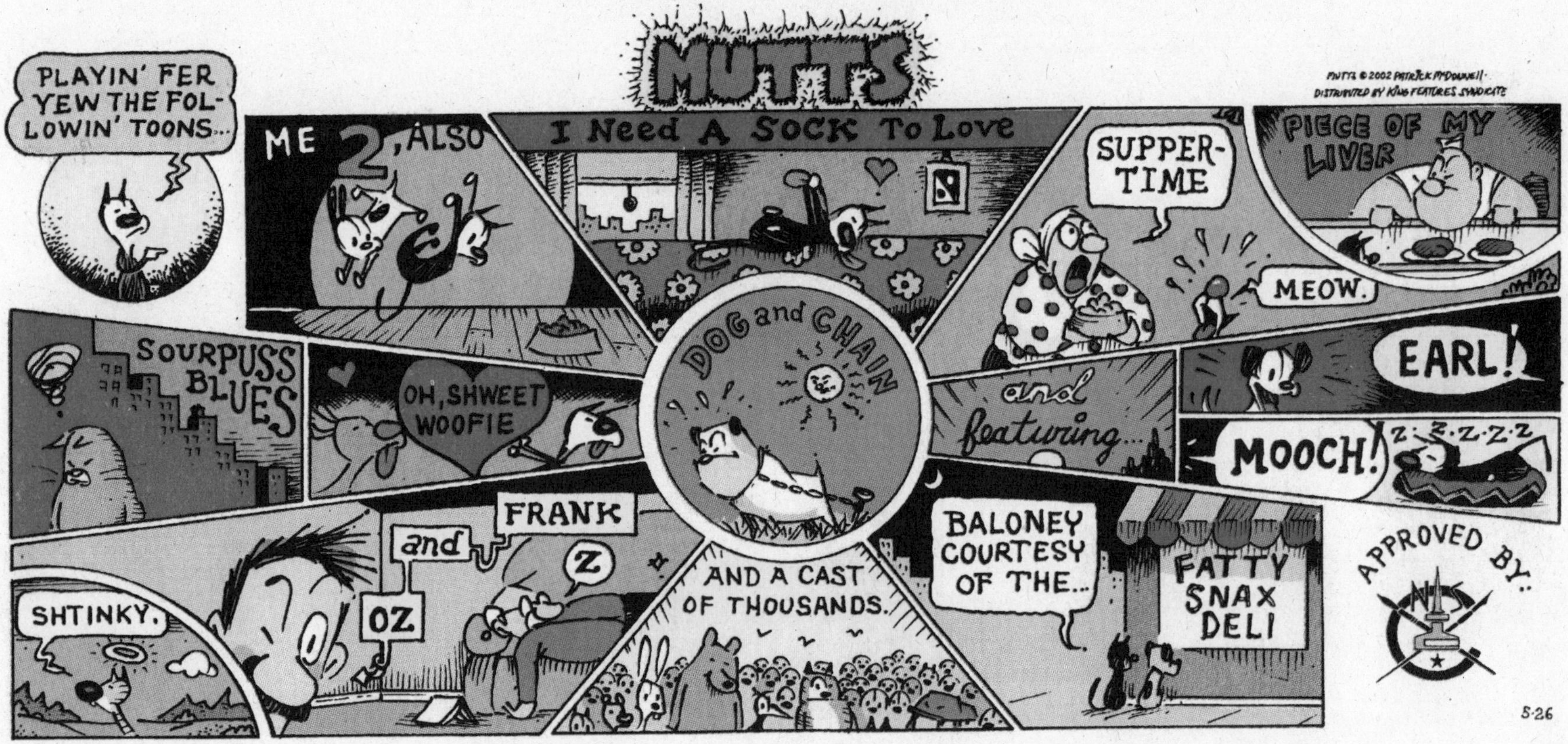
MUTTS
MUTTS © 2002 PATRICK McDONNELL·
DISTRIBUTED BY KING FEATURES SYNDICATE
PLAYIN' FER YEW THE FOL-LOWIN' TOONS...
ME 2, ALSO
I Need A SOCK To Love
SUPPER-TIME
PIECE OF MY LIVER
MEOW.
SOURPUSS BLUES
OH, SHWEET WOOFIE
DOG and CHAIN
and featuring...
EARL!
MOOCH!
Z.Z.Z.Z.Z
FRANK
and
OZ
Z
SHTINKY.
AND A CAST OF THOUSANDS.
BALONEY COURTESY OF THE...
FATTY SNAX DELI
APPROVED BY:
5·26

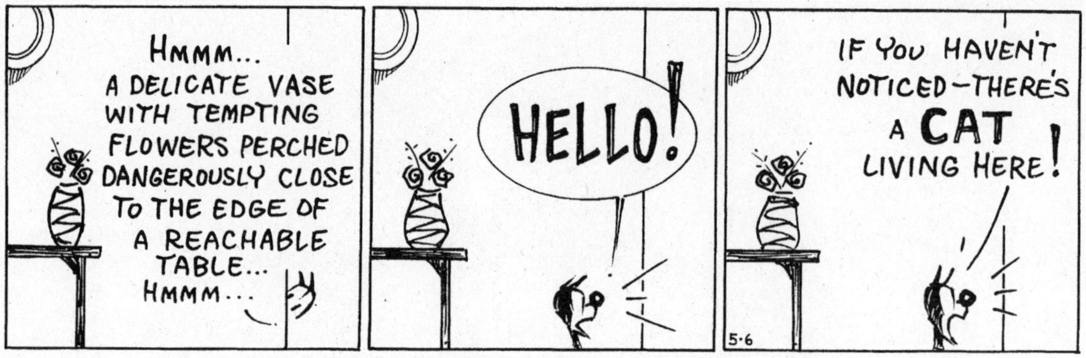
HMMM... A DELICATE VASE WITH TEMPTING FLOWERS PERCHED DANGEROUSLY CLOSE TO THE EDGE OF A REACHABLE TABLE... HMMM...
HELLO!
IF YOU HAVEN'T NOTICED—THERE'S A CAT LIVING HERE!
5·6

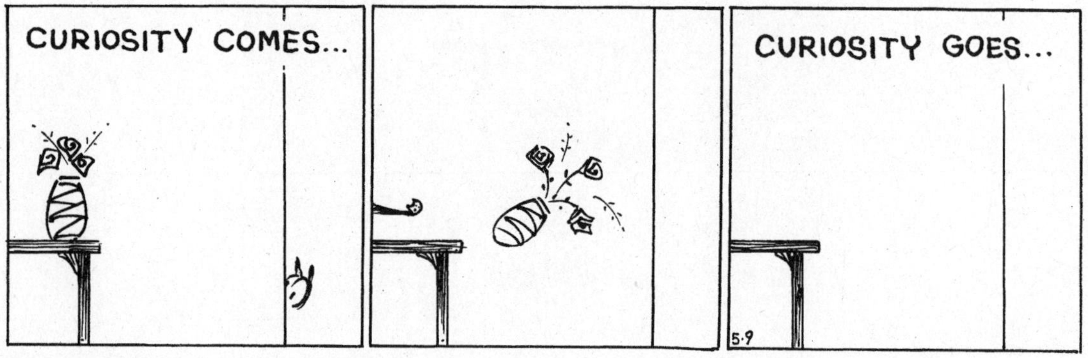
CURIOSITY COMES...
CURIOSITY GOES...
5·9

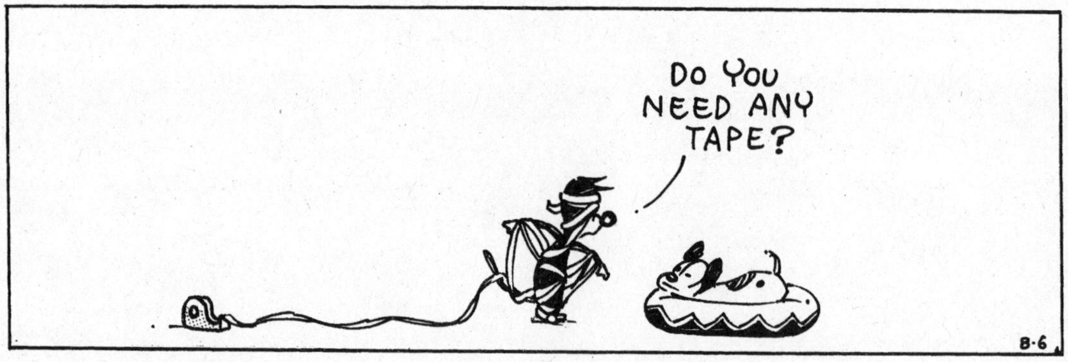
DO YOU NEED ANY TAPE?
8·6

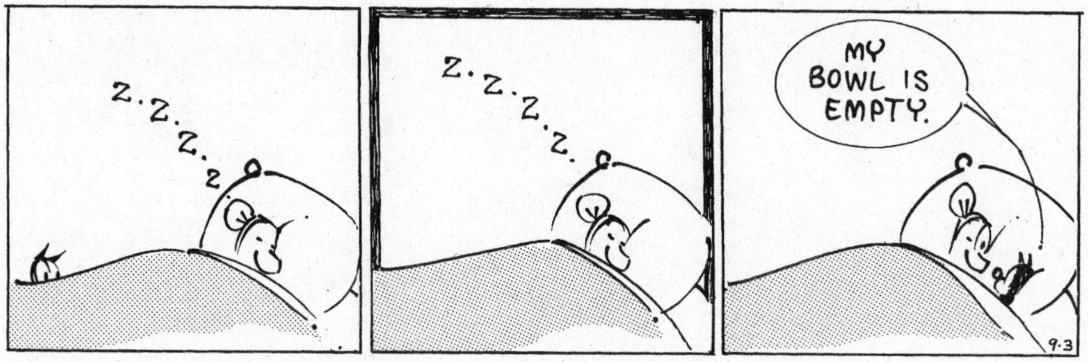
Z.. Z.. Z.. Z
Z.. Z.. Z.. Z.
MY BOWL IS EMPTY.
9·3

EAT. 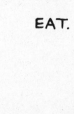 WALK.  PLAY. 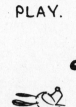 NAP.

I'M A SIMPLE DOG.

5·25

AAUGH! I'M COVERED IN **CAT** FUR!!!

AAUGH! I'M COVERED IN **CAT** FUR!!!

AAUGH!!!

6·7

ANOTHER ROUGH NEWS DAY.

6·10

MY SQUEEZY TOY!

SQUEEK SQUEEK SQUEEK SQUEEK SQUEEK SQUEEK SQUEEK SQUEEK SQUEEK SQUEEK SQUEEK SQUE

FUN FOR THE **WHOLE** FAMILY.

SQUEEK

6·28

BUT THAT WAS YOUR FAVORITE!
"WAS" IS RIGHT.
7·5

HMM...LET'S SEE... A SQUIRREL, TWO BIRDS AND A BUTTERFLY.
LOOK OUT WORLD!
TOP OF THE FOOD CHAIN.
7·8

SIT.
HE'S GOOD.
7·20

I'M BEAT...
I ONLY GOT TWENTY HOURS' SHLEEP.
11·11

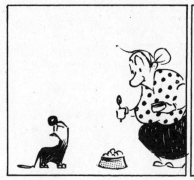

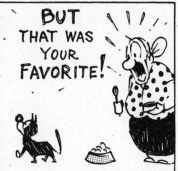

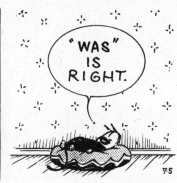

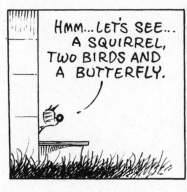

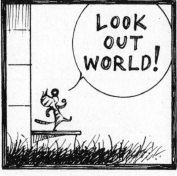

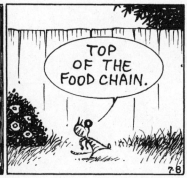

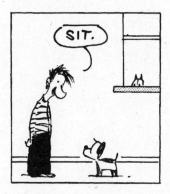

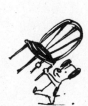

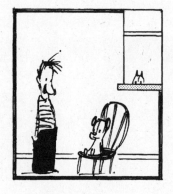

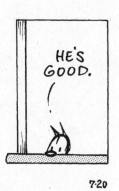

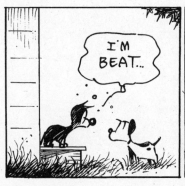

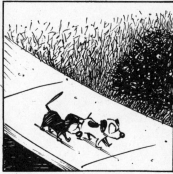

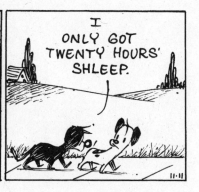

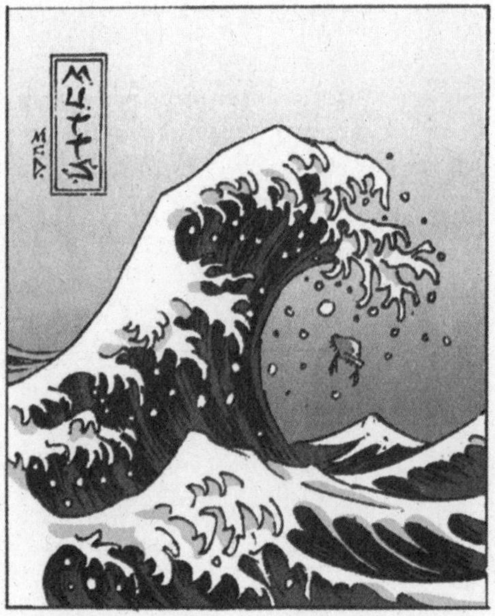
MUTTS

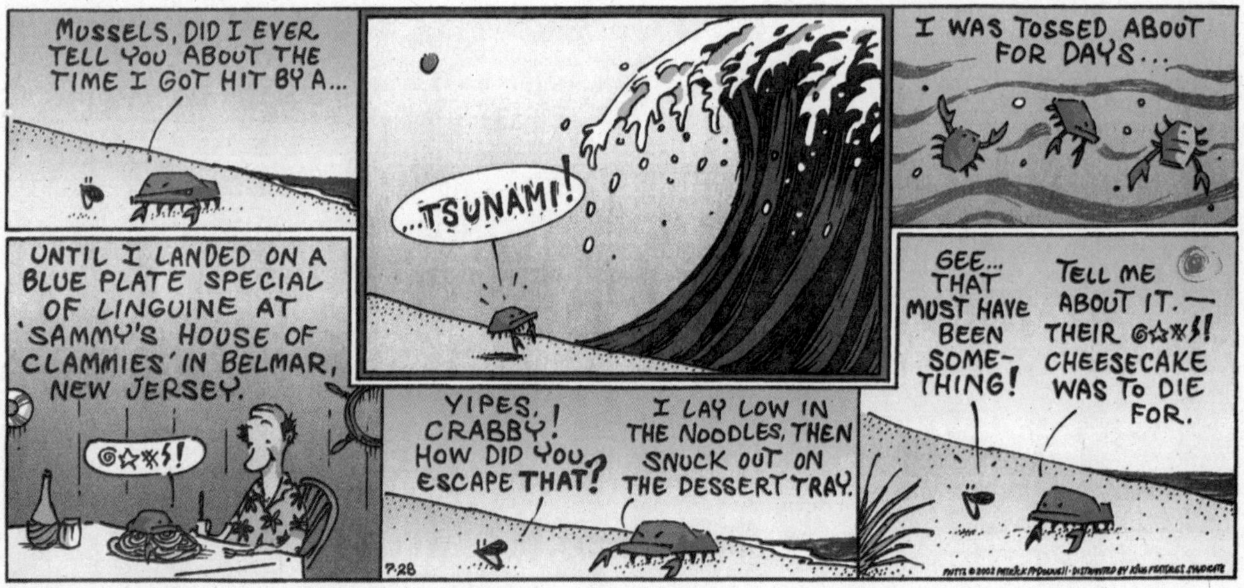
MUSSELS, DID I EVER TELL YOU ABOUT THE TIME I GOT HIT BY A...
...TSUNAMI!
I WAS TOSSED ABOUT FOR DAYS...
UNTIL I LANDED ON A BLUE PLATE SPECIAL OF LINGUINE AT 'SAMMY'S HOUSE OF CLAMMIES' IN BELMAR, NEW JERSEY.
@☆*$!
YIPES, CRABBY! HOW DID YOU ESCAPE THAT?
I LAY LOW IN THE NOODLES, THEN SNUCK OUT ON THE DESSERT TRAY.
GEE... THAT MUST HAVE BEEN SOME-THING!
TELL ME ABOUT IT.— THEIR @☆*$! CHEESECAKE WAS TO DIE FOR.
7-28

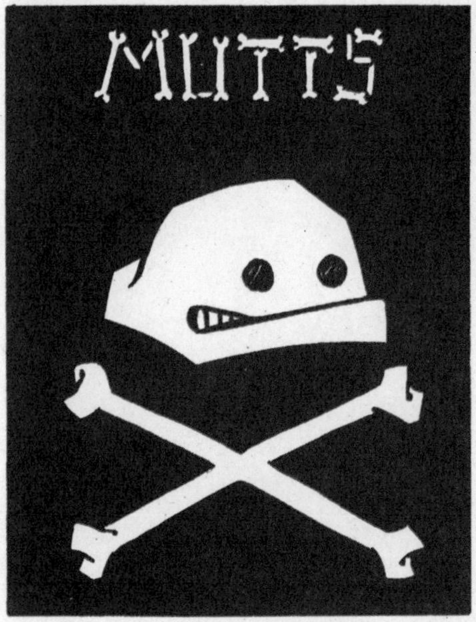
MUTTS

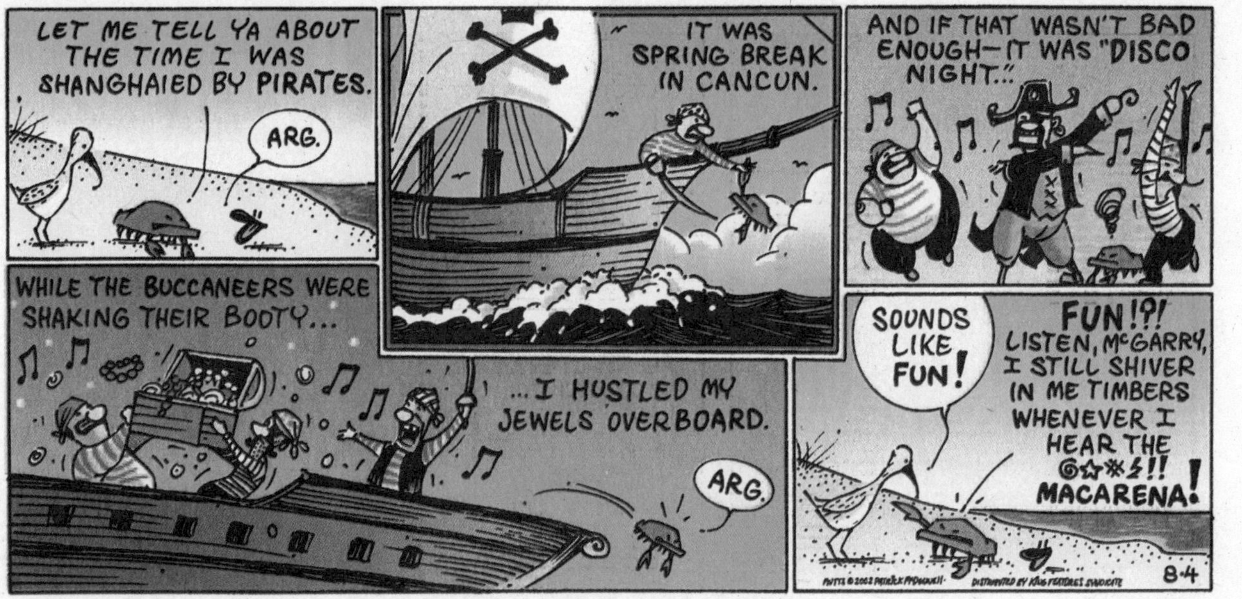
LET ME TELL YA ABOUT THE TIME I WAS SHANGHAIED BY PIRATES.
ARG.
IT WAS SPRING BREAK IN CANCUN.
AND IF THAT WASN'T BAD ENOUGH—IT WAS "DISCO NIGHT."
WHILE THE BUCCANEERS WERE SHAKING THEIR BOOTY...
...I HUSTLED MY JEWELS OVERBOARD.
ARG.
SOUNDS LIKE FUN!
FUN!?! LISTEN, McGARRY, I STILL SHIVER IN ME TIMBERS WHENEVER I HEAR THE @☆*$!! MACARENA!
8-4

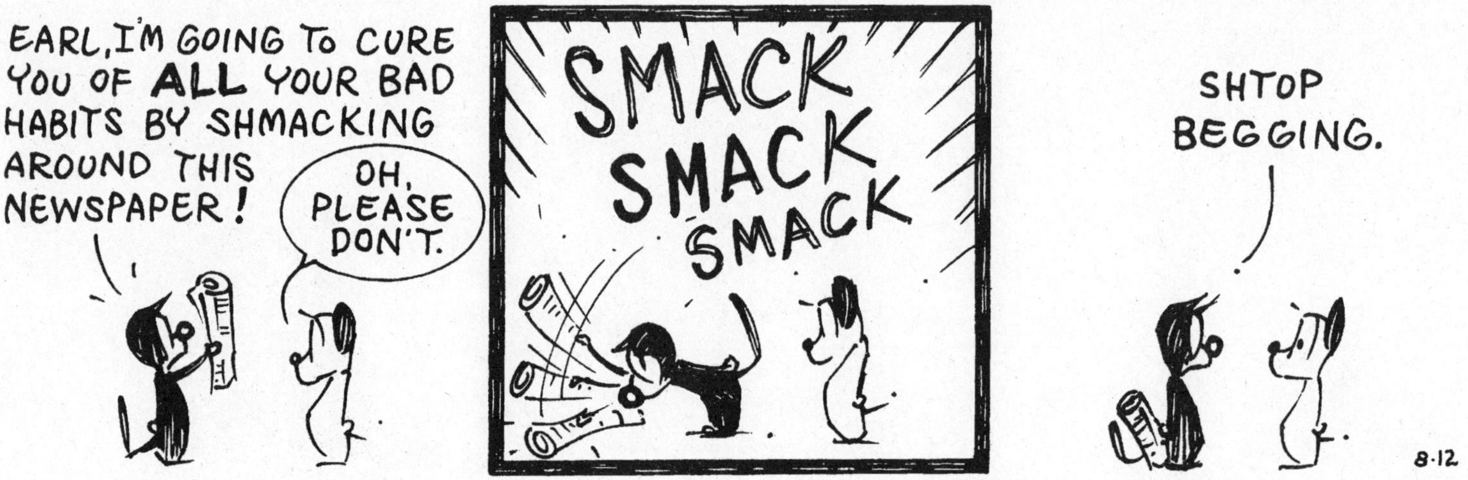
EARL, I'M GOING TO CURE YOU OF ALL YOUR BAD HABITS BY SHMACKING AROUND THIS NEWSPAPER!
OH, PLEASE DON'T.
SMACK
SMACK
SMACK
SHTOP BEGGING.
8·12

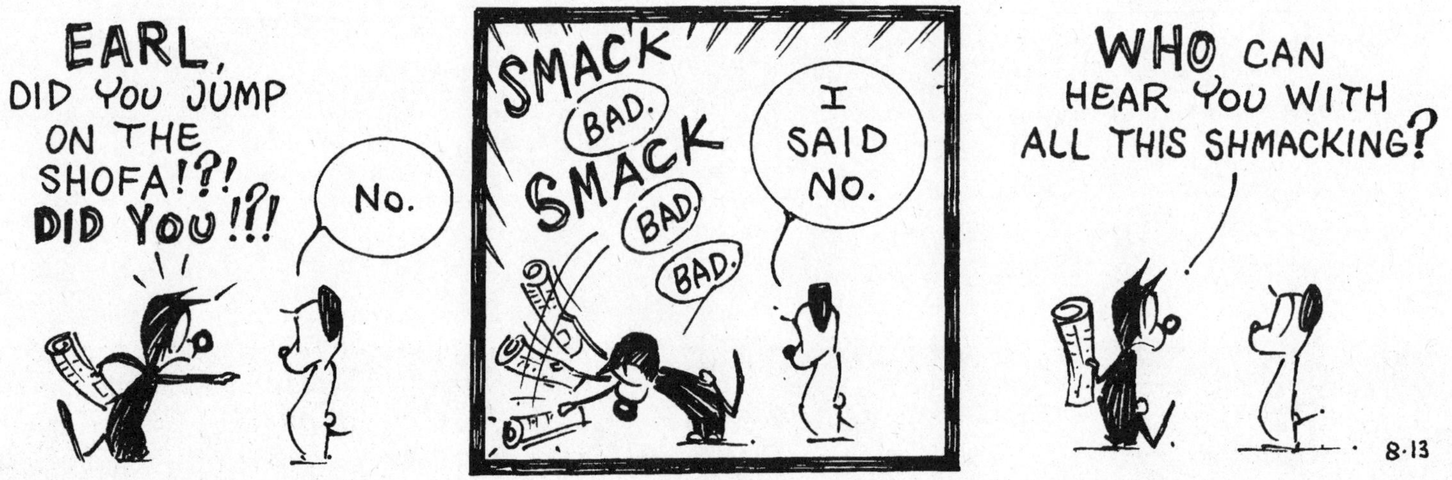
EARL, DID YOU JUMP ON THE SHOFA!?! DID YOU!?!
No.
SMACK
BAD.
SMACK
BAD.
BAD.
I SAID NO.
WHO CAN HEAR YOU WITH ALL THIS SHMACKING?
8·13

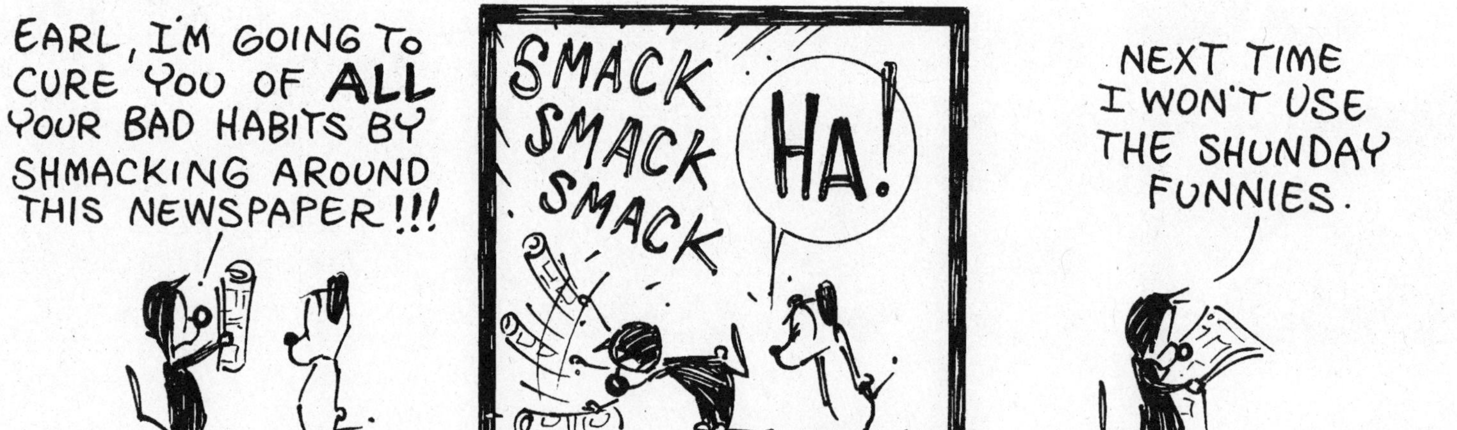
EARL, I'M GOING TO CURE YOU OF ALL YOUR BAD HABITS BY SHMACKING AROUND THIS NEWSPAPER!!!
SMACK
SMACK
SMACK
HA!
NEXT TIME I WON'T USE THE SHUNDAY FUNNIES.
8·24

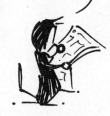

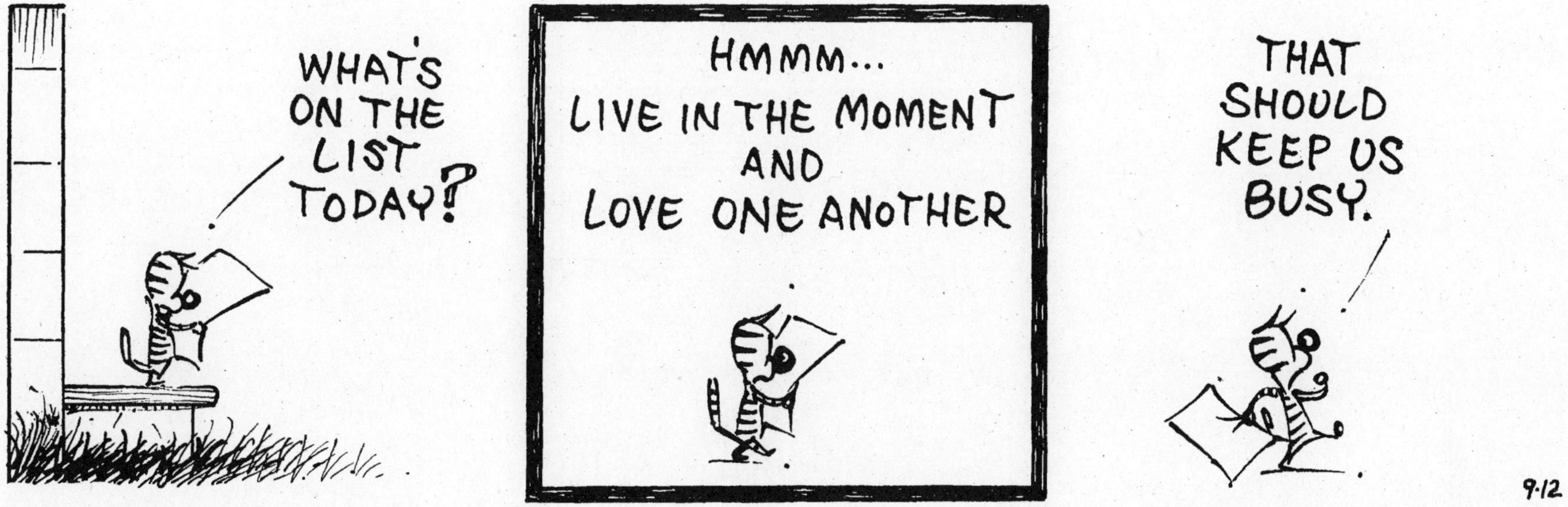
WHAT'S ON THE LIST TODAY?
HMMM...
LIVE IN THE MOMENT AND LOVE ONE ANOTHER
THAT SHOULD KEEP US BUSY.
9·12

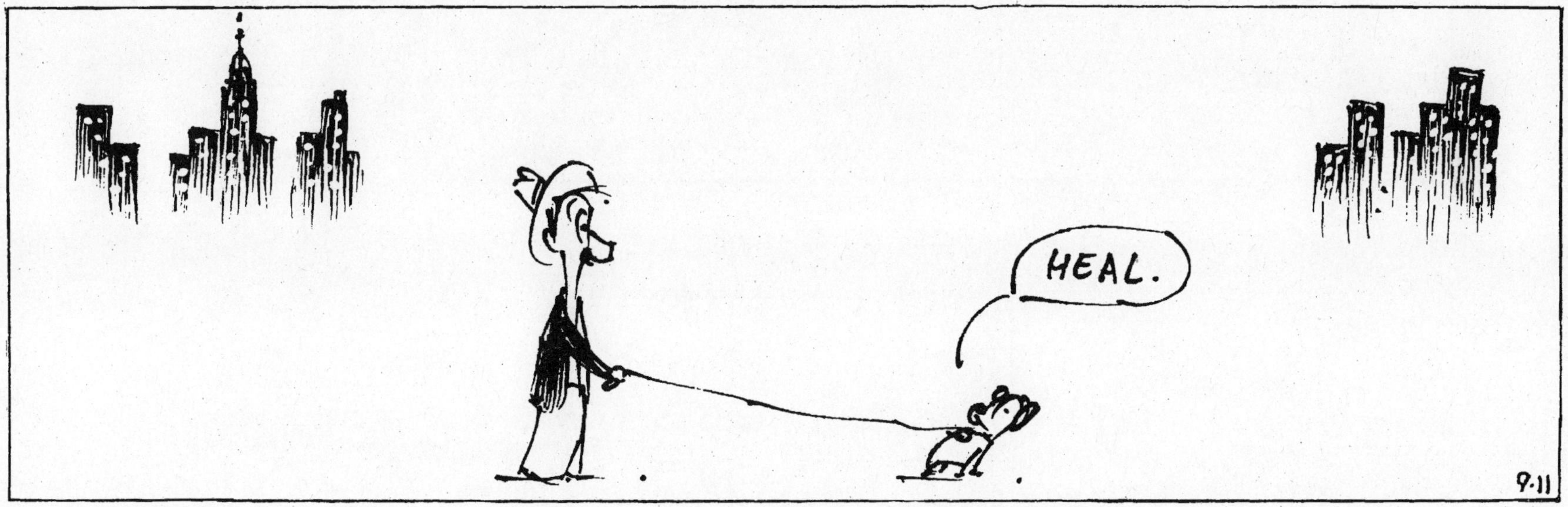
HEAL.
9·11

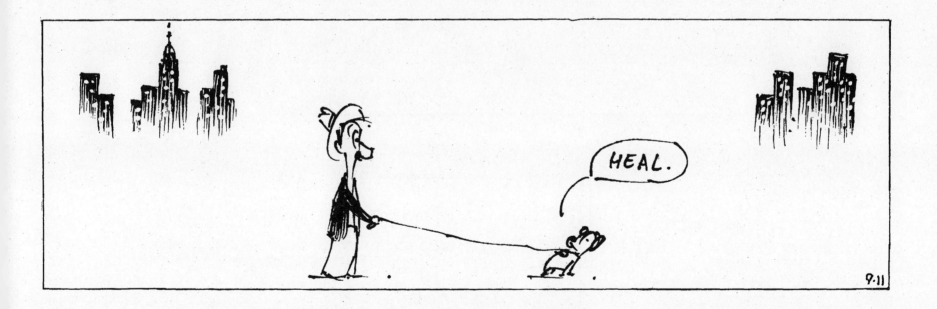

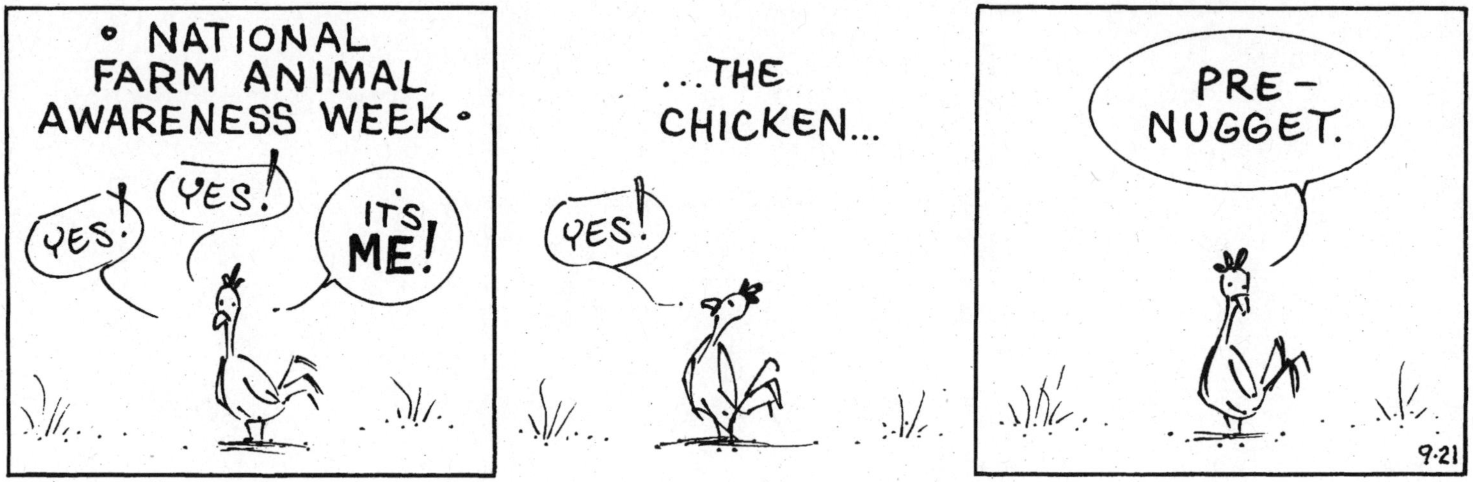
• NATIONAL FARM ANIMAL AWARENESS WEEK •
YES!
YES!
IT'S ME!
...THE CHICKEN...
YES!
PRE-NUGGET.
9·21

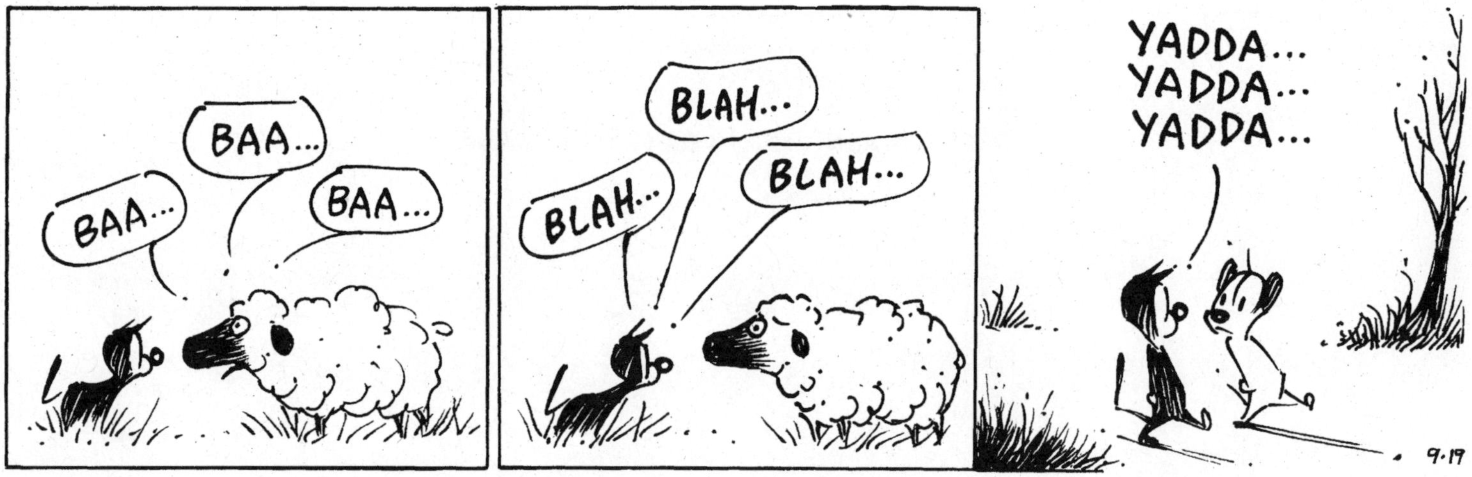
BAA...
BAA...
BAA...
BLAH...
BLAH...
BLAH...
YADDA... YADDA... YADDA...
9·19

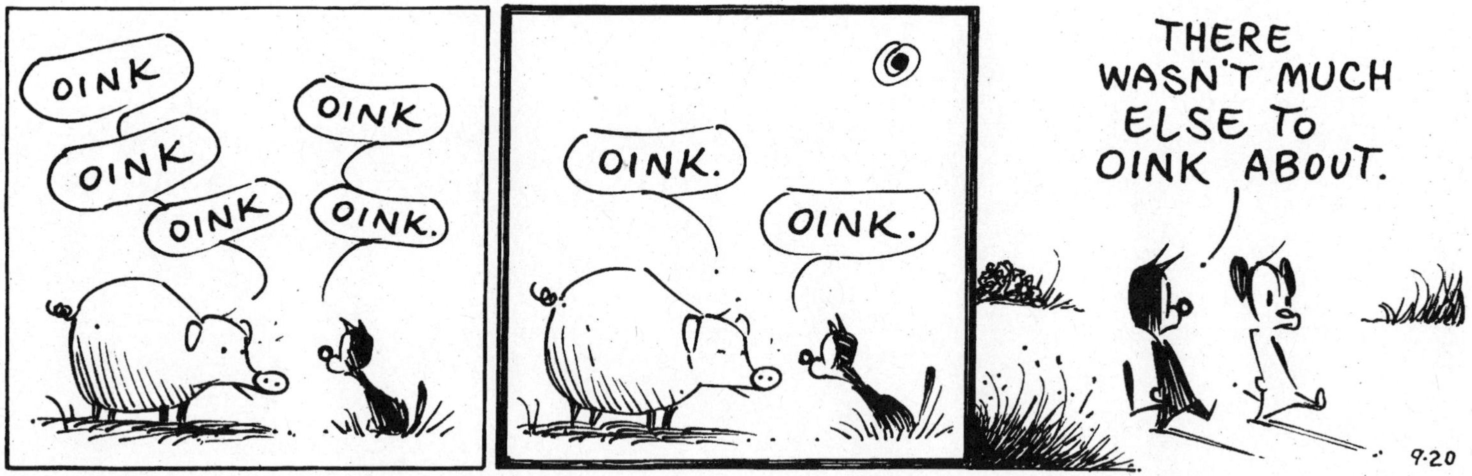
OINK
OINK
OINK
OINK
OINK.
OINK.
OINK.
THERE WASN'T MUCH ELSE TO OINK ABOUT.
9·20

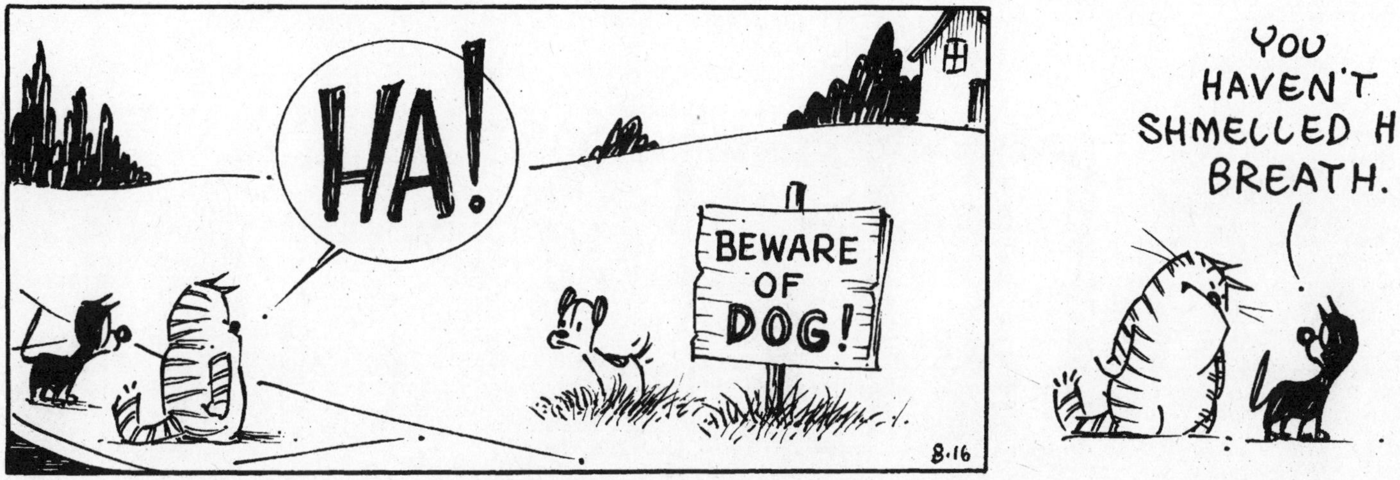
HA!
BEWARE OF DOG!
YOU HAVEN'T SHMELLED HIS BREATH.
8.16

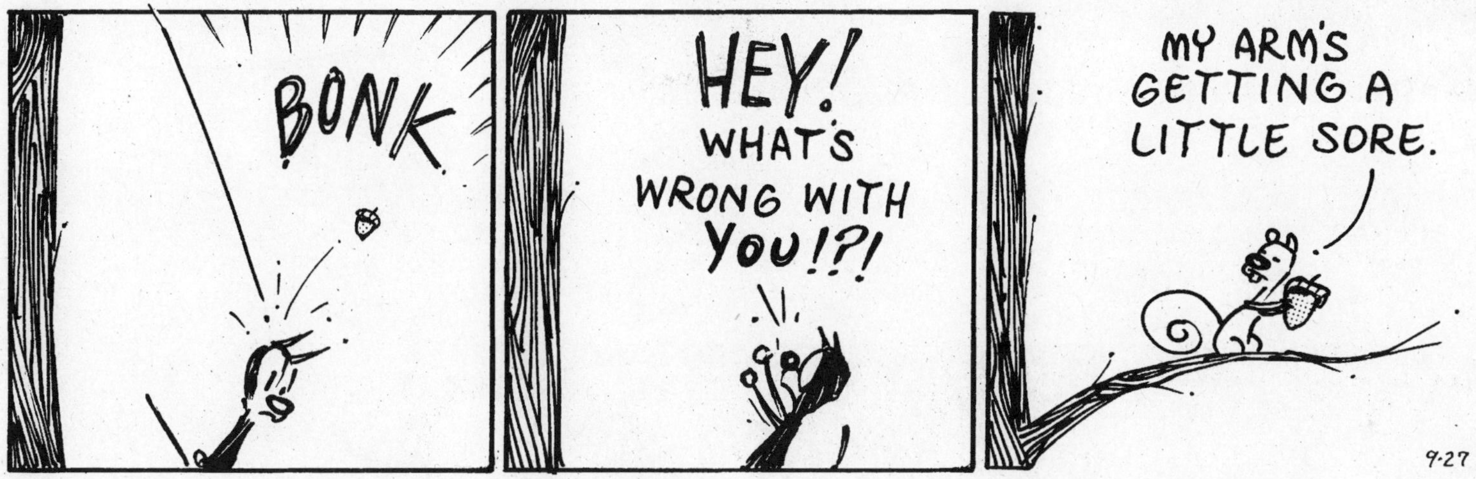
BONK
HEY! WHAT'S WRONG WITH YOU!?!
MY ARM'S GETTING A LITTLE SORE.
9.27

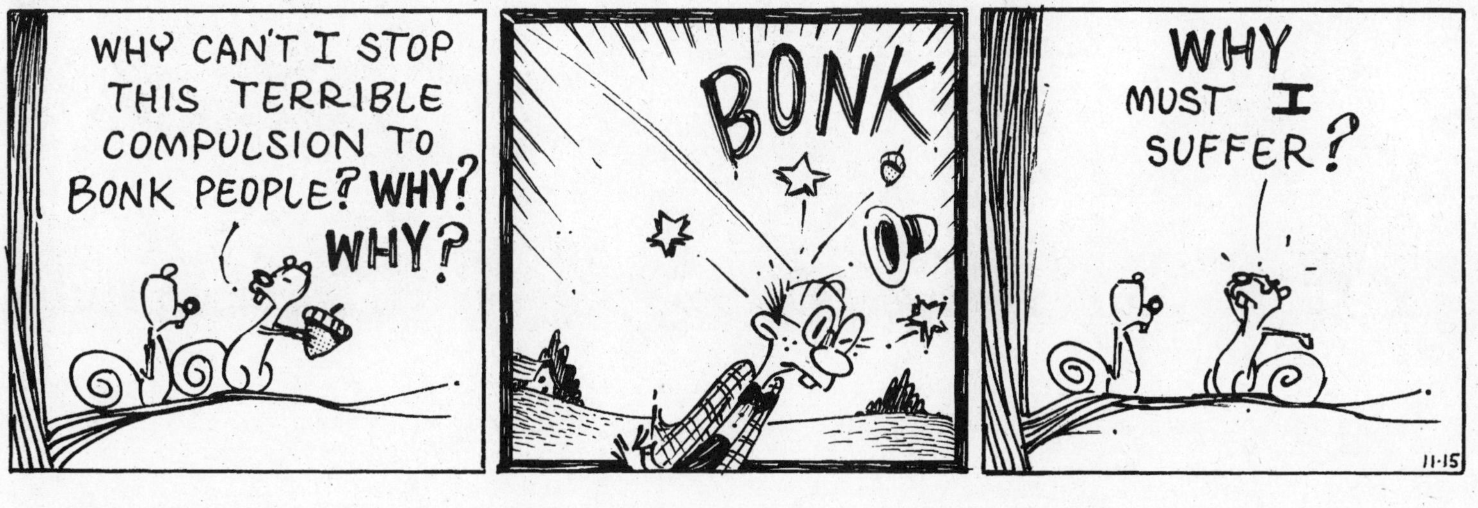
WHY CAN'T I STOP THIS TERRIBLE COMPULSION TO BONK PEOPLE? WHY? WHY?
BONK
WHY MUST I SUFFER?
11.15

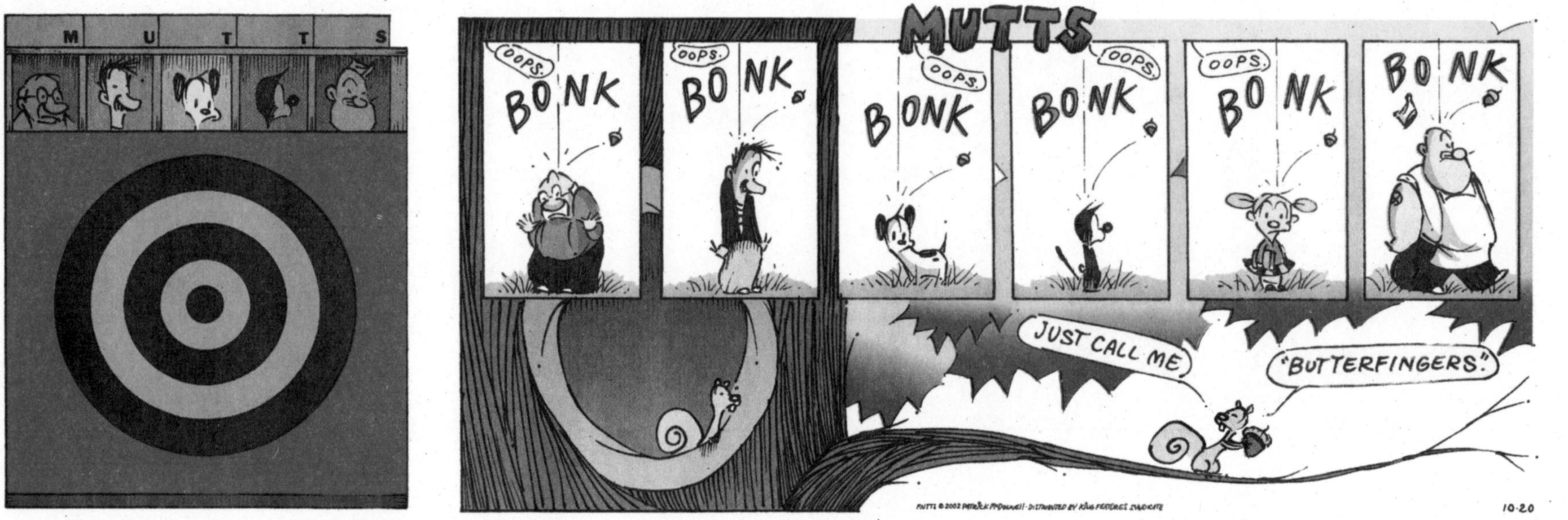
M U T T S
MUTTS
OOPS.
BONK
OOPS.
BONK
OOPS.
BONK
OOPS.
BONK
OOPS.
BONK
BONK
JUST CALL ME
"BUTTERFINGERS."
10·20

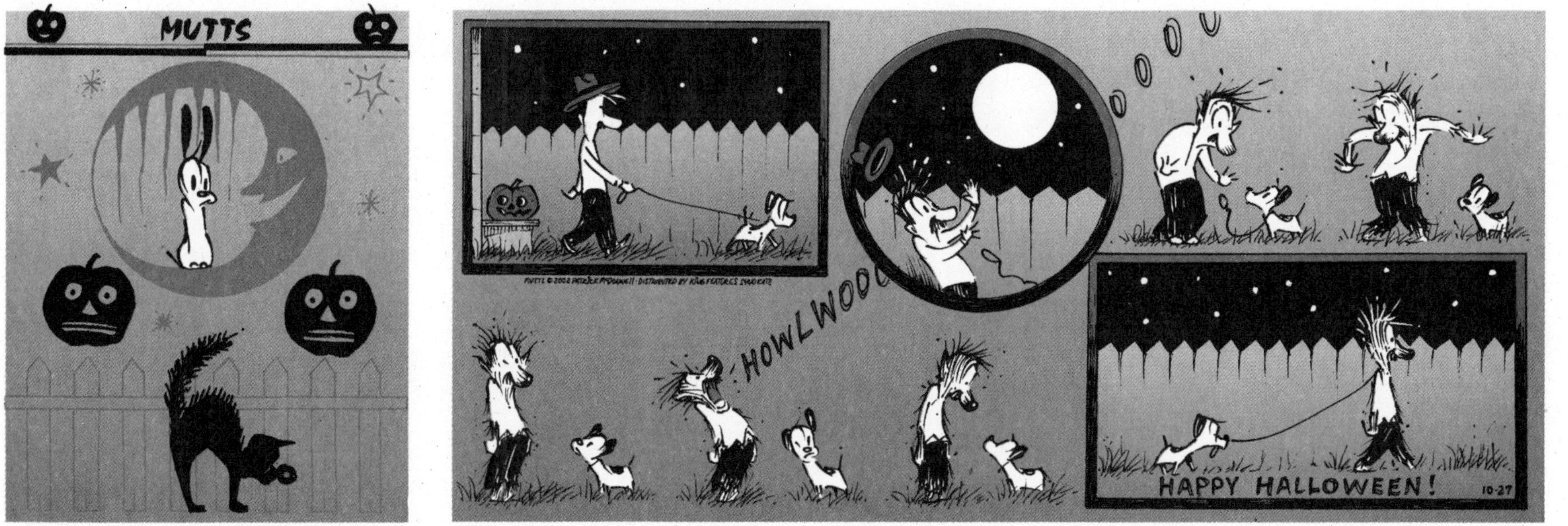
MUTTS
HOWLWOO
HAPPY HALLOWEEN!
10·27

HOWLWOOOOOO
I WONDER WHAT HE'S HOWLING ABOUT?
I HAVE A LIST.
9·5

WHAT'S ON MY LIST TODAY?
10·23
BE TRUSTWORTHY, OBEDIENT, LOYAL AND FAITHFUL.
HEY!
THIS IS YESTERDAY'S LIST!

WHAT'S ON OUR LIST TODAY, EARL?
WELL, MOOCH, LET'S SEE...
FWIP
12·6
Z

DOGGY SWEATER!
?!
DOGGY HAT?
DOGGY BOOTS!?! HOW EMBARRASSING!!!
No PANTS.
12·9

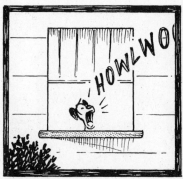

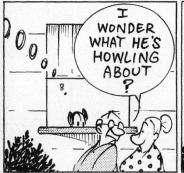

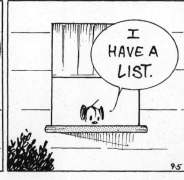

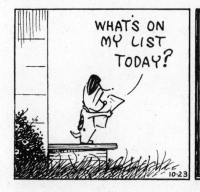

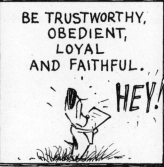

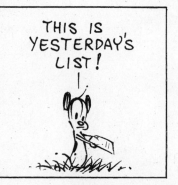

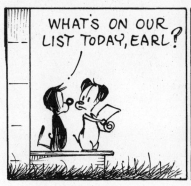

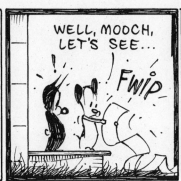

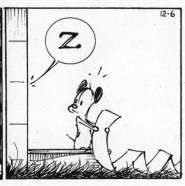

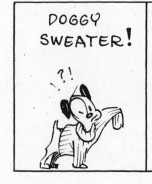

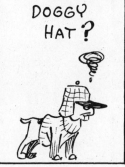

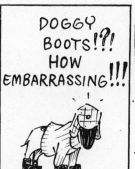

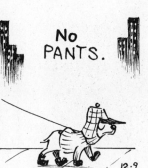

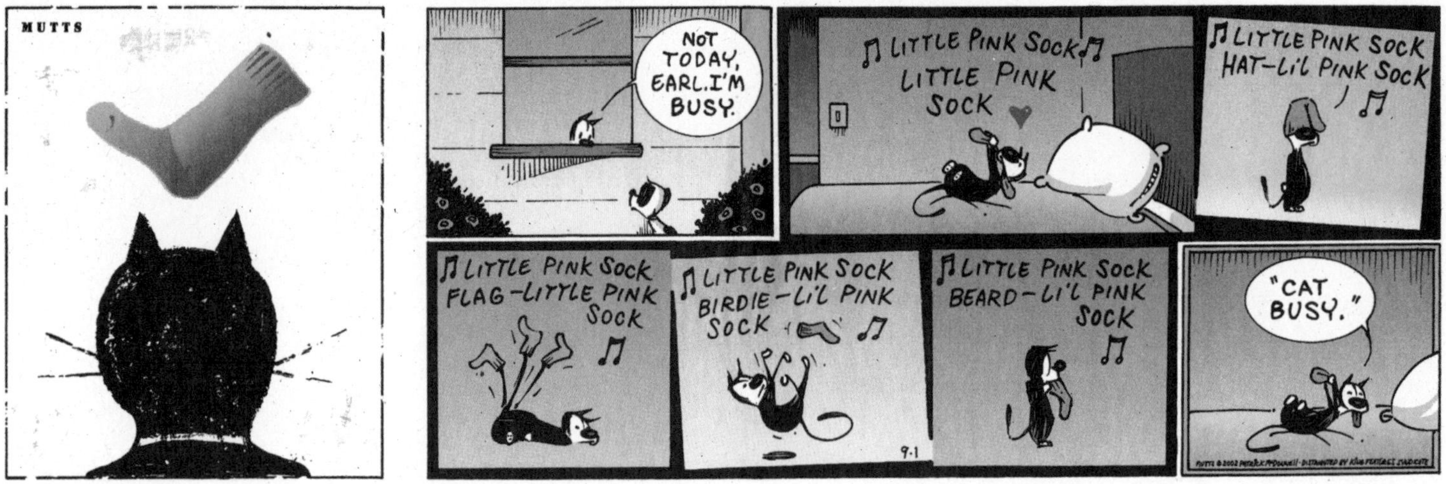
MUTTS
NOT TODAY, EARL. I'M BUSY.
♫ LITTLE PINK SOCK ♫ LITTLE PINK SOCK
♫ LITTLE PINK SOCK HAT—LI'L PINK SOCK ♫
♫ LITTLE PINK SOCK FLAG—LITTLE PINK SOCK ♫
♫ LITTLE PINK SOCK BIRDIE—LI'L PINK SOCK ♫
9-1
♫ LITTLE PINK SOCK BEARD—LI'L PINK SOCK ♫
"CAT BUSY."

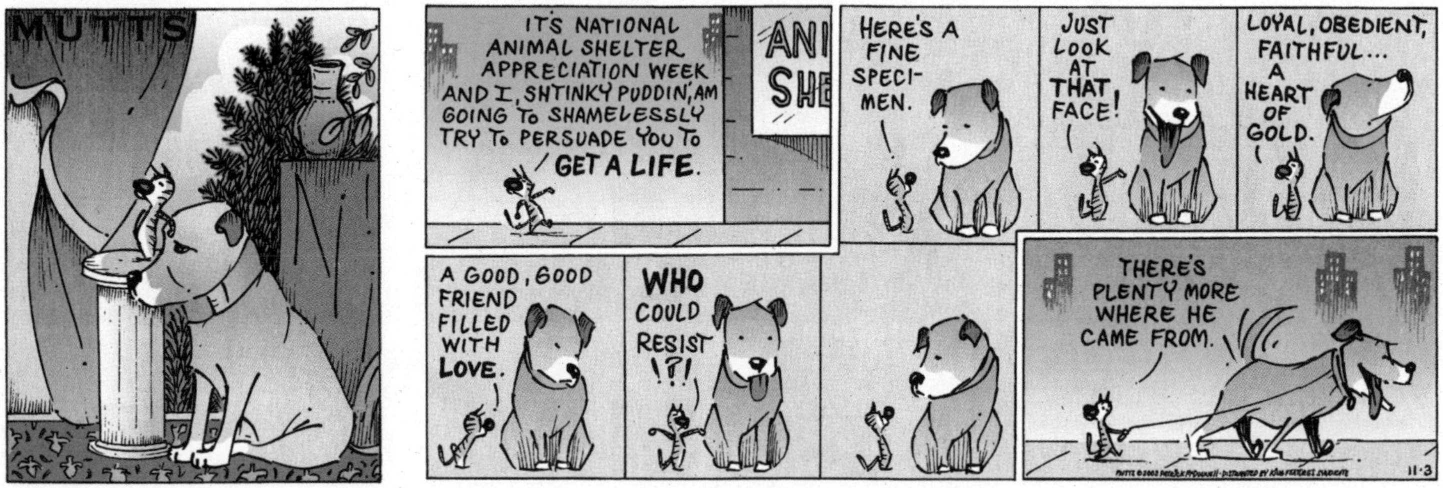
MUTTS
IT'S NATIONAL ANIMAL SHELTER APPRECIATION WEEK AND I, SHTINKY PUDDIN', AM GOING TO SHAMELESSLY TRY TO PERSUADE YOU TO GET A LIFE.
ANI SHE
HERE'S A FINE SPECIMEN.
JUST LOOK AT THAT FACE!
LOYAL, OBEDIENT, FAITHFUL... A HEART OF GOLD.
A GOOD, GOOD FRIEND FILLED WITH LOVE.
WHO COULD RESIST !?!
THERE'S PLENTY MORE WHERE HE CAME FROM.
11-3

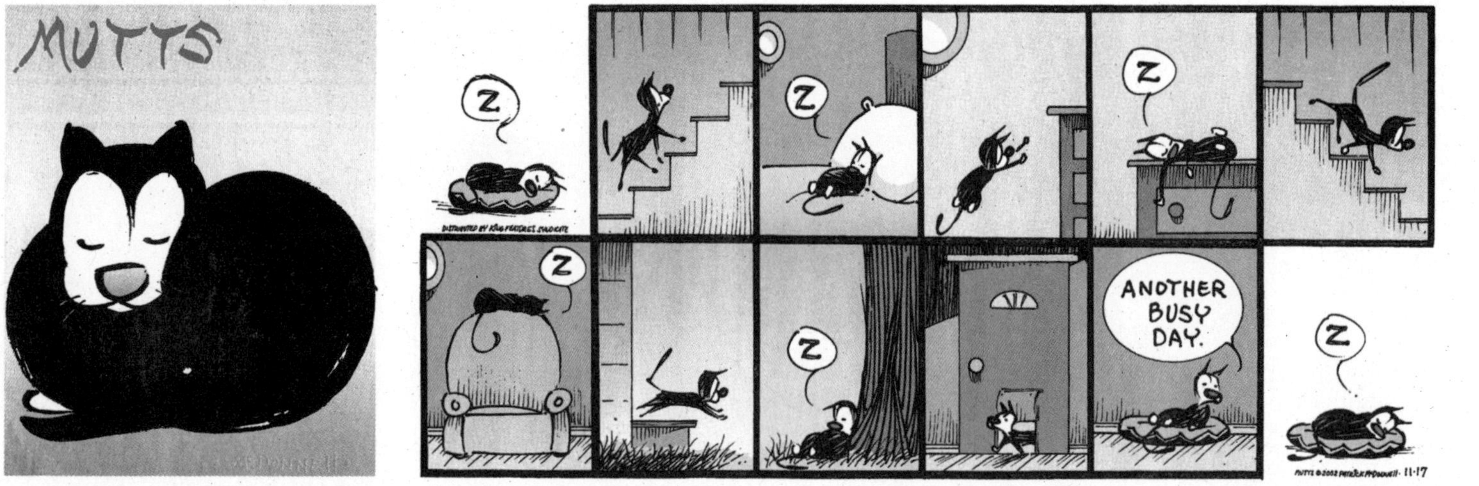
MUTTS
Z
Z
Z
Z
Z
ANOTHER BUSY DAY.
Z
11-17

**Mooch introduced us to his pet,** a snail he affectionately and teasingly named Little Earl. Mooch, being a good guardian, took Little Earl out for long crawls. It was fun to explore how Mooch would behave if he had a pet.

During Shelter Story week, we met Chickpea and Chickpea's Brother, two sibling kitties waiting to be adopted. Many readers took to the duo and were quite worried about them when the week ended with Chickpea and Chickpea's Brother still homeless at the shelter. Due to popular *demand*, I had them successfully adopted as a team the following April. If it were only that easy . . . I hope I inspired a few real-life rescues that season.

The November 16 Sunday page (page 231) is an homage to cartoonist Frank King's *Gasoline Alley*. During autumn he would draw beautiful Sunday pages of his characters, Walt Wallet and his adopted foundling son, Skeezix, going for quiet walks through breathtaking fall foliage. It seemed like a natural to have Ozzie and Earl follow their contemplative footsteps.

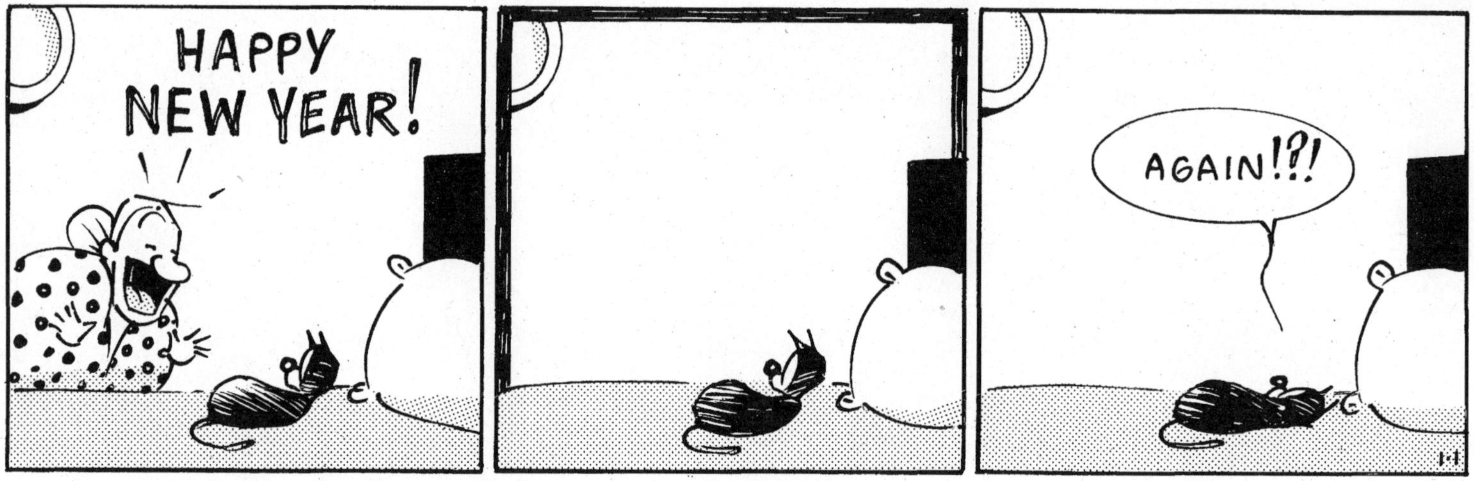
HAPPY NEW YEAR!
AGAIN!?!
1·1

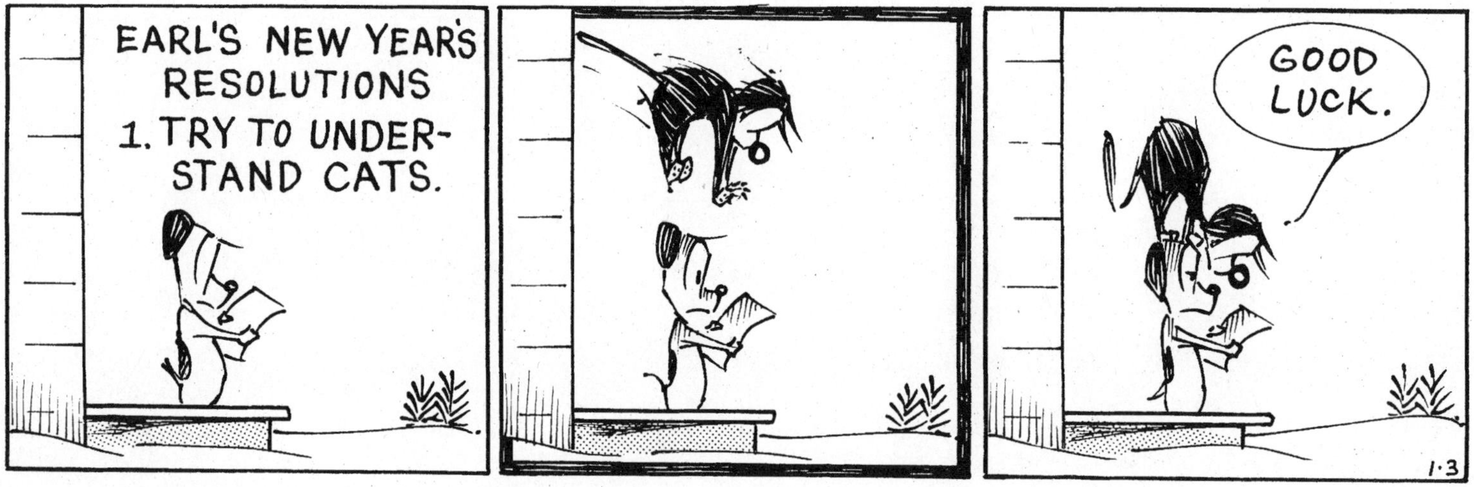
EARL'S NEW YEAR'S RESOLUTIONS
1. TRY TO UNDER-STAND CATS.
GOOD LUCK.
1·3

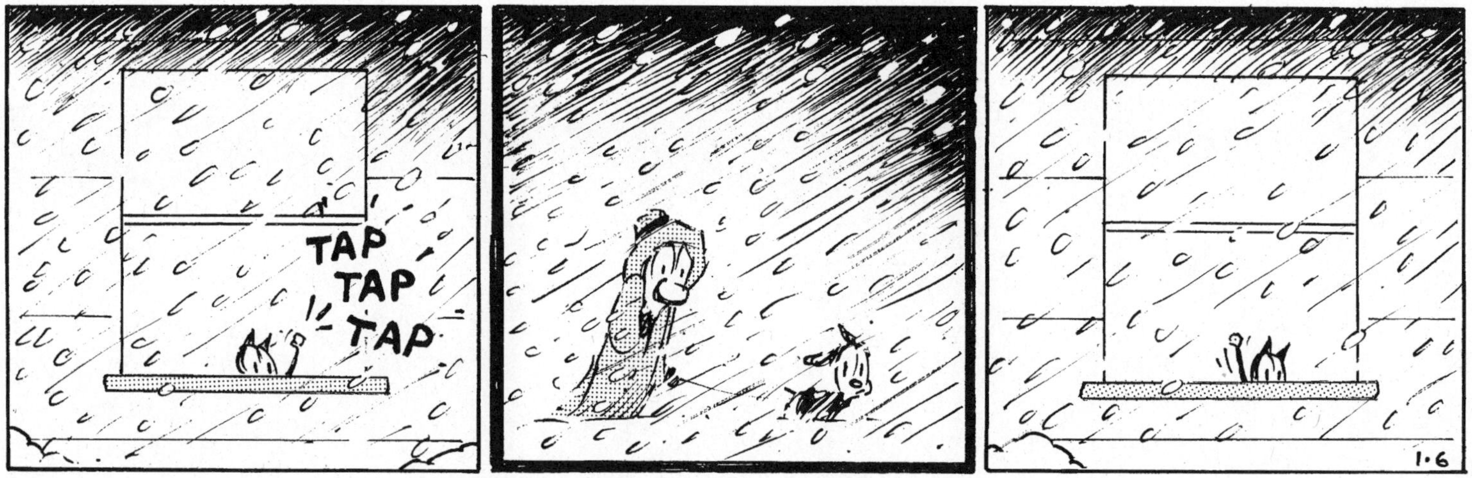
TAP
TAP
TAP
1·6

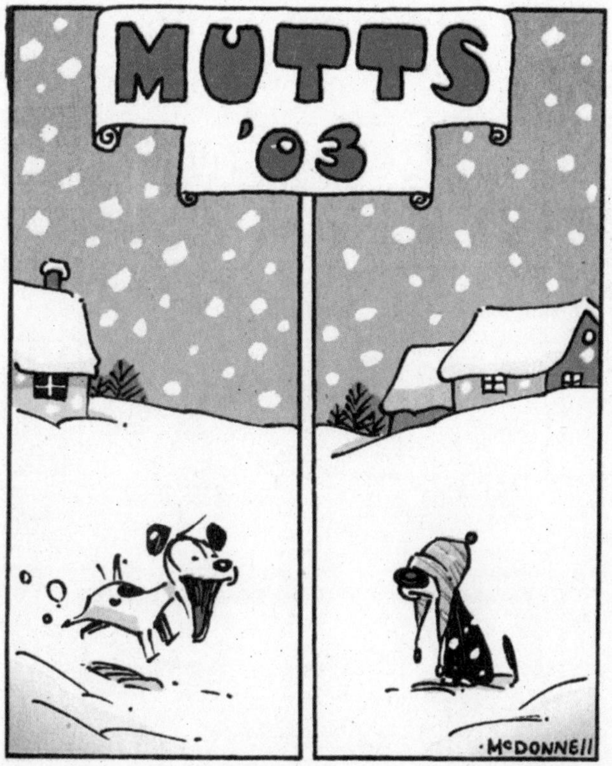
MUTTS
'03
McDONNELL

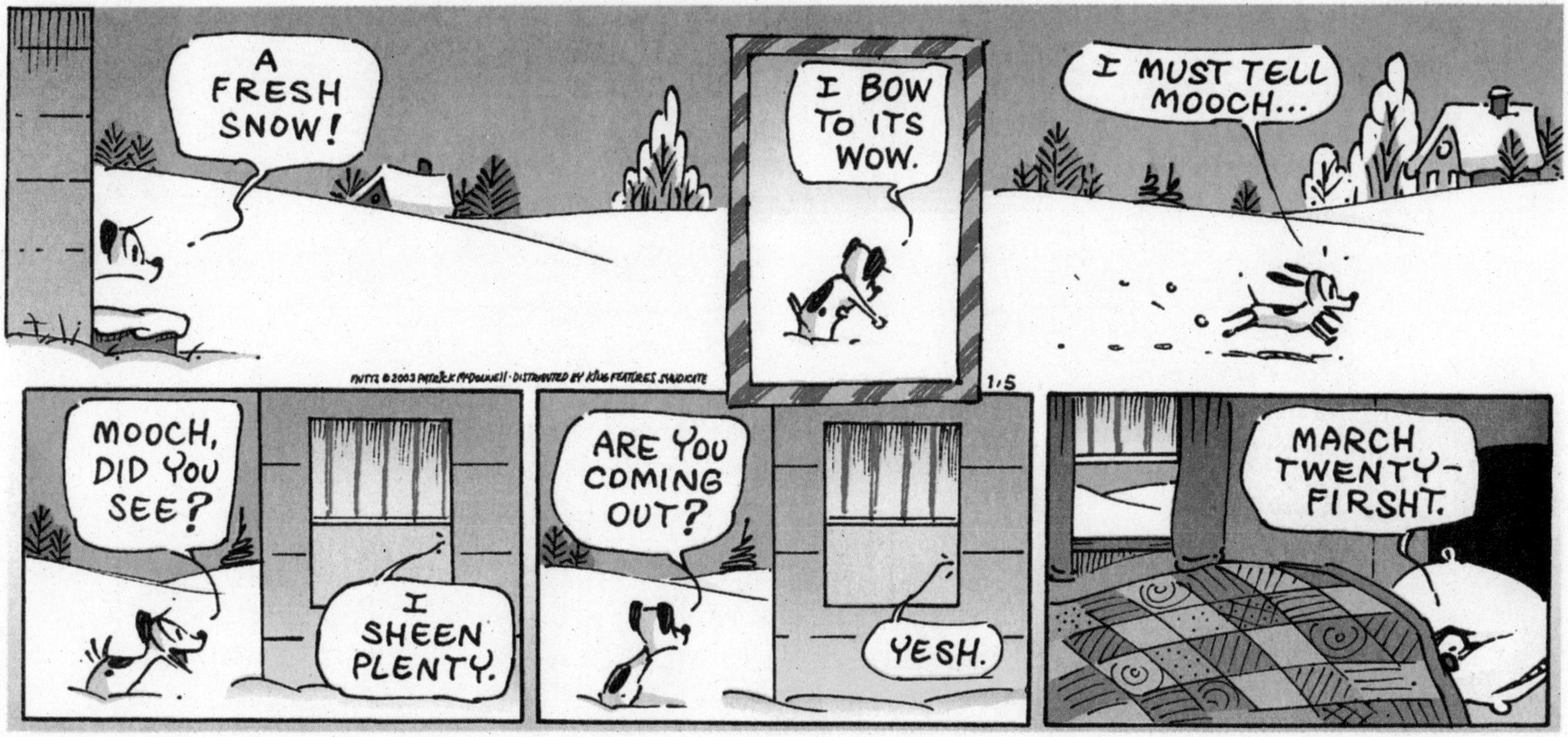
A FRESH SNOW!
I BOW TO ITS WOW.
I MUST TELL MOOCH...
MUTTS ©2003 PATRICK McDONNELL · DISTRIBUTED BY KING FEATURES SYNDICATE
1/5
MOOCH, DID YOU SEE?
I SHEEN PLENTY.
ARE YOU COMING OUT?
YESH.
MARCH TWENTY-FIRSHT.

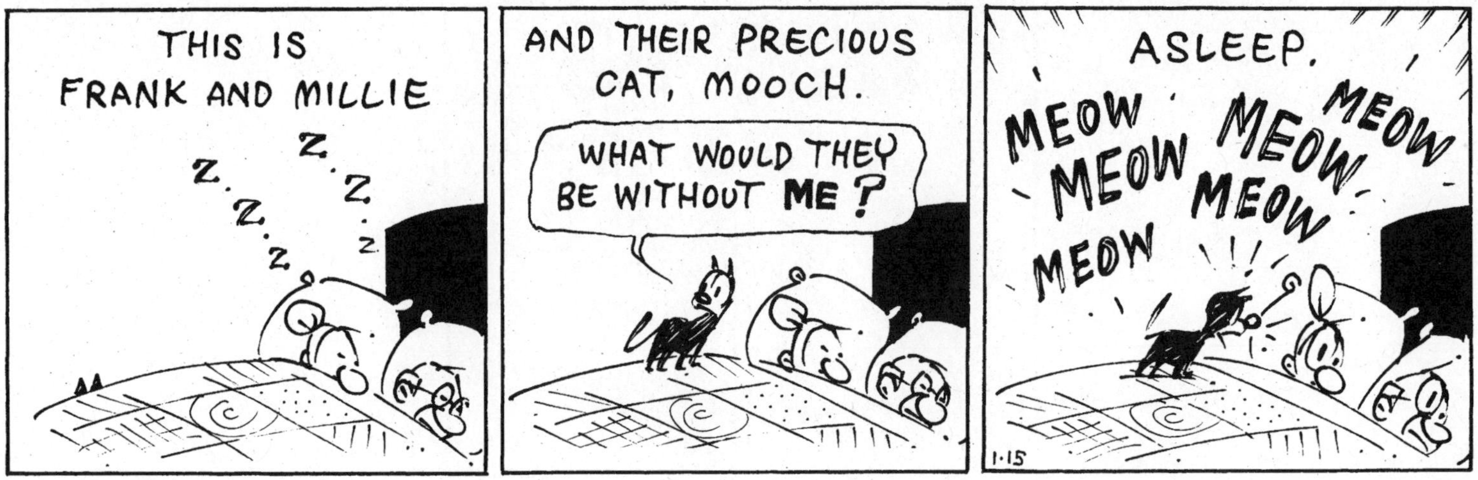
THIS IS FRANK AND MILLIE
Z Z Z Z Z Z
AND THEIR PRECIOUS CAT, MOOCH.
WHAT WOULD THEY BE WITHOUT **ME**?
ASLEEP.
MEOW MEOW MEOW MEOW MEOW MEOW MEOW
1·15

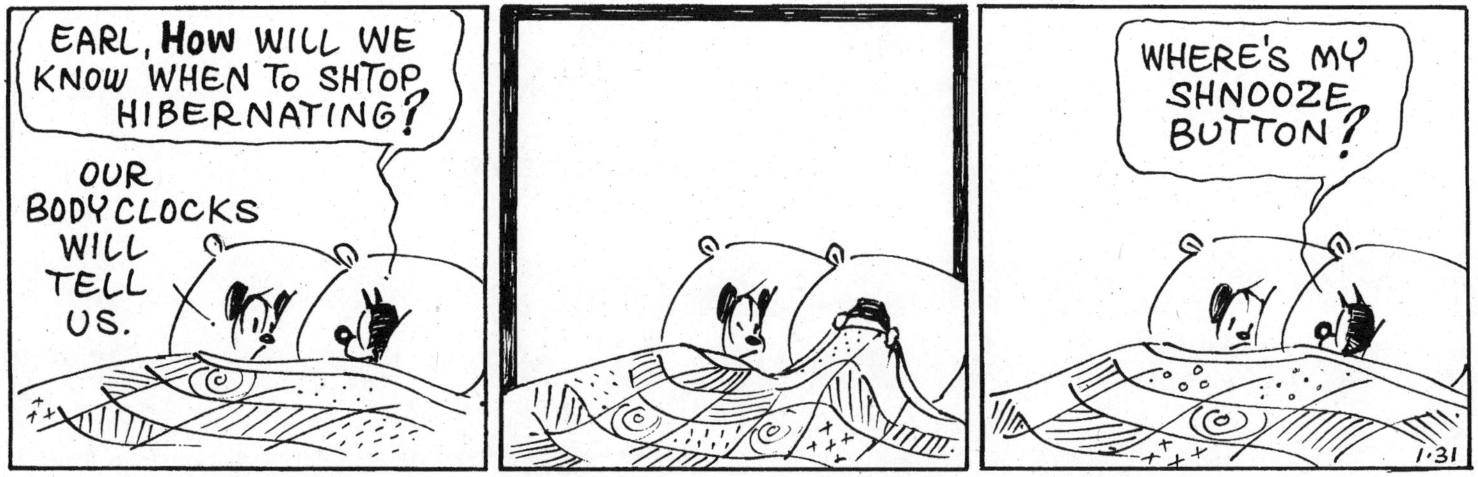
EARL, **HOW** WILL WE KNOW WHEN TO SHTOP HIBERNATING?
OUR BODYCLOCKS WILL TELL US.
WHERE'S MY SHNOOZE BUTTON?
1·31

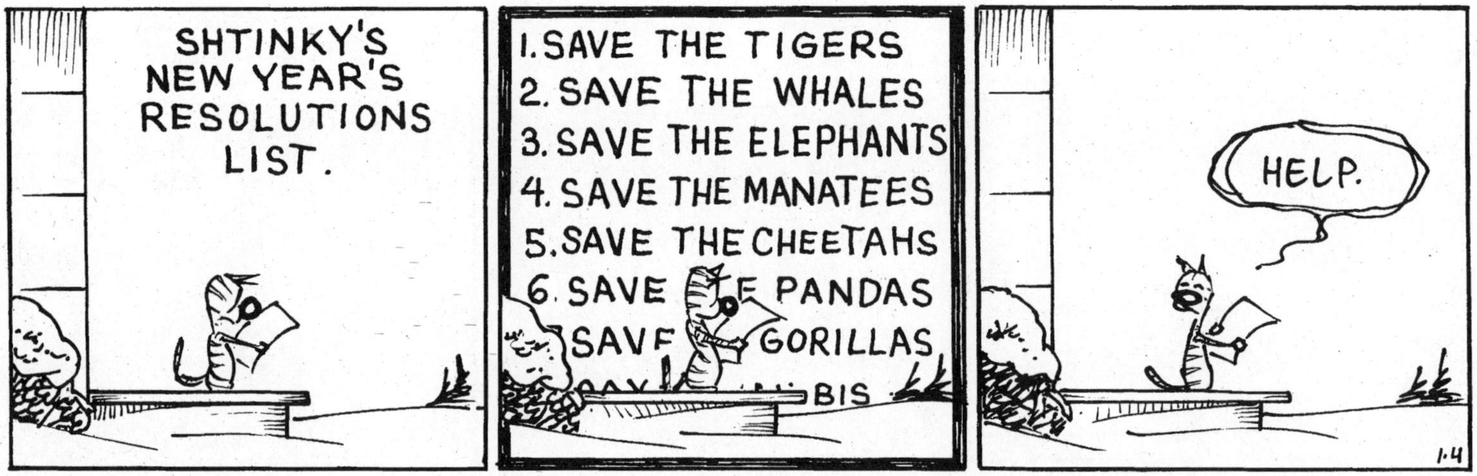
SHTINKY'S NEW YEAR'S RESOLUTIONS LIST.
1. SAVE THE TIGERS
2. SAVE THE WHALES
3. SAVE THE ELEPHANTS
4. SAVE THE MANATEES
5. SAVE THE CHEETAHS
6. SAVE
PANDAS
GORILLAS
BIS
HELP.
1·4

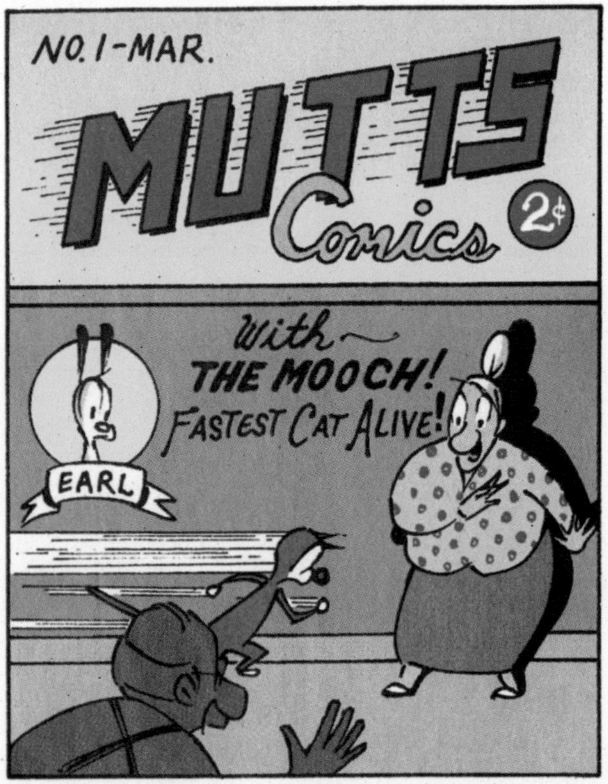
NO. 1-MAR.
MUTTS Comics
2¢
With THE MOOCH! FASTEST CAT ALIVE!
EARL

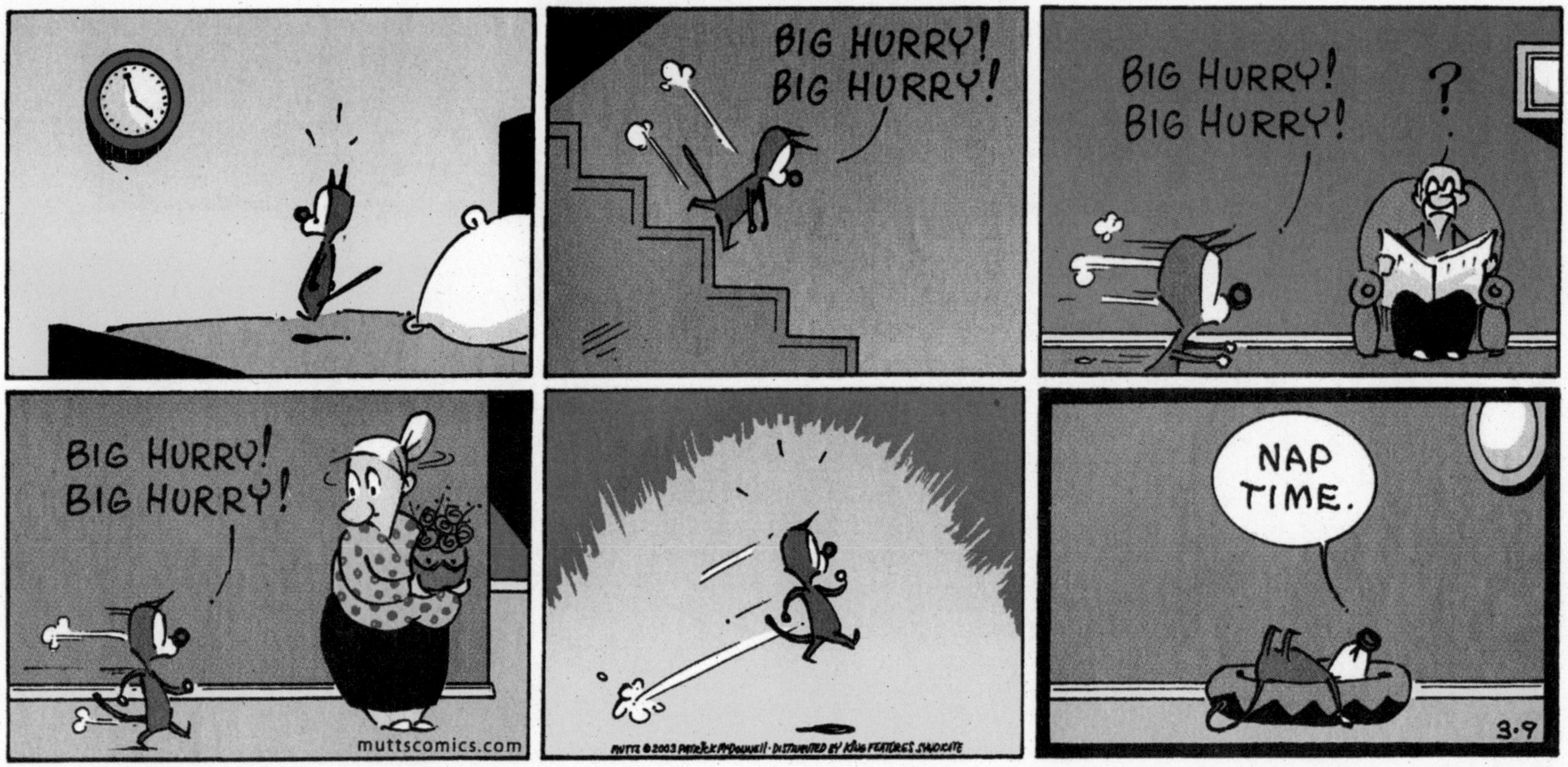
BIG HURRY! BIG HURRY!
BIG HURRY! BIG HURRY!
?
BIG HURRY! BIG HURRY!
muttscomics.com
MUTTS © 2003 PATRICK McDONNELL · DISTRIBUTED BY KING FEATURES SYNDICATE
NAP TIME.
3·9

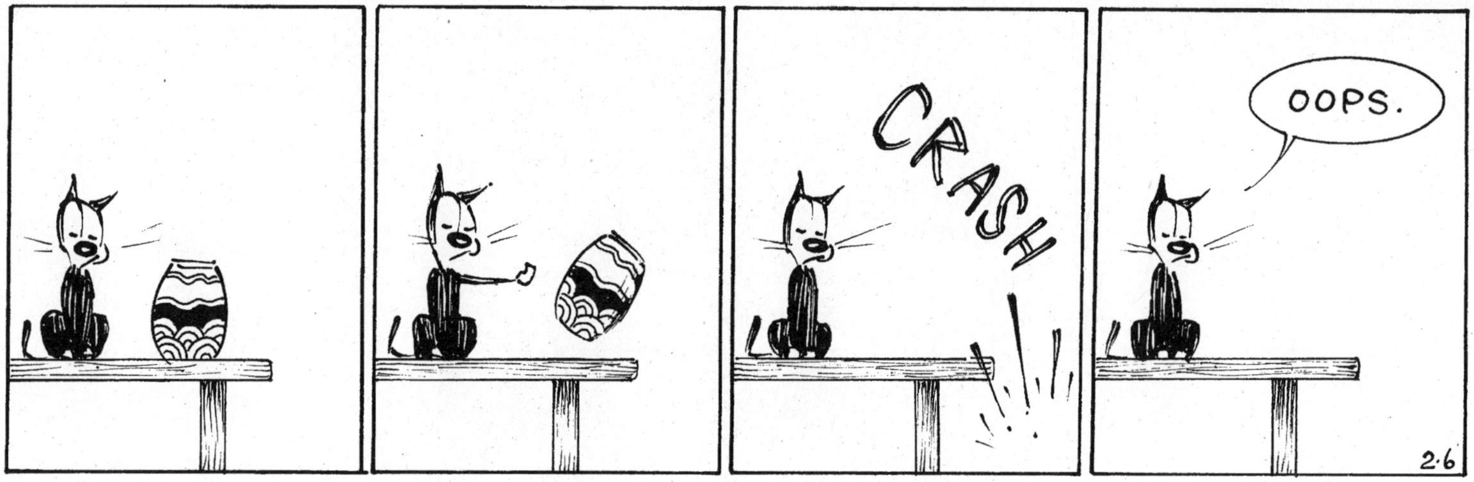
CRASH
OOPS.
2·6

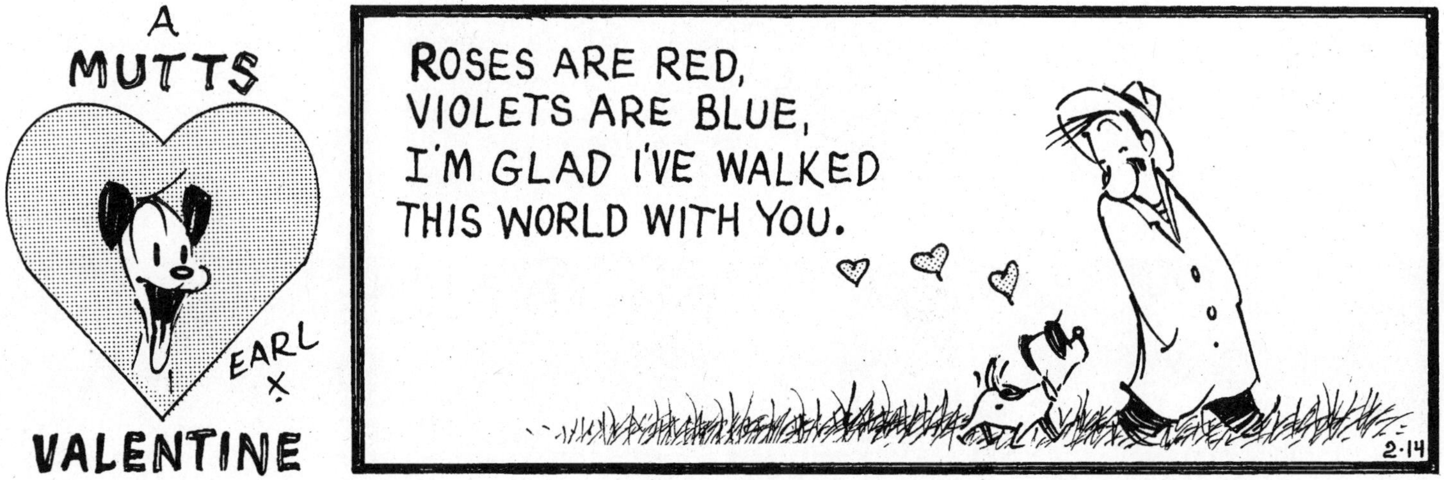
A
MUTTS
EARL
X
VALENTINE
ROSES ARE RED,
VIOLETS ARE BLUE,
I'M GLAD I'VE WALKED
THIS WORLD WITH YOU.
2·14

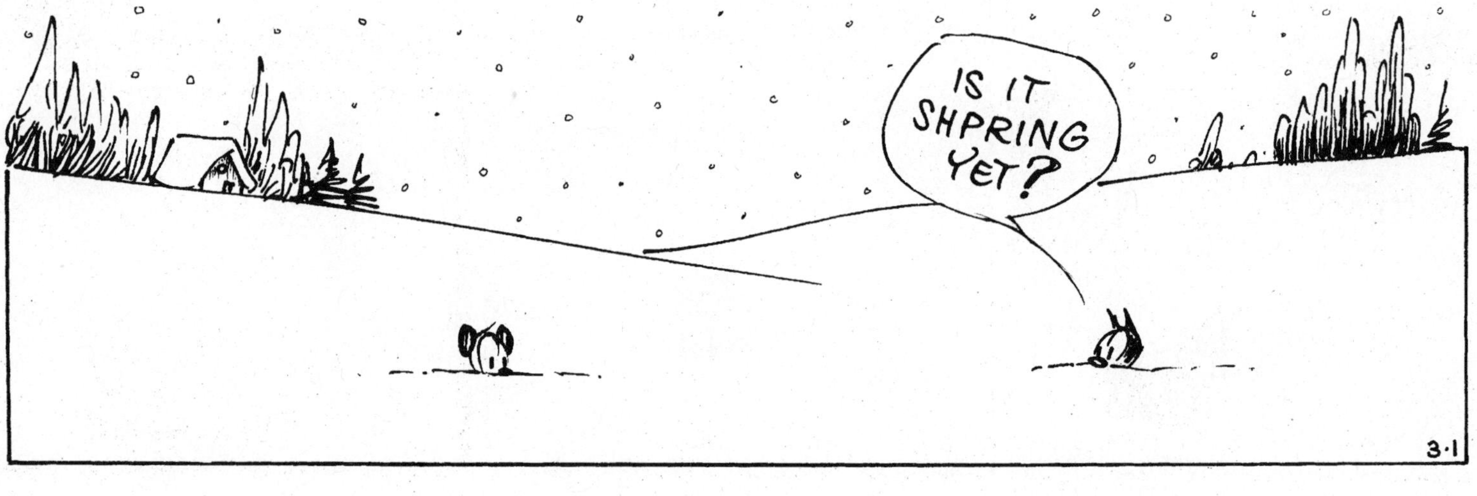
IS IT
SHPRING
YET?
3·1

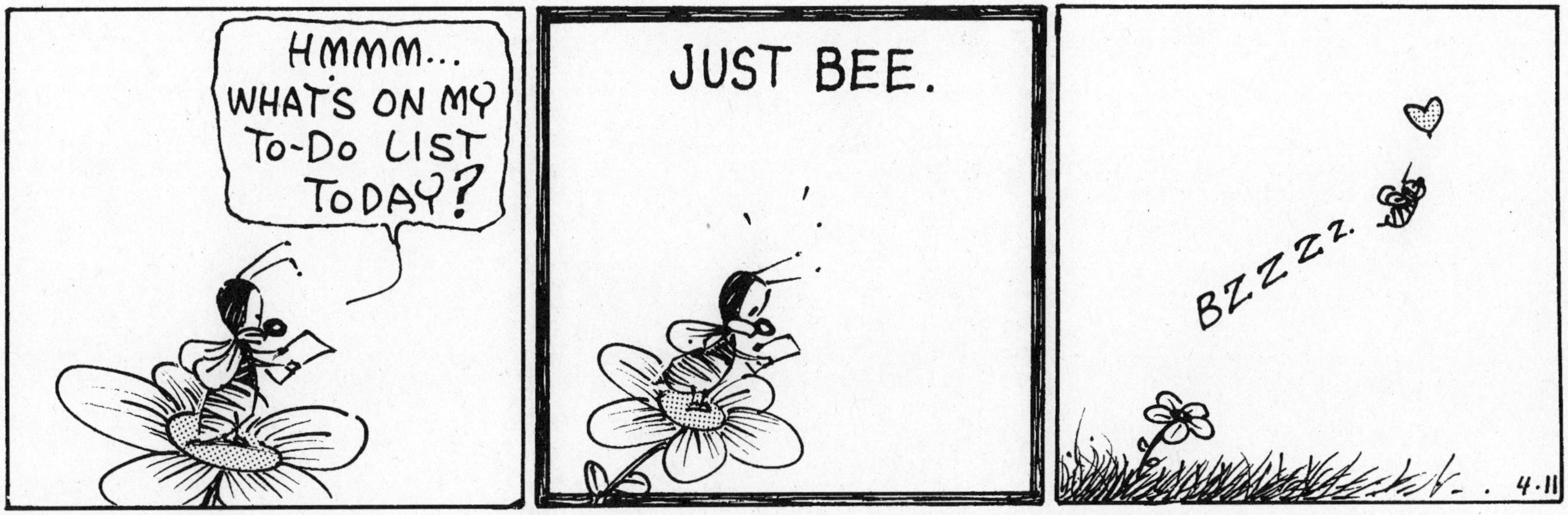
HMMM...
WHAT'S ON MY TO-DO LIST TODAY?
JUST BEE.
BZZZZ.
4-11

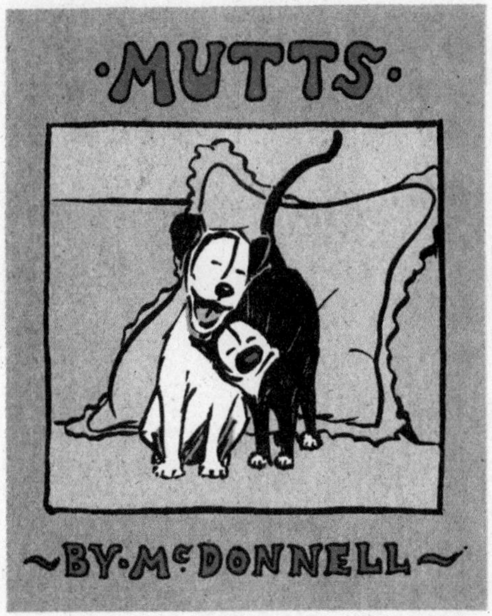
·MUTTS·
~BY·McDONNELL~

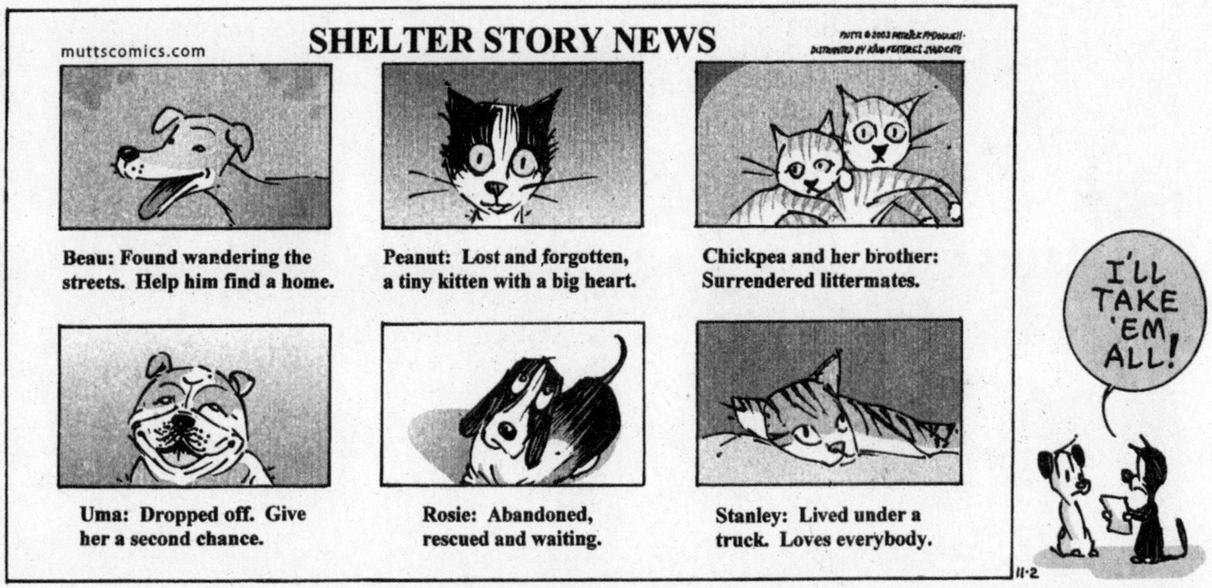
muttscomics.com
SHELTER STORY NEWS
Beau: Found wandering the streets. Help him find a home.
Peanut: Lost and forgotten, a tiny kitten with a big heart.
Chickpea and her brother: Surrendered littermates.
Uma: Dropped off. Give her a second chance.
Rosie: Abandoned, rescued and waiting.
Stanley: Lived under a truck. Loves everybody.
I'LL TAKE 'EM ALL!
11-2

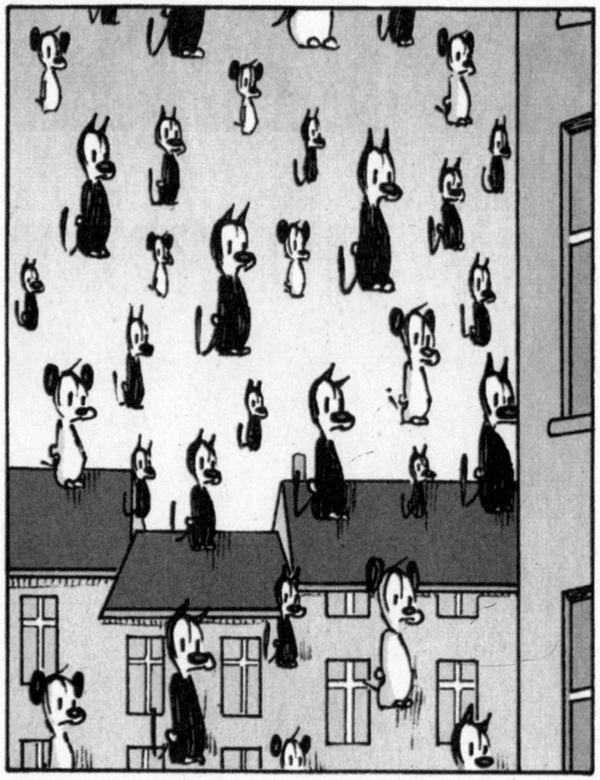

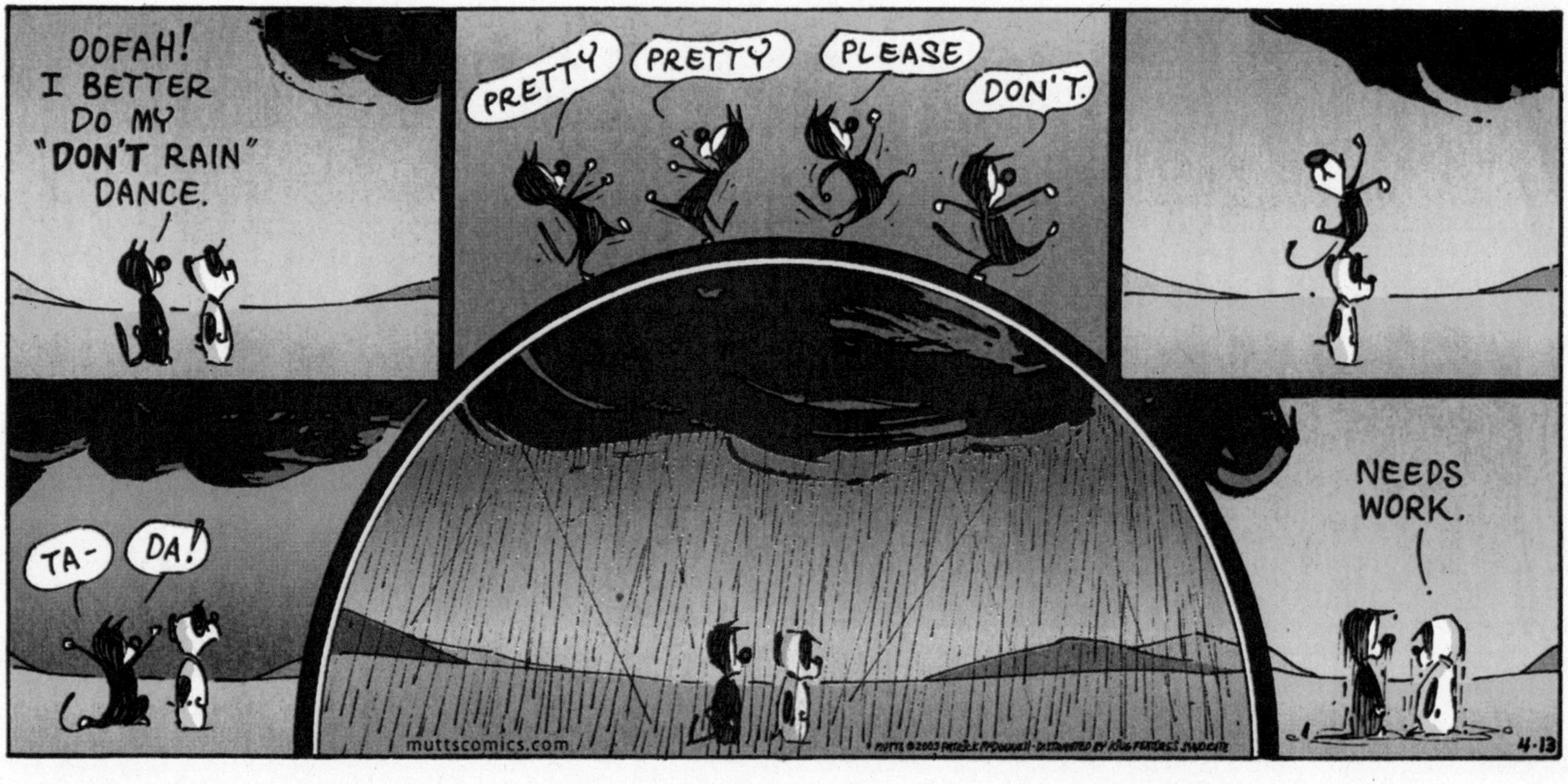
OOFAH! I BETTER DO MY "DON'T RAIN" DANCE.
PRETTY
PRETTY
PLEASE
DON'T.
TA-
DA!
NEEDS WORK.
mutts comics.com
4-13

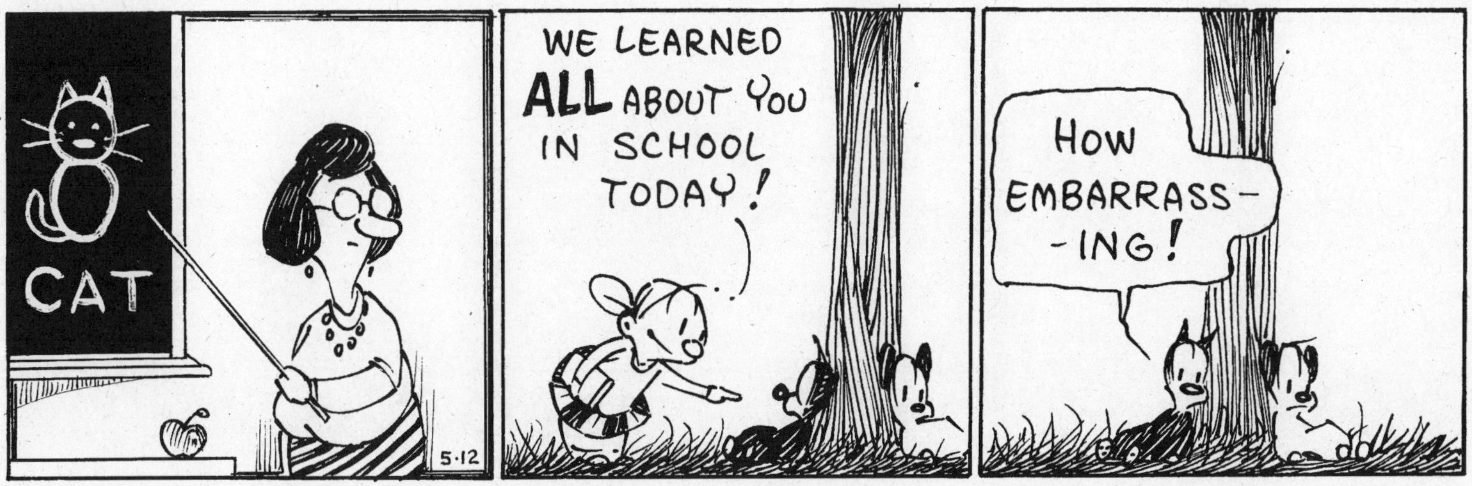
CAT
5·12
WE LEARNED ALL ABOUT YOU IN SCHOOL TODAY!
HOW EMBARRASS--ING!

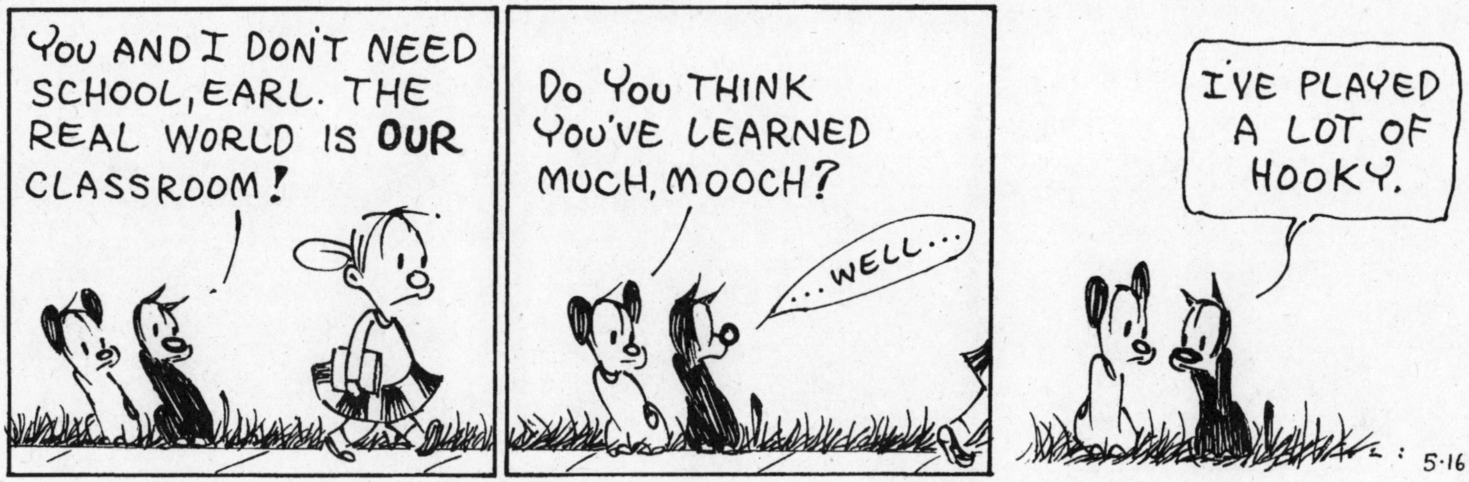
YOU AND I DON'T NEED SCHOOL, EARL. THE REAL WORLD IS OUR CLASSROOM!
DO YOU THINK YOU'VE LEARNED MUCH, MOOCH?
...WELL...
I'VE PLAYED A LOT OF HOOKY.
5·16

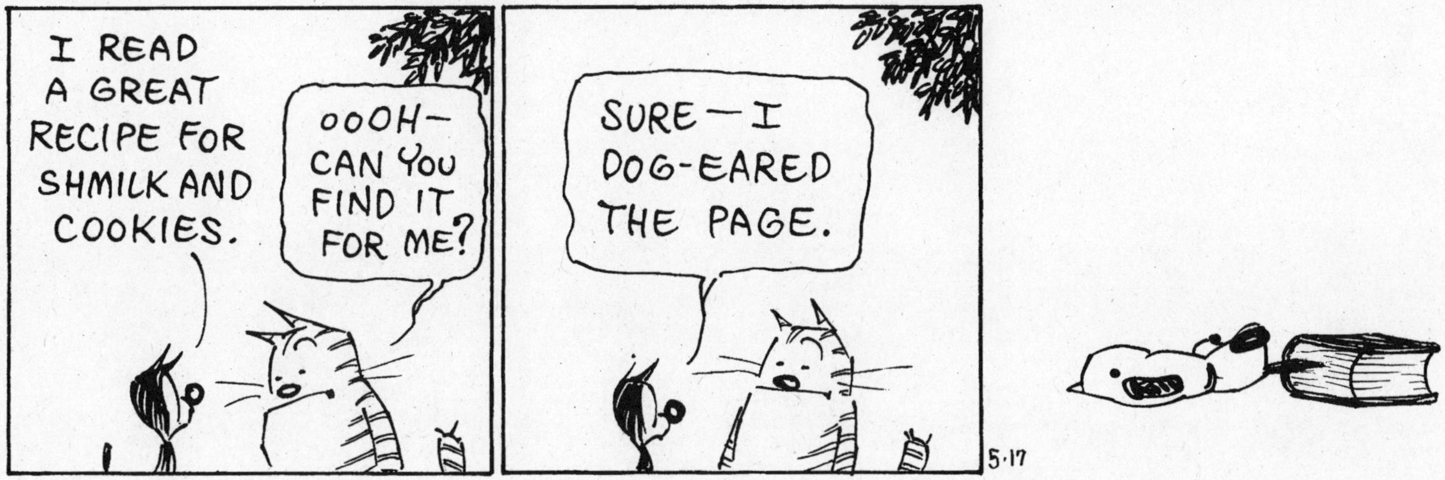
I READ A GREAT RECIPE FOR SHMILK AND COOKIES.
OOOH— CAN YOU FIND IT FOR ME?
SURE—I DOG-EARED THE PAGE.
5·17

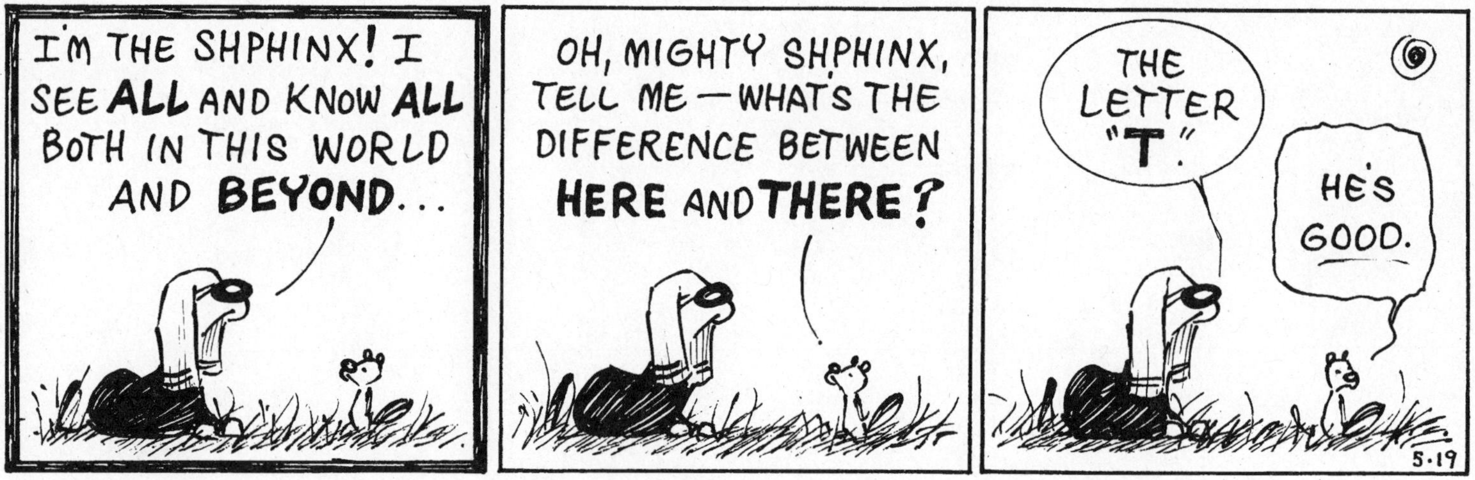
I'M THE SHPHINX! I SEE ALL AND KNOW ALL BOTH IN THIS WORLD AND BEYOND...
OH, MIGHTY SHPHINX, TELL ME — WHAT'S THE DIFFERENCE BETWEEN HERE AND THERE?
THE LETTER "T."
HE'S GOOD.
5·19

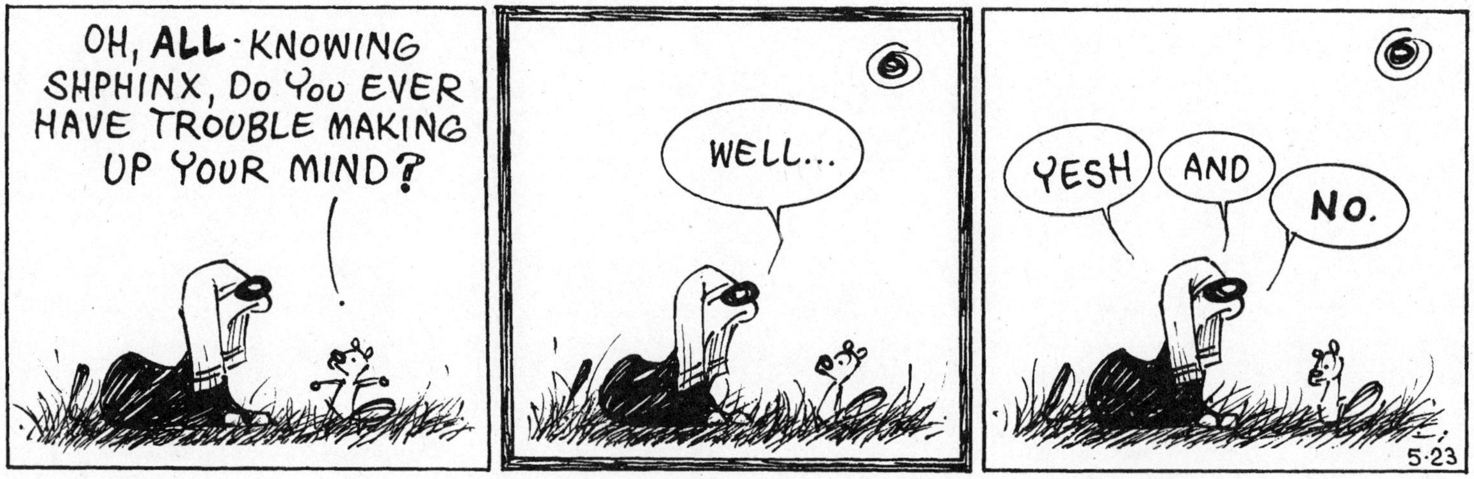
OH, ALL-KNOWING SHPHINX, DO YOU EVER HAVE TROUBLE MAKING UP YOUR MIND?
WELL...
YESH
AND
NO.
5·23

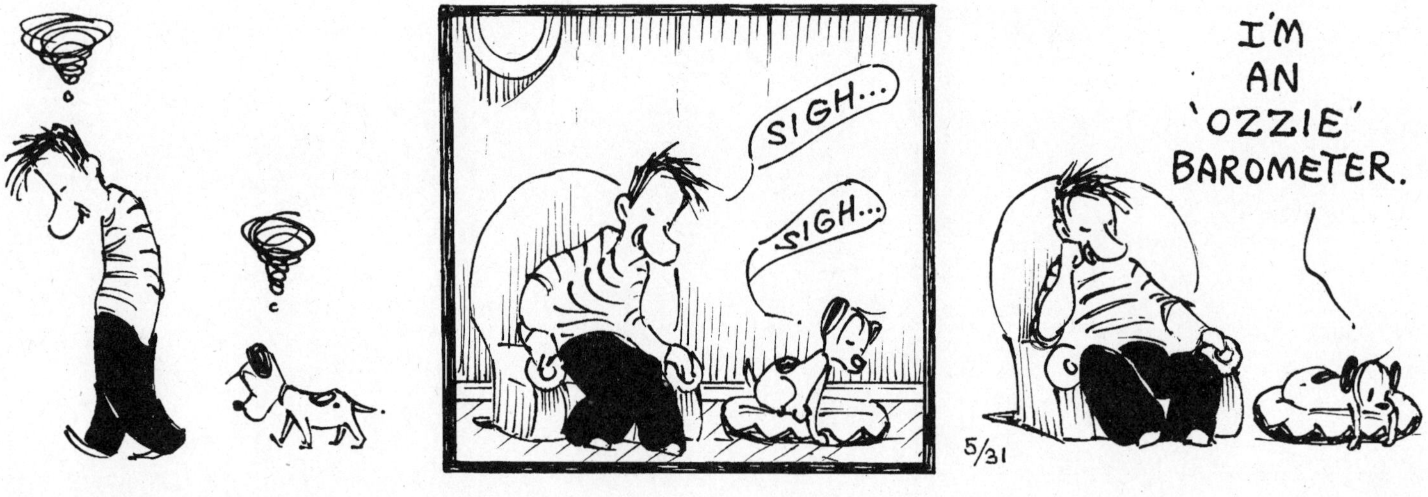
SIGH...
SIGH...
5/31
I'M AN 'OZZIE' BAROMETER.

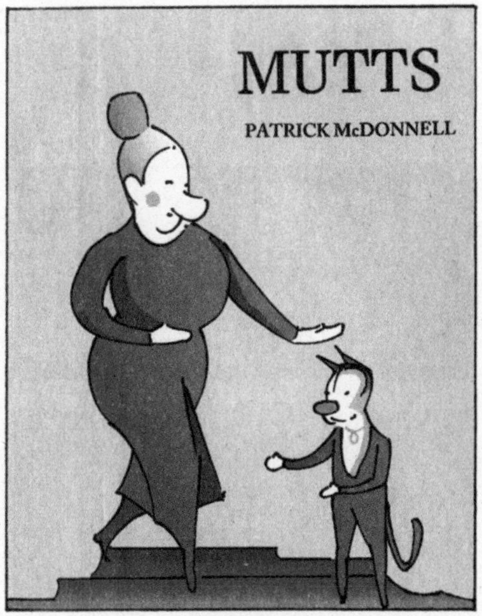
MUTTS
PATRICK McDONNELL

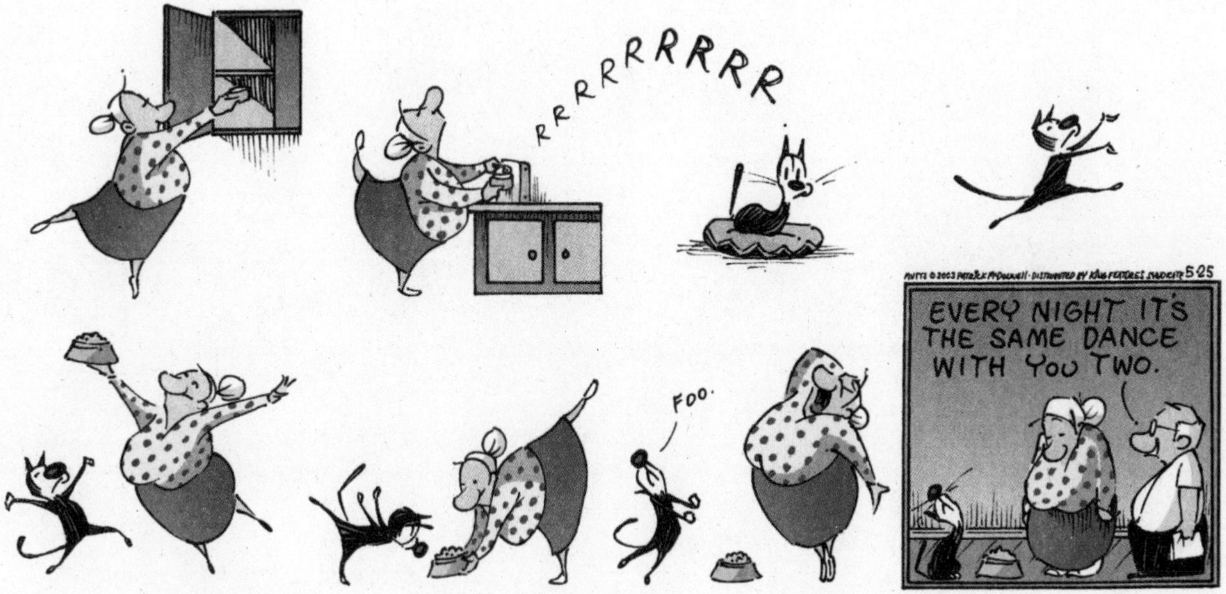
RRRRRRRRRR
FOO.
EVERY NIGHT IT'S THE SAME DANCE WITH YOU TWO.

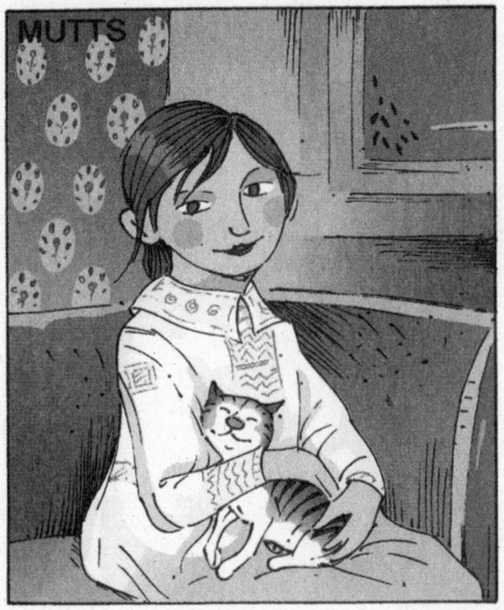
MUTTS

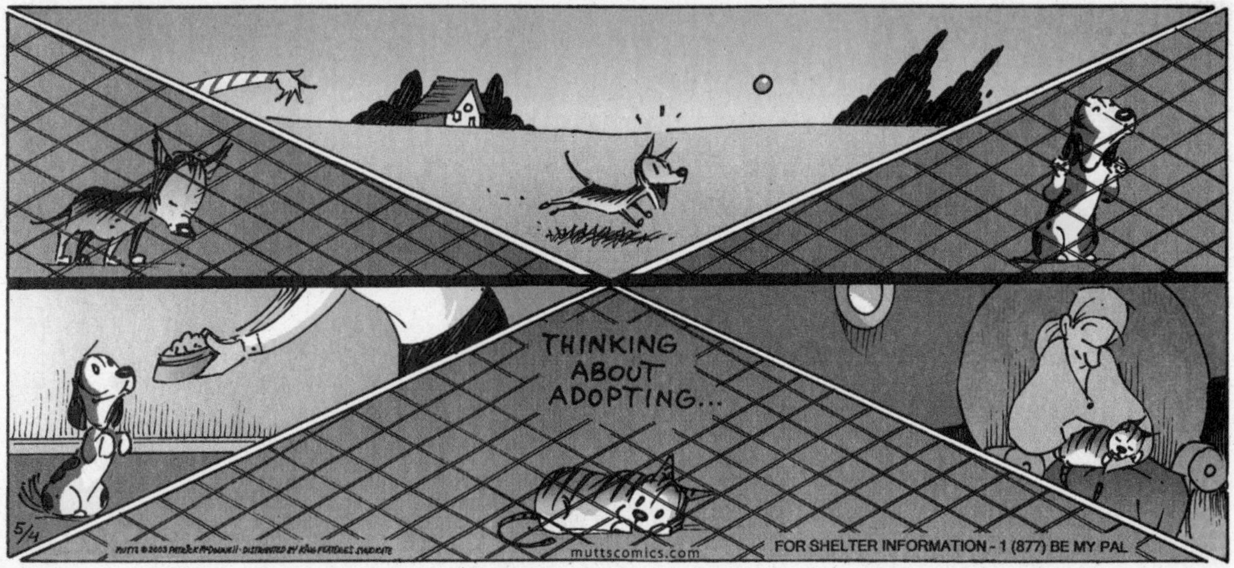
THINKING ABOUT ADOPTING...
5/4
muttscomics.com
FOR SHELTER INFORMATION - 1 (877) BE MY PAL

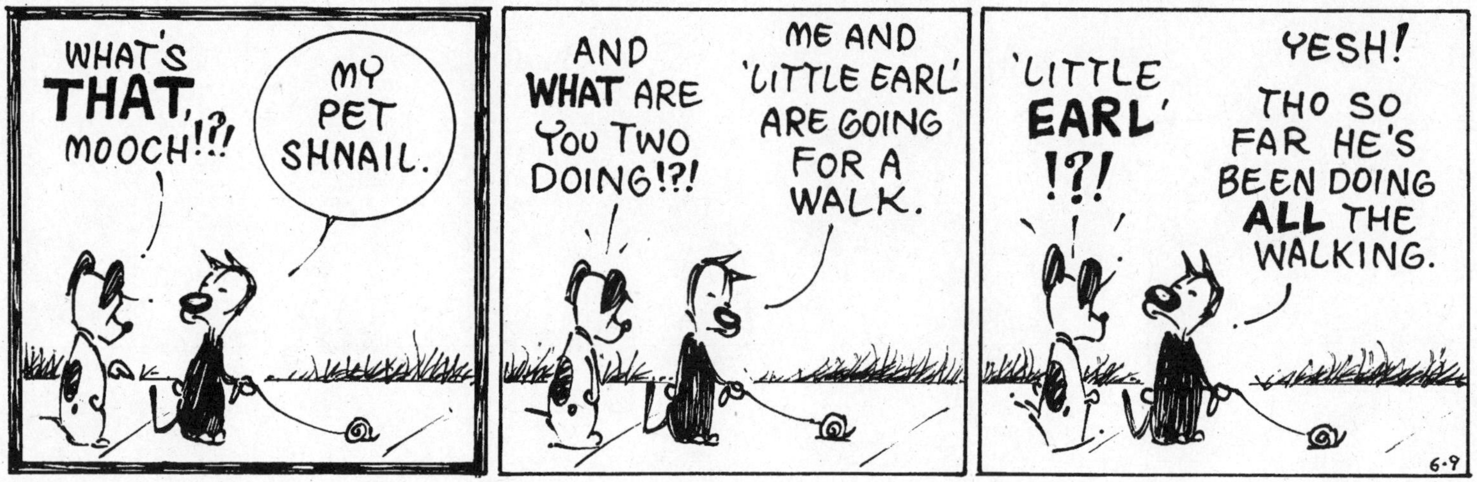
WHAT'S THAT, MOOCH!?!
MY PET SHNAIL.
AND WHAT ARE YOU TWO DOING!?!
ME AND 'LITTLE EARL' ARE GOING FOR A WALK.
'LITTLE EARL' !?!
YESH! THO SO FAR HE'S BEEN DOING ALL THE WALKING.
6-9

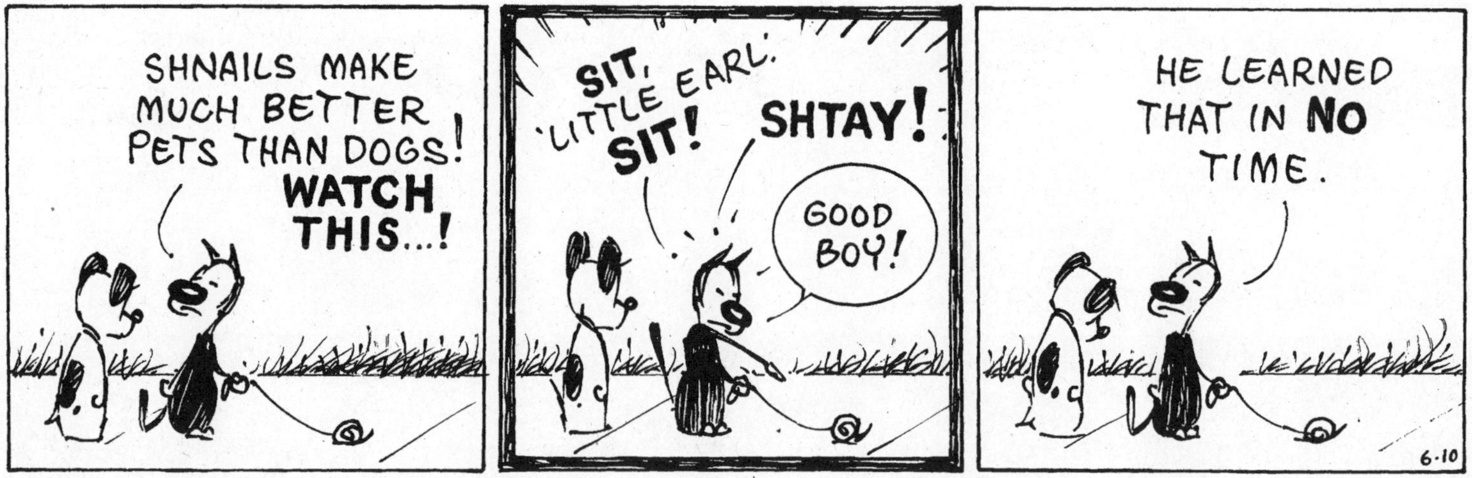
SHNAILS MAKE MUCH BETTER PETS THAN DOGS! WATCH THIS...!
SIT, 'LITTLE EARL.' SIT! SHTAY!
GOOD BOY!
HE LEARNED THAT IN NO TIME.
6-10

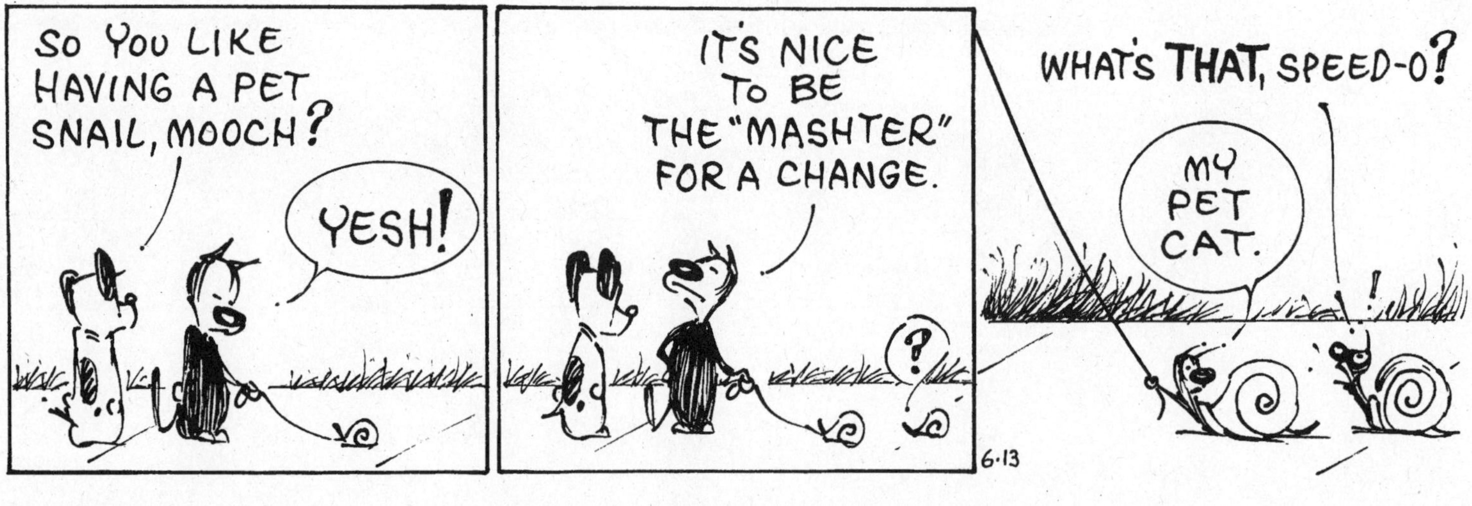
SO YOU LIKE HAVING A PET SNAIL, MOOCH?
YESH!
IT'S NICE TO BE THE "MASHTER" FOR A CHANGE.
?
WHAT'S THAT, SPEED-O?
MY PET CAT.
6-13

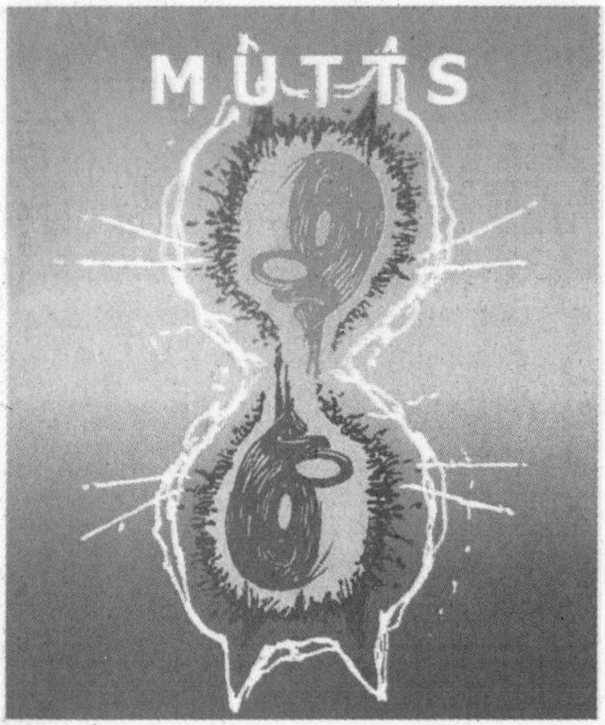
MUTTS

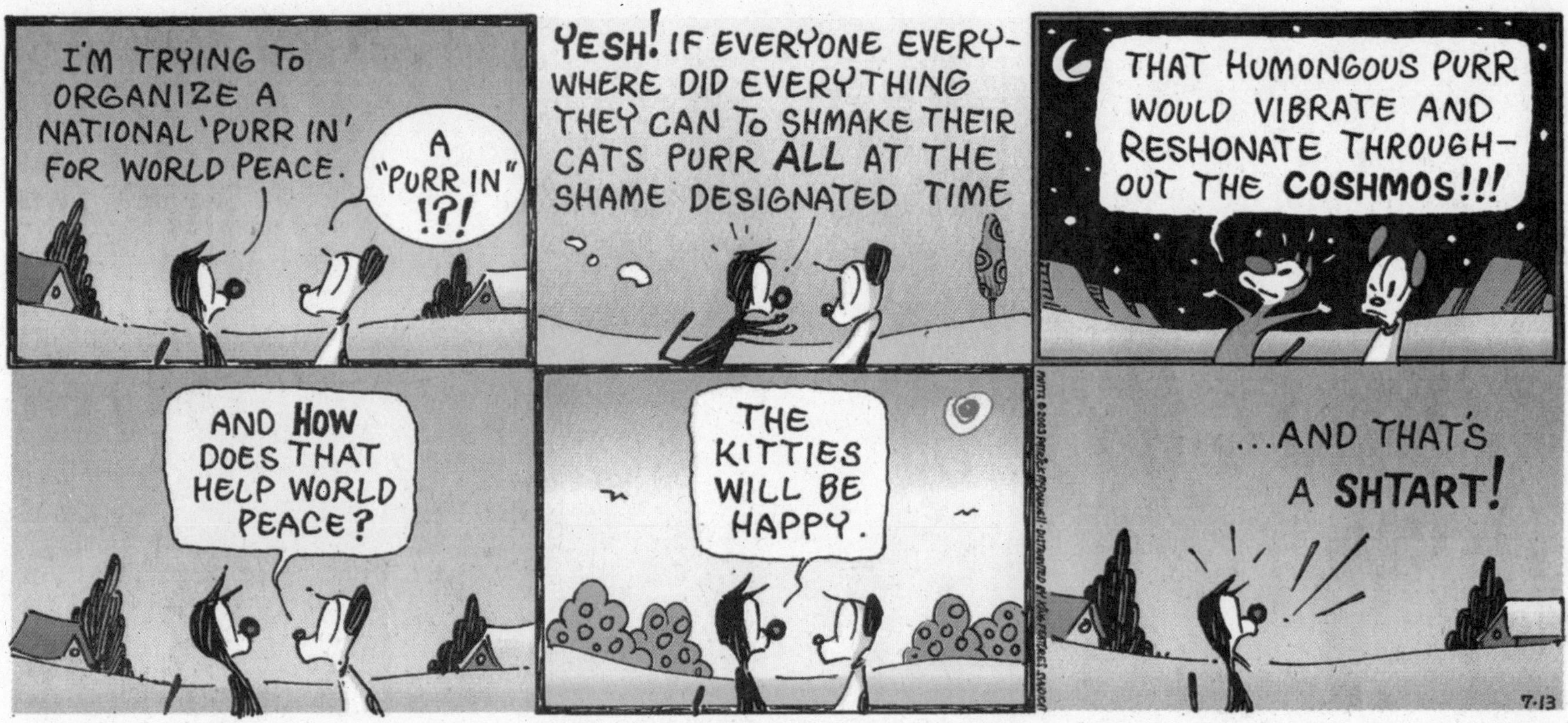
I'M TRYING TO ORGANIZE A NATIONAL 'PURR IN' FOR WORLD PEACE.
A "PURR IN" !?!
YESH! IF EVERYONE EVERY-WHERE DID EVERYTHING THEY CAN TO SHMAKE THEIR CATS PURR ALL AT THE SHAME DESIGNATED TIME
THAT HUMONGOUS PURR WOULD VIBRATE AND RESHONATE THROUGH-OUT THE COSHMOS!!!
AND HOW DOES THAT HELP WORLD PEACE?
THE KITTIES WILL BE HAPPY.
...AND THAT'S A SHTART!
7·13

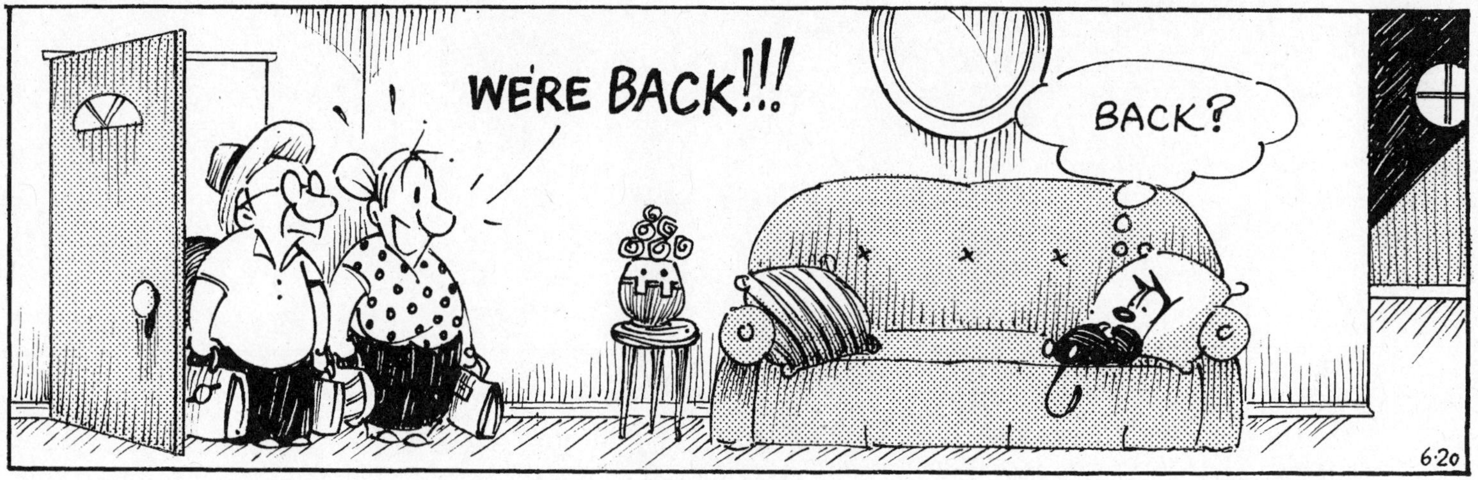
WE'RE BACK!!!
BACK?
6·20

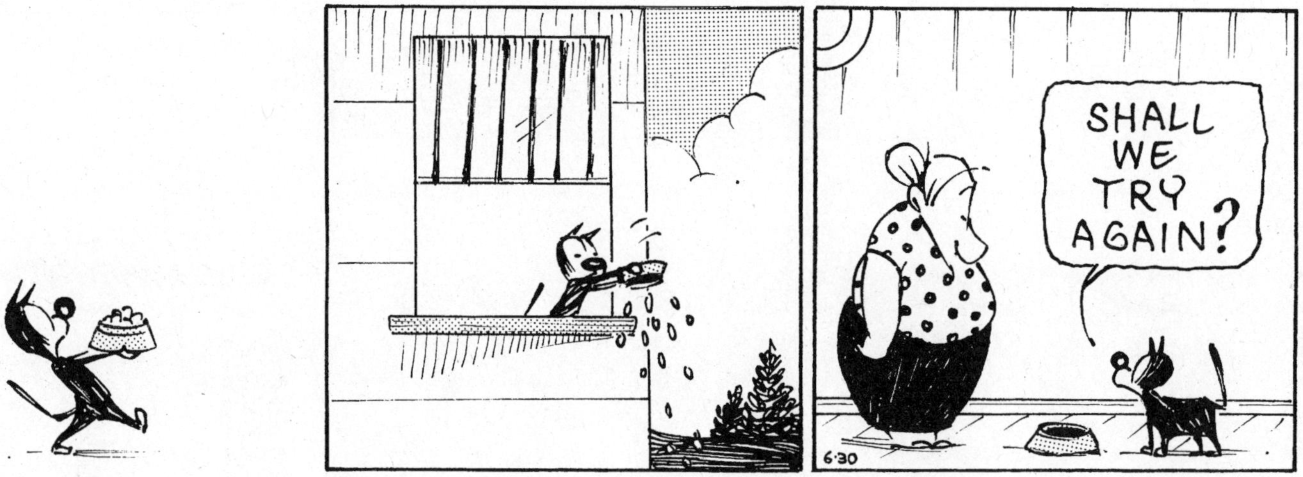
SHALL WE TRY AGAIN?
6·30

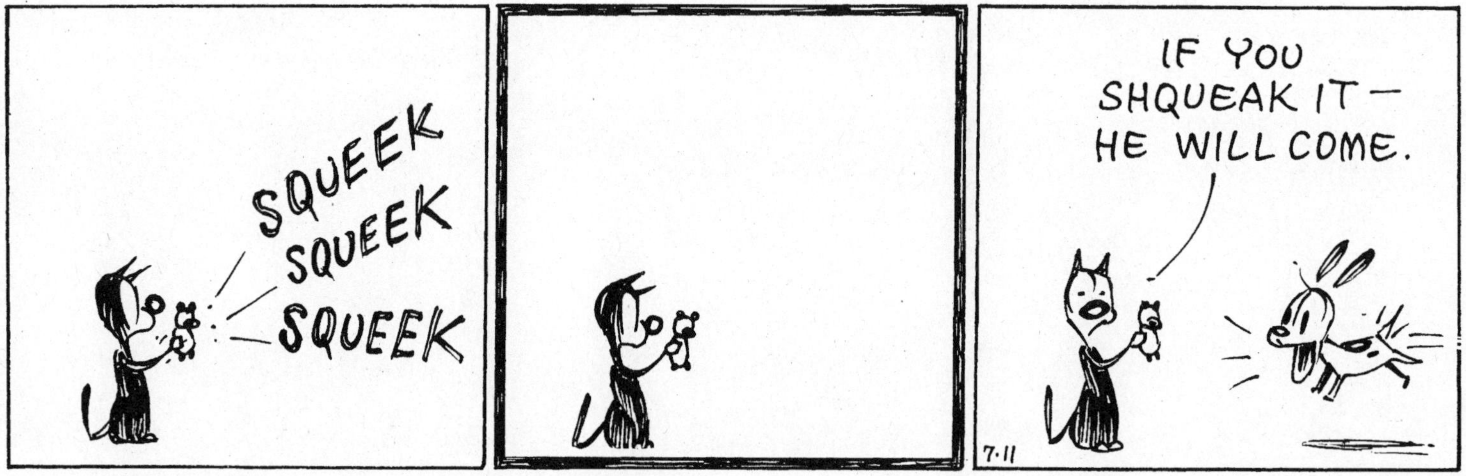
SQUEEK
SQUEEK
SQUEEK
IF YOU SHQUEAK IT— HE WILL COME.
7·11

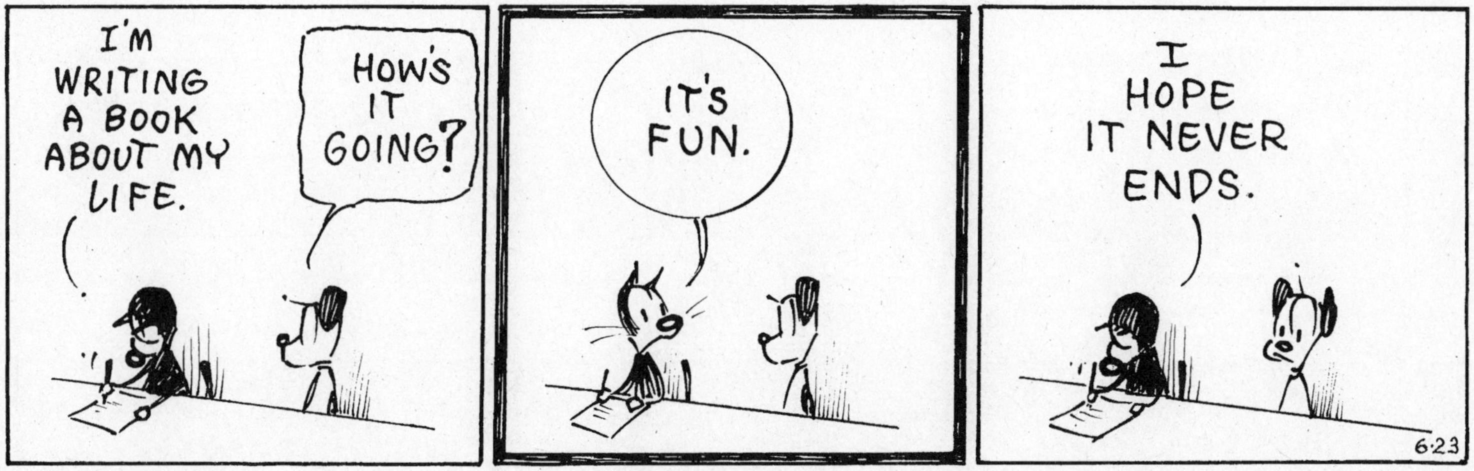
I'M WRITING A BOOK ABOUT MY LIFE.
HOW'S IT GOING?
IT'S FUN.
I HOPE IT NEVER ENDS.
6·23

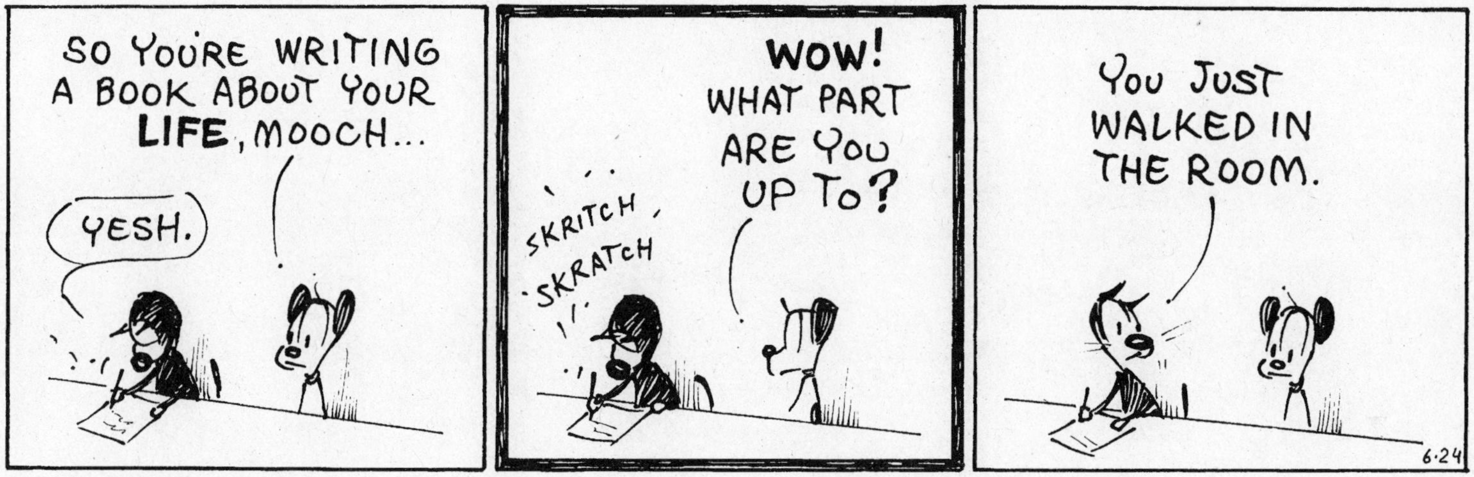
SO YOU'RE WRITING A BOOK ABOUT YOUR LIFE, MOOCH...
YESH.
SKRITCH SKRATCH
WOW! WHAT PART ARE YOU UP TO?
YOU JUST WALKED IN THE ROOM.
6·24

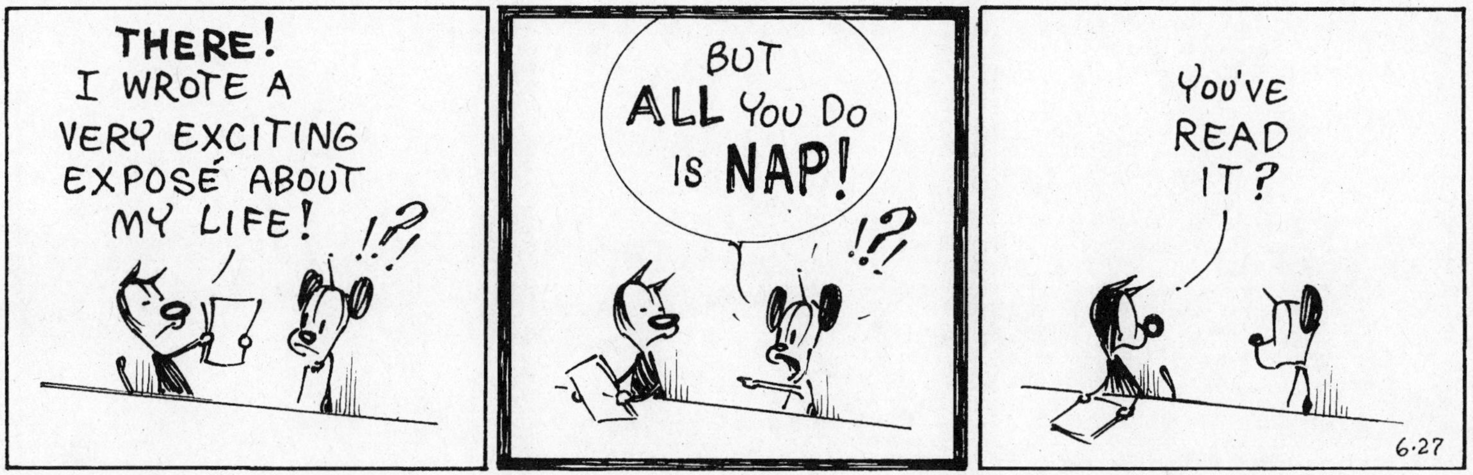
THERE! I WROTE A VERY EXCITING EXPOSÉ ABOUT MY LIFE!
!?
BUT ALL YOU DO IS NAP!
!?
YOU'VE READ IT?
6·27

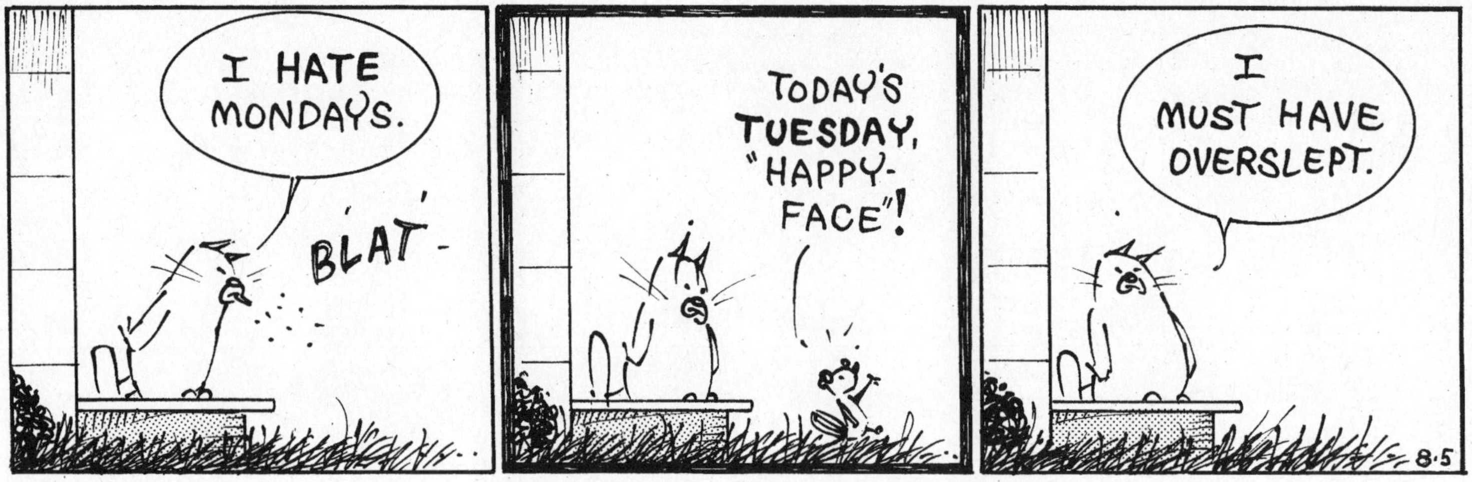
I HATE MONDAYS.
BLAT
TODAY'S TUESDAY, "HAPPY-FACE"!
I MUST HAVE OVERSLEPT.
8·5

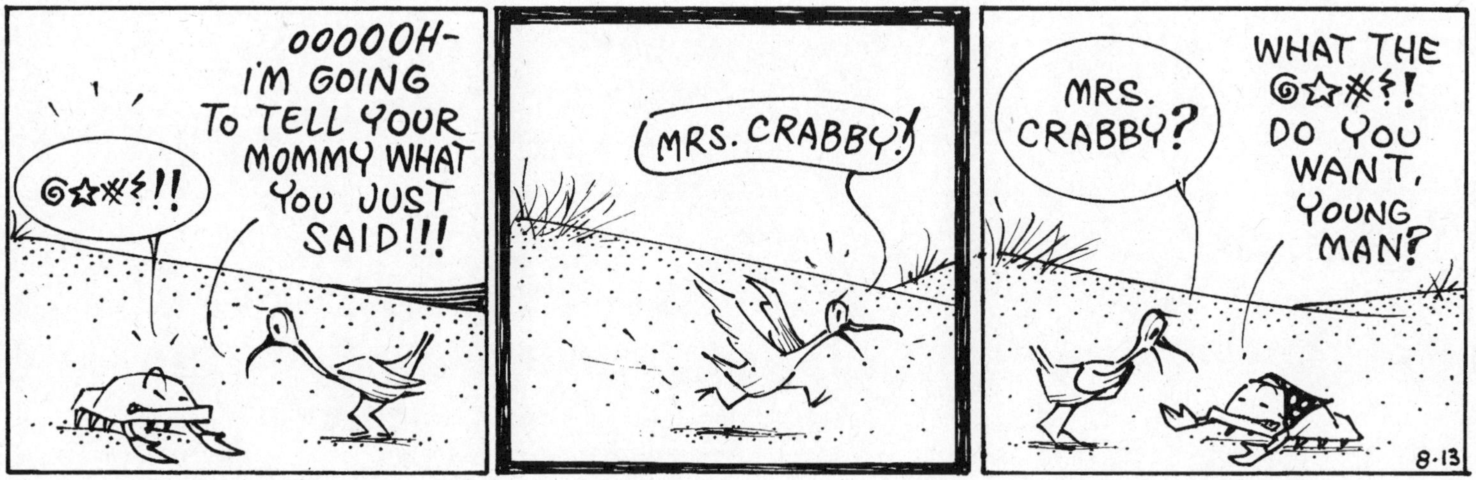
!!
OOOOOH- I'M GOING TO TELL YOUR MOMMY WHAT YOU JUST SAID!!!
MRS. CRABBY?!
MRS. CRABBY?
WHAT THE
!
DO YOU WANT, YOUNG MAN?
8·13

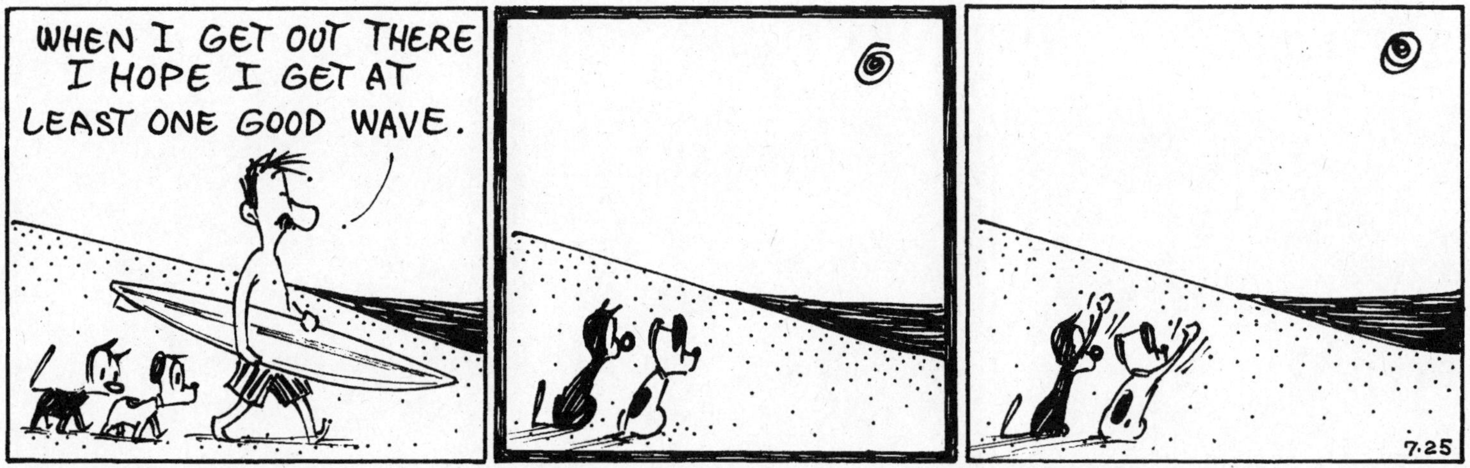
WHEN I GET OUT THERE I HOPE I GET AT LEAST ONE GOOD WAVE.
7·25

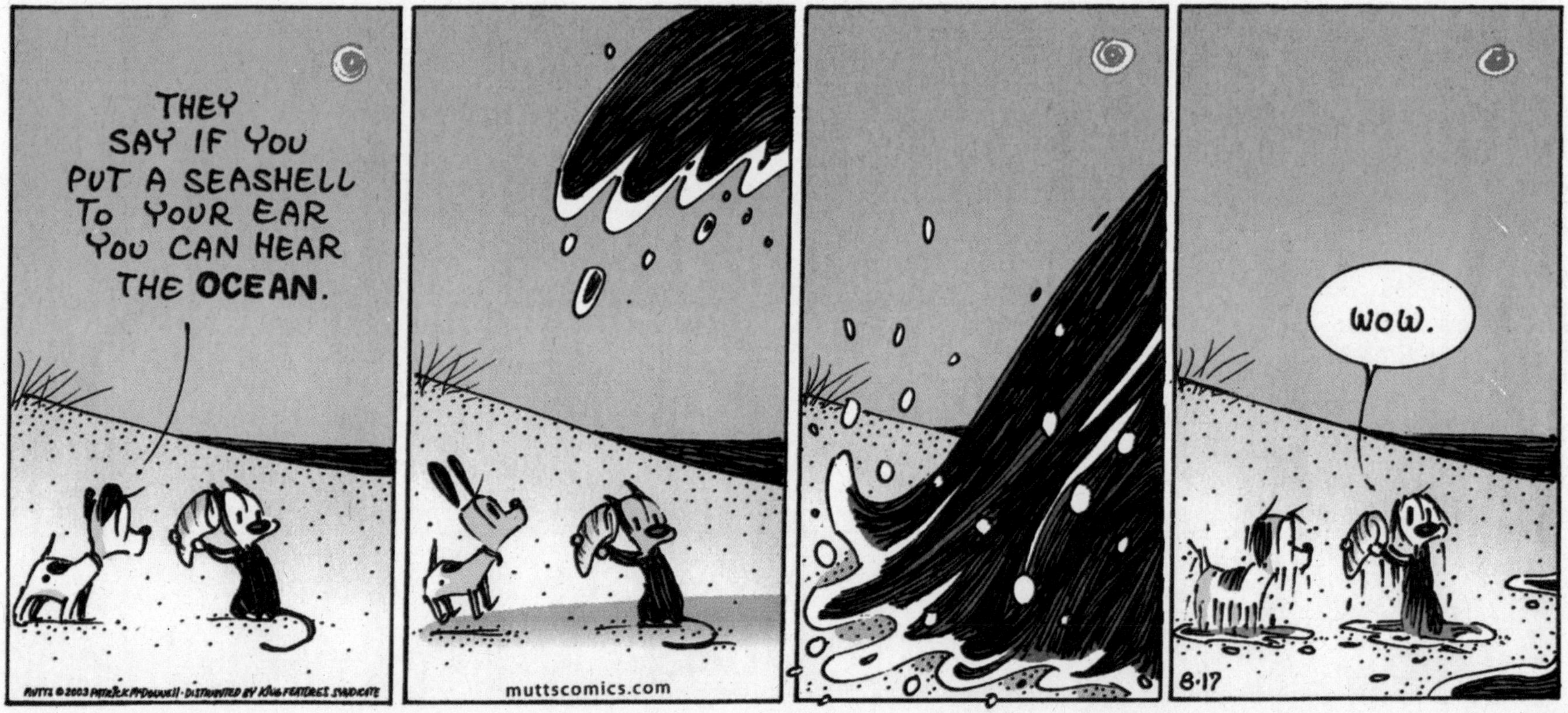
THEY SAY IF YOU PUT A SEASHELL TO YOUR EAR YOU CAN HEAR THE **OCEAN**.
WOW.
MUTTS © 2003 PATRICK McDONNELL · DISTRIBUTED BY KING FEATURES SYNDICATE
muttscomics.com
8·17

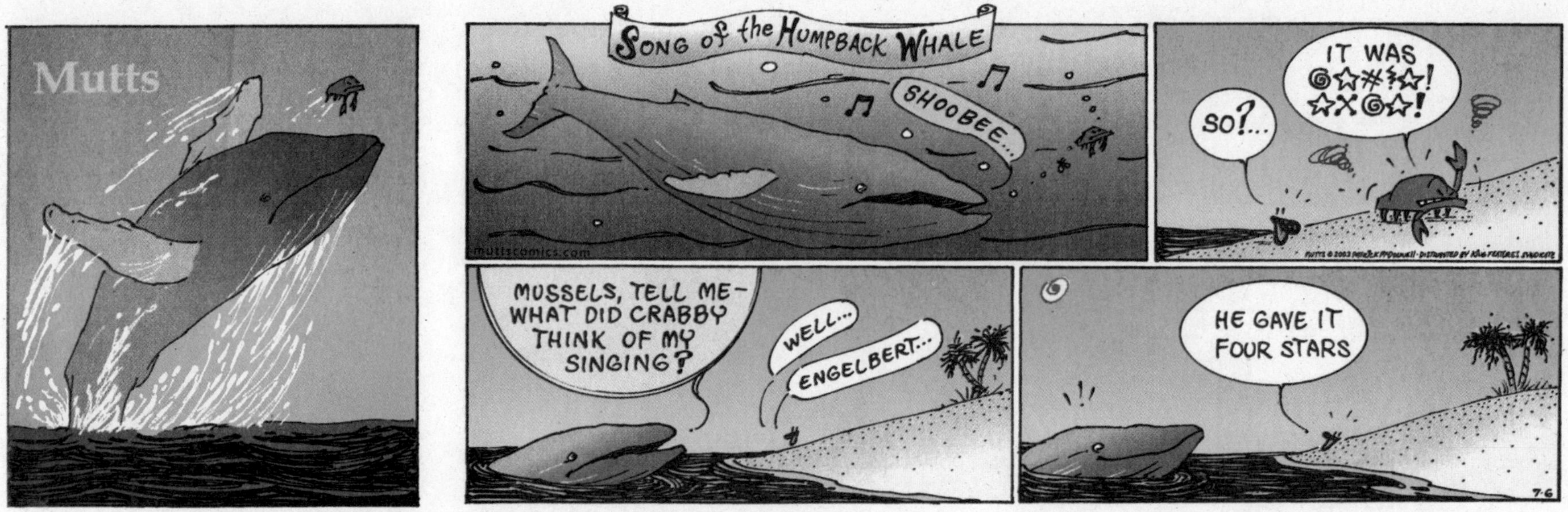
Mutts
SONG of the HUMPBACK WHALE
SHOOBEE...
muttscomics.com
SO?...
IT WAS @☆#!☆! ☆X@☆!
MUTTS © 2003 PATRICK McDONNELL · DISTRIBUTED BY KING FEATURES SYNDICATE
MUSSELS, TELL ME- WHAT DID CRABBY THINK OF MY SINGING?
WELL...
ENGELBERT...
HE GAVE IT FOUR STARS
7·6

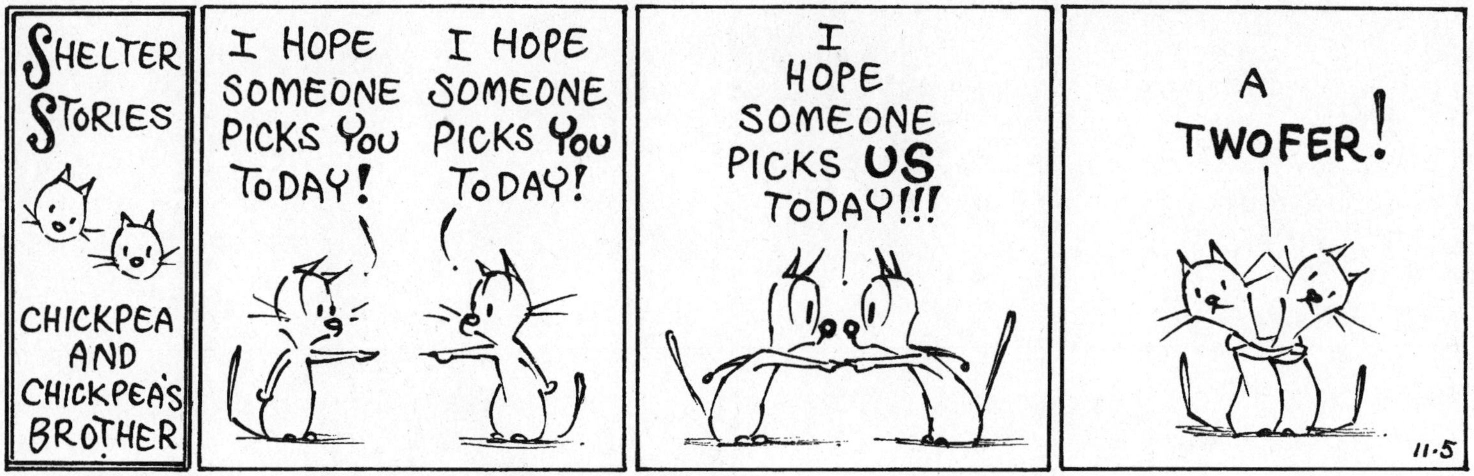
SHELTER STORIES
CHICKPEA AND CHICKPEA'S BROTHER
I HOPE SOMEONE PICKS YOU TODAY!
I HOPE SOMEONE PICKS YOU TODAY!
I HOPE SOMEONE PICKS US TODAY!!!
A TWOFER!
11·5

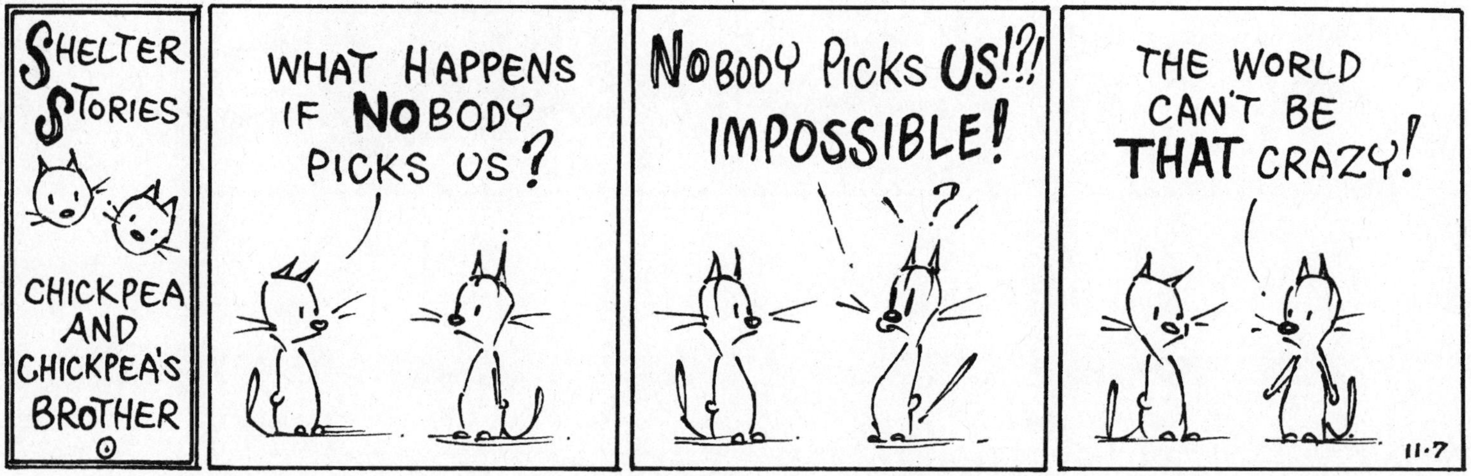
SHELTER STORIES
CHICKPEA AND CHICKPEA'S BROTHER
WHAT HAPPENS IF NOBODY PICKS US?
NOBODY PICKS US!?! IMPOSSIBLE!
?
THE WORLD CAN'T BE THAT CRAZY!
11·7

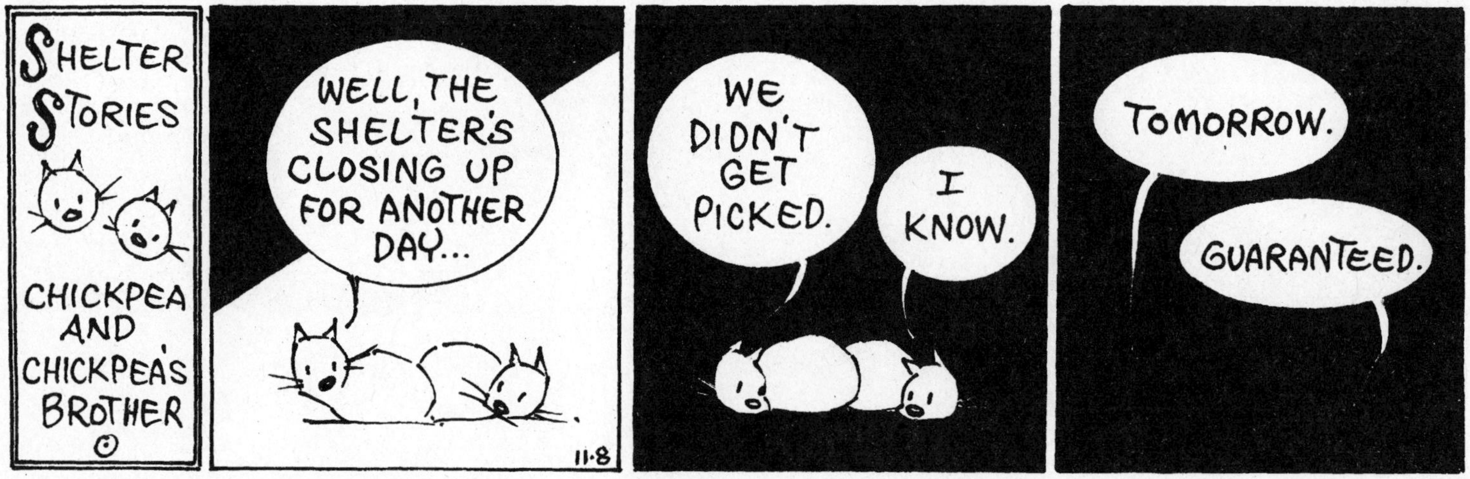
SHELTER STORIES
CHICKPEA AND CHICKPEA'S BROTHER
WELL, THE SHELTER'S CLOSING UP FOR ANOTHER DAY...
11·8
WE DIDN'T GET PICKED.
I KNOW.
TOMORROW.
GUARANTEED.

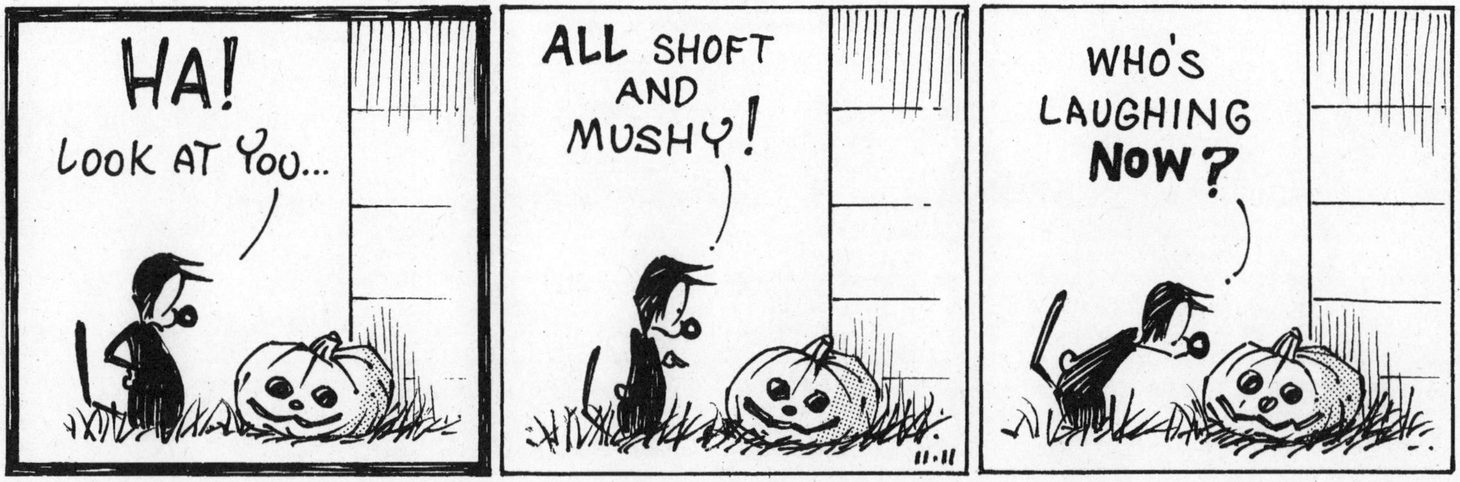
HA!
LOOK AT YOU...
ALL SHOFT AND MUSHY!
11·11
WHO'S LAUGHING NOW?

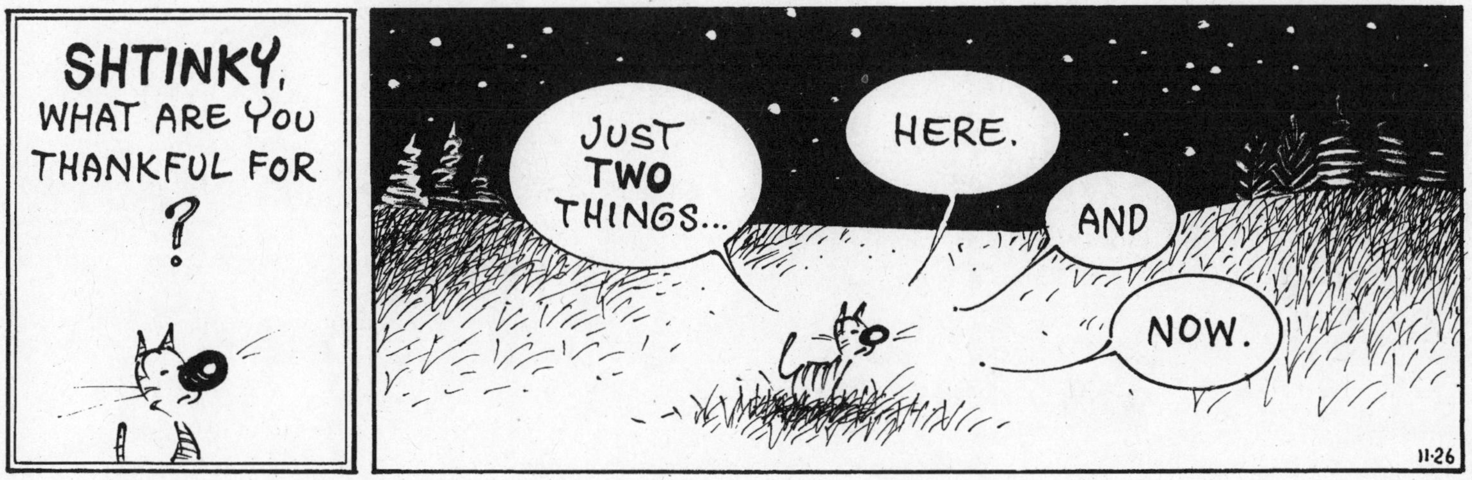
SHTINKY, WHAT ARE YOU THANKFUL FOR ?
JUST TWO THINGS...
HERE.
AND
NOW.
11·26

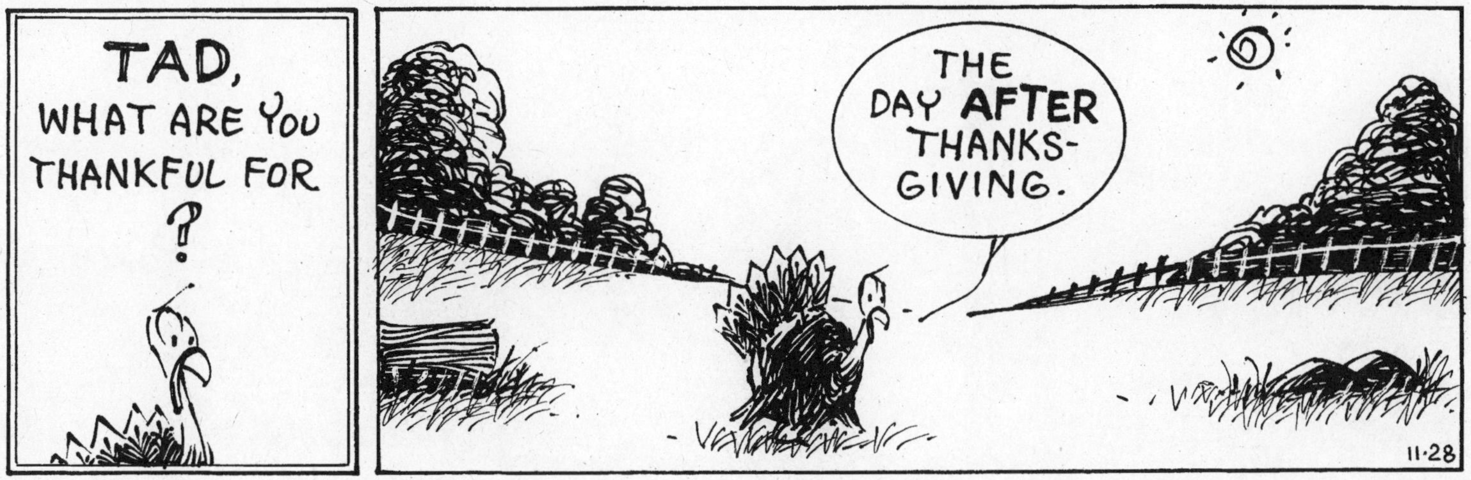
TAD, WHAT ARE YOU THANKFUL FOR ?
THE DAY AFTER THANKS-GIVING.
11·28

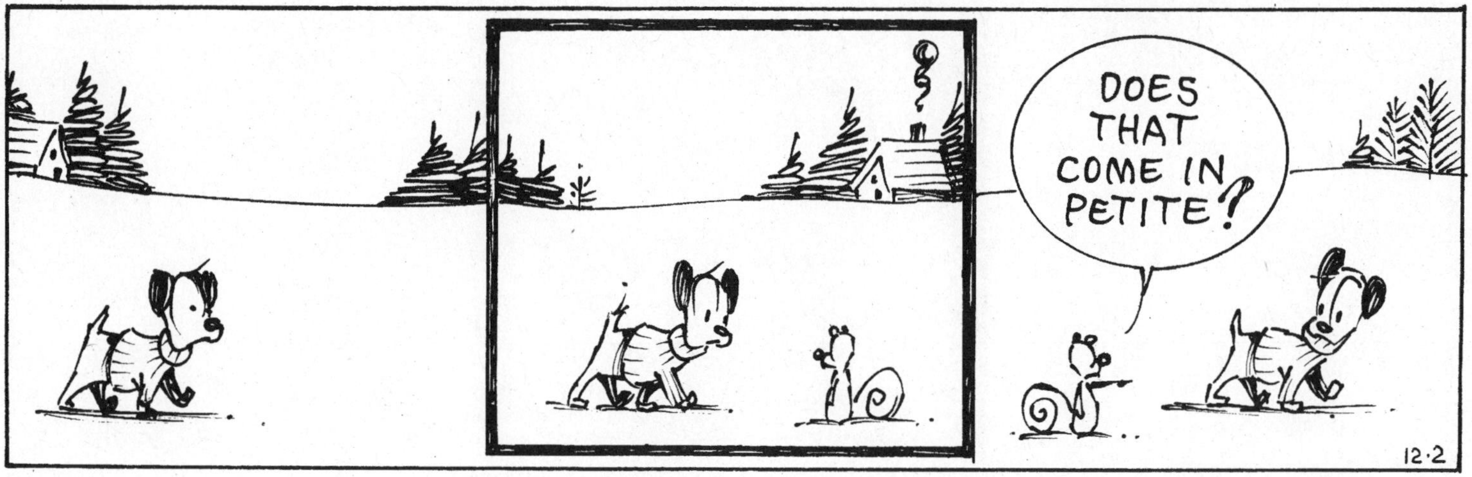

DOES THAT COME IN PETITE?
12·2


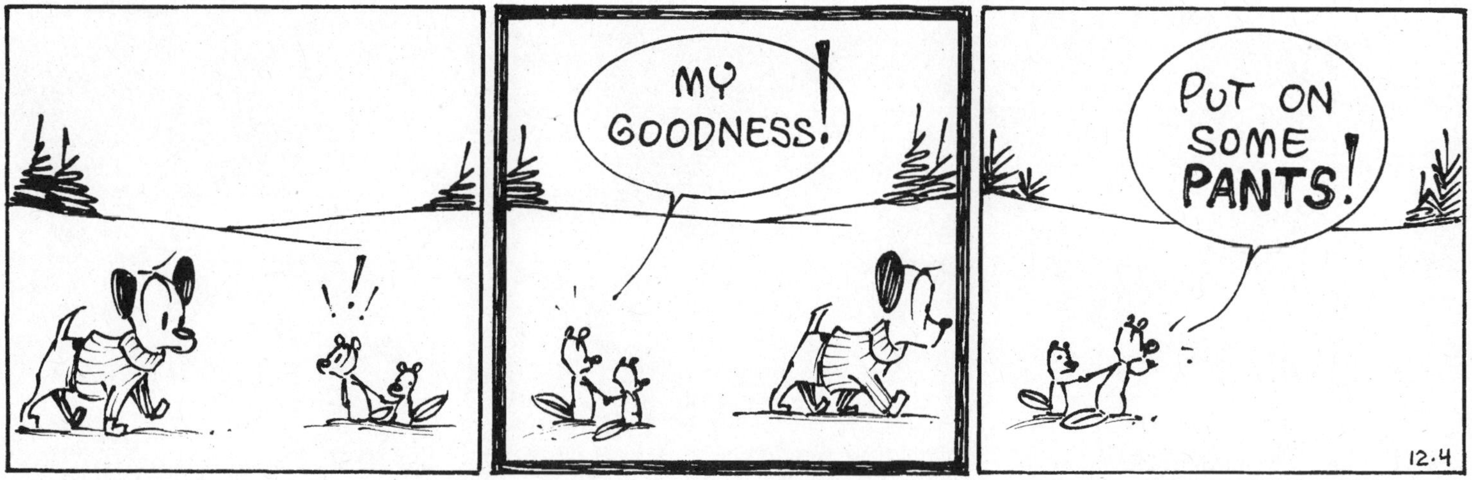

MY GOODNESS!
PUT ON SOME PANTS!
12·4


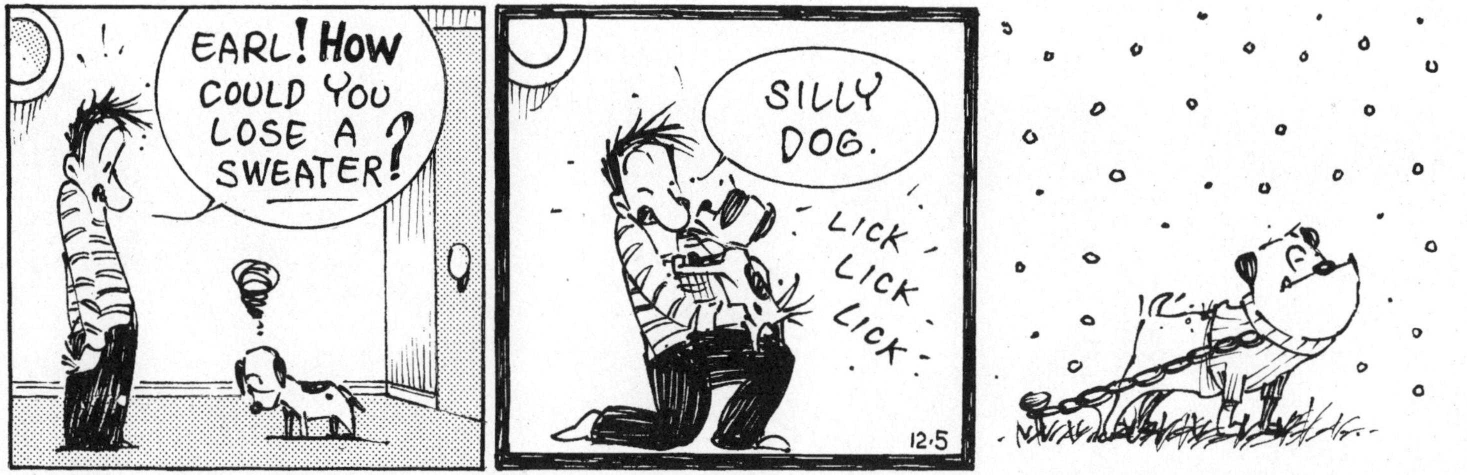

EARL! HOW COULD YOU LOSE A SWEATER?
SILLY DOG.
LICK LICK LICK
12·5

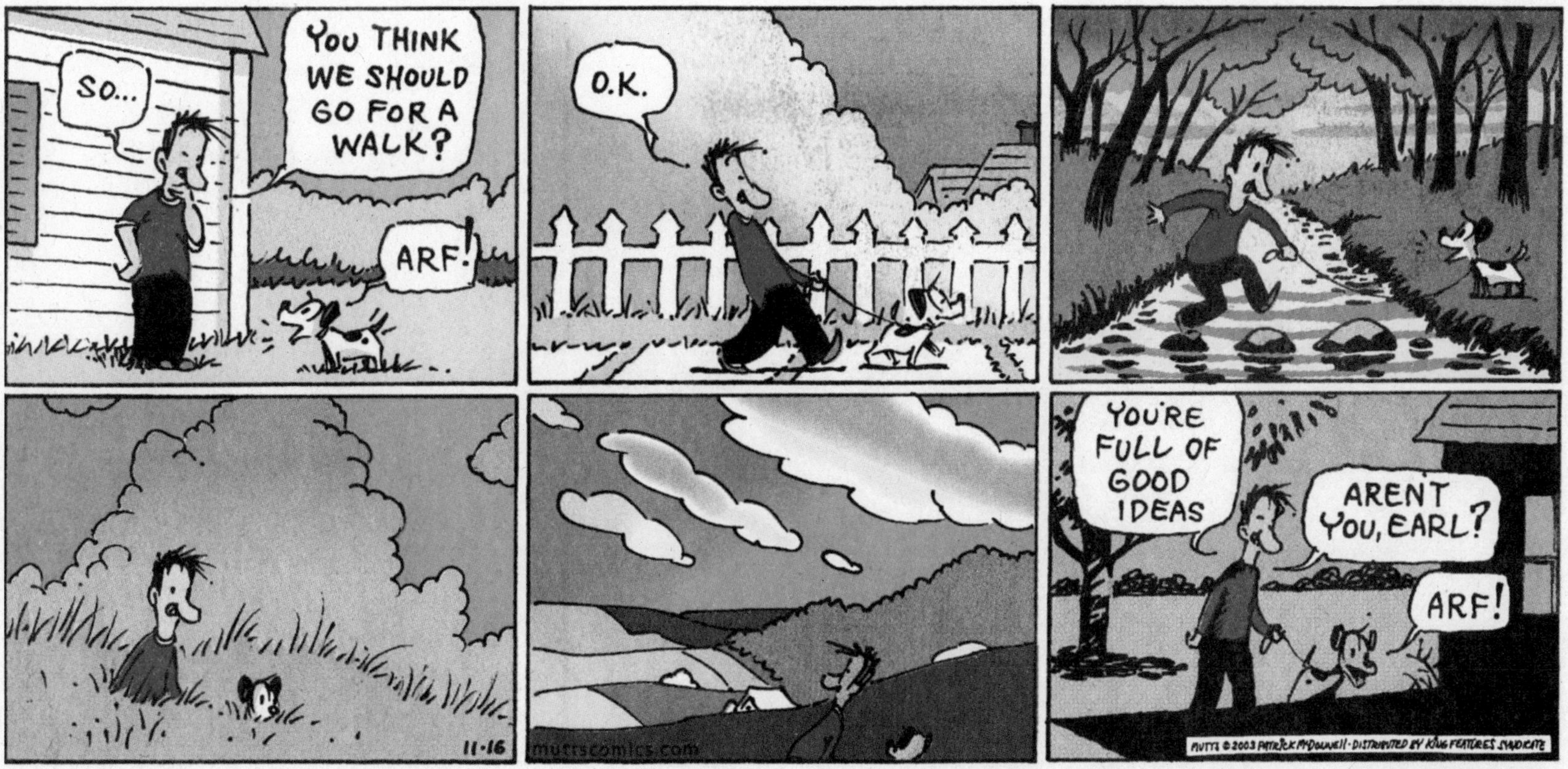
SO...
YOU THINK WE SHOULD GO FOR A WALK?
ARF!
O.K.
11-16
mutts comics.com
YOU'RE FULL OF GOOD IDEAS
ARENT YOU, EARL?
ARF!
MUTTS © 2003 PATRICK McDONNELL · DISTRIBUTED BY KING FEATURES SYNDICATE

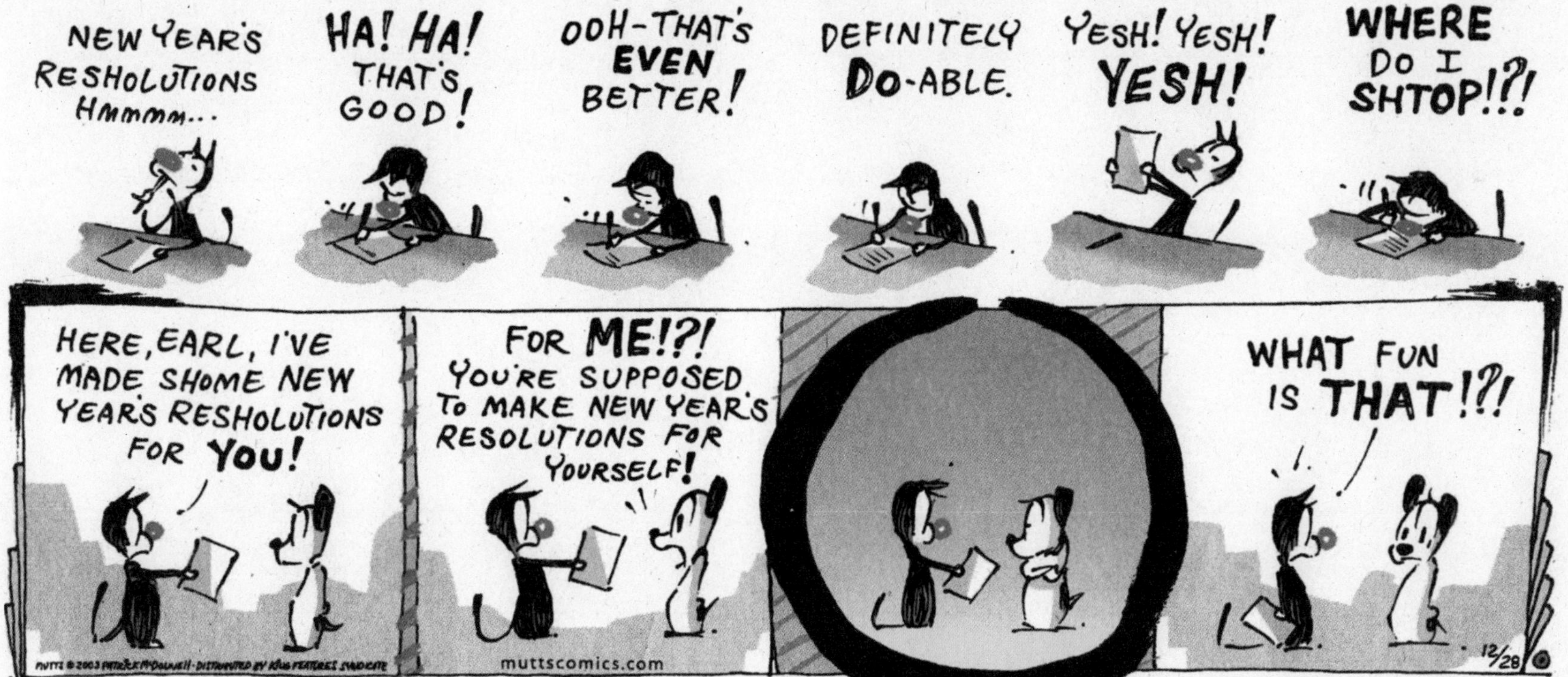
NEW YEAR'S RESHOLUTIONS Hmmmm...
HA! HA! THAT'S GOOD!
OOH-THAT'S EVEN BETTER!
DEFINITELY DO-ABLE.
YESH! YESH! YESH!
WHERE DO I SHTOP!?!
HERE, EARL, I'VE MADE SHOME NEW YEAR'S RESHOLUTIONS FOR YOU!
FOR ME!?!
YOU'RE SUPPOSED TO MAKE NEW YEAR'S RESOLUTIONS FOR YOURSELF!
WHAT FUN IS THAT!?!
MUTTS © 2003 PATRICK McDONNELL · DISTRIBUTED BY KING FEATURES SYNDICATE
muttscomics.com
12/28

! ? !
I LOSHT MY "PURR".
12·15

WHERE ARE YOU GOING, MOOCH!?!
I'M OFF TO FIND MY PURR, EARL!
WHAT'S IN THE BAG?
YOUR LUNCH.
12·19

SHTINKY! WHAT ARE YOU DOING OUT HERE?
THE USUAL. I'M LOST...
YESH. I UNDERSHTAND. I'M OUT TRYING TO FIND MY "PURR".
...BUT NOT THAT LOST.
12·23

I LOST MY PURR, SHTINKY.
I KNOW WHERE IT IS, MOOCH.
YOU DO!?!
SURE! IT'S THAT FEELING OF JOY DEEP INSIDE YOU.
I THOUGHT THAT WAS THE EGGSHNOG.
12·2

HERE, SHTINKY, HAVE ALL MY FOOD AND THEN I'LL CARRY YOU HOME. I CAN TRY TO FIND MY 'PURR' SHOME OTHER DAY.
WOW.
PURRR..
PURRR
WOW!
12·25

SO YOU FOUND YOUR PURR, MOOCH!
NOPE.
PURRRR.
IT FOUND ME.
12·27

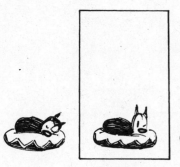

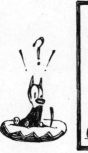

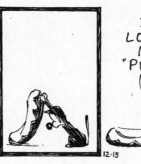

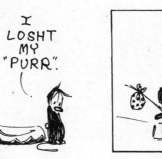

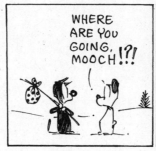

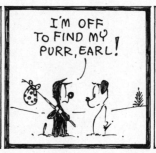

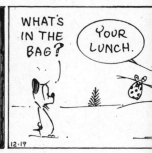

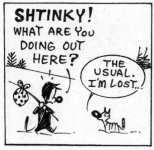

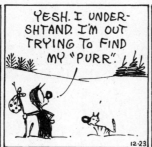

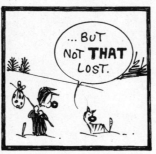

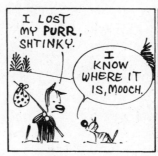

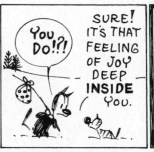

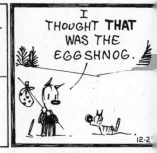

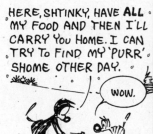

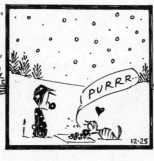

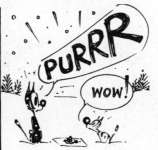

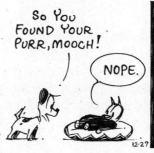

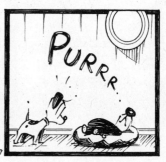

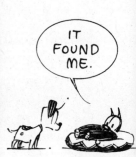

**On occasion, I like to play** with the conventions of cartooning. In the January 25 Sunday strip (page 235) I thought it would be interesting and funny to give the impression that the whole comic was slipping off the newspaper page. The fan in me enjoyed seeing that in print.

In *Mutts*, I often show the human characters enjoying a newspaper or a book to help encourage reading. This year I took it a step further by introducing the *Mutts* Book Club, where Mooch and, occasionally, other animal characters recite from their favorite novels. Reading cannot be promoted too much.

The August 29 Sunday page (page 249) is an homage to Richard Outcault's *The Yellow Kid* (which is generally considered to be the first comic strip). The Yellow Kid was a tough street urchin who expressed himself with commentary on his T-shirt (he was years ahead of his time). I thought the setup would work well for shining light on the feral cats who live in the back alleys of our cities. Comic strips are over a hundred years old, a newcomer to the world of art. I believe this nascent medium will always be a powerful way to tell stories and touch lives.

The year 2004 was *Mutts* 10th anniversary, and today it can be read in over 700 newspapers in over 20 countries. Sometimes I feel like I've been drawing *Mutts* my whole life; sometimes I feel like I just started yesterday. I'm very lucky and blessed to be doing something I truly love. Yesh—10 years, 3,650 strips . . . and still counting.

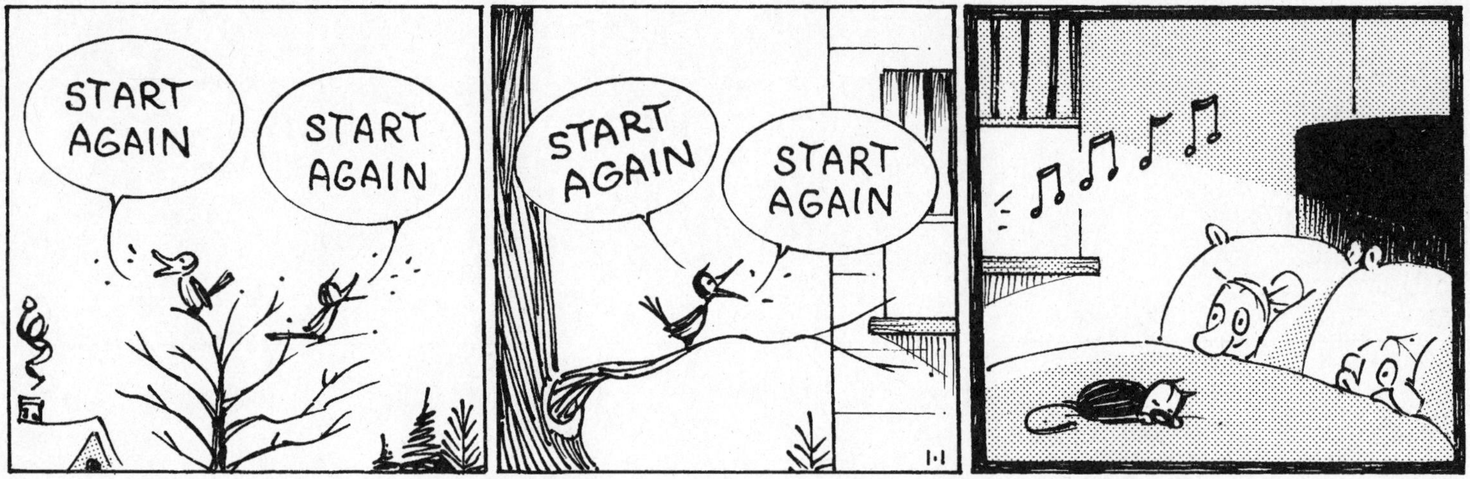
START AGAIN
START AGAIN
START AGAIN
START AGAIN
1·1

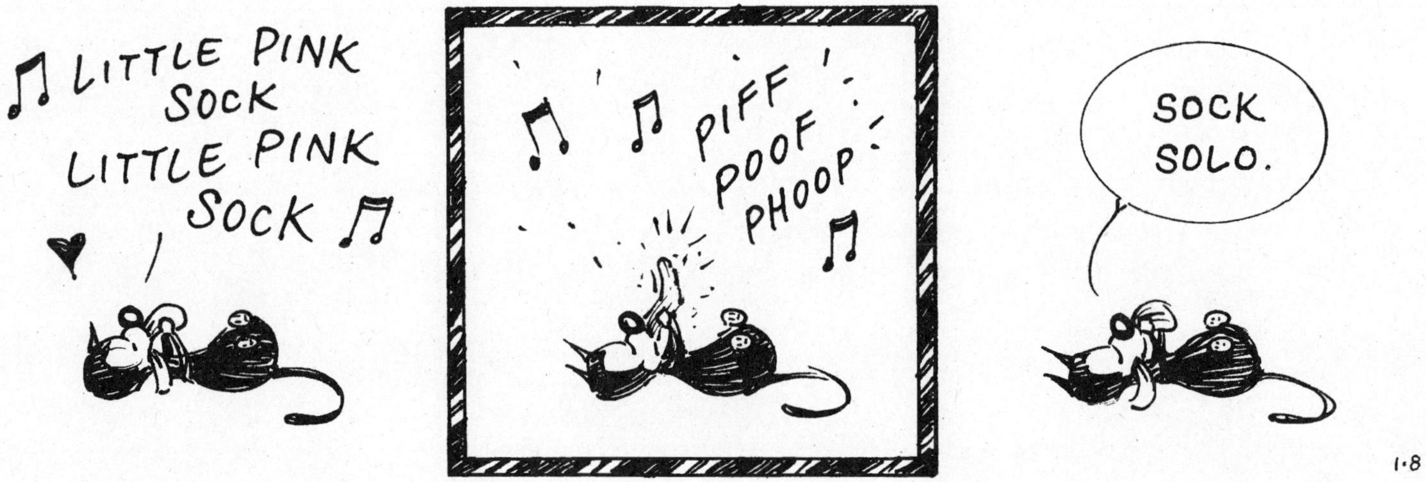
LITTLE PINK SOCK LITTLE PINK SOCK
PIFF POOF PHOOP
SOCK SOLO.
1·8

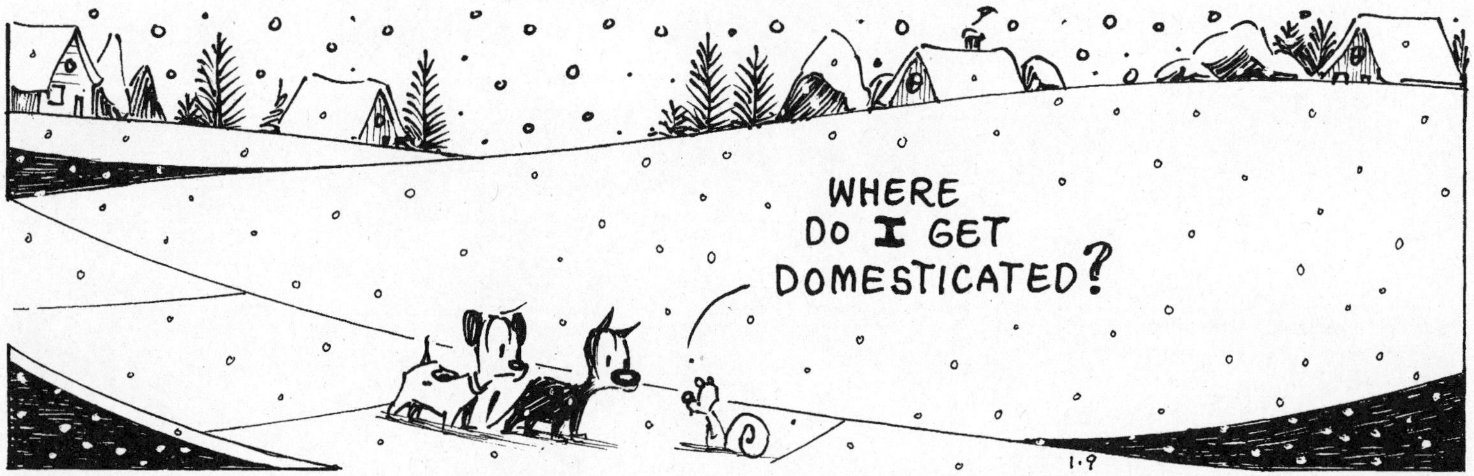
WHERE DO I GET DOMESTICATED?
1·9

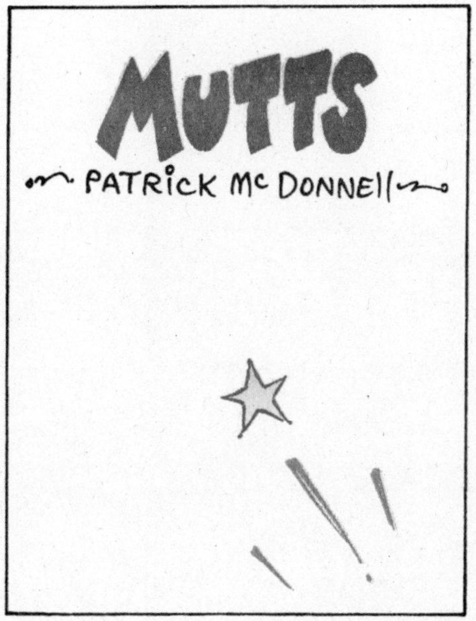
MUTTS
PATRICK McDONNELL

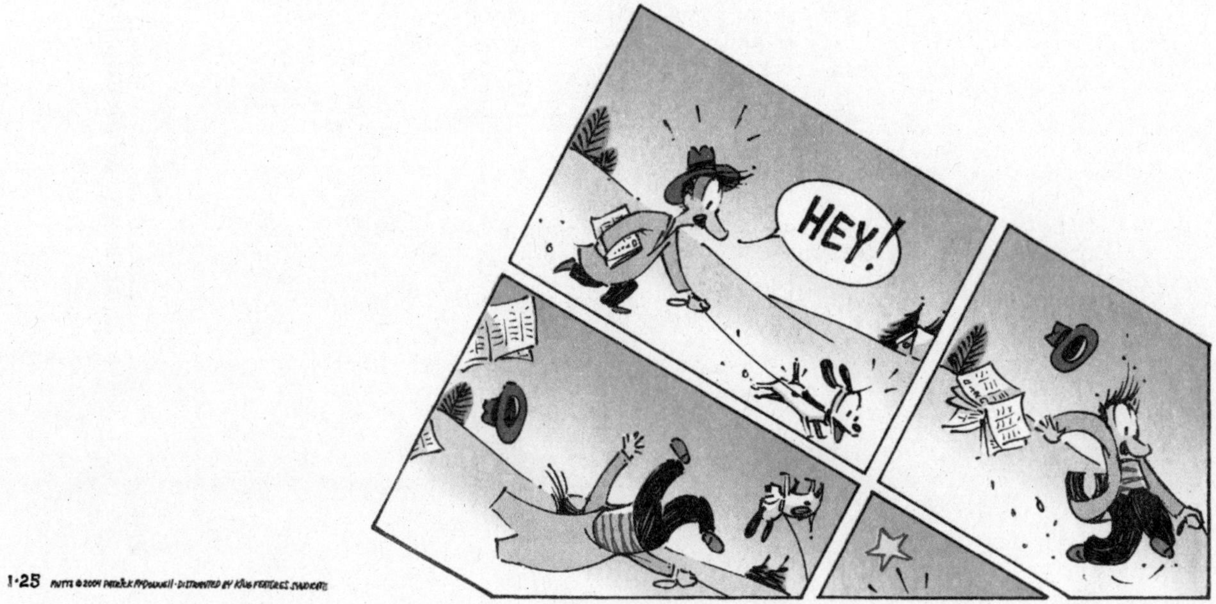
HEY!
1·25

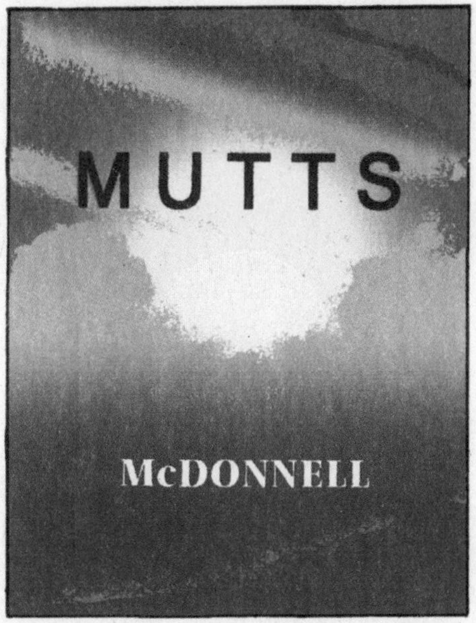
MUTTS
McDONNELL

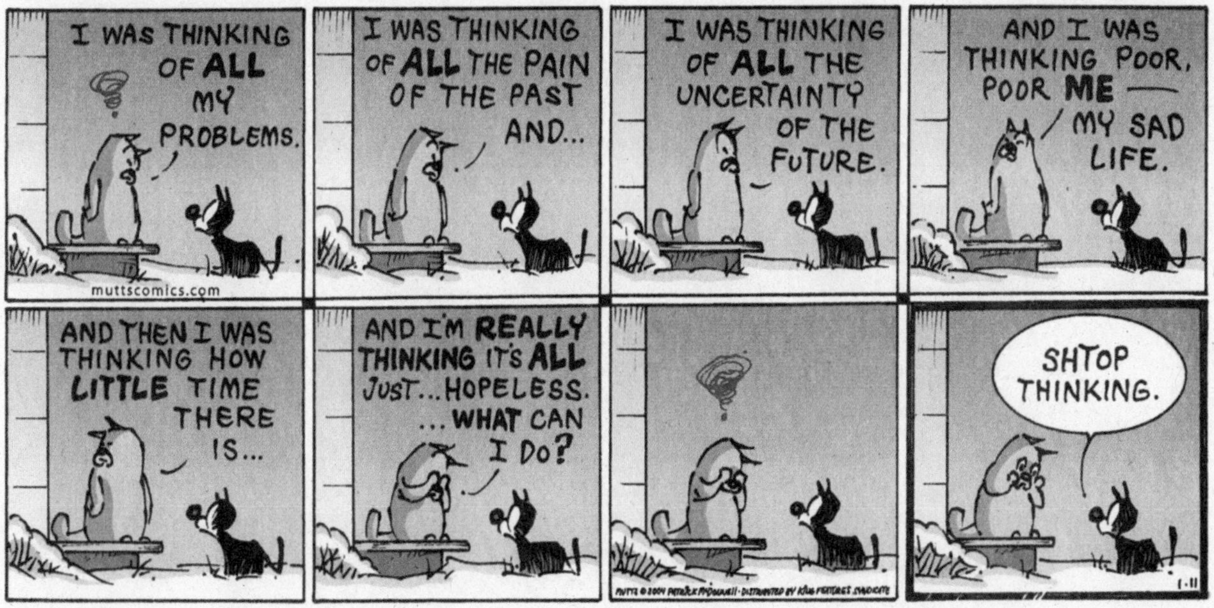
I WAS THINKING OF ALL MY PROBLEMS.
mutts comics.com
I WAS THINKING OF ALL THE PAIN OF THE PAST AND...
I WAS THINKING OF ALL THE UNCERTAINTY OF THE FUTURE.
AND I WAS THINKING POOR, POOR ME — MY SAD LIFE.
AND THEN I WAS THINKING HOW LITTLE TIME THERE IS...
AND I'M REALLY THINKING IT'S ALL JUST... HOPELESS. ...WHAT CAN I DO?
SHTOP THINKING.
1-11

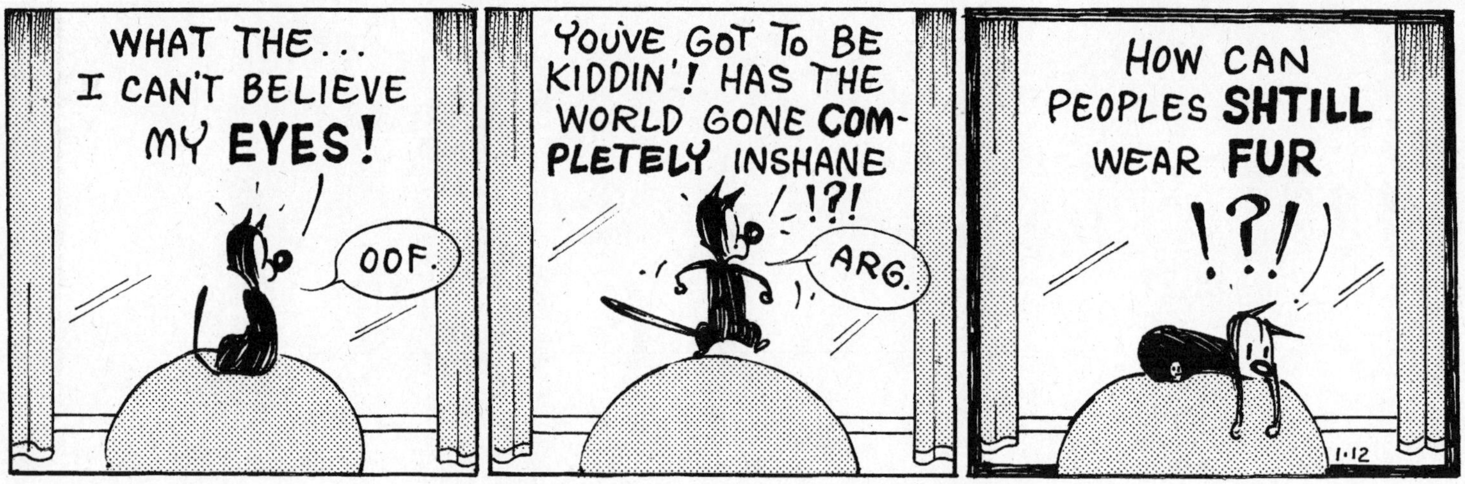
WHAT THE... I CAN'T BELIEVE MY EYES!
OOF.
YOU'VE GOT TO BE KIDDIN'! HAS THE WORLD GONE COMPLETELY INSHANE !?!
ARG.
HOW CAN PEOPLES SHTILL WEAR FUR !?!
1·12

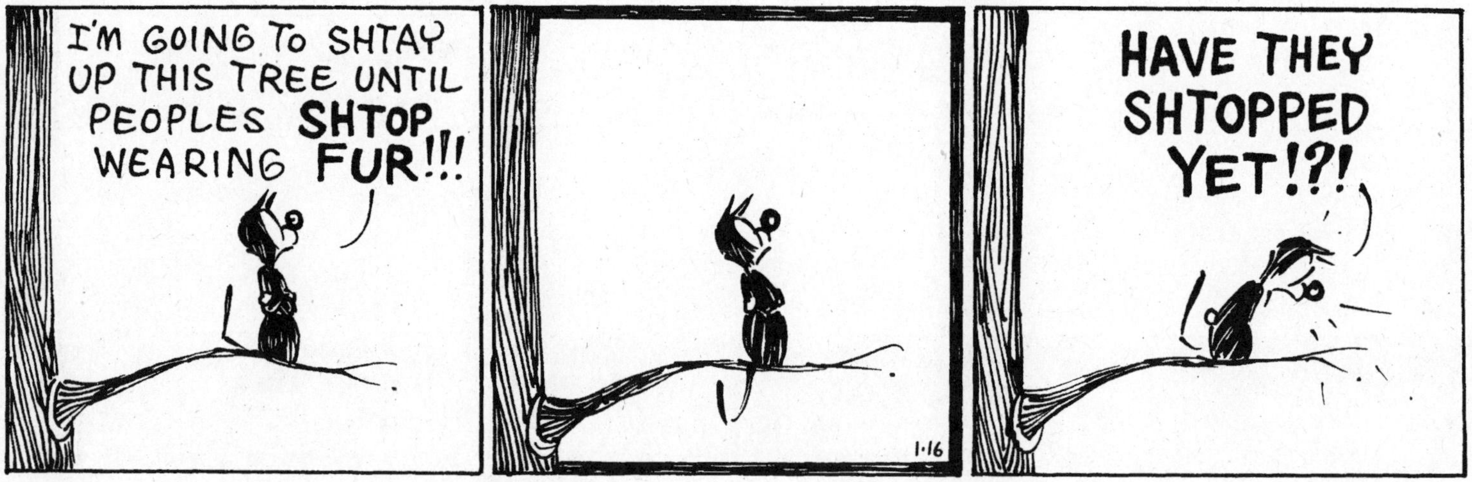
I'M GOING TO SHTAY UP THIS TREE UNTIL PEOPLES SHTOP WEARING FUR!!!
1·16
HAVE THEY SHTOPPED YET!?!

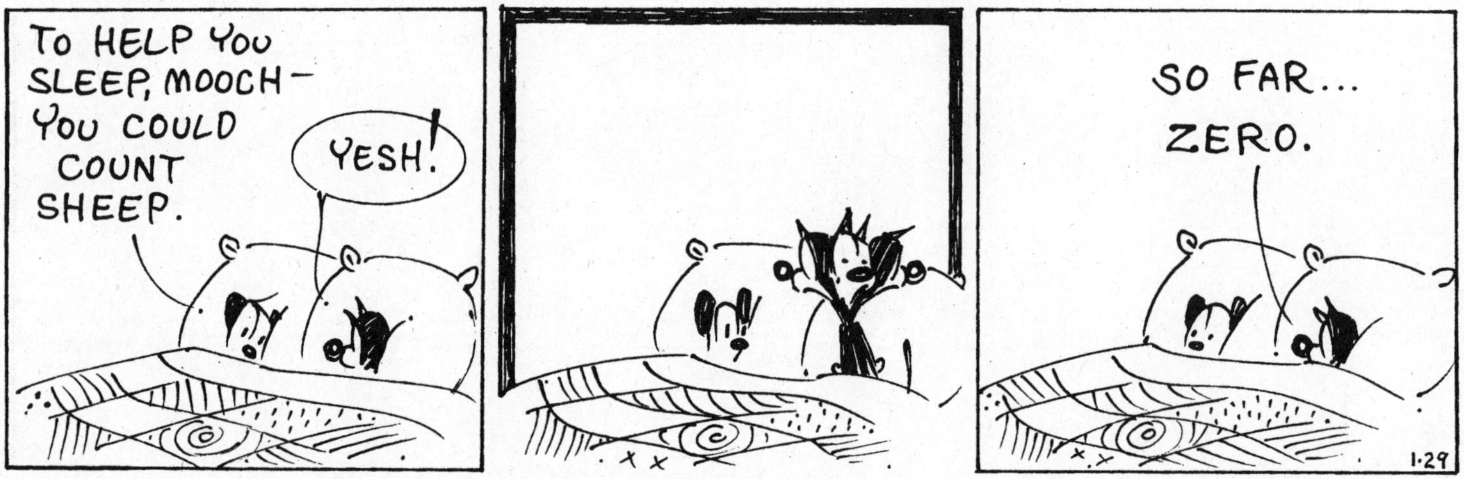
TO HELP YOU SLEEP, MOOCH– YOU COULD COUNT SHEEP.
YESH!
SO FAR... ZERO.
1·29

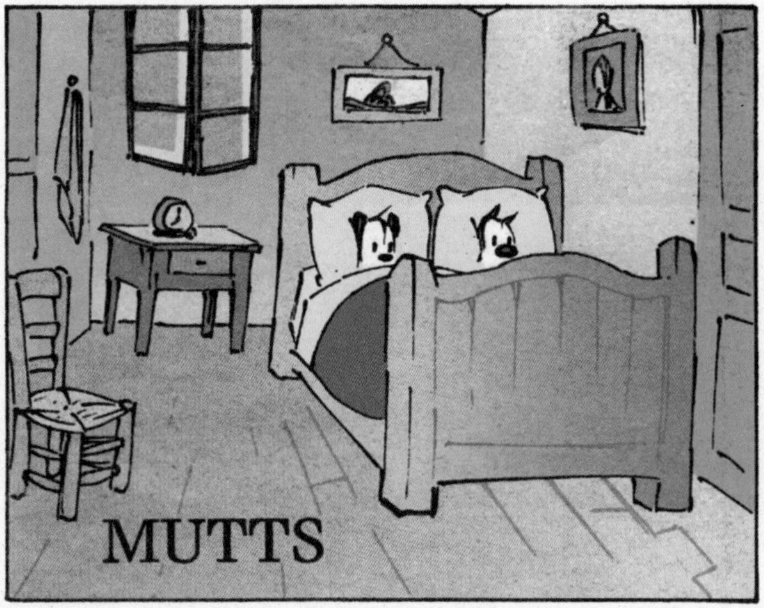
MUTTS

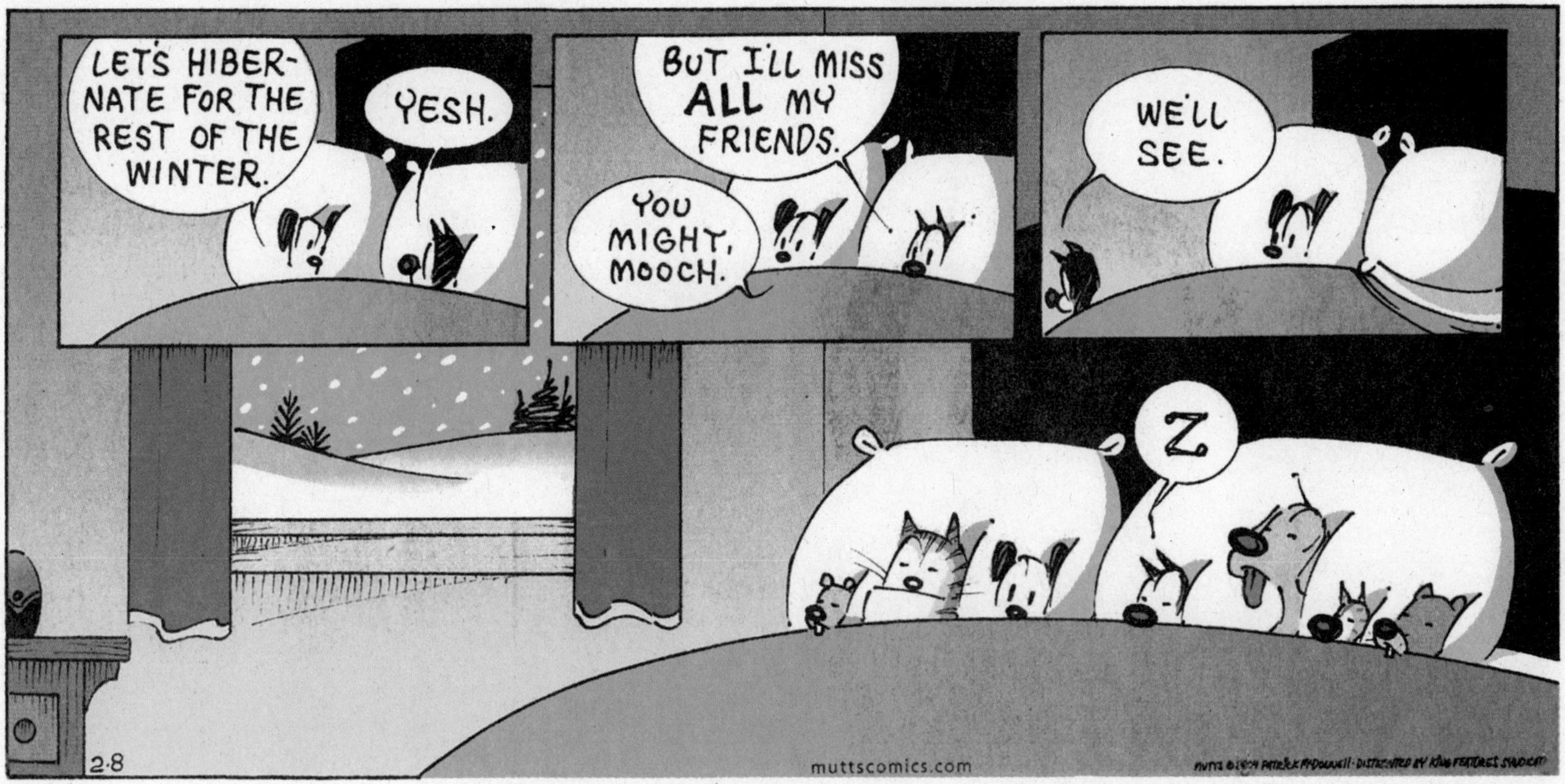
LET'S HIBERNATE FOR THE REST OF THE WINTER.
YESH.
BUT I'LL MISS **ALL** MY FRIENDS.
YOU MIGHT, MOOCH.
WE'LL SEE.
Z
2·8
muttscomics.com

WHAT'S IN MY DAILY PLANNER?

IT'S "HAIRBALL THURSDAY" ALREADY!

SIT. STAY. SHAKE.

GOOD BOY.

WHAT I'D REALLY LIKE TO LEARN IS HOW TO OPEN THE FRIDGE.

SHE SHNUBBED MY SHNUB!

SMAK SHMAK SMAK. SMAK SHMAK SMAK

ALWAYS KISS THE HAND THAT FEEDS YOU.

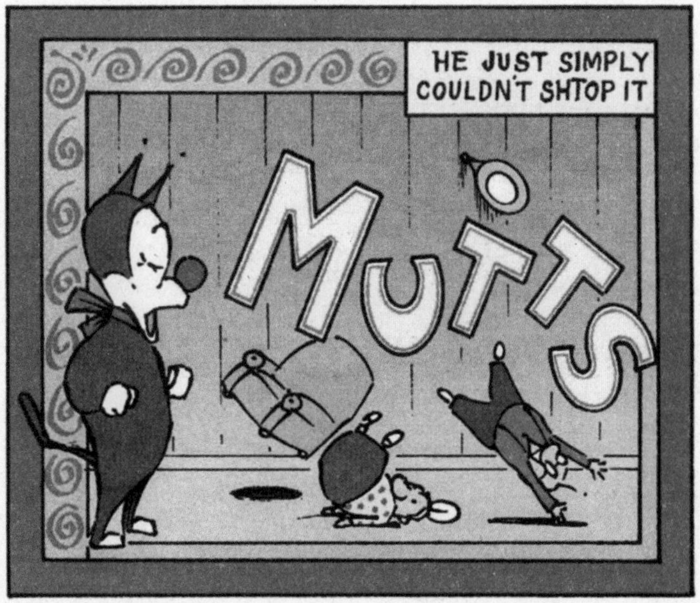
HE JUST SIMPLY COULDN'T SHTOP IT
MUTTS

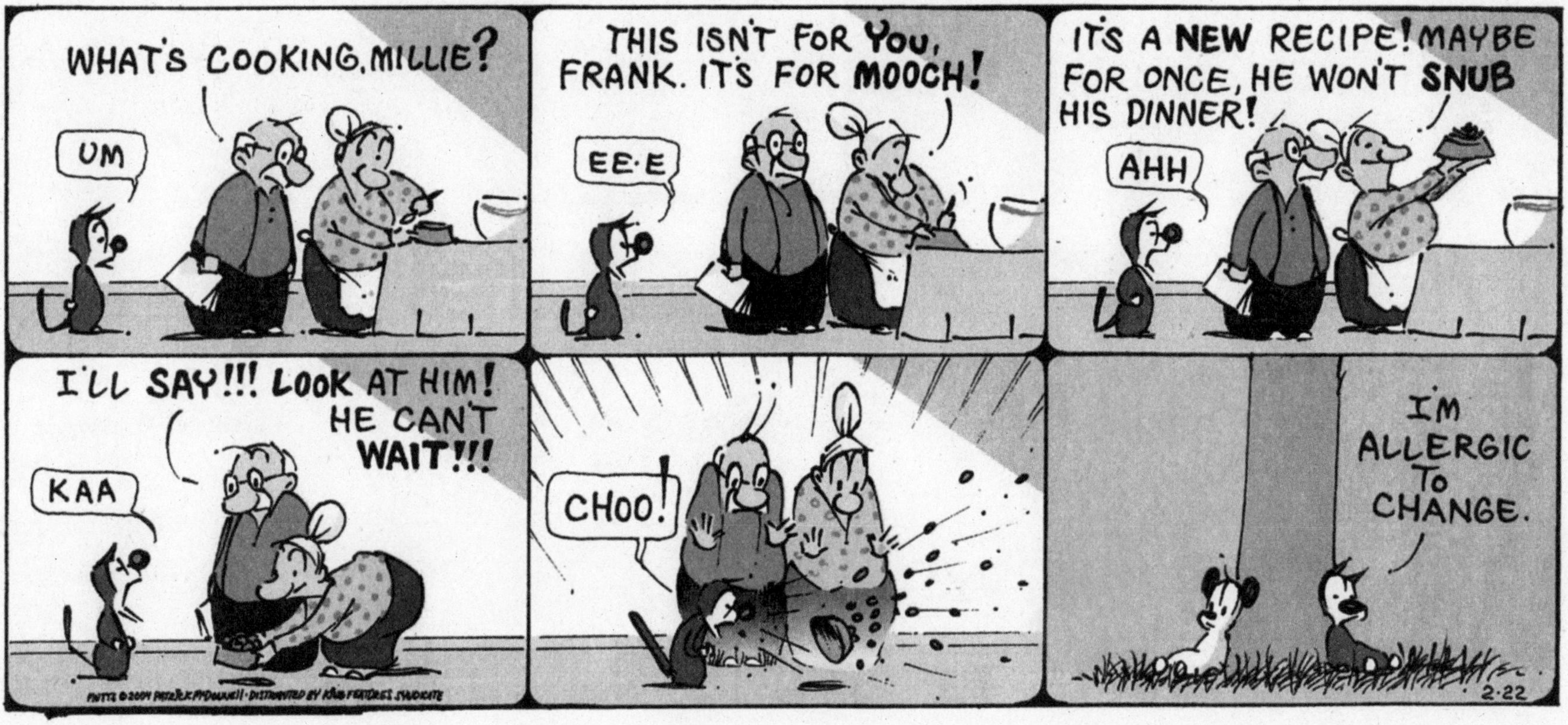
WHAT'S COOKING, MILLIE?
UM
THIS ISN'T FOR YOU, FRANK. IT'S FOR MOOCH!
EE·E
IT'S A NEW RECIPE! MAYBE FOR ONCE, HE WON'T SNUB HIS DINNER!
AHH
I'LL SAY!!! LOOK AT HIM! HE CAN'T WAIT!!!
KAA
CHOO!
I'M ALLERGIC TO CHANGE.
MUTTS © 2004 PATRICK McDONNELL · DISTRIBUTED BY KING FEATURES SYNDICATE
2·22

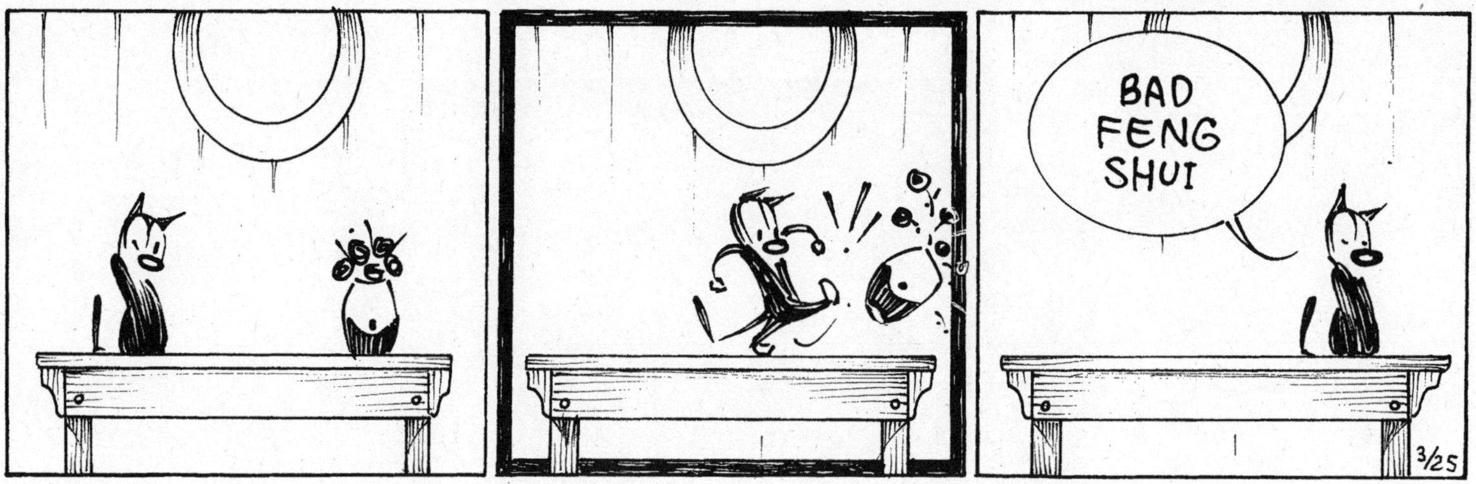
BAD FENG SHUI
3/25

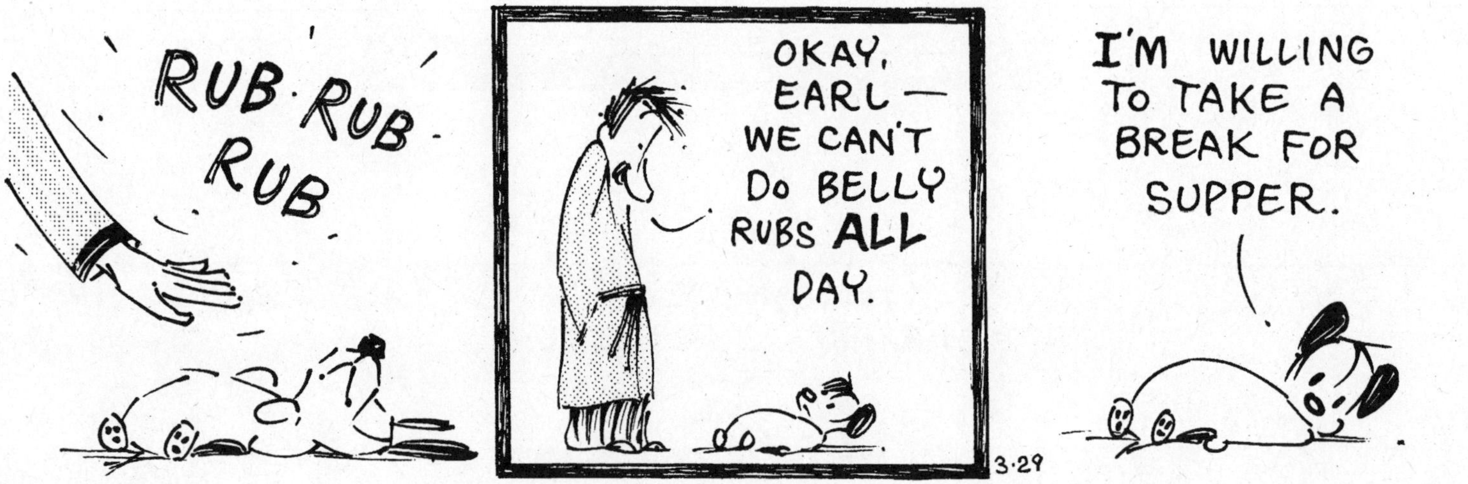
RUB RUB RUB
OKAY, EARL— WE CAN'T DO BELLY RUBS ALL DAY.
I'M WILLING TO TAKE A BREAK FOR SUPPER.
3·29

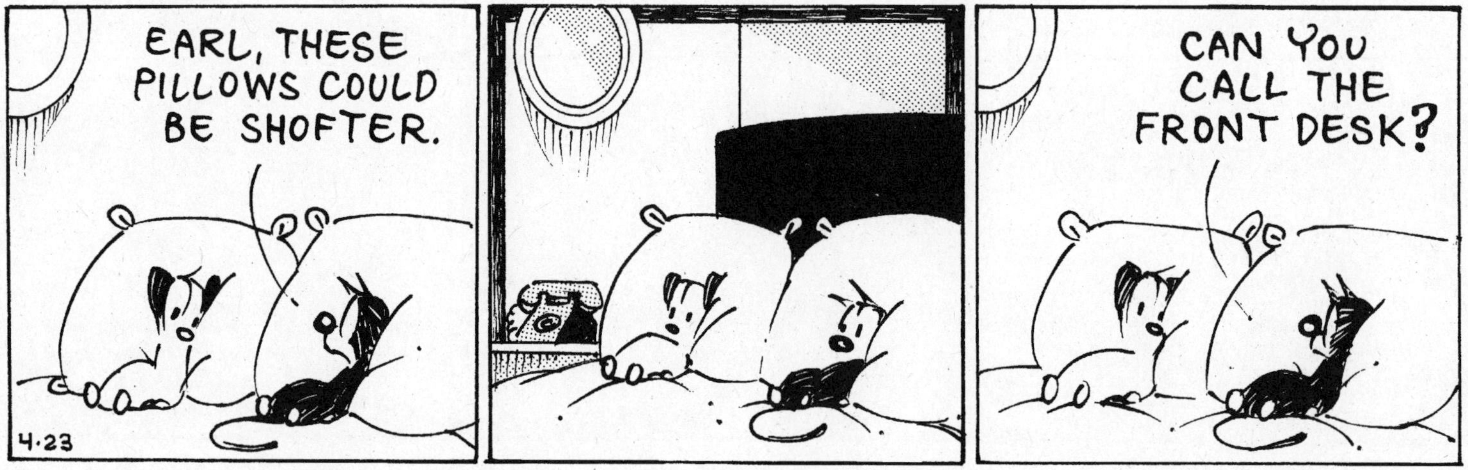
EARL, THESE PILLOWS COULD BE SHOFTER.
CAN YOU CALL THE FRONT DESK?
4·23

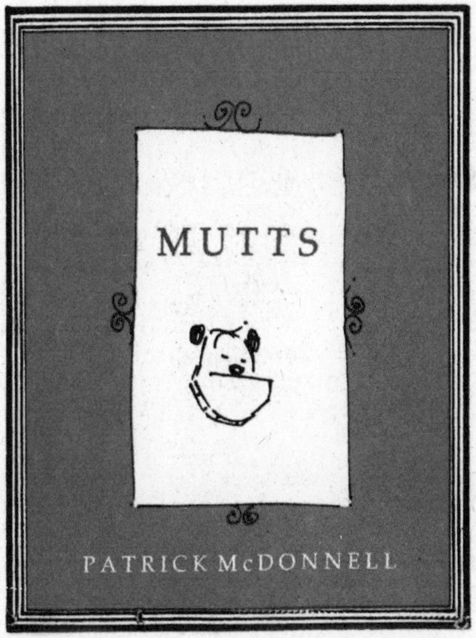
MUTTS
PATRICK McDONNELL

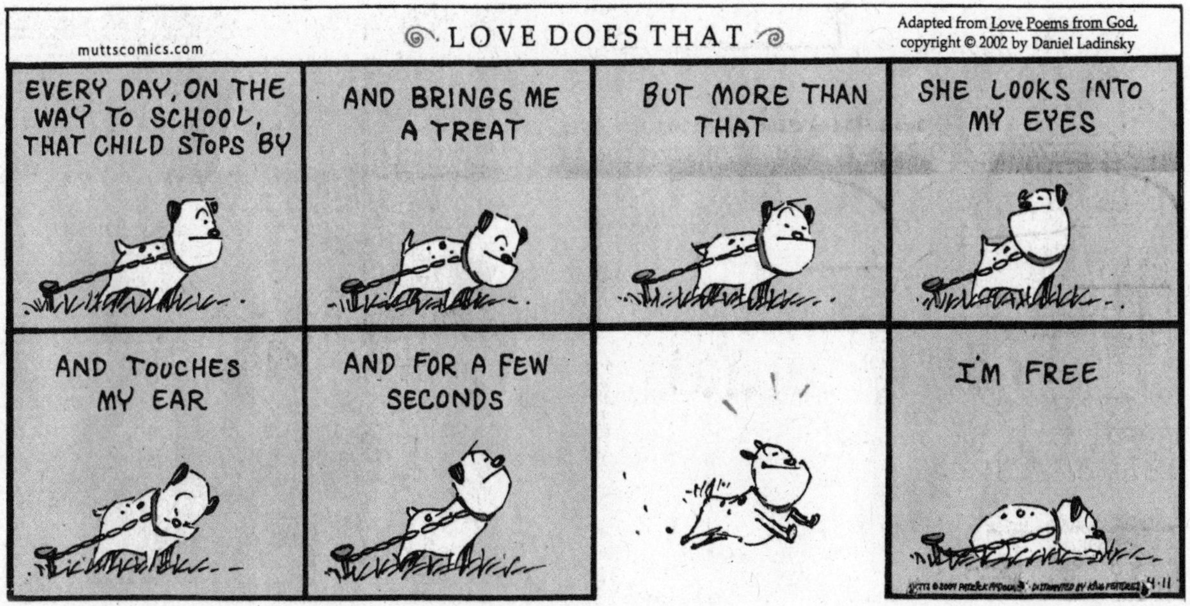
muttscomics.com
LOVE DOES THAT
Adapted from Love Poems from God, copyright © 2002 by Daniel Ladinsky
EVERY DAY, ON THE WAY TO SCHOOL, THAT CHILD STOPS BY
AND BRINGS ME A TREAT
BUT MORE THAN THAT
SHE LOOKS INTO MY EYES
AND TOUCHES MY EAR
AND FOR A FEW SECONDS
I'M FREE

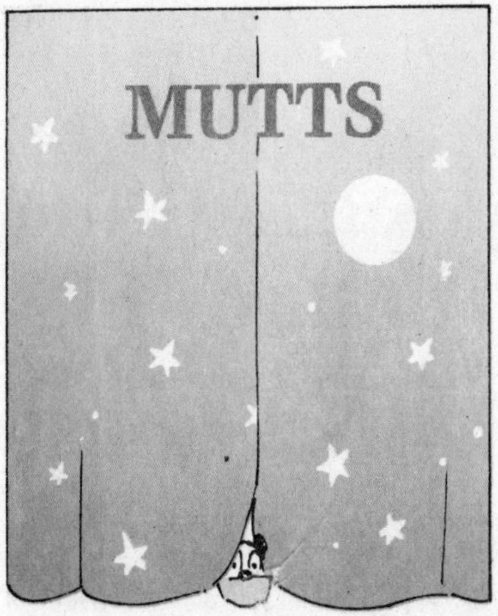
MUTTS

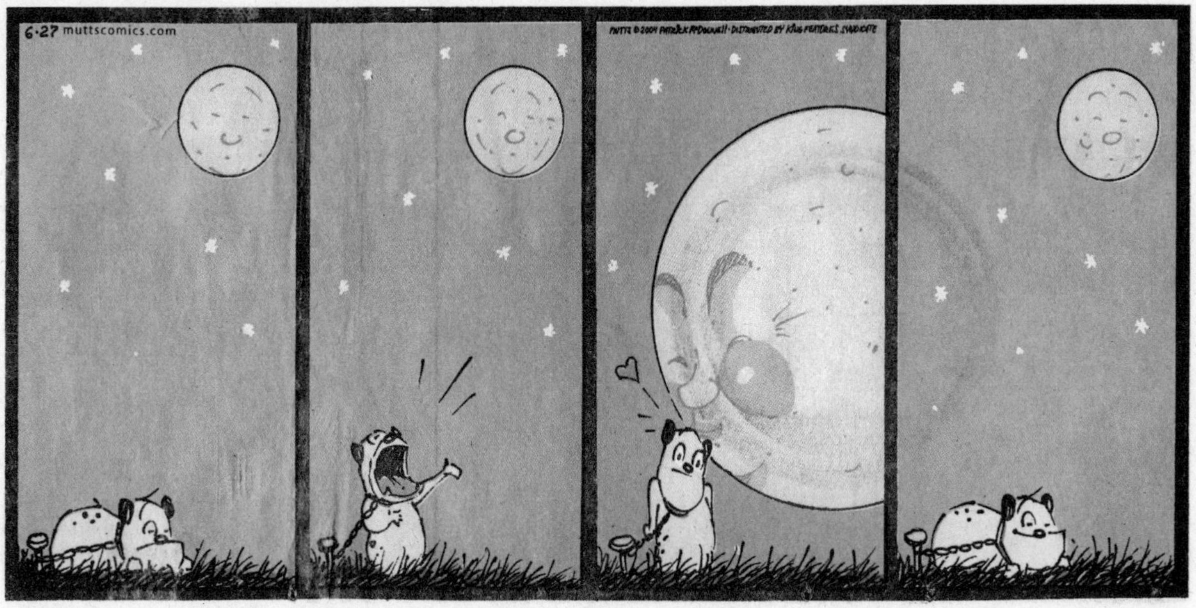
6·27 muttscomics.com

GOING TO A RESTAURANT WAS A **GREAT** IDEA, MOOCH!

YESH! NOW IF ONLY WE CAN GET SHOME SHERVICE.

`AAAAIEEE`

I THINK I CAUGHT OUR WAITRESS'S EYE.

5·31

MOOCH, ARE YOU THINKING ABOUT ORDERING AN APPETIZER?

NO.

I'LL JUST EAT THE FLOWERS.

6·2

THESE BREADSHTICKS TASTE LIKE **DOG FOOD**.

6·3

OUR COMPLIMENTS TO THE CHEF.

SHOULD WE GIVE OUR WAITRESS A **TIP**, MOOCH?

YESH.

6·4

ALWAYS FEED THE KITTY FIRST.

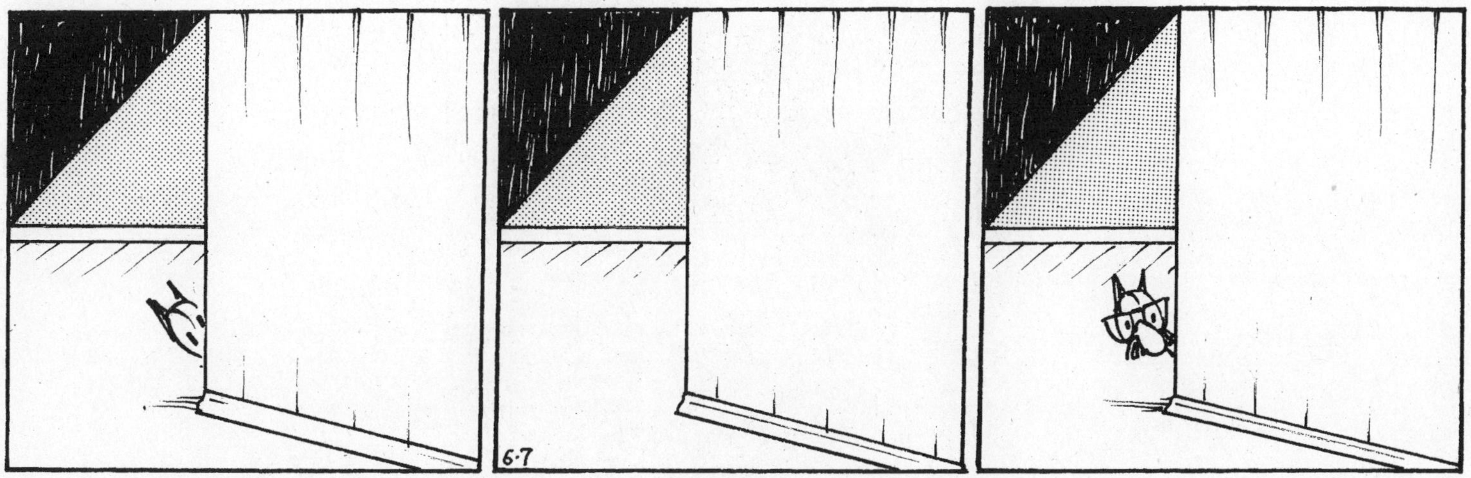
6·7

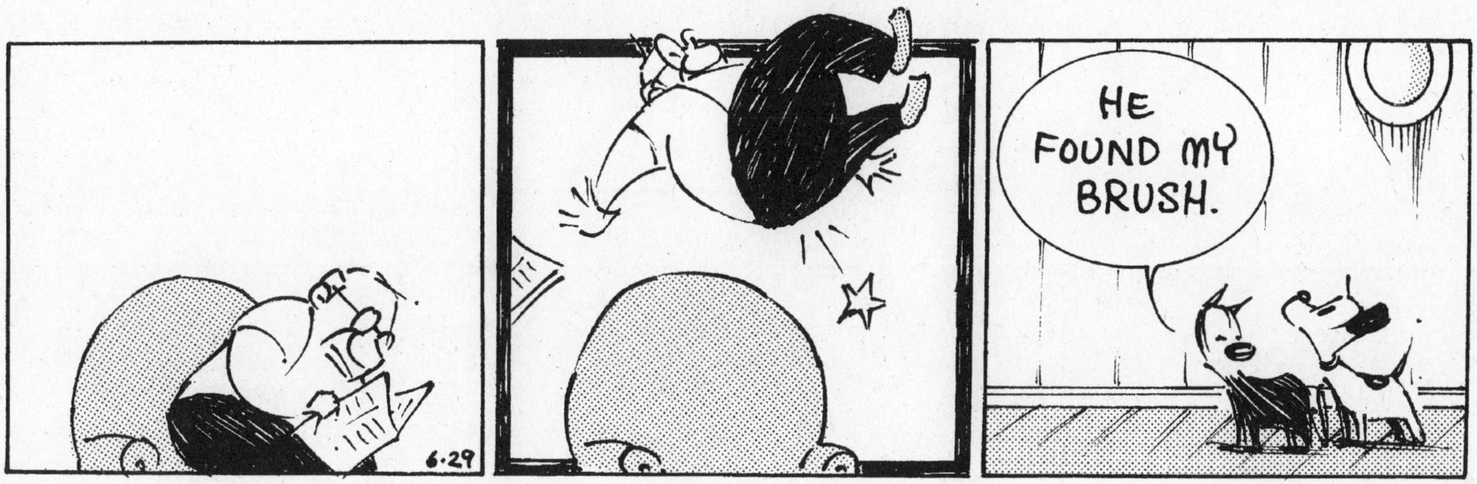
6·29
HE FOUND MY BRUSH.

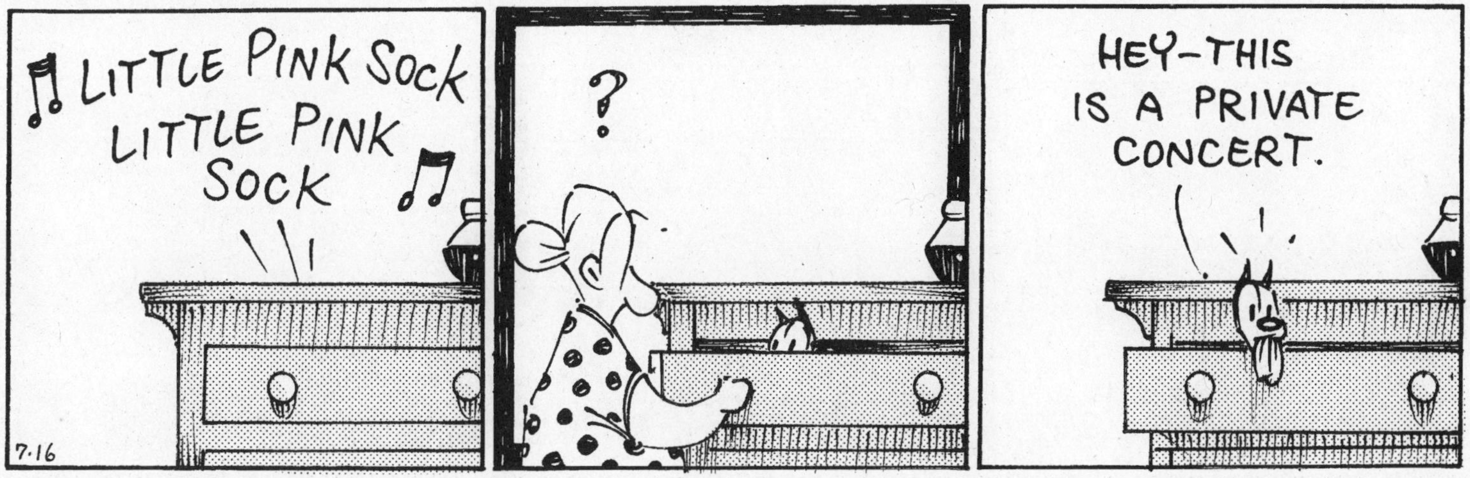
LITTLE PINK SOCK LITTLE PINK SOCK
7·16
?
HEY–THIS IS A PRIVATE CONCERT.

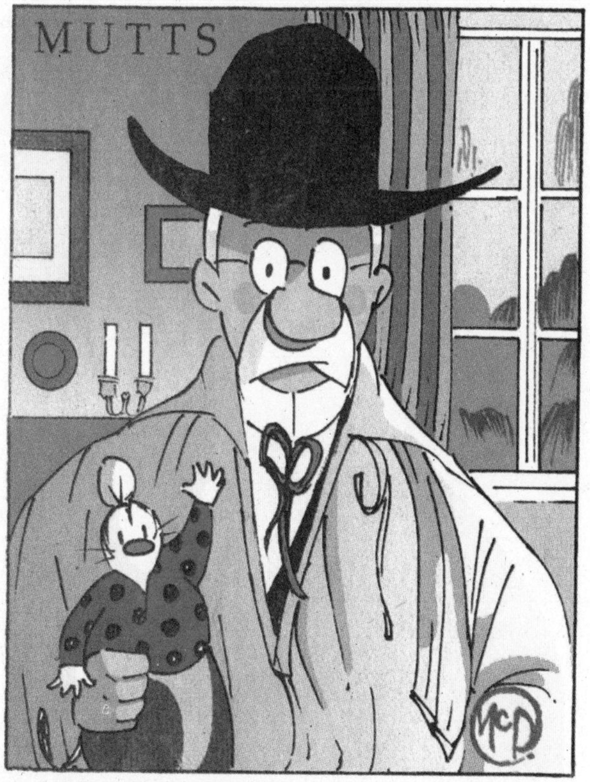
MUTTS

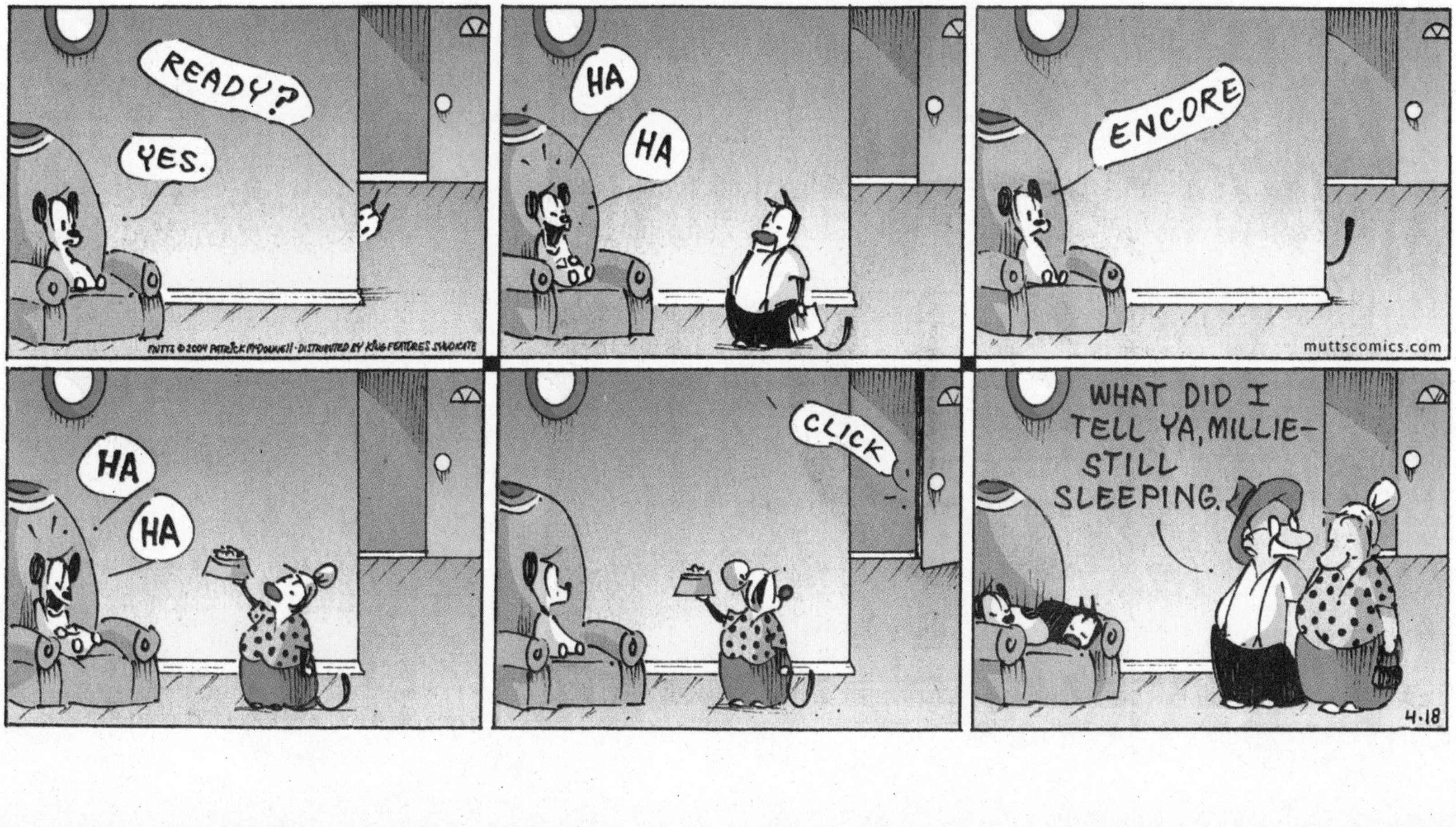
READY?
YES.
MUTTS © 2004 PATRICK McDONNELL · DISTRIBUTED BY KING FEATURES SYNDICATE
HA
HA
ENCORE
muttscomics.com
HA
HA
CLICK
WHAT DID I TELL YA, MILLIE- STILL SLEEPING.
4·18

MUTTS
· BOOK CLUB ·

A TALE OF TWO CITIES bY DICKENS

"IT WAS THE BEST OF TIMES, IT WAS THE WORST OF TIMES..."

7·5

MAKE UP YOUR MIND!

MUTTS
· BOOK CLUB ·

MOBY DICK bY MELVILLE

"CALL ME ISHMAEL."

7·6

CALL ME A CAB!

MUTTS
· BOOK CLUB ·

MR. JOHN STEINBECK'S

"OF MICE AND MEN"

BRAVO!

7·7

WE'LL STAY FOR THE FIRST HALF.

MUTTS
· BOOK CLUB ·

WILLY SHAKESPEARE'S

"AS YOU LIKE IT"

7·8

SHORT AND SWEET, BABY!

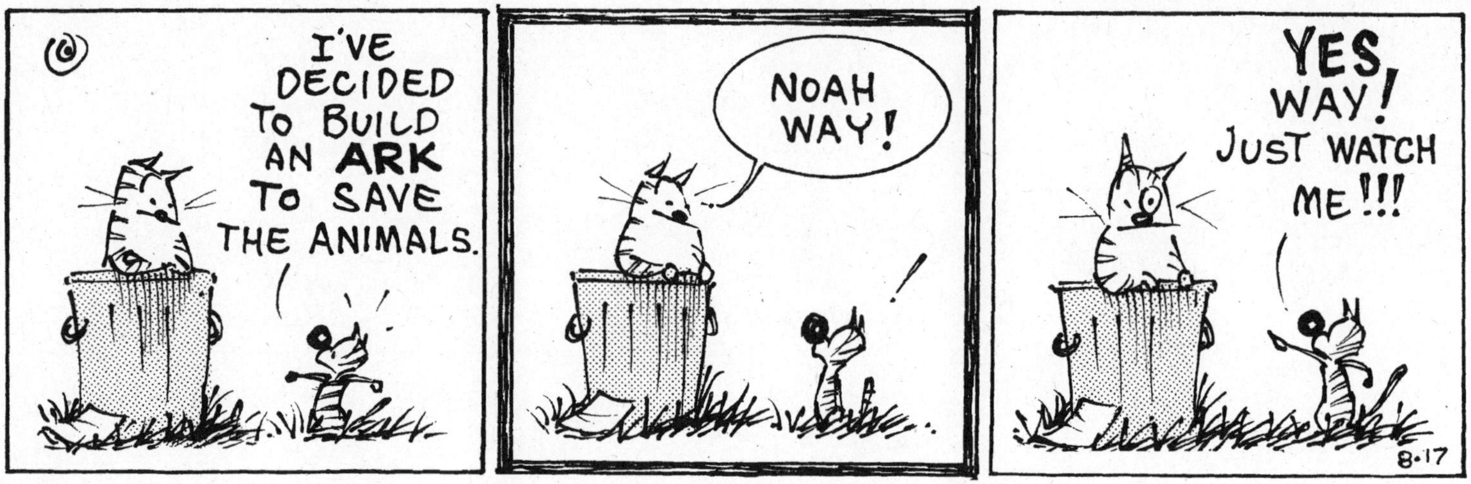
I'VE DECIDED TO BUILD AN **ARK** TO SAVE THE ANIMALS.
NOAH WAY!
**YES,** WAY! JUST WATCH ME!!!
8·17

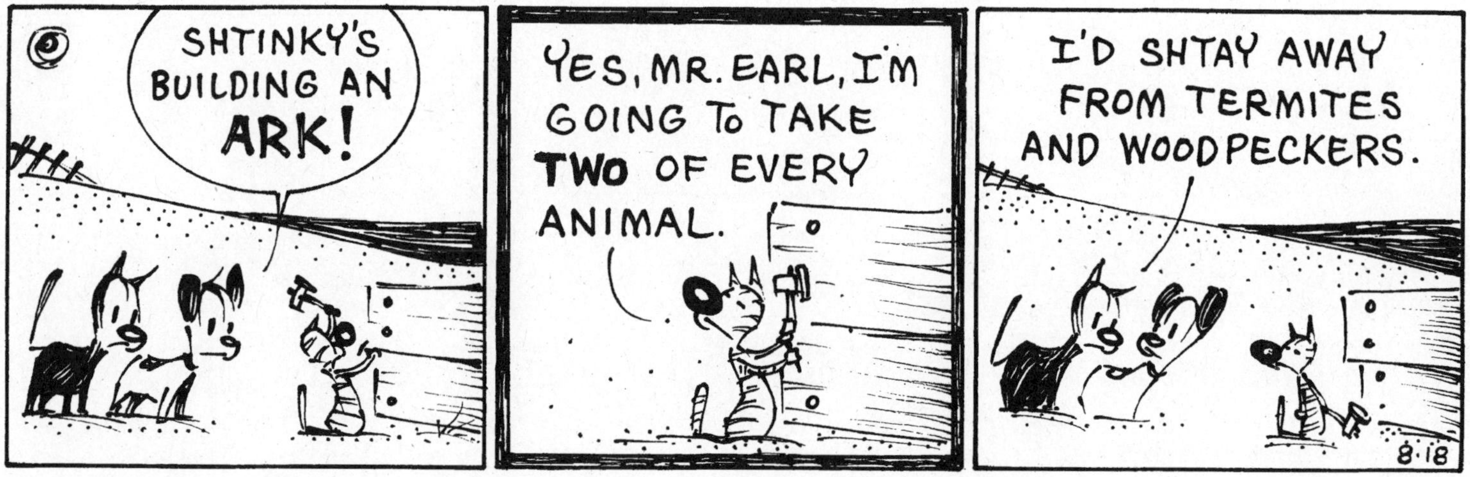
SHTINKY'S BUILDING AN **ARK!**
YES, MR. EARL, I'M GOING TO TAKE **TWO** OF EVERY ANIMAL.
I'D SHTAY AWAY FROM TERMITES AND WOODPECKERS.
8·18

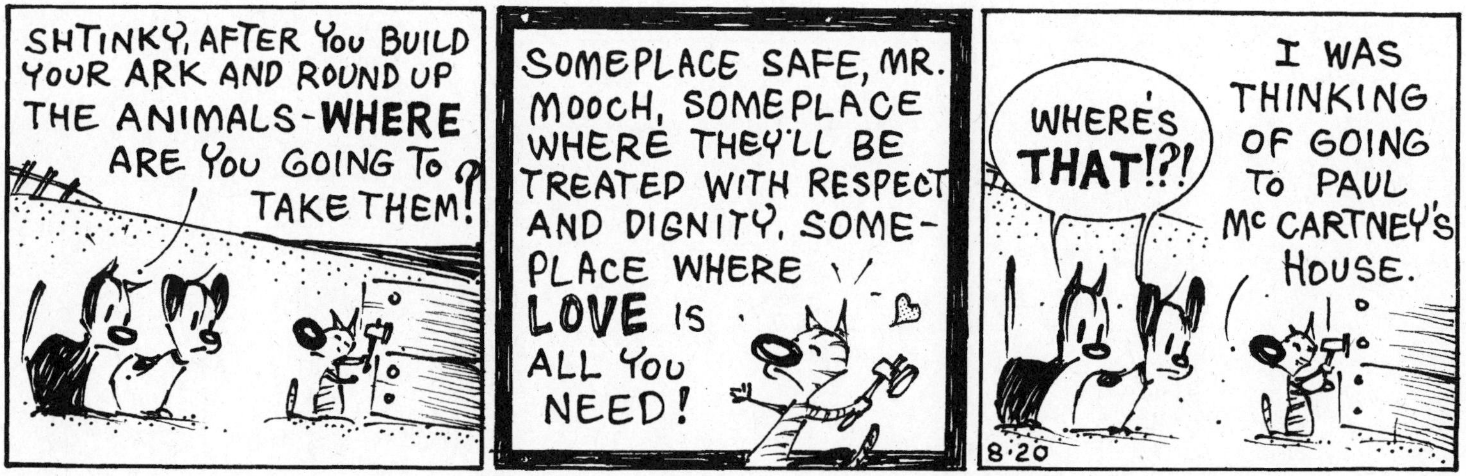
SHTINKY, AFTER YOU BUILD YOUR ARK AND ROUND UP THE ANIMALS-**WHERE** ARE YOU GOING TO TAKE THEM!?
SOMEPLACE SAFE, MR. MOOCH, SOMEPLACE WHERE THEY'LL BE TREATED WITH RESPECT AND DIGNITY. SOMEPLACE WHERE **LOVE** IS ALL YOU NEED!
WHERE'S **THAT!?!**
I WAS THINKING OF GOING TO PAUL McCARTNEY'S HOUSE.
8·20

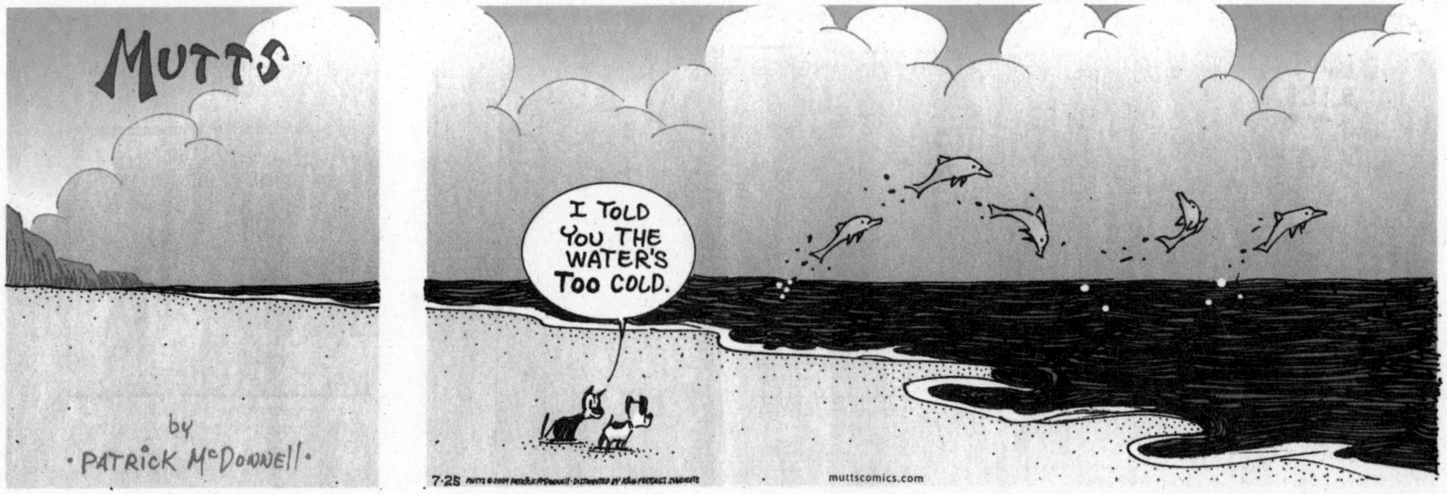
MUTTS
by
PATRICK McDONNELL
I TOLD YOU THE WATER'S TOO COLD.
7-25
muttscomics.com

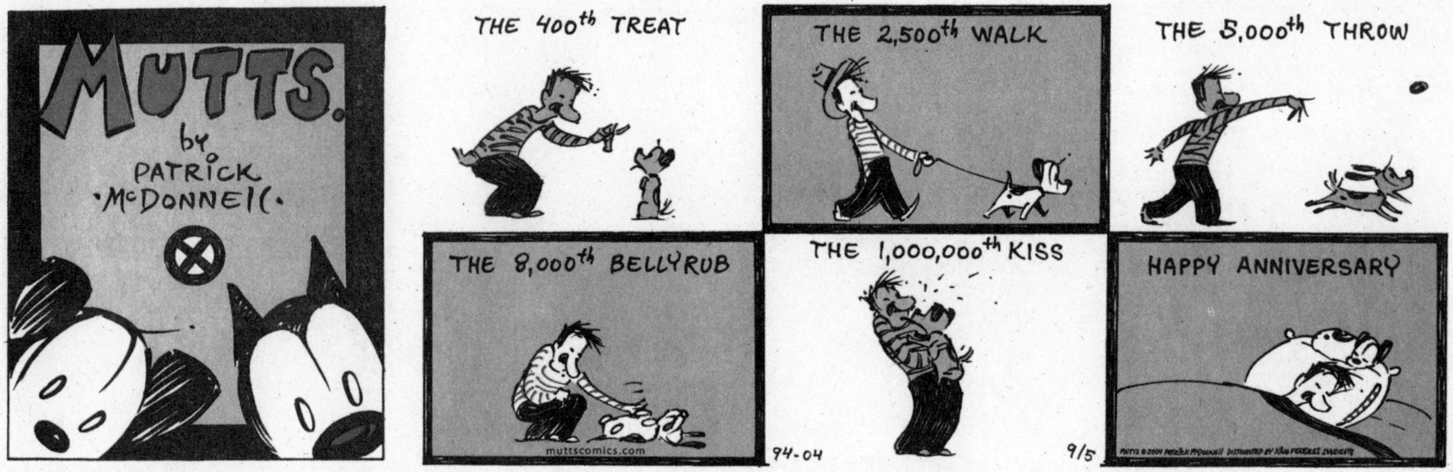
MUTTS.
by
PATRICK
McDONNELL
THE 400th TREAT
THE 2,500th WALK
THE 5,000th THROW
THE 8,000th BELLYRUB
THE 1,000,000th KISS
HAPPY ANNIVERSARY
muttscomics.com
94-04
9/5

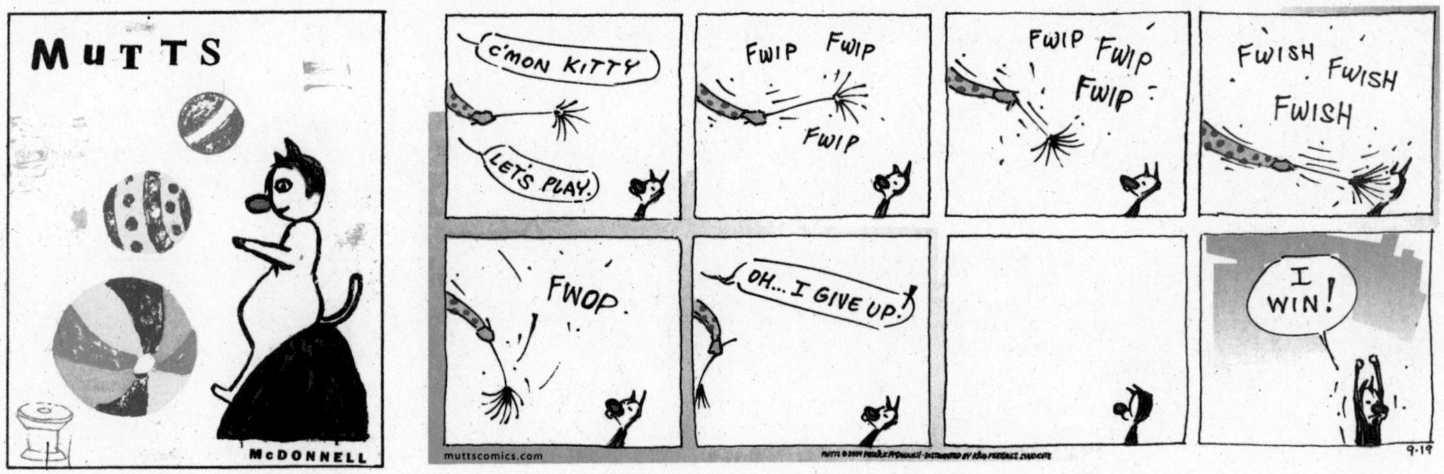
MUTTS
McDONNELL
C'MON KITTY
LET'S PLAY.
FWIP FWIP
FWIP
FWIP FWIP
FWIP
FWISH FWISH
FWISH
FWOP.
OH... I GIVE UP.
I WIN!
muttscomics.com
9-19

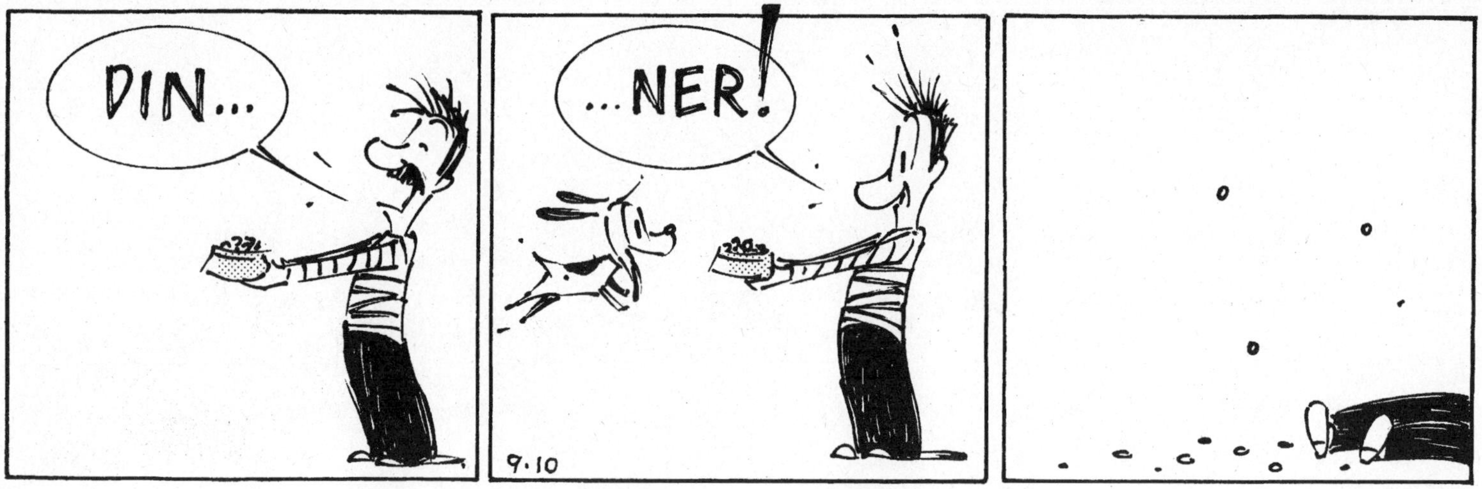
DIN...
...NER!
9.10

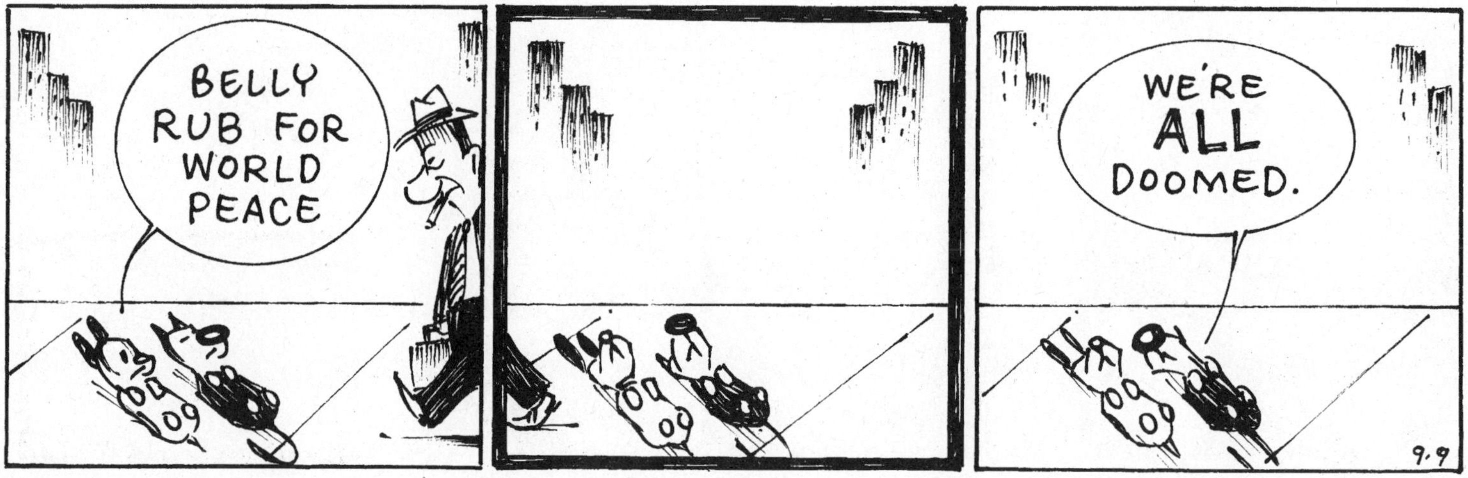
BELLY RUB FOR WORLD PEACE
WE'RE ALL DOOMED.
9.9

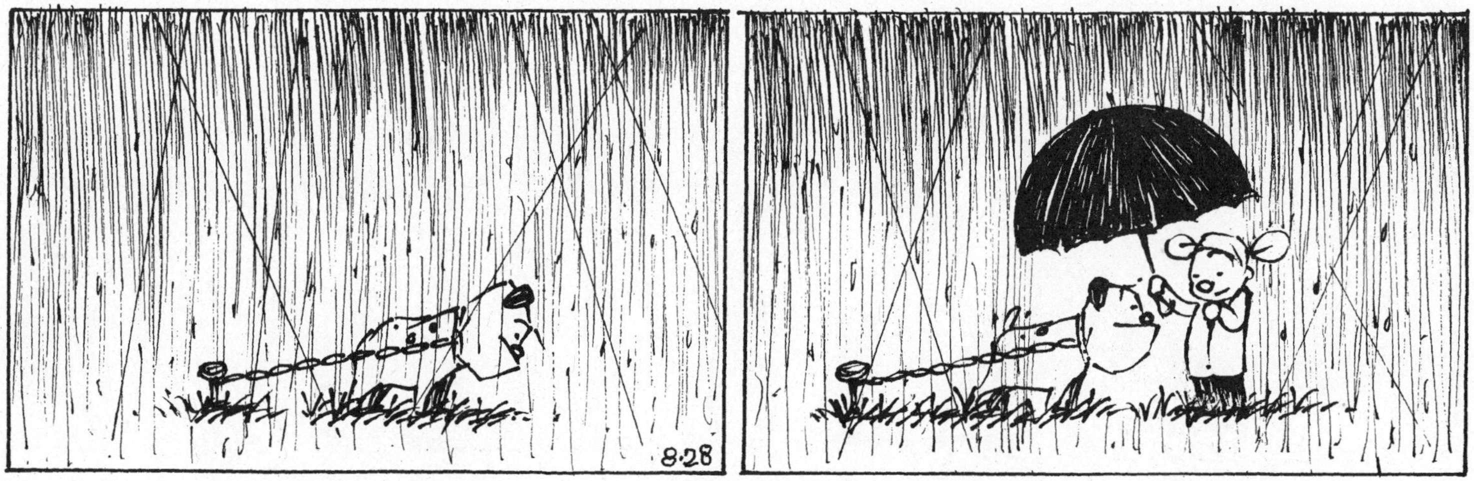
8.28

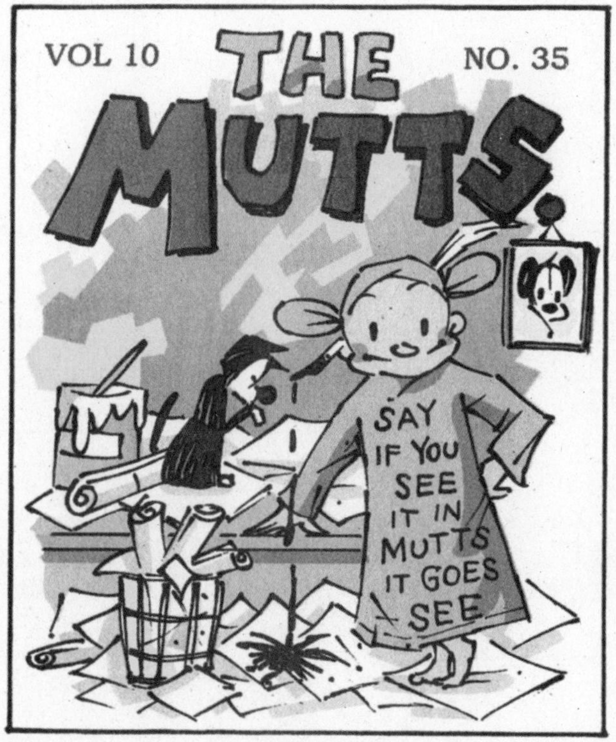
VOL 10
THE MUTTS.
NO. 35
SAY IF YOU SEE IT IN MUTTS IT GOES SEE

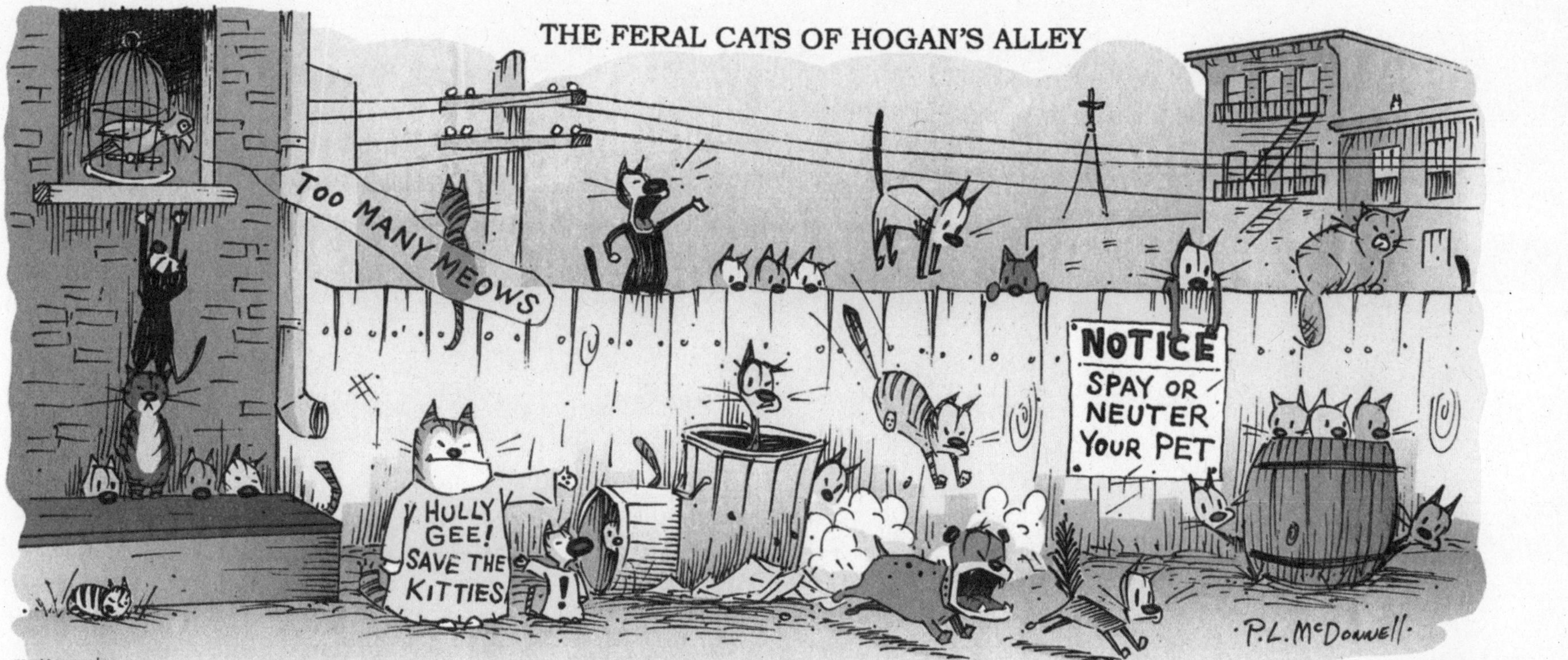
THE FERAL CATS OF HOGAN'S ALLEY
TOO MANY MEOWS
NOTICE
SPAY OR NEUTER YOUR PET
HULLY GEE! SAVE THE KITTIES
P.L. McDONNELL
muttscomics.com
8-29

HEY! LET'S HAVE A SHTARE CONTEST! FIRST ONE TO BLINK IS OUT.
GOOD LUCK.
8·30

SHTARE CONTEST! FIRST ONE TO BLINK IS OUT!
MADE YOU LOOK.
9·1

THE SHTARE CONTEST CONTINUES...
COME CLOSER... ...CLOSER...
OOOH... I SEE MYSHELF IN YOUR EYES!
9·2

STARE CONTEST!
TO BE CONTINUED...
I HATE THAT.
9·4

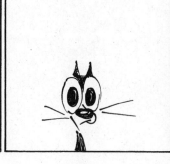

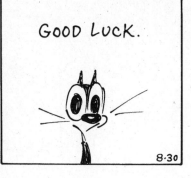

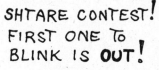

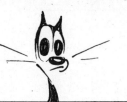

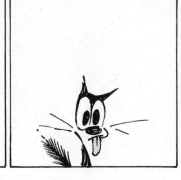

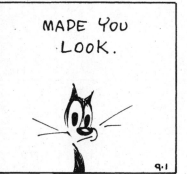

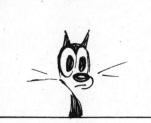

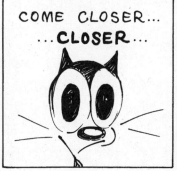

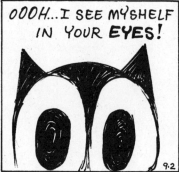

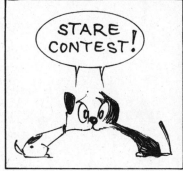

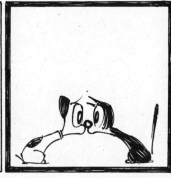

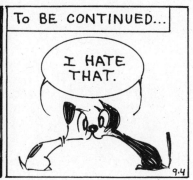

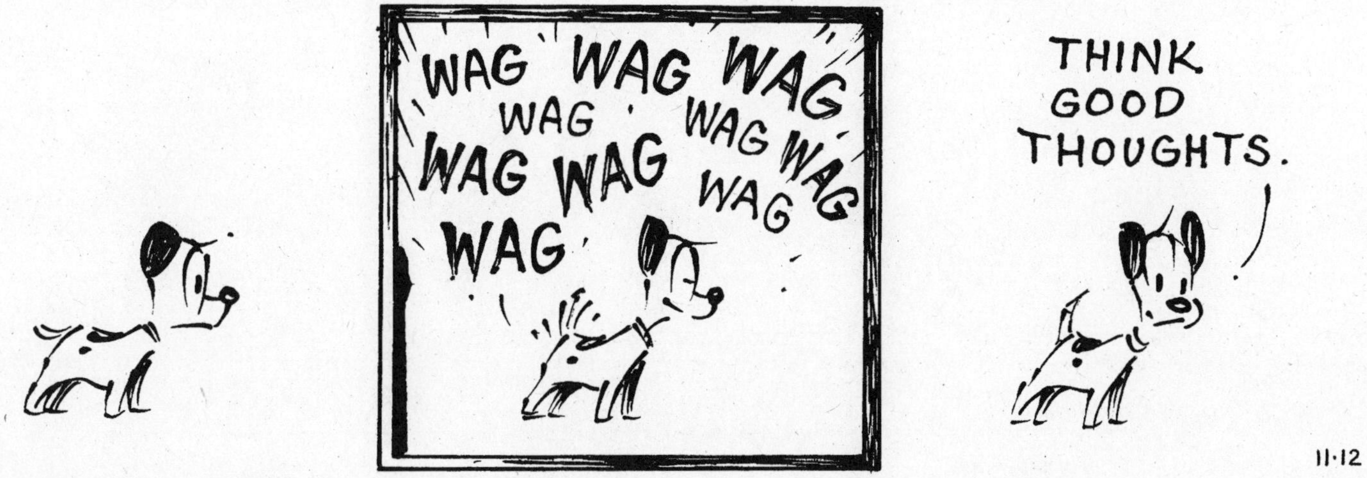
WAG WAG WAG WAG WAG WAG WAG WAG WAG WAG WAG
THINK GOOD THOUGHTS.
11·12

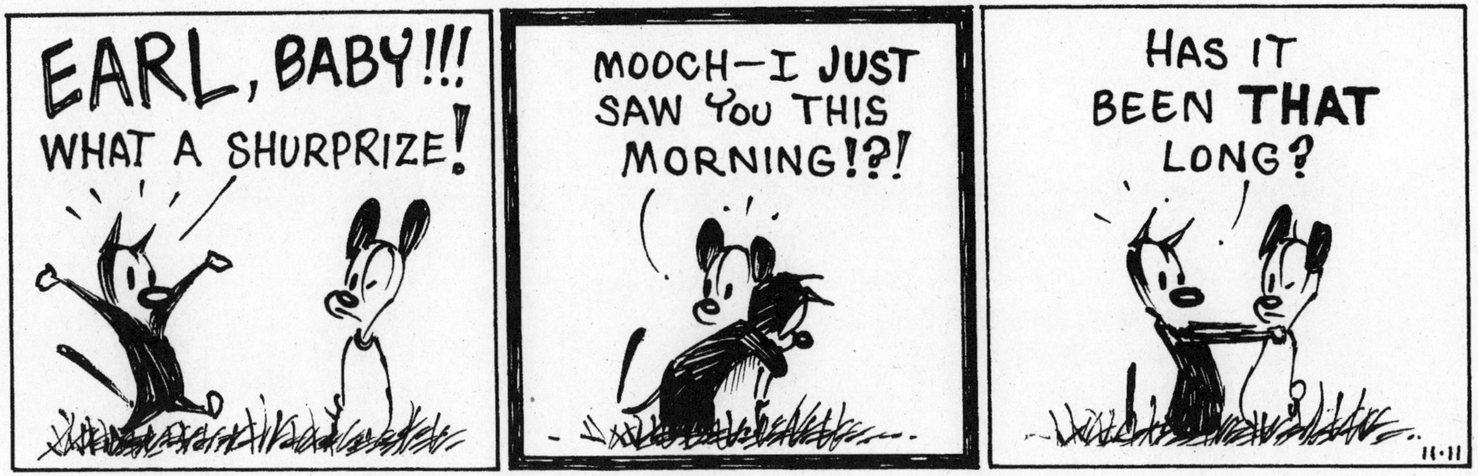
EARL, BABY!!! WHAT A SHURPRIZE!
MOOCH—I JUST SAW YOU THIS MORNING!?!
HAS IT BEEN THAT LONG?
11·11

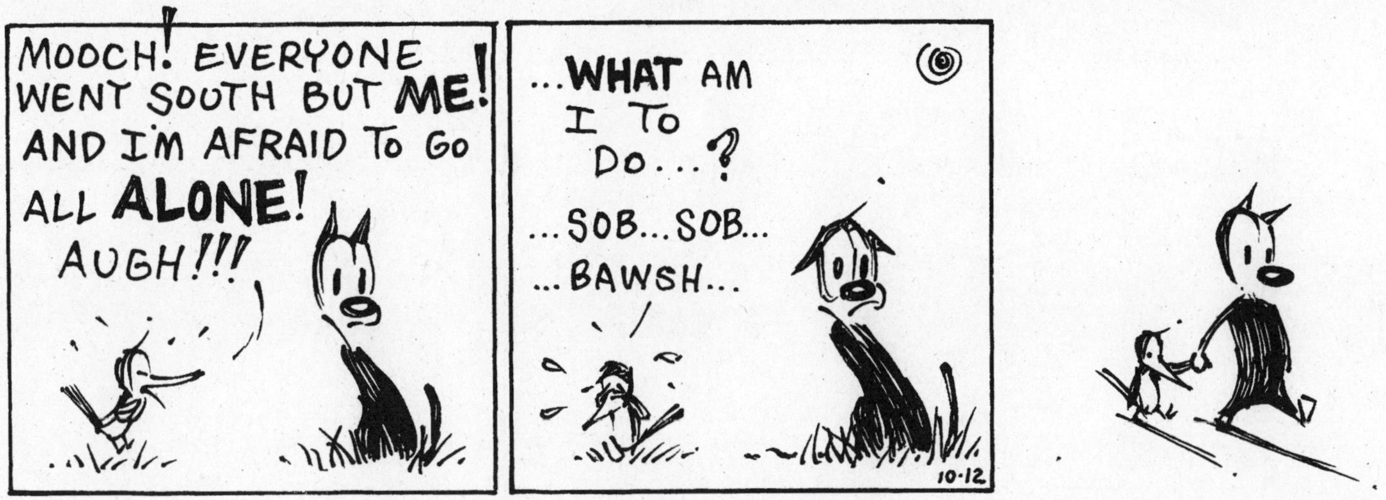
MOOCH! EVERYONE WENT SOUTH BUT ME! AND I'M AFRAID TO GO ALL ALONE! AUGH!!!
...WHAT AM I TO DO...?
...SOB...SOB... ...BAWSH...
10·12

Giving Thanks

...AND BLESS THE TOFU.
11·25

TODAY THE SEAL HUNT BEGINS...
I CAN'T LOOK.
11·15

IT'S SO WARM AND SAFE UNDER THE COVERS.
I WISH I COULD FIT THE WHOLE WORLD IN HERE.
11·19

SHELTER STORIES
"SHEMP"
I GOT PICKED!
WOW! NO MORE CAGES!!!
MAYBE I'LL SEE YOU OUT THERE IN THE "FREE" WORLD...
I'LL BE THE GUY ROLLING IN THE CLOVER.
11·6

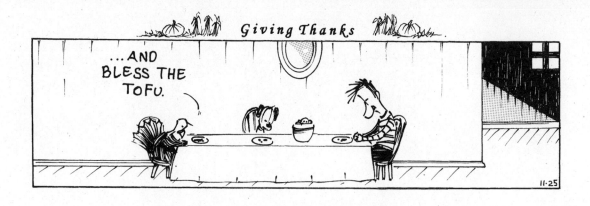

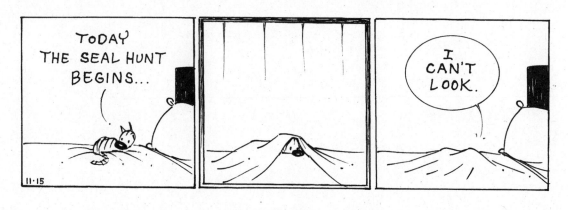

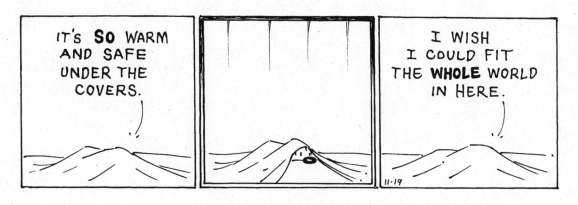

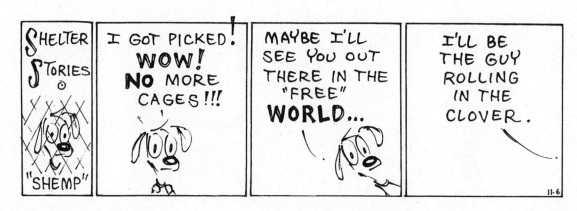

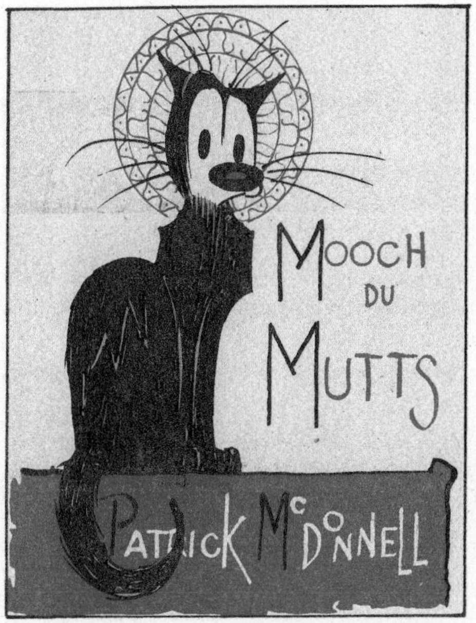
MOOCH DU MUTTS
PATRICK McDONNELL

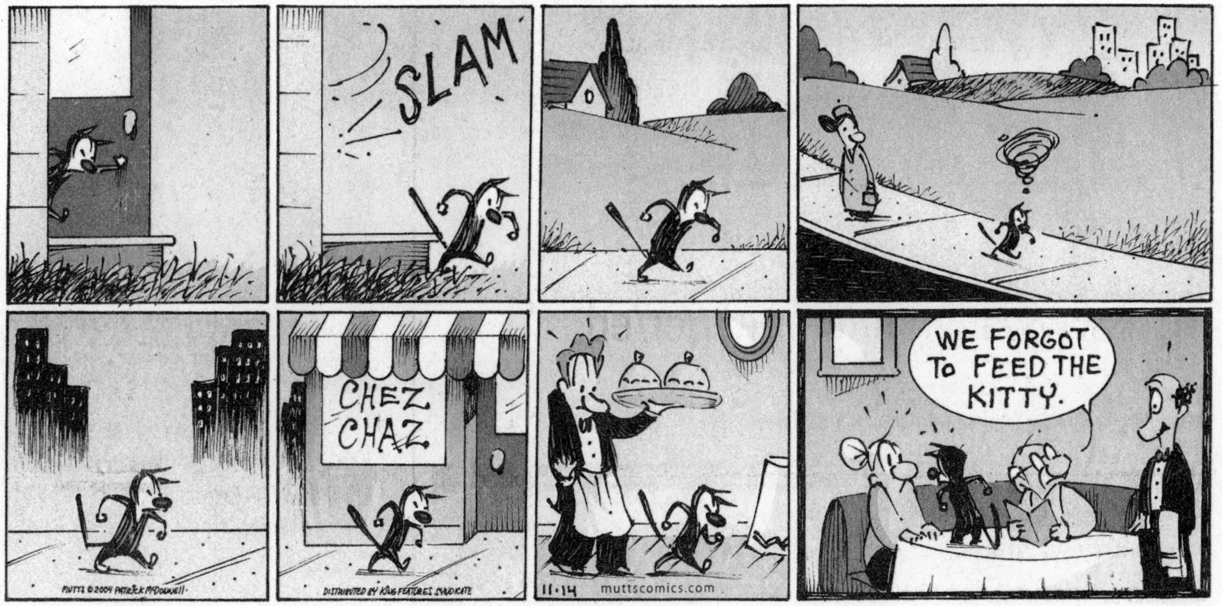
SLAM
CHEZ CHAZ
11-14
muttscomics.com
WE FORGOT TO FEED THE KITTY.

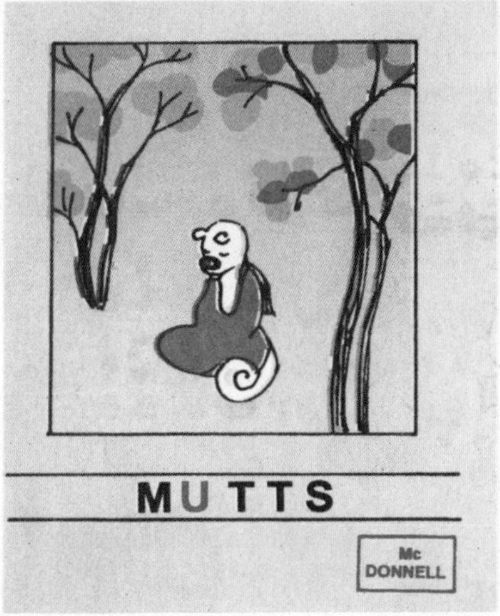
MUTTS
Mc DONNELL

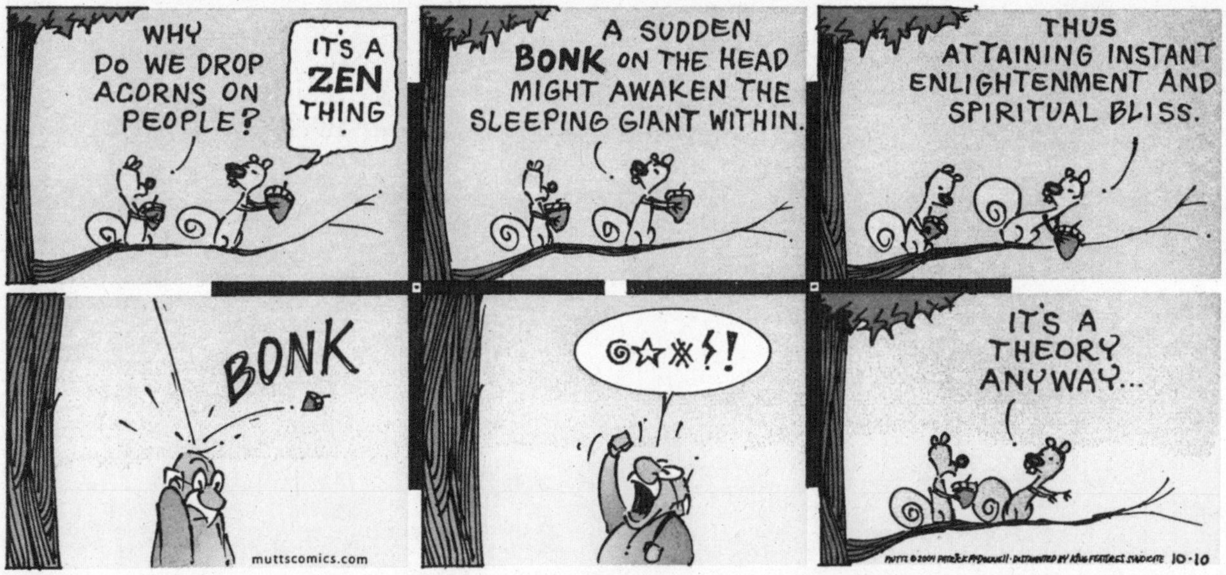
WHY DO WE DROP ACORNS ON PEOPLE?
IT'S A ZEN THING
A SUDDEN BONK ON THE HEAD MIGHT AWAKEN THE SLEEPING GIANT WITHIN.
THUS ATTAINING INSTANT ENLIGHTENMENT AND SPIRITUAL BLISS.
BONK
muttscomics.com
IT'S A THEORY ANYWAY...
10-10

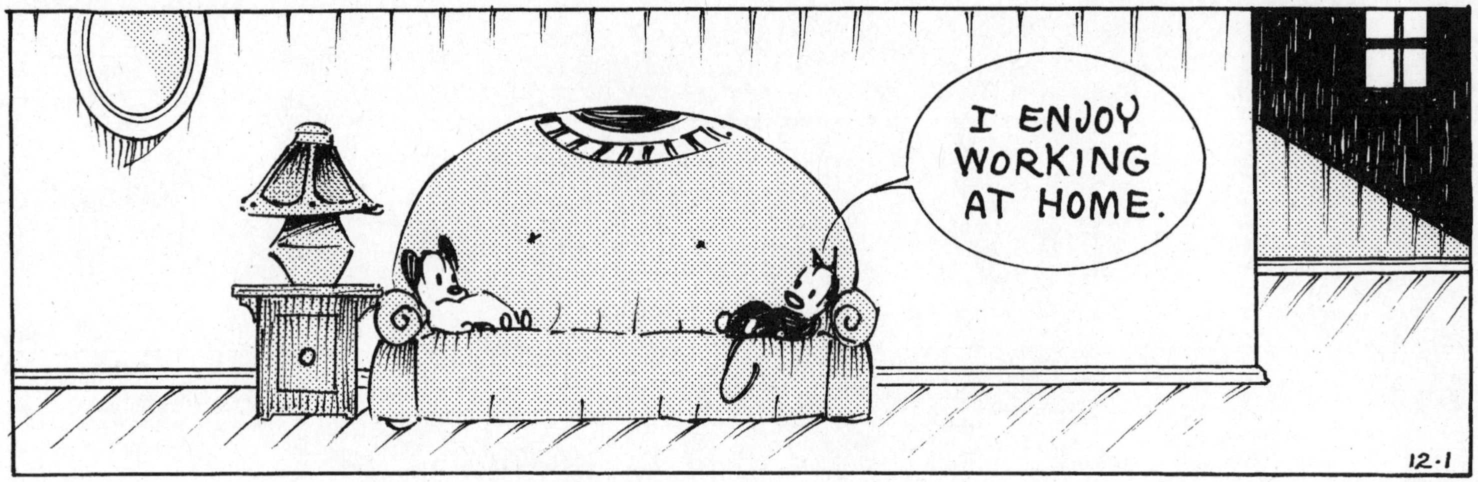
I ENJOY WORKING AT HOME.
12-1

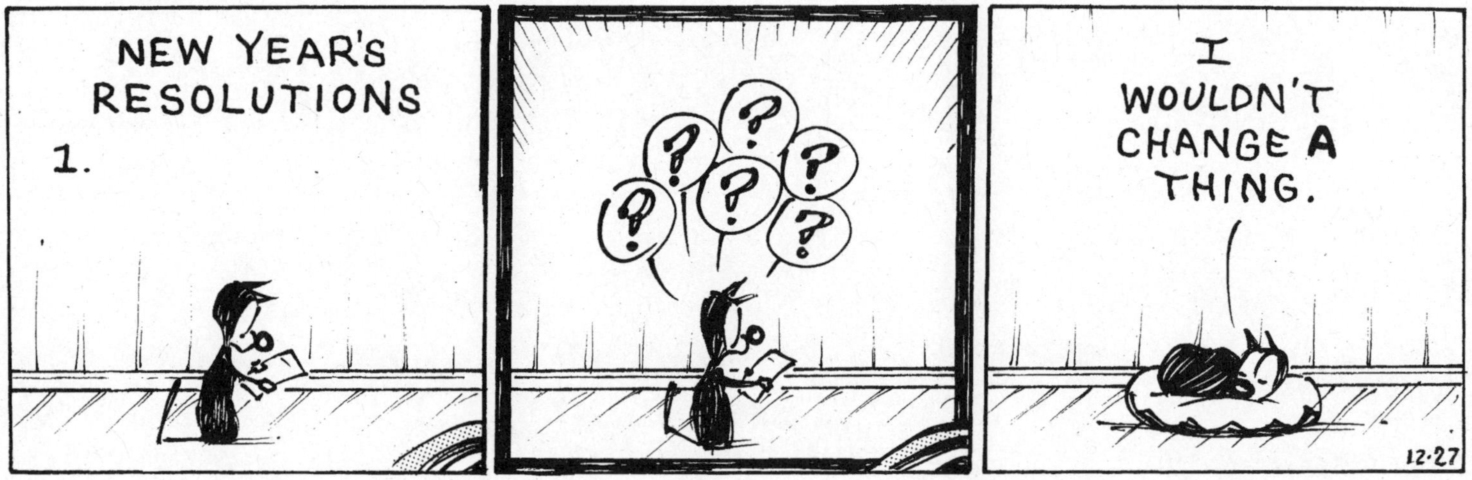
NEW YEAR'S RESOLUTIONS
1.
?
?
?
?
?
?
I WOULDN'T CHANGE A THING.
12-27

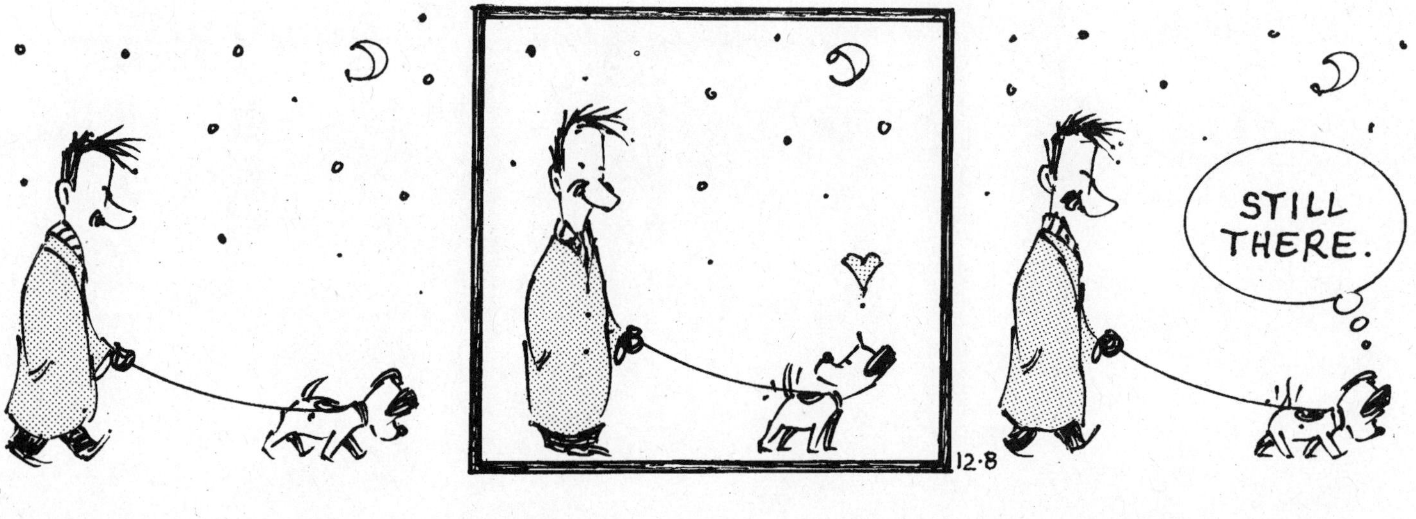
STILL THERE.
12-8

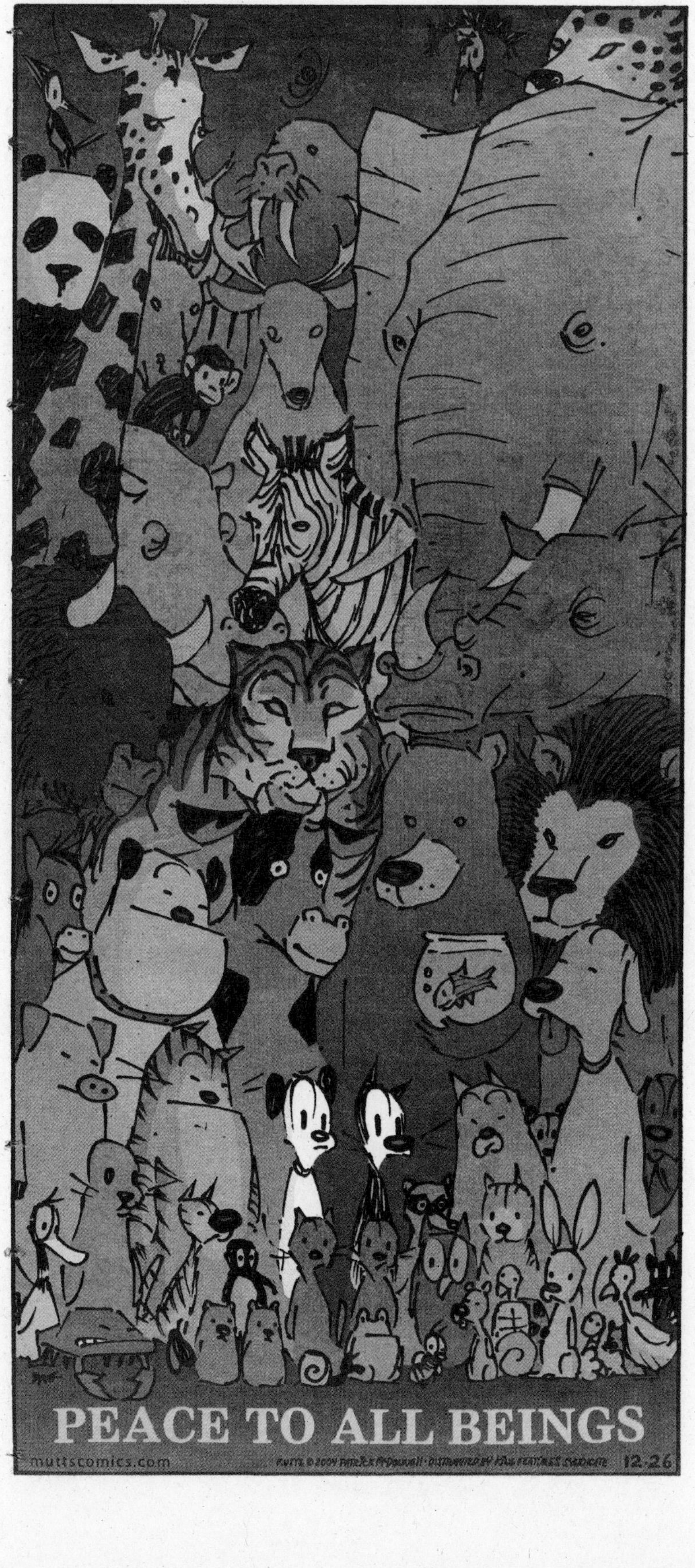
PEACE TO ALL BEINGS
muttscomics.com
MUTTS © 2004 PATRICK McDONNELL · DISTRIBUTED BY KING FEATURES SYNDICATE
12·26

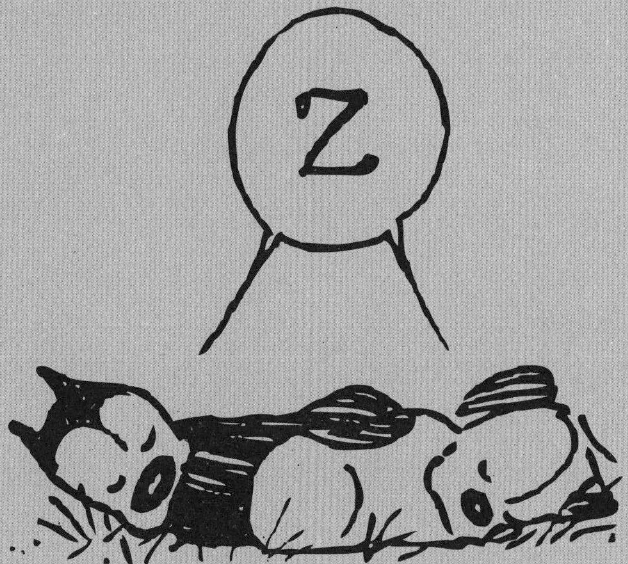
Z

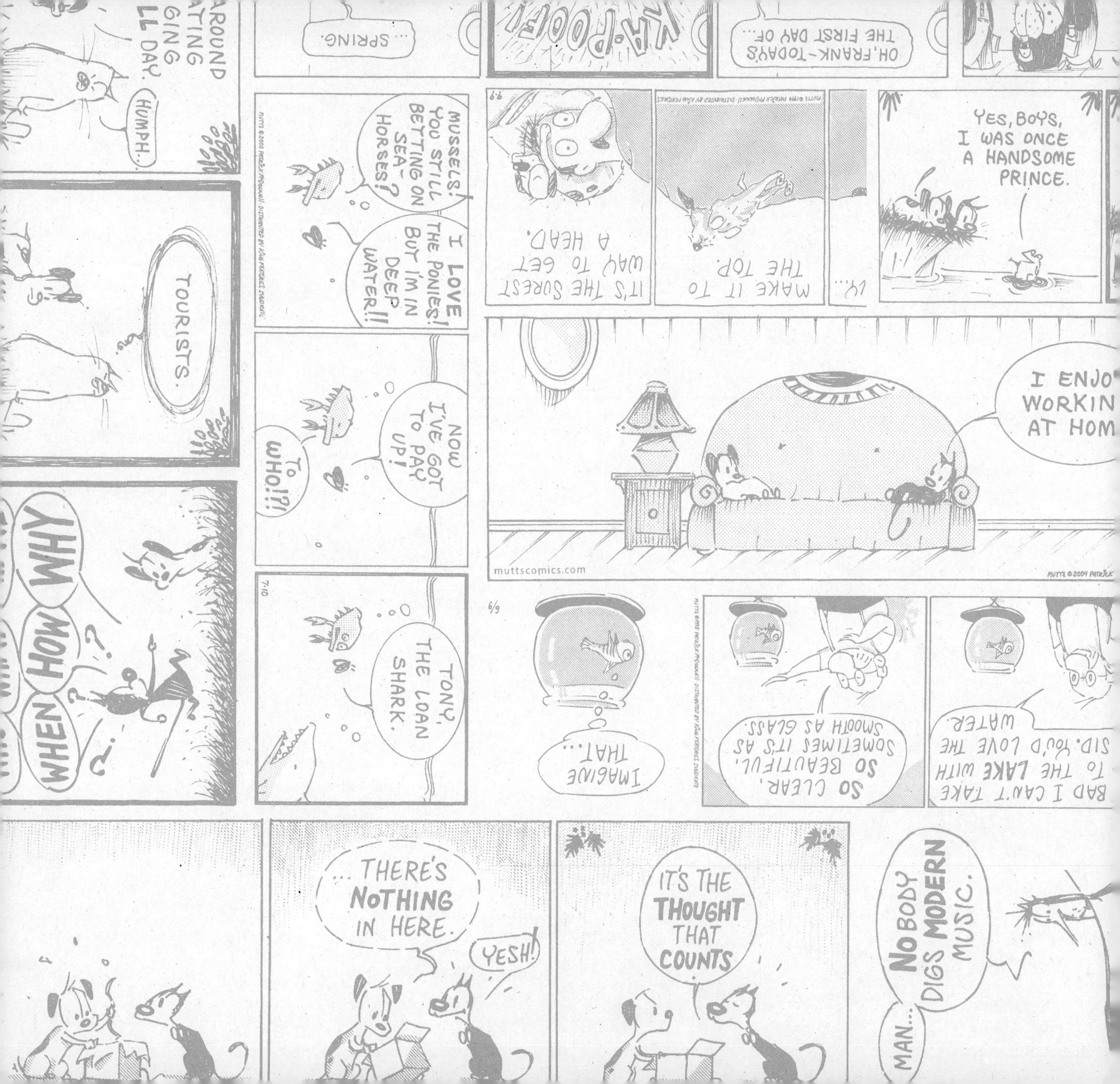

AROUND
ATING
GING
LL DAY.
HUMPH.
TOURISTS.
WHEN
HOW
WHY
MUSSELS! YOU STILL BETTING ON SEA-HORSES?
I LOVE THE PONIES! BUT I'M IN DEEP WATER!!
NOW I'VE GOT TO PAY UP!
TO WHO!?!
TONY, THE LOAN SHARK.
...SPRING.
OH, FRANK–TODAY'S THE FIRST DAY OF...
IT'S THE SUREST WAY TO GET A HEAD.
MAKE IT TO THE TOP.
YES, BOYS, I WAS ONCE A HANDSOME PRINCE.
I ENJO
WORKIN
AT HOM
muttscomics.com
IMAGINE THAT...
SO CLEAR, SO BEAUTIFUL, SOMETIMES IT'S AS SMOOTH AS GLASS.
BAD I CAN'T TAKE YOU TO THE LAKE WITH SID. YOU'D LOVE THE WATER.
...THERE'S NOTHING IN HERE.
YESH!
IT'S THE THOUGHT THAT COUNTS
MAN...
NOBODY DIGS MODERN MUSIC.